*Discovering the*
*North-West Passage*

# Discovering the North-West Passage

## The Four-Year Arctic Odyssey of H.M.S. *Investigator* and the McClure Expedition

GLENN M. STEIN

McFarland & Company, Inc., Publishers

*Jefferson, North Carolina*

LIBRARY OF CONGRESS CATALOGUING-IN-PUBLICATION DATA

Stein, Glenn M., 1962– author.
Discovering the North-West Passage : the four-year Arctic odyssey of
H.M.S. Investigator and the McClure Expedition / Glenn M. Stein.
p.    cm.
Includes bibliographical references and index.

**ISBN 978-0-7864-7708-1 (softcover : acid free paper)** ∞
**ISBN 978-1-4766-2203-3 (ebook)**

1.  McClure, Robert John Le Mesurier, Sir, 1807–1873—Travel—
Northwest Passage.    2.  Northwest Passage—Discovery and exploration—
British.    3.  Arctic regions—Discovery and exploration—British.
4.  Search and rescue operations—Arctic regions—History—19th century.
5.  Investigator (Ship)    I.  Title.

G6651850.S74 2015          910.9163'27—dc23          2015031090

BRITISH LIBRARY CATALOGUING DATA ARE AVAILABLE

On the cover: (top right) Arctic Medal issued by the United Kingdom
(photograph by Spencer J. Fisher); (bottom) H.M.S. *Investigator* trapped in the
ice, lithograph by Samuel G. Cresswell, 1854 (both from author's collection)

Printed in the United States of America

*McFarland & Company, Inc., Publishers
Box 611, Jefferson, North Carolina 28640
www.mcfarlandpub.com*

For my wife Marsha, our daughters Aleah and Rebekah,
and my parents, Edward M. and Dorothy H. Stein—
to all of whom I owe a debt which can never be repaid

and

In memory of my friend,
Theresa Anne "Terry" Ferguson
(1962–84)

# Table of Contents

# Acknowledgments

My debts are enormous, spreading far and wide, and my sense of thankfulness runs deep. I want to especially thank my good friend and excellent professional researcher Peter John, for his vital assistance and unfailing support throughout the long course of this project—his belief in me never faltered.

Barbara Jannasch and Emanuel Jannasch (the widow and son of Niels Windekilde Jannasch, descendant of Johann A. Miertsching) most kindly permitted me to quote freely from *Frozen Ships*. In turn, Emanuel introduced me to Mechtild and Wolfgang Opel, whose friendship and generosity in sharing their original research and interpretations about Miertsching's life and writings brought greater insight into this gentleman.

The friendship, extensive research, and authorship of polar historians Dr. William "Bill" Barr, Dr. Herbert J.G. Dartnall, Dr. Russell A. Potter, Dr. Hal Vogel, and Douglas W. Wamsley, have provided me with energy and support. In particular, Bill graciously offered up his transcription of Carpenter Ford's journal, and Doug kindly allowed the use of images from his superb Arctic collection.

The fine abilities of professional researcher Kevin J. Asplin, and my friend and professional photographer Spencer J. Fisher, were very important throughout, and they are much deserving of my gratitude.

I cannot write enough about the expertise, enthusiasm, and helpfulness of Dr. Jim Molnar, Ryan Harris, and all of the scientists and staff at Parks Canada.

With the gracious permission of Her Majesty Queen Elizabeth II, material from The Royal Archives was instrumental in uncovering the creation of the Arctic Medal 1818–55 (Appendix 7).

The patience, support and encouragement of the following people can hardly be overemphasized, and I owe them all my heartfelt thanks: Robert Gottlieb, and especially my agent Don Fehr, at Trident Media; Scarlett Gragan Bland, Dr. Veena Bush, Dr. Azhar Chaudhry, Dr. Dominique Dirou, David Erskine-Hill, Mark Fowler, Dalia Katz, Marjorie LeVangie, Michael Osbun, Charlie Samaha, John Stewart, Laura Waterman, and Jeffry D. Wert.

## Individuals

Lara Andrews (Canadian War Museum)
Philip Attwood (The British Museum)
Heather Aylesbury

Alan Barclay (Plymouth & West Devon Record Office)
Dr. J.D. Bateson (Hunterian Museum)

William Battersby

Aimee Benoit (Glenbow Museum)

Michael Bevan (NMM)

John Boadle

Naomi Boneham (SPRI)

Mark Bougourd

Martin Brady

Dr. Barbara A. Brannon

Fred D. Calder, Jr. (descendant of John Calder)

Julie Carrington (RGS)

Pamela M. Clark (The Royal Archives)

Lieutenant Ernie Coleman, RN (retired)

M.J. "Peggy" Collins

Sim Comfort

Rory Cook (Science Museum, London)

Rory M. Cory (The Military Museums, Calgary)

Jon Cray

Georgina Cronin (SPRI)

Tony Daly (Coastguards of Yesteryear)

Jennie De Protani (The Athenaeum)

Rachel Edwards (St. Clement's Parish Office)

Dr. Todd Farmerie (Haswell family genealogist)

Frederick Feather (descendant of John Woon)

Martin French (SPRI)

David Hannam

Jane George

Mark Gilbert (SPRI)

Jonathan Gregson (The Natural History Museum, London)

the late Dominick Harrod (descendant of Samuel G. Cresswell)

Henry Harrod (descendant of Samuel G. Cresswell)

Andrea Hart (The Natural History Museum, London)

Robert F. Hartley (Charnwood Museum)

John H. Haswell (descendant of William H. Haswell)

Dr. G.W. Hawkes

Robert K. Headland (SPRI)

Leilani Henry

Christopher Hill (DNW)

Terry M. Hogan

Colin Hulott

Robert Hulott

Avis Hutchins (Warren County Historical Museum)

Sylvia Hynes

Jane Inglesby (descendant of Edward H. Fawcett and James Williams)

Heather Johnson (Royal Naval Museum Library)

the late A.G.E. Jones

Dr. Roger Knight (Visiting Professor of Naval History, GMI)

Susan M. Kooyman (Glenbow Museum)

Heather Lane (SPRI)

Miranda Lowe (The Natural History Museum, London)

Mary Lozier (Warren County Illinois Genealogical Society)

Travis Lutley (Glenbow Museum)

Dr. C. Stuart Mackinnon

Michael Hargreave Mawson

David McCullough

Danna Messer (Borthwick Institute for Archives)

Lia Melemenis (Glenbow Museum)

Dr. Keith Millar

Glenn Minehart

David A.E. Morris

Thelma Mort (Tenby Museum & Art Gallery)

Alexandra Mould (Borthwick Institute for Archives)

Paul and Anne Murawski

Jim Murray

the late Dr. Leslie H. Neatby

Margaret Newman (Royal Naval Museum Library)

Stephen Nicholson

Dr. Dirk Notz (Max Planck Institute for Meteorology)

Richard Noyce (Royal Naval Museum)

Steve Nye (Guildhall Museum, Rochester)

Marg O'Leary

Dr. Dean Oliver (Canadian War Museum)
Theresa Palfrey (Norfolk Record Office)
William "Pick" Pickering
Tim Popp
Elaine Pordes (The British Library)
Sondra K. Pritchard
Dr. Cameron Pulsifer (Canadian War Museum)
Dylan Read (Norfolk Record Office)
Alexa Ress (Nottinghamshire Archives)
Laurie Richards (3R's Used Books, Port Robinson)
Frances Roback (Glenbow Museum)
Tom Russell (local historian, Port Robinson)
Andrés Paredes Salvador (Remembering the Franklin Expedition)
Arthur Satterley
Shirley Sawtell
Robert J. Scarlett
David J. Scheeres
Marlene Schuster (Parish of Stoke Damerel)
Barry E. Scott
Ship Modeler
Willow Silvani (SPRI)
Jack Skead
Thomas Skead
Harry and Laurie Stein
Sarah Strong (RGS)
Kevin Thomas (Tenby Museum & Art Gallery)
Linda Tree (King's Lynn Library)
Cameron Treleaven (Aquila Books)
Clare Valentine (The Natural History Museum, London)
Clifford Walters (King's Lynn)
Becky Wash (Essex Police Museum)
Robert Watt
Jill Wellby (The Old Vicarage B&B, Morwenstow)
Joy Wheeler (RGS)
Frank Whitehead (Morwenstow Church, Cornwall)
Freda M. Wilkins-Jones (Norfolk Record Office)
Dr. Sam Willis
John Wilson (LSARS)
Jeremy F. Wong (SPRI)
Damien Wright
the late David E. Yelverton
Justin Young

## *Institutions and Organizations*

The British Library, Borthwick Institute for Archives, The British Museum, Canadian War Museum, Essex Police Museum, Glenbow Museum, Guildhall Museum, Hunterian Museum, Karpeles Manuscript Library (Santa Barbara), King's Lynn Library, Life Saving Awards Research Society, Moravian Archives (Herrnhut), The Military Museums (Calgary), The National Archives (UK), National Archives of Canada, National Maritime Museum, The Natural History Museum (London), Naval Historical Collectors and Research Association, Orange County Library System (Florida), National Museums of Scotland, Norfolk Record Office, Orders and Medals Research Society, Parish of St. Clement, Parish of Stoke Damerel, Royal Collection Trust, Royal Geographical Society, Royal Naval Museum, Science Museum (London), Scott Polar Research Institute, Seminole County Public Library System (Florida), Warren County Genealogical Society (Illinois), Warren County Historical Museum (Illinois), Warren County Historical Society (Illinois), Wellcome Museum (London)

# Preface

*Carry on wondering, as that is the way to get to the bottom of a story that everybody has taken for granted.*

—Polar historian A.G.E. Jones to
Glenn M. Stein (Oct. 11, 1995)

The story that follows is true.

This is a balanced account of the *human* story behind the four-year Arctic odyssey of the men onboard Her Majesty's Ship *Investigator*, during their search for the missing Franklin Expedition and the North-West Passage. Through an unfiltered lens, I have gone to great lengths to understand and accurately depict the people and the events in which they were involved.

On April 11, 1970, I stood in amazement on a Florida beach, gazing upon Apollo 13 as she hurtled toward the moon. Two days later, hundreds of human and computerized minds melded in a race to save three explorers trapped within the frigid void of space. To the Victorian mind, the Arctic *was* the moon. Like outer space, the polar regions offer life and death—and the difference between them hangs by a thread.

Exploration has always been as much—if not more—about the human species' struggle with *itself*, as its struggle with the natural world.

With the Investigators, I focused on seeking out possibilities, and then finding answers. In the following pages, an understanding emerges through the careful peeling away of the layers of reality these men confronted during the expedition.

As I immersed myself in the journals, documents and letters of the Investigators and other polar explorers of the period, their words washed over me. I delved into naval customs, ship construction, oceanography, ice navigation, and the effects of extreme cold and starvation on the human body—anything that allowed me to inch closer to their nineteenth century world.

At the same time, I strived to understand the indigenous peoples with whom the sailors and Marines came into contact, by obtaining a sense of their culture, and in particular their relationships with Europeans.

I am proud, and yet humbled, to be the caretaker of the Investigators' memories. However, neither these men, nor anyone else, bear any responsibility for any inaccuracies or misinterpretations which may have found their way into these pages. Any faults within this work are mine alone.

# The Frozen Grail, up to 1845

*Ambition leads me not only farther than any other man has been before me, but as far as I think it is possible for man to go.*

—James Cook (1729–79)

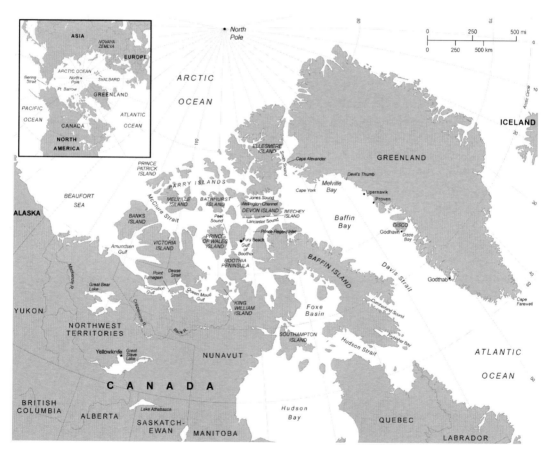

**Canadian Arctic Islands and Greenland Map (LibbeyDesign, Orlando, Florida).**

For a seeming eternity, Her Majesty's Ship *Investigator* was imprisoned in Mercy Bay, "frozen, like an almond in the middle of a chocolate bar."[1] The western Arctic had been the battleground for her crew of Investigators since August 1850, as they continually flung their minds and bodies against a foe far more relentless than any human one.

In the bow of the vessel, coddled by an internal fortification of wood and iron, Able Seaman John Boyle spoke cheerfully from his sickbed, made a slight movement, then faded into unconsciousness. Boyle's song and tap of shoe were to echo through the wooden walls no more—the first Investigator was gone—and the specter of Death hovered over the ship's company. "This melancholy occurrence could not but evince a depressing influence on the minds of all, which was generally manifest throughout the ship, and enveloped us thus suddenly in a mantle of gloom and despondency," Dr. Alexander Armstrong reflected afterward.[2]

At four o'clock the following afternoon, silence reigned in and about the ship. Some 400 yards distant, four men were hacking out a final resting place for their departed shipmate in the frozen earth. Nearer to *Investigator*, her captain and first lieutenant were discussing the depressing business of cutting a grave in the permafrost, when "we perceived a figure walking rapidly towards us from the rough ice at the entrance of the bay."[3]

What happened next that April day in 1853 spun the Investigators' wheel of fate one full turn, making for an unforgettable episode in the tides of polar history.

Until this moment, one mortal held sway over the Investigators and their wooden world: Commander Robert John Le Mesurier McClure, Royal Navy.

Being "one of those unfortunate Devils who lose their Father before they were launched,"[4] McClure was born on January 28, 1807, five months after his father's death, at the residence of his maternal grandfather, Archdeacon John Elgee, Rector of Wexford. Captain Robert McClure, 89th Regiment (The Princess Victoria's Regiment) had married Jane Elgee in 1806. The unfortunate Mrs. McClure "had the singular destiny of being wife, widow, and mother in one year, and before she had attained the age of nineteen."[5]

The elder McClure's ghost guided Robert's younger years. While serving under General Ralph Abercrombie in Egypt during the struggle with revolutionary France, Captain McClure was said to have been at Abercrombie's side when he fell mortally wounded on the field of battle at Alexandria in 1801. During this same foreign service, McClure saved the life of his brother officer—and future general—Captain John Le Mesurier, thus cementing a "peculiar friendship" between the two men[6]:

> From this a promise arose, the general having then no children, that should his friend ever marry and have a son, he would adopt him as his own. Accordingly, when the young Robert was four years old, General Le Mesurier wrote to claim him, in fulfillment of this promise, and he was taken to Alderney by his uncle, the present rector of Wexford, who describes him as being then singularly attractive, and remembers well the fearless pleasure manifested by the child, even at that age, at being on the water for the first time.[7]

Even then Neptune was beckoning, and McClure eventually answered his call.

As a young officer, McClure's godfather and guardian served in Ireland during the whole of the 1798 rebellion, and again from 1802 to 1805. In mid–1805 Le Mesurier left the Army as a major general to assume the hereditary governorship of the island of Alderney, the most northerly of the main Channel Islands between Britain and France.[8]

Robert "resided in the princely residence of the governor, as the adopted child and son of the house" until the age of 10, when his idyllic world was unexpectedly transformed. Since their marriage in 1804, Le Mesurier and his wife Martha had remained childless, but in 1817 a son was born, and another in 1818. Two years later, Robert was sent to Eton, and afterwards the Royal Military Academy Sandhurst, to follow in his father's and godfather's footsteps, and enjoy the latter's support in an Army career.[9]

But the military life didn't suit McClure at all, and "with a rashness of sixteen, he left the college with three young noblemen, fellow-students there, and proceeded to France, determined never to enter the college walls again." The general evidently bowed to McClure's maritime wishes in 1824, securing for him the appointment of volunteer first class, which was one path to a lieutenant's commission. But the lad was now on his own—without "interest" (political support) in the rough and tumble world of the Royal Navy.[10]

McClure must have also been aware that he faced an unmovable obstacle: age. Ordinarily, a "young gentleman" entered the Navy as a volunteer first class around age 12 or 13, so at 17, McClure was well behind the curve from the start. The average time it took to pass through the ranks of volunteer, midshipman and mate, before being allowed to take the lieutenant's exam and actually receive a commission, was *at least* 12 years. However, passing the exam did not guarantee anything, because a commission was to a single ship, resulting from a vacancy; consequently, a very large number of would-be lieutenants never secured a commission.[11]

The realities of his situation may have gone a long way in shaping McClure's resolve for the future, thus welding his determination to achieve prominence, and thereby promotion. McClure was hardly the sort of man to sit idly by and pin his hopes on mere chance; and though persistence and determination are omnipotent in life, they need to be balanced by humanity and diplomacy—qualities which sometimes went missing in McClure's word and deed.

The post–Napoleonic Wars Navy was "spit-and-polish," and the naval officer prided himself in keen ship handling through harnessing the wind. McClure was caught in the midst of the transition from sail to steam propulsion that began in fits and starts during the 1820s and '30s. But the steam engine was inefficient and unsightly: "[S]team, from whose grotesque and clumsy engines, from whose monstrous smoke-stacks, there belched forth the smuts, the concentrated mess from the combustion of filthy Newcastle coal, and the first smell and contamination of Oil."[12]

And it wasn't just the mechanical contraptions themselves which were viewed with disgust, the human machines who operated them—mechanics and stokers—were seen as "the lowest form of adult marine life."[13] In later years, this anti-steam mindset came to permeate some of McClure's professional associations, and his outlook gave birth to startling and unforeseen consequences. And in 35 years afloat, McClure served aboard just one steamship, and that at the very end of his career. A good deal of his sea time was spent aboard smaller ships, like the handy 18-gun sloop *Primrose*, onboard which he got his first taste of action as a midshipman during a five-hour chase that ended in the capture of the slaver *Les Deux Nantois* off St. Domingo in December 1824. The French-flagged vessel was transporting 466 African slaves to Cuba, and *Primrose* was part of the Royal Navy's ongoing attempt at strangling the slave trade on both sides of the Atlantic.[14]

Becoming a mate and then passing the lieutenant's examination in 1830, McClure afterwards wed Mary Mallors on January 26, 1831, in St. Mary's Church (Portsea, Hampshire), when he was still in his early twenties. None of the biographical writings on McClure even mention this first marriage, so very little is known of it. However, prospects for future professional and financial gains were dim. To start with, in January 1832, there were 3,255 active RN lieutenants, but 76 percent were *unemployed* (some of whom were too old to have much hope of getting employment). So, between 1830 and 1836, while waiting for a commission, McClure served nearly all of this time aboard Coast Guard cutters—and in terms of naval advancement, this was by and large backpedaling in one's career. Many a man who took a Coast Guard appointment later found himself unable to resume the track for naval promotion.[15]

To gain a lieutenancy, McClure knew he must aggressively *seek it*. And seek it he did, in one of the most forbidding and unforgiving places on Earth: the Arctic. While on leave from the Coast Guard in June 1836, McClure was on his way to visit his recently widowed mother and half-sister in Ireland, not having laid eyes on them in nine years,[16] when

> the friends that I was residing with knowing Capt. Bowles who is at the head of the Coast Guard Department undertook to introduce me to him with a view to my advancement in the Service, having obtained a strong letter from him to be given to Capt. Elliot who was an officer I formerly served under & one of the Lords of the Admiralty, he very fairly gave me to understand that in my present capacity which was Chief Mate of a Cutter he could do nothing, but the "Terror" was fitting out under the orders of Capt. Back for the purpose of tracing the line of [the Arctic] Coast not hitherto known between Cape Turnagain & the Hecla & Fury Straits, and if I proceeded with it my promotion might be almost reckoned a certainty, so sudden a proposition rather confounded me & I begged a day to consider but for an excellent reason four hours was all that was allowed, so that in the space of that time the whole career of my life was altered.[17]

With the *Terror* expected to leave England in just four days, McClure invoked his family motto, *Paratus Sum* (I am ready), and plunged into his destiny. Captain George Back,[18] a very experienced Arctic traveler, and his crew were tasked with completing the mapping of the northern Canadian coastline by entering through the eastern Arctic.[19] The mission was an element in the long search to discover a North-West Passage, that fabled maritime route connecting the Atlantic and Pacific Oceans through the Arctic.

Beginning just before the close of the sixteenth century, the search for the Passage, into which McClure was now magnetically drawn, eventually spanned 350 years. The motivations for seeking it included Far Eastern trade, the search for mineral wealth, and the fur trade. The first particularly involved Britain, since she was at the end of long trading routes, and paid higher prices for goods like spices, jewelry and textiles from the Orient. The North-West Passage also represented the shortest distance to Far Eastern markets, so the quest was transformed into a British national obsession.[20]

Serious business meant serious money, and the British government was so intent on finding the Passage, it laid down cold hard cash for its discovery. In 1745, Parliament passed an Act which dangled a king's ransom of £20,000 in the public eye—equal to well over two million dollars today. The prize was open to any royal subject, or subjects, who found the Passage through Hudson Strait. A further Act in 1776 flung a similar reward on the table—but the rules had changed. It was no longer a requirement to discover the Passage by way of Hudson Strait; instead, another condition for collecting the prize was put in place. Any passage must be discovered north of the northern 52nd parallel. As an added sweetener, £5,000 went to anyone reaching 89° N latitude by sea. Yet another parliamentary Act was passed in 1818, offering not only the rewards from the 1776 Act, but authorized rewards for partial successes: £5,000 for crossing 10° westward, 110° W, 120° W and 130° W.[21]

Even after all of the Acts were repealed in 1828, the widespread approval of the earlier policy meant that Parliament continued to dole out several cash rewards for Arctic discoveries.[22] Rough comparisons of the value of a person's spending money for these rewards between the years 1830 and 2013[23] are as follows:

| 1830 | | 2013 |
|------|---|------|
| £20,000 | = | £1,600,000 ($2,560,000 U.S.) |
| £5,000 | = | £400,000 ($640,000 U.S.) |

By the early nineteenth century, it was long realized that a commercial water route through the Arctic was not practical due to the yearly shifting ice conditions, but the search continued in order to achieve political and scientific goals.[24] With no way to predict the state of the ice for any given season, the likelihood of success was down to simple luck—good fortune *sometimes* favored the brave.

The British navy had a surplus of men and ships to commit to the goal after the end of the Napoleonic Wars.[25] In that day, sailors signed on for a ship's commission (usually lasting three to five years), since a system of enlisting for specific periods of engagement was still decades away. By way of contrast, men of the Royal Marines were traditionally like other soldiers, being recruited for unlimited periods of service, for life, or until their services were no longer required.

More importantly, the Navy had Second Secretary of the Admiralty John Barrow (later Sir John Barrow). Serving from 1803 to 1845, Barrow was responsible for the inner workings of the Admiralty and for correspondence with naval officers, which gave him great powers of patronage, and the inclination to use them in gaining promotions for these officers.[26]

Barrow feared the Russians would connect their empire through the top of the world with its ongoing exploration of Russian America (Alaska), and this propelled a flurry of British naval Arctic expeditions beginning in 1818. In addition, Barrow felt that it would be somewhat horrifying if a second-rate naval power like Russia "should complete a discovery in the nineteenth century, which was happily commenced by Englishmen in the sixteenth."[27] Barrow had to justify to his Admiralty bosses that expensive Arctic adventures could pay handsome dividends in national prestige.

On the scientific side, there was a direct link between science and exploration, and this is where the Admiralty and the Royal Society of London had vested interests. But there was a far deeper connection between science and exploration: a vibrant guiding belief during the early nineteenth century of the melding of science and economics bolstered the call for Arctic exploration. If relationships between glaciology, oceanography, hydrography, meteorology and agriculture could be understood, scientific *and* commercial benefits would follow. Case in point: Sir Joseph Banks (President of the Royal Society) was interested in recent reports from whalers of decreased polar ice and how this might relate to Britain's climatic changes, since a string of unusually cold springs and summers resulted in a sharp reduction in the cider crop of apples for at least sixteen years. Global warming is not only a modern day concern.[28]

Success was nearly at hand from the start of the renewed naval effort. During an 1819–20 expedition from the eastern Arctic, a tried and true Lieutenant William Edward Parry[29] led two ships through three-quarters of the Passage. He wintered at Winter Harbour, on Melville Island's southern coast—the first deliberate Arctic wintering performed by British naval vessels. "Near the south-western point of this harbour there is a remarkable block of sandstone, somewhat resembling the roof of a house, on which the ships' names were subse-

**"Parry's Rock" in Winter Harbour, Melville Island (*The Illustrated London News*, Nov. 29, 1851).**

quently engraved by [Surgeon Alexander] Fisher." This landmark became known as Parry's Rock. Afterward, Parry continued west, but was stopped by massive ice at Cape Dundas, on the southwestern point of the island, where he achieved his furthest success of 113° 48' W. Having crossed the meridian of 110° W, Parry won the £5,000 award for the partial discovery of the North-West Passage.[30]

Looking to the southwest, Parry glimpsed land, which he named Banks Land. Onboard Parry's ship was a midshipman named James Clark Ross,[31] who, along with Parry, was among those destined to leave indelible marks upon polar history.

Unknown to mariners and mapmakers over the course of the search was that *several* routes connect the northern Atlantic and Pacific Oceans, but the Arctic is a geographical labyrinth. The maze of islands could spin the head of any seasoned seafarer. Navigators had to grope their way along ice-infested shallow coastlines in pea-soup fog and snowstorms, with questions abounding at every turn: Where did a coastline begin and end? Did a narrow waterway lead to a channel or a bay? Did a piece of land connect to the North American mainland or was it an island? Finding a North-West Passage was not like attempting to find a needle in a haystack—it was like trying to find a needle in a *stack* of needles.

In the British public's imagination during the late eighteenth and early nineteenth centuries, the awe-inspiring grandeur and picturesque beauty of the Arctic were intertwined with the dread of confronting the unknown. The resulting national heroes, who endured hardships, achieved victories, and sometimes suffered tragedies, had particular appeal to a Protestant popular imagination in Britain. Travel books, novels, panoramas and art made indelible marks on the British (and American) public mind, which led to stereotyped views of not only the Arctic, but Africa's interior and many other parts of the globe.[32]

For the public, the vast, brooding Arctic landscape offered the perfect backdrop to the tales of extreme hardship and ever-present danger experienced by explorers. A long line of British nineteenth century explorers embodied imperialism, and the public and press turned a blind eye to their failings and human frailties. Notably, there is one defining difference between the American and British heroes of the nineteenth century: "The Americans preferred their heroes living; the British most honored (and used) those who were dead."[33] With a martyred hero, death for a cause allows the individual's "heroic status to be most easily created, interpreted, and manipulated."[34]

Robert McClure was about to begin his first of several dances with Death in the frozen zone. And sharing a first-time Arctic cruise with McClure was one of the men who became wrapped in his destiny years later—Mate Graham Gore.[35] Having joined the Navy just a year later than McClure, Gore was a combat veteran who fought in the Battle of Navarino in 1827, the last major naval engagement in history entirely under sail. His family background was also steeped in worldwide exploration and naval service. Gore's grandfather was born in America, became a Royal Navy officer, and sailed on two of Captain Cook's expeditions; Gore's father was also a naval officer who had his share of adventures at sea and against enemies of the king.[36]

In September 1836, iron men and their wooden ship sailed into Foxe Channel, north of Hudson Bay, and by the 20th the *Terror* was beset (closely surrounded by ice). Within a few days, Back and his crew got just a taste of the unpredictable perils which were to menace them over the next nine months. Violent pressure from an unseen hand toyed with them. Danger lurked everywhere.[37]

Before the year was out, during an excursion on the ice away from the *Terror*, a sailor fell through young ice. McClure helped rescue the unfortunate soul and hustle him back to the ship.[38] The man was oblivious to the danger of hypothermia, during which the core body temperature drops below that required for normal metabolism and functions (95°F), allowing one to float into unconsciousness—and even death.[39]

Over the course of the winter, the movements of the ice pack badly damaged the *Terror* and she drifted southeasterly, so when she got clear of the pack in July 1837, the ship emerged broken and leaky at the western end of Hudson Strait. With the *Terror* in no shape to continue her mission, and with some of her crew attacked by scurvy, Back was left with little choice but to run for home. The ship's condition was so pitiful that only by superb seamanship was the little vessel coaxed across the Atlantic and onto the sands of an Irish beach by early September. Unbeaten, the *Terror*'s twisted timbers were put back into shape by dockyard workers, and her inevitable fate was further polar adventure.[40]

McClure survived his Arctic baptism—and got his lieutenancy in November—but worries about further promotion were not easily swept aside, since one eye needed to be always cast upon the future. Up until now, he had consistent good conduct ratings from his captains, and within two months secured another billet. By April 1838, he headed to North America again, this time to the Great Lakes, and by June was serving aboard the 20-gun sloop HMS *Niagara*, commanded by Captain Williams Sandom, Commodore of Her Majesty's ships on the Lakes.[41]

There were nearly simultaneous rebellions in Canada in 1837: the Lower Canada Rebellion saw armed conflict between rebels of what is now Quebec and the British colonial power of that province, while the Upper Canada Rebellion began in the adjacent colony (now known as Ontario). With regular British troops and local militias committed to the fight, the Royal Navy had only a small share in quelling the series of revolts that extended into 1838.[42]

Still, McClure found himself in the thick of things later that year when the *Niagara* helped save the border towns of Brockville and Prescott from destruction at the western end of the St. Lawrence River. When Prescott was attacked on November 13, "Sandom's force, aiding the troops, was instrumental in driving back the rebels, and forcing them to surrender."[43]

From *Niagara*, McClure transferred to the new 16-gun brig *Pilot* in August 1839, sailing the North American and West Indies Station on anti–slave trade duties. Leaving three years later, McClure acquired his first "command"—the receiving ship *Romney*, anchored in Havana Harbor as a temporary home for freed slaves until they could be transported back to Africa.[44] Receiving ships were typically older vessels that could still be kept afloat, but were obsolete or no longer seaworthy: hardly the sort of assignment that brings career opportunities, especially for a 35-year-old lieutenant.

In September 1843, while McClure was still languishing in a backwater far from England, Captain James Clark Ross[45] returned home with HMS *Erebus* and *Terror*, having made three seasonal journeys to Antarctica since 1839—some of the most successful polar voyages in history. However, in spite of attaining the highest southern latitude up until that time, making astounding geographical discoveries like the Ross Sea, Ross Ice Shelf, Mount Erebus and Mount Terror, sighting extensive sections of coastline, and gathering a wealth of scientific data and natural history specimens, the expedition did not capture the public's imagination as did earlier Arctic adventures.[46]

"There were good reasons for this; the British Empire was in a state of expansion, Antarctica offered no prospect of colonisation or trade [and] there were many more profitable areas for enterprising Britons to develop. The Royal Navy had increasing duties worldwide, and attentions of those interested in polar exploration were soon directed once again to the search for the North West Passage."[47]

The return of the Antarctic expedition immediately ignited notions for a new venture from the seasoned explorer Captain Frederick Beechey, but with a notable difference: steam. Beechey placed great faith in the recently introduced screw propeller, envisioning that such a device "opens an entirely new field of hope," and if *Erebus* and *Terror* could be fitted with propellers, he believed "arctic research might be most advantageously resumed."[48] When adopted, it was only the second time steam power found a place in polar exploration.

Steam had been introduced to the frozen zone when naval officers John Ross and his nephew James Clark Ross took a paddle steamer on a private 1829–33 North-West Passage voyage. Machinery was purchased from the firm Braithwaite & Ericsson. The latter was the same Swedish engineer who afterward designed the U.S. Navy's ironclad *Monitor*, which fought the Confederate ironclad *Virginia* (ex–USS *Merrimack*) in 1862, during the American Civil War.[49]

John Ross, wanting to keep the purpose of the voyage and name of his financial backer secret, misled Braithwaite & Ericsson as to the environment in which their steam engine was to be used, partly resulting in numerous breakdowns of the machinery. In the fall of 1829, the engine was dismantled and abandoned on the eastern shore of Boothia Peninsula (in the south central Arctic).[50] Its failure stamped a lasting imprint upon James Ross.

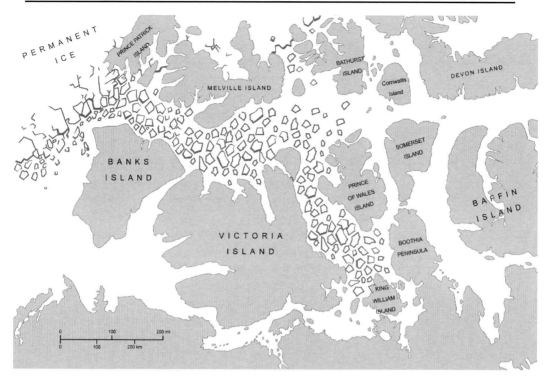

**Arctic Ice Stream Map (LibbeyDesign, Orlando, Florida).**

The overwhelming opinion voiced by British explorers was that a North-West Passage should take priority over a North Pole attempt, and by December 1844, an aging Sir John Barrow presented Lord Haddington, First Lord of the Admiralty, with a convincing document: "Proposal for an attempt to complete the discovery of a North-West Passage."[51]

It was well known that attempting to sail west from Cape Dundas, Melville Island, the farthest point achieved through the Passage by Parry in 1819, was useless due to the thick multiyear ice in the Beaufort Sea. Tides and currents are less able to disrupt the huge expanse of ice that forms in this sea, so it grows into multiyear ice, dozens of feet thick (although near the coast the ice breaks up in August and September). The Beaufort Sea ice stream had a direct effect on all central Arctic water expeditions for the period concerned.[52]

Barrow's plan suggested sailing a southwesterly course from Cape Walker, Russell Island (just north of Prince of Wales Island, eastern Viscount Melville Sound), to around 120° W longitude on the North American coast, and then onto the Bering Strait. The *assumption* was that there was scant land to obstruct the path, as Barrow believed "Banks Land," "Wollaston Land" and "Victoria Land" were only small islands, writing, "It may be presumed, therefore, that a distance of 300 leagues [about 1,000 statute miles] on a clear sea, keeping midway between the supposed Bank's Land and the coast of America would accomplish" the North-West Passage (see Western Arctic Map).[53]

A combination of past good fortune during Arctic expeditions, resulting in few deaths, and blind optimism, now guided Barrow—but there was no reckoning the Arctic's whims, and the ever-changing condition of the ice was always the unknown variable that made going north high stakes gambling.

The decision to proceed was reached just before Barrow's retirement from the Admiralty, and of the three most experienced British polar explorers living—Sir John Franklin,[54] Sir James Clark Ross and Sir William Edward Parry—command eventually went to Franklin.[55]

On being asked to comment on Barrow's plan, Franklin endorsed it, but added, "In case of the Passage not being found in that direction, then, to the Northward by the Wellington Channel."[56] This viewpoint was undoubtedly prompted by a theory that persisted even until the final decades of the nineteenth century, the Open Polar Sea. Some people believed that, while the Arctic was ringed by ice, if one could navigate through the ice it was possible to cross an ice-free Arctic Ocean—and even sail across the North Pole.[57]

With Barrow's plan, James Ross forewarned Lord Haddington about the ships encountering an easterly current and "great pressure of ice from the north or west," between Cape Walker and Banks Land. Ross drew on his unique experiences, as he was with Parry at Cape Dundas in 1820 *and* on the 1829–33 expedition, where he viewed the ice on King William Land's northwest shore in the south central Arctic: "He suspected (correctly) that they were part of the same ice stream" coming from the Beaufort Sea.[58]

But that wasn't all. Ross's negative experience with steam power during his uncle's expedition was reason enough not to seek leadership, as he bluntly penned to Hydrographer of the Navy Francis Beaufort: "I understand also that the ships are to be fitted as steamers, a measure to which I could not consent if the command were placed in my hands & which alone would be sufficient reason for not wishing to undertake the service as it is proposed at present to carry it forward."[59]

One person who stressed the advantages of steam was Arctic legend Sir William Edward Parry, Comptroller of Steam Machinery and Packet Service since 1837; he put forth the idea of retractable propellers, which could be lifted out of the water when the ships were under sail or there was danger of the blades' becoming caught in the ice. *Erebus* and *Terror* became among the first naval ships with bladed propellers, rather than the spiral Archimedean screws fitted on earlier vessels.[60]

Preparations for the expedition moved along at a rapid pace, including the fitting out of *Erebus* and *Terror* with auxiliary engines, using modified 20-horsepower railway locomotives (which under the best of conditions allowed for a humble four knots). With only a small supply of fuel aboard each vessel, official instructions stated that steam power was to be used only in difficult circumstances.[61]

Despite his apprehensions, James Ross became intimately involved with the enterprise, and was largely responsible for the appointment of its two senior officers, Captain Francis R.M. Crozier (*Terror*)[62] and Commander James Fitzjames (*Erebus*, Franklin's ship),[63] both of whom were Ross's close friends. To Fitzjames fell the a good deal of the responsibility for recommending the 21 junior officers, having seen previous service with many of them.

Because McClure was out of touch—still stuck in Havana Harbor—though he would have heard about the expedition, he didn't have the connections to secure an appointment. However, among those chosen was ex-shipmate Graham Gore, first lieutenant on the *Erebus*, who had once served (along with his father and brother) alongside Crozier.[64]

According to Admiralty records, the ships would carry foodstuffs for at least three years, including canned meats, vegetables and soups. And there was nourishment for the mind and spirit in the form of a library of some 1,200 volumes on each ship, everything from narratives of polar journeys and one hundred religious publications, to volumes of *Punch* (a humorous and satirical magazine) and textbooks for schools to be held during the winter months. For

**HMS *Erebus* and *Terror* before leaving England in May 1845 (*The Illustrated London News*, May 24, 1845).**

planned scientific research, all the necessary instruments were supplied to carry out programs in magnetism, geology, botany and zoology. But a recent technological innovation offered to make the Franklin Expedition the best remembered voyage of its age. A complete daguerreotype photographic apparatus was shipped; for the first time a camera was going on an Arctic expedition. "Probably no Arctic expedition had ever been so lavishly equipped."[65]

Out of the euphoria leading up to the Franklin Expedition's departure on May 19, 1845, came a voice of strong dissent from Sir John Ross. He repeated his well-publicized view that the ships and their crews were far too large, and told Franklin that if no news of him was received by mid–January 1847, he would volunteer to go on a search. And in fact, there was no contingency planning, and no written or oral agreement between Franklin and the Admiralty regarding the sending out of a relief expedition after a specified length of time had passed. Keeping in mind the prevailing attitude of almost everyone connected with the venture, this was not the result of negligence, but of a self-assurance that success was just over the horizon. In reality, if something went wrong, ensuring the survival of such a large group in a hostile environment would be daunting in the extreme, and invited disaster for the 129 men who entered the ice.[66]

The expedition's sailing may have transported Sir John back to his youth, when, in 1801, he left his native shores on his first exploring voyage, bound for Australia aboard HMS *Investigator*—the first naval vessel to bear this name.[67] But the present expedition would be like no other Franklin had ever known.

*Erebus* and *Terror* were last seen in northern Baffin Bay by the whalers *Enterprise* and *Prince of Wales* in the final days of July,[68] waiting for the ice to clear so they could enter Lancaster Sound. No one aboard was to ever see England again.

# 2

# Into the Fray, 1846–50

*The Devil to Pay*
*The devil seam on a ship's deck was the most difficult to pay (seal).*
*Paying the Devil is any difficult and unpleasant task.*

The slow funeral procession of sailors and Marines wended its way over a trail of uneven ice, dragging a sled with a casket that bore a heart-shaped tinned plaque signifying the mortal within, formerly a leading stoker aboard Her Majesty's Discovery Ship *Terror*:

JOHN TORRINGTON DIED JANUARY 1st 1846 AGED 20 YEARS[1]

Reaching the sloping, snow-covered gravel of the island, the somber parade then came up to the stoker's last resting place, recently hacked from the iron ground.

Just three days later, *Erebus*'s Thomas Hartnell lost his 25-year-old brother and shipmate John.[2] A warning from the Book of Haggai was chiseled in Able Seaman Hartnell's headboard, and left to moan in the piercing wind:

THUS SAITH THE LORD OF HOSTS, CONSIDER YOUR WAYS.[3]

In the depths of winter, *Erebus* and *Terror* were imprisoned off Beechey Island, in Barrow Strait—a stone's throw away from what became an isthmus of graves. Not even a year since departing England and two of Franklin's men were already dead. Still another followed that April,[4] making for a trio of sentinels guarding the eastern gateway of the North-West Passage.

Well over three thousand miles to the south, the warm Caribbean breeze wasn't the only thing that blew in Robert McClure's face. In Havana Harbor, onboard the receiving ship *Romney*, he also felt the fiery sting of political discontent. In response to a complaint by Vice Admiral Sir Francis W. Austen, Commander-in-Chief of the North America and West Indies Station (and brother of Jane Austen), lowly Lieutenant McClure penned a letter attempting to explain his recent conduct.[5]

The nature of McClure's misbehavior doesn't rise to the surface of his naval service record, but the lieutenant's earlier correspondence to Austen makes it likely McClure became embroiled in the question of the *Romney*'s continued presence in paradise. The Spaniards' "honour takes fire at the bare idea of the British Government possessing an inch of Cuban ground; so it is far from improbable this vessel may be continued."[6]

Towards the end of January, terse words inked upon McClure's record again bespoke of similar straits: "22 Jan 1846. Secretary of State for Foreign Affairs complaining of the improper & disrespectful conduct of Lieut. McClure towards the Consul General at the Havannah."[7] By this date, the ship was sold to the government of Her Catholic Majesty, and McClure had already set sail for home with *Romney's* officers, crew and Marines.[8]

But the dark cloud that hung over McClure concealed a silver lining which only revealed itself that October, when the vicious Great Havana Hurricane sliced through southwestern Cuba. Roaring winds topped 135 miles per hour, and monstrous 30-foot waves wrecked 85 merchant ships and obliterated coastal villages; in a matter of hours nearly every building in Havana lay in ruins. The official butcher's bill was 163, though some disputed reports put the number as high as 600—save one lucky Irishman.[9]

*No hay mal que por bien no venga.*—"There is no evil from which some good may not be derived," flows the Spanish proverb.[10]

Representing the only blemishes on his record thus far, the transgressions McClure committed in Cuba may have kept him "beached" for a full year. He only found employment again in January 1847, as the lieutenant of Camber Coast Guard Station (No. 84), in East Sussex. Some ten miles down the coast from the station, wife Mary was settled in at 6 St. Mary's Terrace, in the picturesque seaside town of Hastings.[11]

Again, McClure's career was going nowhere—but in good time the Arctic opened its doors once more, and invited him back to opportunity.

With still no word from Franklin's expedition, Jane Franklin started worrying about her husband, and had written Sir James Clark Ross the previous month, receiving reassurances of a bright future reply. For Sir John Ross, however, a dark road lay ahead, and he began assaulting the Admiralty in January for a relief expedition. But their Lordships had offered a reward for any news of Franklin, and were quite content to await any information supplied by whalers and fur traders.[12]

Still, the Admiralty had not entirely shut its eyes to looming possibilities, and a three-pronged relief effort slowly began to take shape over many months.[13]

In April, approval came for a plan put forth by Sir George Simpson, the Governor-in-Chief of Rupert's Land (the territories of the Hudson's Bay Company (HBC), a fur trading company comprising nearly forty percent of modern Canada). Upon Sir George's recommendation, a large supply of pemmican was to be manufactured in England so an overland relief expedition could leave caches (stores of supplies) for Franklin. Pemmican was a concentrated mixture of dried meat and fat used by nineteenth- and twentieth-century polar explorers as a nutritious, high-energy (albeit unpleasant-tasting) food.[14]

However, it was November before the expedition leader, Sir John Richardson (formerly surgeon and naturalist, and second-in-command during Franklin's two earlier overland expeditions) had a second officer appointed to him—only after the last of the Davis Strait whalers returned without any news of Franklin. This was Dr. John Rae,[15] a chief trader with the HBC, who came as the result of Richardson's recommendation. An outstanding outdoorsman and hunter, Rae was from the Orkney Islands and was inured to the harsh wilds of North America, having learned the survival skills of its indigenous peoples.[16]

Among the native groups were people historically known as Eskimos (or "Esquimaux" in many original texts). Today, they call themselves Inuit, meaning "people" (plural; Inuk— singular), the preferred term in Canada and Greenland. Conversely, among the Inuit of Canada, kabloona (or kabloonak/kablunak) is the word for a person who is not of Inuit ancestry, especially a white person. The terms Eskimo/Esquimaux and kabloona were in use during the time period concerned in these writings.[17]

By the following August, Richardson, Rae and a party of Iroquois and French Canadian *voyageurs* in canoes, were on the North American coast, with orders to search the central Arctic, between the Mackenzie and Coppermine Rivers, and on the southern shores of Wollaston Peninsula, Victoria Island.[18]

The other two prongs of the search were naval ones, spawning a whole new generation of Arctic officers and men.

In January 1848, the Admiralty sent HMS *Plover* (Commander Thomas E.L. Moore) to act as a supply depot on the northwestern coast of Russian America, and during summers, search the coast in boats as far as the Mackenzie River. Moore, who had served as a junior officer onboard *Terror* (Crozier) in the Antarctic and commanded the *Pagoda* in Antarctic waters in 1845, was to also make contact with Eskimos and learn of any information about Franklin. The *Plover* was to work in concert with HMS *Herald* (Captain Henry Kellett, an Irishman from Tipperary), when the latter broke away from her Pacific surveying voyage to make summer searches through the Bering Strait.[19]

Another expedition, set to follow Franklin's trail, was composed of two vessels, HMS *Enterprise* and HMS *Investigator* (originally intended to be named the *Sir Edward Parry*). Robert McClure volunteered, and was now ushered back onto the Arctic stage to serve side-by-side, and form a lasting friendship with, none other than Sir James Clark Ross.[20]

Ross had been allowed to choose his officers, and so on March 9, McClure was assigned as his first lieutenant onboard *Enterprise*.[21] From now on, Ross became bonded to McClure's future, as did several of the expedition's officers and men who were soon to cut their teeth on the Arctic.

As in all naval vessels, there was a specific hierarchy: officers (captain, lieutenant, mate, surgeon, etc.); warrant officers (gunner, boatswain, carpenter, etc.); petty officers (quartermaster, boatswain's mate, captain of the forecastle, etc.); able seamen and ordinary seamen; and an unclassed group (carpenter's crew, subordinate officers' steward, gunroom cook, etc.). The ship's officers and warrant officers had their own cabins, and the former dined in a wardroom (also called the gunroom), while the crew slept in hammocks and were divided into messes of several men each.[22]

In 1835, the government gave the naval service more overall structure by introducing the registration of seamen with the passage of the Merchant Shipping Act. This allowed for the identification of every registered seaman with a unique number, and acted (very loosely) like a naval reserve, with even those on active naval duty being registered. The Registrar General of Shipping and Seamen initially compiled indexed registers of seamen from crew lists, and then issued each individual with a "seaman's" or "master's" register ticket.[23]

However, it was not until "the Naval Enlistment Act, 1853 (16 & 17 Vict. Cap. 73) was passed in parliament, allowing the Admiralty to draft Coastguardsmen (and pensioners) to ships of the Fleet at times of emergency which rendered—in the Admiralty's opinion—such a course advisable. From this time all members of the Coastguard were in every sense 'Fleet Reservists.'"[24]

*Enterprise*'s navigating (warrant) officer was 21-year-old Second Master Stephen Court, who lost his father at the tender age of five, when the smack *Rhine* went down while sailing from London to Rotterdam. Six years later, Court entered the Greenwich Hospital School to study the art of navigation, afterwards serving in the mail packet service between his native Folkestone and Brazil.[25]

Among the lower deck men, Quartermaster Henry May was a true old salt, who was born in 1800, and first went to sea 11 years later. He sported gray hair and a mermaid emblazoned on his left arm, and not uncommon among sailors, May wasn't favored with the three Rs. Somewhat ironically, Able Seaman Michael Flynn's Irish gait had recently strode the decks of HMS *America*, at a time when droves were fleeing the Irish Potato Famine by emigrating to the United States. Standing five feet six inches, the brown-haired and blue-eyed Subordinate Officers' Steward Mark Sunday Bradbury hailed from Whitechapel, and went by the alias Mark Bradbury. By the 1840s, Whitechapel (the scene of many a gruesome crime decades on) was among several districts, collectively known today as "the East End," that were classic Dickensian London, festering with poverty and overcrowding.[26]

The other expedition ship was to be HMS *Investigator*, commanded by Captain Edward Joseph Bird, Ross's close friend and companion on both Arctic and Antarctic voyages.[27]

Soon to step on her deck was 20-year-old Mate Samuel Gurney Cresswell, who had spent the first five years of his fledgling naval career in the Far East, tangling with Borneo pirates. As a midshipman, he was "in the personal staff of Rear Adm! Sir Thos Cochrane at the destruction of the Forts and Batteries of the River Bruné in Borneo [on July 8], 1846," earning a Mention in Dispatches (MID).[28]

Cresswell's home county of Norfolk was also birthplace to the best-known British sailor of all—Horatio Nelson—who, as a teenaged midshipman, had voyaged on an Arctic expedition half a century before. But it was due to the encouragement of another lustrous seaman that Cresswell volunteered for Arctic service: Sir Edward Parry, in whom Cresswell had both a friend and a mentor. As an observant and gifted watercolorist, Samuel was destined to record Arctic history with a rainbow of realism.[29]

At nearly six feet tall, towering Boatswain's Mate Edward Fawcett had several inches on most men of his day. Brought up to the fishing trade before joining his first Royal Navy ship in the 1830s, Fawcett was a married man who brandished an anchor tattoo on his right arm— so was dually devoted to his wife *and* the mistress of the sea. No stranger to the frozen climes, Fawcett shipped in *Erebus* for the 1839–43 Antarctic journeys. Her surgeon and naturalist, Robert McCormick, chanced upon one of Franklin's officers (Captain Crozier) in London in March 1845, who informed him that Fawcett was going out with Franklin. But Fawcett was a boatswain's mate aboard the surveying ketch *Sparrow* (west coast of Scotland) between 1844 and 1846, so it was his good fortune not to sail with the ill-fated expedition. Still, considering at least 12 Antarctic men from *Erebus* and *Terror* did go out with Franklin, Fawcett likely had an emotional investment in the search.[30]

Shipmate John Calder's hazel eyes had gazed upon a good bit of the world during his globetrotting adventures in the merchant service, far removed from his Somerset farming roots, and the butcher's apprenticeship he served in London from age 14; he abandoned that trade in the spring of 1840 for a seaman's life. Merchantmen took him to South Australia, and from there, he was engaged in different jobs for several months in Van Diemen's Land (Tasmania), with the next two years being divided between China and Bombay (Mumbai), before returning to England. Still having a taste for salt and further adventure, Calder signed onto HMS *Eagle* as an able seaman in 1844, roaming to such places as Aden, the Persian Gulf, India, and various South American ports.[31]

Able Seamen William Carroll, George Olley and Peter Thompson were all in their 20s, and thorough sailors. Carroll and Olley hailed from Greenwich, while Thompson, a Yarmouth man, had very recently served with Calder on the *Eagle*. The sailor's world was a small one—even more so for Arctic men—and former shipmates frequently crossed paths.[32]

*Enterprise* was laid down as a merchant vessel at the Blackwall yard of Money Wigram & Son, and purchased by the Admiralty in February 1848; *Investigator* was ordered built by John Scott & Sons of Greenock and purchased in the same month. *Enterprise* displaced 471 tons empty, while *Investigator* was 422 (both Builder's Old Measurements). Fully loaded, *Enterprise* displaced 530 tons and *Investigator* 480 tons.[33]

In order to harness every breath of wind, sailing ships were necessarily complex and sophisticated craft. *Enterprise* and *Investigator* were barque-rigged vessels,[34] an arrangement which consisted of a bowsprit and three masts—foremast, mainmast and mizzenmast. Two sails were placed fore-and-aft from the bowsprit, whereas the first two masts were square-rigged, having horizontal spars (known as yards) fastened on them, from which sails were set. The mizzenmast handled two sails, set fore-and-aft.

Literally miles of cordage, reminiscent of a den of spiders, attended to the raising, lowering and controlling of yards and sails (running rigging), or supporting the masts (standing rigging). In order to remain as flexible as possible, running rigging did not get tarred or receive any other preparation, whereas standing rigging was generally fixed and tarred to protect it from the elements.[35]

Underlying the operation of a sailing ship were skills sailors developed that fell into two basic areas: (1) navigation—making and taking in sail, steering, trimming sail (adjusting sails and yards so that they properly receive the wind), and carrying out related tasks on watch; and (2) shipboard maintenance—scraping, sanding, oiling and painting wooden planks, tarring and replacing rigging, paying pitch into deck seams, etc. It was a never-ending fight against wind and wave.[36]

The *Investigator* was towed to Greens' Yard at Blackwall, where she (and presumably her consort) were strengthened both internally and externally to resist the pressure of the pack ice. Several inches of English and Canadian woods were laid onto the hulls above and below the waterlines, while two layers of one and one-half-inch African boards were crossed diagonally to reinforce the lower decks. And the upper decks were layered in three-inch fir plank. The ships' bluff bows, and sterns, were strengthened from within by wood sleepers, breastworks and iron crutches. On the outside, the bows were fortified, and galvanized iron plates ⁵⁄₁₆-inch thick fitted overtop. In addition, *Enterprise* and *Investigator* were fitted with iron rubbing plates (a rubbing plate is a false keel for protecting a vessel's keel-plate against damage in grounding).[37]

In spite of the impressive sounding modifications, the eye of "an old seaman who had grown gray amongst the ice" captured the essence of reinforcing Arctic-bound vessels:

> Lord, Sir! You would think by the quantity of wood they are putting into them ships, that the dockyard maties believed they could stop the Almighty from moving the floes in Baffin Bay! Every pound of African wood they put into them the less likely they are to rise to pressure; and you must, in the ice, either rise or sink. If the floe cannot pass through the ship it will go over it.[38]

To form insulation, the ships' sides between decks were covered with felt, and then overlaid with three-quarter-inch fir boards. Arrangements for heating and ventilation were provided by Sylvester's Warming Apparatus (stove). This invention by civil engineer John Sylvester featured "hot-air pipes, enclosed in an outer casing, to convey the warm air throughout the ship; and copper tubes, also enclosed in casing, to carry the foul air to the upper deck."[39]

All in all, through the eyes of Commander Sherard Osborn, the *Investigator* presented a rather dull sight:

> Everything in the shape of outward ornament was of course carefully eschewed, and a solemn coating of black paint, but little relieved by a white riband and small figurehead, added yet more to the appearance of strength and weight of the little, but I am afraid I cannot say <u>pretty</u>, vessel.[40]

With high hopes, Ross sailed on May 12, 1848, and in writing to his parents six days later, Cresswell compared *Investigator*'s sailing qualities to that of her consort: "The *Enterprise* sails a little faster than we do before the wind, but I think on a wind we have the best of it. This I think is because she is not so deep as we are, [her full weight] being 60 tons larger and only having the same stores and men that we have."[41]

On June 20, Lieutenant Francis L. McClintock (third-in-command of the *Enterprise*),[42] who was destined to make a name for himself in the Arctic, noted in his journal: "This day is a notable one to us, as we found ourselves the first time within the Arctic Circle—only 4 persons onboard had crossed the Frigid Zone before."[43]

A fellow Irishman, McClintock was from Dundalk, and of a very different character and background from McClure; still, they shared one commonality—neither enjoyed "interest" in the Navy. McClintock was unemployed in early 1848 when he volunteered for Arctic service, so Captain William H. Smyth (an old shipmate from HMS *Samarang*) recommended him to Ross, and the veteran explorer immediately took to the 28-year-old polar novice.[44]

Ross was of the opinion that the missing ships had sailed southwesterly from Cape Walker, Russell Island (eastern Viscount Melville Sound). If correct, it meant they were stuck in the ice somewhere in the vicinity of Banks Land, and to all appearances, Ross did not expect his ships to make contact with *Erebus* and *Terror*, since following their presumed route would also trap him in the same treacherous Beaufort Sea ice stream. Instead, one of Ross's sledding parties would find Franklin, make him aware of arrangements for his relief, and provide direction if his ships had to be abandoned.[45]

But as it happened, *Enterprise* and *Investigator* met with very unfavorable ice conditions, and it was the end of August before they arrived in Lancaster Sound. All attempts to proceed down Prince Regent Inlet, or reach Wellington Channel and Melville Island through Barrow Strait, were fruitless—everything was jammed with ice. The ships went into winter quarters at Port Leopold (on the northeast tip of Somerset Island) by mid–September.[46]

In order to communicate with whalers in Baffin Bay, Ross was supplied with two steam pinnaces. They "were used to carry provisions and stores to form a depot at Whaler Point, at the entrance to the harbour two miles from the anchorage. Although the initial use of the steam pinnaces had proved satisfactory, the machinery was removed, for some reason not explained, and the boats hauled up ashore." This was the first time in any Arctic expedition that steam pinnaces were provided, and throughout the voyage, Ross repeatedly fed McClure earfuls of stern warnings against ever taking on anyone with a background in steam propulsion.[47] These cautionary words became ingrained in McClure's mind.

In spite of winter's dormant ways, there was an academic flowering; Lieutenant McClintock highlights the scene in his journal:

> The School commenced a few evenings ago, & now boasts of 24 scholars. All can read except one. The clerk officiates as schoolmaster, & initiates them in the mysteries of the three R's. And a young Masters

HMS *Investigator* in Winter Quarters at Port Leopold, 1848–49 (Henry C. Selous, *The Illustrated London News*, Feb. 23, 1850; courtesy Russell A. Potter).

Assistant from the Greenwich School, teaches Navigation to a select few who aspire to become Navigators. The degree of zeal & attention all of these men display is as astonishing as it is praiseworthy. They tuck their sleeves up, square their elbows, draw in a long breath, & go at the pot hooks & hangers, like men bent on conquest. Some get on very well indeed, & all rejoice at the anticipated astonishment of their wives on receiving epistles written in a greatly improved hand. With the most ignorant the grand desi[g]natum is to be able to write their own letters to their wives; They care less about learning to read.[48]

On St. Andrew's Day (November 30), commemorating the patron saint of Scotland, McClintock observed his band of brothers: "Sir James dined with us; on discussing our nationality we discovered our party to consist of 4 Irishmen—M'Clure, M'Clintock, Browne & Mathias, 2 Scotch—Sir Jas. & Robertson, & 1 English—[Acting Paymaster & Purser] Biggs ... an unusual preponderance of Irish for the Navy."[49]

Just seven days earlier, 84-year-old Sir John Barrow, the architect of British Arctic exploration for the first half of the nineteenth century, died in London without ever knowing the fate of the men who were his final instruments in attempting to discover the North-West Passage.[50]

On the other side of the Arctic, on Christmas Day a dinner was being enjoyed onboard HMS *Plover*, snug in her winter quarters at Providence Bay (now Bukhta Provideniya, a fjord along the southern coast of Siberia's Chukchi Peninsula). Blacksmith William Riggs, who had served in the Antarctic under Crozier, asked his shipmates to raise their metal cups in a toast mixed with a sense of foreboding: "Sir John Franklin, the officers and men comprising his expedition; may we find them, and in health and safety, and not in the lamentable condition to which it is feared they have been reduced."[51] Over the winter, one of the creative methods aimed at assisting Franklin during the course of what would become a long search, was put into play. Foxes were captured alive in traps, fitted with special copper collars stamped with the positions of *Enterprise* and *Investigator*, and supply caches (depots), and then released. It was hoped they would at some point be caught by the lost explorers.[52]

When the spring of 1849 arrived, sled parties were organized and dispatched. Ross, McClintock and 12 men formed the main traveling party, searching along the northern and western coasts of Somerset Island, down Peel Sound to 72° 38′ N. Along the way, Ross named not one, but two geographic features after McClure, a bay and a cape, which grace the map to this day, along with Cape Court. Three other parties were sent out: one crossed Barrow Strait to Cape Hurd, Devon Island; one crossed Prince Regent Inlet, reaching near the northern end of Brodeur Peninsula, and a third examined the east coast of Somerset Island south to Cresswell Bay.[53]

All the searching produced ... *nothing.* If the party crossing Barrow Strait had been able to reach Beechey Island (at the entrance to Wellington Channel), it would have discovered the first winter quarters of *Erebus* and *Terror.*

Ross now faced a grave situation. The health of the crews was affected to a great extent by scurvy, combated in part by the regular issue of lemon juice. It was afterwards discovered that the faulty preparation of lemon juice provided to the expedition probably "destroyed much of the anti-scorbutic value of the juice." As a result, a special inspector was sent to Sicily to oversee the preparation of future supplies of lemon juice.[54] Twentieth century research was able to paint a clearer picture of the disease: "Once thought to be a disease carried by the deficiency of one vitamin, ascorbic acid [Vitamin C], Arctic scurvy was probably a group of diseases, perhaps caused not only by deficiency of ascorbic acid, but also other essential factors such as niacin, riboflavin, or thiamine."[55] If left untreated, scurvy is invariably fatal. The early stages of the disease produce any of the following symptoms: gums become soft, tender and spongy, and teeth fall out; internal bleeding, and spots appear in various parts of the body, more so on the thighs and legs, looking like small blood-blisters, red and purple in color; severe joint and muscular pain; skin becomes pale, eyes are sunken, and the victim may be extremely irritable and appears depressed. Exhaustion, diarrhea, fainting, kidney or lung disease follow.[56]

Dr. John Robertson (*Enterprise*) described the salt provisions as "bad in quality and deficient in quantity, and the preserved meats were a disgrace to the contractor." Many cans were found to be underweight.[57]

To add to Ross's troubles, despite the ships' being able to work their way out of Port Leopold at the end of August, within a few days, westerly winds shepherded the ice pack down upon them, frustrating any more searching. *Enterprise* and *Investigator* were carried steadily eastward for some 250 miles (400 km) over the coming three weeks. And even though open water was finally reached, all hope of sailing westward again and finding a safe harbor so late in the season had vanished. Ross sailed for home, arriving November 4. The ships were paid-off three weeks later.[58]

In spite of the disappointing results, the late expedition produced a new crop of experienced Arctic officers and men for the ongoing Franklin Search, along with Ross's development of new sledding techniques.[59]

Four days later, Richardson turned up. He and Rae had covered the coast from the

Mackenzie to Coppermine Rivers, but there was no evidence of Franklin. Rae had continued the search until September, and would begin again the following autumn, under the direction of the HBC.[60]

Just a few weeks before Ross and Richardson reached London, the editors of the *Illustrated London News* captured the mood of the nation:

> But of all the Expeditions which private enterprise or public policy has fitted out for the exploration of the still unknown regions of the globe, the several expeditions for the discovery of the northwest passage are looked upon by the people of this country, and by the world in general, with the greatest interest and anxiety. The failure of one expedition is but incentive to fit out another; and the greater the danger, the greater the eagerness of enterprising and resolute men.[61]

When Franklin departed in 1845, he, his men, and *Erebus* and *Terror*, represented the very essence of the British character, which was wrapped up in one grand package of nationalistic pride and the unshakable belief in man's unquestioned superiority over the natural world. The Americans possessed the same spirit and pride over a century later, when their *Apollo 13* spacecraft blasted off at Cape Kennedy, hurtling three explorers toward the moon—and near-disaster.

Cresswell, for one, wrote to his parents after his arrival, "Thank God I am once more in old England.... We have not discovered a trace of Sir John Franklin or any of his party. I fear they have all perished."[62]

Before this time, Lady Franklin increased a personal reward to any whaler bringing news of the missing expedition to £3,000, and Parliament had announced a reward of £20,000. But now Lady Franklin's thoughts shifted. She wrote to John Rae that she intended to ask the Admiralty to increase the reward offered to £50,000—"not only to finding them living, but to finding any memorials [artifacts or graves] of them, or obtaining any certain intelligence of their fate."[63]

Unrevealed at this point were any doubts McClure may have harbored about the fate of Franklin and his men. However, with two northern winters behind him (being especially fortunate to escape the ice in 1837), McClure *knew* what the Arctic could do to a man's body—and mind.

McClure's most recent Arctic experience put him in an advantageous position; he was at the right time and right place. Having spent the previous year and a half making a good impression on James Clark Ross, McClure also probably fit in well with his superior's reputation as a stern disciplinarian. In addition, Ross's character was shaped both personally and professionally through his nine years of Arctic voyaging with Parry. Both polar legends held deep religious convictions, and throughout his letters, McClure gives the impression that, at the very least, he felt God sided with his ambitions.[64]

McClure was "promoted to be a Commander for his services in the Arctic Expedition" (November 4), and his service record glowed with, "Captain Sir James Ross highly recommending him as an officer of very great merit" (November 26). The promotion meant McClure's monthly wage as a senior lieutenant jumped from £15 to just over £23. By contrast, an able seaman received £1 14 shillings per month, only slightly more than his counterpart in 1815.[65]

Having been intimately involved in the organization of Franklin's expedition, Ross still believed *Erebus* and *Terror* were in the vicinity of Banks Land. Ross, and other experts, recommended an expedition sail through the Bering Strait to find them.[66] This "put" Franklin and the western end of the North-West Passage in the same area of the map, and after spending the past eighteen months as Ross's second-in-command, McClure would have been well aware of his captain's views. McClure's self-made destiny was beginning to come into focus.

With the British public now jolted out its complacency for Franklin's safety, arrangements moved forward for additional official and privately funded seaborne expeditions—including an American one—to leave in the spring of 1850 and search Wellington Channel.[67]

Ross's plan for an expedition through the Bering Strait was put forward by the Hydrographer of the Navy on November 24. It was based on the assumption that Franklin's ships must be trapped somewhere west of Melville Island. This plan was approved, and *Enterprise* and *Investigator* were selected for reequipping in haste, to prepare for sailing on January 20, 1850. While the ships were being refitted, officers had to be appointed, crews selected, and arrangements for provisioning, clothing, sled traveling, scientific observations and communications all needed to be carried out by ships' officers—there was no time to spare.[68]

Captain Richard Collinson (*Enterprise*), received his appointment as senior officer of the expedition on December 14. He hoisted his pennant on that very day, while seeing the ships being sheathed in copper below their waterlines at the Woolwich Dockyard.[69] Copper sheathing helped to prevent the growth of marine plants and organisms. It appears the ships were not coppered for the 1848–49 expedition, but the process was now applied since they were to sail the tropical regions of the Atlantic and Pacific.

In addition, *Enterprise's* barque rigging was altered to ship-rigged, which had some advantages when the wind was behind the ship, or over the quarter.[70] Her mizzenmast was now fitted with two horizontal yards to set a square sail, while having the upper gaff removed. Collinson wrote that since the ships had "recently returned from Lancaster Sound, their fittings were complete, and but few alterations required for our passage through the tropics,"[71] and it would seem that any orders for changes in the sail arrangement must have come from him.

Since coppering increases the speed of a ship, this, along with the altered sail arrangement on *Enterprise*, meant she possessed even more of a speed advantage over the slower *Investigator* (as mentioned earlier by Cresswell). Contemporary images show *Investigator* remained barque-rigged[72]; why wasn't she altered as well?

Unknown to her captain, one more factor added to the *Enterprise's* speed advantage: in the depths of the Arctic three years later, Collinson discovered the stock of coal originally put onboard at Plymouth was *18 tons short*.[73] The even greater disparity in speed between the vessels came to echo with irony, as the difference in the sailing qualities between *Enterprise* and *Investigator* became a strange ally to McClure's ambitions.

Collinson possessed only very limited polar experience, while a midshipman onboard HMS *Chanticleer* in 1829, when the ship spent two months among the South Shetland Islands, off the Antarctic Peninsula. However, it was Collinson's considerable skill and experience in marine surveying which would be so very valuable in the dangerous, uncharted Arctic waters. Collinson, and the *Chanticleer's* first lieutenant, Horatio Thomas Austin, became lifelong friends. Now a captain, Austin was chosen to lead a four-ship naval squadron (*Assistance, Resolute, Pioneer,* and *Intrepid*), set to leave for the eastern Arctic in May.[74]

But the connections to Arctic officers didn't stop there. Collinson's friend and former messmate, Captain Henry Kellett, commanded the *Herald,* and was tasked with resupplying the *Plover* (stationed along the Bering Strait). In addition, Captain Sir Edward Belcher, one of Collinson's former commanding officers, came to lead a Franklin Search expedition in 1852.[75]

The newly promoted Commander McClure became captain of HMS *Investigator* on December 18; it was McClure's first *seagoing* command in 25 years of naval service. Many of his contemporaries were not so fortunate; for example, in January 1848, of the Navy's 873 active commanders, only a mere 148 (17 percent) were employed.[76]

Coupling Collinson's and McClure's experiences appeared to be an excellent match for the arduous voyage ahead, and perhaps this played into the Admiralty's line of thought when making these selections.

At five feet, nine inches in height, topped off by a receding hairline surrounded by wavy brown hair, McClure was taller than the average man of his day. Gray eyes and a slim, prominent nose occupied the center of his thin, fresh-complected features, the whole being sandwiched between a pair of long sideburns.[77] However, time is a thief, and with McClure coming up on 43 years of age, the expedition probably represented one of his last opportunities to make his mark, and send him further down the road to attaining a captain's rank.

Everything was moving at a rapid pace, and paper flew as Collinson attended to the copious details needing to be worked out for the long voyage ahead. On New Year's Day, *Enterprise* and *Investigator* were hauled out into the river, and on the tenth, towed downriver to Greenhithe, where their compasses were adjusted (all compasses are subject to deviation, and for reliable navigation a routine calibration check is essential).[78] Second Master Francis Skead (*Enterprise*) described the scene the following day:

> We were towed through the Downs by steam tugs which were cast off when abreast of Deal. Our passage down the river was greeted by numerous salutes both of guns and right hearty English cheers—impressing us with a deep sense of the universal interest the fate of our missing countrymen had awakened, as well as assuring us of the heartfelt good wishes for our success that accompanied us.[79]

After struggling through bad weather in the Channel, the ships anchored in Plymouth Sound on the afternoon of the 16th.[80]

Meanwhile, the Admiralty Orders (dated January 15) were in Collinson's hands by the 18th, and McClure was supplied with a printed copy of them[81] (see Appendix 4 for extracts from the Admiralty orders).

Following the orders until the expedition reached Point Barrow (the northernmost tip of Russian America) were straightforward—or so it seemed: Supplied with provisions for three years, in addition to a large amount of extra stores, *Enterprise* and *Investigator* were to make for Cape Virgins on the southeastern tip of

**Captain Robert John Le Mesurier McClure, RN** (*The Illustrated London News*, Nov. 5, 1853).

Argentina, where a naval steamship would tow them through the Strait of Magellan. After stopping at Valparaiso and the Sandwich Islands (Hawaiian Islands) for watering, replenishment of fresh provisions, and resting the crews, they were to proceed to the Bering Strait in order to reach the ice by August 1.[82] This last portion was imperative, so as to take advantage of the navigable season before the onset of winter—*time* was of the essence if *any* of the lost explorers were to be found alive. HMS *Plover*, the depot ship and point of relief for Franklin, was to act in kind for Collinson's ships, should any party need to fall back after entering the ice.[83]

Their Lordships' instructions strongly emphasized specific elements, shown in these excerpts:

16. We leave it to your judgment and discretion as to the course to be pursued after passing Point Barrow, and on entering the ice; and you will be materially assisted in this respect by what you will learn from Captain Kellett, if he should be fallen in with at the Sandwich Islands, as well as from the observations of Sir E. Parry and Captain Beechey contained in the memoranda, of which we send you copies.

18. We deem it right to caution you against suffering the two vessels placed under your orders to separate, except in the event of accidental or unavoidable necessity; and we desire that you will keep up the most unreserved communication with the Commander of the "Investigator," placing in him every proper confidence, and acquainting him with the general tenor of your orders, and with your views and intentions from time to time....

20. In case of any irreparable accident happening to the "Enterprize," you are hereby authorized to take command of the "Investigator," and to make such arrangements for the officers and crews as may be most consonant to the rules of the service, and most conducive to the objects of the Expedition.

23. With respect to your search proving fruitless, and your finally quitting the Polar Seas, as well as your securing your winter quarters towards the close of any one season, we cannot too strongly impress upon you the necessity of the utmost precaution and care being exercised in withdrawing in time; so as in no case to hazard the safety of the ships, and the lives of those entrusted to your care, by your being shut up in a position which might render a failure of provisions possible.

24. You will bear in mind that the object of the Expedition is to obtain intelligence, and to render assistance to Sir John Franklin and his companions, and not for the purpose of geographical or scientific research....[84]

No. 20 made reference to "the objects of the Expedition," and although this may refer to the "intelligence" and "render assistance" in no. 24, there is at least the suggestion of something more. And in spite of the additional wording in directive no. 24, as a matter of course, geographical discovery and natural history observations were normal consequences of all Franklin Search expeditions. Along these lines, *Investigator* was identified as Her Majesty's *Discovery* Ship in her Letter & Order Book (and within other official records), and Dr. Armstrong was in part recommended to *Investigator* due to his achievements as a naturalist. Indeed, Collinson was tasked with making various scientific observations, to include the areas of meteorology, magnetism and atmospheric air, with glass bottles being supplied for taking samples in different parts of the globe.[85] Yet it remained to be seen if the line between the intended focus of the expedition and geographical discovery became blurred by the ambitious Robert McClure.

Oddly for a search and rescue mission, "the *Enterprise* and *Investigator* were not well fitted out for sledge travelling." This was evidently a reference to the type, quality, or number of sleds and sledding provisions provided for the voyage, since on March 6 and 12, 1851, just prior to the first spring sledding season, Carpenter Ford noted in his journal that the *Investigator*'s carpenters were "making new sleds." The time available for fitting out was most likely a factor, and (as Ford's writings might suggest) they were expected to improvise during

**Mr. Green's Signal Balloon and Parachutes (*The Illustrated London News*, May 11, 1850).**

the voyage. Neither Collinson or McClure had any sledding experience, so perhaps beforehand they also didn't put sufficient thought in this direction.[86]

Along with fox collars—like those used by Ross—the present expedition (and ones afterward) were provided with other ingenious items intended to alert Franklin and his men of the search for them. Gilt metal clothing buttons (termed "rescue buttons" or "postal buttons"), with wording in relief about the locations of vessels and caches of provisions, were to be given to and worn by Eskimos, in the theory they might come into contact with the lost men and the information would be discovered. Hydrogen-filled balloons carrying small parachutes and batches of messages on brightly colored paper were stitched to lengths of slow-burning fuses for release at intervals. Finally, a certain Mrs. Washington of Woolwich offered up dolls to be given to the Eskimos, so that if members of the Franklin expedition came across them, they would be aware assistance was in their vicinity.[87]

When it came to volunteers, there was no shortage of men willing to go north, and though altruism and adventure seeking played their roles, a financial incentive also invaded men's minds: double pay. It had long since become a common practice to offer double the ordinary wages to volunteers for polar expeditions, and for a voyage to the western Arctic, double pay commenced upon passing the meridian of Cape Horn. Some historians have stated that Royal Marines did not volunteer for polar service, but were ordered to go; and it has been additionally stated that Marines did not receive double pay for expeditions. Research by the author has proved both of these to be false assertions.[88]

Over the preceding month, officers were appointed, sailors signed on, and Royal Marines mustered. Eventually, 64 souls on *Enterprise* and 66 on *Investigator* spent most or all of the expedition in the Frozen Zone.

The noncommissioned officers and privates from the Woolwich Division, Royal Marines, were divided between each vessel into two detachments. Dubbed "Leathernecks," "Jollies," "Lobsters" (due to their scarlet coats), or simply "Boots," the marines fulfilled their traditional role of seagoing infantry.[89]

Though only armed with one light and one heavy brass 12-pounder cannon, shrapnel shells, and a small mortar, *Investigator* also carried "a large stock of muskets, pistols, hand grenades, and Congreve rockets."[90] The muskets were for hunting and rockets for signaling— except the armaments might just as easily be for use against human enemies.

The Admiralty Orders made specific mention of always being mindful of possible treacherous attacks by hostile Eskimo or Indian groups. But what if the weapons fell into the hands of disgruntled crewmen? Marines also provided internal security; they had guard duties, enforced regulations regarding sailors' conduct below decks, and stood by during punishments. Consequently, Marines are often associated with quelling that unthinkable act: *mutiny*.[91]

The sea soldiers had one more (unimaginably benign) role, due to the nature of the voyage. There was a shortage of the normal domestic help onboard, so: "Each officer has a [Marine] servant who keeps his cabin in order, does his washing and mending, etc. ... and for that receive twelve shillings a month in addition to their regular pay."[92]

In command of *Investigator*'s eight-man Marine detachment was Sergeant John Woon, a sturdy 25-year-old West Countryman. Having joined the Corps in 1844, just four years later he earned his sergeant's stripes. From top to bottom, Woon was every inch a Leatherneck, and would prove more than worthy during the severe trials ahead. His junior was a Scot and former blacksmith named John B. Farquharson, who had been promoted to Corporal 3rd Class only six months prior to joining *Investigator*.[93]

Of McClure's command, 14 officers and men had previous polar experience. Nearly all of them came directly from the 1848–49 expedition, including Lieutenant Cresswell (now third in command), Second Master Court, Able Seaman/Quartermaster Henry May, Captain of the Forecastle John Calder, and Captain's Steward Mark Bradbury. Onboard *Enterprise*, Collinson had the same number of people with polar experience.[94]

Two civilians on *Enterprise* and one on *Investigator* were from the whaling and sealing trade, and mustered onboard as ice mates for their expertise in ice navigation. The Royal Navy's use of civilians from these trades for Arctic expeditions stretched back three decades; their titles evolved from merchant master/mate, to Greenland master/mate, to finally ice master/mate. Due to the historical Scottish involvement in the whale and seal trades, such valuable men were invariably Scots; they had seen much ice as ship masters or first mates, and surely this was the case with William Newton on *Investigator*. At about 47 years of age, Newton was—next to May—the oldest man on the ship.[95]

Most intriguing about McClure's crew is the fact that *over half*—39 men—had been ship-mates with one other person onboard (and in some cases more than one) over the nine years prior to the expedition. This meant that the crew possessed a certain unity from the very start.[96]

When *Investigator* was commissioned, as men joined, those crewmembers whose work must be done at all times of the day and night were assigned to one of two watches (the starboard watch and the port watch). When at sea, the 24-hour day was divided into four-hour watches, each with an officer of the watch and 15 to 20 men.[97]

While McClure's crewmen were bonding through the renewal of old acquaintances, a grave fracture in his command was taking place—threatening the ship before she ever left England. And the problem started at the top. During the tow downriver, Cresswell's pen painted an ugly scene for his parents:

> The Capt. continues to be very civil to me but poor Haswell catches it on all occasions. Yesterday the Capt. went on in a most foolish way with him, saying that he should not be in his ship and that he was incompetent to be 1st Lieutenant, and that he would write to I do not know who about him.
> Now this is too bad particularly as Haswell is ten thousand times more of an officer and a sailor than our worthy Captain ever was or ever will be. Haswell would have had a row with the Capt. yesterday about his unreasonable conduct to him, but he is determined to put all he possibly can in his pipe and smoke it, as the saying is.
> I like all my messmates very much, and I think we will be very comfortable notwithstanding our Chief.[98]

Lieutenant William Henry Haswell was second in command, and had been under McClure's authority for just over three weeks. As first lieutenant, Haswell was tasked with seeing to the administration of the ship and upholding discipline. He was the 31-year-old son of a naval commander (of the same name) who was a Trafalgar veteran, as was his father (a Royal Navy carpenter). Haswell's father died in January 1831, the very year after his young son entered the naval service.[99]

Though Haswell was without polar experience, he'd seen his share of action: combat off Syria in 1840; anti-slaving operations from 1843 to 1845 (which entailed much work in ship's boats); active service in the River Plate, South America, in 1845 (promoted lieutenant the same year); and he was credited with capturing 13 slavers during 1847–49.[100]

Although it's uncertain whether either or both knew about it, there was a strange coincidental connection between Haswell and McClure. Haswell was a mate onboard HMS *Talbot* during the allied fleet's bombardment of St. Jean d'Acre off Syria, on November 3, 1840. Haswell's fellow officer onboard was a certain Lieutenant B.G. Le Mesurier—the nephew of McClure's godfather. In about the middle of the action, debris from a bar shot "struck Lieutenant Le Mesurier's watch as it lay in his trousers fob, smashing the works and injuring the Lieutenant's stomach; the officer fell and was carried below. Another fragment cut the leather from the upper part of one of Mr. Haswell's shoes, bruising his toes considerably." Le Mesurier died at five o'clock the following day, and was buried ashore with military honors on November 5; he was the only British officer in the fleet to die as a result of the battle.[101]

In addition to his active service, Haswell also made political connections—from 1846 to 1847, he served under Commodore Sir Charles Hotham, KCB (*Devastation*, flagship of the West African Squadron). Hotham "was a sound, but not a zealous nor brilliant, officer, and he had the misfortune to be exposed to the full glare of publicity during the whole period of his command," being under the eyes of Parliament and the press while he handled anti–slave trade operations.[102]

When Hotham moved his flag to HMS *Penelope* in 1847, Haswell went with him—as his flag lieutenant (personal assistant). Finally, in September 1848, while still in the *Penelope*, Hotham appointed Haswell an acting commander. The ship was paid-off in April 1849, and *Investigator* was Haswell's next ship. It's reasonable to assume Haswell felt (and/or was told) that after the Arctic expedition he would be assured promotion to commander.[103]

So why *did* McClure insist on humiliating his first lieutenant—a man whose support would be crucial during a long and difficult voyage—by declaring Haswell "should not be in his ship," and that he was "incompetent"? To some degree, the answer was wrapped up in Haswell's previous postings: the *Devastation* and *Penelope* were *steamships*. In fact, steam had made its mark against the slave trade, with Hotham reporting in March 1848 "that of fifty-nine slavers captured in the previous year, twenty-three were taken by steamers." Prior to these vessels, Haswell served in several sailing ships, and had been successively promoted, but was now well on his way to becoming the *Investigator's persona non grata*, because of the stern warnings Ross had repeatedly given McClure against ever taking on anyone with a background in steam propulsion.[104]

On January 16, a few hours before arriving in Plymouth Sound, off Devonport, with tensions simmering just below the surface, Cresswell acquainted his brother Joseph with the surroundings onboard:

> The Capt. has put such a rum little "mid" [jokingly, midshipman] in my watch, in the shape of our poor old ice mate, a man that has been to sea for the last 20 years. I would rather have been without him, as I should think he would not like to be under such a comparative youngster as myself, but I will try and make it as comfortable as I can for him.
>
> ...There has not been an open rupture between the Capt. and 1st Lieut. for a day or two, only a little gentle bullying &c. He still continues very civil to me, I think he is waiting until we leave England. I do not care a pin about him so you need not make yourself unhappy about my being uncomfortable.[105]

Over the following few days, Cresswell wrote final letters to his parents. He would not set pen to paper to them again until the ship was in the northern Pacific Ocean, on the verge of entering the Arctic.

*Investigator* took on coal and other provisions, and awaited the arrival of tinned meats at Devonport. "Poor Haswell has 5 sisters living here and as far as I can make out he supports them,"[106] sympathized Cresswell when he wrote of the senior lieutenant's birthplace. In fact, Haswell had 11 siblings in total, most of whom (like Haswell himself) never married,[107] and with his father long since passed away, the first lieutenant must have experienced ongoing financial pressure. Consequently, the strong prospect of promotion after the expedition— and accompanying rise in pay—would have been a particular presence in Haswell's mind.

"We have got about ¼ of our preserved meats on board, the rest have not yet arrived from Ireland.... Three of our men ran [deserted] last night, it was a very foolish thing paying them their six months in advance before leaving Greenhithe,"[108] fumed Cresswell. The *Investigator's* boatswain also slipped away, and the ship eventually sailed with this warrant officer's post vacant.

As he settled into the wardroom, Cresswell's wariness of McClure began to soften, "We have £580 of mess stock on board.... I get on as yet very well with the Capt. and think I shall.

We are <u>most</u> comfortable in our mess."[109] Wardroom officers privately supplemented their mess with various delicacies, wines and beer.[110]

The usual ship's fare over the course of the expedition included bread, salt beef and pork, preserved meat and ox cheek soup, along with potatoes, carrots, barley, rice, beans, dried cabbage, flour, oatmeal and chocolate; sometimes suet (raw beef or mutton fat) was issued in lieu of flour. Peas, pickles and cranberries were also served, along with cocoa for breakfast and tea with biscuit at night.[111]

Rum allowances onboard British men-o-war stretched back about 200 years, and during this time period grog was issued daily to the men, consisting of a gill (4.8 U.S. fl. oz.) of 50/50 rum and water.[112]

For naval crews' pleasure, ships usually carried tobacco leaf, "but in 1850 manufactured tobacco was adopted in Arctic discovery ships, to economise stowage; and *Cavendish*, or flat compressed slabs; or *negro-head*, or twisted sticks, were supplied by the Admiralty to Captains Collinson and Austin's expeditions."[113]

On the 18th, Mr. Gamble arrived from Dublin with his order of preserved meats.[114] Clerk-in-Charge Joseph Cave Paine was there to account for every morsel of food aboard *Investigator*. But that wasn't all: he was also responsible for the stocks of clothing, men's pay, and weekly musters, and he assisted the captain with the ship's books and paperwork.

In the early evening hours, a small boat crawled the three miles through a drenching rain to *Enterprise*. Two gentlemen of the Moravian Brotherhood scrambled on deck and

> found the crew busily taking on provisions, coal, etc.; a good many of them were drunk, and one was seated in irons near the wheel. Captain Collinson and his guest, Commander McClure on the *Investigator*, who had just finished their meal, welcomed me in the friendliest manner. Brother Van Deurs conversed for some time with the two captains, but I understood nothing of what they said. He then got into his boat and returned to Devonport. I was given temporary quarters in the captain's cabin where I enjoyed a good night's rest.[115]

Thirty-two-year-old Saxon Johann August Miertsching was an outsider onboard Her Majesty's ship in more ways than one: his tongue was German and his heart belonged to God. He had only returned to Germany from the Moravian mission station in Okak, Labrador, around the time Ross arrived in London in early November 1849. Miertsching's linguistic skills fated his return to frozen surroundings.[116]

An evangelical Protestant denomination, the Moravian Church has a heritage that stretches back to Bohemia in 1457 (now part of the Czech Republic). The Moravians were able to secure a land grant in Labrador from Britain's King George III in 1769, and they received support from their headquarters in England and Germany. Every year a ship was dispatched to the mission field. Moravian missionaries were the first large-scale Protestant missionary movement, and individuals were carefully chosen, as the mission field meant a lifetime commitment, or until age intervened.[117]

Miertsching's path to God began in Gröditz, Saxony (east of Dresden), in 1817. His father died when he was two, and he grew up with a Bohemian stepfather who was a shoemaker, and who taught Johann the Bohemian language. But humble circumstances did not enable him to provide schooling, so at fifteen, Johann was sent to the nearby Moravian settlement of Kleinwelka (now a subdivision of the city of Bautzen), where the boy followed his stepfather's trade and came to embrace the Lord's teachings.[118]

From 1844 onward, Brother Miertsching served as a missionary among the native people in Labrador. Acquiring the Eskimo language (in this case, Eastern Canadian Inuit) was difficult for Miertsching, since winter was the only period of the year that could be devoted to learning. Even so, by the fall of 1847, the Brother had gained some proficiency in the native tongue, but admitted, "I am not yet fully competent to carry on a discussion in the Esquimaux language." Miertsching did, however, master living and survival skills which were particular to those climes— hunting, dog sled driving, and judging ice conditions.[119]

When the Admiralty determined that an expedition was to be sent through the Bering Strait, their Lordships wrote to Parry, asking him communicate with Reverend Peter La Trobe (Secretary of the Moravian Missions, London) regarding obtaining one of the Moravian brethren to act as an interpreter in the Eskimo language. There not being a suitable person available in England, La Trobe wrote to the Mission Board in Herrnhut, Saxony. The Moravians consented—they were mindful of the protection and assistance provided by the

Johann August Miertsching (Emilian Fehrenbach of the Strand, 1854; courtesy Barbara Jannasch).

British to their missions (especially on the Labrador coast), and naturally saw an opportunity to spread the Gospel to Eskimo people who had not previously been captured by a European faith. La Trobe was then able to write to Captain Hamilton, Secretary of the Admiralty, on January 14 about "one whom I cannot but consider the best qualified for the discharge of its duties that could have been selected from the whole number of missionaries, either in retirement or on visits to Europe from their respective fields of labour in Greenland and Labrador." Thus, Johann Miertsching became the official interpreter of the expedition. He would be treated as an officer, and therefore saluted by the sailors and Marines.[120]

The Admiralty—and perhaps Miertsching himself—evidently assumed the native people of Labrador spoke the same language as those some 3,000 miles away. In fact, despite the differing dialects of Eastern and Western Canadian Inuit, Miertsching came to find he could usually get along quite well.[121]

The morning before the expedition was set to sail, Collinson took Miertsching into Devonport and had him fitted out with the necessary clothing and other articles. Afterward, the Brother "wandered about the town and dockyards until Captain Collinson, having finished his own business, brought me back at 6 p.m. to the *Enterprise*. On arriving there I was straightway transferred to the *Investigator*, because, as they explained to me, there was no cabin for me on the *Enterprise*." Upon the expedition's reaching Valparaiso, Miertsching was to be transferred back to his proper ship.[122]

Though occupied writing letters, McClure extended a warm welcome to Miertsching "and said many things to me which I did not understand," while all around people were hastily scribbling correspondence amid the clamor of provisions streaming onboard *Investigator*. Her decks and passageways were littered with casks, boxes and chests, in addition to all manner of items peculiar to their ultimate destination: sleds, ice triangles, ice saws, and a crow's nest.[123]

As he settled down to write letters in his seven-foot-square cabin that evening, only a bed, washstand, desk and chair occupied Miertsching's snug surroundings. The cabin had been prepared by his servant, Corporal 3rd Class Farquharson; the blond-haired, blue-eyed Perth native was to become the Brother's friend—and fellow evangelist. For the present, they "communicate more by signs than by words."[124]

6:00 a.m., Sunday, January 20, 1850: Anchor chains creaked their chorus and boatswains' pipes shrilled, sending nimble-footed sailors scurrying skyward, to array themselves along great wooden crosses, in order to release spreads of canvas and engulf the wind. HMS *Enterprise* and *Investigator* gently shuttled out to sea.[125]

Brother Miertsching's mind was heavily tinged with apprehension, as he soaked up his surroundings:

> Shall we see England or Europe again? and when? These are the questions which force themselves against one's will on every man; but it is impossible to answer them. Quite indescribable are the emotions that overwhelm everyone when such a ship sails—as on an arctic cruise—to an unknown destination, perhaps for two years, perhaps forever. The future is wrapped in obscurity.[126]

Miertsching went to his cabin and prayed ... alone with God.

# 3

# The Pacific, 1850

*Borders? I have never seen one. But I have heard they exist in the minds of some people.*

Thor Heyerdahl (1914–2002)

"We soon found that in point of sailing, we had the advantage over our consort," wrote Collinson. Even though the sea was kind to the expedition for the first few days, her mood turned ugly while *Investigator* was carrying a press of canvas to keep company with *Enterprise*:

> [A]t about six in the morning [of the 24th] the Fore-Top mast went, carrying with it the two Top Gallant Masts, Royal Masts, Flying boom and Fore Top Gallant yard, together with the After Crosstree of the Fore and Main Top Masts, gave sufficient employment for that day to clear away the wreck, and get another mast aloft, it blowing strong with a heavy sea running; this accident vexatious it certainly was, still, was attended with an advantage [as] it gave me an insight to the disposition of my crew, and a more willing, orderly set of men have seldom been collected.[1]

Collinson shortened sail and offered assistance, which McClure declined, so Collinson again made sail, "thinking that in light winds [*Investigator*] might have the advantage, [so] I determined on not delaying our progress by keeping company."[2]

It was "with great satisfaction" that Able Seaman James H. Nelson and his shipmates soon lost sight of *Enterprise*. Though "Keep a good look out for the *Enterprise*" often rang out on deck, the Investigators were worried their consort would enter the ice before them. Nelson knew *Enterprise* was a faster vessel, and in a sailor's eye, Collinson was giving *Investigator* a bad treatment.[3]

Like many of his fellow sailors, the 21-year-old Nelson initially went to sea as a boy, so when the Hampshire native joined the RN in July 1848, he was rated an ordinary seaman in HMS *President* (in which Passed Clerk/Secretary's Clerk Joseph C. Paine had been serving for three years). At the time, the 52-gun *President* was the flagship of the commander-in-chief of the Cape of Good Hope Station, Rear Admiral James Richard Dacres. Nearly four decades earlier, Dacres had earned a particular place in naval history, when he commanded the frigate HMS *Guerrière* during her close action with the stronger USS *Constitution*, to whom he surrendered after *Guerrière* was battered to a virtual wreck. While on *Investigator*, Nelson came to be warmly praised by Dr. Armstrong as "a young man of good education and ability, a universal favorite in the ship; he by his exertions in hunting, his cheerful character and other good qualities, ever acquitted himself in our trying service in a most credible manner."[4]

But hard feelings about Collinson's command weren't confined to the lower deck, as

Assistant Surgeon Henry Piers's pen suggested: "The 'Enterprise' came down to us, and having taken a look at our misfortune—and perhaps a laugh—stood on ahead of us and to windward." In fact, this son of the Reverend Octavius Piers (vicar of Preston, Dorset) had seen true human misfortune in the time prior to joining the Arctic expedition. The year after graduating with a medical diploma from Guy's Hospital in London, Piers found himself the acting assistant surgeon aboard the frigate HMS *Cleopatra* for most of 1842–47, engaged in anti-slaving patrol along the East Africa coast.[5]

While such accidents as the *Investigator*'s naturally created confusion and disorder, the sailors' past associations began to show themselves. McClure—not one to praise lightly—knew the importance of rewarding good work, so "at the termination of their exertions I directed an extra issue of spirits, which as all were drenched with sea and rain was duly appreciated."[6]

Miertsching had confined himself to his cabin for nearly the entire day, "where the drenching sea water stood two inches deep," and he lamented, "A fine beginning for me, a total stranger to the life and the language of the sea." And though he'd known McClure only a handful of days, Miertsching went on to stress how he "began on this occasion to learn something of my captain's character."[7]

The following day, the rain slackened, but the weather was still foul, as strong breezes came on from the south and west. *Investigator* pitched and rolled in the Atlantic swell, her decks above and below crowded with stores and provisions. Hatches were often battened down, conjuring up a sickening atmosphere within her hull.[8]

At daylight *Enterprise* was spotted and *Investigator* strained to keep in company during the day. Twenty-eight-year-old Carpenter 3rd Class George J. Ford was unimpressed with their sailing companion: "*Enterprise* ahead, to all appearances unconcerned about us. Raining heavy. It's a bad beginning. I hope for better bye & bye a good time coming." In seeking better times, Ford, like Miertsching, regularly immersed himself in the Bible and other religious literature; they also consoled themselves many an evening by playing tunes—the German with his guitar, the carpenter his flute. The latter, true to his nautical culture, also occupied evenings making and mending clothes.[9]

"[M]aking two feet of water during the twenty four hours, the upper Deck leaking very much fore and aft," noted McClure. The pumps were being manned daily in an attempt to keep pace with the intruding sea. All the while, Miertsching recorded "five men engaged in [rigging the new masts] fell overboard but were rescued. A bitter quarrel between the captain and the officers."[10]

A miserable downpour shrouded *Investigator* through January 26 (when she again lost sight of her consort) and on into the coming days. Sylvester's Warming Apparatus was fired up, its warming tentacles throughout the ship were intended to dry her up between decks, "which was damp and unhealthy from the constant thick and rainy weather, combined with leaking from upper deck and sides rendered her appearance below most wretched." At various times since the accident, *Investigator* fired rockets and burned blue lights in attempts to keep in contact with *Enterprise*—all in vain.[11]

*Investigator* fell in again with *Enterprise* on January 31, while they were still being assaulted by rain and rough seas, and she spoke to her consort by signal. She was still battling the effects of Neptune's wrath—and in desperate need of recaulking: McClure had four feet of water pumped out of *Investigator*'s well.

Casting his thoughts to the future, and their mission of mercy, Piers was well aware the

**Sylvester's Warming Apparatus (*The Illustrated London News*, May 13, 1848).**

clock was ticking: "Most adverse winds, retarding our progress so long, will materially lessen our chances of reaching Behring's Straits in time next Summer to make any useful search."[12]

The next day, *Investigator* continued to plod along as waves crashed on deck; amid the bursting wind and rain, the "men, with nothing to do, are joyous, and the fiddle in full play." The strains that invaded Miertsching's ears sprang from the instrument of the captain's steward, Mark Bradbury, whom Nelson described not only as an excellent violin player, but also a good singer, thus proving himself to be a very amusing shipmate. Some two months on, Bradbury's domestic duties were evidently taken over by Private 3rd Class James Biggs, and Bradbury was rerated an ordinary seaman, working about the decks or as circumstances required. Seemingly content in his work, he was later promoted to able seaman, while continuing to unfurl melodies for his fellow Investigators.[13]

Music was more than simple entertainment. The Royal Navy recognized the value of working to a beat and music's morale-building effect. The musician (who could play the fiddle, fife and/or drum) often played well-known and well-liked tunes while men toiled away on deck and in the boats, or while warping (moving a vessel by hauling on lines)—particularly during long and tedious voyages of exploration.[14] In days gone by, peg-legged fiddlers were often depicted afloat and ashore by caricaturists like the well-known Thomas Rowlandson and George Cruikshank.

Even *Punch*, a well known satirical and humor magazine of the day, grinned at the need for lyrical sailors:

GOOD NEWS FOR THE NAVY
    JACK'S ALIVE appears to be the tune just now in Portsmouth, and our other naval ports. And that
Jack may be kept lively, the Admiralty very clearly seems to wish. Else we should not see such an
announcement in the [weekly newspaper] Era as that which we subjoin:—
    WANTED for the Royal Navy, a few BANDSMEN that can Play a Brass and String Instrument.
Also, a few FIDDLERS, that can Play Jing, Reels, and Hornpipes.—Apply, &c.[15]

The weather now eased into a kinder mode, and the wind decreased, becoming more
westerly, so *Investigator* made to follow *Enterprise* to the southwest. But she again lost sight
of her consort, and Piers pointed to his vessel's inferior sailing qualities as the culprit for "not
being able to keep pace with her, although we carry as much sail as the ship will bear."[16]

Hatches were removed and fresh air bathed the lower decks, bringing some relief from
the recent misery and discomfort. During the week, after McClure inspected the cabins, an
attempt to dry them out nearly led to disaster. The Sylvester stove "was heated, and red-hot
cannon-balls were placed in corners and recesses. In the evening a fire broke out and was
promptly extinguished by the deck watch. A number of new sails were burnt."[17]

The incessant leaking was attributed to the pressure and strain of *Investigator's* previous
Arctic journey, but also slackness on the part of the Woolwich Dockyard workers. Caulker
James Evans (an 1848–49 *Enterprise* veteran) led the way in recaulking the ship's sides and
upper works. He bore a tattoo of a man and woman on his left arm, which referred to his mar-
ital status, while the anchor on his left accompanied the word "HOPE"; the former was not
only used a nautical sign, but also spoke of Christian symbolism from ancient times. Evans
served with nine other Investigators in the years prior to the expedition (and twice with Bradbury), including the survey frigate *Columbia* in the Bay of Fundy's frigid waters, between the
present-day Canadian provinces of New Brunswick and Nova Scotia.[18]

The fine and warming weather also allowed the sailors to wash their clothes, but the
Investigators' gay nighttime dancing and singing rattled Miertsching's religious sensibilities
in these still new and strange surroundings. "And now the officers too are quarrelling; the
captain prefers not to notice them."[19]

"From today [February 8] on every third day a keg containing notice of our ship will be
thrown overboard. From today also I am to go every day at 12 noon to the captain's cabin and
drink a glass of wine with him (luncheon). My books and notes, which are all moist and damp,
and also my guitar, I am henceforth to keep in the captain's cabin," wrote the grateful
Miertsching.[20]

Given that McClure was in command at sea for the first time and relations with Haswell
were poor from the start—and grew worse—this situation set the stage for the captain to
befriend Miertsching. As a civilian (and a foreigner), the German did not pose a personal or
professional threat—particularly to McClure's ambitions.

On Sunday morning, "the captain held Divine Service on the upper deck, and read the
Gospel and Epistle for the thirteenth Sunday before Trinity."[21] Miertsching was pleased to no
end that dancing and music fell silent on the Lord's day.

McClure also chose to recite the Articles of War that day. In the Royal Navy, captains
were required to display and read these Articles to their ships' companies, which covered the
penalties for anything from profane swearing, drunkenness and uncleanness to sodomy (with
man or beast), uttering seditious words, mutinous assemblies, and outright mutiny. The death
penalty, which meant hanging, was seldom imposed, excepting for atrocious acts such as

mutiny. The commander of a vessel possessed broad discretionary powers, so in regard to punishments, everything depended on the personality of the captain.[22]

Here too, McClure was at a disadvantage, since the first lieutenant was in charge of the day-to-day administration of the ship, so looking after discipline would fall more heavily on McClure's shoulders.

Invariably linked to discipline was the crew's health, and this was the prime responsibility of surgeon and naturalist Alexander Armstrong, who, at just over ten years junior to McClure, was a fellow Irishman who hailed from County Donegal. Unlike his captain, however, Armstrong had already made a name for himself in the Navy.[23]

Receiving his medical education at Trinity College, Dublin, and the University of Edinburgh, Dr. Armstrong entered the Navy in 1842. From October 1843 to March 1844, while detached from HMS *Polyphemus*, he was an assistant surgeon in medical charge of a party landed from the *Medea* for the exploration of the ancient city of Xanthus, the principal city of ancient Lycia. Situated near the mouth of the Xanthus River (now the Esen Cayi) in present-day southwestern Turkey, the ruins include a theatre, temples, and tombs, and a number of artifacts were spirited away for the British Museum.[24] The commander-in-chief of the Mediterranean Fleet had ordered Armstrong to keep a scientific journal, and for his observations Armstrong received the official thanks of the trustees of the British Museum. He was recommended for promotion by the commander-in-chief, who "trusted their Lordships would give [Armstrong] credit for the intelligence & zeal with which he had fulfilled that order." Armstrong was also complimented on the excellent organization of the sanitary arrangements.[25]

Between 1846 and 1849, Armstrong served as assistant surgeon onboard Her Majesty's Yacht *Victoria & Albert*, and from December 1847 was placed in charge of medical stores onboard. In August 1849, with the disastrous effects of Irish potato famine still being felt, Queen Victoria made her first visit to Ireland. That October, Armstrong was promoted to surgeon on the occasion of the Queen's recent stay in his homeland.[26]

After Surgeon Armstrong volunteered for the Arctic expedition, none other than the highly respected explorer-naturalist Sir John Richardson bore testimony to the doctor's "industry, steadiness & superior professional abilities, and also to his fitness to be appointed to the Arctic Expedition, on account of his attainments as a Naturalist."[27]

Viewed through the eyes of an anonymous future obituarist, the coming head-on collision between McClure and the ship's doctor was unavoidable:

> Sir Alexander Armstrong was a man of striking appearance. His tall, handsome, and athletic figure, together with his bold and resolute look and carriage, indicated a man not to be trifled with by anyone. A highly combative temperament was no doubt one of the features of his character. But it is said of him that he always liked to meet his adversary in the open, and that when the fight was over he never took advantage of his official position to indulge in measures of personal resentment…. But it must be added that he showed little mercy to those who in any way brought discredit upon their profession.
>
> His chief claim to the grateful remembrance of those who served under him was that they felt they could always rely upon him to protect them from injustice, and that he would not tolerate anything in the nature of a job [something done astensibly in the public interest but actually for private gain], no matter where it was hatched or from what quarter it came.[28]

As of February 13, the crew was placed on a daily allowance of lemon juice, "but owning to the special character of the service on which we were employed, double quantity was issued, viz: one ounce daily instead of half an ounce; the latter, the usual allowance issued in the Navy," wrote Armstrong. The lemon juice was issued with an equal portion of sugar. In fact, the Investigators were part of an experiment, and as Armstrong stated, "It was intimated to me by the then Director-General of the Medical Department of the Navy, that I should be called upon to report on the relative merits of the two kinds of acid, and their efficacy as anti-scorbutic agents on my return to this country."[29]

Professor Keith Millar, of the University of Glasgow's College of Medical, Veterinary and Life Sciences, explained how:

> *Investigator* was supplied with lemon juice in two forms from the Royal Navy's victualing yard at Dept-ford. One half of the quantity of juice was boiled, the other half was "fortified" with the addition of 10 percent brandy to allow a simple trial of which preparation might offer the best protection against scurvy. The daily "dose" of one ounce of lemon juice would equate to approximately 12 milligrams of vitamin C, and was thus only slightly above the minimum requirement. But that figure refers to fresh juice. Unfortunately, vitamin C is highly vulnerable to heat so that boiling would greatly reduce its content in the juice. Adding 10 percent brandy to the unboiled "fortified" juice would, obviously, have the disadvantage of reducing the vitamin C content by 10 percent by volume in the one-ounce dose. Armstrong recorded that the juice (boiled and fortified) was also exposed to "the highest degree of tropical heat" during the outbound voyage via the east and west coasts of South America, and this would have further reduced the vitamin content of both preparations. Storage time also results in loss of the vitamin, as does exposure to air, for example while standing in the Deptford storage tanks. It is therefore unlikely that the lemon juice provided adequate vitamin C in later parts of the mission. Arm-strong's claim that both the boiled and fortified juice prevented scurvy was not supported by any pub-lished data that I am aware of, and the conclusion would seem contradicted anyway by the appearance of the disease when the full normal ration of the juice was being maintained. Any supposed benefit of the juice was probably confounded with the variable quantities of vitamin C obtained from some of their other rations—perhaps the preserved potato—and success in hunting. In the mid-nineteenth cen-tury, vitamins were unknown and the antiscorbutic effect of lemon juice was ascribed, variously, to its citric acid content—in fact, citric acid contains no vitamin C.[30]

"The weather is becoming very hot," wrote Miertsching, and temperatures climbed to the mid–80s by month's end, becoming several degrees higher below deck, and going as high as 94° in sick bay. A week later "came the order to wear white socks, jackets, and straw hats."[31]

While the ship nosed toward the Tropic of Cancer, the northeasterly trade winds fol-lowed. Great numbers of flying fish are seen taking their short flights from the ocean runway, while dolphins frolicked about the strange wooden creature. Above, one of the avian greeters to the tropics was the stormy petrel, the smallest of seabirds. With their vibrant blue, green and purple hues, an army of Portuguese men-of-war also acted as companions to the Investi-gators. Dr. Armstrong captured and preserved a fine specimen of this jelly-like marine inver-tebrate, whose tentacles reach an average of thirty feet below the water's surface. Sharks, too, made their presence known, and so, during one of the frequent calms, a sail was rigged from a swinging boom and dipped into the water to allow safe bathing for all onboard.[32]

Beyond the earthbound wonders were other sights to behold, as McClure discovered on the night of the 25th: "At 9:30 observed a most beautiful meteor shot from the Zenith to the SW bursting as a Rocket and illuminating that portion of the Heavens."[33]

In spite of all that filled the eye and ear, ongoing preparations for their mission kept everyone well-occupied with appointed tasks. Carpenter Ford, for example, examined the caulking around the boat davits and chains, only to find them to be "exceedingly slack"—evi-dently not caulked at Woolwich, and one cause of water intruding into the starboard cabins and a leak in the sail room.[34]

To increase his communication skills, Miertsching decided he would devote two hours daily to studying English, and two hours to the Eskimo language. And though he found God's creatures of the sea "most agreeable," Miertsching desperately pined for "a Christian friend or a Christian environment!!!" Still, there were compensations; on the final day of February, the Moravian Brother kept dinner company with McClure, Cresswell, Court and Piers, with the latter commenting that they "formed a very pleasant little party—Capt. McClure being affable & agreeable."[35]

As *Investigator* reached the latitude of Rio de Janeiro, just above the Tropic of Capricorn, she crossed paths with a number of vessels. "One or two of them presented a very suspicious appearance; and from their build, rig, and being without cargo, opinion was unanimous in pronouncing them slavers. They glided swiftly through the water, steering a course for the coast of Africa," remarked Armstrong.[36]

Several onboard had served on anti-slave trade duty, and thus understood the tragic plight of the human cargo forcibly torn from their homes. Royal Navy seamen paid a high price—sometimes with their very lives—to suppress the evil trade. But for two Investigators in particular, the sight of a slave ship may have especially stirred their hearts, since Able Seaman Charles Anderson and Captain's Coxswain Cornelius Hulott were men of African descent.[37]

"Charles Anderson was a very good, well-conducted man, and from his many amusing qualities, a great favourite in the ship. He was a man of colour, represented himself as a Canadian, inured to a hunter's life in North America, and was one of the most powerful and muscular men amongst our crew," wrote Armstrong. And Miertsching "had the opportunity of conversing with our comedian, the Negro Anderson; for two years he had been cook on a vessel carrying German emigrants to America, and he had picked up a few words of German; unhappily he is the most godforsaken of men. He is universally popular because he provides so much amusement."[38]

Blacks often served in merchantmen and onboard warships, especially as cooks. "Black sailors of West Indian, African, American, and East Indian origin became so well known in English ports that when the men of African origin were required for labour, Englishmen sought them in dockyards."[39]

Crispus Attucks—forever linked with the Boston Massacre, and a man of mixed African/American Indian origins—was a runaway slave turned sailor after escaping to Nantucket, Massachusetts, and sailing on a whaling ship as a harpooner. In the latter stages of the War of 1812, nearly 1,000 black American seamen, and 5,000 of their white shipmates, were held in the British Admiralty's Dartmoor Prison.[40]

William Hall, a British naval seaman who received the Victoria Cross in 1859 for the Indian Mutiny, was another notable man of color. Born in Nova Scotia in 1827, he was the son of a black man who was rescued by a British frigate from a slave ship en route to the United States and taken to Halifax. Hall's mother was a black girl whose family escaped Washington when the British destroyed that city in 1814. Such historical example helped Herman Melville introduce a handsome black sailor in *Billy Budd*, and craft him in a masculine mold; he was "the center of a company of his shipmates.... Ashore he was the champion; afloat the spokesman; on every suitable occasion always foremost."[41]

Anderson's shipmate Cornelius Hulott[42] was described by Miertsching as a mulatto (of mixed white-black blood), suggesting he had a lighter brown skin tone. Promoted to captain's coxswain (first-class petty officer) only ten days after joining *Investigator* as an able seaman, Hulott was in charge of the captain's boat and attended to him. McClure must have taken a fancy to the slight, five-foot two-inch, teetotaling sailor, to make him his personal coxswain.

In 1846, Hulott was rated an ordinary seaman, and for two years prior to the expedition, served as a seaman rigger at Sheerness Yard, on the Isle of Sheppey (off the northern coast of Kent), having come from the island's small town of Minster.[43]

Because black sailors stood out and made an impression, officers sometimes detailed them for particular duties. Commodore Perry described one such occasion in 1853, during the presentation of letters from the U.S. President and himself to the Emperor of Japan: "These splendid specimens of American workmanship, were covered with scarlet cloth and carried into the audience room by two of the best looking boys of the squadron, selected for the purpose, who were guarded by a couple of tall jet-black Negroes, completely armed."[44]

Even at sea there was no escaping the Ides of March, which came early—and stayed late. On the fourth of the month, McClure, after complaints about the meat issue, ordered Haswell, Cresswell and Court to survey the meat provisions, and "found some Gamble's preserved meats rotten in consequence of the canisters having holes, apparently made by nails driven in to secure the hoops of the casks. Cleared one of the preserved meat-rooms and found a couple of 8 lb. canisters of Beef rotten."[45]

Three weeks later, during rough and squally weather, Ford wrote of an odd event invading his sleep: "I dreamed a curious dream: I thought I heard peals of thunder & the Almighty speaking through it to the Earth & great lights of fire in the heavens. Also that my Dear [wife] Mary had changed my watch for a useless one & that [I] was in such a passion concerning it that I threw it down & broke it to pieces under my feet."[46] Clocks, chronometers, hourglasses, sundials, and other timepieces are the more subtle symbols of death, as they represent the passing of time and the capriciousness of life, along with *memento mori* (Latin—"Remember your mortality"). A broken watch suggests one's life is running its course. A marine chronometer allows for measurement of longitudes, without which a ship and her crew could well become lost. A broken "watch" in the Arctic could indeed be fatal.[47]

Nautical tradition intervened during this time, as the carpenter cheerfully scrawled, "Lat. 0° 6'; long. 26° 16'. Fine day. Evening preparing for the reception of Neptune having crossed the Equinoctial Line to the south this day [March 5]."[48]

Crossing the Line was a cruel-hearted ceremony in the nineteenth century and before, and sailors were known to have died during the affair. Often times, a pollywog (a person who has not previously crossed the equator) was beaten with boards and wet ropes, and may even have been thrown over the side of the ship, to be dragged in the surf from the stern.[49] However, according to McClure, the scene on *Investigator*'s deck was of a kinder and gentler nature, which, most unusually, was witnessed by outsiders:

> At 8.45 a.m. Hove to for an hour to permit Neptune the usual privelege [*sic*] of initiating the fresh arrivals in the mysteries of the Southern seas, the ceremony was conducted with great good humour, humanity and fun to all. Just as we had finished the Brazillian Brig [Atalante] which had been in company the last two days passed close under our Lee, there was a woman and some children on board, what there [*sic*] ideas of the spectacle presented to them may have been, it is not easy to conjecture, so many half naked bipeds in their grotesque costumes must have conveyed an expression of insanity.[50]

For Miertsching, to see the bodies of pollywogs smeared in tar and then scraped off with a razor fashioned from the rusty hoop of an old keg, was "truly more than any Christian man can comprehend that men such as our sailors exist!" Somewhat understandably, he did not "hold it worth while to give an exact description of this festival which I would be very glad to forget entirely."[51]

But what the torrid zone would *not* allow is for the Investigators to forget the oppressive heat. Until they were able to capture rainwater, the supply onboard remained lukewarm and stale; Miertsching would have gladly sent a sliver of sun to Labrador in exchange for a handful of ice or a cool drink from a pond. Still, Piers struck a note of harmony to accompany the sunshine and iridescent colors reflecting off Portuguese men-of-war that floated by the ship.[52]

On Sunday, March 10, McClure proudly recorded: "Performed Divine Service onboard to an exceedingly orderly and well disposed crew, nearly all join in the responses, and which pay great attention to the Service & sermon." At lunch with the captain afterward, the Moravian Brother pointed out to McClure that for the second time he confused his Sundays, incorrectly making it a Trinity Sunday. The Irishman allowed a rare bit of humor to escape his lips as he "laughed heartily and said: 'We are seafarers, and have fifty-two Sundays—one just like another—and only one festival, Christmas, when Jack must have roast beef and pudding.'"[53]

Though he had a "most interesting conversation" with the captain, Miertsching lamented his poor English, but in the coming days Piers began visiting him daily so they could read together. In spite of Miertsching's linguistic struggles, his eyes and ears took in the coin's other side: "Since we left England, scarcely a day has passed with no one under arrest; today three men are in confinement." At month's end he recorded "another bitter quarrel between the captain and his officers."[54]

Upon reflection many years later, Able Seaman George Brown didn't recall any of his shipmates particularly warming to the captain: "I don't mean to say he was neglectful, unkind or harsh; but I do not suppose it ever entered the mind of one of the hands to call him, 'Father'; as I read they called Captain Nares [leader of the 1875–76 British Arctic expedition]." It's not without interest that Brown and shipmate Able Seaman Frederick Taylor experienced an historical brush with mutiny during their recent service onboard HMS *Calypso*. *Calypso* visited Pitcairn Island in 1848, home to descendants of the 1789 mutiny on the *Bounty*. Only one of the original settlers from the group was still alive, a Tahitian woman named Teraura, who was in her early 70s at the time.[55]

According to Collinson, *Enterprise* and *Investigator* "were never two days' sail apart until 31st March [Easter Sunday], when we obtained an advantage by standing to the southward with a south-westerly wind, while Commander M'Clure, being desirous to hug the coast, stood to the N.W., and this brought us to [Cape Virgins/Cabo de Virgenes] the entrance of the Straits of Magellan eight days before him."[56] Cutting through the Straits was an important time-saving alternative to going round Cape Horn, on South America's southern tip.

For *Investigator*, the wind had been blowing very hard from the northwest, when between "11 and 12 a.m. the wind suddenly lulled and the sails fell to the masts, but the wind, which was observed by the state of the water to be coming ahead, was in five minutes blowing hard again from S.S.W. (8) and continued at a gale for upwards of 30 hours"—so *Investigator* was driven northward by the wind (and current, as Court also informed Piers). On April 3, with the temperature dropping into the 50s, the wind slowly came around from northward again, and in spite of the strong current, *Investigator* was again able to shape a course for Cape Virgins. The consuming monotony was broken by a great many birds dancing about the ship, including albatrosses, often regarded as the souls of lost sailors. All the while, whales in the distance plodded southward on a placid sea, "with their huge cawdal [dorsal] fin, and the picturesque jets of water, which they spouted into the air, as they sluggishly pursued their onward course."[57]

Five days later, the mood onboard turned dark. Subordinate Officers' Steward/Gunroom

Cook Henry Sugden, one of four men then under arrest, felt the lash of the cat-o'-nine-tails across his back. Only in his mid–20s, Sugden was "a strong, wiry fellow," whose conduct had not always been the best since he joined the Navy in 1840. "The first punishment happened this day, the officers' cook, for mutinous conduct, and dis-gusting language, happy to find the Petty Officers are disposed to check it on the lower deck, as they were the complainants," wrote McClure with pride. Piers also commented, "Our cook was punished to day with forty eight lashes for, I believe, blasphemous and thuswise bad language. He had been complained of to the Captain once or twice before, and is undoubtedly a bad character, so that, disagreeable as the sight of corporal punishment is, he met with very little sympathy from any one." "A horrible punishment so to flay the back of a fellow creature, but with a rabble like our crew some such punishment there must be," concluded Miertsching.[58]

The grisly scene would have played out something like this: The Marines under Woon were drawn up on deck—with bayonets fixed—the officers being grouped on the opposite side, while the crew looked on with heads uncovered to show respect for the law. McClure read the Article(s) of War the offender had contravened, and the prisoner was brought forward and asked if he had anything to say in mitigation of punishment. Sugden's shirt was then removed and his hands secured to the rigging or a grating above his head.

At the order, "Boatswain's mate, do your duty," either Edward Fawcett or Henry Bluff stepped forward with the cat—a short rope or wooden handle, to which was attached nine waxed cords of equal length, each having a small knot in the end.

Sugden then felt the full effect of the cat as it whipped across his back, each lash tearing skin and biting into his flesh. In order to remove the clotting blood, the boatswain's mate would run his fingers through the cords after each stroke. For each dozen lashes, the other boatswain's mate stepped forward to continue the punishment. After the beating Sugden received, his back would have looked like raw meat.

The punishment completed, Sugden was cut down and taken to the sick bay to have salt rubbed into his wounds in order to prevent infection.

From 1750 into the nineteenth century, twelve lashes were the maximum authorized for any one offense, but partly due to political reform, flogging was on the decline: 2,007 men were flogged in 1839,

John Woon as a quartermaster lieutenant, Royal Marine Light Infantry, c. 1867 (courtesy Frederick Feather).

and by 1847 that number dropped sharply to 860. At the same time, within the Navy the attitude that flogging was degrading and unnecessary slowly gained momentum. On some decks of Her Majesty's ships, however, the eighteenth century world had altered little—and a captain's *personality* held sway.[59]

With only 91 miles to the entrance of the Strait of Magellan, and at a chilly 47°, on April 14 double pay commenced for the Investigators.[60] Six o'clock the following morning brought their first sight of land since departing England three months before. The right (or northern) side of the strait was Patagonia, while the left was Tierra del Fuego. White cliffs of Cape Virgins slowly rose out of the sea, and soon Armstrong was likening the Patagonian side of the strait, with its high and bold headlands and sandy beaches skirting indentations, to Downs on England's southern coast. The sailors were struck at the sight of great herds of llama (guanacos) grazing about the green hills or running along the beach. Likewise, the seafarers' eyes feasted upon the multitude of birds lounging about the shoreline.[61]

Two days later, the steam paddle frigate HMS *Gorgon* (Commander Paynter) hove into view in Possession Bay. A Gorgon in Greek mythology usually refers to any of three sisters who had hair of venomous snakes and turned to stone those whose eyes were captured by their deadly gaze—but the sight of Paynter's *Gorgon* brought relief to the Investigators. The *Gorgon* had specifically steamed out of Valparaiso to tow *Enterprise* and *Investigator* through the strait. Collinson met up with Paynter on the fourteenth and decided to push through the strait alone, leaving the *Gorgon* to bring up *Investigator*.[62]

In a progress report to the Admiralty, Collinson revealed his intention for the expedition to make directly for the Sandwich Islands, instead of calling upon Valparaiso (according to instructions), "as I look upon our arrival in Behring's Straits during the first week in August to be essential to their Lordships' orders."[63] Collinson obtained provisions from the *Gorgon*, and intended on acquiring additional ones and fresh water while moving through the strait.[64]

Under sunshine and temperatures in the mid–40s, the *Gorgon*'s machinery snorted and her paddles obediently turned, to pull the *Investigator* along the winding, and sometimes uncomfortably narrow, corridor of the Strait of Magellan. After a stop at Port Famine (Puerto del Hambre), which did not yield one speck of provisions, the pair pushed onto Fortescue Bay (Bahía Fortescue) on April 17. "[T]here we saw to our great delight, our long lost Consort, quietly at anchor, in expectation of our arrival," beamed Armstrong. The expedition was again in sync.[65]

The bay's impressive surroundings caught the eye of the British tars, and Second Master Skead on the *Enterprise* was particularly impressed:

> Very fine scenery is met with hereabouts, & from the head of the bay which is formed by a thickly wooded valley surrounded by lofty peaks of bare rock a magnificent view of the mountains of Tierra del Fuigo [*sic*] was obtained. The mountains which were covered with snow appeared to rear their heads & shoulders which were laden with stupendous glaciers, out of the very bosom of the sea.[66]

For the Investigators, the hustle and bustle of procuring a supply of water commenced, and extended throughout the night; though no fresh vegetables could be had, one of the small bullocks obtained by *Enterprise* was sent onboard *Investigator*, and the former also provided McClure with a good supply of fish, freshly caught by the consort's crew.[67]

While the expedition was resupplying and preparing for the second leg of its journey, the Gold Rush was in its third year. Armstrong noted three American vessels in the bay bound for California, which were kept from their destination by contrary winds, and the expedition "therefore had good reason to feel thankful, that wisdom and foresight had placed a steamer at our disposal." The doctor took advantage of the brief delay to add a few geological and botanical specimens to his natural history department.[68]

Meeting the *Gorgon* also allowed for the departure of men who were medically unfit for Arctic duty, and three Investigators left the ship.[69] At this point Miertsching was supposed to transfer to his proper ship:

> I was required (now, in the darkness and rain) to move with sack and pack to the *Enterprise* to occupy a new and comfortably fitted cabin. But this was not a positive order, and my captain, Mr. McClure, put in a good word for me, so I was permitted to remain on the Investigator until our arrival at the Sandwich Islands.[70]

In granting this seemingly innocent concession, Collinson unknowingly altered the course of his future ... and that of the expedition.

But now, the time had come to press on, and anxious excitement filled the air. In the wee hours of the nineteenth, the *Gorgon* took *Enterprise* and *Investigator* in tow and chugged northwest through the final leg of the strait. At one point "the Gorgon slacked her speed and sent on board Mr. Kennedy." Since the *Investigator*'s boatswain deserted at Plymouth, Boatswain's Mate George Kennedy was made an acting boatswain third class by Collinson. Doubtless McClure was unaware the Scot had also previously served for three years with the West African Squadron onboard HMS *Prometheus*—another paddle steamship.[71]

During the early hours of the next morning, a heavy swell from the westward announced the closeness of the ocean, and around 8 a.m., "Cape Pillar [Cabo Pilar] was rounded, and the broad expanse of the Pacific Ocean broke fairly into view." An aquatic roller coaster snapped the cables towing *Investigator*, and though replaced, they eventually parted again, forcing McClure to make all sail and follow as best he could. Around 1:30, the *Gorgon* left *Enterprise*, turned round, and bore down on her consort. Final letters and dispatches for England were shuttled over by cutter, which returned with two hawsers to continue the tow. All the while, *Enterprise*'s outline dwindled, till she was no more.[72]

The barometers had been gradually falling, signaling sinister weather was on the way, and Piers worried—"our ship was plunging 'bows under'—as it is, from the great straining of the ship, the fore part of the upper deck, particularly about 'the bits,' leaks very much, and Court says, that one of the hawsers is reduced by the stretching two inches in circumference." Shortly after midnight, the hawsers parted for the last time.[73] *Investigator* was now on her own in the vastness of the Pacific.

McClure's thoughts turned to his crew's health. He was anxious to fend off the seeds of an insidious disease:

> From our long privation of vegetables and the probability of another three months without being able to obtain any I have thought it prudent to alter the scale of victualling, giving the crew preserved meats and vegetables every alternate day as a preventative against scurvy, and with the hopes of being able to take them to the Sandwich Islands where supplies can be obtained without their health being impaired, so as to render those objects for invaliding instead of prosecuting this voyage, which would be extremely detrimental to the Service.[74]

But he kept uncovering more bad provisions:

> April 29, 1850
>
> Goldners preserved meat is failing us much [since] several cannisters of eight and six pounds have been found rotten, this however is not to be surprised at, they being part of those returned from the

late expedition, which found them not only absent of their contents but also decayed in consequence of the badness of the Tin and inattention in the soldering.[75]

May 7, 1850

> ...and what was of infinite more consequence, three cannisters of Goldners Roast Mutton, two containing only peas, the other, one pound and a half of that vegetable and a pound and a quarter of meat and issued as six pound of Meat these being part what was returned from the late expedition which suffered much from this cause,—am afraid we all bear a close resemblance.[76]

Stephen Goldner was the only contractor who provided tinned meat for Franklin's expedition, and he also "supplied the Navy with tinned meat for several years after Sir John Franklin had sailed. After a time the quality deteriorated, complaints became increasingly frequent, and finally the Admiralty terminated all its contracts with him."[77]

Strangely, neither Dr. Armstrong nor Dr. Piers mentioned anything in their writings about McClure's preventative measures to bolster the crew's health, yet it seems only logical that the captain would have conferred with his medical men in this regard. In addition, Armstrong's subsequent writings on the quality of the meat provisions left a distinctly false impression:

> The provisions consisted of salt beef and pork, and preserved meat, all of which were of a most excellent quality. The two former had been salted only a few days previous to our departure from England, so that we received them under the most favourable circumstances that it was possible for us to possess salt meat. The fresh meat had been but recently prepared by Messrs. Gamble, of Cork, and, from the excellence of its quality, reflected great credit upon that firm. The vegetable food supplied consisted of Edwards' preserved potatoes, pearl barley, peas, rice, and carrots, together with cranberries and pickles, the latter consisting of cabbage, onions, mixed pickles, and walnuts.[78]

Continually assailed by brutal eastern winds, the ship drifted southwest from 50 to 60 miles a day until reaching the latitude of Cape Horn, from whence the winds became more westerly and allowed *Investigator* to take a more direct line of sail. "The almost constant exposure of our men to the united influences of cold & wet, having this long & trying period of boisterous weather such as few amongst us had ever before experienced, and the squalls of hurricane force, necessarily entailed from their frequency the entire strength of the crew in working the ship," wrote Armstrong.[79] The sick list began to grow, with several cases of rheumatism and phlegmon (acute inflammation and discharge of pus, affecting the connective tissue deep beneath the skin), among other ailments.[80]

On April 29, seaman James Nelson witnessed three successive seas, the size of which he'd never seen equaled, rolling toward his little vessel, the wind sweeping long trails of foam from their peaks. The massive arched trio seemed to crash down upon themselves and roll over as they surged onward. Nelson judged the height of the third monster to be 40 feet, and credited a higher power for allowing the wave's base to pass underneath the ship. As she climbed the liquid mountain, *Investigator* heeled over, her yardarms brushing the water.[81]

In spite of Nelson's attributing their salvation to divine intervention, the Investigators seemed to tempt fate during the ongoing gale by capturing several large albatrosses. It was thought very unlucky to kill an albatross, because of the belief that within each one resided the restless spirit of a dead mariner. These birds were snared by means of a line and hook—like that used in mackerel fishing—attaching a piece of salt meat and towing it well astern. "They were really magnificent looking birds; the plumage was white, with a mottled grey back, and dark wings—head and legs of a pink colour," admired Armstrong. Weighing 19 and

21 pounds, two of the fine winged creatures measured upward of 12 feet between outstretched wingtips.[82]

While nature's fury continued unabated day in and day out, Miertsching witnessed human passions boil over, as "there was again a sharp dispute between the captain and the officers." He also experienced considerable angst from being immersed in the "devil of discord" that sprang up among the Investigators: "It is as if each man were himself a devil. Towards me they are friendly and courteous, but it is most difficult to stand alone in the midst of such antagonists." The tense atmosphere only added to the physical discomfort of continually being tossed about, unable to stand, sit or lie down, amidst the miserable wetness and sickening odor within the wooden walls.[83]

Adding to their woes, a fiendish leak in the starboard quarter required three buckets of water to be bailed every hour from McClure's cabin, and the invader destroyed or damaged many stores. It would be several days yet before the Sylvester stove gained ground in drying things out below decks.[84]

Meanwhile, with the ship only halfway to the Bering Strait, Assistant Surgeon Piers eyed the humanitarian mission and pondered the future on April's final day:

> I fear unless we receive, somewhere, considerable aid from steam, that we shall reach the North too late to take up a good position for despatching searching parties in the following Spring, and if that cannot be effected we might as well as had better winter to the south of the Straits. This unfortunate delay, however, of a twelvemonth must do away with any little chance there may have been of our carrying relief to Sir John Franklin and his party; for the Summer of 1851, when we should under these circumstances enter the ice, would be his sixth from England, and, in the following Spring, 1852, when our exploring parties would be sent out, he would be seven years from his Native country, and how, under the most favorable circumstances that we can imagine, can they be supposed to exist so long in their icy prison?[85]

But the raging storm was not nearly done, and on one occasion, as tons of frigid water cascaded down upon the *Investigator*'s deck, her bulwarks were smashed and carried away, as was the head and waist hammock netting.[86] But much worse loomed.

"Last night a terrific squall; everyone, even the captain, feared that the ship was lost. We sailed by some coral reefs, and saw a large fragment of mast floating in the sea," wrote Miertsching.[87] During moderate winds and passing squalls and showers the following morning (May 15), disaster struck "while the first lieutenant, who was officer of the watch, had quitted the deck for a few minutes,"[88] continued Miertsching. Dr. Armstrong relates how "a squall from the west-south-west suddenly took the ship, which carried away her fore and main top masts, and top gallant masts, together with the jib-boom [and flying jib-boom]—a direful casualty under the circumstances of our position." But then everyone was allowed to breathe a sigh of relief: "Luckily for us the squall was of short duration, and the wind subsequently, for a short time fell light."[89]

With the crippled *Investigator* pitching to and fro, the cry of "Man overboard!" pierced the air, as four of the six men who had been on the jib-boom dangled precariously by the bobstays under the vessel's bow. "[A]ll the crew were in immediate activity to save their messmates, the life-buoy was at once let go, and a boat manned in less time I have taken to narrate it," added Armstrong. With only an unwelcome dunking bruising their egos, the sailors were soon gathered up and back onboard. The ship's dinghy was dispatched to collect the lifebuoy as it bobbed a short distance away; meanwhile, whales lumbered about the ship, loudly spouting

**Right Whale (W. Kuhnert; Harter, 1979).**

fountains of water skyward, and causing the Investigators to keep anxious eyes on the leviathans until the dinghy's safe return.[90]

As tangled rigging, yards and the remains of the topmasts hung limp over the ship's side as she wallowed in the early morning light, the zephyrs offered a brief respite. The difficult work now began in earnest, "for each man must hold on with one hand and work with the other, with the ship rolling and the waves breaking in cataracts over all."[91]

And her commander was alight: "The fury of the captain was terrible, positively inhuman," wrote Miertsching.[92] For McClure, the dismasting "was as unfortunate as it was a careless circumstance crippling the resources of the vessel, and proving the incompetency and great want of judgement in [Lieutenant Haswell], which I had long been aware of, a man more unfit for his responsible situation could rarely be met—it took all day to get in order as the topmast crosstrees had to be renewed and picked."[93]

By evening, with stout yards in place of the damaged masts, *Investigator* was again under sail (but within 24 hours, a hurricane-force gale bore down on *Investigator*, and Armstrong knew that "we dared not show a stitch of canvas" as the little vessel was mercilessly driven before the wind).[94]

McClure wasted no time in demanding his senior lieutenant explain the most recent calamity—and the previous incident as well:

It is my direction that you forward to me in writing a detailed report of the circumstances that caused the loss of the Spars named in the margin [fore topmast and jib boom] in which when taken in conjunction with the very heavy Damage sustained on the 24th January last, has to a great extent crippled the resource of this Vessel and rendered her inefficient for the Service she is employed upon, that I may be enabled to give a clear Statement to my L.C.A. [Lords Commissioners of the Admiralty] upon this Subject.[95]

On the morning of May 16, the ship showed itself not fully healed from its recent wounds ... and neither were her human masters. Carpenter Ford reported that the main topmast was sprung about three feet below the trunk truss (which supports the yard), and as no replacement was available, the captain well knew the seriousness of the matter. McClure rightly praised Ford, "who is an exceedingly active intelligent man [and who] fished it aloft with eight substantial oak battens [reinforcing planks of wood], which will permit of a single reefed Topsail and Top Gallant sail being carried, and I believe the spar is strong but not so serviceable as ever"[96]:

> From the activity of the Carpenter, I turn to the Apathy of the Senior Lieutenant (Mr. Haswell) who when the spar was reported sprung contented himself with mentioning the same to me as I was dressing, and then with the most perfect indifference as to the fate of the mast walked into his cabin to his toilette, without having had the energy to go aloft to examine, or give any orders for its security, an act of listlessness I would not calmly submit to [and] upon reproving him sharply for his excessive negligence, he had the Modest assurance to tell me that he knew that he was a very good officer, as he had been told so by those much my senior in the Service.
>
> After such a remark I had nothing more to argue, But only trust I may be for ever exempt from such very good officers. In the course of the evening this very good officer presented me with a letter detailing the loss of the spars and winding up with a very impertinent observation upon my conduct, for which I intend to place this very good officer under arrest, which I trust will teach him a lesson of humility, and discretion. I never met a gentleman who was on better terms with himself.[97]

In detail, Haswell dutifully mapped out how he had relieved Wynniatt (officer of the middle watch) at four a.m. the previous day, the latter having stated the weather was moderate. "In compliance with [the captain's] night orders to carry all sail with safety, at 5.30 a.m. the weather being Still moderate with occasional Showers of rain, [a moderate breeze] from the W.N.W., the Ship close hauled on the Port Tack, I piped make sail."[98] At daylight, just under an hour later, Haswell perceived a squall approaching, and the shrill of the boatswain's pipe followed, calling hands to shorten some sails and furl others. However, "finding there was more wind in the squall than I first expected, I ordered the Topsail Haulyards (halliards—ropes) to be let go which was done accordingly—Main Topsail Yard came down but the Fore Topsail (altho' the Halliards were let go by [Henry] Bluff Bos Mate at the time I gave the order) hung at the masthead in consequence of the Wind shifting to W.S.W. in the Squall & the whole force of it pressing on the body of the sail & binding the yard against the lee rigging, causing the Topmast to go over the side and the Jib boom to [be] carried away."[99]

The lieutenant went on to emphasize his desire to further the mission and McClure's repeated and clearly stated orders to all Watch officers not to take in sail until forced to do so, "in consequence of your expressed wish to reach the Sandwich Islands as early as possible, the Topsail Halliards were not let go until I considered it imprudent to keep them fast any longer."[100]

Haswell then detailed how McClure had twice censured him on April 2, once *for not making sail* during weather that had been consistently squally for many hours (due to the safety order), and a second time *for making sail* in the same weather (in the interests of the mission). As an important clarification regarding the January 24 incident, Haswell pointed out that he was not in charge of the deck on that occasion (it was Cresswell).[101]

Within the last paragraph of his statement, Haswell was barely able to contain his disdain for the captain, as he observed "that from the great inference which I have at all times experienced from you not only as Officer of the Watch but in carrying on the general duties of the Ship as Senior Lieutenant I have found great difficulty and embarrassment in discharging the duties of my Station."[102]

"This morning there was held a solemn inquiry or trial of the seamen and officers; the outcome was that Lieutenant Haswell was placed under arrest; he is under the guard of two armed marines," wrote Miertsching on May 17.[103]

The public deposition of members of the ship's company was an unthinkable act against the honor of a naval officer, not to mention deadly for discipline and morale. McClure was thorough in setting up the humiliation of his second-in-command to further (so he believed) the groundwork for Haswell's expulsion from the expedition. The proceeding would have only heightened Haswell's bitterness.

The captain questioned Quartermaster Henry May, Able Seaman William Carroll (doing duty as Captain of the Maintop), Captain's Coxswain Cornelius Hulott, and Boatswain's Mate Henry Bluff (all of whom signed statements which were witnessed by Lieutenant Cresswell). The last was a seasoned sailor and County Durham man, who held a first-class certificate in gunnery, and had been an acting gunner 3rd class (warrant officer) for the better part of a year before joining *Investigator* in his present rating. During one of his engagements in the gunnery training ship *Excellent*, from October 1843 to April 1845, Bluff served with five officers who were destined for the Franklin Expedition.[104]

McClure carefully probed his men regarding their positions during the incident; appearance of the weather before, during and after sail was made; times orders were given and completed; any notice of the squall's approach and from what direction; time the squall appeared and precautions against it; time from sail being made to dismasting; and which sails were furled or taken in.[105]

May, the old salt and experienced Arctic hand, described the weather during the period as "thick and dirty [and] Wind variable,"[106] and the sailors' testimony backs up Haswell's account—except on two crucial points.

Haswell stated that upon finding there was more wind in the squall than he expected, he ordered the topsail halliards let go, and this was done. When Hulott was asked what he did when the squall hit the ship, he replied he let go the main topsail halliards, however:

McClure: "By whose direction?"

Hulott: "No orders."

McClure: "What induced you to let them go without orders?"

Hulott: "The Ship heeled over and I thought it was time they were gone."

McClure: "Did you think the Mast endangered by not letting them go?"

Hulott: "I had no thought of the Mast at the time but the Vessel heeled over so much that I thought it was time they were let go."[107]

Haswell stated that the fore topsail halliards were let go by Bluff *at the same time* he gave the order for all the topsail ropes to be released, but the last order Bluff heard as a precaution against the approaching squall was to take in the topgallant sails:

McClure: "Was there anyone stationed at the [Fore and Main] Topsail Haulyards and if so, how long before the Squall took the Ship?"

Bluff: "There was nobody by the Fore, I cannot speak as to the Main. I let go the [fore topsail halliards] without orders when too late."

McClure: "From the time sail was made until the Ship was dismasted how many minutes elapsed?"

Bluff: "About Fifteen minutes."[108]

After the depositions, McClure drove home the emphasis on safety by reviewing "Extracts from Night Orders":

January 23

Carry sail during the night so as to keep close company with the "Enterprize" and in the morning Watch make all possible sail, without endangering the Spars.

May 14

Carry all sail that can be made, with safety to the Spars.

May 15

Be careful of Squalls which invariably give ample notice of their approach, therefore require but moderate attention to guard against their probable effect.

*  *  *

I cannot too strongly impress upon the Officers of the respective Watches the absolute necessity there is of the greatest precaution in carrying sail as the whole of the spare Spars are expended—consequently any further loss will compel me to bear up for Valparaso [sic], when the object of the expedition will be entirely frustrated.[109]

Collinson had sent a progress report to the Admiralty via the *Gorgon* on April 10, and with the view of reaching the Bering Strait during the first week of August, he made known his intended deviation from their Lordships' orders by not calling on Valparaiso, but instead sailing directly to the Sandwich Islands. McClure had been informed of the change, and given the *Enterprise*'s superior sailing qualities and his own ship's dismasting, he knew there was no time to spare.[110]

In spite of Haswell's experience in sailing vessels, the strain of being under McClure's constant scrutiny, plus the double-edged orders to squeeze every breath out of the wind, may have conspired to prey on the lieutenant's judgment when handling the ship. Yet, there is still one piece missing from this picture. Miertsching recorded for May 15 that the dismasting occurred when Haswell "had quitted the deck for a few minutes." How Miertsching came by this information is unknown, as one doesn't get the impression he actually observed the lieutenant leave the deck.[111] In addition, Haswell makes no reference to it in his statement, and McClure would surely have asked about such a thing during the depositions.

A wider problem between McClure and his officers now spilled from the captain's pen:

Placed Lieutenant Haswell under arrest as a prisoner at large this unpleasant but necessary duty was occasioned by his addressing to me a letter which contained improper allusions to my character as his immediate commanding officer, I can see extenuating circumstances, but on the contrary trace a spirit of insubordination in this, emanating from my refusal to give up part of what has formerly been the Midshipman's berth to the use of the Gunroom, in preference to fitting it as a Mess place for the Warrant Officers.[112]

However, McClure had already made it clear in a letter to Collinson in April that due to his announced plan to alter the enlarged gunroom, an undercurrent of insubordination already existed among the officers. The officers carried out the enlargement before the ship left England—while McClure was on leave—with the addition of the adjoining midshipmen's berth (part of the ship's original 1848 construction). McClure had a further rude surprise when he returned onboard: "Immediately I understood that the Messes were to be united."[113]

The mixed mess became the crux of McClure's problems, as he afterwards privately related to James Ross. Excepting the ever-dependable Stephen Court, the captain viewed his officers as inexperienced—save Haswell, whose indifference prevented him from being in control of the gunroom. Consequently, Surgeon Armstrong held sway, and was a man who was on unusually good terms with himself. The doctor's attitude would not have endeared him to his fellow officers on any vessel, but even less so during a long and difficult voyage.[114]

Dr. Armstrong had written to McClure on April 22 about six bales of slops (clothing and bedding for sailors), which had been taken from the bread room to make way for 50 bags of bread from the *Gorgon*, and stored in sick bay. Therein, the doctor also questioned the captain's order for the sick men to have their hammocks slung on the lower deck, rather than in sick bay. One week later, the doctor handed McClure the sick report—and asked the slops be removed. The captain responded that this would be done as soon as possible, but his immediate attention was focused on the heavy weather battering *Investigator*[115]:

> Incredible as it almost seems that within an hour after my assurance that when the proper time arrived his requisition should be attended to, this communication was placed in my hands accompanied by a Verbal intimation that he should report my conduct in his Quarterly Return, had it not been for this observation I should have attached but little importance to his letter or trouble their Lordship[s] upon the Subject ... but it remains with me to express my surprise as well as regret that any such feeling of discontent should have been elicited by so trivial a cause, from so young a man and an Officer of such very junior Standing, which may in some measure be attributed to his having previously seen nothing of the Service but its smooth surface, his employment being in a Mediterranean Steamer, and Summer Cruizing for some years in the Royal Yacht, never until this, having been consecutively a week at Sea, or known what was a Ration of Salt Provisions a circumstance in my experience quite unparalleled. Had I not taken these as extenuating circumstances, and willing to hope that the Service upon which we are engaged will have the effect of Showing the necessity of over coming instead of yielding to difficulties whether real or imaginary, I should have deemed it my duty in accordance with the proper maintenance of my authority to have placed this Officer under an Arrest for the improper and disrespectful termination of his letter, accompanied by the remark which I take it as meant to intimidate, upon its presentation,—and having waited until this date to yield an opportunity of its withdrawal, nothing more remains with me but to submit it for the consideration of their Lordships.[116]

In the first two weeks of May, Miertsching "slept little, and that badly" in the swampiness below decks, and then both he and Farquharson became sick. Receiving medicine from Armstrong, the Brother was also given "orders to drink four glasses of sherry daily. The captain was very kind and ordered me to spend the day [May 18] in his cabin. Our conversation was long and interesting; it seems to distress him that he had so forgotten himself on that day and had not handled the affair as a sincere Christian should have done."[117] This was a reference to McClure's "positively inhuman" behavior during the dismasting three days before. McClure was able to let his guard down with Miertsching and relax from the constant strain of command.

With balminess on the rise and the stormy conditions abating, the following day, Sunday, was the first time in six weeks the Lord's book was cracked open for Divine Service on the deck of *Investigator*. "The captain told me that certain officers will be changed when we reach the Sandwich Islands. I also would be glad to bid the *Investigator* farewell,"[118] Miertsching wrote. He breathed easier, assuming a transfer to *Enterprise* at Honolulu was with within his grasp.

McClure was also anxious to catch up with *Enterprise. Investigator* had last had contact with her four weeks previous, so he steered directly for the Sandwich Islands, ignoring a scheduled stop at Easter Island to obtain fresh water. A pint a day was soon fixed as the daily ration of the life-giving liquid.[119]

The now familiar problem with provisions again bedeviled the *Investigator's* commander for the coming weeks. "A couple of Goldner Beef cases bad, this is the most unfortunate affair we can be subject to," penned McClure. A few days afterward, there was "a sad misfortune in issuing the preserved meat, had four 4 lb. Cannisters decayed and unfit for any use." McClure inspected the Gamble's preserved meats and found them in "excellent order," but he was "more fearful of our late contractor [Goldner]." He added that he "threw twelve canisters of different descriptions overboard and expect to find several more," and "a couple of Goldner's cases of Beef, and Roast Mutton condemned." Though some of Gamble's preserved meats were found damaged, Mr. Gamble guarded against any shortage by sending aboard extra canisters.[120]

The last days of May brought more unwelcome news, the crew having "to clear the Port Breadroom and a most deplorable sight the bags presented, nearly the whole which had touched the side or bottom of the Breadroom were damaged, we spread it out fore and aft the decks and carefully picked it, at the termination of their labours, threw overboard eight hundred and fifty pounds, fortunately we shall be enabled to complete at the Sandwich Islands otherwise so large a loss would have been an irretrievable mis fortune [*sic*]."[121]

Despite the fine weather, the end of the month brought a dark cloud over Kentish sailor Frederick Taylor, as McClure recorded: "Had to punish Fred: Taylor a seaman with 24 lashes for disobedience of order and disgusting language to the Captain of the Main Top [Robert Tiffeny]. I am much pleased with the conduct of the Petty Officers, they evince every desire to perform their duty in which I give them every support."[122]

It's no wonder the captain was "much pleased" with his petty officers, providing "every support": of the 16 petty officers, six served on the 1848–49 expedition (three under McClure), and half had served with at least one other shipmate before that time. McClure badly needed their leadership and skills, since—in addition to his troubles with Haswell—nearly all the remaining sea officers lacked vital experience.[123]

Still, McClure's turn of mind toward his crew was that of a benevolent spiritual and academic leader, as he related on June 9:

> This being Sunday performed Divine Service on deck and am much gratified by the great attention of the crew—as this is the day I have appointed for the men to exchange their books from the Library, it was most delightful to observe with what avidity they availed themselves of the privelege [*sic*], no sooner was Divine Service terminated than the library was besieged by anxious applicants—the schoolmaster is certainly <u>aboard</u>; who can see no great change [in] the character of the seaman & still advocate the system of <u>Ignorance</u>.[124]

In with June blew the long-anticipated northeasterly trade winds, and McClure hoped "we may retain it, for I am very desirous to arrive at the Sandwich Islands so as not to detain the Expedition. Enterprize is certain of being before us [since] our [Main Top] Mast presents as much sail being set as might otherwise be carried."[125]

For some days the sailors and Marines had been treated to the sight dolphins and flying fish breaking the surface of a sparkling sea, and the hoarse calls of sleek, white and black-accented phaethons crisscrossing a cloudless sky. Armstrong beamed as *Investigator* was "carrying every stitch of canvas it was possible to crowd on the ship. Under circumstances so favourable, we made an average daily [distance] of upwards of 100 miles [160 kilometers], and on one occasion 186 miles [299 kilometers] in twenty-four hours, the greatest performance the slow sailing 'Investigator' ever made."[126]

The magical island of Oahu and its Honolulu harbor beckoned—but fate's sleight of hand soon transformed the course of the entire expedition.

# 4

# Western Arctic Gateway, 1850

*Human beings are nothing more than frail and fallible creatures—*
*and that's all we are.*

Glenn M. Stein

Beautifully clear and tranquil weather made it "grand to be a sailor"—unless, of course, you were *Investigator*'s second-in-command: "Lieutenant Haswell is still under arrest in his cabin with two [Marines] guarding his door; morning and afternoon he must pace the deck for two hours, but he may speak to no one,"[1] observed Miertsching.

From a different quarter, uncertainties about his officers flowed with McClure's sarcasm:

[June 12]

Today I was rather surprised to have received a communication from the Surgeon of rather an uneasy nature, no less than the mental sensibility of the officers, a subject which I cannot attempt even to touch upon, feeling my utter inability to "minister to a mind diseased" but must leave it like all other cases of the same description to that only "Mollifyer" old Time.

The delicate complaint appears to have originated by my desiring that in walking on the deck the officers [were] not to converse in a loud tone as it was incorrect and opposed to discipline, which certainly is a very hard case—another very weighty grievance appears from the lights being put out at 10 p.m. in the Gunroom, and at 11 p.m. in their cabins. This is doubtless a piece of unprecedented oppression. Surely such frivolity was never heard.[2]

McClure's disdain for the officers was offset by his continuing warm praise for the men, who were

busily engaged at the Holds, sharp work for the crew, who are employed the whole day, a most excellent set of men, not a murmur or an account of discontent, which I shall not fail to remember, the more I see of them the greater my admiration—from the stowage gained I think the comfort and ventilation between decks will be much increased....[3]

Have much work for the crew in restowing the Holds, and am excessively delighted with their correct, obedient and cheerful conduct under very unusual circumstances, they have not had a watch to themselves during a fortnight, the most gratifying part of such work is what struck Mr. Miertsching (a missionary on board with the hope of being an interpreter) that in the evening, instead of being tired & laying down to sleep, the greater part of the first watch is dedicated to singing—surely with such spirits what may not be anticipated, if difficulties arise, I have much confidence in them.[4]

In spite of water restrictions, McClure tried to view the glass as half-full when they "found several cases of preserved meats bad during our removal of them today, but I think all those that are restowed will be found good, if so our loss will not be of such magnitude or importance as was originally anticipated."[5]

On June 15, *Investigator* slid across that invisible equatorial line for the second time in three months. Under extra spreads of canvas, to entice every breath of wind, she drew closer and closer to the Sandwich Islands. Soon the expedition would be whole again. In the meantime, Miertsching busied himself *spiritually* enticing his shipmates: "A sailor asked me for a tract, and I distributed among the crew all that I had. On learning of this the captain laughed heartily and gave it as his opinion that his people were not such simple folk as my Eskimos."[6]

The same day, the usually robust Stephen Court went on the sick list, having "been very unwell the last week; apparently suffering from disagreement of the Liver & Stomach, with soreness of the gums and considerable emaciation for so short a time," commented Piers.[7] Despite continuing illness over the following two weeks, the Second Master's skills didn't falter one iota. Early on the morning of the 29th, with her storm damage repaired and wrapped in a fresh coat of paint, *Investigator* came within sight of the massive, snow-covered Mauna Loa—the largest volcano on Earth—on the Big Island of Hawaii. After a voyage of some 15,000 miles, McClure glowed with admiration for his young navigating officer, the grand sight "yielding evidence unquestionable of Mr Court's ability and niceness of observations in Lunar distances, as those he had taken three days previous determined our exact position."[8]

In the predawn darkness of July 1, two signal guns boomed outside Honolulu Harbor, beckoning a pilot to guide the ship into its narrow mouth. By six a.m. the pilot was in the Investigators' midst, feeding them a breakfast of disappointment:

> Our first inquiry was for our consort "Enterprize," whom we learned, with deep regret, had only left on the morning preceding for the North, having arrived here on the 25th of June, and after replenishing provisions, stores, &c., her Captain, not considering it prudent to wait longer for us, proceeded to sea, having left instructions for our guidance with the senior officer, Captain Aldham, of the "Swift." No time was therefore lost in making preparations to follow her.[9]

The *Enterprise*'s departure "caused our captain no small alarm," remarked Miertsching, and in fact, it had been a wishful sailing for Collinson and his people. As Collinson wrote, "We cast many an anxious look to the leeward in hopes of seeing our consort; but as the season was far advanced I determined on proceeding alone, trusting that our detention in communicating with the *Herald* or at the edge of the ice would give her time to rejoin us."[10] Being the leader of the expedition meant Collinson had to balance his mission's objective with the Admiralty's explicit orders "against suffering the two vessels under orders to separate, except in the event of accident or unavoidable necessity."[11]

Due to the prevailing wind and tides, and narrowness of the harbor entrance, the pilot could not take *Investigator* into the harbor, and she was obliged to drop anchor in the roads, outside the reefs. Keeping the newcomer company were several merchantmen and the *Bayonnaise*, a French corvette, whose captain immediately sent an officer over, offering assistance and congratulations at McClure's arrival. Her Majesty's Brig *Swift* was anchored in the harbor, and had already exchanged acknowledgments with *Investigator*. Commander William C. Aldham and his crew previously assisted *Enterprise* in taking on provisions, water and other stores, so her officers and men could briefly enjoy paradise ashore, and the same generous treatment awaited the Investigators. McClure had the pleasure of writing Aldham and asking that Court be examined for Master, as he completed his qualifying time; Court passed his exam the next day.[12]

Comradeship and pleasant duties aside, before *Investigator* departed the enchanted surroundings, Aldham would be drawn into the ugly rift between McClure and his officers.

In the meantime, on the advice of Kellett, Collinson chose to sail in a northwesterly arc around Attu Island (the westernmost of the Aleutian Islands)—in the belief he could avoid northwesterly gales that were supposedly prevalent in the northwest Pacific—before shaping a course for the Bering Strait. "But in my private letter to Captain M'Clure I stated that Captain Kellett had come through the Straits of Amoukta [Amukta Pass], and that if he was late, perhaps it would be worth while risking the passage [directly through the Aleutian Islands]." Still, Collinson (naturally) assumed *Enterprise* would reach the Arctic before *Investigator*—but the hand of fate had again dealt ironic cards.[13]

After passing through the Bering Strait, McClure was instructed to make his way to Cape Lisburne (northwestern coast of Russian America), and to keep a good lookout for HMS *Herald* and any whalers that may provide information on *Enterprise*'s progress:

> Should you obtain no intelligence, you will understand that I intend to make the pack, close to the American shore, and pursue the first favourable opening west of the coast stream, pressing forwards towards Melville Island.
>
> In the event of meeting land, it is most probable that I would pursue the southern shore; but conspicuous marks will be erected if practicable, and information buried at a 10-foot radius.
>
> As it is necessary to be prepared for the contingency of your not being able to follow by the ice closing in, or the severity of the weather, you will keep the "Investigator" as close to the edge of the pack as is consistent with her safety, and remain there until the season compels you to depart, when you will look into Kotzebue Sound for the "Plover" [Commander Moore], or information regarding her position; and having deposited under her charge twelvemonth's provision, you will proceed to Valparaiso, replenish and return to the straits, bearing in mind that the months of June and July are the most favorable.
>
> Should you not find the "Plover," or that any casualty has happened to render her inefficient as a depôt, you will take her place; and if (Captain Kellett supposes) Kotzebue Sound has proved too exposed for a winter harbour, you will proceed to Grantley Harbour, leaving a notice to that effect at Chamisso Island....
>
> In the event of leaving the straits this season, you will take any weak or sickly men out of the "Plover," and replace them from your crew; affording Commander Moore all the assistance in your power, and leaving with him Mr. Miertsching the interpreter, together with the instructions which you have received with regard to his accommodation.[14]

At first, a misinterpretation of Collinson's orders *seems* to be the culprit of Armstrong's strong feelings about the near future:

> All participated in the feeling of anxiety that no time should be lost, as we had heard that Captain Collinson had expressed his intention, (indeed his orders to us were to that effect, as we learned subsequently,) to take the "Plover" into the ice with him, in the event of our not reaching Behring's Strait in time. This intelligence was received with manifest dissatisfaction—nor could we understand why we, who were all volunteers for service in the ice, should be thus thrown aside to remain in listless inactivity, while others would assume the place in this philanthropic service we could not concede to any, and which it was our undoubted privilege to occupy.[15]

Although Armstrong initially referred to the possibility of Collinson's taking *Plover* into the ice with him as being a rumor (and McClure noted the same rumor in Honolulu), the doctor revealed he afterward learned Collinson's orders "were to that effect." But McClure's book made no reference to Collinson's orders, although it's possible the following portion of the Admiralty orders caused some confusion: "[W]henever you fall in with her [*Plover*], you are hereby directed to take her and Commander Moore under your orders."[16]

For now, the surroundings gave the Investigators a respite from their mission. Piers and Miertsching went ashore, called upon an American mission house (where Piers captured rare butterflies in the garden), and then had a look around Honolulu. Writing that the city boasted a population of over 30,000, Miertsching added that "many English, Americans, Chinese, Jews, and Germans are met here." And Piers formed the opinion that American influence would supersede British influence: "Although the Island is under the protection of the British Flag, and there are American Chapels and Schools and two German Catholic Chapels, there is not one English Missionary in the place."[17]

James Nelson, who frequently went ashore with his captain, noticed a "Sailors Reading Room" and two neat, well-built churches. He had good opportunities to observe the town, which appeared to be well regulated, and almost entirely under the control of the missionaries, who were at the forefront of all of the inhabitants' social matters.[18]

The following day, *Investigator* glided past the bones of several ships resting upon sandbanks that jutted out on either side of the harbor's entrance, and was warped into her anchorage by a swarm of native muscle. These nautical skeletons allowed McClure to breathe new vigor into his ship through the purchase of spars, old topmasts and yards.[19]

After dinner, Court and Piers trotted into the countryside on the main road atop a pair of pack horses, and met up with Sainsbury and Wynniatt:

> Before we arrived here we understood that the ladies of Oahu admired fair men; and Sainsbury, who is particularly fair having dismounted and seated himself by the side of a nice looking, selk [silky], Hawxian girl, I was much amused to see her stroking his face. Among the coloured population (the ladies), it is considered a compliment to be kissed by an European, or white man, and I was further much amused to see Court dismount and salute a young girl who had just supplied us with a Pawpaw [papaya]—it was not however his simply saluting the girl, but my observing at the same time a lady, in a house on the opposite side of the road, watching the flirtation from a window that amused me, and made me laugh heartily. On my telling [Court] of it afterward he said "why did you not tell me?"— but again, to pass it off I said, "Oh, I dare say she would not have minded being in the girl's place."[20]

With the upcoming search looming, any Arctic intelligence was vital to McClure. In this regard, Mr. R.C. Wyllie, Minister of Foreign Relations at Honolulu, had shown Collinson a very important letter from Dr. Rae to Mr. Anthony Barclay, the British Consul in New York, which had been published in New York on April 13. In these writings, Rae outlined his travels with Dr. Richardson, having searched the North American coast from the mouth of the Mackenzie River to the Coppermine River in 1848–49. Due to ice conditions, Rae had not crossed the Dolphin and Union Strait and examined Wollaston and Victoria Lands (both later found to be part of Victoria Island). McClure must have also been made aware of this information by the minister, since McClure made reference in a later dispatch regarding Rae's travels in this area. Now both Collinson and McClure knew what section of the North American coast had been most recently searched for Franklin. In June, Rae received a communication from Sir George Simpson (HBC governor), who "wanted [Rae] to travel farther north than ever before," and this journey resulted in Rae's nearly coming face-to-face with one of the *Investigator*'s sled parties.[21]

On the third day of July, Her Majesty's Brig *Cockatrice* arrived from Mazatlan, and Armstrong noted that she came "with the latest letters and dispatches from England; but as few of the former were received, we assumed they had been sent on to Valparaiso, in the hope of meeting us there."[22] But for Brother Miertsching, it was nothing less than a bountiful feast for his heart—and soul: "Oh, how I rejoiced over the beloved letters and an English *Losung* [Moravian daily devotional manual] and missionary leaflets from Brothers Mallalieu and Latrowe [Latrobe?]. Also the letter from Brother U.A.L. cheered me greatly. Thanks to Thy love, my joy was indescribable."[23]

Several of the Investigators were still busily employed taking on provisions, but in the afternoon, Carpenter Ford was able to go on shore leave: "I took a horse & rode out several miles into the country which I found to be very pleasant & fertile. Every person to all appearance industrious & happy, which was more than I was, as the beautiful scenes around reminded me of my home etc. In the evening at sunset I returned on board & to my great joy I found a letter for me from My Dear Mary & Father. I felt so overjoyed that I scarcely knew where I was, on my head or feet & entirely put new spirits in me. In fact I was [so] happy I could dance, sing or anything else. I wrote a letter home that evening before I turned in."[24]

*Investigator's* brief stay at Honolulu allowed for some changes in the ship's company, with a few invalids leaving for the *Swift*: Able Seaman Joseph Elson, Captain of the Foretop Thomas McClune, and Private 1st Class Joseph Adams, RM. Meanwhile, it also afforded Able Seaman James Jackson the opportunity to disappear into paradise. Consequently, four able seamen joined the expedition from ships in the harbor, plus one Royal Marine: Samuel Bounsall, Ellis Griffiths, John Boyle, Thomas Toy (two naval men and two merchant sailors, respectively), and Private Elias Bow, RM.[25]

There was one person whom McClure was absolutely intent on *leaving* the ship— Lieutenant William H. Haswell. Long before *Investigator* ever came within sight of land, McClure was mapping out a blistering case to the Senior Officer of HM Ships & Vessels at the Sandwich Islands, Commander Aldham, to have Haswell removed from his ship:

[May 27, 1850]

1. I have the honor to enclose copies of my order to and explanation from Lieu[t] Haswell Senior Lieu[t] of this Vessel,— referring to the loss of certain Spars as per Margin [fore topmast and jib boom] which occurred upon the morning of the 15th Instant during his Watch. Upon the merits of this Statement I purpose to offer but a few concise remarks, content to let it rest upon the evidence of Henry Bluff (Bo[s] Mate) & Corn[s] Hullott (Cap[t] Cox[n]) herewith forwarded, this enquiry I felt it necessary to institute as from Lieu[t] Haswell's account it would appear that every precaution was taken to guard against this disaster which prudence could dictate or the regulations of the Service require; having myself heard the opera-

Carpenter 1st Class George J. Ford, RN, wearing his Baltic Medal 1854–55 and Arctic Medal 1818–55, c. 1857 (courtesy of the Karpeles Manuscript Library).

tions of making sail completed, I was surprised to hear it almost immediately followed by the order to take in the [top gallant sails] (therefore to this point I did not doubt the Statement, but beyond it evidence was required to satisfy me) speedily succeeded by an Uproar and confusion which I was at a loss to account for until the damage sustained was reported.

2. As Lieu$^t$ Haswell has thought it necessary to advert particularly to orders given by me to the different Officers of the Watches, which by inference might imply a recklessness upon my part, I beg to submit a few Extracts of my night orders which I hope will have the effect of removing any such impression and shall dismiss this part of my letter without any further observation.

3. Lieu$^t$ Haswell has also added that in consequence of his having been censured by me on the 2$^d$ April for not making sail, he by implication therefore considered it necessary to do so, altho' in the face of a Squall regardless of its consequences, fearful that he should again fall under my displeasure. Surely since the 2$^d$ April considering during that period he has Kept many morning Watches in common with the other Officers; he must have occasionally made sail, or does he wish me to understand that the 15th May was the first time since that date he has attempted anything of the Kind. Unfortunately for that Officer his making all Sail on the 2$^d$ April immediately after my censure without any damage to the Spars is sufficient of itself to show that he had not been too zealous in the discharge of his duty particularly as the log shews the Weather had been moderating since the evening preceding. As to the frequent allusions to the zeal for this particular Service, I have little to add except to remark that it must have had its emanation with the Squall and expired with the fall of the Mast—for the following morning when the Main Topmast was reported Sprung I find that this zealous officer was content with intimating the same to me as I was dressing, and then retired to his Cabin without permitting his Zeal to carry him to the mast head to examine the extent of the Spring, or induce him to give any directions for the security of the Mast, in this I perceive his characteristic apathy and indifference had returned which on many occasions has called forth my displeasure, nothing further remains for me to add to this part of my letter except to express my regret that he had not in this instance abated a little of his Zeal and added a small portion of his discretion which would have had the effect of saving the Vessel her Spars and not reduced her to her present crippled condition.

4. I now arrive at the last paragraph, and that of infinite importance involving as it does a question of discipline, to which I would beg to draw your attention and point out the unbecoming tone which Lieu$^t$ Haswell assumes in accusing his Commanding Officer with interference in his duties. Sir, if this simple principle is once admitted I see no point of limitation for if to day an inferior may tell his Commd$^g$ Officer with impunity he is not to be interfered with tomorrow he will contemptuously spurn his authority. And in conclusion will take leave to state that the result of such conduct was followed by inevitable and necessary consequence in support of discipline, the Officer was placed under an Arrest on the morning of the 17th Inst$^t$ in which he still continues as prisoner at large from which I deferentially urge and most earnestly entreat that he may be removed from under my command.[26]

McClure followed up these writings in another letter two days later:

I beg to forward you a Copy of a letter from L$^t$ Haswell and also to offer any remarks upon the circumstances which gave rise to it.

Upon the morning of the 16$^{th}$ when the [main topmast] was reported Sprung as mentioned in my letter of the 27$^{th}$ Instant, struck with the Apathy of L$^t$ Haswell as therein detailed I gave him a very severe reprimand on the Quarter Deck in the presence of Mr Court (2$^d$ Master) for his utter indifference to his duty, in so doing I doubtless expressed myself warmly, for I can assure you I felt most Keenly that Officer's utter incapacity for his responsible situation and far from my now expressing any wish to modify a syllable that I then uttered it is a source of infinite satisfaction to me to hope what then occurred may possibly have been some effect in stimulating him to some future exertion.

With reference therefore to that letter my reason as communicated to Lieu$^t$ Haswell was that as it was antedated I would not receive it, unless it bore the date upon which it was written, my motive for this—that being compelled upon the morning of the 17$^{th}$ Inst$^t$ to place that Officer under an arrest as reported in my letter of the 27$^{th}$. I was sensible it was in consequence of such arrest and not from any feeling that the reprimand was undeserved that he then addressed me, as otherwise this letter would have either preceded or accompanied that of the 16$^{th}$ Inst$^t$ which he delivered to me at 8:30 p.m.[27]

Nearly a month later—just days before land came into view—McClure set pen to paper for the senior officer at the Sandwich Islands, again bringing the hammer down on Haswell. The captain listed the spars lost in the ship's passage from Plymouth, and asked for help in replacing them:

> The only plea that I can urge in extenuation of any part of this great damage is the case of Lieu.t Cresswell on the 24th of January, who is a very young officer without the previous advantage of Practical experience in charge of a Watch and was more intent on endeavouring to sustain his Station with the "Enterprize" than considering the effect of the gradually freshening breeze upon the Masts which he could not very well ascertain it being still dark. With respect to Lieu.t Haswell I have no such case to allege it being daylight and the Squall which caused the wreck being fully observed was only partially guarded against also being aware of my particular ["orders" is struck through] directions to be prepared against their approach as he witnessed a very severe reprimand which I gave to Lieu.t Cresswell but a few days previous for not taking any precautions against a Squall which would certainly have dismasted the Vessel, had I not given directions for the Sail to be taken in which was barely completed when it reached the Ship. Moreover being informed by Lieu.t Haswell "that he Knows he is a very good officer having been told so by those much my Senior in the Service"—I feel it is perfectly futile offering any further observation after the above modest assurance from this exceedingly well self-satisfied Officer but at once allowed the impression which it is obviously calculated to produce the full weights of its merits.[28]

In his final communication (written the same day), McClure first asked the senior officer of the Sandwich Islands to bring the subject to the notice of their Lordships, while launching in on Lieutenant Cresswell this time:

2  It is with much concern that I have to report Lieu.t Cresswell Junior of this Vessel for conduct evincing a Spirit of insubordination which I was quite unprepared to expect.

3  The circumstance from which it arose is this upon the 17th May I wished to elicit some further facts relative to the loss of the Spars which occurred on the 15th by the investigation of some Petty Officers who had the morning Watch for the purpose of satisfying myself whether every precaution had been taken to guard against the approaching squall that I might be enabled to draw out a statement for the information of their Lordships, the damage sustained in Spars being very considerable and quite incompatible with the fineness of the Weather.

4  In accordance with these intentions I desired L.t Cresswell to attend in order that he might attest the evidence; to this [he] positively objected unless I gave him a written order, as he considered "my conduct quite illegal," I again repeated my order and default of compliance threatened to place him under an Arrest (desiring M.r Paine Clerk in Charge who was present for the purpose of taking down the evidence to attend) upon which L.t Cresswell remarked that is the same as a written order, recollect, addressing M.r Paine, "I do it by order."

5  Sir could I to this date have been able to detect any returning symptoms by L.t C admitting the impropriety of his behaviour or alleging a mistaken view of his duty it would have afforded me

Lieutenant Samuel Gurney Cresswell, RN (after a photograph by Taylor, *The Illustrated London News*, Nov. 4, 1853).

some satisfaction to have overlooked an offence which to a certain extent might be considered unintentional but under existing circumstances (his subscription being under Protest) I do not feel any other course but that which I now adopt could be approved by their Lordships, or indeed in accordance with discipline.

6  Furthermore I would take this opportunity of stating that I trace the systematic opposition of the Senior officers from the time that Mʳ Piers Assistᵗ Surgeon addressed a letter to Capᵗ Collinson, complaining of my having taken part of the accommodation belonging to the Gun Room for the use of the Ship's Stores—those officers having previously claimed it from me as their right, a term I could not admit, or a principle I will not allow, but as the place in question is still contained some private Stores, I did not hurry their removal until after sailing from the Straits of Magellan when I certainly thought the time had arrived for its occupation according to my original intention.

7  In consequence I gave an order for its clearance; from that period difficulties to which I had hitherto been a stranger have arisen which the date equally as the purport of my different letters too palpably but unavoidably illustrate.[29]

On July 3, in responding to Aldham's writings, the *Investigator*'s captain tried his utmost to have Haswell removed from his ship:

In reply to your letter of this date requiring to be informed if the removal of Lieutᵗ Haswell will be attended with any circumstance detrimental to the Service that I am employed upon I beg to state that so far from it being prejudicial, it will be of the utmost advantage both as regards the Service and my own happiness which has been entirely overturned by the conduct of that officer, which as you are already in possession of the facts connected with the Subject of this application I need not again recapitulate, but at the same time will beg to reiterate most emphatically the request that he may be removed from under my command.[30]

Commander Aldham must have been in a quandary as to how to deal with McClure's "problems," and this is the only direct evidence uncovered regarding Aldham addressing them. Rear Admiral Sir Phipps Hornby was commander-in-chief of the Pacific Station (1847–51), onboard the second rate ship-of-the-line *Asia*, in Valparaiso Harbor. A search of Hornby's official correspondence and his journal did not produce any reference to Aldham's situation with McClure. Dr. Armstrong did, however, weave a subtle reference into his published journal: "I am sure the latter gallant and estimable officer [Aldham], should these pages ever meet his eye, will not readily forget the visit of the 'Investigator,' and *the circumstances* which led to his acquaintance with her officers."[31]

How did McClure expect to embark upon his arduous mission without his first lieutenant—the most experienced sea officer onboard—or did he think Aldham would simply offer up the *Swift*'s senior lieutenant as a replacement? The scenario appeared to play out on the same day, with Miertsching witnessing a lengthy proceeding: "Today they held a sort of court-martial or rather court of inquiry on our ship. After a five-hour session and much debate, the officers promised the captain exact obedience, etc."[32]

On July 4, the appointed day of departing paradise, Armstrong lamented the lack of fresh provisions for the voyage ahead:

We failed to obtain an ample supply of fresh meat, owning to several bullocks having been drowned in attempting to land them from one of the native boats, and our stock was consequently reduced to one bullock and twelve sheep. The supply of fruit and vegetables was likewise short, from the scarcity consequent on the briskness of demand. It consisted of water-melons, bananas, pumpkins, cabbages, and other fruits and vegetables; but we could not the procure a single cocoa-nut, abundant as they are on the islands, all having been bought up a few days before.[33]

For Brother Miertsching, it was an overwhelming time, and he confessed:

I am incapable of expressing my emotions on paper; forget them I never will. As soon as I was onboard I went and reported to the captain; he invited me to a glass of wine and showed a composure which was forced. The crew were all busily engaged in making the ship ready for sea, and, as generally happens when a ship is getting under sail, so was it also here: the men were half out of their wits; noise, singing, whistling, and profanity gave me an unpleasant reminder of what lay before me. Everyone was now aboard, including a number of men whom the sergeant and his marines had escorted from the city jail, and whose release the captain procured by paying their fines.... The few letters which I had written for Europe I now sealed and consigned to the English consul. At 5 p.m. we were clear of the harbour and in the open sea, and, as we had a very good wind and sailed fast, the city of Honolulu soon sank from sight. The captain's presence was required on deck, so I went to his cabin and sang to my guitar:

> Give me Thy strength, oh God of power,
> Then let winds blow or thunders roar;
> I need not fear by sea or land,
> For Thou, my God, wilt by me stand.[34]

While *Investigator* sped toward the Bering Strait—gateway to the western Arctic—the true test of her people's physical and mental endurance lay ahead.

The day after leaving Honolulu, Miertsching noticed the "antagonism between the captain and his officers has been changed in a few days into a very agreeable and friendly relationship," but adds warily, "Ah, could it only remain thus!" And the present gentle atmosphere included the spiritual hand of Reverend Samuel C. Damon, of the American Seamen's Friend Society in Honolulu, who "has supplied our sailors generously with books and tracts through my servant Corporal Farquharson. Ah! may these be a great blessing to us."[35]

Over the coming fortnight, the Investigators drew closer to the domain of the ice, and Miertsching observed McClure's religious tenor:

[July 12, 1850]

Every day favourable wind; the weather very fine; we are steering as directly as possible for Bering Strait. The crew are in good humour; a number of them are on the sick list, because they could not refrain from frightful excesses in Honolulu. Daily we note that we are approaching the cold North; for the tropical heat is leaving us. It does not seem right to the captain that the men should read tracts, so ordered the ship's fiddler [Bradbury] to play a tune and the men to dance. A seaman, Boyle, a gifted singer and dancer, received from the captain a large glass of wine as a reward for his skill.[36]

The captain also took practical steps to ensure his crew received extra nourishment in "consequence of the peculiar Service upon which [the] Ship is employed and considering it necessary after any Extra fatigue to the Ship's Company that they should be supplied occasionally with an Extra Meal of (one third Pound of Biscuit, one third Pound Preserved Meat, and a half Allowance of spirits for each man)."[37] Napoleon said an army runs on its stomach—and so does a ship's company.

Miertsching further observed:

[July 19, 1850]

For several days raw, cold weather and fog; wind favourable; five sailors still under the doctor's care and regretting the frightful diseases which they contracted in Honolulu. I often have interesting discussions with the captain about the missionaries to the heathen and civilization itself: we hold very different views on these matters. Today we had a long discussion on the words, "it is easier for a camel to pass through the eye of a needle, [than for a rich man to enter into the kingdom of God.]" I still lack faith in my English, so I advised the captain to refer his mistaken views to his own writings and books; for he has a fine library, and in it some rare and precious works on Christianity. With the officers I associate much more agreeably than formerly. In the last few days we have seen countless varieties of seafowl.[38]

"At five o'clock on the evening of the 20th, land was reported on the port bow, stern looking outline of the eastern extremity of the island of Amlia [in the central Aleutian Islands] could be faintly discerned through the dense haze which enveloped it, then distant about ten miles," wrote Armstrong.[39]

That same day, the captain wrote a letter to the Secretary of the Admiralty (which was later forwarded to England by HMS *Plover*), in which he made the case for his possible arrival at Cape Lisburne *after* Collinson, and so failing to rendezvous with *Enterprise*. McClure outlined very detailed plans for *Investigator* to then enter the ice and carry on alone—all predicated on the narrow possibility *Enterprise* might reach Cape Lisburne first, and that Collinson would take her into the ice without his consort, thus breaking the Admiralty's strict orders against the two vessels separating, "except in the event of accidental or unavoidable necessity."[40] In his writings, McClure reiterated Collinson's instructions, in which McClure recorded he was to:

> proceed to Cape Lisburne, in the hope of meeting him [Collinson] in that vicinity, as he anticipated being detained a day or two by the "Plover" in Kotzebue Sound, it is unnecessary to add that every exertion shall be made to reach that rendezvous, but I can scarce venture to hope that, even under very favourable circumstances, I shall be so fortunate as to accomplish it ere the "Enterprise" will have rounded that Cape, as, from her superior sailing, she hitherto having beaten us, by eight days to Cape Virgins, and from Magellan Straits to Oahu by six. It is therefore, under the probable case that this vessel [Investigator] may form a detached part of the expedition, that I feel it is my duty to state, for the information of the Lords Commissioners of the Admiralty, the course which, under such a contingency, I shall endeavour to pursue, and I have to request that you will lay the same before their Lordships.
>
> 1st. After passing Cape Lisburne, it is my intention to keep in the open water, which, from the different reports that I have read, appears, about this season of the year, to make between the American coast and the main pack, as far to the eastward as the 130th meridian, unless a favourable opening should earlier appear in the ice, which would lead me to infer that I might push more directly for Banks Land, which I think is of the utmost importance to thoroughly examine. [McClure knew there may well be a connection to the western end of Viscount Melville Sound—a link to a North-West Passage.] In the event of thus far succeeding, and the season continuing favourable for further operations, it would be my anxious desire to get to the northward of Melville Island, and resume our search along its shores, and the islands adjacent, as long as the navigation can be carried on, and then secure for the winter in the most eligible position which offers.
>
> 2nd. In the ensuing spring, as soon as it is practicable for travelling parties to start, I should dispatch as many as the state of the crew will admit of, in different directions, each being provided with 40 days' provisions, with directions to examine minutely all bays, inlets, and islands towards the N.E., ascending occasionally some of the highest points of land, so as to be enabled to obtain extended views, being particularly cautious, in their advance, to observe any indication of a break-up in the ice, so that their return to the ship may be affected without hazard, even before the expenditure of their provisions would otherwise render it necessary.
>
> 3rd. Supposing the parties to have returned (without obtaining any clue of the absent ships), and the vessel liberated about the 1st of August, my object would be then to push on towards Wellington Inlet [Wellington Channel, Franklin's proposed alternate route] (assuming that that channel communicates with the Polar Sea), and search both its shores, unless, in so doing, some indication should be met with to show that parties from any of Captain Austin's vessels had previously done so [Captain Horatio Austin left England in May 1850 with a four-ship naval squadron to enter the eastern Arctic], when I should return and endeavour to penetrate in the direction of Jones' Sound, carefully examining every place that was practicable. Sir, should our efforts to reach this point be successful, and in the route no traces be discernible of the long-missing expedition, I should not then be enabled longer to divest myself of the feeling, painful as it must be to arrive at such a conclusion, that all human aid would then be perfectly unavailing, and therefore, under such a conviction, I would think it my duty, if possible, to return to England, or, at all events, endeavour to reach some port that would ensure that object upon the following year [and completing a North-West Passage].

4th. In the event of this being our last communication, I would request you to assure their Lordships that no apprehension whatever need be entertained of our safety until the autumn of 1854, as we have on board three years of all species of provisions, commencing from the 1st September proximo, which, without much deprivation, may be made to extend a period of four years, as, moreover, whatever is killed by the hunting parties I intend to issue in lieu of the usual rations, which will still further protract our resources.

It gives me great pleasure to say that the good effects of fruit and vegetables (a large quantity of which we took on board at Oahu) [not according to Dr. Armstrong] are very perceptible, in the increased vigour of the men, who at this moment are in as excellent condition as it is possible to desire, and evince a spirit of confidence and a cheerfulness of disposition which are beyond all appreciation.

5th. Should difficulties apparently insurmountable encompass our progress, so as to render it a matter of doubt whether the vessel could be extricated, I should deem it expedient, in that case, not to hazard the lives of those entrusted to my charge after the winter of 1852, but, in the ensuing spring, quit the vessel with sledges and boats, and make the best of our way to either Pond's Bay, Leopold Harbour, the Mackenzie, or for the whalers,[41] according to circumstances. [These were, respectively, the whaling station at Pond Inlet, on the northeast of Baffin Island; Ross's 1848 supply depot at Port Leopold, on the northeast tip of Somerset Island; one of the HBC posts along the Mackenzie River in North America; and the whaling grounds in Baffin Bay.]

Finally. In this letter I have endeavoured to give an outline of what I wish to accomplish (and what, under moderately favourable seasons, appears to me attainable), the carrying out of which, however, not resting upon human exertions, it is impossible even to surmise if any or what portion may be successful. But my object in addressing you is to place their Lordships in possession of my intentions up to the latest period, so, as far as possible, to relieve their minds from any unnecessary anxiety as to our fate; and having done this—a duty which is incumbent on me, from the deep sympathy expressed by their Lordships, and participated in by all classes of our countrymen, in the interesting object of this expedition,—I have only to add that, with the ample resources which a beneficent Government and a generous country have placed at our disposal (not anything that can add to our comfort being wanting), we enter upon this distinguished service with a firm determination to carry out, as far as in our feeble strength we are permitted, their benevolent intentions.[42]

In reality, it was all a setup—part of McClure's cleverly devised plan to ensure he could operate independently in the Arctic, and avoid any future official condemnation for doing so.

"For two days we have been experiencing very changeable weather; at times the wind very strong; the weather so foggy that one can scarcely see a ship's length ahead. Gore's Island passed in soundings of 25 fathoms (150 feet; see Appendix 1). Violent tides in this still very poorly known archipelago, full of shoals and reefs, cause the captain and officers much uneasiness,"[43] warily wrote Miertsching. "The seamen are in excellent humour, but the captain is far from happy in these wholly uncharted seas; for a week neither sun, moon, nor stars visible, and the ship has been driven now backwards, now sideways by the current, so that one does not know where we actually are. The land is hidden in fog, and the charts of these seas are most untrustworthy."[44]

The morning of July 27, Armstrong observed, "King's Island [in the Bering Sea] was faintly visible about eight miles distant, where we found a strong easterly current setting into Norton Sound. We altered course a little more to the westward, to keep clear of the land."[45]

McClure now privately related a different scenario to Sir James Ross from the one he had laid out for the Admiralty only one week before:

Collinson wrote me he intended going to 170° E & 30th North before he shaped his course [to the Bering Strait], I mentioned this to several persons Capts. of Whalers, who advised me to steer as I have done & said I should arrive at Bhering Straits a week before him; And from our uninterrupted run to this, I think stand a fair chance, however as he goes to Kotzebue Sound to communicate with Plover and my orders are to proceed to Cape Lisburne & then follow him into the Ice, I stand a good chance of not meeting him, in such an event I shall push on resolutely for Bank's Land....

McClure failed to mention to Ross anything about Collinson's suggestion (in a private letter) of a shortcut through the Aleutians, and even McClure's book stated that it was "an intelligent merchant sailor, who urged him by all means to steer a *direct* course to the northward, and not to fear north-west gales at that season of the year." It appears McClure *purposely* did not attribute the idea of the shortcut to Collinson, in order to further distance himself from his commander. In addition, in spite of the cordiality Miertsching observed between the captain and his officers after leaving the Sandwich Islands, McClure went on to lay bare to Ross the overall inexperience of his officers and his raw feelings about naval officers generally:

> I think of you about ten times a day, I would say twenty only you would observe this is his usual romance.
> But when I mention the cause you will exonerate me from any flights of imagination. Do you remember your often expressed opinion,—never to take a Steam officer or Man, unfortunately the 1st Lieut[n] served all his time in the Penelope & positively is as ignorant of sails and their utility as if he had never seen them, the other officers two Mates [Sainsbury and Wynniatt], just passed [on the gunnery training ship *Excellent*], & young Cresswell had never had charge of a watch before, so you will see what a low ebb the service has come to when not any officer of any standing would volunteer, they count the time when their promotion is due, and wait quietly at home for it.... Mr. Court is the only exception and very attentive and accurate in his navigation, he passed at Wahoa, so is now eligible for his promotion, with your assistance he might obtain it during his absence.[46]

In setting down lines on July 28 to Francis Cresswell (the second lieutenant's father), McClure made a seemingly offhand remark about the Passage, and again commented on the quality of naval officers of the day:

> I am induced to hope that we shall be able to reach some considerable distance towards the N.E., what we shall perform towards the effecting [of] the Passage, I can say nothing of, except that our best exertions shall be given in furtherance of the benevolent object of the Expedition, & the honor of our country, leaving the results to the Great Disposer of all events—I am happy to say that Lieut. Cresswell is in good health & spirits & very diligent in the performance of his duties—rather a rare virtue I am sorry to add among the young officers of the present day....[47]

On the same Sunday, McClure again wrote to the Admiralty, explaining that after leaving Oahu, he "shaped a direct course for the Aleutian Group passing them in 172° 40' W upon the evening of the 20th continued our course with a fine S.E.[ly] breeze, but extremely thick and foggy weather (which retarded the best of our way being made) got fairly out of Behring's Straits upon the evening of the 27th and are now in a fair way of realizing their Lordship's expectations of reaching the Ice by the beginning of August."[48]

He afterward contradicted his recent writings to the Admiralty, in which he set forth the scenario that *Enterprise* might very well enter the ice *ahead* of *Investigator*: "I have not seen anything of the Enterprize, nor is it my intention to loose [*sic*] a moment by waiting off Cape Lisburne but shall use my best endeavours to carry out the intentions contained in my letter of the 20th of which I earnestly trust that their Lordships will approve."[49] If McClure had no intention of "waiting" for Collinson, he was clearly indicating his belief that *Enterprise* was behind him.

At seven o'clock on that morning, *Investigator* slid across the Arctic Circle amid crisp 41° air, and for the second time in as many years, made her appearance upon the polar stage.[50]

# 5

# The Wily Arctic, 1850

*And now there came both mist and snow,*
*And it grew wondrous cold;*
*And ice, mast-high, came floating by,*
*As green as emerald.*

—Samuel Taylor Coleridge,
*The Rime of the Ancient Mariner*

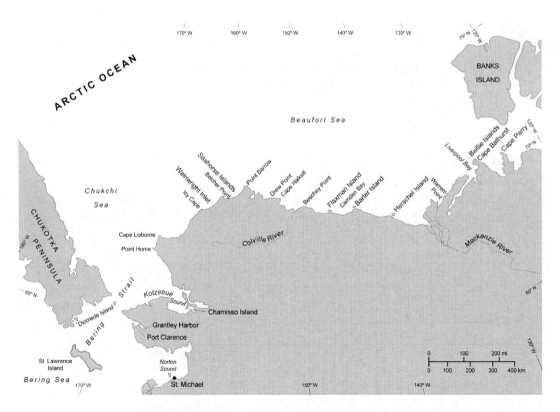

**Bering Strait and North American Coast (LibbeyDesign, Orlando, Florida).**

Through the day the Investigators exchanged colors with two apparently home-bound American whalers. In the distance, water jetted from several whales, while a legion of seabirds gorged themselves on the stripped carcass of a leviathan floating past the ship.

The doctor recorded that the "first issue of the warm clothing supplied [by the] Government for our use, was made; embracing one complete suit of blue double milled box cloth, boots, stockings, boot-hose, comforters, mits and caps; all of excellent quality, and well adapted for Polar service." Acting Captain of the Foretop George Brown recalled how "we had for the rigorous weather thick drawers, and jerseys, thick socks, peajackets and blue trousers, over which we pulled leather boots, reaching to our hips. We never had fur, even in the worst weather, but as the winter came we substituted for the leather boots, snow boots with cork soles and thick cloth uppers."[1]

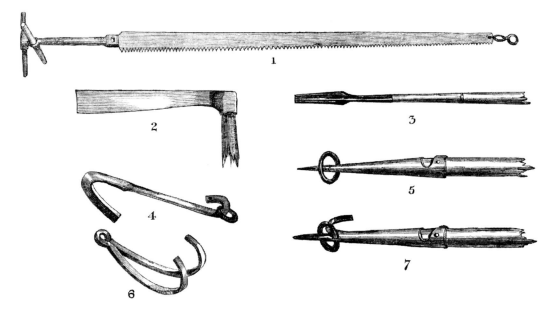

Ice Implements: (1) Ice Saw, (2) Ice Hatchet, (3) Ice Chisel, (4) Ice Anchor, (5) Ice Pole, (6) Ice Claw, (7) Ice Hook (*The Illustrated London News*, May 13, 1848).

The Investigators were "now daily employed in putting in order, and preparing all necessary implements for ice navigation; ice anchors and chisels, hatchets, saws, whale lines, &c., were all duly overhauled and got on deck in readiness for use. In addition, the crow's nest was hoisted into its aerial position at the fore-top-gallant mast head [which was the duty of George Brown]." This hooded, barrel-shaped perch was critical for making observations on the state of the ice in all directions. Its most frequent occupant was ice master, who communicated to the officer of the watch on deck through a long gutta-percha megaphone.[2]

A barrel was thrown overboard at lat. 68° 00′ N. and long. 167° 50′ W.; its positive message detailed, in part, "Fine breeze from the NNE and not a particle of Ice to be seen in any direction from the Masthead."[3]

In the Arctic, summer days grow long, and afterward the sun spends but a brief period below the horizon; during this twilight, a soft glow warms the sky, caused by the reflection of the sun's rays from the upper atmosphere. Two days before the end of July, a sail was spied on the horizon at eight in the evening—it was the *Plover* (Commander Moore). At the time of the encounter, Moore was away with two boats, making inquiries among the natives of Wainwright Inlet (southwest of Belcher Point) regarding an unfounded rumor about a party of white men building a boat along the coast to the northward. Also detached from *Plover*, leading a boat expedition along the coast toward Cape Bathurst (reached August 8), was recently promoted Commander William J.S. Pullen—Lieutenant Haswell's first cousin. *Plover* had just returned from observing impenetrable ice conditions from Wainwright Inlet to lat. 71° 30' N. and long. 164° 28' W. "This was not what I had anticipated from the continuance of the south-east winds," wrote McClure, "but the [navigable] season is not far advanced, and much may yet be accomplished *ere we are frozen up*."[4]

The *Plover* had no word of *Enterprise*, and James Nelson expressed the general sentiment that this news gave everyone great satisfaction. This common feeling toward their "so called" consort had its origins in *Enterprise*'s superior sailing qualities, and the *Investigator*'s early mishap in attempting to keep up. This proved—in their eyes—that Collinson cared very little about *Investigator*, and was firmly determined to do anything he could to be first to enter the ice. With the belief that the tables were now turned, and *Enterprise* trailed many leagues astern, Nelson suggested it was *now* Collinson's people who felt the sting of disappointment.[5]

The next day, the Investigators sent their letters and dispatches for England over to *Plover*, lying nearby. Miertsching warily recorded, "Captain Moore has employed a young Eskimo woman to act as interpreter among the natives; she dwells in his cabin." This was Mary Natalia, who was mustered aboard on April 7, 1850, at the Russian settlement of Gregoria, and was listed among the supernumeraries (extra personnel) to receive "full allowances without spirits." She remained some 27 months before being landed at Port Clarence.[6]

Miertsching goes on, and cannot hide his disgust at what he sees: "A great number of friendly Eskimos have gathered on the shore opposite the ship; unfortunately there is no one on the [*Plover*] to use this grand opportunity of teaching them something of their creation and salvation; rather the men—and this includes high-ranking officers—behave themselves so shamelessly that here one will soon have an Anglo-Eskimo colony."[7]

The European world had long since invaded northwestern Russian America. Three decades before, when the first Russian ship penetrated deep into Kotzebue Sound, the Russians worryingly found several hundred Inuit in a camp—some of whom possessed firearms. Later on, when tensions boiled over, gunfire rang out between the two groups. Another Russian ship arrived in the sound around this time, and the Russians were surprised to witness the arrival also of an American ship. The captain of the latter announced he was on a fur trading voyage, and had with him firearms and ammunition as trade items.[8]

George Brown had sung out, "Sail ahead!" off Cape Lisburne, on the morning of the 31st: it was Kellett in the *Herald*. "He hasn't a spark of religion about him, never goes to Church by any chance, and this, together with his being an Irishman, makes me distrust him," is how the stormy "Jacky" Fisher (later Admiral of the Fleet Sir John Fisher) described Kellett, under whom he later served in China during the 1870s. Though at first disgusted by him, Fisher soon surrendered to Kellett's delightful ways, remarking how "he is so full of kindness to me." As the survey ship closed with *Investigator* and rounded her stern, three hearty cheers sprang from the her rigging and rolled across the water. Nelson radiated with the "capital news" that the *Herald* had recently visited the ice and reported it was fast breaking up. "Captain M'Clure presently went on board, but soon returned accompanied by Captain Kellett and

In the crow's nest (*Our Lost Explorers*, 1883).

some of his officers," wrote Armstrong. Among the officers serving under Kellett at the time were Acting Mates Bedford C.T. Pim and Tathwell B. Collinson (eldest son of Rev. Henry Collinson, Vicar of Stannington—and nephew of the *Enterprise*'s captain). Whether or not one or both of these gentlemen visited McClure's ship is not known, although Pim's name later became forever embedded in the memories of the mortal Investigators.[9]

"The 'Enterprise' had not yet been seen, but the fogs had been dense, and the weather unfavourable for meeting her, so that all conspired to make the impatient men and officers conjecture that she was still far ahead, and waiting for them," deceptively asserted McClure. At the same time, he correctly "pointed out how valuable every hour was to him [in order to reach the ice by August 1], and to the important service he was upon; for he well knew the value of the arctic maxim, that a day lost often entails a whole season of fruitless labour."[10]

In spite of his captain's hubris and calculated lie, Armstrong revealed that neither he, nor those around him, held any such illusions:

We learned with regret that nothing had been seen or heard of our Consort, and having now arrived at the rendezvous, there could exist no doubt that she was still far behind us.... It could not, therefore, for a moment be supposed, that the "Enterprize," (a much slower sailing ship than the "Herald") could even, under the most favourable circumstances, have made the passage in much less time [than the average passage of 50 days]; nor did any of us believe it possible for her to have done so, despite the opinion that was then advanced to the contrary.[11]

Without orders from Collinson as to what to do if *Investigator* should arrive first, two options rise from Armstrong's published account, namely:

either to remain at the rendezvous until the arrival of the "Enterprize," with the uncertainty of then meeting her, owning to the foggy state of the weather, and thus lose the season in the ice; or at once proceed to the northward, and enter the ice single-handed. We resolved on the latter, and cheerfully prepared to encounter all obstacles and dangers, with a firm reliance on a merciful Providence, and full confidence in our resources.[12]

And yet, such confidence failed to flow from Dr. Armstrong's pen the following month, when he wrote to Sir John Richardson, a naval surgeon, naturalist, and veteran of three land Arctic expeditions, pointing out that "the most cooperation of both ships being so essential for our eventual safety & success."[13]

Carpenter Ford also saw no reason for cheerfulness: "The prospect around looking very dismal. As far as information given us the Enterprise had not arrived & very likely would not, considering the route she took, in 3 weeks or a month."[14]

Based partly on rumors, Assistant Surgeon Piers formed his own thoughts as to what was transpiring:

I understand, from hearsay, that Capt. Collinson's orders are for us to call at Cape Lisburne, where, if he had gone on, we should find some written orders: but, not dreaming of our arriving before him, I believe he made no arrangements for such an occurrence. Considering the positive nature of the Admiralty Instructions, with respect to the Ships keeping company, and perhaps also that we are the Junior Ship, Capt. Kellett wants Capt. M<sup>c</sup>Clure to wait here, but Capt. M<sup>c</sup>C. is not disposed to do so without a positive order from him—this Capt. K., I suppose, will not undertake to do.... How Capt. Collinson will regard this course remains to be posed, but, from his parting company shortly after our departure from England and again at our entrance into the Pacific, as also his not waiting for us at Honolulu, where we arrived only the day after his departure, it may be thought that he considered the Ships would act more effectively being separate & independent.[15]

Lieutenant Cresswell laid out the scene of Kellett's visit onboard to his parents: "Captain M'Clure was very strong for pushing on, telling Capt. Kellett that if he liked to detain him he could, but at the same time he must take the responsibility, that as far as he was concerned he would get on. Nearly all that day we were drawing stores from the *Herald*. We also got 3 *good* men that we were short, hearty good wishes and cheers."[16]

All the newcomers were able seamen, unmarried, with the *Herald* having been their first naval ship: Thomas S. Carmichael was a 25-year-old Edinburgh-born man, who had only joined the *Herald* in May at Honolulu. Mark Griffiths stepped aboard in 1846; he was the same age as Carmichael and hailed from Canterbury. Around 23 years of age and standing 5'7½", Irishman John Keefe (or O'Keefe) was the tallest of the trio, and had only been on the *Herald* since March.[17]

After an exchange of complimentary signals the two ships drew apart, and *Investigator* stood in for the towering headland of Cape Lisburne, with *Herald* following astern. Armstrong relates how McClure persisted in his charade that Collinson was ahead of him and bringing the ship close to the cape, with a view of ascertaining if a cairn, or any other landmark, had been erected that might in any degree affect the resolution we had arrived at, of proceeding onwards to the ice; but nothing was visible to afford any indication that it had been visited at any period either recent or remote. We, therefore, shaped a course at once for the ice, and stood away to the N.W. ½ W., with a fine fresh north-easterly wind. The "Herald" still kept ominously astern, which did not at all contribute to our comfort; for, it may now be confessed, we still feared that Captain Kellett would detain us, and that on reflection, he might see the necessity of keeping us at least some days to await the chances of meeting our senior officer's arrival; but as the truth must be told, an opposite state of the case was urged upon him. Captain M'Clure maintained that the "Enterprise" was a-head of us, and in support of which, retained the private letters he had for Captain Collinson for early delivery. The impossibility of such being the case I have already shown—of course, no person could truly entertain an opinion to the contrary, and I am sure Captain Kellett had too much sagacity not to see the true state of things. This I must confess we all rejoiced at, as we were anxious to get on, from a general feeling entertained that our Consort had neglected us. But he was evidently unwilling to assume the responsibility of detaining us.

Our worst fears were excited however, when in the evening we saw the "Herald" make all sail towards us, and rapidly closing from her superior sailing qualities, she made a signal recommending us to wait forty-eight hours for the "Enterprise," to which Captain M'Clure signaled in return, *"Important service. Cannot on my own responsibility!"*

This not being clearly understood, Captain Kellett hailed from the poop, desiring us to repeat the signal, which was accordingly done. She then gradually dropped astern, made no further reply; and at 11:30 p.m. she tacked and stood in for Cape Lisburne. This afforded us an inexpressible degree of relief, as we then considered ourselves free from all control, and the object sought had been obtained.[18]

But this was hardly the end of Captain Henry Kellett's involvement with the Investigators—merely a hiatus. If fact, a recommendation placed in Lieutenant Haswell's service record is directly linked to Kellett: "17 October 1851, Captain Kellett, of the *Herald*," strongly recommending him for his services in the Arctic Seas:= See Memorial stating his services 29 October 1853:=."[19]

*August 2, 1850, lat. 72° 1' N. and long: 166° 12' W.*—Displaying an Arctic veteran's characteristic pride after ice was reported by the lookout high above, Nelson then had the satisfaction of seeing "Old Iron Bows" smashing her way through the heavy drift ice, as the crashing and grinding astonished the uninitiated onboard. Miertsching also took notice of the novices' reactions to the polar ice: "One hears them saying: 'Had I known that the ice was so hard and strong, I would have been only too glad to stay at home.'"[20] The sun's rays played and bounced off the ice field, radiating color far and wide, broken only by the hulking forms of walruses— congregating in herds of 50 or 60—which casually rolled over the ice edge into the darkness of the water.[21]

There was young and old "marine beef," as the sailors' nickname goes. Mothers playing with their cubs provided an interesting sight, even to the old ice mate. A quarter-deck six-pounder gun was loaded with grape and canister, but sympathetic feelings aroused by the females and their young caused Captain McClure to countermand the order to fire, and Piers states before the gun could be brought to bear, the walrus plunged into the water. Even so, the ship glided within 20 yards of some of the herds, and one creature was wounded by a musket ball. At one point, Nelson had overheard Ice Mate Newton describing the scene if these creatures were attacked by a boat's crew. Should the boat become surrounded, the entire herd might rush the craft, and by using their long, curved tusks, capsize her. As *Investigator* crawled eastward, her new hosts gradually melted away.[22]

"On the first occasion when it became necessary to send some of our men on the ice to

**Walrus (Harter, 1979).**

assist us, great was the rivalry manifested as to who should first touch its surface; but after a considerable display of agility, the honour was claimed by the Boatswain [Kennedy]," recorded the doctor.[23]

Throughout the third day of August, as she sailed by floes six to eight feet above the water, a light coating of ice formed on the deck and rigging, transforming *Investigator* into the phantom ship out of Coleridge's *The Rime of the Ancient Mariner*. For the first time, that evening the thermometer dipped to the freezing mark. The ice stubbornly refused McClure any northward progress, and the ship continued to feel her way along the southern extremity of the pack. At nine o'clock on a foggy morning two days later, identifications were exchanged to the westward with the *Plover* (which was evidently expecting the return of her boats with Captain Moore)—but nothing more—as a fair wind kept *Investigator* going about her way.[24]

Upon approaching land, having the appearance of a continuous embankment of shingle with occasional outcroppings of rocks, near the water's edge, northeast of Point Franklin, "we observed several [raised] mounds, into each of which poles were inserted ... the interpreter pronounced them to be graves, it being the custom of some tribes of Esquimaux to mark their places of sepulture in this manner."[25]

Nelson felt the Investigators were not only mindful of finding "the great objects" of their search—Franklin and the Passage—but *sailing* the water route back home. Indeed, Armstrong acknowledged, "[E]ven at that early period of the voyage, [we] freely indulged and expressed the hopes we entertained of quitting [the] Polar Sea by the more legitimate route of Barrow's Strait and Baffin's Bay." And Brother Miertsching declared: "Time and again the question intrudes: How long will we have to cope with these frightful ice-masses in order to make our way through to Greenland?"[26]

But the vicissitudes in the ice had only barely begun.

In addition to the North-West Passage, the alien surroundings caused Assistant Surgeon Piers to ponder using advancing technology in Arctic navigation to discover Franklin's ships:

[T]here are three to one against a sailing vessel—adverse winds, calms and ice—but these three obstacles would be in a great measure overcome by a Steamer.... It would seem as if there were always an extensive "Pack" in about Lat. 71° or 72° N.—off Icy Cape—and which the extent of it is unknown, the navigation of this part of the Arctic Sea must be also dark & dangerous. No one ventures round by the westward of this ice, because they are ignorant where it will lead them and whether they will be able to extract their ships. It may be an immense expanse of ice, reaching as far as Melville Is$^d$ to the eastward and an equal or greater distance to the westward, or at no great distance to the north of it there may be a clear sea, or land—however, from its being so constantly seen in the same latitude, I cannot help thinking it is an immense pack of the Northern Ocean, that it is perennial, and only connected with the shore in the winter. A small steamer, appointed in the Summer months to examine the character of the ice in this Sea, might soon render the navigation of it as safe & familiar as Davis Straits, Baffin's Bay and Barrow's Straits are at present to our whalers. It may be this very "Pack" into which Sir John Franklin has got fixed in forcing a passage to the S.W. from Melville Island or there abouts. Moreover, a surveying Steamer, which could be employed more to the southward in the internals, by examining this unknown Ice for three or four Summer months annually might be the means of either discovering the missing Ships or a passage to Melville Island, should these much desired objects not be very shortly and happily accomplished.[27]

Several years down the road, Piers' suggestion about Franklin's predicament was to prove correct—the Beaufort Sea ice stream certainly had a direct effect on the progress of the *Erebus* and *Terror*—but (understandably) the doctor's geographical bearings were off as to the location of the lost ships.

"We rounded Point Barrow on the 6th of August not without some difficulty and danger, a foul wind and tremendous ice, but we had luck or a merciful providence taking care of us, and in the morning the wind became fair and we made for the land," wrote Cresswell to his parents. "The ice very deep; some floes to all appearance 20 ft. & upwards thick," observed Carpenter Ford.[28]

Piers enthusiastically wrote in his journal: "At noon when Court, the Master, found our position to be to the eastward of 'Point Barrow'—supposed to be a great obstacle to Ships proceeding to the Eastward—a general burst of delight proceeded from the Officers, and every face among them rained with joy. I think we had at least surmounted this difficulty, and advanced in this direction further than any Ship had been known to be before."[29]

*Investigator* now sought to "reach the *land-water*, or the space between the American coast and the line of heavy ice, which from its great draught of water was checked by the shallow nature of the sea, at distances varying from a few yards to sometimes a mile in width, and, once in that land-water, to struggle to the eastward for that open sea off the Mackenzie river."[30] As long as *Investigator* advanced along any uncharted coastline, she faced the menace of shoals (sandbanks or sandbars) lurking beneath shallow waters.

The ship picked her way between immense floes—challenging for the most skilled of seamen. Some fragments of ice were unavoidable, and crashing into *Investigator*'s hull, sent vibrations through the entire vessel, as her human masters struggled to maintain their balance on deck.

Piers set the scene for the following day. With the lightness of the wind, as several large flights of ducks passed overhead and seals frolicked in the ice, at around ten in the morning, five boats were quickly lowered and manned with eight men each. Piers described the warping (towing) procedure: "In ten minutes or a quarter of an hour from 'the pipe'—'hands to tow'—were in a good line a-head of the ship. They sing as they work; as a proof that our men are good, Cresswell said, all the time they were out before they could never get their men to pull so well together as ours did to day."[31] The few men left onboard were hardly idle, since it wasn't only a matter of steering *Investigator* through narrow and tormenting lanes of water, but her progress demanded nearly constant tacking and trimming (maneuvering and adjusting the sails) to avoid the ice.[32] "The Captain 'spliced the main brace,' in consideration of our having reached a position never attained by a Ship before, and the ding[h]y took it, mixed with the lime juice, to each boat in succession."[33]

*Investigator* was towed for the rest of the day through the ice, arriving off Drew Point at eight in the evening. As a consequence of such backbreaking work, that evening Bradbury's entertaining fiddle fell silent.[34] During this period, Miertsching took the opportunity to have "another long talk on Christianity with the captain: he asserted that on a ship at sea no one could hold that form of Christianity which is observed on land: at sea a man must have spirit and not hang his head."[35] McClure knew how to draw the distinction between one's faith and the application of that faith relative to time, place and situation.

At about two a.m. on the eighth, the ship had moved to within three miles of land; she was in five fathoms of water, making it unwise to venture any closer. With the intention of leaving notice of their search, Court, Armstrong and Miertsching were rowed toward the beach by six seamen. Dr. Armstrong states he went ashore, but oddly, both McClure and Miertsching do not include the surgeon in their writings; it seems Miertsching for one should have recalled all the officers present during their first encounter with Eskimos. On the one hand, this could well have been an intended omission, that played into some of the subtle relationships between the officers, which will be discussed shortly. On the other hand, most of Miertsching's journal was reconstructed from memory, assisted by his notes and the captain's personal journal, so this *may* have been a simple oversight (see Appendix 2).[36]

During their approach, three figures were spotted, and anxious uncertainty invaded the explorers' minds—were they Eskimos or their lost countrymen? The question was answered when the figures began to run off, and this was surely the reaction of Eskimos; but it remained to be seen if the Europeans would receive a friendly or hostile reception. Occasionally, the runners stopped to gaze at the approaching strangers, and at one point, warmed to a comforting sight. "We stood up in the boat," Armstrong recalled, "and held up our arms— the usual sign of friendly intentions amongst them. We had no sooner done this then they assembled evidently in consultation, and answered the signal without delay, remaining stationary."[37]

Once onshore, Miertsching called out words of peace, and the three unarmed Eskimo men stood and waited as the sailors moved toward the hesitant little band. In a matter of moments, the Investigators and Eskimos were greeting one another in the latter's customary fashion of rubbing noses. "I believed myself transported to Labrador when I saw these people: the same stature, features, hair; even the same clothes, and boots of sealskin, and of the same style; their speech was also the same, but of a slightly different dialect, so that I could understand them well, as they did me," wrote Miertsching.[38]

The presentation of a little tobacco eased into conversation, and although they answered questions in a cheerful manner, the *Investigator* was the focus of their gazes. Piers was told they "saw the Ship last evening, and wondered what the "three large trees," as they called them, could be, some of them remained on the beach to watch all night."[39] Armstrong related how they had no word in their language to express the size of the ship, "and from seeing her move, thought she was a great living island. From the time of being seen, the 'Investigator' had caused extraordinary consternation amongst the tribe, encamped but a short distance, as they said, from where we were,"[40] wrote Armstrong.

Although the Eskimos had not seen any craft like *Investigator* before during their annual visit to this place, a boat party from the *Plover* (under Lieutenant Pullen) had been seen the previous year—but "no other white men had been seen on the coast."[41] Trading with the Indians was conducted through another Eskimo tribe, and the former dealt directly with the Russian Fur Company.

The tribe were Iñupiat people,[42] who had only arrived in the area a few days before, after a five-day journey from the south, and planned to depart from the coast when winter drew near. It was difficult for the officers to glean sufficient information about seasonal ice conditions, due to the natives' apparent inability to calculate time periods beyond cold and hot seasons. The "ice, they said, never went farther off than at the present time, and at one season there was no water at all along the coast," and "we understood there would be open water on this part of the coast for two moons," so the latter seemed to correlate with the expected navigational season during August and September.[43]

Later on, in his official dispatches to the Admiralty, McClure did not fail to mention "the assistance of our invaluable interpreter," pointing out that "the selection of this gentleman for this important office does infinite credit to the discernment of those who sent him."[44]

After they had erected a cairn and buried a bottle with a record of the expedition ten feet to the magnetic north, a cannon's boom rippling across the water signaled the party's expected return. Consequently, the sailors were unable to concede to the Eskimos' strong desire for them to visit their encampment, which was about a 30-minute walk away, as seen from a small hillock, across a generally flat, grass-covered expanse.[45]

*Habitans du Golfe de Kotzebue*

**The Iñupiat people of Kotzebue Sound in 1816 (Louis Choris; National Library of Australia, 1379737).**

Offering a warm farewell, and inviting the Eskimos onboard, the landing party entered the boat, then slipped off the beach and made their way back to *Investigator*. Arriving before five a.m. and carrying botanical specimens and turf—the result of Armstrong's naturalist role—the party was surprised to find a baidar alongside the ship (a Russian name for an open, wood-framed, skinned-covered boat, called an umiak by the Inuit). "The baidars appear well adapted from their lightness and buoyancy, for river or shallow water navigation, such as the coast presents."[46]

Piers told of its occupants:

> At 3 a.m. Sainsbury came to my cabin, and telling me to get up, as there were several Esquimaux on deck. I at once dressed, and on getting on deck found three men and two women dressed in the usual Seal skin clothes—they appeared to be much pleased at all the novelties they witnessed and much amused—one of the women skipping along the deck with a piece of hide, laughing, and offering it to us to use in the same manner: the men were running up the rigging, mocking the leadsman, turning the pumps & amusing themselves in various other ways, but in the midst of all this, bartering any thing they could find a purchaser for—though all they had were a few ducks, fish and inferior fur dresses.[47]

Presents of knives, mirrors, scissors, beads, and tobacco were distributed among the group, with the most favored being knives and tobacco; sources of metal and wood were crucial to the Eskimos' survival. As a way to communicate the *Investigator*'s passing with anyone who came into contact with the natives, Armstrong suggested that the ship's name should be stamped on all articles given to them. Accordingly, this was done with the blades of knives, while mirrors were cut using a diamond.[48] "The carpenter (Mr. Ford) had also very ingeniously made some copper medals, similarly marked, for distribution."[49]

The captain devised a clever means of discouraging removal of the names from the knife blades through sharpening or polishing: the Eskimos were told for as long as the engraved letters remained, they would be a good luck charm for the hunters. In return the Europeans received some skins and items of clothing, like coats and mitts. As usual, seafaring eyes were drawn to the unfamiliar, and a brisk trade was done for bows and ivory-tipped arrows.[50]

With the promise to be friendly to any white men like the Investigators, the natives left the ship.

The wind was scant and *Investigator* only crawled along, so through the day other baidars came alongside with men and women to ply their wares:

> The Esquimaux we saw to day were rather below our average height; their colour a lightish or dirty brown—partly natural & partly perhaps from want of washing—with a tinge of red on the cheeks; their hair black & straight; their countenance round & plump, with small eyes & high cheek bones. Just before each angle of the mouth the men had an aperture through the cheeks, in which they wore pieces of stone or bone [known as labrets, which were first put in about the time a male reaches puberty[51]]; and the women were all tattooed with several perpendicular lines from the under lip to the chin—more or less according to their rank. Some of the girls were also observed to have of lead or tin, which Miertsching informed us were marks of their being betrothed—they had, too, bangles round their ankles. These people resembled much, and in their faces particularly, the Chinese, except that they were more robust. The men & women were dressed alike, only that the Seal skin frocks, which they drew on over their heads, were worn longer before & behind by the women.[52]

Several of the Eskimos were caught with their hands in people's pockets (including the captain's). In another example of attempted thieving, one fellow made off with a large deerskin from the quarterdeck—where it had been placed after purchase by an officer—and sold it again to Sergeant John Woon. Based on long-term contact with Eskimos of northwestern

Russian America, Dr. John Simpson (assistant surgeon and later surgeon onboard the *Plover*, 1848–54) offers some balance and perspective regarding the natives' behavior onboard *Investigator*:

> Whilst from being frequently annoyed by petty thefts, false reports, broken promises, and evasions, we perhaps too hastily concluded that thieving and lying were their natural characteristics, without attributing to them a single redeeming quality. Yet, as we became better acquainted, we found individuals of weight and influence among them, whose conduct seemed guided by a rude inward sense of honesty and truth, and whom it would be unfair to judge by a civilized standard, or to blame for yielding to temptations to them greater than we can conceive. A leaf of tobacco is a matter of small value, yet the end of it sticking from one's pocket amid a knot of natives at Nu-wuk [Point Barrow], would be a greater temptation there, and would more surely be stolen, than a handkerchief or a purse seen dangling from one's skirt in a London mob.[53]

As the *Investigator* pressed onward through the uncharted waters, keeping the sailors company from afar were large herds of reindeer flowing over the land, while numerous waterfowl such as king eider ducks peppered the water. That evening, in the area of Pitt Point and Cape Halkett (west of the Coville River), at least two conical-shaped mounds were spied ashore, resulting in Lieutenant Cresswell and Dr. Armstrong's being dispatched in the second whaleboat. Just before the boat went ashore, the depth suddenly dropped to two-and-three-quarters fathoms, and with *Investigator* displacing upwards to 15 feet, her keel glided into the soft bottom. "The only thing to be feared was, a sudden change of wind, bringing the ice down, which was then ominously frowning on us, at no very great distance,"[54] cautiously wrote Armstrong. Anchors were laid out, and the capstan cranked round, in an effort to release the ship from her predicament.

Meanwhile, from a distance the atmospheric refraction (the deviation of light due to air density, which causes distortions) had made the mounds appear upwards of 40 feet in height. In actuality, the mounds were only about three feet high, and turned out to be Eskimo storehouses containing animal bones from hunts. Amid the remnants of old campsites all around, in the same manner as before, a record of the Investigators' visit was deposited by the party.[55]

Examining a nearby small crescent-shaped bay (like the ones that are so often featured along the coast), Armstrong was taken aback by several acres of driftwood piled upon the shoreline. With many tree trunks being at least 60 feet long, it struck the doctor that some of them might be the remains of a ship or wreck, but a quick inspection brought no confirmation to his hopes. The journey back to the ship, observed Armstrong, "was rendered pleasant by contemplating the magnificent appearance of the sky to the westward, tinted as it was by the most brilliant crimson I ever beheld."[56] By this time the ship had cheated the Arctic, and was gotten off the sandbar.

At this point, it's convenient to cast eyes forward for a glimpse of Lieutenant Haswell's unfolding fate over the course of the expedition. Save a single sled journey, Haswell was evidently never dispatched to lead or participate in any other boat or sled parties—why? It certainly wasn't for his lack of experience in handling ship's boats, since during much of the previous decade Haswell became well acquainted with small boat duty while on arduous anti–slave trade operations.

Taking into consideration the animosity McClure had toward Haswell, and the lack of faith in his first lieutenant's abilities, it appears McClure sought to limit Haswell's opportunities for personal recognition and honor related to providing relief to Franklin and/or geographical discoveries. In fact, some weighty circumstantial evidence regarding McClure's disparaging intent eventually presented itself in course of the expedition.

In contrast, given the captain's (deserved) admiration for the second master, it's no surprise that Court was frequently in charge of boats and often accompanied the captain in sled parties.

In spite of time's ability to heal all wounds, Miertsching illustrated the smoldering relationship between McClure and his officers, while taking a glance at Haswell's unending tightrope balancing act:

> Aug. 9, 1850—Today the captain entertained the officers at lunch. The painful misunderstanding which earlier embittered the lives of everyone of them is no more; since we left the Sandwich Islands relations have been better; wholly good they can never be; for the captain has no confidence in his young officers. Lieutenant Haswell, who had been under arrest for some weeks, does his best to carry out exactly his captain's wishes. Towards me both the captain and my mess-mates, the officers, have been most friendly and obliging from the beginning of the voyage until now; yet it has often been most disagreeable for me to stand between factions so harshly divided; now conditions are a good deal better; yet one can see the red-hot embers still glowing under the ashes. I keep very much to myself; the management of the ship is no concern of mine; so I often spend a sacred hour alone in my little cabin.[57]

The Brother goes on to relate his servant's sufferings; Corporal Farquharson was "one of those who loves what is good, is faithful and painstaking in his duty, and seeks to influence his messmates with Christian behaviour, speech, and leaflets, and for so doing endures much mockery and antagonism. I have already spent many happy evening hours with him in my cabin."[58]

For Assistant Surgeon Piers, it was "altogether a most interesting & exciting time; for we now feel quite shut out from civilized life ... how long shall we remain in this icy world, for it is almost, in its features, like a new world. Whether we shall return by the East or West. Everyone is delighted with the progress we have made, and all our hopes are high."[59]

As *Investigator* continued to be challenged by heavy ice on one side and shoal water on the other, the already devilish navigational environment was made worse by a combination of thick fog, foul winds and adverse currents. Battling against gale-force winds, and now rain and snow, the ship passed the entrance to the Colville River, constantly buffeting pieces of grounded ice along the way.[60]

Early on the morning of August 11, the weather having cleared, one of the Jones Islands came into view, and "the officer of the watch reported a spar erected as if for a signal, and considerable anxiety was felt."[61] Court, Armstrong, and Miertsching went ashore to find the spar, some 12 feet long, placed in the middle of a small pile of driftwood. Signs of human presence in the area convinced the doctor that Eskimos were nearby. The 500-yard-long, driftwood-strewn island was examined, and a notice buried. Armstrong came away with a fair number of specimens of sanderlings, which were shot as they lounged in several watery indentations on the sand and shingle surface.

Although Armstrong wrote that he and Court were the only officers who went ashore, Miertsching went as well, with the Brother plainly stating he was awoken at three o'clock that morning to accompany the boat party.[62]

There is an unsettling uniformity in the doctor's writings regarding Miertsching, representing an undertone of condescension toward this gentleman. Armstrong's narrative stands alone among the surviving expedition journals in consistently referring to Miertsching throughout its pages, not by name, but as "the interpreter." With the exception of Ice Mate William Newton, this is not the case in Armstrong's writings with any other officer onboard.[63]

Miertsching's anglicized first name and misspelled last name appear—not among the officers in Armstrong's book—but very last in the list of officers and crew. Miertsching is listed in the identical places for the 1856, 1857 and 1865 editions of McClure's book (where the German's last name is also misspelled), and the best explanations might be language differences and the fact that he was a non-seafaring civilian.[64]

Miertsching mentioned several times in his journal how he enjoyed good treatment from the officers. However, his particular closeness to and kind attention from the captain could well have been a constant irritation to Armstrong. In addition, according to McClure, the doctor was very well informed and showed it; the captain described his surgeon as "one of the most conceited fellows I ever met." On still another level, Armstrong's scientific mind did not rebel against Miertsching's religious office—quite the opposite: "I trust the day is not far distant when the light of civilization will dawn on this poor, benighted, but intelligent race of beings.... The laudable example shown by the Moravian brethren on the dreary coast of Labrador, and the good results which have attended their meritorious labours in the work of civilization, is worthy of our imitation, and will, I trust, be followed." In fact, Miertsching and Armstrong must have worked together to some degree, since the Moravian wrote that he gathered and dried thousands of botanical specimens, and it could well have been the arrogant doctor resented any intrusion into his area of expertise.[65]

At the very least, Brother Miertsching undoubtedly sensed the doctor's displeasure, and his writings subtly ignored Armstrong in various ways; for example, as related above, his omission of the doctor's presence in the shore party during the first encounter with Eskimos.[66]

Armstrong served up an identical attitude toward Newton, only once mentioning him by name in his book. Also technically a civilian, Newton is in the musters as a warrant officer, but he wasn't necessarily looked upon by some of the officers with a high level of respect. At the beginning of the voyage, Cresswell roughly outlined him as "our poor old ice mate, a man that has been to sea for the last 20 years."[67] Oddly, Newton's name is absent from the lists of officers and crew in the 1856, 1857 and 1865 editions of McClure's book, and in the first edition is only referred to three times, but never by name. He is, however, listed among the warrant officers in Armstrong's book.[68]

It wasn't long after the shore party was back aboard *Investigator* that two baidars came alongside, carrying 24 Eskimos. Although immediately asked about any sightings of white men off the coast, they did not have any useful information about Franklin and his men. The Eskimos, who in Armstrong's view were "a better class of people than those met off Point Drew,"[69] had come to trade some furs, bows and arrows, and bore small fish and wild ducks in exchange for tobacco. If McClure would stay, a quantity of stored venison could also be offered up for barter. The captain cut tobacco sticks into about three-inch long pieces—the price of each piece being one fish. Feeling he wasn't quite getting a fair deal, one recipient sought to equalize the terms by cutting his fish into pieces, offering one portion of fish for one portion of tobacco! This greatly amused the Investigators, and when the Eskimo found his trick didn't work, he couldn't help but join in on the fun.[70]

Divine Service began when the clock struck the tenth hour, and despite many a sharp eye on deck, some of the Eskimos spirited away items and vanished among the numerous chunks of floating ice before the sailors were any the wiser.

After making little progress, towards evening *Investigator* found herself off a low and flat inshore island, teeming with Eskimos "running to and fro in evident consternation and amazement."[71] So as not to leave anything to chance, a whaleboat with McClure and Miertsching, and a cutter with Cresswell and Armstrong, were manned, armed and rowed toward shore. Leaping upon the beach "with the English flag flying, we landed on the island. Although the Eskimos, with knives drawn, spears and bows made ready, wished to hinder us, and although a few arrows flew past our heads, yet these people, who had never before seen white men (*kablunaks*), soon became so friendly and childishly delighted that the friendly gesture of rubbing noses was offered to each of us, often two or three times. These Eskimos had a very pleasing appearance; they were well clad and clean."[72]

Unfortunately, they had no intelligence on Franklin's ships, and because their main camp was on the mainland, the Investigators' hope of obtaining a supply of venison soon faded.

Thus far, through the Investigators' interactions with the various Eskimo groups, few items of European manufacture had been spotted in their possession, so the sailors were rather surprised to see a gun appear from the unwrapping of skins. "On examining it, the words 'Barnett London, 1840,' was engraved on the lock, and we were informed they had received it in trading with other tribes to the southward."[73]

To their chief, Attawa (or Attua), was given a gift of a White Ensign on a boarding pike, while presents were distributed to others. The chief was also handed a canvas bag containing a letter McClure had written to the chief trader of the Russian Fur Company, briefly detailing Franklin's departure from England and his last reported position. Russian aid was "earnestly solicited," should any of the missing crews reach the continent, by promising rewards to the natives in the form of kettles, saws, knives, beads, etc., for giving relief to any white men appearing along the coasts, and seeing them safely to a local fur post. Upon application, the Admiralty would pay the costs of such rewards. Another letter detailing McClure's progress to date was to be forwarded to the Admiralty.[74]

McClure was indeed genuinely following up every opportunity to uncover traces of Franklin's expedition and provide aid for the missing men. The irony of McClure's humanitarian actions was that the further *Investigator* penetrated alone into the Arctic, the more entangled she became in the very white web which had snared *Erebus* and *Terror*.

By his writings, Brother Miertsching for one seemed oblivious to the abyss toward which *Investigator* was inching closer and closer, although his evangelistic fervor was keen to narrow the cultural chasm that separated his faith from that of the occupiers of this land:

> I conversed with these people a long time, and wished to tell them of God, the Creator of all things, including ourselves; and that it is His will that we should be good and not bad, etc., but to explain even one fact to these simple children of nature, and to make them grasp it, requires a longer period of time than our very brief visit afforded. They have no conception of a high and Divine Being, yet they have a notion of two contrasted beings, one good and one bad, living in different regions where they themselves go after death, many to one, others to the second place, depending on their conduct in this life.[75]

The following day, at a place with many islands in sight, four boatloads of men, women and children came onboard to barter fish, ducks and skins. But the immense attraction of wood and metal was such that two iron winch handles and a small ice anchor made their departures. Upon following the suspected culprit to his boat, the carpenter and Corporal Farquharson recovered the anchor, and the pump and windlass handles, having detected that a woman was sitting on one of the latter.[76]

Foggy conditions, contrary winds and the pounding ice forced the ship to be made fast to a floe about a quarter of a mile long, and 300–400 yards wide, on the 13th. In the 34° air, the most was made of the many pools of fresh water on its surface to take on water in the casks. "We were all extremely glad to take advantage of the exercise which this icy field afforded us, after being so long confined on board, rough and uneven as was its surface, for there was scarcely a square yard of level space. We amused ourselves at archery with the bows and arrows procured from the Esquimaux," enthused Armstrong. Though Miertsching welcomed the sport, thoughts of another place later crept in: "We did some target shooting. The captain gave me a double-barrelled gun which I shall keep and use industriously until we arrive at Davis Strait. In the evening I locked myself in my cabin; I was homesick, and joined the Brotherhood in spirit."[77]

Assistant Surgeon Piers's journal, Aug. 14, 1850

The day being clear & fine, in the forenoon we took up our anchors & made sail, the Captain intending to try for a passage to the Eastward more towards the shore: for where we were, the floating ice was heavy & also it was impossible to do anything on a wind, and outside there was a very high, impenetrable pack, in fact, from the place where we first fell in with the Ice, Lat. 72°–Long. 166°, to our present position, there appears to be one continuous barrier.[78]

In spite of McClure's recorded intentions, several days later Lieutenant Cresswell's pen betrayed the Arctic navigator's conflicted mind: "The Captain says we shall try and push North after leaving Cape Bathurst, but as he alters his mind half a dozen times a day it is impossible to say."[79]

Between Point Anxiety and Return Reef, the crow's nest delivered the disheartening reality—heavy pack ice nearly imprisoned the ship. With the water gradually shoaling and no evidence of the pack offering relief on either side, Court was dispatched in the whaleboat to seek the only hope of getting clear of the perilous position by finding a way around the northern extreme of a low, flat island not far from the ship. This done, Court returned onboard, and sail was again set. Following another boat, which made soundings ahead, around 6:30 in the evening *Investigator* slid onto a sandbank, grounding herself in two and a half fathoms.[80]

Release from the shovelful of sand under the ship's keel ultimately came to exact a far, far greater price from the Investigators than any of them had bargained for.

# The Coldest Crucible, 1850

*Even those whom superior weapons rendered fearless of bears, could not but enter into the feelings of superstitious awe, with which the Esquimaux pointed at that vast and mysterious sea of ice, which lay away to the north-west; a sea which ship could not sail through, nor man traverse.*

—"Land of the White Bear" in McClure's
*The Discovery of the North-West Passage*

To lighten *Investigator*, the boats were lowered alongside,[1] and then:

> The kedge anchor was very soon taken out ahead, with the idea of dragging her over the bank which was only a few yards wide: this attempt failed, and then the stream anchor was taken out astern; a heavy strain was hove—all hands at intervals rocking the Ship by running together from one side to the another—and after some time, no perceptible movement being affected, [at 10 o'clock][2] the "main brace was spliced" and hands piped to supper.[3]

After a 15-minute respite to devour the ration of bread, meat and spirits, every soul onboard again threw himself into liberating the ship.

To lighten her further, all the provisions on deck—amounting to 35 casks, each weighing three hundredweight (336 lbs.; see Appendix 1)—were lowered into the whaleboats. The bower anchors were also taken out of the ship, and placed in the cutters. In the meantime, huge pieces of ice made contact with the cables, and drifted down upon *Investigator* until the ship was mostly on her broadside. Alarmed, the men toiled to keep the boats from being crushed between the menace and their wooden world.[4]

"Orders were now given to have all in readiness for pumping out the [fresh] water, about twenty tons of which we had in the tanks; but previously, the capstan was again manned by all hands, and the powerful effort was then made, brought a cheering report from the leadsman astern, that she had taken two inches off the line, and consequently moved."[5]

Slight as the progress was, the capstan was worked *again and again*—until *Investigator* floated free!

The sighs of relief were but momentary; to keep out of further harm's way from the forceful southwesterly current, which had already brought evil upon *Investigator*, it was necessary to make sail in order to manage the ship. In addition, the provisions and anchors still had to be hoisted back onboard and restowed, and this took until four in the morning.

During this operation, disaster visited the Investigators. Laden with their heavy cargo, most of the boats were being towed along the leeward side of the ship, when, according to Armstrong, the third whaleboat capsized, sending eleven casks of prime beef to the bottom 30 feet below. "We had thus lost no less than 3344 lbs. of excellent meat," wrote the doctor, "which might have been obviated had the suggestion of one of the Officers been adopted, of towing this boat with the others to the leeward rather than to windward of the ship, but from some cause not in my power to explain, this was not acted on." In writing to the Admiralty, McClure indicated it was the first whaleboat—rather than the third—that turned over, and he coldly recognized "this is a serious loss, indeed an irreparable calamity."[6]

The identity of the officer concerned remains unknown, but with his previous experience in such environments, the suggestion may have come from Stephen Court. There was a north-easterly wind blowing that day,[7] so perhaps McClure felt if the boat in question was towed on the windward (port) side, the southwest current could have snugly balanced it against the *Investigator*'s side while unloading. Conversely, it must have been something of a struggle to manage the unloading on the leeward (starboard) side, as the current would have fought to draw the boats away from the ship's side.

In consequence of this accident, the place was named Bull Reef.[8]

Piers now eyed the future with a dash of uncertainty: "In a voyage of this nature, when our return is so uncertain, a loss of this kind may be of serious consequence—though at present I am not apprehensive of one feeling much the worst of it, for we seem to be amply supplied with every necessary."[9]

It wasn't until September 1 that an entry was made in the Letter & Order Book regarding the loss of these valuable provisions. At that time, McClure changed the scale of victualling (which he previously supplied to Paine on April 24): "It is my direction that in consequence of the Loss we have sustained of 11 Casks of Beef that you substitute the issue of Pork for Beef on Beef days and the Beef for Pork on the Pork days—as also their accompaniments of Flour & Peas from this date until further orders."[10]

When the witching hour struck, the ice eased off, and (according to Nelson) the crew volunteered to heave *Investigator* through the thick accumulation of ice that ringed the shoal water. To make ready for this effort, Bradbury turned out with his fiddle, mounted the capstan, and burst into tune! Nelson then recalled how he and his fellow Investigators commenced this hard labor at the capstan with such song and good cheer, that their captain must have glowed with great pride at the scene before him.[11]

For all their straining, the Investigators crawled forward but a few yards ... the Arctic was winning.

Cresswell, Court, Paine, Sainsbury, and Newton traveled to an islet nearby and constructed a cairn, and returned at 7 p.m.[12] That evening brought in a western wind and the hope it would set the ice to flight. With it came a rare phenomenon in the frozen north—a thunderstorm. "The west wind," wrote Captain M'Clure, "was ushered in with rain, and thunder and lightning. The two latter I never before witnessed in such a latitude (70° N.). The thermometer rose to 45°+ Fahrenheit, and the air was quite sultry, with dark heavy clouds rising overhead, resembling those seen in a thunder-storm in our own country."[13]

The considerable light refraction transformed the surroundings, and the pack took on the appearance of an unending row of chalk cliffs, 40 to 50 feet in height.[14]

Over the next two days, from the crow's nest the ice mate guided *Investigator* into leads of water, where sailor and Marine alike cajoled the ship by throwing themselves into rope and oar. Piers observed that "all the Officers, as on several previous occasions, 'lent a hand,' in working the Ship, at the capstan and warping; but I found that we required the belt used by the men, for hauling a long time on the hawsers drags one's arms off nearly—or so affects them that for a short time they seem almost powerless."[15]

After one strenuous session, the hands were piped to supper, and "the Officers were on the ice, which we could step on from the Ship, and Wynniatt set one of his musical boxes playing on it," observed Piers.[16] This miniature Arctic concert no doubt lightened the mood.

When the wind favored, the ship's bones shuddered as her bows met drifting heaps of whiteness. Since *Investigator* may at any time find herself in a position whereby the ice damaged her rudder or even made it useless, the crew "unshipped our rudder to fit gear for unshipping when we wanted it."[17]

On the night of the 17th, for the first time the surface of the sea was layered with a coating of ice—winter was approaching.[18]

Snow fell the whole of Sunday, August 18. Flaxman Island was sighted off to starboard in the late morning, and the open Divine Service was canceled due to the laborious ice navigation and heavy buffeting of the ship. "At 9 p.m. the water appearing pretty clear of ice all round, and the Captain hoping to find an open sea, the Ships' head was directed, and course steered, for Melville Island! Everyone is in the highest spirits," enthused Piers, "but whether Fortune will favour us so much as to allow a straight course to Melville Island remains to be proved."[19] However, the fog and darkness formed a sinister veil, and Miertsching passed an anxious and sleepless night, being twice thrown from his bed by the assaulting ice.

By morning, the Investigators had cruised 90 miles. "At noon they sounded 195 fathoms without bottom; and shortly afterwards the disagreeable fact of the 'Investigator' having run into a trap in the main pack pressed itself on the mind of the captain."[20] The temperature hovered in the mid–30s, and there was a marked change in the character of the ice seen to date. Instead of the rough hummocky ice previously experienced, "we were sailing through narrow lanes of water between immense, flat floe pieces, nearly as high as our bulwarks [the side of the ship above the upper deck]."[21] Should the wind shift and the lanes close, *Investigator* would find herself in a perilous position.

Atop his perch, Ice Mate Newton saw no hope; consequently McClure hauled off and beat 70 miles southward against the wind, only to be confronted with closely packed ice amidst a calm, and thick snowy weather. Five boats were lowered, and the men spent hours putting their backs into the oars, until it was thought prudent to spare their energy and drop the kedge anchor for the night. "A number of things broken by the ice were now repaired, then the ship was cleaned and put in order, as is done daily, and the men were given a chance to rest. Certainly they did not dance," observed Miertsching, who added, "That evening a tranquil silence reigned on the ship."[22] The Investigators had left Russian America behind, and were then off the coast of British North America.[23]

"I believe all Polar voyagers advise Ships to keep to the land; and it is very certain that, whenever we have left it to attempt a direct or short course, we have invariably been driven back and lost considerable time—so invaluable here—to say nothing of the risk incurred of our being impacted."[24] Piers went on to write that being off the Mackenzie River on August 20 was more than any of them had ever hoped for, but since the whole coast had previously been searched, if Franklin and his men had made it to the mainland, something would surely have been seen or heard of them.

But then Piers' ink ran blood red:

> [W]hat is more probable than that for Sir J.F., elated with the prospect of effecting the N.W. passage in the "open season" of 1845, pushed with his screw vessels so far into the alluring interstices of the ice that, if they were not suddenly crushed or run over, they became unable to proceed or retrace their steps from the closing of the ice, and at length inextricably impacted: in which case, the "Erebus" and "Terror" may still be slowly drifting about this perpetually frozen Ocean as the melancholy tombs of their unfortunate crews; for I cannot reconcile to my mind their being otherwise than dead![25]

While Piers privately foretold the Investigators' future, many onboard didn't see it that way. Nelson was sure the spirits of the crew hadn't suffered from past events, and believed his shipmates' expressions could convince anyone that Melville Island had been reached, Franklin found, the Passage explored, and the white cliffs of Dover were in plain sight! However, "many a slip between the cup and the lip." The nights grew dark, and before another moon would smile upon them, the weather was changing, stirring Old Man Winter from his slumber.[26]

As part of a long dispatch to the Admiralty, McClure explained his changed turn of mind about navigating in the pack:

> From what I have observed of the pack I feel convinced that any attempt to reach Bank's Land through it, would only terminate in failure and the consequent loss of valuable time; but by working between its edge and the shore have confidence in making a good advance this season, it is therefore my intention to pursue the latter method, and in so doing deviate from my original purpose of pushing into the ice, as mentioned in my letter to their Lordships dated the 19th July [*sic*—July 20].[27]

And to Ross, McClure wrote how the pack may invitingly open her door—but then suddenly close it again—and may not open it again for the whole season,

> [S]o theorists upon the Polar Sea being annually clear of ice, you may rest assured have made a very great mistake, I am fully persuaded that it never does, or ever can, I have witnessed such tremendous floes not a berg to be seen, but many of the former we have measured average from forty five to seventy feet beneath the water are many miles in extent, and to see these enormous islands in motion, influenced probably by an under current cutting road through that which is less dense and stationary is one of the most frightful sights I ever witnessed, an immense field of this description, once and once only passed by us Just grazing our bow, nothing could have saved the vessel had she been resting against a solid floe, it would have gone through her with as little resistance as a sheet of paper would offer to a musket ball, but all this you know better than I can describe it [to] you.[28]

To his parents, Lieutenant Cresswell weighed in on the Passage, McClure, and their non-existent consort[29]:

> I do not think it is impossible that we may make the North-West Passage if the Capt. will but keep to the land. I am sure it is the only way to navigate a Polar sea. This is not an original opinion, it was Parry's and Sir James Ross's and is I believe our own Captain's, or he says so.
>
> But if he sees open water, he has not strength of mind to keep from running into it....
>
> There have been no chances of sending letters except the Herald. If this should find its way to England you will at the same time get Capt. M'Clure's dispatch, pray keep it for me. It will be a most egotistical production, mark my words for it.
>
> It is quite impossible to say where the Enterprise may be. Poor Collinson. I half fear that he will go mad when he hears the slow sailing Investigator has passed him. Pray tell Sir Edward Parry the news. It is well I did not attempt to give you the whereabouts of our winter quarters. I can't, it will wholly depend on circumstances....
>
> We all fraternize mostly well, altho' I do not like [the captain], but better than I did at the time of our most deadly war.[30]

Proceeding in foggy conditions, and surrounded by islands, shoals and ice, *Investigator* observed Richards Island to the southeast on the afternoon of August 22 (situated among various islands at the mouth of the Mackenzie). The very next morning, *Plover*'s boat party (Lieutenant Pullen) was headed in the opposite direction for Richards Island, then traveled along its northern coast during the day, on the way from Cape Bathurst to the Mackenzie.[31]

Two days later, at Point Warren (between the Mackenzie and Cape Bathurst), having sighted an Eskimo encampment, some of the sailors claimed to see someone wearing European dress among the figures ashore. Six armed sailors (including James Nelson) manned the first cutter, and McClure proceeded with Dr. Armstrong and Miertsching.

The party's friendly approach after landing was met with a hostile reception of passionate yells and wild gestures from two men and a woman. In spite of Miertsching's best efforts at verbal soothing, the men kept bows bent, and then bound back and forth, brandishing knives, while the woman stayed in the background with a bow and several quivers of arrows. Only when the seamen's guns were stowed in the cutter did tensions begin to ease, followed by the presentation of a piece of tobacco to each of the Eskimo men, which had a miraculous calming effect. An exchange of presents afterward ensured warm relations between the two parties.

A young man emerged from one of the huts and hobbled toward the group on two sticks, attended to by the woman (who turned out to be his mother). The settlement consisted of between 80 and 100 people, most of whom ran away at the approach of *Investigator*. Of the ones who stayed, the oldest was Kairoluak, chief of the region, and the other two were his sons; the woman was his main wife (in their polygamist society). Kairoluak and the others had been resolved to defend the crippled son from the strangers. Having been injured while hunting, he was in lamentable condition, as gangrene had invaded the lower part of one leg and foot. With the view of saving his life, the doctor proposed taking him aboard and performing an amputation, which the group ultimately refused to allow.

It was discovered that Kairoluak and his people were at war with the Indians to the south, and Eskimos to the east, but were on good terms and traded with their brethren to the west (those led by Attawa). The mention by the Investigators of their communication with Attawa greatly enhanced the bond of friendship.[32]

Piers was told "the reason of the fear and retreat of the Esquimaux was that one of their party had, at some period recently or not [Miertsching] could not learn from them, murdered a European or White man and they thought this Ship, which they regarded with great dread, had come to take revenge on them."[33] In fact, a mound nearby was seen to have a pole placed in it, with a piece of skin, or something similar, hanging from its top; "this the interpreter pronounced a grave, probably of a European, which coupled with the previous report [of an individual in European clothing] increased our anxiety in no slight degree," wrote Armstrong.[34] Much to the doctor's disappointment, the Eskimos did not permit him to examine the grave.

A button dangling from Kairoluak's ear caught Armstrong's eye, and added to the mystery. When he inspected it, Armstrong found the flat metal button to have been made in England, and featured "London" stamped in a circular fashion on the inside of its reverse. The doctor captured McClure's attention, and there began an inquiry as to the source of the button, "when we heard the startling intelligence that an Indian, *like ourselves*, as they said, *had been killed not far from where we stood*. The name of Indian is applied to all people dissimilar to themselves; and the interpreter concluded it was a European; but when the deed was done, it was impossible to determine, from their inability to compute time with accuracy."[35]

However, the Eskimos did say they had seen two boats going eastward the previous summer (1849), and sometime soon after, returning westward toward the Mackenzie—without either establishing communication with those onshore. This must have been a party from the *Plover*, since the four boats under Richardson and Rae, searching for Franklin on the North American coast in 1848, traveled east from the Mackenzie to the Coppermine River, and did not return westward.[36]

McClure, Armstrong and Miertsching went ashore the following day at the locale where the Eskimos indicated the white people had camped (about 10 miles from the Eskimo village), but only found "the ruins of two Eskimo winter-houses built of driftwood, the fragments of old stone blubber-lamps, and other small articles, but all very old and moss-grown," recalled Miertsching. "We found not the least evidence to suggest that Europeans had lived there."[37]

The days that followed brought snow, rain, and light contrary winds, accompanied by gradually falling temperatures, and the Sylvester's Warming Apparatus was lit so its pipes could air the ship. Fewer birds graced the skies, and most of them flew southward. The continuous daylight had also given way to three hours of nightly darkness, during which guns and rockets were occasionally let go, to alert any of Franklin's people or the *Enterprise*, should they be within earshot. All marked summer's rapid ending. "The captain is often very impatient. The channel here is again very narrow: on the one side great impenetrable ice-masses, on the other very shallow water, although the shore is two English miles distant," warily observed Miertsching.[38]

Nicholson Island was sighted to the south on the 30th, as the ship edged toward Harrowby Bay, at the eastern entrance to Liverpool Bay, close to Cape Bathurst. McClure had to start considering a location for his winter quarters, to afford protection from the coming November and December gales, which would drive the ice down upon his vessel, but found this area just as shoal as the rest of the coast.[39]

Here, Cresswell reached out to his family, laying down his final words to loved ones as *Investigator* prepared to disappear into the unknown:

> I open this to give you a later look at my welfare. We have not made much progress as you will see since [my letter of] the 24th, nothing but foul winds, and some very light, so much so that having a current against us we have made a retrograde progress. But all this easterly wind may be good for us, it must clear the land to the eastward of us of ice. I much fear you will never get this. Should you get, best love to all.[40]

It would be three years before family, friends, or the Admiralty heard again from anyone onboard the wayward wooden home of the Investigators.

Sainsbury, Armstrong and Miertsching landed in the morning to leave a record of the expedition's arrival, and marked the spot with a piece of wood, upon which was cut a broad arrow mark (representing British government ownership), along with the ship's name. The wood was gotten from one of two native sleds found nearby, next to a buried cache of fish and ducks. While the marker was being prepared, the doctor seized the opportunity to attend to his scientific duties by carrying out some quick botanizing, and to obtain a few small birds (sanderling, snow bunting, and turnstone). In doing so, Armstrong gazed upon land that "was more elevated than any we had previously visited, but flat, forming a continuous plain.... I also observed several small lakes or ponds on the surface, containing good fresh water."[41]

After the party returned onboard, *Investigator* stood in as close to land as was safe, sailing northeasterly toward the Baillie Islands, on the north coast of Cape Bathurst. A few miles up the coast, two figures were seen standing on the high plain the landing party had visited in the morning. With the belief there must be others onshore, McClure decided to seek them out and put dispatches in their hands for delivery to a Hudson's Bay outpost, and then on to the Admiralty. Accordingly, the first whaleboat and first cutter were manned and armed at 1:00 p.m. The captain, doctor, and interpreter were propelled toward Harrowby Bay in the whaleboat. The cutter, occupied by some officers out for whatever sport they could find, were not to depart until the first boat reached shore, so their total numbers did not cause alarm. Dressed in garb similar to the natives, Miertsching stood prominently in the bow, where he could be clearly seen; and because the naval White Ensign had previously flown along these shores, so it might be recognized, it drifted from the flagstaff astern.[42]

Before the captain's boat reached shore, its occupants spied two women, attended by several dogs, who gleefully returned the signal of friendship made by the Investigators. After the boat's keel slid upon the soft mud beach, the men commenced a hike up a bank about 80 feet in height, to be greeted at the top by the sight of the same extensive plain viewed earlier in the day. The cutter's landing fared differently, with one of her people initially in dire straits: "On landing one of our officers got stuck in the mud so that it took all a cutter's crew to haul him out with a rope," related Ford. "If he had been by himself he must have perished."[43]

Miertsching was soon engaged in a lively conversation with the two women (one of whom carried a child about 15 or 16 months of age on her back), and it was discovered they were mother, daughter, and grandmother. Miertsching named the adults as Kunatsiak and Kenalik (but doesn't indicate who was older), and the men of their tribe are said to be away to the north hunting whales; from this, it was assumed the men were at Cape Bathurst. The women offered to guide them to the others, which McClure readily accepted, and the captain ordered the boat to follow along the shore, while his party advanced on the beach. "After an hour we arrived at two Eskimo houses, the homes of these two women, and in answer to the question as to how far we must yet go to meet their men who were whale-fishing they said, 'twice as far as we had already gone.' As it was already late in the afternoon the captain decided to return to the ship and visit the Eskimos in the following morning."[44]

They reached the ship at 6:00 p.m. While onshore, the party had shot several ducks and gulls, and the great northern diver (common loon) was spotted for the first time, and many flocks of ducks were seen making their was southward. *Investigator* followed the coastline until night closed in, and the temperature dipped to 27° (the sea water being only one degree higher), while the young ice grew on the rigging and "showered about us plentifully in working the ship." Jack Frost was close at hand. The ship anchored off the Baillie Islands "in four fathoms, the weather looking wild and unsettled."[45]

At seven o'clock in the morning on the last day of August, eight seamen (including James Nelson) manned and armed the first cutter, and were supplied with provisions for twenty-four hours. McClure, Miertsching and Dr. Armstrong set off for shore, while stinging blasts of wind assaulted them from the west, on the coldest day the Investigators had yet experienced within the Arctic Circle, ten degrees below freezing. The character of the land they approached had been transformed overnight—grass, plants and flowers that formerly burst with vibrant hues were now blanketed with seven inches of virgin snow.[46]

Meanwhile, Piers and others also headed toward terra firma: "A cairn or mound being seen from the Ship after the sailing of the Cutter, Cresswell, Court, Sainsbury & I went in a whale boat to examine it—it was situated on an Island—Bailey's I think—about four miles distant from the Ship." The assistant surgeon went on to describe the examination of a three-foot mound of clods of frozen earth, which did not have any deposits in or near it, and may have been a native marker for a fresh water pool nearby. Alternately, it could have been built as a place for one or two hunters to hide from deer which likely frequented the pool (deer tracks were spotted in the area).[47]

To search for the tribe, McClure's intention was to parallel the mainland's coast as close as possible to shore, and he ended up heading toward the small bay they had left the previous evening. At one point the boat grounded amidst an onshore wind and a heavy surf, and it was necessary to cast out the anchor. Kunatsiak and Kenalik had seen the boat's approach, and by words and movements, strongly urged the party to land; but due to the shallow water the little craft was rowed out some distance, and the women climbed to the high ground and gazed at the explorers for a long time.[48]

Armstrong recounted the whaleboat's struggle: "The wind having increased considerably in force, it carried away our main-yard, then sprung the mizen mast, and we grounded repeatedly amongst the ice. The coast line presented a succession of lofty headlands, as if each, on becoming exposed to view, was the last, until we got some eighteen or twenty miles to the northward, when that which appeared to be, as it really was, Cape Bathurst, broke fairly on our view."[49]

Not a soul was seen through the spyglass, and the party nearly gave up the search—thinking the tribe had moved inland—when Armstrong was just able to make out a figure in motion near the farthest point of the cape. Before long, 30 tents and nine winter huts (for housing about 300), plus 13 umiaks (baidars) and a multitude of kayaks, and many people, came into view. However, because of the depth of the water, the boat could not be guided directly toward the encampment, and was instead grounded off what initially appeared to be a large floe that extended between the cape and a nearby island, but turned out to be a narrow, sandy isthmus. Still some distance from shore, the boat had to be tracked in as near as possible before the party could advance toward the cape.[50]

The party was not taking any chances: the muskets were loaded and ammunition passed out. According to Armstrong, five men stayed with the cutter and were given orders not to allow any kayaks to come alongside. Three sailors accompanied Captain McClure, Miertsching and himself (including Nelson, who carried a boarding pike with White Ensign attached, and a bag of presents), then moved off toward the cape, about 700 yards away.[51]

Armstrong's description of what happened next is reminiscent of a scene from a Hollywood epic:

> We had got about half way without observing the least movement amongst them, and matters wearing rather a hostile aspect, we considered that our fearless advance, in numbers so few, would convince them of our friendly intentions. Suddenly one of them was observed to descend the cliff, at the base of which were several oomiaks [umiaks] and kayaks, seized one of the latter, launched it in a small channel of water, separating the isthmus from the Cape, which was in some places quite fordable, and made way towards us. In a moment, all the others, as if by preconcerted signal, followed the example, and in a few minutes the whole tribe advanced rapidly towards us. They left the kayaks at the stream, and ran wildly along the beach, yelling loudly—their long black hair streaming in the wind. Carrying their bows ready for use, they unsheathed their long bright knives, and brandished them in the air as they advanced. All the women followed with supplies of arrows, presenting a picture of hostility, which left little to

be understood of their intentions. Their number rapidly increased, several oomiaks filled with men and women having left the shore to reinforce them, all armed.[52]

McClure "kept asking [Miertsching], 'What is to be done? What is to be done?,'"[53] and the Brother sprang into action:

> I handed the captain my gun, securely fastened my Eskimo frock, and ran as fast as I could towards them; which caused in their ranks a—to me—most disagreeable disturbance. I drew my pistol from my pocket, discharged it in the air before their eyes, and shouted to them to throw down their weapons. But they only shouted all the louder: "Shuitok, shuitok, Kalauroktuta" [evidently agreeing to do so only when McClure's men laid down their guns].[54] I took my stand before them with my pistol in my hand, unloaded—but the Eskimos did not know that, being unaware that one must load a fire-arm before discharging it—and told them that we were friends, brought gifts, and intended to do them no harm whatever; whereupon they became more quiet and peaceful; the captain came forward to join me, and finally, after much debate and giving of pledges, they laid down their weapons, but left their knives within easy reach on the ground. I marked a line in the snow between them and us which no one was to cross, and this also impressed them. They became more friendly, and finally all fear vanished, and they brought wives, children, and sucklings, and laid little ones in our arms that we might observe them more closely.[55]

Through the Brother, McClure proceeded to question Chief Kenalualik and the leading men of the tribe about Franklin and his men, and although they knew nothing, "they promised to be kind to any strangers, 'white men,' who might come amongst them." Dr. Richardson (in two boats) and these people had seen one another in the summer of 1848, and evidently three of Pullen's boats were seen the following season. "With regard to the story told of a white man being buried at Cape Warren, they merely said they knew nothing of it, or of the natives residing there; indeed, they were at variance with them."[56]

The chief "was very anxious for the Ship to winter near the Cape and for us all to come & live on shore—promising to allow the Captain & a few others to reside in his tent. Someone asking Miertsching how the Esquimaux would expect us to sleep in their tents, he drily replied, 'Oh! of course with them, altogether, like pickled herrings—the young dogs and children crawling over you, to find a warm place!'"[57]

Admiration for Miertsching's linguistic and diplomatic talents blossomed during the exchanges. "The perfect ease which this gentleman understands and converses with these interesting people surprises them very much; they were most anxious for him to remain, promising to be very kind. The chief presented his daughter, a very pretty girl of about fifteen, which should be his wife,—tents, and all appurtenances were to be added," wrote McClure to the Admiralty. Miertsching, however, didn't experience the same fluency: "The dialect of these people is somewhat different from that of other Eskimos along this coast; they understand me very well; but to me, especially at the first, it was difficult to understand them—they were almost unintelligible."[58]

Miertsching impressed upon the middle-aged Kenalualik and tribe elders the importance of forwarding the tin case of dispatches and letters to the HBC's Fort Good Hope (and then on to England),[59] which the chief

> promised most faithfully to perform, for which he was to receive a musket and ammunition; and upon his delivering the packet, a further reward, equal in value to a silver fox skin[60] [and also "with a promise of a musket to every man of the party who could kill a whale if we heard of their safe arrival in England"[61]]; he however, said that their tribe do not trade with the "Mackenzie," but with another further south, who, in turn traffic with the Indians who are in the service of the Hudson's Bay Company; so they have to pass through three tribes of the heathen before they come into the hands of civilized

man, I think it extremely probable that they may never reach their destination; Mr. Miertsching, from his knowledge of the Esquimaux character, thinks otherwise, and imagines that the chief himself will carry them.[62]

In fact, by the publication of McClure's journal in 1856, those dispatches had still not reached their intended destination,[63] creating a mystery that wasn't solved until a dozen years after the ink on them was dry.

Roderick Ross MacFarlane was the clerk-in-charge at Fort Good Hope from 1854 to 1861, and "[d]uring this period, the Company was getting few furs from coastal Eskimos at its posts at Fort McPherson and La Pierre House and many of these were through Indian middlemen. The Eskimos traded mostly westward along the coast with the Russians in Alaska. In 1857 Roderick MacFarlane was sent by James Anderson, Chief Factor in charge of the Mackenzie District, to explore the possibilities for trade with the Eskimos by way of the Beghula or Inconnu River. MacFarlane renamed the river "Anderson" after his Chief Factor."[64]

In July 1862, MacFarlane wrote to Sir John Richardson about

the receipt of the Despatches, at this post [Fort Anderson], a short time ago: And I have now the pleasure of enclosing a letter to your address, found among the package. Various causes occurred to retard their delivery by the Esquimaux—at that time, and for a year or two subsequently, we maintained no direct intercourse with these people [around Cape Bathurst], and none whatever with the tribe frequenting this river (the Beghula tesse) until 1857, when I first descended and examined it till within a short distance of its outlet. On that occasion, and on several winter journies afterwards made to them for purposes of trade, I endeavored to ascertain what had become of the Despatches, but from the inability or stupidity of the Indians who acted as Interpreters, I could not make them understand my wishes, and indeed it was only when paying a visit to a party of Esquimaux, at their Winter houses last February, that I obtained information which has resulted in the recovery of the papers—the reason given for the long delay being that the Esquimaux to whom Capt⁰ M'Clure delivered them had died previous to 1857, when they first became acquainted with the traders, and that the papers had been buried with the effects of the deceased, and had been altogether forgotten until they understood that I wanted them.[65]

At Cape Bathurst, Armstrong was impressed with what he saw. "The tribe appeared to be composed of young, active, muscular men, and the women were decidedly better-looking, with more vivacity and cheerfulness than any we had met with.... They said they were about half as many at the encampment as were present; so that we estimated the strength of the tribe at one hundred and fifty persons." One young woman, "in appearance and expression, much the most interesting of the whole, had a good complexion, large, dark, sparkling eyes, beautiful pearl-like teeth, aquiline nose, a most luxuriant crop of raven-black hair, small and delicately-formed hands and feet, and her pleasing features radiant with smiles of cheerful good-humour, much excited my interest."[66]

In turn, the Eskimos were impressed with the Investigators' guns, and Miertsching's discharge of his pistol and the gift of a musket and 100 rounds of ball cartridge for Kenalualik could have only fueled desire. "I don't know what faith is to be placed in a skin clad great man," McClure later wrote to his wife, "particularly after he has received payment as I gave him a gun and ammunition for the exec[u]tion he was going to make." "We fully instructed him in its use, and loaded it in his presence," observed Armstrong. "He fired it with great coolness, amid a general shout of joy from his brethren." Attempts by the Eskimos to "acquire" the sailors' muskets and the black lacquered botanical case slung across Armstrong's back (and a pair of pocket pistols it contained), had to be "firmly resisted; and other attempts at familiarity also required us to maintain an appearance of determination." Another destructive element—alcohol—came down through the trading chain, and the natives "repeated the accusation of the fire-water having been given in barter, and its fatal results."[67]

The Investigators hoped to glean from the occupiers of this land something of what lay ahead, but only came away with the realization that they would be pressing into the heart of the unknown, where humans were true outsiders.

> Cape Bathurst was to the "Investigator," in her long voyage, what Otaheite [Tahiti] was in the olden day to our early circumnavigators. The skill in delineating the outlines of the coast, or chart-drawing, which has been so often mentioned by navigators as existing amongst the Esquimaux, was really found here; but nothing could be learnt of what lay to the North. They did not know whether it was sea or not; but they said, pointing to it with an expression of anxiety, "That is the Land of the White Bear!" They appeared to be much alarmed, too, when the ship for a time stood off towards it. The bears they described as coming from it were said to be very fierce and dangerous; and one of the women, with tears in her eyes, told how lately one of those brutes had carried off her child when playing on the beach at a short distance from her.[68]

Not all animals in the Eskimos' world were to be feared, or serve as prey, as Miertsching noticed the "dogs of these people are of the same breed as in Labrador." Labradors "originated on the island of Newfoundland, now part of the province of Newfoundland and Labrador, Canada. The founding breed of the Labrador was the St. John's water dog, a breed that emerged

St. John's water dog (lesser Newfoundland) (Harter, 1979).

through ad-hoc breeding by early settlers of the island in the 16th century. The forebears of the St. John's Dog are not known but were likely a random-bred mix of English, Irish, and Portuguese working breeds." In fact, an Eskimo dog, picked up on the coast of North America, became the ship's mascot and was named Mongo. It may have been a gift from one of the tribes, and it's possible the name derived from the word *mongrel*—a dog of mixed breed. McClure probably realized that allowing a mascot would be good for the crew's morale, and a doghouse was built and kept on the upper deck.[69]

Brother Miertsching made use of his time with the Eskimos by imparting to them an explanation of the natural world, and the existence of a Divine Being. They "have apparently never thought that the sun, moon, rocks, and water were created by anyone, and were much astonished when I told them of a great, good Spirit, Who can do whatsoever He wills, and to Whom nothing is impossible ... that this Spirit has created everything, including the first men, etc., at which they stared at me in amazement, and frequently cried out in wonder."[70]

> These Eskimos also have their own peculiar conception of the life after death. It is that there are two lands, one good, and one not good. In the good land dwells a good spirit who looks after the wild animals, that they do not disappear from the land. In the bad land dwells also a spirit who is bad and always does men harm. When an Eskimo dies, if he has in life clothed the widows and orphans and given them food, he comes to the good land where the sun shines always and where there is never rain, ice, or strong winds, but always warm weather and countless seal, reindeer, etc., and these are not wild or shy; one can catch them with one's hands. He, on the contrary, who has not had a good character in his life, comes to the bad land which is the complete opposite of the good land. While I was carrying on this, to me, most interesting conversation with these Eskimos whom I was beginning to love, the captain came and summoned me to the boat.[71]

The young men and warriors of the tribe returned to the cape, where they intended to launch their kayaks and escort the landing party back to *Investigator*; whereas the older men and women accompanied the sailors back to the cutter. Along the way, seaman Nelson witnessed his astonished captain seized by two women on either side of him, and whisked through the snow at such a brisk pace that McClure pleaded for mercy! Because he carried a boarding pike draped with the Union Jack (Armstrong wrote it was a White Ensign), Nelson himself was also the object of a good bit of attention, and much to his relief he was ordered to hand over this coveted pole and banner to its ardent admirers.[72]

To keep order, a line was then made on the beach, which the intended recipients of gifts understood they were not to pass. Miertsching then proceeded to hand out presents from Nelson's bag, which contained knives, scissors, files, beads, hatchets, kettles, and boilers, along with needles and pins for the women, who beamed with delight at the sight of them. For a short time, "order was maintained, but the fair sex becoming clamorous and closing round, the line was broken, and to prevent being driven into the water, we were compelled to retreat to the boat which was lying aground about twenty yards from the beach."[73]

Though McClure gave the order to shove off, "about forty surrounded the cutter, and although all the crew were stationed round her to prevent their getting on board, so eager and persevering were the women that several were lifted in, endeavouring to seize everything within their reach; one of them, in the most dexterous manner, slipped the compass out of its box into the breast of her jacket, and with difficulty it was recovered."[74]

With *Investigator* lying about 10 miles distant, the cutter hoisted sail and was obliged to toil through the ice floe against a westerly wind, while a flotilla of 17 sleek kayaks acted as escort. All but one of the little craft reached the ship 15 minutes prior to the cutter's arrival at six in the evening, amid a heavy snowfall. The lone exception "encountered a fresh breeze and rough sea: we shortened sail and took boat and all in,—the poor fellow being drenched, we offered him a little brandy, which he drank at a mouthful, not being aware of its strength; he suffered the sensation to subside without evincing (except by his eyes watering) any symptom of vexation, and then asked for water."[75]

Several of the kayaks, mostly with their owners still seated in them, were hoisted onboard, and two of the visitors commenced profound "transformations." One was fitted out in a Marine's scarlet coat and trousers, while the other was rigged as a sailor. As the thermometer hovered around freezing, "it was most amusing to see them go to the gangway and exhibit their finery, at the same time raising their bodies by the hands and throwing their legs into the air to shew the trowsers. The one dressed as a Marine, was a young man about two or three & twenty and had very lately killed a Whale, for which action he had just been decorated with the customary manner of a blue line tattooed across each cheek."[76]

*Investigator* weighed and moved off to the southeast at 5:40 that evening, to steer clear of the Baillie Islands, and bade her visitors farewell. A few hours later, the ship tacked and stood to the northwest.[77]

**Dr. Anderson's Naval General Service Medal 1793–1840, with Syria clasp, as the assistant surgeon in HMS *Princess Charlotte* in 1840 (officially impressed on the edge: ROBERT ANDERSON, ASS$^{\text{T}}$ SURG$^{\text{N}}$); Arctic Medal 1818–55 (unnamed as issued; Assistant Surgeon/*Investigator*/1848–49 & Surgeon/*Enterprise*/1850–55), posthumously issued in 1857; Turkish St. Jean d'Acre Medal 1840 (silver issue/unnamed as issued). The latter two are genuine representative examples (Spencer J. Fisher, 2014; Glenn M. Stein Collection).**

Elsewhere on that final August day of 1850, Captain Collinson—who had taken *Enterprise* to the east of Point Barrow, but then retreated from the ice—forfeited his last opportunity to keep his ship in the Arctic that winter and/or rejoin *Investigator*. At Point Hope, south of Cape Lisburne, Collinson went ashore with Surgeon Robert Anderson (a friend of Armstrong's), and retrieved a message left by Kellett. Shocked to read that *Investigator* was ahead of them, having been seen by *Plover* off the Seahorse Islands (near Point Franklin) on August 4, Anderson "exclaimed 'For God's sake, Sir, go back—it is not too late.' 'No, no,' said the Captain, 'I must see Kellett.' Captain Kellett had arranged to be in Port Clarence on 4th September."[78]

When *Enterprise* encountered the *Herald* and *Plover* at Port Clarence, after talks with the *Herald*'s officers, Second Master Skead seethed with frustration: "Instead of following our blockhead of a course [McClure] steered straight for the Aleutian Islands, entering the Behring sea by the Amouchta Channel [Amukta Pass], and reached C. Lisburne a full 17 days before us.... What a comment in this passage of Investigator upon our miserable bungle—yet it was just what we had anticipated—not that the Investigator would steer straight—but that if she did she would make a quicker passage than ourselves." Skead also recorded how "Captain Kellett was much surprised to find us in Port Clarence in the very heart of the working season, and one of the Lts. told me that Capt. K. had declared "he would rather have seen us upon the rocks than looking for winter quarters at so early a part of the summer season.'"[79]

Collinson had decided that *Plover* was to remain at Port Clarence for the winter, while *Enterprise* would go south and stay at Hong Kong. Consequently, "no time was lost in completing and storing *Plover* for three years, which with the building of a [store]house occupied us until the 13th.... I determined to go to the north and spend the remainder of the season about Cape Lisburne; so that, in the event of anything occurring to the *Investigator* or any of the missing expedition making their appearance, we should be nearer at hand, and save the boats a trip across Kotzebue Sound." Only tempestuous seas and temperatures well below freezing greeted Collinson off Cape Lisburne, and by September 30, he turned south for Port Clarence, and eventually, Hong Kong.[80]

Meanwhile, the Cape Bathurst Eskimos made a final visit to *Investigator* on the first day of September, with about 20 kayaks and umiaks, containing men, women and children, and stayed aboard nearly all day. Afterward, McClure specified in his writings to the Admiralty that when the natives departed, "several presents were bestowed upon them, which had the effect of eliciting promises of friendship for us or any of our white brethren who might come on their coast." That night, the aurora borealis—which results from a stream of ionized solar particles made visible on reaching Earth's atmosphere—was only faintly seen for the first time, extending from the northeast to the southwest, because a dense haze obscured its heavenly glow.[81]

Over the next several days, *Investigator* struggled to the eastward in light winds, encountering several whales (including two beluga and a narwhal), seals, and waterfowl, until she arrived off the mouth of the Horton River (Franklin Bay) at noon on September 4, amid a temperature spike into the forties. With the rise in temperature the depth of the water had fallen, and soundings varied from 63 to 115 fathoms, while large floes had drifted off from the land, to greet *Investigator* at the bay's entrance. Approaching the river's entrance, the ship passed over several shoals in 10 to 13 fathoms of water.[82] Armstrong sketched the scene:

> The land on either side of this river gradually rises to an elevation of nearly 200 feet, with numerous small mounds and ridges scattered on its surface, which on casual observation much resembled huts. Smoke was observed some distance along the coast to the southward, which was anxiously watched, for any sign that could indicate the presence of human beings, apparently it proceeded from an ordinary fire. As evening closed in, we had not reached sufficiently near to satisfy our curiosity on this point.[83]

Punctuating the scene, a large polar bear was seen swimming toward a piece of ice, but the brute was too far off to attempt a chase.

After a torrential downpour the next morning, the sky cleared and it became calm towards noon. "Smoke was again observed rising vertically against the dark back ground of the land, which appeared about 250 feet high." With Ice Mate Newton reporting "he saw the flame of the fire, huts on the shore, and people moving about in light coloured clothes," Cresswell, Armstrong and Miertsching shoved off in the second whaleboat to examine the strange smoke, which was distant about 10 miles (in his writings Armstrong again leaves out

**Narwhals (Gustav Mützel; Harter, 1979).**

Miertsching in the boat party). During the long row, Armstrong remarked on the "great number of Whales—at one period we counted no less than fifteen above water, several of which came quite close to us." Carefree seals also abounded, who were as unconcerned about the harpoon's tip as the leviathans.[84]

Although the giants close by posed no threat, fear invaded the men in the boat party when they saw "a column of smoke rising from the ship which said to us: 'The ship is on fire!' Slowly, slowly now we went forward; back we dared not go, for no signal was hoisted: were the ship to sink before our eyes, or to be blown into the air, which might well happen with all the gunpowder she had onboard.... The emotions which overcame us no man can describe, nor could he describe our joy as the smoke ascending from the ship was seen to diminish and finally fade away; and the ship lay there quite undamaged."[85]

Fire aboard a ship is one of the most feared of all calamities, and according to Miertsching, an inquiry into the fire was held the following morning. James Nelson pointed to the cause as being a quantity of loose oakum (tarred fiber used for caulking decks or packing the joints of timbers) left by the Woolwich workmen around the back part of the Sylvester stove, which ignited because the person in charge of the stove lit too big a fire in it.[86]

After a two-hour row,[87] "we approached the shore, there remained no doubt as to the entire absence of a fire, and the other creations of the ice-master's imagination; the smoke being entirely the result of chemical action in the soil—slender columns of it emanating from small mounds, were borne along the precipitous coast by a light westerly breeze," runs Armstrong's condescending tone. "These [volcanic] mounds formed quite a little amphitheatre, inclining from the sea at an angle of 45°, and elevated in height from ten to thirty feet."[88] The

**Polar bears (J.W. Orr; Harter, 1979).**

smell of sulfur was so strong, the mounds could not be approached closer than 10 or 15 feet, and the ground so hot the soles of shoes were parched brown by the heat.[89]

This incident, and another in December, both involved Newton's supposedly seeing things related to the lost expedition. It would seem the ice mate was indulging in wishful thinking and/or was the victim of optical illusions. It's worthy to take into account that the Investigators were on a continual hunt for *any trace* of Franklin and his men; and, in this instance, after spending long hours in the crow's nest day after day, Newton's mind may have started playing tricks on him.[90]

Miertsching exclaimed, "Alas, alas! that none of us had knowledge of chemistry; the whole place seemed to me like a huge chemical laboratory," but this was not fair to Armstrong, who had some knowledge of chemistry and displays such in his writings. "We took samples of the particoloured dough or earth with us to the ship," continued Miertsching, "but later to our sorrow we learned that our pocket-handkerchiefs in which we brought the specimens to the ship—and also the wood in which we laid them—were scorched." The samples were spread out before McClure on the fine mahogany table of his cabin, but the captain was afterwards rudely surprised to discover his table full of dark holes. The culprits soon found new homes in covered containers of thick glass.[91]

During the nearly hour-long examination of the area, a "notice of our having landed was left, which could not long remain, as the cliff is evidently rapidly crumbling away."[92]

First discovery of land by *Investigator*, Sept. 6, 1850 (S.G. Cresswell, 1854).

At four in the morning of the sixth, Cape Parry came into view; and by eight o'clock, its high round headland was about 10 miles off to the southeast of *Investigator*'s starboard quarter. "[We] wished to follow the coast by Dolphin and Union Strait, but the coast seemed to be obstructed with heavy drift-ice; so a more northerly course was set, where also, to be sure, much and very heavy ice was met, but there was so much space that the ship could pass through and wind freely in a broad zigzag. We saw many whales and seals, and three polar bears." Seaman Nelson gazed at one of the brutes ... after climbing to the top of a large hummock, he [the bear] was evidently convinced that an 'Investigator breakfast' was a long way off, and swaying side to side, lumbered away, perhaps to try his luck at sealing.[93]

> At 11.30 a.m., the joyful report of "land on the port bow" was proclaimed from the mast-head; and as noon dispelled the haze which hung around its lofty outline, and revealed it to our eyes, it bore from N.E. to E.N.E. distant about thirty miles. I need not attempt to describe the feeling of joy which this pleasing intelligence diffused amongst us ... the feeling of confidence universally entertained that the land before us would prove a certain guide to lead us to the northward—perhaps to Melville Island.[94]

# Decisions, 1850

*Nature is nobody's ally.*
—Herman Melville, *The Stone Fleet*

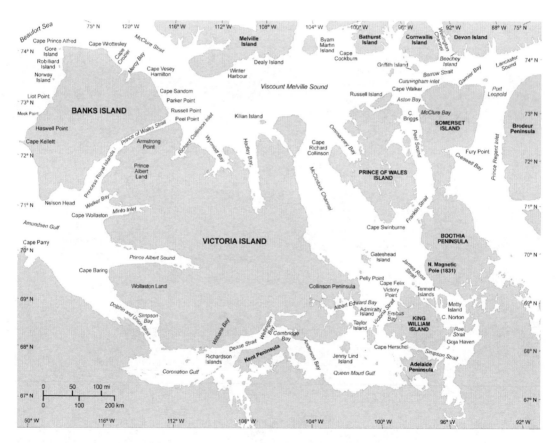

**Western Arctic Map (LibbeyDesign, Orlando, Florida).**

Several times during the night, the ship struck pieces of ice so violently that Miertsching and others were twice cast out of their beds. But the bruises were the sacrifices one paid for success. After all, it was partly due to McClure's boldness in passing through the Aleutians, his shameless deception of Kellett, and his persistence along the precarious North American coast, that "at 8 a.m. [on September 7] we had reached within two miles of the magnificent headland we had just seen, and could obtain no soundings at 120 fathoms. Preparations were at once made for landing, and taking formal possession of it in Her Majesty's name."[1]

At 9:40, McClure and Armstrong departed in the third whaleboat, followed by "as many of the officers as could be spared, in the first cutter,"[2] which included Lieutenant Cresswell (who executed watercolor sketches of *Investigator* approaching the new-found land),[3] Court, Paine and Miertsching—but *not* Haswell. Piers also stayed onboard.[4]

Under a clear sky, and with a fresh northeasterly breeze that accentuated the freezing temperature, Armstrong noted that it was "with joyful hearts we pulled towards shore."

> As we approached, we found the ice still packed on the shore, that obliged us to get out and haul the [whaleboat] over the floes into clear water, which led us on to a fine pebbly beach, eastward of the Cape, extending out for some distance, and it could be distinctly seen to be of great depth from its perfect transparency.
> On landing we unfurled a red ensign,[5] and planting the flagstaff in the soil, took formal possession in the name of our Most Gracious Sovereign, with three hearty cheers, and one cheer more; bestowing on our discovery the name of "Baring," after the First Lord of the Admiralty, under whose auspices the expedition had been fitted out. A scroll containing the ship's name, and those of the officers, &c., was placed in a bottle, and carefully secured in a cask fixed in the soil, with a pole about fifteen feet high attached, to attract the attention of any subsequent visitors to Baring Land.[6]

On the headland's southern side, a vertical cliff rose to around 800 feet above the sea, while behind it loomed an imposing peak, estimated to have been about 1,000 feet or more in height.[7] The grand and imposing appearance of the feature brought upon it the name Lord Nelson's Head (also Nelson's Head or Nelson Head) by McClure, in honor of Britain's best-known naval hero. As the altitude slowly sank on either side of the headland, it ended in a low beach some 18 to 20 miles to the east, "and then rose again in an undulating background, forming a continuous amphitheatre of ill-defined hills [that rose gradually to between 2,000 and 3,000 feet],[8] so close to each face, but which are really separated by tortuous valleys and ravines."[9]

The boats returned to *Investigator* at noon, and "Botanical and Geological specimens were brought on board—everyone wanting a trifle from the 'new land'—some animals teeth were also found & preserved. Traces of animals were observed on there; foot prints resembling those of the Musk Ox, Deer &c," wrote Piers. "We saw several flocks of Brent and Snow Geese, the Fulmar Petrel, a flock of Ducks and a few Snow Buntings, in the course of the day; but failed to procure a single specimen," related a disappointed Armstrong, ever alive to his naturalist duties.[10]

"There is a difference of opinion as to the best course to follow from this point—for it appears to run, in one direction, to the North towards Banks land, and in the other to the eastward towards Wollaston land;—and it may be a separate Island, or it may be connected with one or both of these lands, forming one large Island," wrote Piers. In the midst of these pondering words, the assistant surgeon also takes notice of one of the polar veterans onboard: "Working along the land with a fresh breeze, several of us were amused with a remark of Fawcett, the Boatswain's Mate & an old Polar Voyager, which was: 'go along—go along—cocked hat or a wooden leg this time!' He has been several voyages before both to the Arctic & Antarctic regions; is rather a humourous character, and I believe his society is rather coveted in Strood [Kent County], where his home is, for the sake of the many amusing yarns he can spin."[11]

A "cocked hat" appears to relate to an 18th-century navigation technique where one obtains a ship's location by three position lines, which together form a triangle—resembling a three-cornered cocked hat of the day—at the center of which is the vessel. The term "wooden leg" probably represents the pieces of wood (or timber) that make up the ribs or frame of a ship's hull. Consequently, when Fawcett joked "cocked hat or a wooden leg this time!" he was likely only half-kidding, since not realizing one's position along an unknown coast could easily result in a ship's having its hull smashed in.[12] As for Fawcett's "society," this was surely a friendly society; prior to modern insurance and the welfare state, individuals obtained financial and social services from such societies, that were often along the lines of their religious, political, or trade affiliations.[13]

So, amid fog, snow squalls, and lengthening nights, *Investigator* felt her way eastward:

Yesterday (Sunday) [September 8] we were working along the S. coast of "Baring Island," which the Master says is 60 miles in length, and we concluded it to be a distinct island, because we appeared to have reached the south eastern point in the evening—being unable to see land further to the eastward when close off the point.... To day has been, I think, the most anxious & exciting one with us all, since leaving England. It has been very misty the whole day, with a light air from about S.E.; and in the morning, as we were standing to the N.W. (Compass course—true about N.E. by E.), the eastern part of Baring's Island seen & then appearing as the fog cleared a little—land was seen, not for off, on our starboard bow!—then the opinion, that Court expressed yesterday, of the S. eastern end being only one point of a large & perhaps deep bay, it was feared by us all would prove correct—and the Captain himself, I believe, determined, if such proved to be the case, to return by the way he came and try the western shore of Baring's Island. In this anxious & doubtful state we were kept all day; occasionally getting a glimpse of the land on either bow, the Ship going two or three knots; the water slowly shoaling from 50 fathoms to 35.... In standing on as we are doing, between these two lands one of two things is very probable; either that we are running into a deep bay, and losing, now, valuable time & ground, or else— our good fortune continuing—being led through a Strait or Channel which will conduct us to the much desired Strait by Melville Island—thus accomplishing for the first time, the circumnavigation of America and the long sought passage round its Northern coast through the Arctic Sea!... But in the joy and excitement which will no doubt attend such great success on the part of this Ship, I trust the main object of this Expedition will not be lost sight of—the search for the unfortunate Sir John Franklin and his crews.

We seem to have been Providentially and in an extraordinary manner conducted thus far on our arctic voyage—with almost constant adverse winds; through ice; through shallow and narrow channels of water; through dense fogs, and now the dark nights—and this too in a part never navigated by a Ship before—some of it totally unknown—and without ever stopping night or day, unless becalmed or absolutely obstructed by a barrier of ice. After all this—though we may fail in finding, and returning to their mourning friends, our lost Country men—I believe, as I hope, that our voyage will so far be brought to a successful termination, by our returning to England through Davis Straits![14]

The land Piers described off the starboard bow at lat. 72° 1' N. and long. 119° 25' W., was to be named after Queen Victoria's consort Prince Albert, and the "distance between the two lands was conjectured to be thirty miles." In spite of the intervening fog and snow, ranges of snow covered mountains, and "here and there peaks of a volcanic character and outline were seen, but none that appeared active."[15]

Under studding sails towards noon on the 10th, *Investigator* found herself abreast of two small islands (later named the Princess Royal Islands).[16] "We believe the land on our left hand, which was named by the Captain Baring's Land or Island, to be Bank's Land; and that on our right, [western] Wollaston Land—and for these very good reasons—the land on our left hand is a continuation of what we call Baring's Island," wrote Piers.

At this time,

> observations placed "Investigator" only sixty miles from Barrow's Strait. "I cannot," writes Captain M'Clure in his private journal, "describe my anxious feelings. Can it be possible that this water communicates with Barrow's Strait, and shall prove to be a the long-sought North-west Passage? Can it be that so humble a creature as I am will be permitted to perform what has baffled the talented and wise for hundreds of years! But all praise be ascribed unto Him who hath conducted us so far in safety. His ways are not our ways, or the means that he uses to accomplish his ends within our comprehension. The wisdom of the world is foolishness with Him."[17]

The "good fortune" which had accompanied the Investigators for so many months came to an abrupt end on Sept. 11, 1850, when the temperature plummeted to 21°F, and a NNE gale swept ice down upon the ship. Of sleep the night before there was little, "nothing but heavy shocks, hard grinding of ice against the ship's sides and tacking every ten minutes or quarter of an hour; though, for about two hours, in the middle watch, the Ship was firmly beset—our progress to the N.E. being now completely obstructed by closely packed ice."[18]

On this very day, Captain Austin's eastern Arctic expedition was beset northwest of Griffith Island, in Barrow Strait. Piers and his fellow Investigators "were unacquainted with [the fitting out of Austin's ships] till our arrival in the 'the Pacific.'"[19] Having left England in May and being comprised of HMS *Resolute* (Captain Horatio Austin), HMS *Assistance* (Captain Erasmus Ommanney), and the steamers HMS *Intrepid* (Lieutenant John B. Cator) and HMS *Pioneer* (Lieutenant Sherard Osborn), Austin's expedition was trying to reach Melville Island from Baffin Bay. McClure and Austin were about 400 miles apart—and were entirely ignorant of each other's positions. Just the previous month, Ommanney had discovered the first traces of Franklin's expedition at Cape Riley, Devon Island, and also of Franklin's 1845–46 winter quarters at Beechey Island. At the present time, there were also seven other ships from private and public expeditions searching the eastern Arctic (including two manned by the United States Navy).[20]

The following several days were spent taking advantage of the meager leads of open water afforded to *Investigator*, while alternately staving off destruction from being thrown onshore by westerly gales, by holding on to a large floe with heavy hawsers, stream chain and ice anchors, which, when it grounded, acted as a natural dock or breakwater. Amid "snow falling, with an icy cold blast which froze its flakes together as they fell on our beards and moustache, nearly gluing up the mouth and eyelids," the mercury dropped to a low of 10°F. Ice saws were worked, and at times the capstan was manned by all hands (officers and men) to do battle with the ice by warping; sometimes they toiled for several hours in utter futility. Also, lest it be damaged by ice floes—some of which measured 25 to 30 feet in thickness—the rudder was twice unshipped and suspended over the stern.[21]

In one instance, Piers recorded a near-calamity when "the ship had to make a sharp turn to port, and not doing it quick enough, she ran into a large floe piece with such force that everyone had to look out for himself. I should not have been in the least surprised at seeing the top-gallant masts come down. Fawcett, the Boatswain's Mate, said 'the main-mast went right over the bows!'—meaning no doubt that it bent forward a great deal."[22]

However, the formation of young ice was equally serious to Arctic navigation, and Parry

**Austin's Expedition (left to right),** *Intrepid, Assistance, Resolute* **and** *Pioneer* **(E.W.,** *The Illustrated London News,* **May 11, 1850).**

wrote that a ship stuck in such ice "has often reminded me of Gulliver tied down by the feeble hands of Lilliputians."[23] Armstrong explained how young ice begins

> when a thin film becomes formed on the surface of the water, imparting to it an oily appearance, to which the name of "Pancake ice" has been given. This becomes broken up by the slightest contact with heavier ice; and the fragments sliding under, or over each other, acquire greater thickness. From frequent repetition of the same process, and the continuance of low temperature, they soon acquire strength and thickness, become united with others, and form a frozen surface of greater or less extent, through which a ship cannot possibly penetrate, when thus surrounded.[24]

The Arctic winter had begun.

But in spite of the gloomy and dismal atmosphere, the Investigators were in high spirits, and thanks to "several hollow parts of the floe, where the ice melted in the Summer, there is now capital sliding and tolerable skating—though Wynniatt is the only person who has brought skates with him. Officers and men have all been enjoying themselves in it, for even to get on a piece of ice after so much sea work is pleasant and an agreeable change."[25]

"I have spent the last four days chiefly in my cabin and in bed: I had caught a bad cold. This ship is still fixed fast in the ice," wrote Miertsching on the 16th. "Seals are often seen; the waterfowl are passing from north to south. The captain is growing anxious, and would gladly bring his ship into a good haven for the next winter." For the most part, *Investigator* was drifting slowly northward, and the next day, the Brother continued, "Mr. Court asserts that this is not a bay but a long strait or channel in which we find ourselves, because [the] ebb and flow are regular, and often the tide is very strong." To this passage McClure applied the

**Spotted seals (Harter, 1979).**

name Prince of Wales Strait. The ship reached her most advanced position at lat. 73° 10' N and long. 117° 10' W, "about *thirty miles* from waters of that series of straits which, under the names Melville, Barrow, and Lancaster, communicate with Baffin's Bay." *Investigator* had ceased to drift because the heavy ice of the Beaufort Sea ice stream squeezed into the northern entrance of the strait (see Arctic Ice Stream map).[26]

Curiously, on the eastern side of the strait, Armstrong Point is shown at this location on an Admiralty chart as early as 1853—but is *missing* from the map in McClure's 1856 book. However, the location *does* appear on the map in Surgeon Armstrong's book the following year (see Appendix 6). This is one of the more subtle indications of McClure's antipathy toward his leading medical man.

On September 19[27]—with the temperature having dropped to just 4°F the day before[28]—the time had come for Captain McClure to hold a serious debate with himself: he had to decide whether to "abandon all hope of reaching Barrow's Strait that year, and retrace his steps southward in search of a wintering place, or to hold on, so far as he might, and run the risk of wintering in the pack."[29] As he wrote to the Admiralty:

> I decided upon the latter, for these reasons, that to relinquish the ground obtained through so much difficulty, labour, and anxiety, for only the remote chance of finding safe winter quarters, would be injudicious, thoroughly impressed as I am with the absolute importance of retaining every mile to ensure any favourable results while navigating these seas, the loss of which might frustrate the operations of a whole season.[30]

McClure was certainly not willing to give up ground which brought him so tantalizingly close to discovering *and* sailing through a North-West Passage—which he reckoned he had an opportunity to do during the forthcoming 1851 navigating season.

He continued with the second part of his reasoning for wintering in the pack:

> Above all, being in the vicinity of Bank's Land and in the direction which Sir John Franklin would, in all probability, have endeavoured to penetrate could he have reached Cape Walker, I considered that our position was most eligible for carrying into full effect the instructions of my Lords Commissioners of the Admiralty when the season becomes favourable for dispatching parties upon this important and interesting search.[31]

This was true, and if *Investigator* was forced to winter along the southern coast of the newly discovered land, the capabilities of her search parties during the spring sledding season would have been dramatically reduced. Worse still, if the ship was forced to seek winter quarters along the North American coast, the sledding season would have been lost altogether.

In contrast with the necessity of the commander's hard reality is a scene softened by Piers' sensitive appraisal of the Investigators' home away from home:

> Ship still, fast beset; and from the whole rigging being covered by a very fine, soft snow, which has fallen slowly during the last, still, twenty-four hours, she presents as beautiful a picture as it is possible to conceive of a Ship beset in calm weather in the Arctic regions. She has the appearance of a most delicate & ornamental piece of workmanship; and, like many of the natural appearances & phenomena observed in these regions, I think it would prove beyond the power of painting or words faithfully to describe it.[32]

Beyond this alluring veneer lay hidden nature's sleight of hand. One day, Sainsbury shouted down the skylight, into the gunroom, that a black or brown bear was in sight, triggering Piers and his companions to leap up on deck for a glimpse the animal. A dark object could be seen about a mile or so off, which indeed had the general appearance of being a bear or wolf—"till rising on the wing, it proved to be a dark bird which had been magnified by the ice"![33]

"In consequence of N.W. and westerly winds," wrote Piers on September 23, "the last few days we have been gradually drifting back to the southward, so that this evening the islands, which we had lost sight of for some time and hoped not to see again, are not more than four or five miles off."[34] The floes were freight trains on crisscrossing tracks, constantly on collision courses—and *Investigator* was no more than a wandering vagabond.

Discord existed not only outside the ship, but within her too, as Miertsching tersely pointed out: "Milner, who for some days had been held in irons, was flogged today." The reason for the gunroom steward's severe punishment is not recorded by Miertsching, nor is the flogging even mentioned in any other contemporary source. The 30-year-old Cornwall man's life had taken a bad turn years before. In 1838, he had joined the Navy as George Frederick Luke. From 1841 to 1845, Luke served on the troopship *Apollo* as the wardroom steward and captain's steward, along with future Investigator, Passed Clerk Joseph C. Paine, for the latter part of that time. Up until 1845, he received "Very Good" marks for conduct. But upon signing on with the Arctic expedition, he began using the *alias* George L. Milner, and claimed his last naval vessel had been HMS *Stromboli* (from which he was discharged in July 1845)—these were lies to hide his past. Between the *Stromboli* and stepping onboard *Investigator* in January 1850, Luke held domestic positions in Her Majesty's Ships *Vanguard*, *Belleisle*, *Mariner* and *Spy*, and his conduct was "Indifferent" for all but two months of this period. Like *Investigator*, the gunroom steward was still headed in the wrong direction.[35]

The following morning, Piers put *Investigator* "not more than two miles off the islands and drifting directly towards them—our water having shoaled to ten fathoms, fortunately, just then, the wind shifted more to the eastward and drove the Ship round the western side of the islands, but at the same time towards the lee shore."[36] Around six in the evening she was forced up against heavy ice, and Miertsching knew that although

> we were anchored fast to a great floe with several cables and a chain, yet the ship was so squeezed against the ice [nipped] that her beams began to give. This lasted for a long time and we were all warned that the ship could not hold out for long. The captain hastily assembled the entire company on the upper deck, addressed us briefly, and, in anticipation of an extreme crisis, divided us into two crews—each with its boat, so that we might make our way to land—through that awful ice!! An officer was assigned to each boat—I am in No. 2 cutter. The boats are made ready, each with its tent and some rations. The frightful convulsions in the ice lasted into the night. At 11 o'clock the ship was more than once lifted up by the ice and thrown over on her broadside; but she righted herself as soon as the pressure relaxed. By midnight all was quiet.[37]

After this experience, before wishing him good night, the Brother had a lengthy and intent conversation with McClure, and "opened my *Losung* [Moravian daily devotional manual] and read aloud: 'Be ye therefore ready, for ye know neither the day nor the hour when the Son of Man cometh.'"[38]

By the final day of September, *Investigator* had circumnavigated the islands, and began drifting slowly northward again, receiving several severe nips in the process, and became stationary at lat. 72° 50' N. and long. 117° 55' W.—very nearly her farthest northerly point of two weeks before. She was frequently driven close to shore (as near as 50 feet from a steep, rugged cliff), although the large floe to which she was attached often kept her clear as the water shoaled. The ice mercilessly toyed with *Investigator*: "We came in contact with a large floe piece, which striking the ship on the starboard quarter, swung her completely round, carried away one five inch halser [hawser], and started all the anchors, six in number, off the floe,"[39] observed a stunned Armstrong.

And Miertsching related how one time, for "seventeen hours we stood ready on the deck where each moment appeared to be our last; great massive pieces of ice three and four times the size of the ship were pushed one on top of another and under continuing pressure forced into a towering heap which would then come tumbling down with a thunderous roar." Oakum oozed from seams, casks cracked, and at one point, the captain's door was so affected from the pressure, it would neither open or close. Each moment may have been their last, and "some sailors, with neither hope nor the fear of God before their eyes, burst open the chamber where the spirits were stored, made themselves and others completely drunk and stupefied their senses, so that in this condition they might escape the agonies of death."[40]

Through it all, the rounds of impending doom and invading water leaks did not dampen the men's nighttime animation for kicking up their heels and belting out tunes[41]... except possibly for Able Seaman Charles Steel.[42] "We had only one man who can be said to be at all sick," wrote Piers on the 26th, "and he is laboring under a chronic bowel affection which I think he has scarcely been free of since he has been in the Ship and resulted from Dysentery contracted in the tropics." Steel, who also suffered from a hepatic (liver) abscess, was on the sick list from Sept. 16, 1850 to June 29, 1851: a remarkable *286 days!*[43]

Miertsching wrote how the captain still had to deal with the men who had burst open the kegs of wine and rum a few days before. In addressing his crew, McClure's charisma spilled forth with his adroit handling of men, under very trying circumstances:

> At 9 a.m. [on September 30] the crew was mustered, and after the captain had inspected the ship, he read an extract from the Articles of War relating to discipline on board ship, and the punishment by

which it is enforced. While this was being read everyone stood bareheaded. After this reading the captain addressed the men in terms of vehement rebuke, set before them their disgraceful behaviour, called them a band of thieves, unworthy of the name of Englishmen, and said that he was ashamed that such base robbers, such thievish rabble, should walk the deck of an English ship, etc., etc. He then pronounced against the offenders the punishment which they had deserved and would receive. After this severe rebuke he began to admonish the men; he set plainly before them the danger in which we had been, still were, and still would be, and showed them that all human strength and skill were ineffective in such hours of need; only Almighty Providence had through a manifest miracle saved us from certain death, etc. Even old sailors inured to danger, with weather-beaten faces, could not restrain their tears, and all to a man promised amendment and gave the captain a cheer. In the afternoon the three ring-leaders were punished [no doubt by flogging].[44]

As the mercury hit zero outside, the time had come to make the ship ready for winter quarters: the topgallant masts and yards were sent down, sails unbent, and preparations made for stretching sailcloth fore and aft, and fastening to the repaired bulwarks. *Investigator* eventually came to resemble a huge tent, within which 12 months' worth of "provisions, tent equipage, housing, skins, blankets, clothing, sledges, fire-arms, and such other things as were likely to be useful," remained on deck in the event of any emergency which may force the evacuation of the ship at a moment's notice.[45]

From the time when *Investigator* first entered the ice, until she was frozen in her winter quarters, "the crew were constantly employed at the most laborious and harassing work, and were necessarily much exposed to cold, wet, and fatigue. It was not the physical powers alone that were so severely taxed throughout this period," pointed out Armstrong, but also "the minds of the men were in a constant state of agitation, either elated by hope, or depressed by despair, as the perilous position in which were placed, alternately excited one or other emotion."[46]

At least the calm heavens allowed for an atmospheric optical phenomenon to accompany the aurora and splendid meteors witnessed over the preceding days. The parhelion, which Piers admired, "presented an inverted bow above the Sun, towards the zenith, and at the same distance, as I should suppose, as the superior arch was from the Sun were, what appeared to me, sections of two horizontal bows—one on each side. The colours chiefly visible were red, yellow, and blue." Contrasting this visual feast, Armstrong heard how "the stillness of the day was frequently interrupted by the hoarse croaking of a couple of Ravens which kept flying ominously about us—the sound falling mournfully on the ear." The black birds visited almost daily, crossing the strait from west to east, and then back again a few hours later; before winter was out, only one came calling. McClure nicknamed this lone creature "Ralpho," and it may be imagined the captain was referring to that English clergyman and academic from long before, Ralph Ravens.[47]

Although the ice was relatively calm for the first few days of October, after ordering Haswell, Cresswell and Court to survey the provisions, McClure had to deal with a familiar curse from within; consequently, "no less than 500 lbs. [of preserved meat] was so putrid, as to necessitate its being thrown overboard, a loss mainly occasioned by fractures made in the tins when packing them in England." McClure lamented the loss (which was in addition to the boatload of meat that had sunk in August), but he "consoled himself, however, with the hope that a certain surplus, which the contractor had promised to put aboard to cover such contingencies, would replace this unfortunate deficit."[48]

For the time being, the conditions allowed for Armstrong, Piers and some of the other

Parhelion (Augustus Sonntag; *Arctic Explorations* (vol. 1), 1856).

officers to carry out amateur sculpting by carving out an artificial cave (grotto) in one of the large hummocks, "10 feet high, and 20 feet long, of an elliptical form ... its interior presenting an appearance of extreme beauty, from its ultramarine, semi-transparent structure," wrote Armstrong.[49]

The ice became restless on the morning of the fourth, and heavy pressure began upon *Investigator*, and at eight o'clock that evening, "all being still and silent about the ship, we had evidence of its being in motion; but the suddenness and force of the movement were far different"[50]:

> From the commencement of the movement, nearly all in the Ship were of their own accord, on deck; but scarcely a voice was heard—except that of the Captain occasionally giving an order to the Officer of the Watch or the Ice Mate—every one was silent, looking over the Ship's sides to see, as well as he could, the motion of the ice, and anxiously waiting the result; for the pressure far exceeded anything we had experienced before, and no one could judge how far our good Ship (for such she hitherto proved) was capable of sustaining it. The great motion lasted I should think 15 or 20 minutes, when all was again quiet, but the Ship was left with a very considerable inclination to port from the ice being forced under her starboard side. After it was over, I asked the Ice Mate how a Greenlandman [whale ship] would have fared with such a squeeze:– he replied, "Why, it would have gone clean through her," and he added, "I trembled like a leaf while it lasted; for I have seen so many vessels lost from the same thing." Cresswell & Court, who had remained below some time, said the glass in the skylight shook, and the whole place trembled under the pressure, so much so, that Court, who had been writing, was obliged to discontinue it.[51]

It was times like this when Master Shipwright William M. Rice, of Woolwich Dockyard, would have sprung to the minds of those onboard, as Armstrong noted: "This gentleman's

*Investigator* in the pack, Oct. 8, 1850 (S.G. Cresswell, 1854).

name was frequently mentioned with grateful feelings during our long and eventful journey, when our safety so often depended on the strength of our ship."[52]

The ship was carried southward again, and on the sixth the officers were ordered into five watches, while the men were to start taking daily exercise by themselves and provide their own amusement. The Investigators also began "lighting the Ship's (Sylvester), Gun-room and Sick-bay stoves: the Captain's has been lit some time, the temperature in the Gun-room has lately been 28° or 29°; and in the Officers' cabins 13° and 16° in the day time."[53]

The ship had taken a good deal of bruising thus far, so the time had come to give back by testing the strength and usefulness of gunpowder in blasting ice. Experiments were overseen by Wynniatt, "who had been instructed in its use prior to our leaving England, and under whose superintendence all our subsequent operations with this powerful agent were success-fully and zealously conducted ... accordingly several small hummocks, alongside, were speedily and successfully removed by blasting." Not to be outdone, the invisible forces fought back, and "several large pieces of ice got under the ship's stern, which elevated it considerably, throw-ing her over also on her port side."[54]

Mate Robert James Wynniatt was in his 21st year when he joined *Investigator* from the gunnery training ship HMS *Excellent* in Portsmouth Harbor (where he had been promoted from midshipman only six months before). Assisting in the demolition duties was Gunner's Mate John Kerr, who held a 1st Class Certificate as a seaman gunner, and twice served onboard the *Excellent* (most recently, just prior to the expedition). Kerr had entered the Navy in 1833, at age 15, and was no stranger to difficult service. As a gunner's mate on the paddle steamer *Inflexible* from 1846 to 1849, he served during the waterborne operations against New Zealand's Maori people, and also fought pirates who raided Hong Kong harbor. In the latter action, the steamer's superior gunnery silenced the cannons of piratical junks, and her boats captured eight of the rogue vessels.[55]

During the fitting out of the Arctic expedition, Royal Engineers' First Lieutenant Robert Stotherd "gave a memorandum on the application of gunpowder for blasting ice." Two types of explosive setups were used: (1) using regular tin blasting cases, waterproof powder bags (made of sailcloth), empty preserved meat tins, or wine bottles were tightly packed with black powder and ignited using Bickford's fuse (sump fuse, which burns underwater), and (2) regular tin blasting cases were ignited by electrical charges that were run from galvanic batteries through copper wires covered with gutta-percha (a natural form of rubber).[56]

The use of explosives is something of an art. If the ice was not more than five or six feet thick, the charges may have varied between one and six pounds, and were sometimes lowered through a line of holes bored in the ice, and fired simultaneously. However, "as a rule it has been observed that, firstly, if the blasting charge is too close up to the ice, only a small hole is produced above; secondly, if too far below it, no useful effect is produced. Sea ice has so much elasticity that it will sometimes undulate and lift considerably at each explosion without being cracked or broken, except immediately over the charge."[57]

But it took more than the Devil's distillate to remove hummocks alongside, as men also threw their backs into the battle with the ice. The air was alive with the *Investigator* settling into her white cradle, while the temperature drifted between four and seven degrees below zero: "The crashing, creaking, and straining is beyond description," winced McClure, "and the officer of the watch, when speaking with me, is obliged to put his mouth close to my ear, on account of the deafening noise." Miertsching was pleased the uproar did not include *human* tones, since the "captain and his officers are now on the best of terms and the unpleasantness which formerly existed has not recurred since our departure from the Sandwich Islands." And in fact, every day Miertsching spent "some most agreeable hours with the captain: he seems now to realize that he is not the good Christian which he used to think himself; for some days he has been reading his Bible morning and evening." Even so, the Brother undoubtedly had to console his "servant and friend, Farquharson, [who] is much troubled because the sailors cannot read and instruct themselves by means of books and tracts."[58]

"The days are growing so short that already the sun shines for a few hours only," warned Miertsching of the coming disappearance of the giant star. One of the enduring myths about the Arctic is that the entire region experiences six months of continual daylight, followed by six months of complete darkness. In actuality, after the sun dips below the horizon, there is a soft glowing light from the sky called the *twilight*, which is caused by the refraction and scattering of the sun's rays from the atmosphere. There are three types of twilight: (1) *civil (bright) twilight*—begins when the center of the sun is six degrees below the horizon and ends at sunrise (2) *nautical twilight*—begins in the morning and ends in the evening, when the center of the sun dips to 12 degrees below the horizon, and a sea horizon becomes difficult to discern, and (3) *astronomical twilight*—begins in the morning and ends in the evening, when the sun's upper rim is fewer than 18 degrees below the horizon; this ends on November 13 with the fall of total darkness, and remains so until January 29, at which time the twilight cycle begins again.[59]

The morning of October 10 marked 48 hours of general quiet by the ice, and McClure, Cresswell, Armstrong, and Miertsching, accompanied by four men, left the ship at 8:30 for the eastern side of the strait, to take possession of the land. Some toted guns, others boarding pikes, and "the men with the apparatus for cooking their dinner, pick-axe, shovel, flagstaff, &c.—all necessary implements for the service we were going on." This small band made its way some five miles from the ship, until it reached the top of a cliff, about 150 high, and Prince Albert Land was taken possession of and named. At the same time, the ribbon of ice-choked water which held *Investigator* prisoner was named the Prince of Wales Strait.[60]

Leaving the seamen to erect a cairn, the officers continued on, and after struggling through deep snow over rough terrain for a further two hours, they reached the 1,200-foot summit of what was dubbed "Mount Adventure." "We could clearly trace the termination of the western land, or that of Banks', to a headland or cape of considerable elevation," related Armstrong, "Everything, therefore, was fully confirmatory of the opinions previously formed, *and no doubt could remain as to the existence of a Passage.*"[61]

After rejoining the sailors at three o'clock, it was discovered "the men were unable to cook their dinner, for on opening the tin of preserved meat, it was so hard and frozen, that it could not be pierced with a boarding pike, and they had not the spirits sufficient to thaw it [with fire]."[62] After a quick survey of ice conditions, the party started heading back to *Investigator*, for what became a long and disagreeable journey. Soon a channel of open water many yards wide barred their path.[63] After climbing up and down over the rugged ice in an attempt to find the gap closed, and then firing off several rounds to attract the attention of the ship, the men were stranded in darkness—wearing inadequate clothing and with no usable provisions—in a temperature of 15° below zero. Miertsching recalled how he and the surgeon "had slipped on the ice and fallen into the water; the others hauled us out, but now, drenched through, we could barely endure the cold; our clothes were frozen into icy sheets."[64]

On *Investigator*, two lanterns were hung at the head of the mizzenmast, and guns, rockets, and blue lights were fired at intervals to guide the lost men back to the ship. Shortly after 6:00 p.m. Lieutenant Haswell sent Court and a few men out to look for the missing party. About an hour later, he sent out parties under Wynniatt and Sainsbury, both carrying a Halkett's portable boat and paddles. This inflatable boat was invented in the 1840s by Lieutenant Peter Alexander Halkett, RN, the son of John Halkett, one of the directors of the Hudson's Bay Company. When *Enterprise* and *Investigator* were fitting out at Woolwich, Halkett rowed to and went onboard the former in his own boat, having inflated it in just one minute. Carpenter George Ford, who accompanied Sainsbury's party, explained how a Halkett boat was "made of canvas covered by a solution of India rubber, can be stowed in a box 3 ft. sqr. & 9 inch deep & when used blown up with air so as to carry 6 men & weighing about 20 or 30 lbs [so two were sent], thinking they were prevented by water to get on board."[65]

When the lost band was finally found towards midnight, Court's handling of the rubber boats proved invaluable, amid (newly formed) bay ice nearly an inch thick, the current, and moving ice, allowing everyone to be ferried across the black water and on their way to safety— and not just from the elements. Armstrong confessed to hours before, "having fired our last charge of ammunition, our entire strength for attack or defence, if we met with Bears, which we knew were prowling about, lay in boarding-pikes."[66]

By 2:30 a.m. the next morning, Piers was relieved to report:

> [A]ll were safely on board—and very glad I am sure everyone in the Ship was to see all his Shipmates safe on board once more. Several however were much exhausted, and Sgt. Woon, who had received one or two heavy falls was obliged to be assisted to bed and relieved with hot tea, for he was so weak that he either could not or cared not to undress himself; his circulation was languid, and the heat of his extremities below the natural standard. On his return to the Ship Paine told me the Sergt laid down several times, and he had much trouble, with Corpl [*sic*—Private] Parfitt, in getting him along—he also told me himself, when a little recovered, that he felt faint, drowsy, and careless about himself, and all he wanted was to lie down.[67]

On the ice, Woon had been suffering from hypothermia, and his core body temperature dropped as he floated into unconsciousness. It may have gone below the 95°F required for a normal metabolism and functions—and the sergeant could have died if Paine and fellow Marine George Parfitt hadn't kept him moving along. Of all the men in the various parties, only Woon and Sainsbury were admitted to sick bay (for exhaustion), the former returning to duty on the 12th, and the latter the 13th.[68]

Private 1st Class George Parfitt joined the Royal Marines in 1837, and although he was court martialed the following year for being absent without leave for 10 days, afterwards he was a model Marine. In fact, Parfitt had two Good Conduct Badges to his name upon joining *Investigator*, and earned a third during the expedition. Having served ashore during the Syrian campaign in 1840, he spent 1842–47 in the paddle steamer HMS *Columbia*, during her tedious survey of the Bay of Fundy and the Saint John River (Nova Scotia, British North America). Also onboard *Columbia* were three future Arctic officers, Mate/Lieutenant William J.S. Pullen, Master's Assistant John P. Cheyne, and Volunteer 1st Class Murray T. Parks (afterwards a mate and acting lieutenant in *Enterprise*, under Collinson).[69]

**Private George Parfitt's Naval General Service Medal 1793–1840, with Syria clasp, for service as a Royal Marine private in HMS *Powerful* in 1840 (officially impressed on the edge: GEORGE PARFITT.). Issued in 1849. There is every reason to believe Parfitt carried this medal with him on HMS *Investigator*, as it would have been required adornment on formal occasions (Spencer J. Fisher, 2014; Glenn M. Stein Collection).**

Out of the search and rescue of McClure's party came an exceedingly rare instance of praise for Haswell in writings during the expedition, this coming from the hand of Henry Piers: "The 1st Lieut. (Haswell) acted I think very promptly & judiciously in the measures he took and I hope those who were thus timely relieved are grateful to him and the other Officers & men who saved them from passing a night on the ice; for what the result would have been in that case it is impossible to say, but it would doubtless have been very serious."[70]

The vessel was frozen in so tight "that a knife could not be put down between the ship & ice." The Investigators had much time on their hands, and the

sailors and Marines were cheerful and content, and their evenings filled with exercising, dancing and singing. Everything seemed right in their world—but was it? The observant
Miertsching, who was closer to the captain than anyone else onboard, casually pointed to a
curious activity by McClure: "The captain is very busy writing: he is making a good copy of
his daily journal."[71] Why did McClure feel the *need* to make a copy of his journal? Was it a
*faithful* copy? And *which one* had he planned to hand over to the Admiralty for inspection?

Over the coming days, visits were made to the islands by most of the officers (but not
Haswell). They saw tracks of hares and foxes, as well as animal bones, and "brought back a
hare and three snow-grouse [ptarmigan]—the first we had seen." A grave, and a few small
stone structures were also encountered, the latter intended (according to Miertsching) as fox
traps and for storing provisions. They were "sufficient to prove that we are not the first people
who have visited these islands, but have been preceded by Esquimaux, most probably, many
years ago." The traces of animals and taking of game excited the Investigators, because their
provisions would have to be supplemented through hunting in the course of their journey—
thus keeping the scourge of scurvy at bay. And McClure was increasingly aware he would need
to add to his stocks of food, since the "preserved meats furnished to the ship by Messrs.
Gamble were constantly found decayed to an alarming extent; and between the 12th and 18th
of October no less than *four hundred and twenty-four pounds* of it were thrown overboard as
unfit for food."[72]

On the 14th, Armstrong recorded a temperature spike at 24°F, with a northeasterly wind,
"from which we concluded that there was still a large expanse of water to the northward. This
change we knew would only be temporary." There now being only about eight hours of sun
each day, before the darkness of winter enveloped them, McClure planned a sled journey to
the western end of Viscount Melville Sound, so as to officially confirm and record the existence
of a North-West Passage.[73] On the 17th, he and Dr. Armstrong reconnoitered the best route
for the traveling party. The following morning, at 9:00 a.m., McClure, Court, Armstrong,
Miertsching, and two men, left the ship and walked to the larger of the two islands, ascended
a summit of about 500 feet, and took formal possession of the islands, naming them the
Princess Royal Islands.[74]

McClure determined to start a few days afterward with a sled and five men, commanded
by Stephen Court (who was detailed "for the purpose of taking observations"[75]), and leaving
Haswell in charge of the ship. A sixth man was added after the journey began, and so made
the team: Captain of the Forecastle John Calder, Quartermaster Michael Flynn, Captain of
the Foretop Peter Thompson, Captain of the Maintop Robert Tiffeny, Able Seaman George
Brown, and Private 3rd Class James Saunders, RM (sled parties often included at least one
Marine). Calder, Flynn, and Thompson were 1848–49 expedition veterans, and of the six
men chosen by McClure (and approved by Armstrong), four were first class petty officers, the
captain having previously written: "I am much pleased with the conduct of the Petty Officers,
they evince every desire to perform their duty in which I give them every support."[76]

McClure prudently drew up specific instructions for Haswell, in the event *Investigator*
was driven southward by the ice while the sled party was away. Cresswell and Wynniatt were
to take the third whaleboat (fully provisioned) to one of the Princess Royal Islands for the
party's use (if the ship was gone upon return). Haswell was to come back to the islands after
the ice broke up, but if *Investigator* did not arrive by mid–August, McClure and his party
would sail the whaleboat to Port Leopold, and the ship should find a harbor or sheltered bay

for the winter. At the entrance of Port Leopold was the depot left in 1848 at Whaler Point, and McClure could afterward seek the whalers in Baffin Bay. If *Investigator* was unable to return to the islands, Haswell was to sail for England, communicating with *Plover* at Kotzebue Sound along with way.[77]

The clothing of sledders consisted of thick drawers and jerseys, thick socks, pea jackets, blue trousers, deerskin moccasins, sealskin boots or snow boots. Sealskin caps and "Welsh wigs," woolen or worsted caps originally made in Montgomery, Wales, were issued as head coverings. Also issued were "snow spectacles," to reduce the glare from reflected sunlight off the snow and ice—the cause of snow blindness. Sledders made whatever clothing they liked, probably of duck (a durable, closely woven, usually cotton fabric) or canvas, overlined inside by fearnought (a thick heavy wool overcoating, often mixed with inferior materials), and made solid with leather. Other self-made items included mittens, which hung around their necks like handbags.[78]

*October 21, 7:00 a.m.*—Before the parties departed, three cheers pierced the air, which were answered by the same, amid a light southeasterly breeze and overcast sky, in a temperature of 4° below zero.[79]

**Captain McClure in Arctic dress (Smyth, after a photograph by E.A. Inglefield, *The Illustrated London News*, Oct. 7, 1854).**

"The Captain, with Court and five men, started to the N.E. for the purpose of ascertaining whether or not the strait we are in opens into Barrow Strait [*sic*—Viscount Melville Sound]. They took with them fourteen days' provisions. Wynniatt [and Armstrong, with] another party accompanied, and dragged the sledge for them about ten or twelve miles," continued Piers, adding, "The 1st Lieut. (Haswell) with 'all hands,' going with them to the edge of the smooth, shore ice, carrying everything separately over the rough ice."[80] By five in the evening, Wynniatt and his party reached the ship, having left McClure about noon.[81]

McClure's team, harnessed by broad canvas belts and using drag ropes, pulled a loaded sled weighing some 700 lbs.[82] The sled was packed with a tent (8'3″ × 6') and five boarding pikes as tent poles, Mackintosh (tarpaulin) floor cloth, buffalo robes and raccoon skins, blanket sleeping bags, alcohol stove for melting snow and heating food, kettle, navigational instruments, muskets and ammunition, food, rum, cocoa, and a few medicines. Consequently, the six-man team, each with a knapsack on his back, pulled about 116 lbs. to start, and 133 lbs. per man at the conclusion of the journey, because of the ice that accumulated on the tent, furs, blankets, and sled, due to vapors from the men's bodies and the stove having condensed and then refreezing on contact. "In the British expeditions 200 lbs. per man, dragging, was considered a fair weight, though this may be raised to 250 lbs. per man for a short distance and on smooth ice ... the average daily march being about 10 miles."[83]

Typically, McClure and Court would have each carried double-barrel guns, telescopes and compasses, and scouted ahead of the sled for the best path through the ice.[84]

Sherard Osborn, editor of McClure's journal, specified: "'Investigator' had left England but little prepared for extensive sledge-work, and few if any improvements upon the [man-hauling] system of sledge-travelling originally laid down by Sir James C. Ross. The consequence was, that in all her sledge-parties there was, if possible, a greater amount of hardship and privation than in those of the 1850s expeditions under Captains Austin, Kellett, or Belcher, who each improved upon their predecessors' experiences." Preparing for sled traveling required careful forethought, and McClure didn't have any sledding experience. However, Court had done some fatigue work during 1848–49, and it's possible Calder, Flynn, and Thompson were sledders during Ross's expedition as well.[85]

Sled traveling during British Arctic expeditions stretched back to earlier 19th century North-West Passage expeditions, and often featured techniques and dogs acquired from the Eskimos, although some sleds were hauled by manpower. "Most of the drivers were British seamen who had acquired the necessary skills 'on the job.'" The dog sleds were used primarily as "couriers," i.e., for communication between various wintering ships. The importance of the boost to the men's morale provided by the presence and behavior of the dogs should not be underestimated.[86]

Two factors may have influenced Ross's man-hauling decision: (1) there was a large number of unemployed manpower existing in his crews, and (2) the areas to be searched were largely uninhabited, so it would have been difficult to obtain dogs in sufficient numbers.[87] Also, according to one historian, there

> seemed no reason to cultivate a corps of specialists in native travel methods, since it was expected that the Franklin search would soon be over. As the senior service in the top power in the world, the Royal Navy can be forgiven for thinking that, in most circumstances, British was best. The alternative to manpower for hauling sledges would have involved the use of hundreds of dogs. The problems of selection, feeding, disease and training could not have been quickly overcome.[88]

"No sledging equipment was taken from England [by Ross] and all of it was made on board according to Ross's designs.... Ross used flat sledges on soft deep snow. They proved to be inconveniently small.... For long journeys performed by one officer and six men, Ross used sledges which were modified forms of the Greenland Eskimo sledges. With only slight alterations they remained in favour for many years, and were entirely different to the flat sledges which have just been described. Both ends of the wooden runners were curved upwards and the under surfaces were shod with iron [to reduce friction on the snow surface]."[89]

This sled was a large wooden runner-sled. Its average size was three feet wide and 10 feet long; it carried cargo about a foot off the ice, and it had three-inch-wide runners. It had been constructed with just enough strength as absolutely necessary, since every pound saved in wood and iron meant the ability to carry more provisions. This description also matches that made by Miertsching of the sleds used by the Investigator's traveling parties in the spring of 1851.[90]

Because many polar explorers were wedded to the sea and ships, it was only natural they viewed sleds as extensions of their vessels (much the same way as ships' boats). Indeed, during the long years searching for Franklin, sleds were fitted out with masts and sails to take advantage of the wind. Some were even ceremoniously "launched" from ships' gunwales onto the ice! And like ships, sleds were adorned with names, which "were an aid to esprit-de-corps and competition; they also made life easier for readers of reports giving an account of particular sledge journeys." In addition, sleds carried distinctive flags; "having been carefully prepared beforehand by some fair hands at home," these banners featured mottos and personal badges of the officers commanding the parties.[91]

Since Collinson's sleds carried names, it's reasonable to assume McClure and his junior offices must have also christened their sleds and possessed sled flags, although no details can be found in surviving records.[92]

Soon after parting with Wynniatt, McClure ran into rough and densely packed ice, which damaged his sled. Though it was repaired, it broke down entirely, so he sent Court and the Norfolk sailor Thompson back to *Investigator* for a replacement. Early on the following morning, amid fresh blowing wind and snowdrifts, "Court, Thompson and another man started again to join the Captain, accompanied by Wynniatt [and Carpenter Ford] with a fatigue party [of six men] to draw the sledge; and all hands in charge of the Boatswain, to carry the things separately over the hummocky ice to the smooth in-shore ice." By the early afternoon, about 15 miles from the ship, McClure resumed his appointment with destiny.[93]

The day's ugly weather reflected darker happenings onboard, as Miertsching wrote how "some more spoiled meat [was] thrown overboard; already [in October, more than] seven hundred pounds of this preserved meat have been thrown away as unfit." However, the Brother's intellectual pursuits tempered the gloominess: "Every day I am busy with my chart and comparison of old Eskimo words with new ones recently acquired."[94]

There was no shortage of activity among the remaining Investigators while McClure's party was away. Boatswain Kennedy and a party busied themselves erecting a signal pole and building a cairn on one of the Princess Royal Islands, while the rest of the ship's company was occupied restowing provisions. On Saturday, October 26, amid snow all day and the thermometer dipping to nine degrees below zero, the party completed its work on the island. Later, it was Saturday night at sea, accompanied by the traditional wardroom toast after a meal: "Our wives and sweethearts."—and the retort by the youngest officer present—"May they never meet!" The balance to the evening's gaiety came the following day with the muster to perform divine service.[95]

Armstrong also made fruitful use of his time, which he recorded with characteristic British understatement: "I occupied myself for some days in examining and removing from these islands, specimens of their formation, and I can affirm that geologizing at a temperature from 15 to 20 degrees below zero, is not the most agreeable occupation."[96]

With the view of having a picnic upon the blanket of snow on October 29, Paine, Sainsbury, Newton and Miertsching walked over the rough ice for two hours to reach Prince Albert Land, taking with them "coffee, bacon, and various tasty items such as sardines" to enjoy before a roaring fire of driftwood.[97] Miertsching wrote that, after a time, what was originally thought to be a group of Eskimos approaching in the distance,

were no men but five big black animals.... The first thing that we did was to load our guns with ball instead of birdshot, and then awaited whatever fortune might bring. Mr. Sainsbury was not in a condition to load his gun, for his finger was frozen stiff, white as an icicle, and quite without feeling. It was for the three of us whom remained to receive these five strangers with coolness and determination. As they were coming straight for us without seeing us, we lay flat on the snow twenty feet from one another on the side of a smooth-sloping knoll.... they were the size of an ox—with frightful horns curved like those of an ox—and their bodies were covered with hair so long that it brushed the snow, and their feet were scarcely visible; sixty paces off, and they were aware of us; they stopped suddenly and stood there, snorting, stamping on the ground with their fore feet, and tearing up the ground with their horns: we in the meantime lay quite quiet, but ready for battle. The beasts huddled together with their heads towards us; one, the largest ox, now came alone towards us slowly, snorting, while the rest stayed motionless in one place.[98]

At some 30 paces, the first ball crashed into the defiant musk ox's head; as he turned away, a second ball pierced his ribs, and he rejoined the herd, and still stoically faced the human threat. Spread out in order to fire from three sides, the men crawled 15 paces closer; a volley erupted from all the double-barreled guns, enraging the mortally wounded creature, who was now surrounded by a trio of dead companions. But Miertsching still faced a lone survivor, who

charged blindly at me; I pulled the trigger; my gun [misfired]; the priming had fallen off; I leapt aside, tripped, and fell flat on the ground. The ox, no less frightened than I, dashed by me and without looking around ran on, leaving a trail of blood behind him. In a moment I was on my feet, adjusted my weapon, and ran along the blood-stained trail of my fugitive.... After a short run I found my fugitive standing deep in snow and bleeding from several wounds; one more ball, and that stretched him lifeless on the ground.[99]

**Body of a musk ox (Karst, after a photograph; *Three Years of Arctic Service*, 1894 edition).**

He continued, "But amidst our joy at our good fortune in obtaining so rich a booty we now first realized in what danger we had been; to the Lord Who had so graciously protected and guarded us everyone freely acknowledges that this is a Divine Providence and above all a gracious gift of God; for now we have a prospect of enjoying more *fresh meat* in the course of the winter."[100]

To assist in bringing back the musk ox, Boatswain Kennedy and Carpenter Ford commanded two fatigue parties (a total of 17 men) on October 30, and joined a sled party of Cresswell, Piers, and three men dispatched the previous day. There were four bulls and one cow, the largest of which supplied 420 pounds of meat, and the five combined equaled 1,296 pounds of meat. The balance of the crew was occupied cutting a smooth road to land.[101]

"As the weather was daily becoming colder, we were anxiously looking out for the return of the party from the northward, burned blue lights, and threw up rockets nightly, to point out our position," worried Armstrong; and then the morning of the 31st, "we were astonished by the arrival of Captain M'Clure, unaccompanied by any of his party."[102]

# 8

# Jack Frost, 1850–51

---

*Nothing burns like the cold.*
—George R.R. Martin, *A Game of Thrones*

---

The afternoon before, when the party was still several miles from the ship, McClure went ahead with the intention of seeing that a warm meal was ready for his men when they arrived. McClure later described his experience to his half-sister:

> Shortly after quitting them it came on a thick mist, but as long as it continued daylight, and I could see my compass, I got on pretty well; but at five o'clock darkness set in, and I very soon lost my way, got entangled amidst heavy ice, rough and uneven as a stonemason's yard, having much snow, through which I was tumbling and floundering at the risk of breaking my legs, arms, or neck, so of necessity I was obliged to stop, and being much exhausted, having had nothing since a scanty seven o'clock breakfast, I made myself a comfortable snow bed under the lee of a large piece of ice, burying my feet up to the knees to keep my toes from being frostbitten, soon fell into a doze, and about midnight was aroused by a bright meteor flashing across the heavens, so got up and found a fine starlight night with a brilliant aurora, and, starting in the direction of the ship, was in hopes of getting on board. However, having expended all my ammunition, I could not attract the attention of those in the vessel, and so, to make a long story short, I wandered about until daylight, when I had the extreme satisfaction of finding I had passed her about four miles.[1]

"The Captain, looking thin and much exhausted, returned on board by himself & most unexpectedly, for he was not seen till coming up the Ship's side, shortly after 8 a.m.," wrote Piers.[2] Wynniatt was dispatched at once to assist the rest of the men,[3] with "Court and the men arriving about noon, when all hands turned out on a large hummock of ice to give them three hearty cheers on their safe return, and The Discovery of the 'North West Passage' from the Atlantic to the Pacific!!!"[4]

> They could not discern any sign of a wreck, habitation, cairn or other object leading them to suppose that Sir John Franklin had ever reached this part of the Arctic regions: but failing as we have, thus far, in obtaining even the melancholy satisfaction of meeting with some remains of our lost Country men, we shall at any rate have [six or seven words are scratched out] discovered the long sought "North West Passage"!
> All on board now look forward with hope and pleasure at meeting their friends in "Old England" next Autumn![5]

The ten-day roundtrip of the sled party—a total of 156 miles (in a direct line), during 7° to –15° temperatures—had brought it to the northwest corner of the strait on October 26. Here McClure constructed a cairn and placed a record in a copper cylinder, and named the location after the prime minister, Cape Lord John Russell (Russell Point on maps). And it was atop a hill dubbed "Mount Observation" that a surveillance of the broad expanse was made: the northern extremity of the Prince Albert Land side was judged to be about 35 miles away (named Peel Point, after statesman Sir Robert Peel), and McClure observed that the "Melville Island shore could not be discovered, but in that direction the ice appeared to be very heavy and the floes exceedingly large."[6]

The scene must have been described in more detail to Piers: "They had an extensive view of the Barrow Str. Ice [*sic*—Viscount Melville Sound], but the atmosphere was not clear enough to allow of their seeing Melville Isᵈ. They thought they saw the loom of land [shadowy form], but could not be positive."[7]

But behind the achievement, jubilation, and anticipation of the Investigators' first sled journey, lay hidden dark truths.

After having started out with their replacement sled on the 22nd, McClure and his men alternately encountered patches of rough and smooth ice, until darkness compelled them to pitch their tent and prepare a lowly supper—"one pint of melted snow and a piece of frozen pemmican!"[8]

Aside from chocolate and rum, Armstrong gives the total of 57 lbs. of food consumed by the party, while McClure and Piers both state 51 lbs. Armstrong breaks this down as 18 lbs. pemmican, 31 lbs. biscuit and 8 lbs. oatmeal consumed, and McClure being at variance with only 2 lbs. of oatmeal (Piers does not provide a breakdown). In addition, Piers correctly notes the party traveled for 10 days, while Armstrong and McClure evidently calculated the party's start from receipt of the new sled on the 22nd, so both state nine days of travel.[9]

Interestingly, Piers recorded a man's [intended] daily allowance for this journey[10]:

| | |
|---|---|
| *Cocoa* | *½ pint* |
| *Biscuit* | *½ lb.* |
| *Oatmeal* | *½ lb.* |
| *Pemmican* | *1½ lbs.* |
| *Rum* | *1 gill* |
| *Water* | *¾ pint* |

The daily pemmican, biscuit and oatmeal consumption *should* have been 2½ lbs. per man, or about 200 lbs. of solid food for all eight men after 10 days of traveling—*nearly 75 percent more food than they actually consumed.*

"The reason of this small consumption of food," related the assistant surgeon, "was they took so small an allowance of Spirit of Wine for fuel [for the alcohol stove]. I thought before the party started that this quantity of spirituous fuel was very small, and mentioned my opinion of the whole thing to Court." It seems certain the captain would have been deeply involved in choosing the type and quantity of provisions taken with the party, but whether or not Court ever said anything to McClure about the fuel situation is unknown. In addition, the party was only able to melt snow for five gills (20 ounces) of water a day per person; and "the consequence was that thirst, which seems to oppress travelers in these regions almost as much as it does in the Tropics, proved to them a source of considerable suffering."[11]

One man was so exhausted a few days after starting that he fell from the sledge ropes and held on the side of the sledge—which was obliged to be stopped—and begged for more refreshment. They all ate some considerable quantity of snow, although the practice was checked, and its injurious effects pointed out, by the Captain and Court; but at the same time, Court tells us he suffered so much himself from thirst that he could not help indulging in the same hurtful practice; always however taking care when he did so to get behind the sledge, where he would be free from observation.[12]

The men suffered so severely from thirst because of the considerable evaporation from their lungs into the dry, cold air. For this reason, thirst in the polar regions is equal to that of a desert environment. Attempting to quench one's thirst by eating snow is dangerous, as this can damage the lips and tongue, and leads to inflammation of the throat, as well as digestive and bowel troubles. What's more, such relief is only temporary, since snow does not provide an adequate volume of drinking water. Although putting a small amount of snow in your mouth will not represent a significant hypothermic risk, these sledders faced a very different situation. They were continually fatigued and poorly nourished, so their consumption of quantities of snow drained away much needed heat from their bodies.[13]

Piers continued, and eased into a lighter vein:

Court also tells us an amusing story of the Marine [Saunders], one of the chief sufferers, who came and asked him one day if his Rum would but melt some snow, so as to give him more water to drink; Court told him certainly it would, and as he suffered so much from thirst recommended him to do it: shortly after, he saw the man with his half gill of Rum in one hand and a lump of ice in the other, which the Marine gave him to understand he was about to mix for the purpose of melting the ice! Court of course laughed at the man, and told him how to melt the ice; but the love of grog prevailed, so that he would not expend his Rum for the benefit of a good draught of water.[14]

The party traveled during the day and camped at night.[15] In fact, preparing for sleep brought on extreme difficulties of its own, as Piers explains:

[W]hen the eight travellers laid down at night in the closed tent, which was only 8 ft. 3 in. long by 6 ft. wide, the vapours arising from their bodies [and stove] rapidly condensed, causing the atmosphere of the place to be very thick, and everything in the morning to be quite damp—with a coating of frost in the inside of the tent; then during the day the tent, skins & blankets froze quite hard on the sledge, so that before the skins could be spread out again they had to be laid on to thaw them out: daily the moisture accumulated—freezing on the sledge and thawing again at night: by the repeated moistening & freezing of the skins they shrunk so much as to be too small to cover the whole of the party; and the weight of everything was considerably increased.[16]

The final effect, as McClure and Armstrong point out, was the sled weighed 793 lbs. upon its return to *Investigator*, "being an *increase*, upon what we started with, of upwards of 100 pounds." And as a consequence of their privations, the men "had all lost considerably in flesh, and were more or less frost-bitten, but no other casualties occurred. Although the result of this journey had been anticipated," continued Armstrong with admiration, "we hailed it with the greatest satisfaction, and the perseverance, energy and zeal with which it was performed, must ever redound to the credit of Captain M^cClure and all engaged in it."[17]

On November 1, the young ice was found to be 20 inches thick, and one month later, the new floes reached thicknesses of two feet and six and a half inches. Temperatures dropped to –15° to –20°F (with the nightly temperature below decks being seven degrees). While Ford layered on 20 lbs. of clothes to combat the invading cold, various stove fires were lit, and final winter preparations were made for the ship—and he wrote the "travelling party are very weak from their expedition, therefore they are exempt from duty this week." And even two weeks later, Miertsching pointed out McClure's shaky condition: "Since his return from discovering the Northwest Passage, the captain has not been in good health, and today [November 16] he became so ill that he was forced to stay in bed; his body is also covered with sores."[18]

"A bed of snow about sixteen inches deep was laid on the upper deck, over which a [compacted] covering of sand and gravel was spread, and an embankment of snow about eight feet [thick] was built around the ship; both of which contributed largely to maintain warmth in the interior." "On either side of the ship is an ice stairway—ten feet from the upper deck to the ice."[19]

Ventilation of the lower deck was also a key health concern within the Investigators' canvas and wooden cocoon. To promote a good air current and the escape of foul air, copper tubes from 10 to 16 inches in diameter penetrated the deck, "were attached to canvas funnels, and then [went] through the housing cloth to the open air." In addition, the men were not allowed on the lower deck for so many hours during the day, but "notwithstanding our best efforts, it was humid and impure, from the rapidity with which the vapour that could not escape was condensed by the coldness of the deck."[20]

The second of November, Miertsching looked on as

> the captain gave the crew a good dinner to celebrate the discovery of the Northwest Passage. In the morning the captain mustered the crew and gave a speech in which he expressed his satisfaction with their conduct and exhorted them to behave well in the future and preserve cheerfulness and good humour. Sports and recreations would be organized, and to these he would contribute as much as he could; for they were the surest means to good health, and also through them could the long, cold, dark winter be made agreeable. He promised that when they returned to England he would not forget to recommend his crew to the Admiralty as favourably as he could.[21]

These were not hollow words—McClure meant what he said, and tightly tucked this pledge away in his memory cells: *personal loyalty* occupied a very special place in McClure's psyche.

That evening, Ford listened with pride as

> our gallant Captain made a short speech concerning his travels stating his or our discovery of the NW Passage which had been tried for 400 years & the honor it added to our native country, being the greatest maritime country in the world. Therefore we spliced the main brace, gave supper, & drank with 3 cheers success to dear old England. After 3 cheers for the Captain, 3 for all the officers, 3 for the [blank] or our gallant little barque & last of all "Saturday night at sea," "Health to wifes & sweethearts," the latter what a true-hearted sailor would never refuse. I must confess I feel no small pride in being one that has assisted to add another laurel (if I am allowed the expression) to my native country. There is a feeling of love for his country existing in a true-hearted sailor that I think a landsman is ignorant of in consequence of his never leaving it or seeing a contrast.[22]

A few nights later, Piers was talking "with Lt. Cresswell, who was Officer of the Watch, [and] as we walked the deck by the dim light of a single lantern, [Cresswell] remarked; 'Well, I think this voyage ought to make anyone a wiser and a better man, for it is certainly extraordinary; and we seem to have been wonderfully favoured!'... C[resswell] also told me that the Captain, talking to him of the voyage, had express[ed] himself with much more modesty than he would have expected of him: having said; 'The world may speak of me or the Ship as having done this, but a higher Power than me has directed us.'"[23]

Easing down from the height of their geographical achievement, the Investigators settled into winter by November 11; barely a whisper of wind rippled through the -26° air when the Sun bid farewell on this brilliantly clear and calm day. Looking around, Armstrong saw that everything "wore a truly wintery aspect; snow had fallen in considerable quantities, and nothing but a uniform white surface met the eye wherever it wandered. The ship was completely embedded in it, and appeared as if she could never move again. A death-like stillness reigned

**Arctic fox in summer and winter coats (Harter, 1979).**

around, which it was delightful to hear interrupted by the sound of a voice or the tread of a footstep, on the frozen surface of the snow."[24]

Though the ice slept, the rest of the natural world was not dormant. Two ravens visited the ship nearly every day, "the hardiest of the feathered tribes, and the only one that appears willingly to brave a polar winter, was seen in the depth of the season to flit through the cold and sunless atmosphere like an evil spirit, his sullen croak alone breaking the silence of that death-like scene. No one shot any of these ravens; and they seemed to know they were secure." On the snow, a pure white prowling female fox wandered into a trap; it was decided to try to tame her, so she was put in the ice house. "Our Esquimaux pup [Mongo], although twice the size of the vixen, will not face her. He must either be a bad specimen of his breed, or else they are not dogs of any pluck." Within four days the sly creature effected her escape from captivity.[25]

A combination of daily exercise (totaling five hours), sports, education and entertainment encompassed the winter's daily routine. Hammocks were slung at 6:30 a.m., followed by cleaning the decks, exercise on the ice, breakfast, and muster, followed by more exercise and games of football and rounders (bat-and-ball) on the ice until 11:30 (which the officers actively participated in). To help ward off scurvy, the men then came back onboard for their allowance of lime juice (in the presence of an officer), this being a mixture of one ounce each of lime juice and sugar. From August 1850 until October 1851, the scale of provisions for *Investigator* show the issue of *lime* juice, but thereafter, *lemon* juice. And Armstrong later remarked: "The Lemon-juice with which we were supplied was of the most excellent quality.... The juice was kept in bottles, each containing 64 oz., with a stratum of olive oil, about half an inch in thickness, on its surface, and the bottles were carefully corked and sealed."[26]

"[In 1919, Alice] Henderson Smith was the first to show that substitution of West Indian limes for Mediterranean lemons in naval rations from about 1860 onwards had created a potentially dangerous situation. Naval surgeons and others were already in the habit of using the term 'lime juice' as a synonym for 'lemon juice' and there was no reason to suppose that there was any difference between one variety of citrus fruit and another. In fact the lime has only half the ascorbic acid content of the lemon, but its relative inefficiency as an antiscorbutic was masked for many years." It seems Armstrong knew this in 1858, when he wrote the "present Service allowance of Lime-juice, I should like to see increased; and I should recommend double the quantity to be given, in all cases where the regulations of the Navy call for its exhibition."[27]

Dinner lasted from noon until 1:30, before the men were again piped onto the ice for exercise until 4:30 p.m. and were aboard at five o'clock for supper, followed by "a grog, issued by the Master-at-Arms, and a pipe of tobacco." "Life on board ship is, so to speak, a sort of machine: one day is like another; every task is done every day at the same time in the same way," drearily wrote Miertsching of the winter routine.[28]

A schoolroom was established, and Mr. Ford lent his hand to education by making tables for the pupils. Mr. Paine was the head instructor, and five evenings a week, throughout the winter, they would learn reading, writing and arithmetic. "Mr. Court has four students in navigation. There are sixteen scholars in reading, thirty-seven in arithmetic, five in spelling. The school is held from six o'clock to half past seven; after that, frequently, recitations, dancing, or a concert last until half past eight; but now," Miertsching related approvingly, "the bounds of decorum are never exceeded."[29]

For the "dancing & singing near the main hatchway," wrote Piers, "some sort of railway dance is a great favourite, and the music is certainly very like the noise of the engine during its different rates of speed, which it is intended to imitate; so that as one walks the upper deck and listens to the train below he may almost fancy himself rattling along at some thirty miles an hour on an English railroad."[30]

Dr. Armstrong recorded his admiration for the men's efforts at self-improvement in the evening hours:

> It was really astonishing to witness the number of tradesmen that were to be seen at night, on our lower deck, all actively engaged at their respective pursuits; tailors, bootmakers, and knitters: a great variety of needlework, everything, in fact, that a needle is capable of doing, was, at least, attempted; and it was no less laudable than strange to observe the progress which ingenuity, and industry enabled them to make, and the degree of perfection which they ultimately attained, as they were, I may say, all self-taught. Nor was reading, and improvement of the mind generally forgotten; for while engaged at work in groups, they generally had the best scholar (as he was termed), engaged reading to them aloud.[31]

While the ship slumbered, it was important to be prepared against that dreaded villain—fire. Through the winter months, the quartermasters appointed night watchmen (Brown, Flynn, May and/or Ross), were ordered to keep a hole through the ice about four feet square from freezing over by hourly removing the young ice. The far from pleasant duty was made even more somber by the distant howling of wolves hanging in the air.[32]

A road hewn from the ice to the Princess Royal Islands, and marked with guide poles, made easier the completion of the cairn, and afforded Dr. Armstrong opportunities to collect geological specimens. Able Seaman James Nelson generally accompanied the doctor, and took a keen interest in the many retrieved fossilized remains. Returning with a sled party from his final visit, they were caught in a snowstorm and heavy southwesterly gale, and Armstrong's right hand was so frostbitten that he "had not the slightest ability to bend it.... I lost the use of it for a period of two months, and was, for a time, apprehensive of its safety."[33]

The last day of November, "Capt. M^cClure came out of his cabin to day for the first time since his illness; and walked on deck & outside the Ship—he was looking better than I expected to see him after such a long confinement," remarked Piers.[34]

Temperatures outside ranged from –23° to –37°F for the first two weeks of December, while between decks was a comfortable was 40°+ to 50°F+. Outside, gales of wind swept over *Investigator*, and in company with a blinding snowdrift, kept the men bottled up. "Our Ship's company continues exceedingly healthy," pleasingly wrote Piers, "having for the last month or more, seldom more than one man on the Sick List—this man is Charles Steele [*sic*—Steel], who is suffering from the effects of abscess of the Liver & Dysentery contracted in the Indian Seas two years or more ago, from which he has been free only for short intervals since; and which, if they do not directly or indirectly lead to a fatal termination, will I think entirely preclude his joining in the active duties of the Ship, there is doubtless much arduous work awaiting this Ship next Spring and Summers."[35]

"The men themselves," continued Piers, "appear cheerful & contented: they say (as Newton told me) 'The Ship is as different, to what she was [on the 1848–49] voyage, as possible; there is no "humbuging" [phony] work outside as there was the last time'—alluding to the constant employment in building snow walls &c: their spirits too are no doubt considerably

influenced and preserved by the pleasing anticipation of returning to England next Autumn, and that after no ordinary voyage."[36]

However, not everyone was bathed in holiday cheer. Captain of the Hold James Williams found himself the recipient of his captain's displeasure, after "11 bottles of Port Wine in charge of M^r JC Paine, Clerk in Charge, were found missing from a case whilst stowed in the Hold (and 1 Bottle broken), which had been broached for the use of the Sick, supposed to have been stolen, and that in consequence I have disrated the Captain of the Hold." Neither Williams's service record, nor any of the unpublished or published journals, note this disrating, and his conduct (excepting one "Good") is listed as "Very Good" for the whole of his RN and Coast Guard service between 1843 and 1869. Most likely the wine was found, and McClure restored Williams's rating in a relatively short period of time, so the incident did not affect his career.[37]

In the early 1840s, the first naval vessel for the five-foot nine-inch New Brunswick native was the 50-gun HMS *Vindictive*, in

James Williams, taken at Yarmouth, c. 1880s (courtesy Jane Inglesby).

which Williams served as an able seaman and "went by the name of James Anderson" (the seaman's register ticket issued to him in June 1845 bore his real name). Williams was present onboard the *Vindictive*—along with Lieutenant Edward Little, future first lieutenant in HMS *Terror*—when none other than Lieutenant Governor Sir John Franklin and Lady Franklin stepped aboard for a party at Hobart, Tasmania, on the afternoon of December 28, 1842. "At half-past two, the Governor's barge, with several other boats, were seen riding over the waves in their approach to the frigate, which testified its acknowledgement of the honor conferred upon it, by a salute of thirteen guns, and as the Governor neared the ship, the yards were manned [no doubt including "Anderson"], and with a celerity [speed] and order characteristic of the high discipline which is maintained on board the *Vindictive*."[38]

Able Seaman Williams had another brush with history onboard the *Vindictive* in the spring of 1844, when anchored at Callao, Peru. The ship was in company with two American warships, the frigates USS *United States* and USS *Constellation* (flagship of the U.S. Pacific Squadron), when the former made a challenge for a race out of the harbor. With Ordinary Seaman Herman Melville on the main royal yard, the *United States* handily bested her opponents. As it happens, Melville only served in the U.S. Navy for just over a year (August 1843– October 1844), and during the entire time, his hatred of naval discipline seethed within him, eventually resulting in the writing of *White-Jacket*. When Melville published the novel in March 1850, his graphic depiction of flogging led New Hampshire Senator John P. Hale to renew efforts to have the outdated cruelty banned by Congress. Consequently, in September of that year, flogging was outlawed on all U.S. naval vessels (and finally banned from all military branches in July 1862).[39]

James Williams's encounter with Sir John Franklin came full circle on December 26, 1849—nearly seven years to the day after the festive affair in HMS *Vindictive* at Hobart— when Williams appeared on *Investigator*'s deck.[40]

Piers wrote of a curious event on the 18th, which pointed yet again to McClure's lack of confidence in his second-in-command—not to mention his lack of respect for Haswell as a Queen's officer. It also darkens the character of Newton. At the same time, McClure's response demonstrates his continued vigilance in not leaving any stone unturned to find any trace of Franklin:

> A few days back Newton, the Ice Mate, in the course of conversation with the Captain, while keeping watch on deck, and without considering, I should imagine, what he was saying or the importance of it, told him [McClure] that among the pieces of fire wood that the Sergeant & he saw on the shore, some two months ago, there was one that looked like a part of a top-gallant mast; and on the Captain further questioning him he said that he reported it to the 1st Lieut. when he returned on board. Of course matters of such consequence to the expedition led to an immediate inquiry and spread through the whole Ship: the result of the inquiry was, that the Sergeant remembered Newton turning over a piece of wood which he said looked something like a piece of a top-gallant mast, but he could see no resemblance himself and thought nothing of it: the 1st Lieut said he had received no such report; nor had he or any one else in the Ship heard anything of the kind before. We all remembered hearing Newton speak of the fire-wood, but not a word about a piece of a top-gallant mast, which must at once have excited attention; and we of course concluded he had been—as is familiarly said of sailors—spinning a silly yarn to the Captain, and either not thinking of the importance of what he was saying or imagining that the thing was past & could not be investigated. To day however, the 1st Lieut., Newton, the Sergeant, a Carpenter's Mate [either Carpenter's Mate Henry Gauen or Carpenter's Crew William Whitefield], and I think another man, were sent by the Captain to the eastern shore to look for the piece of wood and examine it: they found nothing at all like a piece of a worked spar, but the Sergeant pointed out a piece which he said was the one Newton made the remark about to him; Newton however did not agree with him, and as we expected the search was a failure.[41]

Miertsching added to the story that the men "came back at five in the afternoon with faces and hands frozen, so that they were all put in the doctor's care. They had hunted for several hours, and had found plenty of driftwood, but no mast: a piece which Newton designated as a ship's plank was a stout piece of driftwood five feet long, and this Newton was compelled to drag to the ship. Now convinced that this was a pure fabrication on the part of Newton which could easily have disagreeable consequences on his return to England, the captain degraded him from his post and required him to offer public apology for the lies he had told."[42]

Come their first Christmas in the Frozen Zone, everyone onboard had reason to celebrate his good fortune thus far. And celebrate they did—in fact a little *too much*, as told by Piers:

> Our men seem to have commenced their festivities somewhat prematurely and boisterously, for many of them last night were so noisy from the effects of liquor, that the Captain & some of the Officers could scarcely sleep at all: [One officer kept watch on the upper deck, and one on the lower deck, to make sure that no drunken seamen wandered onto the ice to meet their deaths.] the consequence of which is, that the Captain has, this morning, before mustering by "open list," given the Ship's company a smart lecture, which will probably throw a damper over the rest of the day; disrated Quarter Master Ross to "A.B." and stopped several others' grog. There was no Church Service on account of the state of several men.[43]

The officers (excepting the warrant officers) dined in the evening on beef from the Sandwich Islands, musk ox sirloin from the Princess Royal Islands, English mincemeat, delightful Irish preserves, and an assortment of Scottish delicacies. Everyone spoke of home, and allowing for the time difference, what their loved ones would be doing, whether attending church, a ball, or retiring for the night. "We drank the health of the Queen," continued Piers, "health and success to Capt. Collinson; the Officers & crew of the Enterprise; health & success to Capt. Austin and the Barrow Strait Squadron ... the men passed the evening quietly and, I should say, pleasantly, dancing, singing & 'skylarking'; but they missed 'a splice of the main brace' on account of last night's disturbance."[44]

As for the 40ish Ross, the illiterate Scot had concealed his past upon joining the expedition, by claiming it was his first time in the Royal Navy. In truth, he was most likely a merchant seaman before his true first entry into the service in March 1842, as an able seaman on the paddle sloop HMS *Phoenix*. By that November, Ross found himself serving onboard the royal yacht *William & Mary*—but just under one year later he was discharged from the "Service for misconduct."[45]

Ross's loss in rank and status were immediate *gains* for George Brown, who was promoted to quartermaster the same day. One wonders if his good fortune was the result of McClure's gratitude for Brown's conduct during the October sled journey. Looking back on it many years later, Brown mused: "This was another era of my life, one which I valued, and one which I gladly accepted the congratulations of my Officers and comrades, [and] listened to the kindly advice given me by Dr. Armstrong." At least partly as a natural consequence of his position, the surgeon had a greater rapport with the crew than the other officers, and Armstrong's congenial ways remained impressed in the newly promoted petty officer's memory cells for the balance of Brown's life.[46]

The day after Christmas, Carpenter Ford celebrated his 29th birthday, and "had a good dinner of roast beef brought from Woahoo [Oahu], wine, etc. & a bottle of wine presented by our gallant Captain, with his compliments: 'Wishing me many happy returns of the day,' to drink my wife's health, which I did from my heart & no mistake, hoping she was in as good health as myself. A year makes a great alteration in [a] man's life.... We all live in hopes to spend our next Christmas with our dear friends [in England]."[47]

"The last days of this eventful year closed on us," wrote Armstrong, "presenting a picture of wildness it is difficult to conceive. A heavy, north-westerly gale and dense snow-drift confined us to the ship." And for the mortal preservation of all onboard, in his journal McClure justly honored the efforts of the medical men: "Every credit is due the medical officers, Drs. Armstrong and Henry Piers," and he particularly mentioned in dispatches the "extreme attention of Dr. Armstrong (upon our monthly inspections) to the state of the crew."[48]

The gloomy and rough weather continued into New Year's Day, but was tempered by the sights, smells and sounds Miertsching witnessed below decks: "After the [9:00 a.m.] muster we went, led by the captain, to the men's quarters, and were astonished to find a hall elegantly decorated with flags, pictures, seas-paintings; the tables laden with excellent puddings and roast beef, all arranged in a clean and appetizing manner; the sailors, neatly and tidily dressed and with friendly faces, received us with three cheers as we entered." Following the meal and coffee, the sailors gave a display of public speaking and sea songs that appropriately concluded with "God Save the Queen."[49]

The officers' afternoon meal was courtesy of Gunroom Steward George Milner, with much of the fare coming from the provisioner Mr. Gamble[50]; Miertsching ably described the sumptuous scene:

> On the table stood 6 bottles of dinner wine, along with porter and bitter ale; at first, turtle soup was brought; trout and eel; roast beef, mutton and musk ox; baked ham, smoked tongues, soused crabs, chicken meatballs, roasted ptarmigans;—
> vegetables: potatoes, green peas, carrots, white turnips, asparagus with pickled cucumbers, cauliflower, capers, onions, green walnuts.—
> Second course: plum pudding with a weight of 24 pounds; rhubarb pie, gooseberry pie, jam pie, damson pie; custard and jellies;—
> Des[s]ert: a big tart, ginger, raisins, almonds, gingerbread biscuits, pears, Seville oranges and olives.—
> 2 bottles of Port, 2 bottles of Sherry;—at last strong coffee.[51]

According to Piers, the steward "exerted himself to do the thing well, having been up all last night cooking the dinner &c—he was for some time, before he entered the Navy, with Peter Green of Weymouth." As for the ship's company, they had taken a warning from the captain at morning muster to heart, and "appeared cheerful & happy, and all perfectly sober."[52]

By the third of the month, the weather had improved, and three days after that, Able Seaman & Sick Berth Attendant John Ames returned from a walk and reported seeing three reindeer (caribou) near the islands, and that the darkness allowed him to get within 20 yards of the creatures. Armstrong wrote that he and McClure left the ship on the morning of the seventh to look for deer; they "failed to discover any trace of the Deer, [since] they probably went to the opposite side of the Strait. However, as no doubt existed of their having been here—their tracks being still visible on the floe ice—it raised hopes amongst us of early sport in the coming season."[53]

The 28-year-old Ames had gone to sea during his youth, mainly serving in warm climates, where he suffered considerably from intermittent fever and dysentery in China. The unmarried Kentish sailor then entered the Navy in 1843, as an able seaman aboard the frigate HMS *Castor*, spending the next four years in the East Indies. *Castor*'s crew was very active during

**Reindeer, also known as caribou (Harter, 1979).**

1846, during the First New Zealand War of 1845–47, and several of her men served ashore with the naval brigade. Throughout his naval service, Ames carried with him a personal secret: his real first name was Moses. His surname name may have been a contraction of "Eames," which would account for this spelling appearing in some sources.[54]

"My cabin is open to all, and to my great joy I often see men coming," wrote Brother Miertsching, "to whom I read aloud and then amuse myself and them by holding a discussion on what has been read." Outside the wooden walls, the temperature hit −45°F—for the first time the mercury in the thermometer froze; and by month's end, the ice reached four feet and nine inches in thickness. Meanwhile, Armstrong was relieved to pen that towards "the middle of January there was a perceptible increase in the amount of light at noon, and the stars appeared less brilliant, which indicated the approach of the sun ... [and the] beautiful pale light of the moon, with an occasional halo and parasellenæ [multiple luminous spots on a lunar halo], and in her absence, the Aurora Borealis, tended to disperse some of the gloom of winter.... More frequent excursions were made to the islands, since the appearance of the Deer, in the hope of meeting them."[55]

With the increased hours of light, and weather permitting, together the men and the officers took their share of "falls and thumps" on the ice, playing bat-and-ball, among other games. Two men were unable to join in the fun, the ailing Steel and James Williams. Williams was entered on the sick list on January 15, with pleuropneumonia (pneumonia complicated by pleurisy, being inflammation of the pleura, the moist, double-layered membrane surrounding the lungs and lining the rib cage[56]). By January 23, Piers wrote how "Williams [was] in a very critical and dangerous state, but I hope will yet do well and return with us to England." Two days later, after "the remedies employed, the acute symptoms of Williams' disease appear to be subdued and the expression of his countenance and his own feelings indicate a decided improvement." Despite this, Williams's recovery was slow, and he stayed in sick bay well into the month of May—a total of 123 days.[57]

Despite the overall happy tone onboard, an old villain again paid a visit, and Piers wrote that "74 lb. of preserved meat were condemned to day [January 28], a considerable addition to our previous los[s]es. The ends of the cases were convex from the formation and pressure of gases within. What is a loss to us in this particular [situation] is [a] gain to the dog, and this morning he received [from] us a present, the contents of an 8 lb. tin: he ate as much as he could, and the remainder he carefully deposited under snow near the Ship." Mongo had a number of such secret spots around *Investigator*, and if anyone should wander too near to them for his liking, "he gives them a gentle, admonishing grasp of the leg or foot; and if they go direct to the spot he puts his nose down over it, with a slight turn of the head, so that he may observe any motion of the intruder—signifying at the same time 'paws off.'"[58]

In his dispatches to the Admiralty, McClure wrote that one of the reasons their first winter passed "without our sanitary state being in the slightest degree impaired" was due to the "excellency of every species of provisions."[59] McClure had previously recorded instances of bad provisions in his journal and Letter & Order Book, but he knew the official dispatches would eventually be published, and therefore probably chose to omit any mention of the faulty provisions.

"On the 30th we were gladdened by the re-appearance of our Raven, which for some days had been absent.... I cannot describe the degree of interest with which we watched for this daily visitor, and his return was regarded as an important event," enthused Armstrong.[60]

February commenced with heavy gales and drifts so severe that, in just one night, a wall of snow was thrown around the ship that reached eight to ten feet high.[61]

Three days into the month, late in the morning, nearly everyone was on the floe with eager eyes. Then, after a slumber of 83 days, the sun peeked "through the openings of the dense clouds over the south eastern hills, and continued more or less bright for an hour or an hour & a half after noon." The event must have particularly cheered sick bay's two occupants, who by now also had Mate Henry Hubert Sainsbury to keep them company. The son of a Romsey physician, Sainsbury was in his early 20s and had only passed for his current rank just over a week before joining *Investigator*. He had suffered a severe injury to his right shoulder joint, and as Piers wrote, "from his description of the accident, which happened at rounders, he appears to have been very near sustaining a dislocation of the joint."[62]

That evening, while attending to Sainsbury's arm in his cabin, Piers casually asked Sainsbury's Marine servant, Elias Bow (who had joined at Honolulu), where in England he was from, and discovered both hailed from Dorset County. A conversation followed about mutual places and people. Private Bow was another combat veteran from the 1840 Syrian campaign, who afterward fought Borneo pirates while serving in HM Brig *Royalist*, and then spent ten months onboard the *Agincourt*—at the same time as a certain Volunteer 1st Class Samuel Cresswell. Bow told Piers he had only been home once since joining the Marines in 1836. When the Marine returned from the Far East, he sported such a dark tan that his father didn't recognize him. He held out his hand, asking why a man wouldn't shake hands with his own son, and the "old man replied, 'Ah! I wish you were my Son; I would indeed shake hands!'" Bow's mother then appeared, but she too did not perceive her son's face, until finally a brother came up and at once recognized him, and shook his hand.[63]

Private Bow had been absent from England for six years, and "although he always received plenty of letters from England, [he] got tired after the first year of answering them, so that his Parents had thought for some time that he must be dead; and this circumstance, together with the change which a six years cruise in China had produced in his appearance, was," wrote Piers, "I think sufficient excuse for the 'old people' doubting the reality of their Son."[64]

A few days afterward, some of the men returning from the islands were followed by a wolf, the first seen so far. The creature boldly approached within 20 yards, and being without arms, the men ran to their vessel, as did the wolf after them—and a game of cat and mouse ensued. A group then rushed out from the ship, but the crafty visitor melted away into the ice, until found by Mongo, hiding under a hummock. Off Mongo went with the wolf, and "so that it was thought we should not see her again; for it is a well known fact that the Arctic Wolves are in the habit of enticing away Esquimaux dogs, and then drowning them." Shortly afterward, Mongo returned with the new acquaintance, but the latter kept his distance, so a line was fastened around Mongo's neck in hopes of enticing the wolf into a good position for shot. But as Piers pointed out, the wolf was "too wary, and the scheme failed—great excitement & fun prevailed all this time, the scenes & remarks on deck being the chief source of amusement—even a trifling incident of this kind does good out here."[65]

The pursuit of the wolf continued in the days that followed, but his cunning outwitted, among others, Mr. Kennedy and Mongo, although "Newton, the Ice Mate, got a shot at him, but missed."[66]

As the sun increased in its altitude, the rays again painted a picture of light and shade on the jagged and broken surface of the icy surroundings; the parhelia also shown more brilliantly and with more frequency than any other period of the year. During the month, the Investigators experienced the severest cold to date, varying between –9°F and –51°F. Such temperatures brought with them clearer and calmer weather, and ushered in the tranquil coming of Saint Valentine's Day. Surely this holiday warmed more than a few hearts onboard, as Piers wrote how Cupid's prance was "not forgotten out here, for it was remembered that the postman in England had had a busy morning." Even their solitary winged visitor seemed to be in the spirit, and lonely no more, since three days afterward, two ravens were seen flying near the ship.[67]

The contrasting warmth of the sun and plunging temperatures caused Armstrong to frequently have one side of his face enlivened by the Sun's rays, while the opposite side was frostbitten, and had to be constantly massaged to restore life![68]

Miertsching noted the surgeon felt more than the Ice Queen's pinch in February: "Dr. Armstrong, who is not the best conversationalist, was thoroughly humiliated by the other officers today. The captain was informed of the whole affair, but took not the least notice of it. The captain has suffered from poor health in the last days and has now started taking medicine." Due to his pompous ways, it appears Armstrong's fellow officers sought to bring him down a peg or two. While McClure respected—and very much needed—Armstrong's medical abilities, this incident points to the captain's low personal regard for his surgeon. On the other hand, clearly McClure was ill, and so probably lacked the willingness to deal with the situation. In the meantime, the Brother was gratified to record that his ministerial ways bore fruit during the idleness of winter, as Williams, Able Seaman (either Ellis or Mark) Griffiths, and Paymaster & Purser's Steward Wilcox gathered nightly in his humble abode. Such visits caused Miertsching to proclaim, "Oh, how much pleasanter it is now on the ship than formerly, when grossness still had the upper hand."[69]

Ellis Griffiths was a tallish, hazel-eyed Welshman who first went to sea as a boy in 1837; he had joined *Investigator* at Honolulu from the brig *Cockatrice* (tender to HMS *Asia*, flagship at Valparaiso of Rear Admiral Sir Phipps Hornby). The story of Miertsching's other visitor is more varied. As a newlywed in his mid–20s, he was John *Willcocks*, and tied the knot with Martha Hobling Jewell, in East Stonehouse, Devon, just six months before signing onto the expedition. Before that, under the same name, he served onboard the 80-gun HMS *Superb* as a boy 1st class and paymaster and purser's steward's mate between 1844 and 1848. Also on *Superb* from December 1844 to March 1845 (on his appointment to *Erebus*) was one of Franklin's officers, Devon native and Opium War veteran, Lieutenant Henry T.D. Le Vesconte. Only beginning with the *Investigator*'s Muster did Willcocks appear as "Wilcox"—and it transpired this sailor may have altered his name when he returned to the sea in hopes of evading his new wife.[70]

"The approaching travelling season, the exploring parties and the probabilities of reaching England next Autumn, begin to excite more than usual interest," commented Piers. Excepting the convalescing Williams, the ship's company made it through the winter in good health, though the ship's interior still bore marks of the extreme conditions—condensation caused large quantities of frost to be collected from the beams and floor cloth of the lower deck, and in the officers' cabins. Outside, the assistant surgeon heeded change in the air: "The ice has, lately, been cracking very much, and the noise attending it is sometimes sharp like a single musket, or continuous like distant thunder. A continued low temperature seems to increase the fracturing of the ice."[71]

And Miertsching revealed the Investigators' moving with resolve on February's final day:

> The sun now rises at 8 a.m. Barrels and chests have been taken from the ship and placed on the ice in order to convey them later to [the larger] Princess Royal Island. The captain fears a terrible disturbance when the ice breaks up in Prince of Wales Strait, and as a precaution will place clothing and provisions for the whole crew for three months on the island, and also [the 30-foot whaleboat], so that in case of disaster all will have a chance of escaping and reaching the shore of the mainland [and eventually reach the *Plover*].[72]

With the expected work on the ice, to protect the men's eyes from the sun's gaining strength, and reflection of its rays off the ice and snow, crape veils were issued to the ship's company, and the men also wore green-tinted glasses or goggles.[73]

March began with the breaking up of the evening school, "but instead of holidays, work has commenced. The first whaler is put on two sledges, ready for running down to the islands on Monday morning (3$\underline{d}$)." More transport was needed, and a few days later, Ford, Gauen, and Whitefield were busy making new sleds. The whaleboat and provisions were conveyed to the larger of the Princess Royal Islands, "as well as the transporting another whale boat, besides one of Halkett's [boats] to the eastern shore, distant five miles, for the facility of allowing the travelling parties going along that coast to reach the islands, should the ice break up and carry the vessel away during their absence." By the time this arduous labor was completed on the tenth, a record placed in the cairn that was built at winter's start, and the emergency provisions and clothing placed on the upper deck in the autumn, were taken below and stowed.[74]

During this time, a small fox examined one of the empty meat tins which marked the tracings of a road, and came quite close to the toiling men. Mongo had sprung into action—closely followed by the Investigators. The little creature paid the ultimate price for its boldness, and Piers described the action, when Mongo "caught [the fox] by the back, threw her over his head and killed her. The chase lasted ten or fifteen minutes, and was seen by all the party, of which the Captain was one." These animals "became so tame, that they were frequently caught in the traps on deck, having voluntarily come on board, and were more numerous, judging from the number of captures which were made, than at the beginning of the season," wrote Armstrong. Some became objects of entertainment, being trapped within a giant human ring on the ice, while Mongo gave chase. Armstrong, Piers, and Nelson tagged the foxes generally with the name "Reynard," evidently an allusion to Reynard the Fox, the folk hero of several Medieval poetic tales that satirize contemporary human society. "Though Reynard is sly, amoral, cowardly, and self-seeking, he is still a sympathetic hero, whose cunning is a necessity for survival. He symbolizes the triumph of craft over brute strength."[75]

On March 22, a hare was shot on Prince Albert Land, and Armstrong wrote that "this was a great event, no less from its having been the first killed, than from the pleasing evidence it afforded us of the presence of such game." Miertsching also recorded an "event" on that day in his journal—one not mentioned in any other contemporary source for that date: "The captain, Cresswell, Court, Piers, and I, with two seamen, were on the Westland, which until now had no name; the flag was hoisted, and the captain took possession of the land in the name of Queen Victoria, and named it 'Baring's Land'; we remained for several hours, tramped around in various directions and found traces of wolves, reindeer, foxes, and hares, and saw a few ptarmigan but shot none." In reality, McClure, Armstrong, Piers, and Ford all wrote about parties going ashore and claiming Barings Island (or Land) *seven months earlier*—on September 7, 1850. It's difficult to account for such a huge discrepancy, particularly in consideration of Armstrong's writings on the last day of the month: "Captain M'Clure, Lieutenant Cresswell, and myself, proceeded to the western land, (Baring's), it never having been visited since we took possession of its southern extreme, when first discovered."[76]

"The officers and crews assigned to the journeys to be made next month were named today [March 27]," recorded Miertsching: Lieutenants Haswell and Cresswell, and Mate Wynniatt were chosen to command the sleds. "The men are busy making ready sledges, and those assigned to travel are working on clothing and boots," and at the same time, Sailmaker Joseph Facey had set to work on tents and gear, while Blacksmith and Armorer Henry Stone (nicknamed the "Jolly Tinker" for his tinsmithing skills and jovial ways) prepared lamps, kettles, and cooking apparatus.[77]

The unmarried Facey had joined the RN in 1836, at about age 16, and sported a tattoo of a Freemasons symbol on his left arm, and a crucifix on the right, as well as being marked by the telltale pitting of smallpox. He served on two ships and rose to able seaman by 1842, but when Facey signed on for the Arctic in January 1850, he stated it was his first time in the Navy. Yet, to have been rated a sailmaker meant Facey no doubt showed proof of seamanlike abilities, and so must have been at sea in the years previous. As for the 26-year-old "Jolly Tinker," it was the Kent County man's first time venturing into the deep blue, but there was salt in his veins: Stone's father Edward had been a naval cook from 1796 to 1831. Years later, Henry told the story of how his father was wounded during the attack on Trinidad, and "carried a bullet in his head for more than forty years"—a reference to that island's capture by Rear Admiral Henry Harvey's squadron on February 17, 1797, which included Edward Stone's 16-gun ship HMS *Thorn*.[78]

The Investigators prepared to break out of their prison of solitude, on a quest for their countrymen over unknown shores ... while the Arctic lay in wait.

# 9

# The Grand Sledding Chorus, 1851

*I have been a long time at sea, and seen various trying services but never have I seen (for men) such labour and such misery after. No amount of money is an equivalent.*

—Captain Henry Kellett, RN, on service with sledding parties

Excitement shot through the ship as "Bruin"—an Old English word for brown bears, and a character from the tale of Reynard the Fox[1]—arrived on the scene. After surveying to the southward, Court and Wynniatt returned in the morning, reporting they had come across fresh bear tracks. And then, on March 29, around "4 p.m. Newton and one of the men came running on board, saying there was a bear just the other side of the "bull ring" [about 400 yards away][2]: all hands were quickly on deck, guns & lances were got ready," wrote Piers, "but no one at first was allowed to go in pursuit, I suppose as the Captain was at dinner and wished to have a start with the rest."[3]

Armstrong takes up the story, which played out against the backdrop of a gale whipping up dense clouds of drifting snow: "The dark appearance of the fox traps on the ice, had first attracted his attention. To them he proceeded, doubtless attracted by the smell of the bait, which must have agreeably assailed his keen scent; after tossing the trap about for some time, and finding all efforts vain to obtain the modicum of meat it contained, he wandered to and fro—evidently fearful to approach near the ship." Piers then saw McClure, Cresswell and Armstrong advance toward the bear, a lofty hummock blinding the creature's view of the approaching hunters, but the bear evidently spotted the threat and quickly shuffled off. The trio "hid themselves for some time behind some high hummocks, and bruin returned to the trap; they then attempted to steal towards him under cover of some other hummocks, but 'John Bruin' again eyed them and retreated. Several others now left the Ship and followed him some distance, but it was very evident he would not face such strange characters, and from the rate he went over the ice, there was not the least chance of overtaking him. He appeared to make for the western shore and was soon lost sight of."[4]

The bear was spotted again, prowling around *Investigator* on April's first day, at about 5:30 in the morning, and Lieutenant Haswell, with three or four others (plus Mongo) took off after the beast. Ford and Sergeant Woon aimed ... fired—and missed—but Mongo was close on his heels! The dog followed the beast for some time after the pair were out of sight; "however, (predictably on this day) the bruin again made *fools* of his pursuers...."[5]

Though the day's average temperature was –20°F, in the sun it rose to a balmy +21°F by two by that afternoon, and through the growing daylight and declining cold the ship was roused from her slumber—even though the "ice was found to have increased 9½ inches, and was then 6 feet and 5 inches thick." The deep snow embankment came down, contrasting her dark hull against the enveloping white surface; the snow was also removed from the upper deck, so one could again feel the planks beneath his feet, while light once more seeped between decks.[6]

Two weeks later, a strong northeasterly wind ushered in a late visit from Old Man Winter. "Today is Palm Sunday, but here are no palm trees for us: from early in the day until evening snow fell so thickly that already it is two feet deep, and we are very thankful that we have a housing over the ship, and sheltered by it can walk back and forth on deck. In the afternoon I was with the captain and read him a sermon for Palm Sunday delivered by an old bishop in Scotland in 1685."[7]

However, with the Investigators being entirely dependent upon their own resources, "the exact quantity, state and condition of the provisions on board" had to be thoroughly surveyed and inventoried. During this process, the spirit room was cleared, and it was discovered that "nearly all the rum casks were found broken in the stave [strip of wood] which contains the bung [cork]: they were all stowed very close, with the bungs uppermost, and on being placed on their sides now they nearly all leak from the damage they have sustained. It is thought that these staves must have given way when the ship underwent the very heavy pressure on the evening of Oct. 4th."[8]

The *Investigator* herself required attention, and in the middle of the month, the "men to day are digging a trench about three feet deep round the ship," wrote Piers, "preparatory to caulking her. Her sides for two three streaks [planks] above the copper, are as bare of paint as if they had been planed [shaved smooth]." An Arctic veteran, Caulker James Evans was assisted by Carpenter's Mate Henry Gauen and Carpenter's Crew William Whitefield (and perhaps Carpenter Ford as well) in caulking "the ship outside, and with the truck round her quarters, the boiling and smell of the pitch, and the hammering, one may almost imagine himself in Woolwich dock again."[9]

Like a dozen of his current shipmates, Evans hailed from Kent County. Illiterate and a caulker by trade, when about 20 years old he stepped aboard HMS *Columbia* in July 1842, for service lasting five years as a caulker's mate. During this time, he was in company with future Investigators Bradbury, Olley, and Parfitt. Evans left home again in 1848 onboard the *Enterprise*, and probably due to being a married man, he had tattoos of a man and woman emblazoned on one arm, and an anchor and the word "Hope" upon the other. By contrast, the towering 6'½" Gauen was Wiltshire-born, and though *Investigator* was his introduction to the Navy, he first went to sea in 1846 in the merchant service. Whitefield was reared in Hampshire, and had tasted naval service during 4½ years onboard HMS *Carysfort* in the early 1840s.[10]

April 17 brought an unexpected change, with the thermometer reaching 38°F in the sun at noon—a increase of *70 degrees* in just four days and eight hours! The snow all about the ship had melted, transforming it into a swamp-like landscape. The considerable and sudden change created a lethargy among the men "that is common on a hot summer's day in England. The dog too is down, quite depressed and listless; with her eyes closed allows herself to be pulled about and turned over without her usual playful resistance, and is with some trouble only made to get on her legs and rise."[11]

As a consequence of the marked change, McClure determined he needed to get his sled parties away as soon as possible, rather than waiting (as Sir James Ross had done) until May 15. In the evening, three sleds were each packed with equipment and provisions for six weeks, and weighed eleven hundredweight (1,232 lbs.) apiece, so that with six men dragging a sled, each would be pulling 205 lbs. On the trail, the "officer goes in advance of the sledge to find the easiest way through the rough ice, and carries a double-barrelled gun, telescope, compass, and a notebook for recording the observations made with the instruments."[12] The sleds were then dragged out onto the ice for a short distance, in preparation for their departure the following day.[13]

Just two days before, Lieutenant Francis McClintock (McClure's old shipmate and Captain Ommanney's first lieutenant on *Assistance*) had set off in command of HM Sled *Perseverance* (motto—"Persevere to the end") from Captain Austin's eastern Arctic squadron, situated at Griffith Island, in Barrow Strait, south of Cornwallis Island. His destination was Melville Island.[14]

Unlike McClure, McClintock had obtained considerable sledding experience during the 1848–49 expedition, traveling over 500 miles (804 kilometers) in 39 days—unprecedented at the time. After his return home, McClintock then "spent the winter of 1849–50 experimenting on the best form of cooking-gear and of fuel, resulting in the almost perfect travelling equipment of 1851. He had the advice and assistance of Prof. [Samuel] Houghton [*sic*— Haughton]." With these experiences behind him, McClintock was put in charge of organizing sledding operations by Austin, and the enthusiastic lieutenant set about designing sleds, tents, and other equipment to be as light as possible. Of course, none of the Investigators had known anything about McClintock's newly developed equipment, which McClintock incorporated into a strategy composed of two systems, in order to allow for wide-ranging searches.[15] The first system

> was to lay a cache of provisions about fifty miles from the ship, from which an outward-bound sledge crew could top up its supplies and leave the balance for the last lap of the return journey. The other was a system of supporting sledge journeys by which one or more sledge crews accompanied the main party for a certain distance, feeding both it and themselves, and then returned to the ship, and if deemed advisable, went out again to establish a depot for the returning party.[16]

On McClintock's outward bound journey, Surgeon Abraham Rose Bradford[17] (HMS *Resolute*) accompanied him in command of HM Sled *Resolute* (motto—"England Onward to the rescue"),[18] before they separated so the doctor could search the east coast of Melville Island. Just then the profoundness of being on the sledding trail in the vast Arctic rose to the surface:

> After [Bradford's] departure I could only give vent to my reflections by inscribing them in my diary, and at once wrote down this passage:—"When our isolated position is considered, how completely we were exposed to all the vicissitudes of a rigorous climate, and dependent upon our own efforts, and the accidental condition of the ice for advance or retreat, had not hope come to the rescue our farewell would indeed have been a painful one." That Bradford felt something of this sort is evident from this passage in his diary:—"We shook hands and wished each other success. I must admit that when the Perseverance (M'Clintock's sledge) was lost sight of in the distance, I began to have some little feeling of the loneliness of our position, almost as if the last link connecting us with the living world had been severed. That these feelings were participated in by the men of the two parties, was evidenced by the manner in which they cheered and shook hands with each other."[19]

**On the sledding trail (Walter W. May; courtesy Douglas Wamsley).**

Meanwhile, on *Investigator*, among the six men in Lieutenant Haswell's party were Quartermaster George Brown and Able Seaman Mark Griffiths, and their assignment was the western and southern coasts of Prince Albert's Land. Some of those in Lieutenant Cresswell's party included Captain of the Forecastle John Calder (sled captain), Sailmaker Joseph Facey, and Able Seaman Ellis Griffiths, who were headed for the northeastern coast of Banks Land. Mate Wynniatt's party was detailed for the northwestern shore of Prince Albert's Land, and then to search eastward, in the direction of Cape Walker.[20]

McClure issued instructions to his sledding officers, specifying that "such service may possibly render their rejoining [*Investigator*] doubtful," although the likelihood of the ship drifting away was "a circumstance only barely possible." Their primary objective was to look for any traces of shipwreck and any wood fashioned by mechanical means, and to "search upon the elevated ground a little above the beach, where parties would be most likely to encamp, for any cairn, preserved meat cases, or other indications of civilised man." At the same time, they were tasked with tracing the coastlines and taking careful geographical measurements,[21] while keeping in mind that "we have no accurate knowledge at what period the ice breaks up in these Straits, [so] you will keep a very vigilant eye upon it for any symptom that would lead you to infer such an event was probable." If it appeared the ice was likely to break up, then spare stores and provisions were to be left at a higher elevation, and "you will use your utmost exertions to rejoin the ship." Finally, McClure instructed that if *Investigator* was found to have drifted away, every effort was to be made for all three parties to rendezvous at the Princess Royal Islands (which may not happen), and "equip yourself with two months' provisions, and make the best of your way to the 'Plover,' as Fort Good Hope upon the Mackenzie cannot be depended upon as a station, where you would be certain of obtaining a supply of provisions in the event of having to winter there; and any attempt to reach Port Leopold without the knowledge of a ship being there to receive you, or of the difficulties which may impede your progress in navigating an unknown coast, is very likely to be attended with obstacles which would place you in a most embarrassing situation."[22] McClure was making reference to a house James Ross built before leaving Port Leopold (Whaler Point) in August 1849, in which he left fuel and provisions for 64 persons for 12 months, along with a steam launch (lengthened by six or seven feet), which would have been capable of carrying both of Franklin's crews to whale ships.[23]

McClure continued: "You are to keep a Diary, from which, upon your return, you will be required to draw up a detailed account of your proceedings for my information." Besides a record of day-to-day observations and events (and sometimes even drawings), the names of each member of a party, the sled's name, flag and motto, were recorded in a sled journal. There is every reason to believe these diaries were kept and the accounts written—and handed over to McClure (see Appendix 2).[24]

It will be remembered that Franklin's planned primary route in 1845 was to sail a south-westerly course from Cape Walker, Russell Island (just north of Prince of Wales Island, eastern Viscount Melville Sound) to around 120° W longitude on the North American coast, and then onto the Bering Strait. The *assumption* being that there was scant land to obstruct the path, as Second Secretary of the Admiralty Sir John Barrow believed "Bank's Land," "Wollaston Land" and "Victoria Land" were only small islands. In addition, Franklin added an alternate route, "in case of the Passage not being found in that direction, then, to the Northward by the Wellington Channel."[25]

McClure of course already knew some information about the search in the southern area he assigned to Haswell. During *Investigator*'s stay at Honolulu, McClure had obtained details of Rae's travels with Dr. Richardson along the North American coast from the mouth of the Mackenzie River to the Coppermine River in 1848–49; ice conditions had prevented Rae from crossing the Dolphin and Union Strait to examine Wollaston and Victoria Lands. It appears that, through a misinterpretation of this information, Armstrong criticized McClure's decision to send Haswell southward, as the doctor believed "we were fully aware that the duty of searching [Wollaston Land's] southern and [western] coast was, at that time, being performed by Mr. Rae."[26]

The doctor went on to insist there was "another reason of even great import—in the event of Franklin having gone up Wellington Channel as was then very generally supposed, and being obliged to abandon his ships to the northward or westward, nothing was more probable than that he would endeavour to reach the locality where Perry [*sic*—Parry] had spent a winter [at Winter Harbour, Melville Island] in the hope of meeting with succour." "Our south-eastern party could have been made available for this service; for it was only in a geographical point of view that any results were expected." The latter was not wholly true. McClure didn't know what lay between his ship and the North American coast to the southeast, and as will be seen, sending Haswell in that direction partially solved a geographic puzzle by testing Barrow's beliefs, and therefore imply an answer as to whether or not it was even possible for Franklin to have sailed a southwesterly course from Cape Walker, Russell Island, to around 120° W. longitude on the North American coast.[27]

However, Armstrong did point out a crucial (and strange) mistake by McClure. The doctor wrote that it was "a matter of the most vital importance to connect our Expedition with that of Captain Austin—thus completing the circuit of search from either side of the American continent—to make that officer aware of our position, that we might be able to afford each other mutual succour and support, and that the efforts of search might be directed elsewhere."[28]

On the one hand, a combination of McClure's political cunning, daring, and good fortune allowed him to achieve remarkable results in just one season. On the other, despite his risk-taking thus far, it's difficult to believe that in his careful planning of the spring sled parties, McClure would make such an obvious and serious mistake—one that came to place everyone onboard in peril. But was it *really* a "mistake"? Evidently no one has previously contemplated this question. It seems entirely possible—given McClure's political maneuverings up to this point and afterward—that he *purposefully* did not send someone to Winter Harbour. Through eluding Collinson, McClure had already discovered a North-West Passage, attempted to sail through it, and planned another attempt when the ice broke up. If he made contact with Captain Austin's expedition, it could well have resulted in McClure's coming under the orders of this superior officer, who in turn may have issued instructions contrary to his ambitions. As a result, McClure may have had to in some way *share* the glory of his discovery, which would have been unthinkable to the *Investigator*'s commander.

However, at the end of the day, whether Haswell's party was assigned to the specific task of sledding the approximately 200 miles (321 kilometers) to Winter Harbour, or someone else, in terms of safety and the primary aim of all involved, it was imperative to get a message to that place. Perhaps more importantly, if McClure *had* sent a party with a message to Winter Harbour, would McClintock have found it? Yes. By comparing the distance a sled party from *Investigator* had to travel to Winter Harbour from the Princess Royal Islands to Winter Harbour to a round-trip journey of a similar distance taken one year later from Mercy Bay to Winter Harbour (18 days out, bad weather and rough ice, and 10 days back, better weather and flat ice), any message from McClure would have been placed at Winter Harbour well before McClintock visited on June 5–6.[29]

And what of Collinson? After deciding to take *Enterprise* to Hong Kong for the winter, Collinson was returning northward, and around this time was in the vicinity of Raza Island (southeast of Okinawa).[30] In the end, McClure's previous actions effectively forced Collinson into the equally dangerous situation of entering the Arctic alone.

April 18, 1851

Today on Good Friday we had Divine Service in the morning, after which the travelling parties were warned to be ready to set out at 4 p.m. They made their preparations with strange feelings, for every one of them seems to feel that they will not find the ship here on their return, but that she will have been swept away or utterly wrecked; it was therefore a mournful parting for a sailor to make. All partook together in a midday meal, and then at 4 p.m. the travelling crews assembled on the quarter-deck and were addressed by the captain.[31]

My lads, you are going on a long journey, and I must say a very interesting one,—interesting, because the ground you are about to go over has never before been trodden by Europeans, at least to the best of our knowledge. The people of England imagine that Sir John Franklin might have reached Cape Walker. Now, my Lads, if we had the choice of the whole polar regions, we could not be placed in a more convenient spot, therefore I trust you will use your utmost endeavours to discover traces of the missing Expedition. I must now hand you over to the All Disposer of events, and pray that He may watch over you; feeling confident you will never abuse the trust reposed in you.[32]

Amid temperatures dipping into the 20s, the parties finally departed around seven o'clock; sled travelers during the spring and summer seasons march during the night, allowing them to take advantage of the warmer daylight hours to rest, and also avoid the effects of snow blindness. When "the ensign was hoisted, the sailors harnessed themselves to their sledges, and with a triple hurrah from those who remained behind they set off," observed Miertsching, "each party in its appointed direction. We accompanied them for an hour." A fatigue party accompanied each sled party for some distance.[33] Armstrong commanded the fatigue party that assisted the northern travelers.

"Immediately after the departure of our travelling parties, the weather assumed an unfavourable aspect, became foggy, with a heavy gale from the north-west. The temperature at the same time fell [and six days later dropped to -16°F][34]: we became anxious about the northern parties, as we feared they might be compelled to return; but, fortunately, the gale ceased in the course of a couple of days with every prospect of finer weather."[35]

In the days that followed, nature provided a measure of excitement for the Investigators, firstly through a bear chase on the 23rd of "a huge fellow, with a pale cream coloured coat; and his legs like immensely stout pillars under him." Then the 27th saw "the appearance of the first of the feathered tribe that had visited us—the hardy little Snow Bunting (*Emberzia Nivalis*) was seen chirping about; it is considered the certain harbinger of spring." However, the more mundane tasks of maintaining Her Majesty's vessel did not escape the explorers, for two days later, a fresh coat of paint was applied to the interior of *Investigator*, "and to assist the drying, I believe more spirit of turpentine than usual was mixed with the paint."[36]

It was also a time for spiritual reflection. After divine service one Sunday, Carpenter Ford spent the afternoon as he usually did, reading his Bible and other religious works, "as I am happy to say I have learned more of my duty towards my Maker since I left home than all my life before & I hope the Almighty will strengthen me to seek more every day." That same afternoon, Brother Miertsching "held a private gathering which many attended, and when it was over they begged me to hold another soon. This was not the first meeting of its kind; and although neither the captain nor the officers attend them, they seem in no way opposed to them."[37]

The ice, measured on the first day of May, was an inch shy of seven feet in thickness, having had a growth spurt of six inches during the last month. This turned out to be the full extent of Old Man Winter's maturity. That morning, Newton, Sergeant Woon, Kerr, and Ship's Cook Isaac Stubberfield, started off with the dog during a heavy snow, on an excursion to the northwestern shore, distant about five or six miles (with the roughness of the ice increasing the walk by a mile to a mile and a half). Though Stubberfield had only recently reached his 28th year, the 5'9½" Sussex man was affectionately known as "Old Stubber" by his shipmates, and had previously spent over two years as an ordinary seaman aboard HMS *Ocean* with one of them, fellow Sussex native, Able Seaman Samuel Relfe.[38]

Stubberfield had hardly been a mile from the ship before, and was wearing thick sea boots and flushing trousers. Both the cook and "our steward [Sugden]—a strong, wiry fellow—who, when he returned from the S. eastern shore, said he never wished to go on shore again," were deceived as to their foot traveling capabilities over the ice and snow[39]:

> In the evening all hands were on the look out for "old Stubber": Newton & the Sergeant came on board first and reported "Stubber" very tired, so several of the men started off with a sledge to carry him on, while others set to and dug a pit in the form of a grave in the snow to bury him in on his arrival. When the sledge party met him—with his boots over his shoulder, for he had been obliged to relieve his feet of their weight—they laid him on it, lashed him fast and dragged him to the ship: here he was met by the other party who pitched him into the pit and commenced covering him with snow, but having still

sufficient animation he managed to extricate himself, remarking very good humorously, while he shook the snow of himself, "well there are not many who are honoured so much as to be drawn on board on a carriage." It was a most amusing scene; enjoyed by all on board and by "old Stubber" himself. It is besides a good sign to see the men disposed for a little humour of the kind; and they are indeed, all of them, in capital spirits and condition.[40]

The following evening, one of the quartermasters lanced a seal after it appeared through the fire hole close to the gangway. The skin and skeleton of the 60–70 lb. creature were destined to become part of the natural history collection, and its flesh, liver, heart and kidneys found their way onto to the officers' dining table, while the blubber was kept for Mongo.[41]

Hunting to bolster the food supply continued to be one of the main tasks, so Newton and another man headed southeast on the fifth, while Fawcett, Corporal Farquharson, Private Saunders, Anderson and Hulott struck out northwest. The parties were away about 13 hours, with the latter group bringing back four hares and three ptarmigan for its effort. Afterward, Piers saw the opportunity to compare the endurance of a teetotaler to a grog man. Piers asked the teetotaling Hulott if he was tired after the walk, and

> he replied, he felt able to start again at once. The water system appears to agree very well for I think the water drinkers will do as much as any of the grog-men on board, I said; to which he replied, yes Sir, we had a specimen of that to day—he then told me that Saunders, a young, powerful Marine, was saying, just before he took about a quarter of a gill of rum, how well he felt and that he could walk all day, but very shortly after he was quite knocked up [exhausted] and would have laid down. This is just what one might naturally expect to follow the stimulus of spirits in cold weather when taking a fatiguing walk.[42]

"At 1 a.m. May 6th I was much surprised to see M$^r$ Wynniatt (Mate) who having broken his Chronometer at the distance of one hundred & twenty miles from the Ship[43] injudiciously returned," wrote McClure.[44] Miertsching recounted the captain's displeasure: "Mr. Wynniatt, fell from a hummock and broke the chronometer that he carried, without which he could not make correct reckonings [determine longitude], so he thought it best to return. The captain gave him no friendly reception when he came on board, but reprimanded him so bitterly for his foolish conduct that he went back covered with shame."[45]

Except for the cold weather for the first few days out, the party was doing well until the accident. The men were able to sleep every night onshore, and found plenty of firewood, so did not suffer from lack of water or hot meals. However, Piers was told of an odd encounter with polar bear:

> A bear, one day, came up within ten or twenty yards of them: the reason of near approach was the diffi-culty of getting off either of their muskets or Wynniatt's gun; and while their pieces were [misfiring] and some of the men were preparing to receive him with the boarding pikes, bruin was leisurely walking up to them, taking up the snow with his tongue and licking his chops as he came along: at last Wynniatt got off one of the barrels of his gun, which was loaded with shot, and peppered "Master John" in the face; at which he retreated some distance to a hummock, where he sat down and wiped his face with his paws. I think they would have had some rough work if not serious injury, with "John Bruin," had not Wyanniatt succeeded in firing his gun; for before they could have done him any great harm with their blunt boarding pikes (used for setting up the tent) he would in all probability have mauled some of them severely.[46]

Wynniatt made it to a little eastward of Peel Point, and really had no excuse for returning: as long as he obeyed orders and kept to the coastline, the young officer would easily have guided his party back to *Investigator*; after all, his primary mission was to look for Franklin, not to make charts. He "brought with him a piece of a small Esquimaux sledge and a pair of antlers; both were old and found on the beach among the drift wood—he also passed the skeleton of a whale."[47]

All of the party were in good health, and after a rest and resupply with provisions for 30 days, set off again at six in the evening; Dr. Armstrong commanded the fatigue party. Since another chronometer was not available, Wynniatt went without one. His orders were to go as far as Cape Walker and return by June 7.[48]

At the same time, Sainsbury led three men for the western shore, while Newton and three others headed for the eastern coast (all were to return Saturday evening). The next morning, Miertsching, with Kerr, Whitefield, and Private Bow, departed for the western shore to visit Sainsbury's tent and a day of shooting, but later on, the dangerous fickleness of the Arctic again showed itself, as the dropping temperature, increased winds, and dense snowdrift nearly sealed Whitefield's fate. While three of the men were in the pursuit of hares, the heavy snowstorm cut Whitefield off from his companions (who were about 160 yards distant, and retreated to the tent). Whitefield "felt himself become suddenly cold, was seized with headache and giddiness, and fell down insensible ... for at least two or three hours." Meanwhile, the men in the tent repeatedly braved the swirling gale, and risk of being lost themselves in the snowdrift, to find their missing comrade.[49]

After regaining consciousness, Whitefield crawled for 400 or 500 yards, and collapsed within six feet of the tent between one and two o'clock in the morning. His companions inside were "suddenly arrested by a noise outside, as if something slow and heavy in its movements was approaching," and prepared to possibly defend themselves against a bear attack, "the tracks of several having been observed close to the tent in the morning." One of the men cautiously ventured outside, and was met with the shocking sight of the last ounces of life rapidly draining from Whitefield—"he could not speak, his body rested on his hand and knees, the head thrown back, the eyes fixed and immovable, the nose, mouth and ears filled with snow, which was fast accumulating about him; the jaws and limbs rigid. A few minutes more might probably have terminated his earthly career, when by the interposition of a merciful Providence, he was thus rescued from the jaws of death."[50]

Whitefield was immediately whisked into the tent, and Sainsbury grasped the man's wrist—but no pulse—and with "a slight movement of the chest being the only indication of life. They set about to resuscitate the almost lifeless body, by means of warmth, friction and the judicious use of stimulants." Miertsching, Kerr and Bow set off for *Investigator*, reported the incident to McClure, adding that their shipmate had "considerably recovered, but [was] unable to return to the ship." The captain at once dispatched Piers, Carpenter Ford, Caulker Evans, Carpenter's Mate Gauen, and two others with a sled. In the face of a strong northwesterly wind and snow drift, the ship and shore were soon lost to sight, so Piers chose to follow Sainsbury's sled track, "instead of resorting every few minutes to the pocket compass with which I was provided."[51]

After reaching the tent, Piers discovered Whitefield suffering from rheumatic pains, but he had recovered enough for traveling, and following a rest for the party, he was placed on the sled for the trip. The relief party arrived onboard about six in the evening. Dr. Armstrong "found the poor fellow much exhausted, suffering from reactionary fever and snow blindness; he was likewise extensively frost-bitten—from all which, he in due course recovered, but frequently told me he never after felt himself equal to the same amount of exertion."[52]

Shooting parties had continued to come and go, "but the sailors and marines, with one or two exceptions, were poor sportsmen, the sum total of their contributions to the general stock being in four weeks but 156 ptarmigan and seven hares." However, the first bear kill of the season was a high point, when Sergeant Woon and another man (part of a party of four that included Ford), came upon a bear asleep at the base of a large hummock, the creature having recently killed and eaten a seal. No sooner had Woon and his companion signaled the others to close on the scene, than the six-foot, four-inch bear was stirred from his slumber, and advanced toward the hunters, until the sergeant of Marines put a ball in the animal's forepaw and he fell. Immediately recovering from the blow, the bear made off for the eastern shore. "The others poured in their fire with effect, and followed up the chase for a considerable time, until the ferocious, but now frightened animal, sank to rise no more." He had taken nine balls before collapsing.[53]

On the same day (May 13), the thermometer dropped below zero for the last time, as the sun's rays worked to thaw the surroundings; the sudden loud noises of the extensive cracking ice (so often heard throughout the winter) gave the impression of an early breakup. In the days after, the "crew were busy repairing cables, sails, etc., and painting the ship and boats. Whitefield has recovered so well that he goes for walks on the ice near the ship."[54]

A week later, the last remnants of snow on the western shore had disappeared, while the strait's eastern coast was still painted a winter's scene. With none of the sledders yet due to return, the approach of men from the northward caused great commotion on the morning of the 20th, and a fatigue party struck out to assist. By 8:30 a.m., Lieutenant Cresswell's party again felt the wood of *Investigator* underneath its feet—excepting the two poor invalids on the sled—the reason for an early return.[55]

Cresswell and his men were absent 32 days, and during that time searched Banks Land, extending from the ship northward, and then to the northwest for about 80 miles (128 kilometers)—for a total of 170 miles (273 kilometers) in all. Particularly severe weather greeted them for the first two weeks in the form of sweeping northwesterly gales, and temperatures as low as 20° below zero, causing frequent frostbites. Cresswell described the northern limit as "presenting a very bold rocky front 1000 to 1200 or 1300 feet high, nearly perpendicular, with very heavy ice thrown or rather pressed some way up its side; and having this character, without bay or indentation, like a tremendous barrier for a distance of 60 or 70 miles [96 or 112 kilometers]" and "from the northern heights of Banks' land saw the loom of Melville Island."[56]

On May 5, Cresswell halted for two days to see if two very ill men would improve, but the poor souls languished. On the morning of the 7th Cresswell reached lat. 74° 16' N. and long. 117° 30' W., and then reluctantly began his retreat that evening. Before starting back, he and Calder ("his chief man") climbed up some high land and could see at about 10 miles distant, the coast veered more to the southward, and nothing but the ice of the northern sea. Overall, Cresswell could see the unknown coast running to the southward and westward, and so formed the opinion that he was traveling upon an island. The trusty Calder was ordered to oversee the erection of a cairn on the spot (which was in the vicinity of what were afterward named Cape Vesey Hamilton and Mercy Bay).[57]

Years later, McClintock recounted his experiences with the sled *Perseverance*, while on Melville Island in mid–June 1851, and wrote, "At the very time when I was upon the summit of Cape Dundas [directly across from the northeastern face of Banks Land], and anxiously scanning with my telescope the distant cliffs of Banks' land, a party from M'Clure's ship, the *Investigator* (then wintering in Prince of Wales's strait), was actually exploring them!" However, this was long after Cresswell's party had returned to *Investigator*.[58]

"For some days the two sick men took it in turn to ride on the sledge, but for about a week before their return to the ship both had to be carried, and Cresswell himself did work at the sledge." Armstrong related how the lieutenant spoke "in the highest terms of the patience, fortitude, and heroic endurance of these two brave sufferers Joseph Facey, (sail-maker) and Ellis Griffiths, (A.B.), who, when suffering intensely, still persisted in doing work; and it was only when rendered utterly incapable of walking that they consented to be placed on the sledge."[59]

> Their state on arrival was truly pitiable. Both were incapable of walking, and had to be carried on board. Facey had his feet and hands so severely frostbitten as to be quite unable to use either; mortification [gangrene] had set in, in nearly all the toes and fingers. Portions of several were subsequently removed by amputation; and the feet were in such a state, that it was only with the greatest difficulty they were saved. Griffiths, who was a most excellent man, was similarly, but less severely afflicted; and the removal of some of his toes became necessary. Both suffered much from low, irritative fever; and, from the effects of eating ice and snow ravenously, to allay the burning thirst then present, the mouth and entire [esophagus] were excoriated and inflamed to a high degree.[60]

Armstrong recalled how the "patience and resignation which [Facey and Griffiths] subsequently manifested throughout a long course of treatment were such as to call forth the warmest expressions of my admiration." It was 132 days before Facey was released from sick bay, while Griffiths spent 57 days in medical hands.[61]

The night after Cresswell's return, a large bear, measuring seven feet, nine inches and weighing an estimated 700 lbs., fell victim to the Investigators' guns. It was Dr. Armstrong's "custom to have the stomachs of all animals examined, in the hope of obtaining some trace of the object of our search, knowing that they would swallow anything when impelled by hunger." When the bear was opened up, "a few raisins, small pieces of pork fat irregularly cut, some tobacco leaves, and two pieces of common adhesive plaster" were discovered, "and the Captain, fearing that he would have got them from some other ship, and that the casualty may have happened to the 'Enterprise,' although a great distance from us, determined at once on despatching Cresswell and a party of men to the S. west tomorrow evening at 6 o'clock."[62]

Armstrong expressed the opinion that the items found in the bear's stomach were "so perfect and fresh" that they could not have been swallowed more than an hour or two beforehand. "No further investigation was made into the matter," added Armstrong. But Piers was also confident that[63]

> they must have come from our own ship. The Bear came up from the southward where, to and from the islands, Officers and men are going nearly every day; and what is more probable than that, since we have been in this position, raisins and pieces of pork may have been dropped or thrown away as bad, and the other things thrown away also. The Captain's measure may be prudent and on the safe side, but I have no apprehension for our lost consort from what "Bruin" had taken for supper.[64]

The next evening, Cresswell and his men departed, accompanied by a strong fatigue party, led by the captain and Armstrong, as far as one of the Princess Royal Islands. Though McClure showed (unusual) concern for Collinson and his men, and made what was evidently his only attempt to find the *Investigator*'s consort, oddly the captain's sensitivity did not extend to the second lieutenant and his sled crew. After only two days' rest, they had been detailed—

with two fresh hands and 20 days of supplies—for the new mission of following the coast as far as Nelson's Head in search of *Enterprise*.[65]

On the 24th, Queen Victoria's birthday saw an ensign run up at noon (for the first time since *Investigator* left the Bering Strait), while a 21-gun royal salute was fired from the ship's two guns and a small mortar. Three hearty cheers followed, and the ship's company was given a holiday, with the main brace being spliced that night.[66]

Fifteen minutes before midnight, the mystery surrounding the items discovered the other day was solved, when a party that had gone to the islands in pursuit of two bears returned onboard with, according to Armstrong, "a preserved meat tin, one of those used to point out the sledge track. To this [the men] were attracted by a Bear's track, when they found it capsized, and containing a few articles similar to those found in the Bear's stomach on the 21st, with marks of where the animal had been tossing it about." However, Henry Stone (the blacksmith and armorer) related a different explanation that was closer to home: "The captain's steward [Biggs] had thrown a tinful of refuse over the side, and the bear had sneaked up and done himself very well."[67]

Three days afterward, the first gulls were seen—being "a sure sign of cracks in the floe having already begun to show themselves. An early season it was; and officers and men longed for the open water that was to lead them, as they hoped, to Lancaster Sound."[68]

In the late morning of May 29, Haswell and his party returned all well to three hearty cheers after traveling about 600 miles (965 kilometers), "having remained out his forty-two days, thereby fulfilling his instructions to the letter." Seeing plenty of Arctic wildlife along the way, the party traced the continuous coastline, and "very nearly established the fact of the land on the S.E. side of the strait being part of Wollaston land." By May 14, Haswell was well along the northern shore of Prince Albert Sound "to latitude 70° 38' N., longitude 115° W., from which point, the day being remarkably clear, [he] observed the outline of land to the distance of [a] full forty miles trending to the S.W.; but having advanced twenty-five days, he considered it prudent to proceed no further." Just ten days later, John Rae—who was on his second Franklin search expedition—reached Cape Baring at the mouth of the sound, after exploring the southern coast of Wollaston Land. "Another proof," complained Armstrong, "if any were wanting, to show the necessity of searching expeditions acting in concert, and with a previous knowledge of each other's plan of operations." Of course, the good doctor ignored McClure's deliberate changing of plans to suit himself, and—as will be seen—inaccurate geographical awareness caused misconceptions.[69]

During Haswell's return journey, he came across many old remnants of Eskimo encampments, and when about six or eight days from the ship, encountered a group of some 18 Eskimos at the southern head of the strait (camped near what was afterwards named Berkeley Point). The sailors were unable to communicate with them, but presented them with a few uniform buttons, and in return they received a few well-prepared sealskins. According to what Piers was told, they "appeared to be of a different tribe to those we met along the coast of America, as they did not understand the nose-rubbing [method] of salutation, neither did they wear pieces of stone or bone below the angles of the mouth. They had ten tents pitched on the ice, six or seven miles off the land; were employed catching seals; and it is supposed from the number of tents that others must have been absent, probably hunting on land." These were Copper Inuit, and "were among the very last Canadian Inuit groups to be contacted by the outside world."[70]

McClure wasn't in the mind to leave the scope of any geographical discovery to chance, and "immediately decided upon proceeding to these people for the purpose of obtaining information that might determine the question relating to 'Prince Albert's,' 'Wollaston, and Victoria Lands,' as to their forming part of the American Continent, or whether each was an island."[71] In addition, Piers plainly stated that expectations regarding the outcome of Haswell's humane mission had been formed before he ever left:

> As to finding any of poor Sir John Franklin's people along the coast traversed in this direction, leaving the time of absence out of the question, no one expects [that] if he reached a position to the southward of [our] ship he might, without much difficulty, have reached Behring's Str. by the sea, or Canada by the Coppermine or Mackenzie rivers; and we know now that on these lands, and particularly to the southward, there is plenty of game of all descriptions.[72]

Taking 12 days' provisions and presents of red and blue flannel, knives, saws, needles, beads, etc., the captain left at six o'clock in the evening, accompanied by Miertsching ("our invaluable interpreter") and six men, including Captain's Coxswain Hulott, Carpenter's Mate Gauen, Able Seaman Carroll, Carpenter's Crew Whitefield. That night, due to Hulott's wearing canvas boots which were too tight and walking through pools of water on the floe (causing them to contract), his feet froze, so by "the following morning, when they encamped, the toes of both feet were quite rigid and frost-bitten." Despite his condition, he agonizingly dragged the sled until forced to give this up and walk, but was not carried on the sled until much later, due to the pace of travel.[73]

Restoring warmth to Hulott's toes was vital, but instead of rubbing them with the hand, "directions [surely from McClure] were most injudiciously given to rub them with concentrated spirits; this produced such violent local reaction, that inflammation set in of such an acute, unhealthy character, mortification [gangrene] ensued."[74]

McClure sighted the band of Eskimos in the early morning hours of June 3, camped in five tents on a small hill, some 10 miles north of where Haswell had encountered them. "I was in joyous excitement at the prospect of soon again seeing Eskimos, and could scarcely wait until I could speak to them," fondly penned Miertsching, "We drew ever nearer wondering whether these people would understand me and I them." The Brother shouted that they came as friends and brought rare gifts, but then—momentarily—his heart sank[75]:

> I drew near and took it as already certain that they did not understand my words, because they uttered no sound; then they raised a universal cry: "Sivoravogut! erksidlarpogut!" ("We are afraid!"). These were the first words which I heard from these folk and to my no small joy I also understood them.... Their language, nature, features, dress, and tools, etc., and, as it seemed, also their character, are just the same as in Labrador. Their harpoons, knives, hatchets, arrow-points, sewing-needles, etc., are all of good copper which they obtain pure from Eskimos dwelling farther east in exchange for seal-oil, walrus tusks, etc.[76]

These natives were taken aback when told other lands exist that are populated by human beings, and believed themselves to be the only men. "In all probability," wrote anthropologist Richard Condon, "McClure had encountered a group of Kangiryuarmiut (Prince Albert Sound people) [a Copper Inuit subgroup]. These people often traded with their southern neighbors, the Puivlirmiut, during the summers." To Miertsching's understanding, they "know nothing of a universal Creator. They have the same theory of the stars as the Cape Bathurst Eskimos: namely, that while they rest at night the sun looks down on the earth through little openings. Of a life after death they have the same idea as the Eskimos on the mainland shore, of Greenland and Hudson Strait: that there are two different lands—a good and a bad."[77]

After the Eskimos gained a level of comfort with the strangers, and had their curiosity satisfied through answers to many questions, Miertsching

> laid a large fold of paper on a great outstretched sealskin. On this I [had sketched] the position of the ship, the coast, and our route as far as their tents; and requested them now, after much explanation, most trying to the patience, to trace the coast from there on to the limit of their accurate knowledge. After about an hour the sketch was finished, and by the men as well as by the women who knew the coast it was declared good and perfectly correct. The shorelines indicated reached as far as Point Parry [in the vicinity of Cambridge Bay][78] on Victoria Land; also the two longest known islands of Sutton and Liston in Dolphin and Union Strait were marked quite correctly; according to their assertion, many Eskimos dwell on the coast to the south and southeast, and this they confirmed by naming capes and the families living there.[79]

"They described a large land opposite Wollaston, called 'Nunavak Saraluk'; this of course is America, to which they had never been, as they only trade with the Esquimaux to the S.E.," wrote McClure, and "I am also of opinion that 'Prince Albert's' Land is part of the continent of America, and that Point 'Peel' is its north-west extremity, and that the land from thence in continuous to Cape Walker."[80] The latter part of his opinion is evident on the chart (with Osborn's corrections) in McClure's 1856 book—and is misleading.

Being without one item of European manufacture, and having no knowledge of iron, the Eskimos used tools that were fashioned of copper, as were spear and arrow points. Understandably, the discharge of one of the guns satisfied their curiosity, while alarming them at the same time. An invitation was extended to visit the ship, and "a gun was offered to each of the men who would visit us, and other presents to the women. They promised to come, but perhaps the state of the ice subsequently prevented them."[81]

Miertsching was saddened when McClure gave the command to start for *Investigator*, not wishing "to part after so short a time from these simple folk who were so dear to me," as the weather was fine and the interpreter sought to stay a further half-day. McClure was certainly in the mind to stay longer, but "could not consent because of the ailing [Hulott], whose frozen feet were growing worse and more painful, so that he sat on the sledge in his stockings and had to be carried in and out of the tent."[82]

Miertsching distributed gifts, and among them, a small looking glass (mirror) particularly captured the Eskimos' fancy. They could not grasp the idea of gift-giving, and when Miertsching gave something away, the receiver invariably asked its value, with the intent of offering various homemade articles of copper in return. According to the Brother, McClure was "so grieved at leaving these loving people helpless in this frightful region of ice that he could not refrain from tears; he took off his thick red shawl and wound it around the neck to a young Eskimo woman who was standing near by with a child on her back." The shocked and embarrassed young woman said she had nothing to give in return, but then took from her hood her little child, and while still smothering the infant with kisses, presented it to McClure as payment. When Miertsching "declared to her clearly and emphatically that it was a gift, she looked at the captain in a very friendly manner and laughed, delighted that she could keep her child."[83]

These people only knew clothing of skins, and anything cloth or of similar materials were foreign to them, so they naturally assumed tent canvas, woven garments, papers, and the like, were the skins of different creatures. The shawl's "red skin" piqued the woman's curiosity—but any possible forthcoming explanation fell victim to the shortage of time, as the sailors took their leave at half past nine that morning. Despite bouts of gale-force rain and snow amidst temperatures that hovered in the low thirties, McClure made rapid progress back to the ship. During the final leg of the journey, with Hulott growing worse by the hour and squalls of rain frequently slamming into the party, the sailors often waded through knee-deep water.[84]

"On the evening of the 5th of June," wrote Armstrong, "we were much surprised on observing the approach of Captain McClure and party from the southward." The captain's party came onboard at seven o'clock with his coxswain suffering terribly, with advanced gangrene in the toes of the right foot. Hulott endured amputations on June 30 of all these toes, plus the big toe and part of the second toe on the left foot, and remained on the sick list for five months; for him, lamented Nelson, "this journey will ever be sadly remembered, for it has left him a cripple the remainder of his life, having to lose seven toes from frostbite." Whitefield was so exhausted from the experience he spent five days recovering in sick bay. Two days later, Miertsching recorded, "The captain caught a severe cold on his last journey, and now lies confined to his bed," so McClure paid a price for his kindness in giving away his warm shawl. And Miertsching continued with, "[T]wo of our travelling sailors, Dawn [Gauen?] and Caroll [sic—Carroll], are quite ill." The latter is difficult to understand, as neither man appears on the sick list.[85]

Dr. Armstrong laid down blistering words concerning the commander's recent travels: "[W]e could scarcely have believed until assured of the fact, that the journey was accomplished in somewhat less than half the time taken in its performance by Lieutenant Haswell—this, however, appeared to answer no other purpose, than that of instituting a comparison at the expense of the men." Armstrong accused McClure of wearing out and exhausting his men by the "rapidity and harassing nature of the march, without sufficient rest," for no other reason than to show his superiority over the slower-moving Haswell, who had returned with his men in good health and, if necessary, ready for additional service. And the doctor backed up his claim by distorting the truth, when he wrote "that one half were placed on the sick list on their return—(one of whom was severely frost-bitten)—and the remainder told me that they could not have continued the journey for six hours longer, at the same rate of travelling." Of course, of the six men, only two were admitted to the sick list, including Hulott.[86]

Miertsching made it clear that McClure did not stay longer at the Eskimo encampment because of Hulott's worsening condition; consequently, the captain understood it was critical to get his coxswain back to the ship as fast as possible. Armstrong must have realized the need for the speedy return (albeit through the sacrifice of the rest of the party), but by pointing out McClure's incorrect treatment of Hulott's frostbite, the doctor still placed blame for the whole situation on the captain's shoulders. For McClure's part, his official dispatch carried a self-assured gloss, while downplaying the injury to frostnip (the first stage of frostbite): "exceedingly gratified by the result of our pleasant excursion, our only misfortune being Cornelius Hullett, my coxswain, having both feet badly frost nipped." More telling is the absence in McClure's book (due to editor Sherard Osborn) of any mention of Hulott's sufferings.[87]

While the captain was away, the frequency of bear sightings increased, but they often could not be brought within range of the gun. Meanwhile, hunting parties continued to trawl the surroundings, netting ptarmigan, plovers, ducks, geese, hares and foxes. Wistfully thinking of home, Piers compared the western land before him to the arable land in England: "I was observing the furrowed [plowed] character of the land one day when Fawcett, who was with me, remarked it also. Moss and flowers grow on the hills; and the valleys are covered with the long, dead grass of last summer, and in a very short time will afford excellent pasturage." Four days later, on the fifth day of June, "we experienced the first rain of the season, which lasted for some hours."[88]

Also during this period, Carpenter Ford measured the ice, and found it at seven feet, a one-inch increase over the previous month. Despite this, with temperatures ranging from the low 30s to the high 40s, plus intermittent rain, it had very much decayed. Due to the rapid thaw and considerable water on the ice, in the days following, the whaleboat, tent and gear were collected from the eastern shore, and a tent from the western side, while McClure put a halt to the hunting parties.[89]

Wynniatt and his men made their appearance at five o'clock on the morning of the seventh, having been under the tent for 50 days. On May 26 they reached Reynolds Point, on the eastern side of what is today Wynniatt Bay. According to McClure's dispatch, Wynniatt's farthest position was determined to have been lat. 72° 6' N. and long. 107° 42' W., "from whence the land was observed for about fifteen miles tending to the N.E." Remembering that Wynniatt did not have a chronometer, McClure stated *dead reckoning* was used, which entails calculating one's position by using a previously determined position, or fix, and advancing that position based upon known or estimated speeds over elapsed time and course. Although this method can give the best available information on position, it is subject to significant errors due to many factors, since for position to be accurately determined, both speed and direction must be precise in all instances. How was this possible when pulling a sled over and around uneven ice? Piers twice left blank spaces in his journal for the coordinates of Wynniatt's furthest attainment—indicating uncertainty on this point.[90]

Up until Peel Point, the terrain remained flat, but "when upon crossing a deep inlet [later named Richard Collinson Inlet], the land then assumed a north-west aspect, when it became high, precipitous, and barren; no driftwood of any description was met with, but the ice lay against its base in heavy and unbroken masses." The party continued further east, and Wynniatt Bay was walked around, "having in it several small islands, with its southern shore formed of stratified cliff, having an elevation of about 800 feet." Despite their going around this bay, its outline on contemporary charts does not compare favorably at all to modern maps, and no doubt the lack of a chronometer was again at work. Finally, although not a single trace of Franklin was found, their experiences did include touches of comedy: "On the way, once or twice, foxes had emptied their provision sack while they were sleeping in the tent, and polar bears had walked off with shoes and clothing.[91]

Remembering McClure's misleading opinion about the land area between Peel Point and Cape Walker, there were some distorted views about sled journeys during this time, Wynniatt's being one of them. Ford wrote that Wynniatt "searched nearly to Cape Walker [on Russell Island], but could not reach it for want of provisions." Miertsching also stated Cape Walker was beyond the mate's grasp due to a shortage of provisions. In truth, Cape Walker was still hundreds of miles to the northeast of Wynniatt's furthest point, and even sufficient supplies would not have made the difference when crossing rugged sea ice. In McClure's 1856 book, editor Sherard Osborn stated that while he was commanding a sled party (the sled *True Blue*, HMS *Pioneer*, Austin's squadron at Griffith Island), he and Wynniatt came within only 50 or 60 miles (80 or 96 kilometers) of each other's turnaround points—however, this can

**A visitor in camp (George F. McDougall; "Facsimile of the *Illustrated Arctic News*," 1850).**

now be shown to be incorrect. Osborn wrote in his 1852 book that he decided not to continue his westward advance over rough sea ice, due to concerns the severely strained *True Blue* may break down. In addition, when his party again reached land, it was hit by another severe storm on May 21, and was held up in the tent until starting back on May 23. A study of Inglefield's 1853 chart, and the chart Osborn corrected in 1856, showed that the lack of geographical knowledge between what are now Prince of Wales Island and Victoria Island caused contemporary maps to be skewed, thus placing Wynniatt's and Osborn's turnaround points deceptively close to one another. The two points were really something like 160 miles (257 kilometers) apart; however, the distortion has survived in writings up until the present day.[92]

> Cresswell and his party returned about 8 a.m. [on June 10] and were received as usual with three hearty cheers. From the wet state of the ice everyone had been most anxiously expecting them the last few days, for it was very certain that they must have been wet both night & day for some time; so indeed it [was] found that they had been, and were all considerably exhausted, particularly Cresswell who had been obliged to get on the sledge for a few hours the last day or two; his voice too I perceived was feeble, notwithstanding all effort he made to appear in his usual state. [Private 3rd Class Thomas] King,[93] a Marine, has one of his legs much swollen & hard, and is placed on the sick list [the next day, where he remained for 76 days with periostitis, being inflammation of the periosteum, a layer of connective tissue that surrounds bone][94]: it has been inflamed & swollen some time previously, and will no doubt do well after a few days rest & support. Cresswell's feet & ankles are also swollen. They walked out two and a half days, Cresswell going six miles beyond Cape Lambton, the S.W. point of Baring's or Banks' land [just beyond Nelson Head], and in Lat. 71° 4,' Long. 123°[95] A day or two before reaching their farthest they had to ferry themselves, sledge & gear, by means of Halket's [*sic*] valuable portable boat, across two or three openings of the ice—one 25 or 30 feet wide—and the season otherwise, appeared much more advanced there than with us, although that was nine or ten days ago, and the weather here has been very warm during the last week.[96]

In writing to the Admiralty, Captain McClure gave proper credit to Cresswell and his men: "This party, with much spirit and zeal, performed their return journey of upwards of one hundred and sixty miles, in nine days and a half, under circumstances reflecting much credit upon them, the lateness of the season being unfavourable to so rapid an advance."[97]

In mid–June, large pools of water covered the ice, and streams constantly ran toward *Investigator*, forming the beginnings of a liquid cradle around her; except within the depressions of surrounding lands, the snow was no more. The air was alive with ducks, geese and gulls, and rain fell with greater frequency. Summer was well in the works.[98]

For George Ford, the future was clear: "We have now searched all around the part of the Arctic Sea that the Admiralty wanted us, therefore we have nothing more to do than go home, as if we are not so fortunate to find our countrymen we have discovered the N. West Passage & plenty of land." Henry Piers put the future to "one of our Quarter-Masters, the oldest man in the ship, and who was out in the last expedition; well May, what do you think of it; shall we get home or not this season? he answered, with a confident smile, 'get home sir! to be sure we shall: if we don't get through (or home, I forget which) this time we never shall.'"[99]

# 10

# The Trap Is Sprung! 1851

*The Ice Queen, wearing her crown and a wry smile, controls all.*
—Glenn M. Stein

Initially, Henry Piers focused on "simply" getting through the passage and going home:

[I]ndeed, if we have such weather for the next two months as we have been favoured with lately, the season bids fair for our accomplishment of "the North West Passage" and return home before another winter—which seems to be the anxious hope of every one on board.

This evening everyone is on board; watering & other work outside the ship is completed; spars &c are all in-board & stowed; royal masts are aloft; the decks are clear & clean; and with the exception of bending sails and shipping the rudder we are all ready for sea:—though I suppose it will be six weeks or two months nearly before sail will be of any service to us, for after the breaking up of the ice and before there is sufficient sailing water we shall have to experience driving, grinding, squeezing & rubbing, similar to what we had in the Autumn—but we have a good stout ship to stand it all, and if we only have water sufficient I have no doubt that this year will see us in England.[1]

Though he understood the dull and tedious nature of Arctic service wore on everyone, Piers pointed out that the officers had many comforts and resources the sailors and Marines lacked, "besides, the latter, being more or less ignorant of the true position of the ship [and] the prospect & chances of the voyage, are apt to conjure up imaginary dangers or adverse circumstances, or magnify real dangers; so that it is not surprising to find the men more anxious than the officers about our return to England this season."[2]

In recounting the highlights of the spring sledding season, the assistant surgeon's mood abruptly changed: "In the chief object of the expedition, however, we have as yet entirely failed," while McClure left no doubt in his writings to the Admiralty: "I am fully confident that the missing expedition under Sir John Franklin has never penetrated towards the Polar Sea in this direction." But as Piers continued, there was a realization of obligations left unfulfilled: "In the instructions to these ships ('Enterprise' & 'Investigator') attention is particularly directed, if I remember correctly, to [search] Melville Island and the west coast of Banks' land." In fact, Admiralty orders left it to Collinson's "judgment and discretion as to the course to be pursued after passing Point Barrow, and on entering the ice." More than likely, when Piers was made aware of McClure's intentions concerning Banks Land and Melville Island, he understood these to be Admiralty instructions.[3]

On a different level, the assistant surgeon insightfully revealed the politics of the Franklin Search—along with prophesying the inevitable:

Then, if instead of returning home this season we should winter more to northward, Melville Is. itself might form our quarters; or if we should be situated any where in Barrow's Str. [*sic*—Viscount Melville Sound]—not too far eastward—it is very probable that a party will go next Spring and examine it. But after all, in searching these places, I cannot but think, as I believe most others must, that it is to be done less with an idea of finding or saving Sir John Franklin and his unfortunate companions than of satisfying anxious relatives & friends and the public mind that all that is possible has been done to rescue them; for if they are not now known to be safe I fear it is long past with them.[4]

Events during the remainder of June played out in and around the Investigators' confined world. The summer solstice came on June 21 (the longest day of year), and by month's end the average temperature hovered in the low to mid-thirties, while the thickness of the ice shrank to 4'9½"—a decrease of 2'9½" over a mere 30 days. Presents of jackets, trousers, drawers, guernsey sweaters, Welsh wigs, comforters, mitts, boots and boot hose, were made to a welcoming ship's company. Ice Mate Newton's perch, the crow's nest, was put aloft to further ready *Investigator* to break out of her icy prison. From still loftier heights, the month's final Sunday service may have made a strong impression upon a higher power, as it certainly did so with Carpenter Ford: "I am happy to say I never saw so much attention by seamen in my life before, in fact, to take them generally they all conducts themselves very well when compared with other ships, an oath seldom heard among them."[5]

At night, Miertsching, Ford, and Sergeant Woon entertained one another through the strains of the flute, octave and guitar, while others amused themselves by sailing little home-made boats of cork or light wood and paper sails. One sailor, Able Seaman Samuel Relfe, turned "pirate" among this group of miniature yachtsmen, and "was chased by two or three men over the ice till between 10 and 11 p.m.—he however managed cleverly to destroy the whole fleet and elude his pursuers," chuckled Piers. "I saw him the next day going about half a mile off on the ice to fetch his boots which he had taken off in the chase. The fleet has not been rebuilt; and the mimic yachting is succeeded by kite flying and [the game of] pitch and toss." Miertsching painted the scene: "Because the sun, which never sets, makes night day, one sees as late as midnight twenty or thirty men on the ice busy flying paper kites of various form and colour; each one naturally asserts that his own is the best."[6]

But the sun surely *had* set on one of Relfe's former officers. When the Sussex-born Relfe joined the Navy in September 1841, he stepped on the deck of HMS *Formidable* as a boy 1st class, and within four years worked himself up to able seaman. Also onboard was Midshipman John Frederick Hornby, who was employed as mate on the 84-gun vessel until April 1844—a little less than a year later he found his destiny with the appointment as mate aboard the *Terror*.[7]

A promising omen appeared on July 7, when open water, about a mile wide, was spotted from the crow's nest, extending for some distance along the eastern shore. Two days later, a lane of water was spied extending from the large island to the western shore. Combined with temperatures that worked their way up to as high as 52°F in the days that followed, and aided by rain and sleet, the ice rapidly rotted in every direction; the currents and tides pushed great masses up on one another, until the pile toppled down. "The captain, who is sufficiently recovered to come on deck [on the 14th], mustered the crew and spoke to them earnestly: he bade each one to be ready, in the event of disaster, to leave the ship; the boats were to be kept ready, and supplied with necessities; and each man was ordered to have ready a travelling-bag containing woolen underclothing, two pairs of socks, gloves, scarf for the neck, needle, thread, and biscuit."[8]

*Investigator* cast off the floe and made sail late in the morning of the 17th for the first time in ten months. Rudderless among loose ice, due to several large floes being in the area, she found her freedom to be short-lived—by two o'clock she was made fast to another floe between the islands. Light southwesterly winds loosened the ice three days afterward, and McClure hoped the passage was within his grasp, so that he might carry out his original intentions of "proceeding to the northward of Melville Island, as detailed in my letter to the Secretary of the Admiralty on July 20th 1850, or should such not be practicable, return to England through the [Barrow] strait. The ship was cast off [with the rudder shipped for the first time[9]], and a mile gained when the wind died away and we were again beset on the morning of the 22d."[10]

Throughout the night and the morning, the drifting ice held the ship fast in its grip. About eleven o'clock, the sound of distant rolling thunder reached the ear, "but it was below, not above us—it was the ground-swell; and in its wake the great ice-fields were broken into smaller fragments. Soon the ice as far as we could see was in great commotion; pieces were thrust one upon another to a height of 34 feet, then collapsing like a house of cards." Sail was again made on the 24th, reaching a spot named Cape Armstrong (see Appendix 6) on the eastern side. There was so much driftwood here that a cutter was dispatched to collect a load; all American pine, some so fresh that Carpenter Ford believed it must have drifted from forests along the banks of the Mackenzie or Coppermine River in the last two years. "A serious and alarming difficulty now added to the anxieties of our navigators. The compasses, without any apparent cause, became exceedingly sluggish, and varied to such an extent in the dense fogs then prevailing, that it became impossible to tell which way they were going."[11]

Near July's final days (for the second time that month), another experimental ice blasting took place. A cask containing 46 pounds of powder was sunk under the approximately three-foot thick floe, to which *Investigator* was made fast. Eleven minutes after the match touched a Bickford's fuse, water and ice cascaded upwards to 100 feet in the air, leaving a gaping 25-foot hole in the floe, along with cracks snaking outward from it for 60 to 100 yards. "The blowing up concern is a complete failure," sighed Ford. "Beset and drifting all day north." The following day, July 29, "the captain requested a concert again, for—he said—to dispel the whimsies and boredom among the crew. The musical group consists of 6 men; 2 flutes, a violin, a concertina [similar to an accordion], guitar and a triangle."[12]

Sailing ... warping ... gradual northward progress. "Great anxiety seems to prevail," wrote Piers, "and there is also considerable fluctuation of opinions, in consequence of our slow progress through this strait; we certainly appear to have reached the [northerly] part of "the Passage," but there is yet plenty of time before us, and that the best; and I think if we can only get round point Peel into the easterly current of Barrow's strait [*sic*—Viscount Melville Sound] we shall never return the way we have come."[13]

The tedium—usually broken up by journal writing, drawing, and taking up musical instruments—was unexpectedly relieved one day, when a dramatic comedy unfolded:

A laughable scene occurred on deck this afternoon [August 6]. Our Captain, whilst walking the quarter deck, observed to the Officer of the Watch that he felt he heard a grinding noise & felt the ship shake. Thinking a piece of heavy ice was forcing itself under our bottom, this officer & several others immediately began to look round the ship in order to ascertain from whence the noise proceeded, when behold, on looking on the port sponson there lay our worthy son of Vulcan [Roman god of fire, i.e.— Blacksmith Henry Stone] fast wrapped in the arms of Morpheus [Greek god of dreams], snoring which proved the source of all the consternation. It made a fine joke for Jack to see his officers deceived in such a manner.[14]

A week later, McClure must have been feeling particularly optimistic when he announced to the crew that he hoped they would be in Lancaster Sound by September 15. Gunpowder finally helped things along: "It was by far the most satisfactory blasting operation performed by the ship, exhibiting the power of extensively fracturing large, heavy masses of ice ... and about 1 p.m. a light air springing up from about E.N.E., all plain sail was made on the ship, and with the assistance of warping for about an hour & a half, we were in clear water."[15]

The fog, which had accompanied *Investigator* on and off over the previous few days, cleared a little on the morning of August 15, very close to the base of cliffs on the eastern shore. Sail was made for open water to the west and gained the middle of the strait; but by 11:00 a.m., fog again blinded the explorers. *Investigator* was made fast to a large and heavy floe, after having her spanker boom carried away while maneuvering through a narrow bit of ice. Ford labored for nine hours to fish the spar out and reposition it on the mizzenmast.[16]

The following morning, with the ship not more than a tantalizing 25 miles from Viscount Melville Sound (lat. 73° 43' 43" N. and long. 115° 32' 30" W.),[17] the Arctic had won again— *Investigator* could go no further. The ship was about 12 miles to leeward of Point Lady Ross,[18] when McClure realized

> at 9 a.m., all hopes disappeared, as [Newton's[19]] clear view from the crow's nest discovered the ice to be closely packed, resting upon Point Lady Ross, extending one unbroken line to the opposite side of the strait. This determined me to give up all idea of prosecuting our search in this direction, having been foiled in attempting this passage the latter end of one season, and commencement of another.... accordingly, at 9:30 a.m. we bore up with the intention of running to the southward of Nelson's Head, and continue our search along the western side of Baring's Island [Banks Land], with the hope of reaching the entrance of Barrow Strait [sic—Viscount Melville Sound] by that route; as from the report of Lieutenant Cresswell, I felt convinced that by Bank's Land there is a passage from the Polar Sea.[20]

According to Miertsching, "The captain made up his mind in a moment: he put the ship about, hoisted all the sail he dared, and away we went to the south, ploughing through so fast that the water foamed around the bowsprit and washed back over the foredeck."[21]

But Dr. Armstrong observed that all wasn't carefree: "As we were about to bear up, two ravens made their appearance. Some thought they were our visitors of the winter—they continued for some time ominously hovering over and about the ship, describing circles in their flight, and uttering their harsh, discordant croak, which did not, in any degree, tend to produce comfortable feelings amongst the more superstitious portion of our crew, their presence being considered an ill omen; and in our subsequent days of adversity, the event was often alluded to as proof *that we should not have abandoned the Strait of Prince of Wales.*"[22]

It was only two and half hours before the Princess Royal Islands came into sight; the ship passed them at four o'clock. The clear weather allowed for magnificent views of both shores, which for Miertsching reminded him very much of the hilly country about Herrnhut,[23] in the Görlitz district of eastern Saxony. Even Armstrong's mood had changed: "How different were our feelings as we sped gaily along,[24] through a large expanse of water, with every stitch of canvas set to a fine, fresh and fair breeze, compared with a period still recent, when we were either immoveably beset, helplessly drifting, or boring our way inch by inch through a heavy ice pack that had entirely disappeared."[25]

Very early on the morning of the 17th, *Investigator* cleared the strait, and was greeted with a strong southeasterly breeze and accompanying heavy swell; in the distant south, a narrow ribbon of ice was stitched into the horizon. Making six to eight knots, the ship rounded Nelson's Head at 11:00 p.m., where the ocean's swell brought on several cases of seasickness. McClure described the land being "remarkably bold and lofty" for about 25 miles to the westward, "from which it gradually recedes to the N.W., where it loses this bold character, partaking more of that remarked in the Prince of Wales' Strait, being ranges of hills gradually sloping from the interior to the shore, having valleys and extensive plains, several small and one considerable river, the water from the latter discolouring the sea two miles from its mouth." During the night Cape Lambton fell astern.[26]

At this point in his translation of Miertsching's journal, historian Leslie H. Neatby commented that McClure intended to "sail through the Passage and circumnavigate the Americas after all—a questionable choice: the continental shore lay not far to the south, offering reasonable assurance of a safe exit by [the] Bering Strait, and at the worst a safer refuge than the islands if the ship came to grief; on the other hand the extent of Banks (Baring's) Land was quite unknown, its northern shore likely to be infested with "the frightful polar pack."[27]

However, McClure had written to the Admiralty that he intended "proceeding to the northward of Melville Island, as detailed in my letter to the Secretary of the Admiralty on July 20th 1850, or should such not be practicable, return to England through the [Barrow] strait."[28] His ship was in good condition and his crew healthy, so to retreat through the Bering Strait could well have been seen as unacceptable—not only to naval authorities, but perhaps also in the public's eyes. In addition, McClure had already been part of two failed expeditions, so this was his last opportunity to make his mark in history, gain promotion, and achieve fame and (possibly) fortune. McClure's ego would have never let him pass up the opportunity to sail the North-West Passage. No, retreating through the Bering Strait certainly was *not* an option for Captain Robert John Le Mesurier McClure!

Without once being opposed by the ice, the *Investigator* had an extraordinary run of 300 miles on the 18th. Waterfowl by the thousands, especially white snow geese, littered the shore, and telescopes scanned the coast, hoping to discover anything connected with the missing expedition. McClure did pause for Court to examine what turned out to be "an excellent and commodious harbor" at the newly named Kellett Point (afterwards Cape Kellett), occupying the southwest corner of Banks Land. A cask containing a notice in a bottle was deposited here (lat. 71° 56' N. and long. 125° 29' W.).[29]

As the ship worked her way up the western coast, the land changed, becoming high and rugged, with steep cliffs, and crisscrossed by deep ravines and waterfalls. But as Piers described, it also eventually included ground that was "tolerably wooded and has an exhuberant [sic] vegetation"; this among temperatures ranging from 43° to 51°F. Armstrong wrote the character of the ice changed as well, becoming much heavier, with many bergs grounded inshore, and "the soundings had increased considerably, [so that] we could not feel otherwise than convinced, that we had got into water which would lead us to Melville Island." The ship then went from having all her studding sails set to Court's sounding ahead, the Investigators warping their ship, or on several occasions, using poles to keep away from grounded ice: they were coming face to face with the Beaufort Sea's unrelenting ice stream (see Arctic Ice Stream Map). When McClure reached the northwest tip of Banks Land on August 20, he graced it with the name Cape Prince Alfred (in honor of His Royal Highness); along the way, Meek Point, Liot Point, Norway Island and Robilliard Island were among the places that found their way onto the map.[30]

One place name between Kellett Point and Meek Point has a curious history—Haswell Point. One source indicates it first appeared on an 1854 Admiralty chart, and though it can still be found on maps and in references today, it *did not* appear in McClure and Armstrong's books, or on the maps within them. While McClure named various features after people, the fact he didn't name anything after his first lieutenant is further evidence of his disdain for the man. So, how *did* Haswell Point come to be on the map? One clue may be Captain Kellett's recommendation in Haswell's service record (see Haswell Point, Appendix 6).[31]

Further up the coast, Cape Collins first appeared on the same Admiralty chart, although neither McClure nor Armstrong mentioned it in their writings. Situated east of Norway Island, this cape was probably named in memory of Second Master Henry Foster Collins, of HMS *Erebus*.[32]

In the naming of Gore Island off Cape Prince Alfred, McClure memorialized his former Arctic companion, Mate Graham Gore, from the 1836–37 expedition in HMS *Terror*. Afterwards, Gore was first lieutenant on Franklin's *Erebus*, having been promoted to commander following the expedition's departure.[33] When McClure inked his old shipmate's name on the chart, Gore had already been dead for over three years.[34]

With the shore ice blocking the way ahead for *Investigator* on the 20th, and heavily packed to the northeastward along the coast, the ship secured to an iceberg at 5:10 that morning; grounded in 12 fathoms (72 feet) of water, it was about 20 feet high, and around seventy yards from the beach. "Mr. Sainsbury discovered on shore a small mountain with trees covered in sand on its summit, about 300 ft. high, some petrified into stone. We got one piece 6'10" long, mean girth 3'8"," observed Ford, who also marveled: "The scenery inland is really beautiful, hills, vallies [*sic*] & lakes all round, as bare as a rock."[35]

Written on the reverse of Wynniatt's calling card from HMS *Nimrod*: "Petrified Wood from the Fossil Forest in the Arctic Regions. Brought Home by RJ Wynniatt, [illegible] of the Investigator Ship—<u>August —1853</u>—" (Marsha P. Stein, 2015; Glenn M. Stein Collection).

Piers was ashore for some time, "with Paine & Wynniatt; then Wynniatt having gone on [back,] I met with Court ... [and] Sainsbury having come up & told us of his having found a quantity of petrified wood, showing at the same time some he had collected, we started off in search of some for ourselves after the direction of the place had been pointed out to us. While in search of the place, a Marine came to us with a couple of haversacks, and directions from the Captain to bring off all we could find of the wood or as much as we could carry."[36]

The assistant surgeon also provided the merest taste of what the ice stream offered the Investigators: "In the evening a very heavy pressure came on the berg we are fast to, forcing it 8 or 10 ft. higher out of the water [and the ship with it], and of course nearer to the shore. Among other ice which drifted against our berg was a very large floe which made it roll and surge greatly, so that it was only by nice attention to the slackening & tightening of the hawsers that we held on; and had we been parted from the berg we must doubtless have been forced on the shore." And then the white giants paused their assault.[37]

The following afternoon, a bear was seen coming toward the ship, and McClure gave permission for two officers to go ashore and shoot him. Piers and Sainsbury volunteered, landed, and laid in wait behind a mound of shingles. The beast was about 70 or 80 yards from its executioners, when

> Sainsbury—although I had been urging him not fire till the bear came within 20 yards of us, so that there might not possibly be any failing in our knocking him down at once—would fire; his shot struck him in the neck, but only grazed him; for turning round a little he saw us, and, shaking his head & grinning, ran towards us. We were now, both of us, standing on the top of the mound, and seeing us

**Critical position of *Investigator*, Aug. 20, 1851 (S.G. Cresswell, 1854).**

awaiting his approach with our guns presented—for whatever Sainsbury did, I was determined not to fire till he came within ten or 20 yards of us—bruin altered his mind when he had advanced about 20 yards towards us: he then stopped & turned, and knowing he would now beat a retreat I let go at his broad side which then presented itself; Sainsbury fired his second shot a moment afterwards, and was followed by two or three shots from the ship: he then fell; either from the last shot from the ship (Haswell's I believe) being more fatal than the rest or the effect of the several which he received. Sainsbury then ran up & thrust a pike into poor bruin's chest, which however was perfectly useless as the brute could not move: [Sainsbury] was called to from the ship, as I also did myself, not to do so, but he persisted in making bruin's dying moments short, and placing his death beyond a doubt.[38]

Seals, deer, musk ox, wolves, foxes, and hares, as well as a variety of birds, were among the wildlife that presented the summer scene, and in an effort to cope with the idleness onboard, McClure sent 37 men with a large net about a mile inland toward two or three freshwater lakes. However, after five hours of labor, the Investigators returned cold and wet, having netted only a few fish. In spite of the active surroundings, strong northwesterly winds, snow and sleet at intervals, and average temperatures hovering at 30°F or below, hinted at the approaching gloom: "Young ice forms at night now, and we shall soon have the dreary winter coming on us again," sighed Henry Piers.[39]

The crew having been deprived of fresh meat for some time, hunters went abroad. Ford and Boatswain Kennedy went ashore, and shortly afterward saw a musk ox. The pair were within 70 yards of the animal, when Dr. Armstrong joined them. "The doctor & boatswain fired but missed. I gave chase to cut him off & after chasing him about 12 or 14 miles over hill[s] & valleys he beat me fair. I was running & walking from 1 p.m. to 8 p.m. which made me pretty tired when I returned on board." Having joined a different party, Kennedy shot at another musk ox, and in the process of "reloading his gun, having put the powder in the barrel carelessly, he placed the muzzle against his abdomen, and searched for a ball. The powder exploded, burned his clothes, and scorched him severely, to his extreme alarm and that of his companions, who discontinued the chase to bring, as they supposed, a dying man on board— he believing his last hour was at hand. They reached the ship in a most affrighted state, and it was with difficulty he could be persuaded that his wound was not mortal."[40]

But August 29 nearly brought *Investigator* to *her* mortal conclusion. For Miertsching, "it was a day filled with anxiety and terror such as neither I nor anyone aboard has yet experienced." The stillness of the ice during the previous week was replaced at eight o'clock that morning with its sudden movement to the eastward, and within half an hour, all hands were required on deck to keep *Investigator* moored to the iceberg. Then, "at 9, heavy pressure came on the berg to which we were attached, carried it from its grounded position completely round, and raised it some twenty-five feet out of the water; presenting a most frightful aspect, overhanging the ship nearly as high as the fore-yard," marveled Armstrong in trembling awe. Breathless moments followed. The ship could have been dashed to pieces, but "the floe split, and the berg giving one or two appalling rolls, bore us with it into deeper water, and into the midst of heavy ice in the wildest commotion—both were driven onward with the moving masses, the berg being then afloat and incapable of resisting further pressure." *Everything* depended on *Investigator* remaining connected by rope and chain to the berg—otherwise she would be driven ashore. So the ship "was still further strengthened by one nine inch, three six and two five inch [hawsers], and a stream chain, two of which were passed round it and secured."[41]

"During the day, tents and all necessary implements were put into the boats in case of renewal of the pressure, and any accident, requiring an immediate abandonment of the vessel, happening to us: a 'whip [crane]'[42] was also ready on the main-yard for hoisting provisions &c out on the ice, and after the men's supper all hands were called on deck; every one stationed to boats and ordered with his allotted clothes, to be ready to leave the ship at a moment's notice."[43]

The ship had withstood considerable pressure, especially upon her stern and rudder (the latter being severely damaged), and several huge masses of ice became submerged underneath *Investigator*. She was cradled in ice at about a 15-degree list; her bow had risen three feet, and her stern nearly five. Helpless, the crew waited for the Ice Queen's next move. In the meantime, it was imperative the rudder was unshipped from around several heavy blocks of ice so it could be repaired—an extremely difficult task only accomplished after hours of labor by pickaxe and ice chisel—and ultimately, blasting. The rudder was then "laid upon a large floe piece, where by 8 p.m. owning to the activity of Mr. Ford, the carpenter, who is always ready to meet any emergency, it was repaired just as the ice began again to be in motion."[44]

A specific threat was directly in the *Investigator*'s course astern. It was a piece of floe, grounded in nine fathoms, among debris gathered at a river's mouth. If this threat wasn't dealt with, the ship would be crushed between this piece of ice and the one she was fast to, so McClure had to take action[45]:

> I sent John Kerr, (gunner's mate,) under very difficult circumstances, to endeavour to reach it, and effect its destruction by blasting. He could not, however, find a sufficient space of water to sink the charge, but remarking a large cavity upon the sea face of the floe, he fired it there, which so far succeeded that it slightly fractured it in three places, which at the moment was scarcely observable from the heavy pressure it was sustaining. By this time the vessel was within a few feet of it, every one was on deck in anxious suspense, awaiting what was apparently the crisis of our fate. Most fortunately the sternpost took it so fairly that the pressure was fore and aft, bringing the whole strength of the ship to bear a heavy grind which shook every mast and caused beams and decks to complain, as she trembled to the violence of the shock, plainly indicated that the struggle would be but of short duration.[46]

"[The] bells rung or chattered," remembered Piers, "the Boatswain, who was confined to his bed, dressed himself and came on deck, for he told me afterward he could not remain below, as he expected every minute 'a visitor' in cabin—and we all know when there is any great pressure on the ship, the cracking, creaking and various noises attending it are much more distinct below than on deck. Biggs too, a Marine and Captain's steward, thinking the cabin was coming in, seized the Captain's packed carpet bag and ran to the ladder with it."[47]

McClure was bitter with resignation: "'Our fate seemed sealed.'" He ordered all the ropes let go, having made up his mind that in a few minutes *Investigator* would be thrust onshore, "where she could still afford us food and shelter for the coming winter," wrote Miertsching. "Before this order could fully be carried out—in the most awful moment of our lives—the ice became silent and motionless. This memorable moment was almost too much for us; each man rested against the bulwarks of the listing ship, and, pale and trembling all over, stared at his comrade, who stared back at him; not a sound or a word could be heard, so that on the ship there reigned a death-like calm."[48]

It was then that McClure believed "a merciful providence interposed, causing the ice, which had been previously weakened, to separate into three pieces, and it floated onward with the mass, our stern still tightly jammed against but now protected by it." *Investigator* then swung upright and settled into the water, and "the only damage sustained were several sheets

**Using an ice saw to cut out of winter quarters during the 1875–76 British Arctic expedition; note the additional ice implements in the right foreground (William H. Overend,** *The Illustrated London News,* **May 29, 1875).**

of copper ripped off and rolled up like a sheet of paper, but not a fastening had given way, or does any leakage indicate the slightest defect."[49]

After a night of comparative calm, the next day the Investigators set to work "by blasting, by pickaxe and all the usual ice implements, with the view of making a good bed for the ship, in the probable event of her being thrown on it; and likewise a road to shore, then not sixty yards distant." To Armstrong, "the appearance of our men on the ice, like so many engineers, sapping and mining, presented a feature of some novelty."[50]

The final day of August 1851 brought the report of a small space of water outside the floe from Ice Mate Newton in the crow's nest—but that was all. Winter now stalked the expedition, and it seemed *Investigator* wasn't going anywhere. "Since this occurrence," penned Brother Miertsching, "I have had long and pleasant conversations with several of my shipmates: the captain told me yesterday and again—openly—today that he has arrived at the genuine conviction that a Higher Power, an Almighty Providence, is watching over and shielding us, and that under this protection none of us will lose our lives, but all will safely reach our fatherland; of this he felt certain."[51]

On the commencement of September, McClure spoke to his assembled crew at length, and "reminded them of the gracious protection granted the ship and with much kindness and the deepest sincerity admonished them to keep this miraculous deliverance in mind, and not to be despondent or lose heart at the onset of another winter season.... In conclusion he said that he would do his utmost to make life happy for everyone of them."[52]

In a collective voice, Piers wrote:

[F]rom our peculiar position and the circumstances under which we ran into it, many are inclined to think that we shall not have a chance either of advancing or retreating any more this season; and if so, that our prospect of getting out of the ice next summer by Behring's Str.—for it is presumed any further attempt to force "the Passage" will not be made—is less promising than was that of last season with respect to our making "the Passage" this year—the idea being, that if the ice does not leave the shore again this season—and the chances are it had not been off it far, or long, before the 20th Aug., when we were stopped—it either may not release us at all next summer, or till so late in the season that we cannot round P^t Barrow before the setting in of a third winter.[53]

With the expectation of possibly wintering, so that his men could be afforded rest here-after, McClure ordered that ballast for the ship be collected from the beach; consequently, this part of Banks Land acquired the name Ballast Beach (lat. 74° 25' N. and long. 122° 32' 15" W.). "[E]verything spoke of winter; yet the position of the ship was too insecure a one to justify the Captain in making any of the preparations for sheltering the men from its rigour, such as clearing decks and spreading housing, lest some fresh movement in the ice should require the vessel to be again placed under canvas." Over the next week and a half the temperature dropped to a low of 16°F, and the aurora borealis peeked through the night sky for the first time. "We go ashore daily to get game for our winter supply, but in these icy regions there is little or nothing to be found. The climate must been milder here formerly," pondered Miertsching, "for everywhere one finds very old bones and skulls of wild animals, and the ruins of houses; tenting-laces and caches are proof that this region was once popu-lated."[54]

All remained quiet until the tenth, when a "raven was seen flying about here today." Then, the wind shifted from the east to the south, sending temperatures rising from 25° to 39°F, with rain squalls. The change eventually developed into a dark and sinister night of gale-force winds. Just before midnight, the officer of the watch and Quartermaster Henry May went out to examine the tide pole (which was planted on the beach, through a hole cut in the ice). May found it could not be steadied, and upon looking around the dark surroundings, discovered open water only a few feet away, extending to the land—the ice holding *Investigator* had broken away from shore![55]

The brutal winds spirited *Investigator* off into the darkness—and towards the pack—keeping the apprehensive and helpless souls onboard in suspense until daylight. Solemnly, McClure wrote in his journal, "Thus we launch into this formidable frozen sea. *Spes mea in Deo* [God is my Hope]."[56]

When the first rays of sunlight stabbed the morning sky, they revealed the ship still beset and drifting a knot per hour eastward, about a mile offshore in 107 to 134 fathoms (642–804 feet), and only 20 or 30 yards from the pack's inner edge. Water was seen from the crow's nest, extending along the land to a point in the distance later known as Colquhoun Point (just west of Cape Wrottesley); offshore of this point, it was supposed the ice packed up due to a shoal. No land was seen further on, but there was a strong ice blink,[57] and from this it appeared the coastline took a southeasterly trend.[58]

In recounting the day, Ford was not shy in his admiration for McClure:

[W]ith blowing & blasting the ice we extricated the ship just in time to get inshore again having gone 20 miles. Evening (dark) just as I went to bed the ice closed & began to nip the ship, therefore it was all hands secure & save the ship. We secured her all safe, but next time I turned in all standing (cloth[e]s on) as it don't give time to put on cloth[e]s & was it not for the good judgement of our Gallant Captain & a strong ship we should not stand it a minute, as his cool, deliberate manner in hours of danger would win the heart of every well-disposed sensible man & if danger gave riches we should be Jews as danger is looking at us in the face pretty often but our consolation is there is one above watches over all our movements & unto Him I trust for my safety. We are now close to the shore in 7 fathoms water, fast to a heavy floe aground, not knowing a minute where we shall go or where we are going to spend a long dreary winter.[59]

The cat-and-mouse game continued between ship and ice—with liberal amounts of powder having been used by the Investigators. "The person that was going to blow up fifteen miles a day in this country speculated rather too far as there is a difference between fireside plans & speculations in England & practical operations in the Arctic regions," pointedly commented Ford. In addition to the sailors and Marines being mocked by the ice, Armstrong notes that "we were again visited by the ominous croaking Raven, which some of our men affirmed, had followed us from the Prince of Wales Strait."[60]

On the 15th, Court and Newton were sent to Colquhoun Point (nine miles distant), to determine the amount of inshore ice further to the east: "They returned in the evening with the report that beyond the cape the coast takes a south-easterly trend and is beset with heavy ice ["but no appearance of bay or harbour was to be seen"].[61] The captain has long believed that this Baring's Land must be an island between which and Melville Island a broad channel leads into Barrow Strait [*sic*—Banks Strait]; should this prove true we have discovered *two* Northwest Passages."[62]

Three days later, it required only 66 lbs. of powder to shake the loose ice from around *Investigator*, and she floated free at four in the afternoon. With no ice on the lee or seaward sides, all that was needed was to set sail—or so it seemed. That evening, according to Armstrong, preparations to get under way were suspended, "the wind being considered too strong to effect much in working to the eastward, although the water at the time, with the exception of its surface being rippled by the wind, was as smooth as a pond."[63]

At this point in his book, Dr. Armstrong was biting in his egotistical criticism of McClure:

Thus was another splendid opportunity of making easterly progress lost. Our proceedings, in not taking immediate advantage of the chances we had of creeping along the coast, since the 10th of September, appeared, at this time, characterized by a degree of indecision, entirely at variance with our previous operations. We seemed willing to go, but loath to depart. Had we promptly taken advantage of all the favourable circumstances that presented, and which I have truthfully narrated, exactly as they occurred, we must have been many miles distant from the position we then occupied. There was no safety in this position we could not have enjoyed, in a greater, or at least, an equal, degree, on any other part of the coast, which could not have been much worse; indeed, I am sure there was nothing in the locality that should have made us so attached to it. I am firmly of opinion, that our tardiness on these several occasions, where an easterly advance, however trifling, was of vital consequence, and when opportunities occurred for making it, exercised a fatal influence on the voyage of the "Investigator."

...[I am] deeply regretting our lost opportunities, when every foot of easterly advance was invaluable, but utterly unable to explain the reason why.

Our situation was then extremely exposed and dangerous—so is every part of this coast—from being quite unprotected to seaward, whence the ice might at any moment assail us, from any slight cause.[64]

Although Armstrong was indeed a very intelligent man, he was not a sea officer, nor did he possess the previous Arctic experience of McClure, Court, or even Cresswell. In addition, without even taking into account the varying conditions of wind, rain, fog, tides, and currents, the character of the Beaufort Sea ice was altogether different from that of the ice thus far encountered by *Investigator*. This was specifically remarked upon by Piers: "Where is the heavy ice, like that we saw along the N.W. coast of Banks' land, formed? We have witnessed nothing like the formation of heavy ice on any of the coast."[65]

Though there was indeed a sense of urgency in getting *Investigator* as far as possible to the east to suitable winter quarters, perhaps McClure also knew he had pushed his luck as far as it would go when rounding Banks Land, so *caution* was the word of the day.

Miertsching and Piers's writings offer comparisons to Armstrong's thoughts about the situation on September 18. The former wrote: "At 7 a.m. it began to blow hard, and so lasted all day, in consequence of which the ice began to churn up, and we had the joy of seeing open water in the distance." And Piers: "This morning the same wind is blowing a good double-reef topsail breeze, and there is a sea of water two miles or more in width outside us, extending as far as can be seen.... At 2 p.m. it was commenced to ship the rudder and blast with powder an outlet for the ship, which was all done before 4 p.m.... We are still holding on to our fender [of ice], ready to take advantage of the wind becoming more S[ly] [southerly] so as to get on to the E'ward, and with the intention of starting tomorrow morning at daylight if the same wind continues."[66]

Two days later, *Investigator* rounded the some 80-foot-high Colquhoun Point, but "progress was slow from many causes; the copper being torn, and projecting from four to twelve inches from the bottom, light winds, and an ice-encumbered sea.... Our day's work did not exceed fifteen miles, when we were compelled to make fast to the land ice, which along the whole of this coast is of the most massive and terrific dimensions I have ever witnessed," explained McClure in his dispatch. At about 100 feet in height, the somewhat higher Cape Wrottesley—the most northern point on Baring Island (lat. 74° 30' N. and long. 121° 30' 50" W.)—was named the next day.[67]

On Sunday, September 21, an open lane of water inshore beckoned the explorers, and between sail and warping, the some 400-foot Cape Austin boldly came into view (in honor of Captain Horatio Austin—see Appendix 6). Miertsching wrote, "[T]oday Divine Service made a great impression, not [likely] to be forgotten, on everyone."[68]

Cape Crozier—subsequently named to perpetuate the memory of the much traveled polar explorer Captain Francis R.M. Crozier, of HMS *Terror*—was a 250-foot perpendicular headland that *Investigator* was secured under the following day. This cape featured "amongst its debris many interesting geological specimens," wrote McClure. "It is composed of lime and sandstone, having fossiliferous shells imbedded; also pieces of coal and petrifications of wood, identical with what has been met with upon other parts of this large island, and upon the 'Princess Royal' Isles." Piers's observations pointed the way forward: "Land can now be seen about 25 or 30 miles distant in an E.S.E. direction—supposed to be about Cresswell's farthest [during his sled journey last spring]." Cresswell's farthest point (later named Cape Vesey Hamilton) was at least twice the distance, and along the way the coast changed direction, trending to the northeast.[69]

During this period, Dr. Armstrong set down in his journal a seemingly oddly worded objection to *Investigator*'s sailing along this coast:

It would be foreign to my purpose, to speak here, of what the nature of our purpose along this part of the Coast, which affords neither shelter nor refuge from the terrible foe (ice) and those elemental forces which so ruthlessly assailed us. Suffice to say that difficulties were encountered, obstacles overcome, and perils and dangers threatening momentary destruction, were happily and Providentially averted, such, I am sure as the actors in this eventful crime [emphasis added], can never cease to remember, and of which the annals of Arctic voyaging can furnish no such parallel.[70]

Shortly afterward, in reference to discoveries in the Prince of Wales Strait, Armstrong used a very similar phrase, but this time was all-inclusive:

Having now taken a hasty glance at the general features of the land which it was our good fortune to discover, it only remains for me to note the existence of two small islands, in the center of the Strait on which the name of the "Princess Royal" was bestowed, and which occupy a prominent place in the history of our eventful crime [emphasis added], from the triple collectivity they have attained. 1st From the fact of our having spent the first winter in their vicinity. 2nd From their having on several occasions threatened the utter destruction of the ship from our proximity to their adamantine precipitous [unbreakable and dangerously steep] sides, having been on two occasions carried toward them when assailed by ponderous ice floes in wild and terrific motion, and 3rd From their great Geological interest, as affording ample evidence of the fossiliferous character of the lands, which I was not afforded an opportunity of personally examining, but which I assume to be similar to the specimens obtained at these islands.[71]

At 3:30 in the morning on the 23rd, the horizon's darkness to the seaward told of open water, and *Investigator* was cast off. The wind fell off by about 10:30, so the boats were lowered and the ship was towed for the next hour, until a west-southwest breeze came to the rescue, allowing studding sails to be set and *Investigator* to speed along at about eight knots (which dropped to five later on). "The prospect is the most cheering we have had for the last five weeks," beamed Piers, "though I fear from the wind hauling so quickly round towards W. that the pack will again soon close & stop our short [cruise]. A thick fog has come on with the S.W. wind ... and about 5.40 [p.m.] we ran through a passage, between the land ice and a point of the main pack—all very heavy stuff—not much broader than the ship herself." What appeared to be three good harbors were passed, but a line of thin ice hugged the shore, blocking their entrances.[72]

"The sea before us and on all sides covered with ice was still opening up ahead. Finally the ice-pilot [Newton]," according to Miertsching, lost his nerve, and "quitting his post aloft without leave, apologized to the officer of the watch and said that he could no longer endure to be aloft: all was ice ahead and not a spoonful of water to be seen, yet the ship was speeding on without hindrance, as could be plainly observed from the land features which we were leaving behind us; he could not bring himself to ascend again to his post aloft."[73]

McClure noted that "the shore shortly trending more to the southward, increased our water, but snow and thick weather, with the night coming on, rendered the land, not two hundred yards distant, barely discernible. Most anxious, however, at the close of the season to embrace every opportunity of getting to some place of security, our course was continued with easy canvas, when under other circumstances we should have most assuredly secured for the night."[74]

To Piers's understanding, "At 8 p.m. we were to have borne up for Melville Island."[75] But before that time came,[76] and just after the leadsman reported 15 fathoms, *Investigator* ran onto a shoal during a thick snowstorm, which McClure named Providence Point.[77] With her bow elevated eight feet above the surface, the water's depth was "only six feet under the bow, and

*Investigator* nearing Mercy Bay (Smyth, after S.G. Cresswell, *The Illustrated London News*, Oct. 29, 1853).

at the distance of ten feet from the stern only eighteen inches, while the stern was in five fathoms; the stream anchor and cable were laid out, which service," penned McClure, "was well performed by Messrs. Wynniatt, Sainsbury, and Court, it requiring four boats in consequence of the freshening N.W. gale, and pieces of loose ice with snow, which, caking as it reached the water, formed so thick a coating over its [surface], and offering such resistance, that it was scarcely possible to pull through."[78]

After the boats were brought in, for some time all of the Investigators' strength was thrown into the capstan—but to no avail. Next, the forehold and warrant officers' storerooms were cleared (all of this weight being brought to the after part of the ship), and water pumped out forward. These tasks were "very nearly completed, when at 9.50 p.m. a large floe piece of ice struck the ship on the port side, [on which] she was inclining, and she immediately fell back [from] the bank; she was then anchored in 6½ f'ms."[79]

In the morning, "still wishing to see if any possibility remained of getting down Barrow Strait [Viscount Melville Sound], we weighed and stood as far as the ice would allow to the N.E., when observing from the crow's nest no water in that direction, I determined to make this our winter quarters," decided McClure. "We were in a great degree acting under the direction of Lieutenant Cresswell, as his observations led us to believe that we had passed the point of the coast reached by him and his travelling party in the spring, and were following the trending of the coast, which, as we supposed, led uninterrupted by bay or inlet, to the southeast. This error was subsequently accounted for," continued Armstrong, "by an alteration in the rate of the chronometer, when the observations were made; caused perhaps by the low degree of cold to which it had been exposed."[80]

Indeed, what daylight revealed to the Investigators, was that by keeping to the shore they had run well into a bay, Armstrong estimated was "some twelve or thirteen miles in depth, its north-eastern boundary running directly across our course; its entrance, (Point Back), being exactly opposite to our position, and distant about seven miles [it was named in honor of Captain Sir George Back, McClure's Arctic commander, 1836–37]." Court was sent in the whaleboat to sound, and *Investigator* followed until she dropped anchor.[81]

The Investigators "that night were firmly frozen in what has since proved a most safe and excellent harbour,—which, in grateful remembrance of the many perils that we had (during the passage of that terrible Polar Sea) escaped, in reaching, have named it [Mercy Bay]."[82]

# 11

# "The fatal error of our voyage,"
# 1851–52

---

*Some say the world will end in fire,*
*Some say in ice.*

—Robert Frost

---

With Melville Island only some 70 or 80 miles away, Dr. Alexander Armstrong had his own "thoughts" about wintering in Mercy Bay, as he related in his book:

> We were thus doomed to spend a second winter in the ice, after all the anticipations we had formed of reaching Melville Island; and, I must say, it was a sad and bitter disappointment to us all. Entering this bay was the *fatal* error of our voyage. This opinion I formed at the time, personally expressed it, and recorded it in my Journal; therefore, I could not be, in any degree, influenced by subsequent events; and, that the decision then arrived at, of entering this bay, was a hasty one, was fully established by its results.
>
> We had, previously to our entering this bay, made no attempt to reach Point Back, although an open sea was before us. The reported existence of shoals, (which we did not examine), and the appearance of the ice, setting down on it from the northward, caused it to be considered not prudent to do so. Nor did we make any attempt to reach the pack edge, with the view of pushing to the north-east: although the wind had become more northerly, and was bringing the ice down with it. It was nothing more than what is termed loose sailing ice in our immediate neighborhood, through which a ship might for some distance have worked her way, as the sea is at this time of the year, clearer of such impediments, than at any other; more may, therefore, be accomplished in a few days, than in as many months at any earlier period. By doing so, we would have got fairly with the influence of the current setting to the eastward through Banks' Strait [later named McClure Strait], and would have been further aided by the prevailing winds from the north-west....
>
> Wintering in the pack, all Arctic navigators had hitherto viewed with the utmost dread; and though I admit it to be perilous and dangerous, our experience of the previous winter was satisfactory evidence that it could be done with safety; and this was, I believe, the first time the experiment had been made....
>
> I am, therefore, firmly convinced, that had we not entered this bay, but boldly pushed into the pack, it would have led to a consummation of all our ardent hopes and wishes....

Not to be altogether negative, at least the doctor made congratulatory space for the expedition's most recent accomplishments:

> It was, however, satisfactory to reflect that, although the ship had only been actually under weigh for five days during the season, we had prosecuted the search over a wide extent of coast line, and added largely to Geographical science by establishing the insular character of Baring Island, besides discovering a *second* "North-West Passage" between the Atlantic and Pacific Oceans, in a direct line through Banks' Strait, in a voyage that stands unparalleled, as the most perilous ever made in the Polar Sea.[1]

But Armstrong's arrogant rant laid bare his fallacies and ignorance.

Firstly, Armstrong's journal held in the National Archives is not the same journal referred to in the above passage from his book (see Appendix 2). The former, written in *retrospect*, presented a toned-down and altogether different picture of the initial encounter with Mercy Bay:

> The morning following, the 24th of Sept[r] disclosed to our view a fine capacious bay, at the entrance of which we now lay, when it was at once determined to enter it, and take up our quarters for the winter, which was accordingly done about 9 miles from its entrance and about 500 yards from its western shore. This bay, subsequently called the "Bay of Mercy," has from the circumstance of its being the region of our dreary abode for nearly two years, within whose icy precincts we were from this date immoveably imprisoned, been well remembered by us all, and as being the locality where necessity compelled us to abandon our ship, will for ever remain one of the memorable spots in the records of Arctic voyaging.[2]

Armstrong flatly stated he verbally expressed his "opinion" (to whom—McClure?) at the time the bay was entered and made a record of it. Nor was he influenced to change his mind by the events that followed, still believing the decision to enter the bay was "a hasty one." In part, Armstrong contradicted himself, having already written that the morning "fully revealed to us our position; from which it appeared that by keeping close to the land, we had been running into a deep bay."[3] In this regard, it's important to keep in mind that McClure had for a long time been looking in vain for a safe anchorage, and believed he had found it.

Next, Armstrong indicated that McClure made no attempt to reach Point Back (at the eastern entrance to the bay), or attempt to reach the pack's edge and try to push to the northeast, claiming that the ship only had to deal with loose sailing ice in her immediate vicinity, and that favorable winds and currents would have aided *Investigator*. According to McClure, in the morning, "still wishing to see if any possibility remained of getting down Barrow Strait [Viscount Melville Sound], we weighed and stood as far as the ice would allow to the N.E., when observing from the crow's nest no water in that direction." Court's contemporary chart of discovered land supports McClure's claim of ice to the northeast of the Mercy Bay, showing ice extending across three-quarters of the bay's mouth (surely *not* representing Armstrong's "loose sailing ice").[4]

Ford's writings support his captain: "At daylight we found we had run into a bay, or rather found & run ashore on a shoal in its entrance which, if we had not run ashore where we did, the wind blowing so heavy & so dark & thick, we should very likely [have] been lost as we could not have cleared the opposite side of the bay. At about 4 o'clock we weighed & stood out & found the ice pack close & on the other side of our shoal a place to all appearance safe for to winter. Therefore we went in & anchored & cleaned up the ship, which took us until 1 o'clock."[5]

Mietsching's account is imprecise: "In the clear light we now saw for the first time that we were in a bay near the west end [*sic*—about midway[6]] of Banks Land; to the north we had a clear view of Melville Island. As there was no possibility of going farther by any means, the ship was anchored in a cove of this bay, where she lay in perfect security, sheltered by the great sandbank from the drifting pack outside."[7]

Piers's writings are also imprecise, but certainly indicate ample *time* therein for McClure to have investigated the ice conditions:

> At 3 a.m. hands were piped to breakfast, a basin of hot cocoa having been made for each: after this they returned again to the work, and at daylight sail was made—wind about the same, strong, W[ly] and

squally. The morning being clear it was soon observed that we were about to run into a deep bay, and the bank the ship ran on extended off from its W'ern point. The bay being large and deep, and appearing to offer very good shelter inside the spit, Court was sent in a whale boat to sound—the ship following—and finding sufficient water in the part the Captain thought of as a secure place for the ship, all idea of proceeding farther for the present or for this season was given up, the vessel was worked up to the desired position, and anchored at 7.50 a.m. in 4 fathoms of water. Cocoa was served out again to the men at 6 a.m., and shortly after breakfast was piped. All hands are pretty well fatigued with work, cold & wet, having been employed almost constantly since daylight yesterday morning, and in the forenoon of yesterday they were towing the ship between one & two hours....

It is clear Cresswell could not have been so far as this or he must have seen the bay, and our meeting with it just as this part of the voyage & season is another circumstance in which we appear to be greatly favored: it was indeed, at the time the ship struck, quite unlooked for and seems now most providential....

The assistant surgeon then followed with a chilling—and credible—projection: if *Investigator* had not been stopped by the mud bank,

> but have had advanced by this morning 20 or 30 miles further to the E.'ward, where we are aware of there being a continuous range of perpendicular cliffs of 60 or 70 miles in length and of 1000 or 1200 ft height, and under which we should probably have been this forenoon when a N.W[ly] wind brought "the pack" on the land. There is no doubt had we not met with this shelter the ship [would] now be jammed by the polar pack against [that] part of the coast, and, judging by time & distance, most probably the bold range of cliffs seen by [Cresswell] in his journey last May.[8]

Finally, despite the danger wintering in the ice pack presented, Armstrong felt it could be safely accomplished, and cited the *Investigator*'s previous experience. But McClure would have known better. The Beaufort Sea ice stream would in no way permit the ship to winter in the pack with the slightest degree of safety, as she had (luckily) done in the Prince of Wales Strait.

The *Investigator* and her mortal masters were—in more ways than one—between the Devil and the deep blue sea.

Many years on, Quartermaster Brown was reflective about Mercy Bay: "And though I grant you, we were there and had to make the best of it, that philosophical argument—true as it is—is not everything, and [if] not everything to us men, how much less to our Commander, on whom all responsibility lay and on whose true courage rested two weighty matters—our lives and the success of the undertaking."[9]

Just the very next day (the 25th), Piers was upbeat when he wrote how "we have reason to be thankful for good health & spirits—our ship's co[mpany] are remarkably healthy," but cautiously added, "and while I hope that all, even on the reduced scale of rations we are going on next month, will get [on] well over this winter, as we did the last, trust at the same time we shall be more fortunate next season.... unfortunately we are going "six upon four" [⅔ rations] on the 1st Oct, which will not tend to strengthen or further us in this cold, hungry region." He went on to pen a retrospect of the navigable season, which included the probability of "our communicating by travelling party with Melville Is. next spring (which will complete 'the N.W. passage,' even if the ship fails in going through)."[10]

James Nelson and his fellow sailors and Marines had known for some time there was going to be a reduction in provisions, in order to guard against any "contingencies" of a third winter. However distasteful this news was, he and the others understood the necessity for such an arrangement.[11]

Armstrong pointed to "the loss of beef we had sustained on first entering the ice, and the depot left at the Princess Royal Islands having very considerably curtailed the quantity on board." The Investigators had gone through one Arctic season, and for a man to maintain physical strength and ward off the invasion of scurvy, it was "an experiment more or less hazardous" to reduce provisions. "The full scale of victualling allowed on Polar service, has for its basis, one pound of meat daily—salt beef, pork and preserved meat on alternate days, with a fair proportion of flour and preserved vegetables. This in a *temperate climate* [emphasis added] is sufficient to maintain the body in a health and efficiency, even engaged in labourious occupation."[12]

The doctor's experience taught him that it takes a *greater* allowance of food in successive winters for a man's body to generate sufficient heat. "If the supply is not equal to the demand, the body wastes, and debility and disease of a scorbutic character ultimately ensue. I am, therefore, of opinion that one pound of animal food daily is not sufficient for men employed in Polar service. For one year, its effects may not be much felt, but to enable men to go through a second year and remain efficient, a larger allowance, I consider, an absolute imperative."[13]

McClure issued the foreboding order on October 1 to Clerk-in-Charge Paine:

> The return of HM's Ship under my command to England being quite uncertain I have deemed it necessary that a reduction should be made in the present Scale of Victualling, in order that the Provisions now onboard may last two years from this date.
>
> It is therefore my direction that you substitute the accompanying Scale of Victualling for that at present in use commencing from this day, and continuing the same until further orders: you will keep a correct account of the Quantity of Provisions so stopped in order that payment may be made for them the first opportunity.[14]

Return home "being quite uncertain"? Possibly a third *and* fourth winter? McClure *knew* he was in trouble.

According to a scale of victualling accompanying McClure's order, and signed by him, each crewman was to receive the following quantities of food and drink[15]:

| | |
|---|---|
| Bread | ⅔ lb. (daily)[16] |
| Preserved Meat | ½ lb. (alternating days) |
| Salt Meat | ½ lb. (four times over two weeks) |
| Flour | ½ lb. (three times over two weeks, at the same time as the suet) |
| Suet[17] | 1½ oz. (in lieu of flour; three times over two weeks) |
| Soup | ¾ pt. (twice over two weeks) |
| Potatoes | 2 oz. (six times over two weeks) |
| Carrots | 4 oz. (once every two weeks) |
| Peas | ½ pt. (four times over two weeks) |
| Pickles | 6 oz. (weekly) |
| Scotch Barley | 2 oz. (six times over two weeks) |
| Currants or Cranberries | 1 oz. (once per week) |
| Sugar for Cranberries | 1 oz. (once per week) |
| Mustard | 1 oz. (once per week) |
| Pepper | ½ oz. (once per week) |
| Salt | 1 oz. (once per week) |
| Tea | ⅛ oz. (daily) |
| Chocolate | ¾ oz. (daily) |

| Sugar | 2 oz. (daily) |
| Lime juice | 1 oz. (daily, mixed with ½ oz. sugar) |
| Spirits | ⅔ gill ( daily—3.16 U.S. fl. oz. of 50/50 rum and water) |

The above does not include fresh meat supplied through hunting game—which could vary considerably from month to month—and was divided between all officers and men onboard. For example, in October 1851, nine deer (852 lbs. of meat), 50 hares (average weight 7½ lbs.), and 42 ptarmigan (average weight 1½ lbs.) were brought in, but November and December combined amounted to only one hare and four ptarmigan. All told, the supplement of meat was simply not enough to make up for the reduction in rations, and certainly not any additional reductions.[18]

Due to better accommodations, purer air than found on the lower deck, and—for the moment—due to the quality and quantity of their diet, during his inspections, Armstrong found the general health of the officers to be better than that of the crew, "and they were the last to manifest any symptoms of scurvy."[19]

By the first days of October, the aurora borealis had already stretched its brilliance from east to west in the southern sky for the first time, while a parhelion also showed itself to the westward. The mercury had fallen to a low of −4°F, and even though *Investigator* was all housed over for the winter, so the decks could derive as much benefit as possible from the light and air, the hatches remained open. It was cold and uncomfortable between decks, from −8° to −10°F (and lower at night); consequently the cabins turned into ice caves. In the daytime, Armstrong "was often unable to write from the ink freezing in my pen, and water or lime juice kept standing on the mess table became immediately frozen."[20]

"Sylvester's stove is to be lit four times a-week," wrote Piers, "commencing to day [October 1]—allowance of coal, 40 lb a day. Our [gunroom] stove also is to be lit daily—allowance 8 lb a-day—Sick bay, 4 lb a-day." To conserve fuel, all were sharp drops from the daily coal consumption from the first winter.[21] Especially with the lack of warmth, exercise became the order of the day, while hunger began to stalk the men. Miertsching warned of even darker clouds on the horizon, "should examination of supplies show that more of them have been spoilt through damp—as suspected—our future portion will be even smaller."[22]

And portents were not confined to the tangible—as recorded by Carpenter Ford: "I dreamed a curious dream last night [October 3], that I was home & that Mother was missing & that Sam overheard her say she would drown herself. The fright awoke me."[23]

The fourth day of October, Court, petty officer John Calder, and five other men, provisioned for six days, sledded northeast to find Cresswell's cairn (the building of which Calder had superintended). McClure stated the cairn was 18 miles away. Piers wrote that Court needed "to determine the position of it, as, from some error in [Cresswell's] chronometer, there appears to be a mistake in the longitude," and recorded the same mileage in his journal. The party returned at 3:30 in the afternoon of the seventh to temperatures in the teens and falling snow, not having been able to find the cairn, despite reaching the area concerned, even though Calder had been certain as to the position. Armstrong, Piers and Miertsching suggested evidence of recent landslides may have accounted for the cairn's disappearance.[24]

By contrast, Ford wrote: "Travelling party returned having been 10 miles from the ship & could not go farther in consequence of open water toward the island (Melville) & to all appearance some landslips recently." Armstrong recorded a similar distance, and that "Mr.

**John Calder, c. 1880s (courtesy Fred D. Calder Jr.).**

Court intended to have gone further to the eastward, but his progress was entirely cut off *by an expanse of open water, extending from the shore to the northward and eastward, as far as he could see. The distance embraced by his range of vision from an elevated position he estimated at eleven miles, with a water sky beyond it, and no trace of ice to be seen in that direction* [original italics]. The water was within eight miles of our position, extending off Point Back to the westward also for some distance, until finally lost in the pack."[25]

As far as Armstrong was concerned, this fully justified his previous comments about entering the bay, and so afforded another opportunity to vilify his captain:

> This was indeed tantalizing, if not vexatious [annoying] intelligence, as we were frozen in within eight miles of it. The most sanguine [hopeful] amongst us were astonished, as we could not possibly have expected such a favorable state of things. It more than verified the opinion I had some days before recorded in my journal, and have already made known in these pages. It may, therefore, readily be supposed how sad were our reflections, as we were bitterly conscious that had we taken advantage of the easterly current, and entered the pack, we should then have been on our way to England—instead of wintering in Mercy Bay.[26]

Disappointing as it was to discover open water was so close, its existence *at that time* in no way indicated the same conditions were present *two weeks prior*, when *Investigator* was entering Mercy Bay. In fact, McClure could not have known anything about the ice conditions at Point Back on September 24.[27]

It was thought that area wildlife migrated south for the winter, but it was discovered that they "never, in fact, left the neighbourhood of Mercy Bay even in the depth of winter; and it was only the cold and darkness which prevented their being shot at that season." And even though the Investigators were not, at times, the most skillful of hunters, during one of the earliest hunts, Newton had the good fortune to be the first to bring down a deer. It was a fine buck and weighed 240 lbs. when brought onboard, yielding 160 lbs. of venison.[28]

When prey was stalked and brought down, wolves and foxes represented another threat. If a deer was shot and left where it fell, by the time the time the hunter was able to gather assistance to bring in the kill, Mr. Wolf might not have left much beyond the head and shin-bones behind. He then cleverly stayed out of the gun barrel's range, and mournfully howled, as if to mock his human competitors.[29]

But four-legged creatures weren't the only hindrances to the hunt; human companions could also present serious problems, as Piers found while out with Caulker James Evans, who became delusional following an injury on October 9. After chasing and bagging a deer as the sun was setting, the men realized they could not haul the animal by themselves, so Piers intended to send Evans to fetch more muscle, while he guarded the 100 lb. prize. The doctor decided to accompany the petty officer until the bay could be seen from the hills,

> but had not proceeded more than a mile or thereabout when looking back from a hill I had just mounted I saw Evans sitting down on the snow some distance behind me: I called to him & got him up, but he told me that in chasing the deer he had fallen [& hurt] one of his knees, and also that his hands were nearly frost-bitten. There was now nothing for me than [to make] the best of my way on board with the man; and I [realize] how fortunate I was I had come this distance with him and discovered his weakness before turning back again; as otherwise I must certainly have been out the whole night, and he also most likely—knowing indeed how stupid sailors are it might even have cost him his life, for afterwards he would sit down every now & then till I made him rise again; he then threw off his shoes, as he said he could get on better without them; and I have altogether great difficulty in get-ting him along, but succeeded best I found by putting him on his mettle [by] telling him I would not mind walking all night without resting, and what others had done: then he would say, ah! If my knee was only right I would walk with every man in the ship. At last at 8 p.m. we reached the ship, and, although not so bad as poor Evans, I was very glad to sit down, and presently to make a good din-ner.[30]

"In the morning [Haswell and I] saw from the hills—(the day being bright & clear)—what several for some days have said to be the cliffs & high land of Melville Is. partially covered with snow: we were doubtful as to it being land—thinking it more like ice thrown up by the refraction," wondered Piers, "but whatever it was, it was in the direction of Melville Is., and the only object of the kind on the horizon." Two days later, while out hunting, Piers was at the identical spot and again saw what he thought was Melville Island, "only the character of the land was much more distinct—I had no longer any doubt as to its being land; and from its position to the N. and E'ward believe it to be Melville Island."[31]

At 8:00 a.m., Sainsbury started southward with a sled party to investigate what appeared to be an inlet running from the south side of the bay to the southwest, while "Cresswell & another party started to go inland, to the W'ward, on a week's shooting for the ship; and I [Piers] left with a third party to bring on board the deer killed yesterday." Two days later, Wynniatt headed up a shooting party of seven men, and took a week's provisions. After eagerly pursuing two musk ox, one of his men went missing for about 20 hours. During this time he was visited by three wolves one time, and a bear at another—although having previously used up his ammunition, he was fortunately able to fend off the creatures by every now and again firing off the few percussion caps on hand.[32]

Sainsbury returned the day after he left, having found the "inlet" was only a river bed that extended 12 miles and ended in a marsh.[33] A transcribed cairn note contained in the *Investigator's* Letter & Order Book is most likely attributable to Sainsbury's party:

> This Cairn was erected by a travelling Party from HM's D Ship Investigator which is Anchored in this place having taken up this position for the Winter on the 25th September 1851 after having circumnavigated this Land which is called "Baring's Island"
> No mark or Intelligence whatever has been found which could throw the least light upon the fate of the missing expedition under Sir John Franklin
> Crew all in Excellent health & Spirits
> Dated onboard HM's D Ship Investigator
> 10th October 1851. Lat: 74°6'N Lon: 117°54'W
> /sig^d Rob^t M^cClure Comm^r.[34]

Having withstood the monotony onboard as much as he was able, Piers volunteered to lead a week-long shooting expedition, and left the ship at 9:00 a.m. on October 17, with two tents, Quartermaster George Brown, Able Seamen Samuel Bounsall, John Davies and James McDonald, and three other sailors, plus Sergeant Woon, Corporal Farquharson, Private Biggs, and four additional Marines.[35]

At 21 years of age, Teignmouth-born John Davies first served in the Royal Navy, spending a few months during 1842 as a well-conducted ordinary seaman in HMS *Poictiers*. In early 1845, he joined HMS *Herald* as an able seaman, and by August 1846, future Investigator Mark Griffiths became a shipmate. For whatever reason(s), Davies's behavior became so poor that Captain Kellett discharged him to the six-gun brig HMS *Pandora* in May 1849 for passage to England—with the conduct rating of "Bad" noted on his service certificate. Just two months later, *Pandora* visited Pitcairn Island, home to descendants of the *Bounty* mutineers; how strange it must have been for the Pitcairners to be called on by the namesake of the very vessel the Admiralty sent to hunt down their ancestors all those decades ago. Davies left the *Pandora* in November, but hadn't soured on the Navy, and the following month volunteered for the Arctic expedition at Woolwich. His last ship shown on the *Investigator's* muster was *Pandora*, but Davies no doubt concealed his previous service on the *Herald*. No matter—Able Seaman John Davies eventually came to prove his unusual loyalty to Captain McClure.[36]

When 5'8" Able Seaman James McDonald volunteered at Devonport for *Investigator*, he too came face-to-face with old shipmates like Cornelius Hulott, with whom he served for nearly four years onboard the frigate *Thalia*. During their 1841–45 servitude—when Hulott was merely a boy sailor—both had only "Fair" conduct. Six months later, in May 1846, the Scot joined the naval schooner *Constance*, where Ordinary Seaman/Gunroom Cook Henry Sugden and Able Seamen Robert Tiffeny and James Jackson also found themselves.[37]

Though Tiffeny's conduct on the *Constance* was "good & then Indifferent," when he later joined *Investigator* as an able seaman, the Yorkshireman was promoted to the captain of the maintop (first class petty officer) by April/May 1850, and afterward served in McClure's North-West Passage sled party. In sharp contrast, Jackson's blue eyes evidently masked a rotten apple, as he was discharged from the *Constance* on December 4, 1849, with "Very Bad" conduct, and sent straight to the Exeter jail! It was January 18, 1850, when the illiterate Londoner joined *Investigator* (with *Constance* shown as his last ship on the muster), but just six months later he deserted in the Sandwich Islands.[38]

"At 12, noon, we pitched our tents about 4 or 5 miles from the ship, towards the head of the bay," recorded Piers. The next day, fog enveloped them, and McDonald commented to

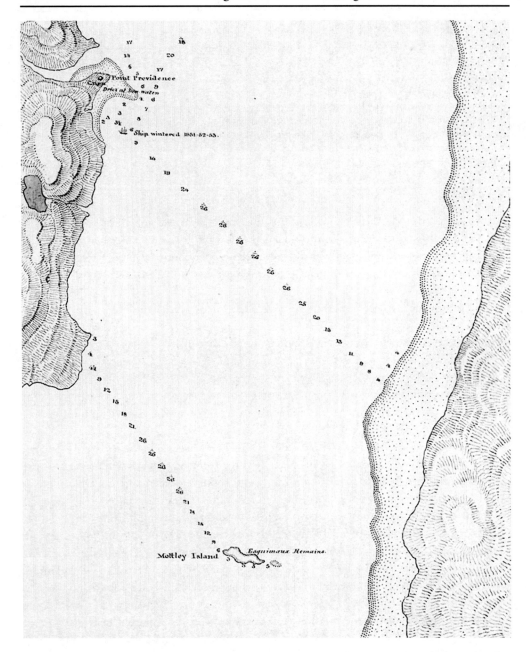

**Chart of the Harbour of Mercy (detail), showing *Investigator*'s 1851–52-53 winter quarters, southeast of what McClure named Providence Point (Stephen Court, 1853; UK Hydrographic Office, www.ukho. gov.uk).**

the assistant surgeon how "it is as thick as a hedge." With vision limited to only 100 yards, Piers "never before witnessed anything like an approach to the ocular deception, as to objects & distance, so common in this part of the world, particularly during thick weather." The fog, and afterward the darkness, conspired to cause two groups who had gone in different directions (all the Marines in one, and three sailors in another), to become lost. By 7:30 in the evening, all were safe at the tents, "but even then the Corporal (Farquharson) was so much exhausted that one of the men had been obliged to carry his musket for some distance, latterly—the Sergeant, on his return, came & told me [Piers] that they had had a very narrow escape; that he had quite made up his mind to be out all night, and that they certainly would have been, had they not met with Davis; and he was afraid that some of them would not have lived to see the morrow."[39]

The nights during Piers's time away were desperately cold, the temperature having plummeted to as low as –23°F, causing everything in the tents to be covered with frost; and when the men exhaled, the vapor was "seen glistening in its frozen state by the light of the lamp." When the party returned to *Investigator* on the 23rd, McClure "enquired how we all were, and appeared pleased to learn we were all well & had not suffered from frost bites: he said he thought we should have been back on Monday (20th) on account of the cold—the question of game seemed quite a secondary consideration, and he was perfectly satisfied with the 25 hares & 11 ptarmigan which we brought on board."[40]

The first anniversary of the discovery of the North-West Passage fell on a Sunday (October 26), and that evening the main brace was spliced for the commemoration, and Piers pleasingly wrote that "the men, with permission, gave three cheers, and one more." Nelson too recalled that the speeches on this occasion were responded to with many shouts of approval from the audience.[41]

The next day, Armstrong's examination of the ship's company during the last few rays of daylight afforded the Investigators, showed "them in a state of health and efficiency—a few appeared to have lost flesh a little, but there was an entire absence of anything of a scorbutic character. I felt it my duty, at the same time, to represent that such a favourable state could not possibly exist long, on the reduced allowance of provisions on which they had been placed."[42]

The ominous transformation was in fact already under way.

Carpenter Ford recently recorded personal changes he keenly perceived taking place: "I have weighed [myself] this evening & weighs 128 lbs naked & 143 with cloth[e]s, which shows I have lost 12 lbs since the 1st of last November.... I have employed myself making a tin cup to eat & drink out of as I am drove nearly to extremities, little to eat what & nothing left to eat what we have on. I was forced to make a spoon of a piece of musk ox horn & a cup out of an old soup tin (Arctic pleasures). Necessity the Mother of Invention." He then went on to describe the new menu of rations.[43]

When November dawned, Piers revealed more dark clouds blowing in with the winds of change, as the average thickness of the new ice crept toward two feet:

> The weather is cold; and with hatches off, the housing as yet unfinished, and very little fire below—light also—it is most cheerless in the gun-room, so that till 1 or 1.30 p.m. when the fire is lit, scarcely any one visits it, preferring to walk the deck or wrap themselves up in their cabins....
>
> Light too is becoming very valuable, of which we cannot boast much in the gun-room—candles, which cost me nearly 4/- [four shillings] a lb at Oahu and were then considered very dear are now invaluable....
>
> I know of an argument of one Officer to give a bottle of Rum every alternate week to another, for his weekly tallow mould candle which he is allowed by the ship; and the value of spirits on board now may be [also] imagined from my hearing of an officer giving [up one] sovereign [equal to one pound sterling] for a bottle—though I think this, if it really was the case, considerably above its present value [of the] spirits....
>
> Fresh meat is now served out on salt beef days—instead of that meat—1 lb a man, a hare being reck-

oned at 6 lb. Saturday, the 1st, was the first day. A pound of fresh meat is a great benefit to all, though only once in four or five days; for even in the gun-room, where we still have a little more than our ship's allowance remaining from the mess stock & savings, the ⅔ [rations] begins to tell a by no means pleasant story—for we are on an allowance of everything, of course, and plates & dishes leave the table clear, and pretty well polished.[44]

However, celebrations still found their way to the table, and with the fifth of November came the 25th birthday of Ford's wife Mary: "I hope [God] has blessed her, even as he has blessed me, with health, strength & happiness & a heart that can look back & see my misspent life. Evening my messmates took a glass of grog together & I have a roasted leg of venison for dinner so that even in this remote part of the globe I could & did keep up the Old English custom on a birthday."[45]

"As cold and darkness increased, and the absence of the sun rendered it unsafe for the crew to leave the vicinity of the ship, the wolves, pressed by cold and hunger, used to haunt her to a disagreeable extent; and the sad prolonged howl of these gaunt creatures in the long nights added, if possible, to the dismal character of the scene." Piers observed how they almost nightly visited *Investigator*: "The dog goes out & plays with the one which we consider as a sort of scout or decoy: the wolf every now & then runs off as if to lead the dog to his friends who are waiting a short distance farther; but 'Vesty' [Mongo] says, no!" When not consorting with his four-legged counterpart, Mongo played cat and mouse with two cunning ravens, who had become part of the Mercy Bay clan.[46]

The usual operations of housing over the deck and "cementing" it with a combination of fine gravel, gravel and earth, and snow and water, plus banking the ship with snow, were completed while temperatures during the month often ranged into the negative 20s and 30s— and even reached -40°F. Within the wooden walls, each officer, sailor, and Marine attempted to make himself comfortable for the long winter months, helped along by a good library onboard. Well-practiced from the previous winter, tailors and cobblers abounded, and Miertsching saw fit to make McClure a pair of warm bedroom slippers; not to be neglectful of her subjects, presents of blankets and cloth boots were also served out on behalf of Her Majesty the Queen. Various other tradesmen became established, and the lack of traditional money gave rise to gun wads (used to keep ammunition in the gun barrel) being accepted as coinage—"the sum due was marked on one of them, with the initials of the officer who con- tracted the debt, which ensured its being negotiable throughout the ship."[47]

In addition to intervals of the aurora, three days of meteor showers (from the 12th to the 15th) decorated a clear and cloudless sky, and Court kindly offered to acquaint anyone interested on celestial bodies. In the midst of this colorful display, the Investigators' shipmate since May, the "other fox—'old Adam'—took his departure, without saying 'good-bye' to any one," penned the assistant surgeon. He gained his freedom to roam far and wide ... but not so the Investigators, who were becoming mental prisoners for want of food. Miertsching related how "the crew must daily spend [a total of] five or six hours off the ship, and employ themselves as they please, but, as it seems, the two-thirds ration is the cause of their apathy."[48]

Toward month's end, Ford's spirits dipped with the mercury: "Very cold & dismal as its been scarcely light all day. Stars shining & the only sound to be heard is the howling of wolves. Last night I dreamt that I was safe home & kissing My Dear Mary on our first meeting."[49]

A monstrous, five-day long southerly gale, the likes of which the Investigators had never before witnessed, roared through with December's onset, as one massive "moving body of snow rolled along higher than the topmast heads." A wreath of snow piled 13 feet high around the ship to windward, causing the embankment to give way from her side, as the ice floe sank under the weight.[50]

Within the *Investigator's* hull, Piers and his shipmates

> still manage to keep up some sort of conversation; but of course it is the same old, oft told story, and any one may guess the usual subjects: England; when & how shall we return, &c; the "Enterprise"; her whereabouts &c; Capt Austin's Ships; and latterly the "two thirds" has been a frequent & interesting topic. Poor Sir J. Franklin & his unfortunate crews are much less spoken of than they used to be; for when they are, it is with the general feeling that they have all long ceased to exist, and that the period for search, with the essential prospect of finding them alive, is also past.[51]

Meanwhile, Miertsching's December 6 entry included critical information attributed to McClure—but very strangely, cannot be found in any other contemporary source (see Appendix 2):

> The captain made it known that as a great amount of provisions must be discarded as spoiled and injurious to health, utmost economy must be practiced, and he had decided gradually to reduce the two-thirds daily ration to one-half, which admittedly small portion would be maintained only for those months when the ship was frozen in, and no work, heavy or light, wad demanded of the men, and as soon as the ship was under sail, or any strenuous effort required, the full daily ration of food would be restored.[52]

Did an inspection turn up more bad provisions, and had McClure privately discussed another reduction with Miertsching, but then decided against it more generally known? Surely Armstrong, at the very least, would have recorded the further discovery of bad provisions.

As if the melancholy surroundings were not depressing enough, on December 9 Able Seaman Mark Bradbury, who had eased many an ear with his voice and violin, got drunk—and was thrown into a severe, 20-minute-long epileptic fit, which no doubt left his shipmates aghast. Under Dr. Armstrong's care, "by restoring the sensations which had become considerably deranged & improving the general health, there was no return of the attack & the case terminated favorably." Bradbury was released from sick bay after 12 days—but the curse remained within him, as the doctor was aware the young sailor was prone to overindulgences in life, especially that of spirits. Bradbury claimed he had never suffered such an attack before, "but from his statement [to the doctor], he has a sister subject to the disease, so how far this can be depended on it is difficult to say."[53] Bradbury had a married sister and this could be the same person (see Appendix 3).

To add to the ever-present wolves, little foxes nightly (and sometimes during the day) visited the ship. Probably urged on by hunger, they boldly came aboard several times at night, when one or two people were on deck, and then fell victim to traps laid out for them.[54]

With the approach of the Yule holiday, the Arctic seemingly offered a reprieve from the physical and mental assault on the Investigators, and moderated its weather; the average temperature on Christmas Eve "warmed" to –10.2°F. In preparation for Christmas Day, Cresswell and Court "were employed decorating a lamp shade with prints of bullocks, sheep, pigs &c, taken from some old illustrated London news' of 1849—portraits of cattle at the Smithfield show [London livestock market[55]]—to the great amusement of all the mess: so that if we are denied the pleasure of partaking, we are at least reminded, of the "good old English fare" so general at this season."[56]

Merriment aside, an undercurrent of apprehension ran through Henry Piers' account of the following day:

Dec. 25th_ Xmas day! After divisions this morning prayers of the Church service were read by the Captain. At noon the men went to dinner, which from all accounts was a good one: my friend Fawcett, Boatswain's Mate, said for the 21 years he had been in "the Service" he had not had such a good dinner—it consisted of Reindeer, which was in prime condition, fat & delicately tender, cooked as the men pleased; roasted or made in puddings or a sort of stew with vegetables, pudding &c. I have no doubt it was a good dinner, but in estimating the quality of food out here, allowance must be made for the circumstances of our case, for everything is not good with us now, and I know "old Fawcett" seldom gets "a good dinner" or any other meal; and it will [be] still harder with him & the rest now the venison [is] all gone. At 4 p.m. all the Officers sat down [to a] capital dinner with the Captain in his cabin [and the] evening passed very quietly; the men appeared very happy and to be enjoying themselves, all singing and chatting in their messes. Absent friends are not forgotten.[57]

When measured on the morning of New Year's Day 1852, the ice was 3'8" thick, while the mercury showed an average temperature just beyond −46°F ... and dropping.[58] The day passed pleasantly for the crew, as they were permitted to stay onboard because of rough weather, and treat it as a holiday. No Divine Service was held, and following morning muster, Captain McClure congratulated the men on the New Year, and "thanked them for their good conduct hitherto, encouraged them to be of good and cheerful heart, and promised them extra rations and grog."[59] An examination of the ship's company also found them to be in good health,

> they evidently having derived much benefit from the excellence and nutritious properties of the fresh meat, which has thus been issued every fifth day for a period of two months. There were only four men on the sick list, and the diseases that had hitherto occurred were chiefly those which resulted from the effects of cold and exposure, such as frostbites, local inflammations, and a few others; all were yet free from any scorbutic taint, although then three months on a reduced allowance of food.[60]

The officers invited McClure to lunch, but animosities boiled over during the meal, "and everyone was glad when it was over on account of the disagreeable relations between the captain and the doctor: yesterday the handle came off the jug," revealed Miertsching, "for the deceitfulness of the doctor which had long imposed on the captain was brought to light and openly revealed; and today at muster there was also bitter contention between the captain and the clerk-in-charge [Paine]. These disagreeable relationships aggravate the wretchedness of our life on board."[61]

Still, the bluejackets and Marines were thankful for their extras (in addition to currants in the pudding), and possessed a sense of pride amidst their tastefully decorated home away from home. During the men's evening "concert," the captain and all the officers paid a visit, and listened intently to singing, recitations, and the like, being much impressed with how such a show was put on given the limited means at hand. Only when the shrill of the boatswain's pipe commanded "Up Hammocks" did the officers retire from the scene.[62]

The outside temperature hit a low of −51°F on the third day of the month, and a strong gale and thick snow drift followed; it was January 8 before the wind (temporarily) subsided, accompanied by something of a warming trend, with the thermometer showing a high of −30°F. It was hoped the exhausted stock of venison could be replenished, but the entire month was notable for its intense cold and boisterous winds, with but a few days without them at gale force. "We have been kept on board, under the housing or below, as long, I think, as a fortnight at one time," remarked Piers. The shrieking wind must have been particularly oppressive for those confined to sick bay, like Private George Parfitt, who was laboring at the beginning of his 85-day treatment for pneumonia and bronchitis—only to be inauspiciously released on April Fool's Day.[63]

At month's end, according to Miertsching, the "daily ration seems to grow smaller and smaller; the men are complaining of hunger. Three sailors have been severely punished [flogged] for stealing and devouring the dog's food."[64]

Many deer were seen, and some wounded, but meager reward for frostbitten faces and fingers was 205 lbs. of meat from two deer, plus two hares and 13 ptarmigan—the sum total of January's concerted and energetic hunting efforts. Ford and Sergeant Woon brought down a deer, and the carpenter proudly recorded how he "went away for a bit of a ramble over the hills & saw 6 [deer] altogether & was fortunate to shoot one, the first this year, weighing 87 lbs, for which I was congratulated by our Captain & presented with a glass of wine on the occasion."[65]

Sergeant Woon especially distinguished himself as a hunter, and Dr. Armstrong wrote glowingly that he

> cannot mention the name of Sergeant Woon without here recording the high opinion entertained of him by the Captain, officers and crew. He proved himself invaluable, was always a ready volunteer for any service, most correct and soldier-like in his conduct, ever promoted what contributed to the hilarity and cheerfulness of the crew, and was one of our most indefatigable and successful hunters. In short, he was brave and intrepid on every occasion, which fully tested the man, and he proved himself a credit to his corps.[66]

And so it was on the night of February 4-5,[67] that Sergeant John Woon displayed the qualities which fully justified the admiration and gratitude of his fellow Investigators, and spoke to his strong sense of humanity in the most precarious of situations.

A deer was spied on land during the morning of the fourth, and several officers and men left the ship, hoping to have a shot at the creature. Although many other deer were eventually chased and fired upon, success eluded the hunters. All returned by dusk—except Woon and the black Gunroom Cook Charles Anderson,[68] who were last seen apart, but not very far from one another.

The heavy fog that rolled in every evening began to descend through a windless sky, and soon the land could not be seen for more than about a mile off. At 8:00 p.m. a mortar and rockets began being fired at intervals, but with no result, and misgivings mounted for the safety of the lost men. At ten o'clock, amidst a fresh breeze blowing and a temperature of −25°, three search parties were dispatched, each carrying muskets, ammunition, rockets, blue lights, and food and drink. Haswell and three men went southward down the coast, and Court and three men traveled northward along the coast, while Ford and his two men proceeded straight inland. The officers were under orders to return to the ship by four in the morning to be relieved by other parties.

That afternoon, Anderson broke the foreleg of a deer, and after chasing it for a while, when fog came in, he realized he was lost, as he paid no attention to the direction he was going during the excitement of the chase. Anderson became frantic, and desperately wandered about for the route home, when Sergeant Woon happened upon him walking in the wrong direction around 2:00 p.m. The pair then sighted some deer and were going after them, but about 15 minutes later, Woon looked around, and saw his shipmate sitting in the snow some distance behind him. When the sergeant came up, he found Anderson half-crazed, overcome with fear and fatigue: the Marine immediately thought only of getting his shipmate back onboard *Investigator*.

Through much persuasion, Woon was able to induce the man to slowly walk with him, but Anderson would occasionally sit or lie down, and then Woon had to pull him up and help him on his way. Since Anderson was much heavier than his rescuer, Woon was dragged or pushed down whenever Anderson fell onto the snow. The sailor grew weaker and weaker, and before he became partly insensible, blood ran from his nose and mouth as he partially convulsed, began muttering to himself, and afterwards said he had felt as if he was drunk. The sergeant realized they were still miles from the ship, so leaving the poor man and going for help was out of the question—the distant howls of wolves foretold of Anderson's being eaten alive before freezing to death.

Only one option remained. The Marine threw both muskets over his shoulder, and then supported and half-dragged the sailor along; the only relief Woon had was rolling Anderson down the descending sides of hills and ravines. Lethargy overtook him, as the sailor begged many times during the journey to be left to die in the snow, but the Marine soldiered on.

Finally, at about 10:00 p.m. Woon estimated they were only a mile from the ship, but he could drag Anderson no more. In spite of Woon's attempts to cheer the sailor by pointing to signal rockets fired from the *Investigator*, Anderson was resigned to his fate. Thus, Woon laid the sailor down in a deep bed of snow, and set off for help; Anderson was just short of extreme bliss, feeling the deadly delight of hypothermia. By good fortune, the Marine quickly fell in with Carpenter Ford's party. The latter was still within hailing distance of Court's party, so the two joined forces and set off with Sergeant Woon to rescue Anderson. Meanwhile, Able Seaman Davis (one of Ford's men) was sent back to the ship with the news.

"I knew the tragic scene must soon come to an end if relief did not speedily reach him; and I at once started in pursuit of the party, having previously left the necessary directions with my assistant (Mr. Piers) to meet the emergency, on Anderson's arrival." When Armstrong met the two parties about three-quarters of a mile from *Investigator*, Anderson was merely hanging on by threads. The surgeon found him "in a state of insensibility, arms and legs stiff and rigid—the former extended, could with difficulty be bent—hands clenched and frozen, eyes fixed and glassy, jaws rigid and both so firmly clenched, that we could scarcely separate them to pour down restoratives. The pulse was imperceptible at the wrist, the heart barely acting; and in a few minutes he must have terminated his existence. A sledge had been dispatched with me, on which I had him placed, and speedily brought on board."[69]

Arriving at about half an hour before midnight, Anderson was not able to say much, and when he did speak he was generally incoherent. "[T]he temperature of the whole surface of his body was lower than natural," wrote Piers, "and his pulse was slow (about 48) and very feeble. Being laid in a cot, by means of friction and warm tea the circulation was soon improved; his hands & feet became warm; and about 2 a.m. he went off to sleep." What Piers did not record in his journal, but James Nelson wrote about later, is that all onboard witnessed the torturous resurrection of Anderson's animation, accompanied by his piercing screams. He afterwards told James Nelson the agonizing return of warmth was comparable to molten lead being poured over his arms and legs.[70]

"Reactionary fever with delirium ensued," wrote Armstrong, "but from these, he in a few days recovered. He was, however, extensively frost-bitten, which ultimately entailed the loss by amputation of both great toes, with portions of others, and also the fingers, together with a part of the nose. He was ever afterwards high[ly] susceptible of cold, and remained much debilitated, and became subsequently affected with scurvy." On this occasion, Anderson earned 44 days in sick bay.[71]

The medical men took the opportunity of Anderson's case to "prove" the "racial superiority" of the white race in such circumstances. "This incident furnishes a striking proof of the differences in moral and physical powers of endurance of the dark and white races," wrote Armstrong, "for not withstanding his arduous exertions, the sergeant returned on board apparently as fresh as if he had had only an ordinary walk." Piers wrote along these same lines the following month, regarding McClure's experience in October 1851, and similar cases involving Stone, Brown and Gibbs. These four cases, compared "with Anderson's, seem to shew a remarkable superiority of spirit & energy in the white man over the black: for the latter, notwithstanding his colour, was born & bred on the Lakes of America, is a much more powerful man than the Captain and Stone, and quite strong as, if not stronger than, Brown & Gibbs: he had too only been out a few hours—six or seven—before he became exhausted."[72]

These assertions about race helped push open a mysterious door, which revealed intriguing circumstantial evidence as to a possible *alternative* identity for Charles Anderson—a fugitive American slave.[73]

Anderson stated he was born in Port Robinson, British North America (Canada), when he signed on to *Investigator* on December 26, 1849 (his first Royal Navy vessel); he repeated this information for his seaman's register ticket, issued onboard three weeks later. Port Robinson was (and still is) a small community in the southernmost part of Thorold, Ontario, along the Welland Canal, which connects Lake Ontario to the north and Lake Erie to the south, and is fewer than a dozen miles from Niagara Falls. Between about 1820 and 1860, well over 20,000 (some sources state tens of thousands more) runaway slaves and free blacks sought refuge in Canada through the Underground Railroad. The majority of these refugees crossed over into what is now southwestern Ontario—and Port Robinson became the heart of clusters of refugee settlers. And in fact, Canada's Colored Corps was headquartered in Port Robinson during the building of the Second Welland Canal in the 1840s, so as to keep order between two feuding groups of Irish canal workers. Not surprisingly, the unit was composed of "some four sergeants, four corporals, one drummer, and eighty privates, the commissioned and non-commissioned officers were white men; the Black privates were former escaped slaves from the United States."[74]

Whether he was a slave on the run or a free black, Anderson would have had every reason to claim his birthplace as British North America, since slavery had been outlawed throughout nearly the entire British Empire by the Slavery Abolition Act of 1833. It also seems quite unlikely he was a free Canadian black, since black slaves had not existed in the large numbers in Canada as they did in the United States, with nearly all of the ones in Canada having been brought from the American colonies. All of this suggests that at the very least Anderson's parents were probably American slaves or former slaves.[75]

Then there is the question of Anderson's way of life. Dr. Armstrong wrote that Anderson "represented himself as a Canadian, inured to a hunter's life in North America," and Piers also noted the man was "born & bred on the Lakes of America." True? For one thing, Anderson stated for his seaman's register ticket that he first went to sea in 1832—when he was about seven years old. And despite his supposed hunting background, in all of the contemporary sources, he is only mentioned as a hunter during the expedition on just three occasions (his near-death experience and two times thereafter). And it also seems odd that an experienced woodsman did not handle himself better when he lost his way. On the other side of things, Anderson's seaman's register ticket shows that he stated his qualification was that of a "Cook," and so matches Miertsching's conversation with him, in which he said that "for two years he had been cook on a vessel carrying German emigrants to America." Finally, it is evident from his shipmates' references that, along with sailor-like chores, the able seaman's duties included cooking.[76]

After 91 days the sun displayed its brilliance on February 7. "His reappearance was anxiously looked for, it constituting one of the greatest events of the year," radiated Armstrong, "and brought the assurance that the days of darkness had passed." But even the power of that mighty star could not obscure the gloom on the Investigators' horizon. The ship's company was inspected prior to Charles Anderson's brush with oblivion, and though all were found to be in good health, several men said they lost flesh and felt a decrease of strength since last summer. This strongly predisposed them to scurvy, which was now closing in on the Investigators.[77]

For the moment, venison was again able to be issued three times over two weeks, and offered some comfort. The fresh meat came with "numerous daily incidents of daring and adventure," during another month of intensely cold and violent weather, where the average temperature was nearly -26°F. Often, however, hunters spent many a long hour trudging through severe conditions, only to return to the ship empty-handed. One day, Ford went some 21 miles, "with nothing to eat or drink but a pint of coco & about 5 oz of dry bread this morning, walking 7 hours over hill & snow vallies with cloth[e]s weighing 20 lbs, musket about 9½, & 10 round of ball cartridges. I have dragged a sledge on a bill of biscuit, pork, a basin of coco & slept on the ice, but this shows what a man can stand in this regard."[78]

Back onboard, Henry Piers painted a ghostly scene:

> [L]et anyone imagine a ship frozen up, with the deck covered with snow a foot or 18 inc. deep, and covered over exactly like a booth, a temperature of—30 or—40 with strong wind, and, notwithstanding every part being closely stopped [sealed] to keep out the wind & snow, the fine snow drift still finding its way through & covering everything—the wind howling through the rigging at the same time: let him picture to himself then this covered deck lit by a single candle in a lantern.[79]

Piers went on to note the striking difference in the men's spirits between the last winter and this one:

> [T]hen, nearly "all hands" [would] rush out to play "duck" or the more popular game [of] "rounders," and these when the summer advanced [were] succeeded by others," but this winter they "proceed to their daily, and monthly, monotonous exercise and then may be seen 20 or 30 men, 2 or 3 abreast, most of them with duck outside coats & trowsers or gaiters, and muffled up with only their noses & eyes, or the eyes alone, peering out, pacing a beaten track out or inside the ship: a word is seldom spoken by one of them, though very probably much of personal interest may be revolving in some of their minds— each silently follows the other, looking down at the heels of the man before him....
>
> "Hands to dance & skylark": now [became] a humdrum form, for no one responds to it, and the men remain in their messes making or mending clothes, reading, talking, lying down or otherwise occupied: and in this again the listlessness of the voyage, accompanied as it is now by the reduction of provisions, is evident when compared with last winter....
>
> [W]hile there were 20 or more at school last winter there are only 3 this.[80]

As a snowy owl graced the sky on March 1, below the frozen surface, the ice had grown to 5'5½" in thickness. Wolves prowled and howled around *Investigator* all day, while within her hull Dr. Armstrong examined the sailors and Marines. They had very noticeably lost flesh, and a majority of them said their strength was diminished—"although in good health, otherwise, they felt themselves becoming gradually weaker."[81]

"Shooting was prohibited last week; but to day being fine and the restriction removed, plenty of sportsmen went over the hills; and although they saw and fired on plenty of deer nothing was killed." In the days that followed, Whitefield, Woon, Newton, and Haswell all brought in deer or hares, the first lieutenant managing to creep up on and kill a hare hidden by rising ground between them. "This mode of killing game might not suit the ideas of sportsmen at home; but out here anything is allowed provided one can only bring home something for the good of the ship or his own mess," reasoned Piers, "particularly in these sharp times."[82]

And they were—indeed—"sharp times."

# 12

# Starvation, Madness— and Mutiny, 1852

One morning a loaf of bread went missing from the cabin of Paymaster & Purser's Steward John Wilcox ... the thief's identity went undiscovered.

Piers initially wrote sympathetically about this event, "the third or fourth case of theft of provisions since we have been on reduced allowance; but if the crime can admit of any extenuation, I think it should be in the case of this ship."[1] Then his tone hardened:

> [T]o be slowly, yet perceptively, losing flesh, [weight,] and spirits, must, when added to the other circumstances attending such a long, dreary & monotonous voyage, be very trying to many fore-mast men, and doubtless would tempt some to steal a piece of bread or meat who, at other times, would not dream of such an action. But on the other hand it might be said that every one fares alike, and the thief is not robbing the well fed, as might be the case under other circumstances, but is depriving his shipmates & messmates of what they can ill afford,—thus aggravating the crime.[2]

The ongoing desperate need to supplement the food supply apparently even forced a turn of mind for the "Jolly Tinker" (Blacksmith & Armorer Henry Stone); up until he killed a hare on March 15, Stone was innocent of shedding blood, never wishing to be labeled a "sportsman." Characteristically superstitious, his shipmates considered Stone's action something of a good omen, which predicted success for their hunting expeditions.[3]

It is impossible to fully understand, without experiencing them, the hardships, privation, and fatigue endured by those hunting in the early months of the year. "If we fired, reloading could only be accomplished after much difficulty and delay, with the certainty of frost-bitten fingers. A zealous hunter could always be recognized by his disfigured face—the result of frequent frost-bites."[4] And by this time, the perils of losing one's way while ashore were well known, as were the apprehension and strain suffered by would-be rescuers.

Such situation again reared itself on March 17, after Henry Stone, Quartermaster George Brown and Able Seaman George Gibbs departed for a hunt at 9:00 a.m. Nelson wrote that the trio headed for a mountain chain about seven miles inland, bordering "a large Inlet" [which must have been Castel Bay]. By evening, except for these three, all the other hunters had returned onboard, so everyone became very anxious, and signals were made by firing blue lights and the mortar at intervals. With no sign of the lost men by midnight, McClure dispatched Cresswell, Sainsbury and Court, each with four men and appropriate weapons and supplies.[5]

"Shortly before 5 a.m., the flash of a musket was seen off the point ahead of the ship, and at 5, Stone came aboard [after 19½ hours' absence]. The Corporal of the watch [Farquharson?] having called me I instantly jumped up & met our 'jolly little tinker' on the lower deck; and, however he may have felt during the night, he had then his usual cheerful expression of face and manner."[6]

Sainsbury and his party returned at 6:45 in the morning, but the mate was so worn out, one of the men had to carry his gun, while two others supported him while walking. Piers commented that Sainsbury, "although apparently in good health, seems delicate and unable to bear fatigue & cold." Cresswell and Court arrived back two hours later, without having discovered any trace of the missing men, and Piers commented how "our greatest fears were entertained for their fate. At 10 a.m. Haswell & Wynniatt were dispatched, with a party of four men each, to continue the search."[7]

> Just after 1 p.m. I was speaking to Fawcett, Boats. M., a messmate of Brown's and a resident of Strood, adjoining Chatham, to which latter place Brown also belongs, and saying I have feared he would have sad news to carry to Chatham. He said, he feared so too; but added, he had yet some hope for them, for he knew B. was a stout going fellow & could bear an immense deal of fatigue. After this I only had time to go to my cabin when two men were reported coming round the point towards the ship: the Captain, most of the Officers & the greatest part of the men ran out to welcome them back again....[8]

Many years later, Brown recalled the predicament he and Gibbs found themselves in, and how it resulted in a providential twist of fate:

> It was early in the morning when we left, and meaning to be back not much after noon, we had not taken any provisions with us.
> We soon shot two hares, and were looking for whatever other game might present itself, when a herd of deer crossed our path. The place, the time, and the future were all forgotten and the herd became to us everything, till a blinding snow storm drove them from sight, and to us, to thinking where we were.
> The thought was easy, but the reduction from the thought, as far as utility went, absurd.
> The storm continued without intermission all that night, the livers, hearts and blood of the hares, our food and drink, and food and drink we needed as we toiled and toiled on, in vain hope of reaching the ship.
> I do not remember whether the night was dark or light, but I do remember a splendid dawn, and fierce contention between my companion and myself.
> He positive, continued on his course, I resolute, climbed an ice hillock, and watched and watched him till he faded out of sight and then...
> Consciousness returned with a confused murmur of threats in my ears, and a numb feeling of blows (of a musket) on my body. Roused to exertion from my pleasant and dangerous torpor, I found my companion had returned. Said he, "I think after all you are right" (about the position of the ship).
> That position had been our contention.
> He discredited me, and went; but in returning to me and my opinion, we mutually saved each other's lives.[9]

At any other time, the first week of April would have seemed to have been smiling on the *Investigator*. The gloom and harshness of Old Man Winter was but a memory, and every evening the moon was wrapped in a glorious circle of dazzling brightness and delightful color

... but it was all a cruel illusion. Though the serving of fresh meat somewhat counteracted the wicked progress of flesh loss, the sick list's daily average gradually rose. At the end of March, Mr. Paine had entered a 99-day stretch due to rheumatism and debility, and he was joined that first week by Private Thomas King (debility, 83 days), Private Thomas Bancroft (debility, 29 days),[10] and Able Seaman Charles Steel (dysentery, 29 days). Chatham-born Able Seaman Thomas Morgan, who first went to sea in 1823 around the age six, as an apprentice, had it worse than most—at month's end Dr. Armstrong had to cut a tumor out of him, thus beginning 118 days under medical care.[11]

Although the seventh was the most successful day of acquisition, wherein no less than 300 lbs. of venison were added to the *Investigator*'s stock, it was also the day "Pipes" (Boatswain Kennedy) came face-to-face with those predatory actors of the hunting stage—wolves. The boatswain left in the morning to look for a deer he had wounded the previous day, before darkness intervened; the same one others had chased for two days and also wounded. Following its tracks, he reached a deep ravine, only to find a pack of five wolves devouring the deer's remains. Intent on at least recovering something of his rightful kill, Kennedy moved forward while very loudly shouting, in hopes of frightening the poachers away. Four of the wolves moved off a few yards, sat down, and began woefully howling—but one very large brute stood its ground. The boatswain, who held his musket in one hand, seized one of the deer's hind legs, while the wolf stubbornly pulled at the other end. Hoping to keep the wolves at bay, while at the same time attracting help, Kennedy continued his chorus of abuse. Meanwhile, the spectators sat snarling at this peculiar tug of war.[12]

All the commotion attracted the attention of Johann Miertsching, who came over an adjacent hill and joined the much trembling and excited boatswain, who feared an immediate attack by the wolves. But with Miertsching's arrival, the wolves hurriedly retreated to a hill about 200 yards away; it was just then that Dr. Armstrong also came on the scene. The boatswain threw the remnant of the deer over his back, and the trio made their way to the ship. Kennedy ended up bringing in 20 lbs. of meat—instead of what would have been 120 lbs.—and he was given a portion, while the general stock was increased by 14 lbs.[13]

With April came rapidly rising temperatures, which encouraged McClure to prepare a sled journey to Melville Island, in the hope of finding some of Austin's ships, or if a depot of provisions had been left by the same, "in the event of any accident occurring which would render it necessary to quit the [*Investigator*]." Dr. Armstrong was asked to choose an officer and six men for the sled party: Second Master Stephen Court, Captain of the Forecastle John Calder, Captain of the Foretop Peter Thompson (from the North-West Passage sled party), and Able Seamen Samuel Bounsall, John Davies, and George Gibbs, and Sergeant John Woon.[14]

Before leaving the ship, McClure prepared a dispatch for the Admiralty.[15] This was an abstract of proceedings since parting company with HMS *Herald* on July 31, 1850, off Cape Lisburne, and included a chart with routes of the 1851 sled parties. In these writings, he slyly played up successes, and downplayed difficulties, by twisting facts.

McClure noted the discovery of a North-West Passage route, and by implication, a second route. He stated that a "ship stands no chance of getting to the westward by entering the Polar Sea, the water along shore being very narrow and wind contrary, and the pack impenetrable"; he continued disingenuously, "but through Prince of Wales' Strait, and by keeping along the American coast, I conceive it practicable." What a ridiculous statement, especially having ear-

**Melville Island from Banks Land, May 1852 (S.G. Cresswell, 1854).**

lier written how he *twice* attempted to penetrate the ice in the strait and sail into Viscount Melville Sound, but found it impenetrable because of the heavy floes from the Beaufort Sea ice stream. McClure was simply trying to enhance his discovery of the first North-West Passage route—and after all, he knew virtually no one outside of the *Investigator* could argue with his assertion.[16]

The commander deceptively stated the "health of the crew has been and still continues excellent, without any diminution of number, nor have we felt the slightest trace of scurvy." He went on to relate how no traces of Franklin's expedition had been found, and that it was his belief Franklin never reached any of the shores the Investigators visited or searched. But then McClure coated the end of his dispatch with an opaque veneer of truth by writing, "nor have we been more fortunate with respect to the 'Enterprise,' not having seen her since parting company at the Straits of Magellan, the 20th April 1850." Of course he hadn't been "more fortunate" in keeping company with his commanding officer—he deliberately eluded Collinson at the Bering Strait![17]

It had been nearly two years to the day since *Enterprise*'s outline faded from sight into the vastness of the Pacific Ocean, and in April 1852, she came out of winter quarters at Winter Cove, on the southeastern side of Walker Bay, Prince Albert Land. On the previous September 26, at Cape Wollaston (the southern entrance to Minto Inlet), a sled party led by the *Enterprise*'s Second Master Francis Skead discovered a cairn left by Haswell. Skead's journal entry afterwards was tinged with envy: "Our consort had thus done more in the way of search than we had given them credit for.... I consoled myself with the hope that our consort while reaping a rich harvest in the fields they had explored, had left the deep inlet that lay before us as gleanings for the 'Enterprise.'"[18]

Collinson prepared to dispatch three spring sled parties, each with eight men and provisioned for 40 days.[19] Lieutenant Charles T. Jago, in HM Sled *Victoria*, left on April 12 to examine the southern coast, and determine if Prince Albert Land was joined with Wollaston Land.[20] Two northern sled parties left on April 16, comprised of Captain Collinson in HM Sled *Enterprise* and Lieutenant Murray T. Parks[21] in HM Sled *Resolution*, with the intention of pushing through the Prince of Wales Strait and separate at the northern end: Collinson to head east, along the northern coast of Prince Albert Land towards Cape Walker,[22] while Parks[23] would make for Melville Island.

Five days before the departures of Collinson and Parks, McClure left with his men and at least 28 days' provisions, bound for Winter Harbour, Melville Island. "This event in itself produced an agreeable amount of excitement throughout the ship, and appeared to exercise a cheerful influence on the minds of all," pleasingly wrote Armstrong. The fatigue party moved out with the captain's sled at six in the evening, amid their shipmates' cheers, and accompanied McClure for about four hours.[24]

While the Investigators' hopes accompanied their captain, the business of hunting and bringing in additional meat continued, along with clearing the ship's deck, removing the housing, and taking down the snow bank from her sides. "In the last half of the month the weather has been consistently foggy,"[25] wrote Miertsching, so that "often the returning hunters must be shown the whereabouts of the ship by the discharge of cannon and rockets." Though the store of venison climbed to 1,155 lbs.—the highest monthly mark since rationing began, or any month thereafter—the endless gnawing feeling that plagued George Ford was no doubt all too familiar to everyone onboard: "I feel sometimes [so] hungry that even when my belly is full I want more, which is through not having sufficient substantial food to keep up the body as when I say (belly full) it's only with tea or soup, which we make in boiling our venison, not much better than water. It's here I have felt hungry & would turn from nothing that can be eaten. However, I trust in God for our preservation & contentment & release this summer."[26]

Boatswain's Mate Edward Henry Fawcett entered the sick list on April 29 with scurvy and great debility—*evil* was among the Investigators. Professor Keith Millar, of the University of Glasgow's College of Medical, Veterinary and Life Sciences, explained that this first case of scurvy, and the five further cases by June, "would suggest that the dietary intake of vitamin C was below the 10-milligram daily requirement to avoid the disease in adult males (but note that substantially greater intake is required by those involved in heavy physical labour). As the onset of scurvy typically follows some four to six months of a deficient intake (but can appear earlier), it would suggest that the crew's diet was becoming deficient in the vitamin in late autumn or early winter of 1851." This coincides with the reduction in provisions McClure ordered in October, and the declining availability of fresh meat throughout the winter.[27] On the same day, the men began the backbreaking work of collecting stones for ballast,[28] which was accompanied by several cases of snow blindness, and continued through May 25, to complete the needed 100 tons. Procuring water then commenced, and otherwise preparing for *Investigator*'s expected liberation—even though the ice measured 6'8½" at the beginning of

the month, a menacing increase of 4½". Ford explained how, on the second day of their strenuous labor, they were "[p]ut on full allowance of grog & lengthen the time for work from 6
to 6. Breakfast at 7, dinner at 12 & supper at 6 o'clock. We have 14 men in the [sick] list with
pains in the body & bad eyes, not having sufficient food to keep up their strength."[29]

Just after McClure's party left *Investigator*, the temperatures sank once again, and combined with the thick weather, snow, and abominable traveling conditions over the pack, the
men "were frequently brought to a complete halt, so that it was only by the greatest exertion
that they could bring the sledge, foot by foot, over the heavy ice that was everywhere met with."
Winter Harbour was not reached until April 28, and the small band entered the harbor[30]:

> I went to Winter Harbour in confident anticipation of finding one of Austin's ships or a depot of pro-
> visions and great was my mortification in meeting neither but a short notice left by McClintock saying
> provisions were at Cape Spencer [southwest coast of Devon Island, near Beechey Island], this was con-
> clusive that all hopes of Franklin were given up and it was never contemplated our penetrating so far,
> I expected a vessel would be left there to cover fronts with the time for which the Plover was ordered
> to remain out, an assignment either side of the Polar Sea would have made the service perfect, for had
> any accident occurred making it necessary to quit the ship when we were nearer to Melville Island than
> Plover, I should most certainly have perished for it, and I think Collinson will be inclined to do the
> same.[31]

"The captain himself said that when, after long search, he had convinced himself that neither
the one nor the other was there, he had wept like a little child," lamented Miertsching. Nothing
greeted them but a small, flat tin case among a few small stones, atop Parry's Rock. The case
contained McClintock's message, dated June 6, 1851, from Captain Austin's expedition, in
which he stated that it spent the winter of 1850-51 between Cornwallis and Griffith Islands,[32]
and according to Armstrong, "a depot of provisions with a boat, were at Port Leopold, (of
which we were aware) and a small depot, likewise, at Cape Spencer, distant nearly 600 miles,
(by travelling)—with some other intelligence connected with the party." Much later, McClure
was able to write whimsically to his half-sister about the "few lines left upon a large block of
sandstone at Winter Harbour by my friend M'CIintock, of 3, Gardiner's Place, Dublin. It is
curious that two Irishmen, one coming round the world by the east, and the other by the west,
should leave a notice upon the same stone."[33]

Two months after McClintock had put pen to paper and scribed the note he left at
Winter Harbour, Austin's four-ship squadron was released by the ice, and sailed for England.
Jones Sound was briefly examined by the steamers *Pioneer* and *Intrepid* during the return.[34]

There was nothing to do but deposit the notice (dispatch), and head back to *Investigator*.
This was accomplished in ten days due to improved weather and flat ice nearly the entire journey, and the party came onboard May 9; "with the exception of the frost-bites they had
received, and a few of the men being afflicted with snow blindness, they were well; but all
were considerably reduced in flesh." In spite of the first case of scurvy having appeared,
McClure later wrote in a dispatch that he "had the gratification of receiving the most satisfactory reports concerning our sanitary condition," following with, "and likewise that the supply of venison continued abundant, having twenty head of deer on board; in consequence,
the ration of venison was increased to a pound and half thrice a week."[35]

Back on Melville Island, Lieutenant Parks made landfall on May 16 at 12:30 a.m., under
Cape Providence, about 40 miles southwest of Winter Harbour. All hands were exhausted,
four of the party were partly snow-blind, and one was almost disabled. The weather being
fine and calm, Parks decided to push on to Winter Harbour with Boatswain's Mate James

Rich and Able Seaman William French, but

> immediately after leaving the people, and getting on the ice, I saw sleigh tracks, and marks of three men's footsteps going toward Point Hearne [at the entrance to Winter Harbour], but they were too much defaced to make out whether they were European or Esquimaux. I then told the people to move up the coast to a place I pointed out, after they had slept. I had given them the raccoon skin, and the only gun I had with me. After going a short distance I saw other sleigh tracks, but older than the first, and going in the contrary direction. 7.30 went on shore to sleep; lat. 74° 33'. 12.30 p.m. started again on our road, when I again saw sleigh tracks: road very good for walking. 6 p.m. fine weather, with a breeze from the S.W., being within 4 miles of Point Hearne, having large hummocks of ice between us and the shore. Heard the howling of Esquimaux dogs,[36] as if being put into harness. Having no arms, and being so far from the people, I was not in a fit condition to have any communication with the natives. Although very loth to do so, I was obliged to turn back. 11 p.m. came up to the point where I had told the people to move to, and found they had just arrived, and that they had managed to thaw some water in a pemmican tin, but had shot nothing. Had they done so I would have taken them on to Winter Harbour, but having only half a tin of pemmican left, the only thing I could do was to erect a pile of stones on the point, and leave the captain's cylinder, which I did, scratching the ship's name on a large stone on which the pile was built.[37]

And so, even after Captain McClure and Lieutenant Parks missed one another, Parks came very close to discovering the notices left at Parry's Rock. If Collinson and McClure had again made contact, one wonders what course the Investigators' future would have taken. Later that year, Collinson made a note in his journal about one of Parks's men—William French—writing that the able seaman, "having been with Mr. Parkes [sic] on Melville Island, may be said personally to have connected the link between discoveries of Sir E. Parry and those of the American Continent." French also possessed a curious "link" with one of the Investigators, for the 25-year-old sailor hailed from King's Lynn, Norfolk—the hometown of Lieutenant Samuel Cresswell.[38]

Celebrations of any kind were becoming thin on the ground, but like any good British subject, James Nelson noted that Queen Victoria's May 24 birthday was not allowed to pass without a 21-gun salute being fired in honor of the occasion.[39]

On May's final day, two snow geese (the first of the season) were seen making their way northward, followed by a few gulls on the same path. Before then, the little snow bunting had appeared in late April, "whose cheerful warbling told us of the approach of a more genial season." The North American crane followed in mid–May, and Armstrong was pleased to acquire two good specimens for the expedition's natural history collection. The common and king eider ducks, brent geese, great northern, black- and red-throated divers, came along next, followed by the pintail and long-tailed ducks. "Short as the period of their stay is," wrote the surgeon with gratification, "it is impossible to describe the cheerful aspect which their presence imparts to regions hitherto so deserted and dreary, and over which the most death-like stillness universally prevails."[40]

But all was *not* still, for the ice that trapped *Investigator* had continued to grow, as Carpenter Ford recorded: "I measured the ice which was 6'10"; increased 1½"."[41] "[I]ndeed, the land is as much covered with snow as in the depth of winter," commented McClure, "nor was it until the 25th of the month that any alteration took place, when small streams commenced trickling down the sunny slopes of the ravines, and little ponds formed upon the ice.—On the 30th we had an entire day of heavy snow, with one of the most severe northerly gales that I had ever witnessed at so advanced a period of the season." And with the toil of watering the ship, dragging sleds through the soft snow, Armstrong grimaced as he observed how the men "began to present an altered and haggard aspect, and to complain of a feeling of general languor, weakness and debility."[42]

Because of rampant snow blindness among the hunters, McClure had ordered the search for game switched from daytime to night only, when the sun's rays were not so strong. The golden plover, phalarope, and purple sandpiper frequently fell victim to the Investigators—but not all winged creatures were destined for the dinner table. "A specimen of the North American Crane was shot on the 3rd," to Armstrong's delight; "—it was a noble looking bird, was 2½ feet high, had an expanse of wing of 4½ feet, and weighed 8 lbs." This, along with Miertsching's having "gathered and dried 3,785 specimens of plants, grasses and moss from various lands," up until early July, demonstrated the resolve to continue carrying on with scientific work.[43]

Eight reindeer were brought in during June—including three shot by Charles Anderson, weighing a total of 223 lbs.—but many of these animals had disappeared by the middle of the month (presumably to migrate inland). Early on, Boatswain Kennedy had another adventure with wolves, which according to Nelson were so numerous they were overrunning the land. While pursuing a deer, the boatswain saw it suddenly halt atop a hill, some 300 yards distant—"at the same moment [10–12] Wolves made their appearance in quick succession, none of which had been previously seen. They formed a circle around the affrighted Deer, and in a crouching position gradually closed on him. Suddenly, as if by some preconcerted signal, they all sprang on the animal, and immediately brought it to the ground, when the work of devouring it commenced." After firing two shots at the pack, Kennedy advance towards the grisly scene, and the wolves moved off—only about 15 minutes had passed from the time the predators were first spotted. Little was left of the poor creature, but "the skin, with the spine, antlers, part of the head, and bones of a hind leg—the rest having been devoured. The bones he brought on board—they were cleanly picked, with small shreds of flesh adhering."[44]

On June 22, fate seemed to draw a line in the snow when Miertsching penned: "With the inspection of the provisions, much of the preserved meat was rotten and thrown away. Our stock of provisions will last to August 1853 on the present half ration [*sic*—two-thirds]."[45] There is no way of knowing exactly how much meat was found to be bad, but the good fortune that was to soon smile upon the Investigators attained even greater meaning.

Somber news again led off a new month, as July found the ice had increased in thickness four inches over the previous month, to reach seven feet two inches. A "most unusual circumstance ... during the month of June, the temperature likewise was very low, showing an average of 31½°," wrote the *Investigator*'s increasingly concerned captain. This was nine degrees *lower* than the previous year.[46]

"The appearance of the crew at their monthly inspection elicited a more unfavourable report from the surgeon than I have hitherto received," McClure penned to the Admiralty, "evident symptoms of debility amongst the generality of them, and sixteen having a decided scorbutic tendency, *plainly the effect of the late heavy labour in ballasting and watering* [emphasis added]; but as all our work is now on board, their gradual return to perfect health may be anticipated without encumbering the sick list."[47] McClure cleverly sidestepped the fact that the lack of sufficient food was the root cause of his people's weakness, which grew worse with heavy labor, and then allowed scurvy to attack. The captain knew there would be no "gradual return to perfect health."[48]

"I felt it my duty strongly to represent [to Captain McClure] the great necessity there existed of placing the ship's company on a more liberal scale of diet," Armstrong wrote in earnest, "and on a larger proportion of vegetable food, with the view of arresting, if possible, the progress of that disease, the germs of which were now so generally manifest amongst them." The surgeon pressed his commander still harder, asking if, indeed, a full allowance of provisions were not available to carry them through a possible third winter, then make the allowance for at least three months, so the men may better endure the arduous work following the ice breaking up. Armstrong explained that, should *Investigator* get free, there was every reason to hope she could make her way eastward, and come within grasp of some of the depots in that direction. However, "assuming that, should we be so unfortunate as not to succeed in either, at least recruiting the strength of our men, and fortifying them in some degree, against the rigour of another winter, which would I feared prove fatal to some, and be most severely felt by all." McClure made no mention of his surgeon's pleadings in his official dispatches, nor in the pages of his book.[49] Armstrong concluded, "To these recommendations Commander M^cClure refused to accede, or make any addition whatever to the allowance of provisions, on which they were then placed, and I could not but feel much regret at this, his expressed determination."[50]

James Nelson felt that, if it were not for keeping the men busy preparing the ship and hunting, the health of many of his shipmates would have suffered to an even greater extent. "Shooting was becoming very trying to men already much debilitated," wrote Armstrong, "from the quantity of water everywhere met with on the floe and the land, through which we were necessarily obliged to wade." Even though the broken state of the ice near the ship offered hope for an early release, "gloomy forebodings as to the future" invaded Nelson's mind, not the least of which was the stock of venison having run out. The Investigators were then dependent on what small game could be brought in.[51]

It was just at this time that one man's sheer raw courage proved to be the salvation of all: Sergeant John Woon, Royal Marines.

Around noon on July 8, Sergeant Woon left the ship to go hunting. Some hours later, while chasing a wounded deer, he unexpectedly came upon two musk ox bulls lying down (one of which was asleep). Advancing to within 120 yards of them, the Marine fired and wounded the larger of the pair, both of which then got up on their legs. "On receipt of the first wound, which did not appear to affect him in the least, the animal approached with a most ferocious aspect until distant about forty yards, when he stood as if about to make a charge." Woon fired again, but the second wound did nothing to alter the bull's attitude. The other beast had come closer by this time, and Woon decided to try to secure both animals by disabling the second, so fired and wounded him as well. Becoming enraged, this bull advanced on Woon. "The Sergeant, in the mean time, reloaded and fired his fifth and last ball at his first antagonist, who still remained in the same position—the missile struck him in the centre of the forehead, passed through his brain and he fell to the ground."[52]

"Having expended his ammunition as one of the wounded and infuriated monsters rushed toward him, he fired his 'worm' [ramrod screw] when at a few yards, but without much effect, as he continued his advance, evidently, however, weak from loss of blood, till he had reached within six feet, when, putting his head to the ground previous to his final rush, the sergeant, as his last resource, fired his iron ramrod, which, entering behind the left shoulder, passed through the heart and out at the right flank, dropping him dead at his feet."[53]

The following morning, two sleds were sent to gather the prizes, but the much-exhausted crews did not return to *Investigator* until five o'clock in the evening, there having been a serious accident. A sled slipped off the bank along the shore into the water, taking with it one of the men. "He tenaciously clung to the sledge, which floated in deep water, and in about fifteen minutes they succeeded in bringing all in safety to land. The man was nearly lifeless from this short immersion in icy cold water, and it was only with difficulty that they succeeded in establishing reaction after the lapse of a considerable time." The poor soul in question was surely Able Seaman Samuel Bounsall,[54] as he was the only patient admitted to sick bay that day; suffering from debility, he took 19 days to recover. Once onboard, the larger musk ox was measured at 7½ feet long, and 6½ feet in circumference, and both proved to be "fine animals, whose gross weight is 1,330 pounds, and yield, after deducting offal [inedible parts] and hunters' perquisites [privileges], 650 pounds of excellent beef, which providential supply was most opportune, as our reindeer were expended last week."[55]

Another very close encounter with Mercy Bay's native inhabitants occurred on the evening of the 12th. Carpenter's Crew William Whitefield had ventured to the bay's entrance, when he suddenly found himself face to face with a bear standing a mere 20 feet away. Thinking it unwise to attempt a retreat, Whitefield raised the musket's butt to his shoulder and prepared to defend himself against the anticipated attack, when ... *another* bear came up at a lively pace, and stopped within about 40 yards of the sailor! The trio stood in each other's company for several minutes, before Whitefield felt joyful relief when the bears simply turned around and ambled off toward the sea—sending the sailor jubilantly off as fast as his legs would carry him, back to the ship.[56]

Also in the middle of the month, Ice Mate Newton "reported the floes outside to be in motion. All heard a rumbling noise, as if the pack were driving along, and the joy was great, until upon further examination it was found that the *débâcle* from a ravine was pouring its strong current over the floe." Still, areas of rotting ice were dangerous for those going to and from land, and one time, when close to shore, Court and two sailors broke through the ice and all of them lost their guns.[57]

However, some dangers were not from without—but from within: Mark Bradbury suffered a second epileptic attack on July 19. Over the seven months between his first and second attack, Bradbury was in "comparatively good health." Both attacks "were severe, of great intensity, and recurred at short intervals" for the first 16 to 18 hours; during them, an excessive quantity of blood rushed to his brain, his heart pounded rapidly and his face glowed purple—while both eyes nearly popped out of their sockets—and small amounts of blood ran from his mouth and ears. The overindulgence in spirits was believed to be the reason for the first episode, and although no cause could be traced for the latest seizure, "for a month or two previous, it was observed that he had become very silent and taciturn, with marked peculiarities in his manner & conduct from having previously been one of the most cheerful & loquacious of our crew." The doctor engaged in a prolonged course of treatment for the next 174 days, and although much weaker than before the attack, Bradbury's health remained good. He never suffered another seizure, but his mind remained like that of a child, and he was tasked with only light duties.[58]

In the meantime, the ongoing battle to shore up the Investigators' health found allies springing up from the harsh soil: sorrel and scurvy grass. Common sorrel has been cultivated for centuries, and the flavor of the leaves resembles that of kiwifruit or sour wild strawberries. Scurvy grass was widely recognized in British folk medicine for its worth in treating the disease, and was taken on voyages by fisherman and sailors; it has also been suggested that the plant may have even been used by the Vikings. Miertsching found "a kind of sorrel" growing in abundance on a hill, and "brought a whole handkerchief full to the ship, washed it, seasoned some food with it, and presented this salad to the captain and the officers. The doctors said that it was very good for the health and also both a cure and preventive of scurvy." But Dr. Armstrong simply wrote the sorrel and scurvy grass "made their appearance on the land," making no mention of Miertsching's find, and took credit for himself: "I represented the necessity there existed of using our best efforts in procuring them, and the good effects which would certainly attend their regular issue to the ship's company."[59]

During July and the early part of August, 12 to 15 men were daily employed gathering sorrel. They usually brought 8 to 12 lbs. back to the ship from the hills, which was eaten as a salad with vinegar at midday meals, or boiled (causing it to resemble spinach). Seaman James Nelson was so comically impressed with Haswell's daily display of lying down flat and grazing on sorrel, he likened the first lieutenant to a sheep![60]

Dr. Armstrong at least had the sincere satisfaction of recording the abundant evidence of positive change,

> for on 1st of August, I could clearly discern an improvement in the general appearance of the men, and the majority expressed themselves as feeling generally better than they had done a month previous. I should also mention that during this time, they were able to procure Ducks, Geese, and other birds occasionally, each man being allowed to retain for his mess the small game he shot, which ever proved a most acceptable addition to it. For a short period, therefore, the evil which threatened us appeared to be partially arrested; clearly proving the necessity there existed for fresh vegetable and animal food.[61]

"Our worst trouble for the moment is that it is impossible to find employment for the seamen," worried Miertsching, "for neither on land nor on the ice is there anything to be shot, and though sea-fowl seeking open water are often seen near the ship, every time a dozen men rush out, not to shoot but to scare; and sports on the ice are not carried on as last year, for hungry stomachs take all the joy out of the men, and even the desire to live." Miertsching went on to record how temptation overwhelmed at least one man, Able Seaman Frederick Taylor, who—for the second time in just over a year—felt the searing pain of the cat-o'-nine-tails slicing across his back. Taylor earned three dozen strokes for stealing a loaf of bread from the oven; this for a man who had recently spent 24 days suffering with debility in sick bay.[62]

The state of the ice was watched every day with increasing excitement—and apprehension. Open water was spied from the heights, reaching for some distance beyond the mouth of Mercy Bay, "and as the ice was entirely detached from the shore by a narrow lane of water [50 feet across[63]], we earnestly hoped for an early release." Those going ashore had to use Halkett's rubber boat after reaching the edge of the floe. The "ice around the ship has been blasted away, so that its fragments may be carried out of the bay with the tide as soon as the ice breaks up, and open a way for the ship."[64]

By mid–August, open water could be seen in the straits; "the bay opened at the outer end, and the imprisoned navigators saw with delight that a broad lane of water extended along the southern shore for ten miles to the eastward. Their hope of reaching it lay in a strong south wind blowing the ice of the bay and the ship out with it to seaward." Using ice saws to cut a path between *Investigator* and the open water was not in the cards, since winter would be upon them before such could be accomplished. There being a possibility of a southern wind, the top gallant yards were put in place, sails bent, and the tide pole taken in. A record of the expedition's accomplishments, and where the ship expected to go, was placed in a cylinder; this was attached to a pole to act as a beacon, in McClure's words,[65] "in the hope that it may meet the eye of some future explorer of these sterile regions, and throw some light upon the fate of those who perhaps may never reach beyond these limits."[66]

But the Investigators' reach exceeded their grasp.

On August 21, the high was only 38°F (down six degrees from 11 days before), and temperatures kept falling thereafter, so that the part of Mercy Bay that had been open froze over three days later. The land fast became covered with snow, and what little vegetation there was, shriveled away. Northerly winds still prevailed, and all the ice was perfectly still, with "no water visible in any direction, that along the cliffs of Banks's Land being frozen, so that [McClure] felt assured that the winter had fairly set in, and all hopes of any release this year totally annihilated, the young ice being five inches thick."[67]

Hints of a further reduction in the scale of provisions (from two-thirds to one-half) reached the ears of James Nelson and his shipmates, only adding to the gloomy news that Old Man Winter would once again be their jailer. Nelson also noticed a striking change in the men's temperaments—they became irritable and easily offended, so that one had to be careful as to *what* subject was brought up in conversation. And scurvy attacked again, this time crippling Able Seamen John Davies and John Ramsay for two months; Joseph Paine's rheumatism also returned, and it was 127 days (on Christmas Eve, no less!) before he was well enough to return to duty. By the end of August, Bradbury was under close watch, as "he is quite distracted, and makes a terrible noise at night"; having the deranged sailor in their midst would have made the wretchedness of life onboard all the more unbearable.[68]

"The captain, oppressed with anxieties, seeks comfort by wandering alone on the hill," sympathetically penned Miertsching. "He always, especially in the presence of officers and men, assumes an air of cheerfulness and hope; but in his innermost self it is far otherwise; as a voyager of experience in the frozen seas, which he is now sailing for the third time, he knows and grasps our situation better than anyone on board; his many prayers and sighs uttered in his cabin or on lonely walks on land declare much more than he reveals in words."[69]

"Having previously determined what course I should adopt under circumstances thus unfavourable, upon the 8th September I announced my intentions to the crew." Miertsching recorded McClure's speech, which only added to the Investigators' agonizing downward spiral[70]:

> Today he assembled the crew on the upper deck and addressed them in a solemn and impressive speech: he declared frankly that after careful observation it was his conviction that the ice would not break up this summer, and therefore they would be compelled to pass a second winter in the same place; he would do everything in his power to make their lives throughout the long winter as pleasant and comfortable as possible, and he urged them not to lose heart, but with firm faith to trust in God, under Whose protection they all were, to discipline themselves and behave like British seamen, whose steadfast courage never yet had failed; for himself, he had a firm, unshakeable conviction that not one of us would be left behind, but that all would safely reach their fatherland. In conclusion he said that for a year we had received rather more than half a daily ration; and still through God's good favour found ourselves in good health; and now, to make our small reserve of provisions last until next summer he felt compelled to make another small reduction in the daily ration that we might in a period of complete inactivity remain in health: he had some food, his personally, and this he would share in common on appropriate occasion.[71]

Armstrong knew the reduction was

quite inadequate to maintain health in an Arctic climate, our condition fully proved; much less is it able to sustain life for any lengthened period, if laboriously engaged and exposed to the rigorous severity of intense cold. The Lime juice, the regular issue of which had been attended with so much previous good, was at this time, likewise, reduced to one half the quantity [½ oz. lime juice mixed with ½ oz. sugar daily]; and to my great regret, no extra food was allowed for the sick under any circumstances— the same scale of diet being ordered for all. We had previously felt much the want of food. As our private mess stock had been long exhausted, the officers were in the same position as the men.[72]

But there was more. McClure went on announce that in the following spring, he would send away half of the crew in two divisions.[73]

The larger party, consisting of Lieutenant Haswell, Assistant Surgeon Piers, Mates Sainsbury and Wynniatt, and 22 men, was to strike out for Cape Spencer, via Griffith Island (Cape Spencer is along the southwest coast of Devon Island, close to Beechey Island—see the Western Arctic Map for locale). Armstrong wrote that what Haswell had to cover, "making due allowance for ice travelling, could not be estimated at less than between 5 or 600 miles[74] [804–965 km]" to the cape, with 45 days of provisions, where it was understood a small depot and boat had been left. In editing McClure's book, Sherard Osborn added a telling footnote: "To the best of the Editor's knowledge, this [depot] consisted of a boat so heavy that no sledge-party could have launched her; the provisions were two casks of salt meat and a bale of blankets." As soon as the season permitted, Haswell would attempt to find a whaler along the western shore of Baffin Bay or try to reach Greenland, from where he and his party could hope to return to England.[75]

Knowing all too well the debilitated condition of the men would only be worse with the passing of eight months, the doctor was blunt: "To enable men to undertake such a journey as that by Cape Spencer, it would require them to be in a high state of health and vigour; even then, the risk attending it would be considerable."[76] What's more, the distance Armstrong stated from Mercy Bay to Cape Spencer certainly could not take into account a *precise* route and distance, which involved traveling over several areas of sea ice. Nor could one possibly know the variable ice and weather conditions, which may considerably slow down—or even delay for days—a large party of half-starved men. It was a death sentence.

The second party was to be led by Lieutenant Cresswell, with Miertsching and six men, also traveling many hundreds of miles. He was to have 13 days of provisions for going eastward, along the shores of Banks Island, then move south through the Prince of Wales Strait to the Princess Royal Islands, where *Investigator* had left provisions and a boat. When the ice broke up in three months' time, Cresswell was to attempt to reach the North American coast, travel up the Mackenzie River to the HBC post Fort Good Hope, and then on to England (see Canadian Arctic Islands and Greenland Map). Interestingly, in McClure's instructions to his three 1851 sled parties, if *Investigator* was found to have drifted down the Prince of Wales Strait, every effort was to be made for all the parties to rendezvous at the Princess Royal Islands, and "equip yourself with two months' provisions, and make the best of your way to the 'Plover,' as Fort Good Hope upon the Mackenzie cannot be depended upon as a station." But McClure dare not hope Cresswell could reach *Plover* in the spring of 1853, and may have assumed she would have left Port Clarence by this time (but in fact, *Plover* was on station until September 1854).[77]

"The weakest men were to proceed by this route," warily wrote Dr. Armstrong, "some of whom would be unable to walk; and in their condition, a sojourn of three months under canvas, while waiting for the breaking up of the ice, followed by the severe labour necessarily entailed in transporting a boat through ice encumbered sea, when barely able to guide themselves, could not but excite the gravest apprehensions amongst us." The surgeon stressed how he had previously "fully informed" McClure of the state of the men's health, but "nevertheless, I felt called on again, to represent their condition, and to express my opinion of their unfitness for the performance of this service, without entailing great and inevitable loss of life. It had no result."[78] Another death sentence.

Captain McClure, Second Master Court, Clerk-in-Charge Paine, Surgeon Armstrong, Boatswain Kennedy, Carpenter Ford, Ice Mate Newton, and the rest of the crew, were to remain onboard *Investigator*, in the hope of breaking out of Mercy Bay in the summer of 1853, or if unsuccessful, proceed by sleds to Port Leopold in 1854. Port Leopold, at the entrance to Prince Regent Inlet, is where Sir James C. Ross left a hut and ample supply of food and clothing for Franklin's men in 1848–49. Reaching that place would have involved taking a route from along the (still largely unknown) southern shores of Viscount Melville Sound. Remembering McClure's misleading opinion about the land area between Peel Point and Cape Walker, such a journey would be much longer and more hazardous than McClure expected.[79]

In his official dispatch, McClure explained that his intentions were the result of "our provisions admitting of no other arrangement, although we had already been a twelvemonth upon two-thirds allowance, it was necessary to make preparations for meeting eighteen months more, a very severe deprivation and constitutional test, but one which the service we are employed upon calls for." In explaining to his old commander, James Clark Ross, he wrote that "this is the only plan I could adopt in the hopes of saving the ship"; and to his half-sister, "I hope this measure, which I have adopted solely upon my own responsibility to endeavour saving the ship, as well perhaps as a little pardonable vanity in wishing to bring her as a trophy to England, will be approved of by the Admiralty." The emphasis was on "the ship" and his "vanity"—and even at that, McClure surely realized the extreme uncertainty of ever breaking out of the ice. Of course to the Admiralty, he also cleverly presented the *Investigator*— and the *glory* of sailing the North-West Passage—as convenient justifications for his way forward[80]:

> [T]he vessel being as sound as the day she entered the ice, it would therefore be discreditable to desert her in 1853, when a favourable season would run her through the Straits, and admit of reaching England in safety, where the successful achievement of the long-sought-for and almost hopeless discovery of the North-West Passage would be received with a satisfaction that will amply compensate for the sacrifices made, and hardships endured in its most trying and tedious accomplishment. This statement was well received [by the crew], and its execution will, I hope, be carried out without difficulty.[81]

McClure's positive twist regarding the crew's reaction to his announcements was mirrored for public consumption in his book, with additional gleeful bits: "This arrangement was cheerfully received by this excellent body of men; and those who thought they would be the first to go home, were soon heard speculating, with praiseworthy generosity, upon immediately volunteering to come out again in the first ship to the rescue of their messmates, and with lighthearted jocularity promising to bring out a good stock of tobacco pipes for them."[82]

But the dark and sobering reality of the crew's reaction was revealed in confidence to James Ross, with a finger pointed directly at the captain's nemesis onboard—Dr. Armstrong— whose "remarks upon the occasion of my telling the men last September what were my intentions with respect to sending them home, & consequently a slight reduction of provisions, so as essentily [*sic*] created a mutiny, which might have attended with unpleasant consequences, but the Marines with their gallant & energetic serjeant behaved like good men and true."[83]

McClure appears to have had his Marines "stand to" (stand ready for an attack). This would explain Miertsching's seemingly cryptic words, when he "could observe many gloomy and anxious faces, but in this situation there was nothing to do but submit"—as one must do when staring down the barrel of a gun and point of a bayonet![84]

McClure continued afterward to Ross: "Pray do not mention any thing about my crew being disaffected, although I have detailed the circumstance to the Admiralty; for in all other occasions I never met a finer or more energetic lot & so well disposed, but they were panic struck by being told [by Dr. Armstrong] their provisions were not sufficient to support them & that the vessel ought to be left [this] year &c &c."[85] McClure had long been in a severe bind when it came to dealing with his quarrelsome surgeon. Dr. Armstrong's skills were essential, and with him being on warmhearted terms with the crew (even more so during this time of growing sickness), the captain had to be careful about suppressing the doctor. What's more, McClure needed a medical man to stay onboard *Investigator* for the duration, and he dared not send him away with one of the parties in the spring, for fear of the possibility (however slight) that Armstrong might make mischief with the Admiralty before McClure could get home.

Winter came on rapidly, and although the wind shifted on September 17, and blew hard from the south-southeast, the ice was firmly set at eight inches thick; there was nothing to do but unbend the sails and prepare to begin housing in the ship. The 24th was the anniversary of the ship's arrival at Mercy Bay—when it was 33°F and a completely ice-free bay—but on this day the mercury stood at two degrees, the ice solid in place, and there were signs a very severe winter was in the making.[86]

With the animals having returned farther inland, or retreated to large valleys, the Investigators lacked the strength to reach them, but were encouraged to continue trying to hunt, rather than be inactive and brood about their situation, over which they had no control. Consequently, no deer were brought in during August or September, and according to Armstrong, not until the last day of October did the first deer of the season fall. During the space of these three months, only 14 hares, 61 ptarmigan, 55 wild fowl, and one seal were shot, the water-loving birds having departed around mid–August. Worse still (in the eyes of the crew) a survey of the spirits supply at September's end found a shortage, so the issue was reduced to half a gill (2.4 U.S. fl. oz.) per day.[87]

"The doctors have examined all members of the crew, and report that the general health is fairly good, but," noted Miertsching, "warn the captain that the daily ration is insufficient and must have evil consequences." Surgeon Armstrong's gentleness and unfailing kindness had made such a deep impression on the sailors and Marines, that James Nelson prayed for God's mercy to spare the doctor to them. And so the sick list continued to grow, with the more notable cases in September having been: Able Seaman David Harris (scurvy, 43 days); Able Seaman Richard Ross (stricture and irritable bladder, 144 days); Able Seaman Samuel Relfe (rheumatism and debility, 42 days).[88]

McClure knew (as Armstrong had told him more than once) that without game being added to the provisions, they would not make it through winter on the current allowance of food, and all hands would have to abandon *Investigator* in the spring—"but nothing," wrote McClure, "but the most absolute necessity will induce me to take such a step." Miertsching "notices symptoms of grumbling and discontent among the men; one even sees hungry sailors burrowing in last winter's garbage-heap, which still lies on the ice, in the hope of finding some discarded morsels to still their nagging hunger." The captain ordered that all small game shot will be turned in to the common stock, with half saved for the sick, and the other half returned to the hunter. When larger game started to become available, venison would be issued in place of regular rations.[89]

With the men consumed with a desire for food, and experiencing even more intense cravings during this period, on October 4, Armstrong witnessed how they "came on the quarter deck in a body, to ask for more food, and to be placed on a more liberal allowance of provisions, but to their application, Commander M$^{c}$Clure peremptorily refused to accede."[90] Miert-sching provided a more detailed picture of the scene—but with a very different out-come:

**Engraving of Robert McClure (after a painting by Stephen Pearce, 1855; courtesy Douglas Wamsley).**

> Today at midday the entire crew gathered on the upper deck and demanded, through the officer of the watch, a few words with the captain. As he appeared, four sailors approached him, requested his pardon for their unauthorized assembly, and stated that the crew had resolved to present a collective request for a small increase in rations: they could not exist on the present allowance; they could not sleep for hunger, etc. The harassed captain listened of necessity to this petition, and after an earnest conference dismissed the men with a promise to grant their request.[91]

McClure's published account *leads one to believe* he did increase the rations, since towards "the close of September ... they were on a bare two-thirds of rations," and at the start of November, he wrote that, "hungry we all are; but, with a little management, the two-thirds allowance, now that we have nothing to do, keeps us from losing health." Neither Armstrong, Miertsching, nor Nelson mentioned anything about a return to two-thirds rations. Miertsching did write on October 26: "Today in memory of the discovery of the Northwest Passage the captain out of his own stock gave a meal and extra grog to the whole crew," and on November 26: "The captain supplies an extra ration of grog weekly to the whole crew, and this is received with gratitude and greedily devoured; everyone is cheery and good-humoured."[92]

As the thermometer's highs and lows settled into negative numbers, even though double the quantity of clothing was piled on, the emaciated bodies could not produce the warmth to fight off winter's onslaught. On deck, no one exercised more than required of the usual daily routine, which was shortened by an hour from previous winter routines. The hatchways were still kept open, and housing in and snowing the upper deck were postponed, in an attempt to conserve the already scarce supply of candles and oil. The men constantly complained of the cold, as they endured sitting, eating, and sleeping in the damp, frigid atmosphere below decks, which extended an invitation to disease.[93] "The whole week I have suffered great pain from rheumatism in all my limbs and have been plagued with a violent tooth-ache," glumly wrote Brother Miertsching on October 7, adding "[T]he doctor drew two of my teeth yesterday on account of a bad ulcer. All day long I shiver with cold, and must then at night lie in a damp bed, where I find little repose because of pain."[94]

Quartermaster Henry May was struck with scurvy for nearly three months, beginning October 5; and the sick list numbers mounted throughout the month. Nearly all of the rest were rheumatism and/or debility, under treatment between 12 and 41 days (cases related to the cold): Anderson, Batten, Bounsall, Bow (dysentery), Boyle, Evans, Keefe, Tiffany, Toy.[95] One additional case mirrored the unfortunate Bradbury's situation, as Miertsching recounted another Investigator who had become unhinged:

### October 14

For a short time now we have noticed in one of our officers, Lieutenant Wyniatt [*sic*—Wynniatt], strange actions that have puzzled everyone. Yesterday they took shape in complete madness, and he, like Bradbury, must now be watched day and night lest he do violence to himself or to his ship-mate. He passes the night with frightful shouting and raving, today he slept a few hours and then began again to jest, laugh, weep, sing, and whistle; neither threats nor kindly admonition have the least effect on them. I went to him and begged him in the most affectionate terms, as one who occupied the cabin next to mine, to sleep a few hours at night, or at least to remain quiet that others might be permitted to sleep, but he seemed not to understand or to grasp the meaning of my words.

### October 16

Our two distracted comrades are no better yet; they sleep by day; by night they weep and rave. Today I again visited Mr. Wyniatt; he kissed my hand and wept without speaking a word to me. Today in memory of the discovery of the Northwest Passage the captain out of his own stock gave me a meal and extra grog to the whole crew; the officers were invited to dine with the captain; unhappily the poor stricken Wyniatt could not be one of us. A quite unwonted animation prevails onboard; everyone is cheery and good-humoured.

### October 31

The men are building new sledges for those who are to travel next spring.... The deranged seaman, Bradbury, has grown quite peaceful; he speaks little and sleeps much; Mr. Wyniatt, on the other hand, raves and jests frantically as ever. I visit him in his cabin daily, but he listens to no advice, takes no medicine, and says that not until the captain and Dr. Armstrong are dead will he cease from his raving.

### November 5

The poor sick Wyniatt is causing much trouble with his raving and babbling. I am the only one besides his servant whom he allows to approach him, but his mind seems utterly unsettled. As often as the weather permits, I go abroad, just to escape from the ship.[96]

Dr. Armstrong, indulging in the age-old belief that the moon triggers strange behavior, remarked how Lieutenant Wynniatt's emotional outbursts coincided with "Lunar changes," and Nelson noted how the officer had to frequently be confined to a strong room below decks. But on a more scientific course, the doctor probed his patient for possible answers as to the origin of his condition during "occasional intervals of lucidity" (sometimes occurring after treatments with medicines), when he again became "quite rational"[97]:

From all that I have been able to learn, there exists in his family a hereditary predisposition to the occurrence of the disease, of which I had no knowledge prior to his illness, he was occasionally guilty of slight eccentricities, to which no particular attention was ever paid, as they appeared nothing more than the offspring of an enthusiastic and excitable disposition, but kind and good natured to a degree.

He was passionately fond of music,[98] prone to indulge in habits of ease & luxury, had an opportunity in our cruise ever afforded him the means of doing so, we might be expected from one of his phlegmatic [calm] temperament, in which there likewise existed much of impulse & excitement, but not of a permanent nature, he had a dislike to his profession, but particularly to the service in which he was then engaged.[99]

For some time Wynniatt had been having dark premonitions "with respect to our probable and ultimate fate," wrote Armstrong, "which had much increased when it became evident that we were destined to spend another winter in the ice, which together with other causes, more immediately connected with our internal economy & to which it is here unnecessary to allude, had for a long time previous rendered him very unhappy in his mind."[100]

Robert Wynniatt's family appears to have been established at Dymock Grange (Dymock, Gloucestershire), and held estates there, since the times of Henry VII and Henry VIII. In this regard, lands were passed to the family at the dissolution of Flaxley Abbey, during the reign of the latter.[101] The son of a minister, Robert was the eleventh of 13 children (he had five brothers and seven sisters), and when he was just 11 years old, his older brother Wenman died under mysterious circumstances an ocean away.[102]

At age 22, Wenman Wynniatt was commissioned (by purchase) an ensign in the 83rd Regiment of Foot in December 1837, and gained his lieutenancy (also by purchase) two years later. The regiment had been ordered to Canada in February 1834, and saw active service after rebellions in Lower and Upper Canada broke out in late 1837, and extended into 1838—when one Lieutenant Robert McClure was also involved in battling the rebels.[103]

Horse racing was a very popular sport for British officers in Canada during this period, and Lieutenant Wynniatt had two horses: a grey foal named Cinderella, that evidently had a jittery nature, and another mount named Beatrice. In 1839, while Wynniatt was on garrison duty in Kingston, Ontario, he broke his femur during a race, and was out of commission for a month. At the time, he was riding another officer's horse. The following year, Wynniatt raced in London, Ontario, during a two-day event at the Newmarket Racecourse, on November 2–3. After a fine start, Cinderella made a poor showing at the rails, and bolted off the track, leaving Major (Mr. Maitland's horse) the victor. On the second day, Wynniatt was riding Beatrice in a hurdle race, but was again denied a victory.[104]

In the spring of 1841, the lieutenant was invited to a ball on the evening of Friday, May 14, to be given at Eldon House, the nearly 10,000-square-foot Georgian mansion of John and Amelia Harris, leaders of London society. Wynniatt had been in a steeplechase race attended by Sarah Harris, the Harris's eldest daughter, and having spied Sarah carrying a rose before the race, he suggested that it be awarded as a prize to the winner. Lieutenant Wynniatt afterward became the proud possessor of the rose, and placed it in the buttonhole of his jacket. Encouraged by his success, the young officer asked Sarah for another prize—several dances at the upcoming ball—and she agreed.[105]

Friday evening, Sarah waited for Wynniatt to join the party. Arriving late and wearing ordinary evening dress, the lieutenant looked at her intently, but said nothing as he continued through the library (being used as the ballroom), and proceeded into the dining room. Sarah followed Wynniatt into the latter, but found he had simply disappeared. Evidently, his presence in the library was also noted by three soldiers Sarah was standing with, in addition to Mrs. Harris. Lieutenant Wynniatt was not seen again until Sunday morning, when his body was found in the Thames River, close to the bottom of deep water in the middle of the river, nearly entirely covered by sand. The hands of his ruined watch were frozen at 10:15 p.m.—the exact time he had appeared in Eldon House; and his buttonhole still contained Sarah's rose. Evidence seemed to suggest that he fell, or was thrown, and hit his head, while wading a shallow portion of the river on horseback.[106]

A dozen years later, younger brother Robert was facing his *own* ghost, and Armstrong "felt disposed to form an unfavorable opinion of his state, as there was no possibility of either obviating the causes which existed or removing him from the sphere of their influence, and there was consequently every possibility of his disease assuming a more permanent character."[107]

Even though venison again began being issued in November (three times every two weeks, in lieu of provisions), Armstrong listed only three deer were shot for October and November, so the venison could not have lasted very long. Sadly, because the portion of food was so small, and then shrank when it was cooked, "the practice of eating the salt beef and port raw, and the preserved meat cold or in a half frozen state, was almost universally adopted by both officers and men." Armstrong told McClure this would only further the deterioration of health, and encourage the onset of scurvy, but nothing changed. And on the fifth, another sailor went on the sick list for 48 days with scurvy.[108]

Two weeks later, Able Seaman Mark Griffiths was admitted with debility for just over a month, but Henry Gauen went under the knife a few days afterward for a contracted tendon, and endured a three-month recovery.[109]

The officers felt the time had arrived for each of them to take turns dividing up the daily rations as Paine issued them, and then draw for them by lot. Generally the portions were eaten during one meager meal, unless "a mouthful of bread for a little weak tea or cocoa" could— by self-restraint—be saved for morning and evening. They also had a daily ration of 8 to 12 lbs. of coal under the care of the officer of the day, who ensured it was burned during the times of day they could afford to have a fire. Likewise, the quantity of oil being small, lights glowed only at certain hours of the day.[110]

The sun deprived the Investigators of its company on November 7, and the banking up of the ship's sides, and other outside work, was completed the following day. A few days afterward, Carpenter Ford sustained a hernia while helping to prepare for housing in.[111] On the 18th, the upper deck was layered with 18 inches of snow. "This winter there is no school," wrote Miertsching. "[T]he men employ themselves by reading books from the ship's library and other private books, and by sewing, knitting, crocheting to shorten the fearful long hours." Most of the sailors and Marines had lost their will to hunt, "with one or two laudable exceptions," like the ever dependable James Nelson. It was therefore up to the officers, and though the weather was fair, they braved temperatures that sank to the—30s and 40s to bring in what they could; the humble figures amounted to a mere 1 deer, 3 hares and 16 ptarmigan for all of November.[112]

Heavy gales, continual storms, and snow drift greeted December; even so, daily exercise on the upper deck remained a requirement, and (according to Seaman Nelson) the captain led by example, despite his lower tolerance for the cold, with the least bit of exposure causing severe frostbite. Nelson also had an appreciation of how such physical demands only added to the mental strain of command. Outside, the hunters' persistence paid off, and several deer fell to the Investigators—though at a price. In the darkness, Armstrong fell down a steep snow bank and suffered a hernia. Miertsching "wounded a buck reindeer with very large antlers; he charged at a sailor who stood by, but the latter struck him a blow on the forehead with the butt of his gun and dashed him to the ground; the gun broke into three pieces, but we shared the proceeds of the deer." Other successes followed, and the victors drank the blood of their victims, "as it flowed fresh and warm from the wound"; but the deep crimson hues froze on the hunters' faces, and they greeted their shipmates with ghastly masks when they came onboard.[113]

Fine and clear weather then smiled on the Investigators for at least some of the time, before it turned foul again as the holiday approached. It mattered not. The crew had voluntarily slightly reduced their food allowance, so that full meals could be provided for Christmas and New Year's days. Given that it was the last Christmas the entire ship's company was to spend together, particular care was paid to decorating the tables, and McClure admired how "each mess was gaily illuminated, and decorated with original paintings by our lower-deck artists, exhibiting the ship in her perilous positions during our transit of the Polar Seas, and divers[e] other subjects." Miertsching admired how "flags and rhyming aphorisms were sprinkled on the walls. On every table was a plum pudding, posing as a hill, from which the small English pennants and flags, handmade by the seamen from silk, were waving."[114]

Divine Service was held Christmas morning, followed by the midday meal, which was consumed with passion. Marveled McClure: "The grand features of the day were the enormous plumb puddings, some weighing six and twenty pounds,[115] haunches of venison, hares roasted, and soup made of the same, with ptarmigan and sea pies."[116]

"A seaman disguised with a long beard, represented Zero; he gave a long speech in the presence of the captain, in which he, in the name of all his comrades, gave thanks to the captain for facilitating such a jolly day; thereupon the captain responded with a long speech and promised another such jolly day with a joint meal with plum pudding before the parting in the next spring."[117]

The poets amongst the crew drew vibrant laughter from verses of their own sufferings, while comic actors added to the hilarity. One of the "poets" was James Nelson, whom Miertsching described as a "young sailor, once an evil-doer, whom I had later won over, had learned to read and write, and had begun to write poems; this man, previously so coarse, but now, through the grace of God, reformed," may well have recited this (undated) original poem for the occasion[118]:

Arctic Cooking
I'll chant you a song that puts out of time
Modern inventions of every clime
And zero himself must confess it's a plan
That beats all the Inventions of wonderful man
Then hasten right merrily!
Bring the Mills cherrily!
And endeavour to frighten black hunger away.

Such grinding and clankering you never did hear
Oh! you'll find the very best of economy here
And so well is it practiced that in one fell swoop
It silenced for ever the old cry of "Pea soup!"
Then hasten &c

French Cooks coming here would stand a poor chance

For would soon turn their brain from that cook shop France
And Jellies-a-la-mode would fly from their minds
And with their usual politeness—ask—"donne moi a la grind"
Then hasten &ᶜ

So gentlemen have I again to repeat
That the grinding the peas gives an excellent treat
And so reccommend you all with a polite "if you please"
The new plan of the arctics—to grind all your peas.

Then hasten &ᶜ

And to England I'll go as soon as I can
And induce the M.P.ˢ* to take up the plan
And then if I don't—may I stop here to freeze
Get a Polar Act passed for grinding all Peas.
Then hasten &ᵍ[119]

[*Members of Parliament]

When recounting the scene in his official dispatch, McClure was inclined to "stretch" the truth about the condition of his men: "Any stranger to have witnessed this scene could but faintly imagine that he saw a crew which had passed upwards of two years in these dreary regions, and three entirely upon their own resources, *enjoying such excellent health* [emphasis added], so joyful, so happy."[120]

All the same, it was most unwise for starving men to have gorged themselves, and afterwards Nelson and his shipmates became miserably ill. This only added to the never-ending mortal reminders of their insane predicament. Bradbury was quiet, but deeply depressed, and continually wept. Wynniatt was also quiet while onboard, but only rambled during his numerous visits with Miertsching. Yet the lieutenant "is left on the ice daily where he [is] free to vent his rage against the captain. Thrice already he has made murderous attacks on him."[121]

Even Wynniatt, with his demented mind, knew who was responsible for their dilemma.

# 13

# Infinity's Brink, 1853–54

*Strange—is it not?—that of the myriads who*
*Before us passed the door of Darkness through,*
*Not one returns to tell us of the road*
*Which to discover we must travel too.*

—*Rubáiyát of Omar Khayyám* (FitzGerald's translation)

Brother Johann August Miertsching left behind 1852, comforted by the knowledge that the Lord had "so inclined the hearts of my ship-mates that they gladly listen to my weak words spoken for the good of their immortal souls; and show by their conduct that they have found the better way and seek to walk in it." Starvation humbles the soul.[1]

Gale-force winds from the southwest continued unabated New Year's Day, and thus kept everyone bottled up within their wooden walls, and protected from temperatures that dropped to a staggering –65°F during January. The *Investigator* herself cried out: one could hear bolts, nails and fastenings crack from the frost and contraction. The subdued holiday celebrations began with Divine Service in the morning, followed by the midday meal, and a private assembly in the evening. "Thoughts of the future and of what the Lord has in store for us this year have caused a very serious frame of mind among the men." They wondered who of them would the captain decide should leave the ship with the sled parties under Lieutenants Haswell and Cresswell—and who shall stay onboard?[2]

Though Miertsching naturally believed that "to Him alone is that possible which seems impossible to us," the Moravian brother could not escape a *realistic* assessment of his upcoming spring traveling with Cresswell. "When I contemplated the proposed journey, its difficulty, and ourselves, humanly speaking according to my understanding, there is not the faintest possibility that any one of us should reach England."[3]

Mierstching recorded how McClure "is continuously busy and much concerned to provide what best serves the health and comfort of the crew; and his care is acknowledged by many with thanks." The brother had lost 35 pounds since the previous New Year's Day, and was fortunate in preserving his health, never appearing on the sick list for the whole of the expedition. Still, with a medical survey showing the men growing weaker, and scurvy spreading and appearing in a more aggressive form, the number put on the sick list rose to 16 during January—double the admissions for either of the two previous months. The effects of cold and hunger were grinding the men down.[4]

Doubtless Private Thomas King and Able Seaman John Ames were thankful to have recovered by January 1 from 22 days of dysentery and four days of intermittent fever, respectively, but it was several more days before Batten's rheumatism and Hulott's frostbite allowed them to be released to duty, and another two more months before Keefe's ascites was resolved. A new round of scurvy attacked Facey, McDonald, Saunders, and Davies, laying them up for one to three months. Charles Anderson suffered with ascites for 84 days, plus a case of frostbite that resulted in a further amputation. Eleven more souls labored under dysentery, debility, diarrhea, rheumatism, and fever.[5]

Armstrong was fighting a losing battle against scurvy and he knew it: "My resources were so limited that when scurvy advanced to a certain stage, I was obliged to discontinue the treatment, so as to be able to extend it to more urgent, recent cases, the consequence was, that the disease was never thoroughly eradicated, but only temporarily subdued." And since the causes of the disease were not only still present, but became stronger every day, when scurvy reappeared, it did so in an even more severe form. The disease was closing in on all of them.[6]

As sick bay filled up with occupants, in order to keep their growing numbers warm to some degree, Dr. Armstrong had them stay in hammocks along the majority of the lower deck. "A few hours illness would produce the most alarming degree of prostration I have ever witnessed,—fainting and syncope [from low blood pressure] were constantly present on making the slightest exertion." *Investigator* must have come to resemble a hospital ward struggling to cope with an epidemic. In the meantime, Wynniatt had become quieter by mid–January, but was still watched with a close eye, because of his threats to murder the captain and the officers, and also to set fire to the ship. Afterward, his return to crazed behavior necessitated his being tied up. Then, both he and Bradbury took to incessantly howling and raving day and night.[7]

The bitter cold seemed to have caused the reindeer to forsake high elevations for the coastal regions; therefore a dozen deer fell prey to the Investigators' guns during January (for 866 lbs. of meat). Even for the weapons themselves, "the cold is so severe that the ordinary double-barrelled guns crack when discharged, and the spring of the lock snaps ... and all have become unusable; only the best English firearms stand up in this climate." With a renewed regular supply of venison, the six hares and 10 ptarmigan shot were allowed to become property of the individual hunters.[8]

But rations were still tightly controlled, and unceasing hunger often became the denier of sleep. Miertsching witnessed how actions resulting from such overwhelming cravings brought fearful punishment: "The ship's baker was reported to the officer of the watch for thieving; when his chest was searched, meat, flour, and dough were discovered; after stubborn denial he finally confessed to the officers and received two dozen of the cat on his naked back." Considering his previous flogging, and that his overall conduct during the expedition was only "Fair," this was most likely the Subordinate Officers' Steward and Gunroom Cook Henry Sugden.[9]

"The ebbing courage of the men seems to have revived with the return of the friendly sun [on February 3], for every man begins afresh to hope that this year he will succeed in escaping from the ice and come back to his beloved fatherland." The life-giving star's companions during the month were dense fog, frequent gales, snowdrifts and nearly intolerable cold, which averaged—38.5°F. On the lower deck, "particularly from about twenty feet before the main hatchway to the gun-room bulkhead, has been very damp and wet; we cannot afford [to burn] more coal to dry it up," wrote a frustrated McClure. Even though the weather permitted hunting for only a few hours for two days of the first week, four deer were shot; six more fell in February, for a total of 706 lbs. of fresh meat.[10]

In preparation for his plans, McClure employed the strongest men in carrying sand on sleds, and had it spread in a broad strip for 800 yards from *Investigator* toward the mouth of Mercy Bay. Miertsching wrote that McClure did this "in the hope that through it the ice may melt earlier in the powerful rays of the sun than if under a white blanket of snow. The intention is, when summer comes, to tow the ship through this canal nearer to the open sea. The men thus employed are to draw a larger daily ration." By month's end, after Armstrong and Piers examined the crew, a report was made to the captain: not a single man was fit for heavy work. As their bodies became steadily weaker, so did their spirits.[11]

> Twenty-one men are now in hospital,[12] and the recovery of some is despaired of; truly a gloomy prospect for us, for in six weeks we must, with those judged unfit to remain longer with the ship, harness ourselves to sledges laden with supplies, and drag them through snow and ice for hundreds of miles. How many of us will in this way see Europe? The answer is: "No one."
>
> But what if we should leave the ship in a body, whither could we go? In this icy region we know of no ship but our own.[13]

As dark and sinister as the future appeared, it was still taken in hand by Miertsching. Since the Blacksmith and Armorer Henry Stone was in sick bay with intermittent fever, the multi-talented interpreter turned his hand to metalworking, and had set about making three dozen small mess tins ordered for the spring sledders. And not one to be ungrateful, the man of God was thankful for the few *positive* changes around him: "Mr. Wynniatt, who now visits me frequently, has become much more tranquil, and often has a lucid hour."[14]

Armstrong observed how during the long winter, nearly the entire crew worked on preparations for the spring departures[15]:

> We had as yet remained in ignorance of the men who would be detached from the ship, as no communication had been made to me or others on this subject, and as each mean appeared to think himself unable to go through another winter, and preferred running the hazardous risk of the journey, rather than again experience the privations & sufferings of the past winter, which bordered on a slow system of starvation, so that with this feeling, so unusual amongst them, everyone had persuaded himself that he would certainly be sent, conscious of their own debility, and so anxious were they to depart from the ship, when hunger & want had been so severely felt.[16]

From this feeling the men's spirits were somewhat raised, allowing for the hope among them that they may again see home, "without in any great degree reflecting on the perils of the journey which awaited them, until the period of departure began to draw nigh."[17]

On March 2, the long-awaited announcement arrived, and Armstrong carefully recorded the event in his journal: "Captain McClure made known to me his intention of dispatching the weaker half of our crew from the ship, and retaining the most efficient, at the same time that he gave me a list of those men he wished to send, and who really were the weakest of our crew, but desired me to make any change I might consider necessary, provided the most efficient men were retained." There is a notable difference between the wording in Armstrong's journal and his book, as the latter states: "he requested me to make the necessary selection." To all appearances, Armstrong wanted to publicly give the impression that McClure *ordered* him to select the men for the sled parties, instead of the captain doing it himself. The doctor's journal continued: "There was however but little alteration to be made in the original list, and with one or two exceptions, it was returned as it had been received."[18]

The next day, the names on the list were called out, much to the joy of some chosen for the sleds, although Mietsching knew "many of those appointed to travel have visions of their corpses lying on the ice, [as] prey for wolves and foxes. Yet there are many who, having experienced the wondrous works of God, in all times rely on the aid of the Lord, our true Helper, and show a cheerful spirit." It was a bitter disappointment for the men remaining onboard *Investigator*. Dr. Armstrong then returned the list to McClure, and considered it his "duty to place on record (by letter)" the combined opinions of himself and Assistant Surgeon Piers, concerning "the unfavorable condition of the men and the absolute unfitness of several for the performance of the journey." Armstrong went on to state in his journal how several times he pointed out the men's growing debility, and the need to combat it by issuing more food— in addition to McClure's refusal to listen to the recommendations.[19]

In his official dispatch, Captain McClure wrote with cool deliberation how the crew "appeared extremely well satisfied with the arrangement, as I explained to them my object was to send home all who had suffered the most from the severity of the climate, and to which another year might prove exceedingly trying, as well as to retain the most effective men in the event of being detained another winter." And he continued further on in the most deceptive way: "On the 15th [of April] it is my intention to start to the parties destined to make their way to England; and from our good sanitary [healthy] condition I feel but little doubt but all will safely arrive."[20]

At the time, James Nelson seemed to have been the exception to the rule regarding the feelings among those who were to remain behind. He very much wanted to stay onboard to see things through, and felt *Investigator* may even eventually make a victorious passage up the River Thames. But two of his shipmates were devoid of all comprehension as to what was happening around them. The minds of Wynniatt and Bradbury were so altered, they could not be made to understand they were going to leave the ship; Bradbury "is perfectly docile and must be handled like an idiot child."[21]

Around the same time, the departures of the two sled parties were planned for on or about April 15, and McClure had previously indicated both would be placed on the full allowance of food for one month beforehand; this actually began on March 15. As summarized by Miertsching, a previous survey of provisions showed that supplies for everyone onboard could not last beyond November, "and because it was neither possible or practical to desert the ship in a body, [McClure] would send away only enough to ensure that supplies for those who remained with the ship would last until the following spring, in case the ship again failed to get out of the ice."[22]

Game had become uncommonly scarce, and only 8 deer (equaling 436 lbs. of meat) were shot for all of March, plus 19 hares and 4 ptarmigan. When deer were spotted, they were often so erratic that it was impossible to get sights on them. Up until this time, wolves had been too crafty to allow themselves to fall victim to the Investigators' guns, but on the 24th, as one of the beasts gorged on the carcass of a prize, Sergeant Woon put a ball through its heart from 100 yards. A few days after this encounter, Court met with a pack of seven brutes, one wolf closed in from the front, while the other cut off Court's retreat from behind—howling as they advanced. Their companions hid behind the ridge of a hill. Court tried to frighten the threatening pair off by shouting, waving his arms, and running toward them, but almost too late, he found the one before him only 20 yards away. Careful aim was taken, and a ball smashed into the predator's neck; undeterred, the beast continued to crawl forward, while it gnashed and showed its teeth. By the time Court reloaded and let go the fatal round through the wolf's head, the brute was only within three yards; this was too much for his accomplice and he made off.[23]

Although March had brought to light only seven new sick cases—the Reaper lurked in the shadows.

Among the newest patients was a 30-something Kentish seaman named George Gibbs— who just in early February had recovered from a 30-day bout of rheumatism and debility— only to go back on the sick list for 32 days with debility. Scurvy attacked Richard Ross and Thomas Morgan, and Morgan also suffered from scrofula (tuberculosis). Mate Hubert H. Sainsbury was in the worst condition. This officer struggled under bronchitis (as he had previously for 31 days in May and June 1852), catarrhal (inflammation of a mucous membrane, especially of the respiratory tract), and the beginnings of phthisis (pulmonary tuberculosis); his condition was also complicated by scurvy.[24] Fortunately, Armstrong had a "Jeffreys's Respirator" (a small face mask with a wire grid, which helped retain moisture from the breath) on hand, which made Sainsbury's breathing considerably more comfortable.[25]

As April drew closer, Dr. Armstrong saw outward improvement in the men; not only had their faces become healthier looking, "but more animated in expression; the dull, haggard stare of former days had become more generally cheerful." The travelers continued to prepare for their journeys in earnest, while those who were to remain onboard occupied themselves by writing letters to be carried home. This façade briefly obscured the Investigators' reality, until a grim reminder reared its ugly head: Sick Berth Attendant John Ames was seriously stricken on the second day of April with pericarditis (swelling and irritation of the pericardium, the thin sac-like membrane surrounding the heart) and dropsy (now called edema, which occurs when an excess of watery fluid collects in the cavities or tissues of the body).[26]

The newly built sleds were put through their paces during the first week of April, amidst fickle weather, with strong winds, snow squalls, and temperatures averaging well below zero, then stowed away. Nelson overheard shipmates who were anxious to take their departure, speaking assuredly of reaching England. All their personal possessions were packed up and addressed, before being handed over to Second Master Court for safekeeping, to be returned to them if *Investigator* made it home. McClure also issued a directive that has had a lasting impact on the history of the expedition[27]: "Through a written order of the captain's it has been announced: That all journals, sketches, charts, and other documents, written, drawn up, or prepared in connection with our expedition must, by the 5th of this month, be sealed, marked with the proper address, and delivered to the captain, who will turn them over to the Admiralty whence we may recover them"[28] (see Appendix 4, no. 22).

On April 5, McClure completed a long dispatch to the Admiralty, which detailed events starting off Cape Bathurst on August 30, 1850, up to this April day, and stated near the end: "To this period we have not lost an individual of our crew, either by accident or disease." He attributed "our excellent salutary state to the causes previously alluded to in this narrative, in conjunction with the bountiful game which a merciful Providence had aided us with, and has so materially added to our provisions, which are certainly of the best description I ever met with." Two days afterward, Miertsching wrote: "The captain spent the morning [of April 6] preparing for the Admiralty letters and dispatches which we [Cresswell's party] are to carry." It is telling that McClure planned to entrust important official dispatches to Cresswell—his *second* lieutenant—and not Haswell, his *first* lieutenant. Neither one had any real chance of

getting through to England, and McClure even wrote to James Ross that Haswell's party probably would have starved. The unspoken proof rested with Cresswell and the dispatches, of the
captain's undiminished dislike for Lieutenant Haswell—he saw no reason to give his first lieutenant any opportunity for personal recognition.[29]

McClure also took the opportunity to write a long letter to his first Arctic commander,
Sir George Back, in which McClure made reference to dispatches he assumed would get
through to England: "As you are in Town, you will see at the Admiralty, the tracing of our
discoveries, shewing a considerable addition of new territory." He gave an account of his proceedings, and curiously wrote that "in searching for poor Sir John Franklin, we have accidentally tumbled through this long sought for 'North West Passage':– indeed, two of them." He
stated this as though it were all by chance; and further on, McClure conveniently stated: "As
regards Sir John Franklin, I have arrived at the conclusion that, all hopes expired in 1850:–
when it was far from expected that we could have penetrated so far to the East."[30]

Very skillfully, McClure made sure to minimize the true seriousness of the state of his
crew's health, and this played into the conclusion of his letter, in which he prepared for possible
problems with his superiors, *and at the same time*, laid the foundation for advancing himself:
"Up to the present, I have much to be grateful for, in the freedom from serious sickness of the
Crew, and though some few cases of scurvy and dropsy have been prevalent, on the whole,
they are tolerably well:– and those intended to leave us, are already in high spirits for their
journey. As all my actions were on my own responsibility, I must beg of my friends at home
to give me a little support at the Admiralty—if they are not approved: and if they are—should
their Lordships think my services worthy of promotion—an influential word might get it
dated back to the 26th October[31] 1850, to commemorate the discovery of the "Passage"—
provided Enterprise is not before us, which I do not think." This is McClure's self-
congratulation for not waiting for *Enterprise* in the Bering Strait, and reveals that, even though
McClure achieved independent command, Collinson was undoubtedly viewed as "the competition."[32]

The night of the fifth, 29-year-old Able Seaman John Boyle spoke cheerfully from his
sickbed, made a slight movement, then faded into unconsciousness around 10:10 p.m., the
victim of dysentery, acting on a scorbutic tendency. A man of a rather small build, Boyle went
to sea in the merchant service as a boy, afterwards dealing with much hardship and privation.
During an 1849 voyage from the East Indies, most all of the crew came down with a severe
form of scurvy, and upon arrival in England, he was successfully treated onboard the hospital
ship *Dreadnought*. He signed on to another merchant vessel soon after being discharged, and
eventually found himself at Honolulu, so in July 1850, he volunteered for *Investigator*.[33]

Something of a mystery surrounds Boyle's death. On the evening of April 4—without
any specific cause besides cold, hunger and want—he experienced vigorous attacks of diarrhea
and much weakness. Boyle's condition ebbed and flowed. The next morning, with a weak
pulse and scorbutic symptoms, Dr. Armstrong immediately took him under his care and put
him to bed. The sailor steadily improved through the day and into the night, right up until
the time of his sudden passing.[34]

The quiet and inoffensive Boyle was appointed an extra sick berth attendant the day he
became ill. According to Nelson's understanding, Boyle was to clean empty acid bottles and
instead swallowed the remnants of their contents; Miertsching had a similar understanding.
Operating on an already weak body, the dregs caused diarrhea, followed by severe cold, and

a fatal outcome. According to McClure's 1856 book, the death "was occasioned by the thoughtlessness of the poor fellow himself, who, by way of a joke, went into the surgery and drank off the washings of several medicine bottles." The following year, Armstrong's published account stated, "[I]t was reported to me that he had taken some medicine out of a bottle which caused his death. I at once fully investigated the matter, and found it without the slightest foundation." However, Armstrong did not record this piece of information in his handwritten journal, and it seems probable the doctor was reacting to the revelation in McClure's book. It is also worth noting that Armstrong entered Boyle out of order on the (COPY) sick list, having placed him *after* Facey's and Gauen's entries on April 13.[35]

Boyle's song and tap of shoe were to echo through the wooden walls no more—the first Investigator to perish was gone—and the specter of Death now hovered over the ship's company. "This melancholy occurrence could not but evince a depressing influence on the minds of all, which was generally manifest throughout the ship, and enveloped us thus suddenly in a mantle of gloom and despondency," reflected the surgeon.[36]

At four o'clock the following afternoon, silence reigned in and about the ship. Some 400 yards distant, four men were hacking out a final resting place for their departed shipmate in the frozen earth.[37] Nearer to *Investigator*, McClure and Lieutenant Haswell were discussing the depressing business of cutting a grave in the permafrost, when "we perceived a figure walking rapidly towards us from the rough ice at the entrance of the bay," wrote McClure. At first, the pair thought it was one of their men being chased by a bear, but as they continued their approach, the manner of the stranger's dress struck them as odd. At about 200 yards, with arms overhead, the person made gestures that reminded McClure of those used by the Eskimo, and shouted "at the top of his voice, words which, from the wind and intense excitement of the moment, sounded like a wild screech; and this brought us both fairly to a stand-still." Then, the stranger quietly advanced, and McClure and Haswell "saw that his face was as black as ebony," so wondered if he was an inhabitant of this or some other world.[38]

"[W]e could hardly have been more astonished than when the dark-faced stranger called out,—'I'm Lieutenant Pim, late of the "Herald," and now in the "Resolute." Captain Kellett is in her at Dealy Island!'"[39]

Unable to utter a sound—for the sheer joy of relief being so close at hand had overwhelmed his tongue—the astonished McClure rushed forward and seized Pim's

Bedford Pim as a naval captain, c. 1883, wearing the China Medal 1856–60 (Lieutenant & commanding/*Banterer*), Arctic Medal 1818–55 (Midshipman & Acting Mate/*Herald*; Acting Mate/*Plover*/1845–51, and Lieutenant/*Resolute*/1852–54), and Baltic Medal 1854–55 (Lieutenant & commanding/*Magpie*), plus his judicial neck badge (Cooper, 1883; courtesy Douglas Wamsley).

hand. As news of Pim's arrival spread onboard, the *Investigator* exploded with human fireworks: "The sick, forgetful of their maladies, leapt from their hammocks; the artificers dropped their tools, and the lower deck was cleared of men; for they all rushed for the hatchway to be assured that a stranger was actually amongst them, and that his tale was true. Despondency fled the ship, and Lieut. Pim received a welcome—pure, hearty, and grateful—that he will assuredly remember and cherish to the end of his days."[40]

And yet, the realization that they were *actually* saved seemed beyond their comprehension. "The shock was to a degree overpowering to most on board, the men in particular," a stunned Lieutenant Cresswell wrote that day. "It struck me most forcibly that so far from having the effect of elevating [the mind], on the contrary had rather the effect of depressing or rather paralyzing the mind & faculties. The men might be seen walking about the decks with grave stupefied faces. Several that I spoke to seemed alive to the goodness of an ever masterful providence but at the same time their minds did not appear to be able fully to grasp the extraordinary, almost miraculous change in our circumstances."[41]

McClure and his Investigators had no way of knowing that it had been nearly one year to the day since Captain Sir Edward Belcher left England in command of a five-ship Arctic squadron—the Royal Navy's last attempt to find traces of Franklin. Although Belcher had overall command of the squadron, Admiralty orders essentially divided the expedition into two parts, an eastern division and a western division. In the eastern Arctic, HMS *Assistance* (Belcher) and the steamer HMS *Pioneer* (Commander Sherard Osborn) were to search the Wellington Channel. Meanwhile, in the west, HMS *Resolute* (Captain Henry Kellett) and the steamer HMS *Intrepid* (Commander Francis L. McClintock) were tasked with the region of Melville Island. If possible, they were to also leave provisions, fuel, and clothing at Winter Harbour (or failing that, Byam Martin Island, in between Bathurst and Melville Islands) for *Enterprise* and *Investigator*, since nothing had been heard of either since they passed through the Bering Strait in 1850 and 1851. Finally, HMS *North Star* (Commander William J.S. Pullen, Lieutenant Haswell's first cousin) was to act as a depot ship and base for the expedition at Beechey Island.[42]

Francis Cresswell (Samuel's father) had very much shaped his son's rescue. Through a letter he wrote to the Admiralty on March 23, 1852, he suggested that Belcher's forthcoming expedition could support Collinson and McClure by leaving supplies via steamer at Winter Harbour, and if "the Admiralty thought proper, in case of the steamer reaching Melville Island, she might winter there, and in the spring send searching parties to the westward. They might be so arranged as to command a wide field of research, and possibly cross Captain Collinson or Commander M'Clure."[43]

The *Resolute* and *Intrepid* parted company with the rest of the squadron on August 15, continued westward, and established winter quarters at Dealy Island. From there, during late September and early October—in preparation for longer journeys the following spring—sled parties set up supply depots at several points on Melville Island's southern shore. After sled parties under Lieutenant George F. Mecham[44] in HM Sled *Discovery* (motto—"Per Mare, per Terram, per Glaciem"—"By Sea, by Land, by Ice") and Mate George S. Nares[45] in HM Sled *Fearless*[46] put down a depot in Liddon Gulf, they went to Winter Harbour and found the note left by McClure.[47]

On March 10, 1853, the first party to strike out from Dealy Island was Lieutenant Bedford C.T. Pim, HM Sled *John Barrow* (motto—"Hope on, Hope ever"[48]) and seven men, accompanied by Surgeon William T. Domville, commanding HM Sled *James Fitzjames* (motto—"Deo Volente"—"God be willing") with Dog Driver (Able Seaman) Emanuel Bidgood and Sailmaker Robert Hoile,[49] and six Eskimo dogs (including a puppy). It was 160 miles to Mercy Bay as the crow flies, and they had a difficult start. Scarcely half a mile from the ship, the larger sled fell on its side and broke while crossing hummocks, and a replacement had to be gotten from the ship. Then, during the night a gale blew in, and the parties were confined to their tents for three days. "Fortunately," wrote Pim, "the temperature rose from—51° to—36°F, at which it remained." On March 29, the *John Barrow* broke down about 25 miles (40 km) from Cape Dundas (on the southernmost part of Melville Island).[50] Pim transferred his sled and crew to Dr. Domville, with orders for to go to Cape Dundas and wait for him. Pim then carried on with the *John Barrow*, Bidgood and Hoile. When Pim arrived at Mercy Bay at 10:30 in the morning on April 6, he did not see any sign of the ship, and convinced she had left the bay, determined to cross the bay, so as to trace the coastline in search of McClure's cairn. At 2:00 p.m. when already halfway across, "Hoile reported that he saw something black up the bay; upon looking through the glass, [Pim] made out the object to be a ship, and immediately altered course for her."[51]

Below decks on *Investigator*, Pim was so overcome by the half-starved faces and extreme sparseness of food on the mess table that "he rushed to his sledge, then out on the ice, brought a large piece of bacon, placed it before us, and gave us the only breakfast we had known for many a long day." Armstrong also witnessed how Bidgood and Hoile's "manly cheeks became moistened with tears" as they saw the men drawing lots for their evening 'meal'—a small cup of tea and a little biscuit.[52]

**Departure of the Travelling Parties from *Resolute* and *Intrepid*, April 4, 1853, by McDougall (courtesy Douglas Wamsley).**

The week following Pim's arrival onboard *Investigator*, Captain Kellett himself had returned to *Resolute* from a 10-day sled journey with a crew of seven men having pulled HM Sled *Erin* (motto—"Auxilium ab Alto"—"Help from above"). He wrote movingly in a private dispatch to John Barrow, Jr., Keeper of the Records at the Admiralty, and called attention to the toil of man-hauling heavily laden sleds, which caused him to ponder the idea of an "Arctic Medal" for sled travelers (see Appendix 7).[53]

Lieutenant Pim had brought dispatches from Kellett, and in his writings to the Admiralty, McClure offered only a vague explanation as to his actions regarding them: "In consequence of the purport [substance] of the despatches received from Captain Kellett, I deemed it preferable to communicate with him personally than by letter." Later, his published journal merely added a veneer of truth: "Captain M'Clure decided now at once upon going to see Captain Kellett, and making arrangements with him for having all his sickly hands sent to Dealy Island, and thence home, whilst he, still adhering to his original plan, endeavoured to carry home the 'Investigator.'" Consequently, at 6:00 a.m. on April 8, McClure, with Court and six men (including Able Seaman Nelson and Captain of the Foretop Thompson), left to see Kellett. Pim and his crew followed an hour and half later, taking the scurvy sufferer Able Seaman McDonald on the *John Barrow*. Later that day, a solemn funeral procession made its way over the ice to the shore, and John Boyle was laid to rest.[54]

Two days out, the Investigators were trying to drag their sled over a hummock, when it suddenly slipped down the side and capsized, severely injuring Nelson's right leg, which afterwards turned black and very stiff. According to Nelson, Thompson, and then McClure, became "very unwell"; but when Kellett greeted his fellow Irishman afterward, he wrote that McClure "looks well, but is very hungry." Dr. Domville was met up with at Cape Dundas, and given charge of the *John Barrow*. All three teams arrived at Dealy Island on April 19.[55] In spite of being barely able to crawl onboard, the very sight of *Resolute* wiped away all of Nelson's physical pain; still, Dr. Domville said he needed to be confined to a hammock for two months. On that same day, nearly three years since passing his qualifying exam in balmy Honolulu, the much deserving Stephen Court was promoted to acting master.[56]

Though the Investigators' circumstances had dramatically changed, Captain McClure's *mindset* had not. McClure still had absolutely no intention of abandoning his ship, and this flowed from his pen to the Admiralty.[57] In case he did not break out of the ice and return home in 1853, McClure laid out his intentions during 1854, so as to aid a coordinated relief effort. Among the possibilities, McClure may take on provisions from the depot at Port Leopold and then winter in the pack, or if he was detained at that place, he may take the boat stored there and make for the western shore of Baffin Bay, and fall in with whalers or their boats. If this failed, the plan was to cross Baffin Bay to Disco Island, Greenland.[58]

To James Ross, McClure recapped events upon entering the ice in 1850, and indicated that his wife Mary would relate the *Investigator*'s proceedings to the ship's 1848–49 commander, Captain Edward J. Bird. Predictably, McClure again minimized his crew's dire health, and as already revealed, boldly recounted the mutiny of September 1852—but when it came to his officers, the ink boiled over[59]:

> I have had a wretched time and will be truly glad when it is over, the dissensions among the officers themselves, and the impertinencies that I have been subjected to from a set of the most young inexperienced men I ever met with, has astounded me beyond measure, owning I believe in the first place to the baneful Union of the messes where Juniors had the majority & consequently carried everything

their own way, as none but the senior Lieutenant had ever been entitled to Gunroom rank before, whose apathetic disposition unfitted him for keeping order, the Surgeon consequently ruled the roost who is one of the most conceited fellows I ever met, having been three years in the Royal Yacht, which has given him ideas of self importance which is not at all reconcilable with his position, he has given me much trouble, opposing every arrangement which I have made.... Court is the only officer whose conduct has been exemplary, you my old James could scarcely credit what I have had to submit, I will only mention that Lt. Cresswell had the cool impudence to tell me that "my censure or commendation was a matter of the utmost indifference to him" now really I was not prepared for this from a youngster whom in the last cruise I was aware was not considered competent to take charge of a watch.[60]

In responding to a letter from his uncle (the Reverend Richard W. Elgee), which was delivered "through [Pim's] travelling party dispatched by my excellent friend Cap.[t] Kellett," McClure continued the charade regarding his men's health. Although he did admit to "having only lost one man who accidentally poisoned himself," he wrote to both his half-sister and his wife that he had not lost anyone "either by disease or accident," and to Mrs. Reynolds (Cresswell's aunt) that everyone was enjoying good health, and not a man had died since leaving England. In common within his writings to Ross, his half-sister, his wife Mary, and Mrs. Reynolds he (convincingly) gave credit to a higher power for the *Investigator*'s harrowing Arctic passage, through which God's hand alone safely guided them. McClure also paid homage to the Eskimos first encountered by Haswell on Prince Albert Land in 1851. As they had never before seen white men, he wrote to his uncle that he was struck how "they gave me a pleasing idea of man taken fresh from his maker's Hand and uncontaminated by intercourse with our boasted civilization, [while] all those [Eskimos on the mainland] who traded with the Hudson's Bay Company we found the greatest reprobates [thorough scoundrels]."[61]

It must have been known to McClure before he left in 1850 that his mother was unwell: "My dear Mother's demise I was prepared to hear and indeed from Jane's account view it as a happy release, for when reason was gone a more deplorable state of existence cannot be conceived, the mind irretrievably darkened what a sad spectacle." He finished with his uncle on how every effort was being made by the eastern Arctic search expeditions "to follow up the traces of poor Sir John Franklin"—and added almost as an afterthought, "I know nothing of the Enterprise & can only regret her leaving us."[62] McClure truly had no idea if Collinson had met with good fortune *or* misfortune, and so in planting a seed with his family that it was *Enterprise* that left *Investigator* behind, he cast a shadow on Collinson—and absolved himself of any blame if things went badly for his superior officer.

In writings to his wife Mary, McClure carefully laid out financial arrangements in a page-long postscript. He had already instructed his agent, Hallet & Robinson, regarding the distribution of any money that may accrue "in the event of my never returning to torment you"—as McClure quaintly put it. By writing this, McClure was privately acknowledging that the chances of *Investigator*'s breaking out were slim—and his chances of making it to safety even less so if this failed (and *Resolute* and *Intrepid* already went home). McClure believed the government might grant the £20,000 reward previously offered for the discovery of the North-West Passage, and further felt it was only canceled because nobody really thought it could be done. If this came to pass, he surmised his share would amount to £3–4,000. Added to this was the pay due him, from £5–600, which was in Hallet & Robinson's care. The firm was directed to pay Mary McClure the full *interest* from the total monies during her lifetime; added to this would be a yearly government pension of at least £100, making for an annual income of nearly £300 (with an extra £200 to set her up in her widowhood). Upon Mary's death, the whole amount would be equally divided between McClure's half-brother, half-sister, and his agent (the latter in compensation for various difficulties McClure caused at different times), "or to the survivors of any of the parties now alive."[63]

Back on *Investigator*, joyfulness gave way to the melancholy of John Boyle's burial the day McClure left for Dealy Island: "The procession wending its way over the ice to the adjacent beach—where we laid him in his cold and icy grave—presented a picture of the most touching solemnity." For several days, Able Seaman & Sick Berth Attendant John Ames had been suffering from dropsy resulting from heart disease, when he gradually lapsed into a coma, and then all life slipped from him at 1:00 a.m. on April 9. Three days later, Gunner's Mate John Kerr, who "spent the best part of his life at Sea and had fully indulged in the usual indiscretions incidental to a sailor's life," and had struggled for two months with ascites, dysentery and debility, gradually fell into a coma (broken only by occasional convulsions), and died in the morning. Both men carried the taint of scurvy with them to their graves.[64]

Kerr's touching funeral ceremony was described by Miertsching:

> [T]he coffin, wrapped in black cloth and draped with the English flag, was placed on a sledge and drawn by eight sailors to the open grave on shore; the marines in military order preceded the coffin, and the rest of the crew followed it; on the ship the bell was tolled and her ensign lowered to half-mast. The English burial service was read at the graveside, and at the words "earth to earth" the coffin was lowered into the grave. At the conclusion of the service the marines fired three volleys over the grave, which was then closed. The marines marched slowly back to the ship with colours flying.[65]

The two parties originally intended to leave for Cape Spencer and the Mackenzie River were combined into one, and included Mate Wynniatt, Assistant Surgeon Piers, Miertsching, and 26 seamen and Marines[66] (see Appendix 5 for the full list), with Lieutenant Cresswell in command. Cresswell—*not* Haswell; as Armstrong wrote, "[T]he Senior Lieu⸢ was detained to take a party of invalids across at a later period of the season"; the reason for these specific arrangements was soon to become obvious. Mate Sainsbury was the only other officer left on *Investigator*, but he was in a bad way, being bedridden with hemoptysis (spitting up blood or blood-tinged sputum from the respiratory tract) and in the early stages of pulmonary tuberculosis. When examined the following month, Sainsbury was determined to also be mentally unbalanced ("general derangement"). Two days before the sled party's departure on April 15, scurvy attacked sledders Joseph Facey (who also had a contusion of the ribs) and Henry Gauen. Able Seaman James McDonald was ravaged so badly by the disease that he had to be hauled on a sled the entire way to *Resolute*.[67]

During the journey, Cresswell was forced to stop and send someone to look for a missing man, who was found about a mile and a half back in a pool of water, and his "extraordinary conduct confirmed me in an opinion that I had long held that the man was not sane."[68] This may have been Bradbury, who, along with Wynniatt, Miertsching wrote "have caused us a great deal of trouble on this journey." By April 30, poor Charles Anderson could not walk any further and had to be put on a sled; the evils of dropsy and edema were at work. After 170 miles, Cresswell's party arrived at *Resolute* at 4:00 in the afternoon on May 2, and the lieutenant was struck by the irony that Captain Kellett was the last person he had seen on *Investigator* in the Bering Strait, and the first he shook hands with at Dealy Island. "We found

*Opposite, top:* **Cresswell's sled party leaving *Investigator* in Mercy Bay, April 15, 1853 (S.G. Cresswell, 1854).** *Bottom:* **Sledding Over Hummocky Ice, April 1853 (S.G. Cresswell, 1854).**

the *Resolute* and *Intrepid* nearly deserted, all available strength of both ships away travelling."[69]

Captain Kellett initially agreed with attempts to save *Investigator*, and even wrote in a private dispatch to John Barrow, Jr., that "I must stay here myself another winter if Investigator does not break out this year but Intrepid will go please God direct to England with half Investigator's Crew & the portion of mine sent to Beechey." But the arrival of Lieutenant Cresswell's pathetic band of Arctic castaways changed everything. Cresswell, Wynniatt and Piers were already much debilitated when they left, though the thin Miertsching was in fair health.[70] There was certainly no hiding Wynniatt's insanity, nor McDonald and Anderson on the sleds, and the child-like Bradbury must have looked all the more lamentable with his severely frostbitten fingers. Dr. Domville carried out a medical survey of the men, with predictable results: Scurvy had more or less invaded everyone, and among other issues, several were debilitated by edema.[71]

As senior officer, Captain Kellett was ultimately responsible for the health and welfare of not only his men, but the Investigators as well. Kellett knew exactly what he had to do: "Order № 2" was issued on May 5 to Captain McClure *and* Surgeons Armstrong and Domville:

> You are hereby directed and required to proceed on board H.M.S. Investigator, and there hold a strict and careful survey on all the Officers, Seamen and Marines remaining on board her, accordingly.
>
> The report of your proceedings herein is to be made out in duplicate and contain information under the following heads. Name, age, Rating, State of health, whether fit to undergo the rigours of another winter in this climate, and whether volunteer or not.
>
> Before deciding on their fitness or otherwise to remain another winter in the ice, the Medical Officers will duly consider the advantages to be derived from placing the Crew on a full scale of Provisions (of which for the last 18 months they have had but two thirds or less) together with the addition of any game that may be procured—not forgetting that they have already been three winters in this climate, and you will perform this surface [sic—service] with such care & accuracy that you may be ready, or required, to make solemn declaration to the impartiality, and correctness of your proceedings.[72]

"This course was adopted from the fact of Captain Kellett being but ill informed of the actual state of health remaining on board," pointedly wrote Armstrong, "for in the dispatches brought by Lieu.t Pim, he had ordered Com.r M.cClure to send him a report from the Surgeon (myself) of the actual state of health of the Crew, but this order was withheld from me, and no intimation whatsoever was made to me on the subject." Armstrong added a stinging comment in his published account, that Kellett "had already a specimen of our *diplomatic skill* in Behring's Strait, in 1850—the remembrance of which, may, doubtless, have influenced him, in receiving Captain M.cClure's verbal report of our state of health and efficiency with great caution, as he had ample reason to distrust us."[73]

At the same time that "Order № 2" was sent, Kellett "sent orders, *at the request of Com.r M.cClure* [emphasis added], that if the latter could procure twenty volunteers (Officers & Men) the number he considered necessary to work the ship, and whose state of health was approved of by the Medical Officers, he would allow them to remain on the ship, and await the chances." Unrecognized at the time, this was McClure's coup of foresight—he had cleverly done everything possible to avoid giving any orders on his own responsibility, that would lead to the abandonment of *Investigator*. Kellett's "Order № 1," which dealt with this very subject of volunteers, is curiously missing from Armstrong's journal.[74]

McClure left *Resolute* under a cloud of suspicion, on the same day of Kellett's explicit order, with Acting Master Court, Dr. Domville, two sleds and five men from *Investigator* and seven from *Resolute*. The doctor was concerned Nelson's leg injury was not properly healed, and despite Domville's objections, the sailor got in the drag ropes, wishing to see the ship one last time. Before departure, McClure made a particular promise to Miertsching: "My good Captain McClure has promised to send me my journal which he has had in his keeping since April 4, with Dr. Domville when he comes back, or, in event of the ship being abandoned, to bring it himself." As far as is known, this was the first time McClure openly expressed the possibility that *Investigator* might be forsaken to the ice.[75]

Captain Kellett sent Cresswell, Mate Richard Roche, Boatswain Thomas Chandler (both of *Resolute*), the deranged Wynniatt, and ten of the least fit men from his two ships, to the depot ship *North Star* at Beechey Island. Not surprisingly, Cresswell was perfectly placed to carry McClure's dispatches—and later his journal—to the Admiralty (see Appendix 2). According to McClure's book, the dispatches would "inform the Admiralty of the safety of the 'Investigator,' should the 'Intrepid' or 'Resolute' fail to escape from their advanced position in the forthcoming autumn." More importantly for McClure's personal and professional future, the Lords of the Admiralty must read news of the North-West Passage discovery and *McClure's version* of the voyage as soon as possible. After Cresswell's party arrived at the *North Star* on the morning of June 2, it was then a matter of waiting for the expected supply ship from England.[76]

McClure arrived back aboard *Investigator* on May 19,[77] but since he had not allowed for any increase in daily provisions[78] when he departed over six weeks before, his men's weakness and debility had grown even worse, and spring's daylight gave full view to the walking dead about the deck. Scurvy's handiwork during the last week of April laid low Boatswain's Mate Henry Bluff. Then May 2 and 10, the disease reached out to Able Seaman Ellis Griffiths and Blacksmith & Armorer Henry Stone; by month's end the sickness enveloped Ship's Cook Isaac "Old Stubber" Stubberfield, and he joined his shipmates on the sick list.[79]

On Sunday, three days after the captain's return, Kellett's order regarding the requirement for volunteers was read by McClure on the quarterdeck. Carpenter Ford recalled within Kellett's writings, that "every man had done his duty and if he would not volunteer we were to bear in mind it would be thought no disgrace whatever as we had done all that was expected of us but as it would contribute to the honor of our country to get the ship home. If 20 men on the examination from the doctor of the Resolute was found fit, to stop [and] they may volunteer, if not it would be no dishonor. After reading it [McClure] told all hands to consider on it." Armstrong then observed the men in groups of two or three, weighing their options in earnest for the rest of the day.[80]

Ford narrated what came next: "On the Monday [May 23] we were all examined by the doctors. On my going before the Capn. & doctors, after examining he asked me to volunteer. I (knowing that all hands had agreed to leave & being the first asked) told him that under the present circumstances [I] would rather go home. He told me in a harsh tone I had deceived him & "You can go, Sir. I'll not keep you."[81] Only four men volunteered to stay with their captain[82]:

- *Captain of the Forecastle John Calder*—"Tumidity [swollen], lividity [discoloration] & recession of the gums, which bleed on pressure with general Scorbutic taint is in apparent, and maintains health. Vol":

- *Corporal James Biggs, RM*—"In apparent health—but tumidity, ulceration and lividity of gums. Vol":
- *Quartermaster John Davies*[83]—"Has been 93 days under treatment for Scurvy, 55 days in 1852 and 38 days in 1853.—the gums are now tumid and supporating. Unfit" [volunteered]
- *Gunroom Steward George Milner*—"In good health—but has slight anemia of the gums. Vol":

Quartermaster George Brown wrote years later:

It was a bitter moment to Captain McClure.

Sanguine of success, trusting in the good will of the men, he had hoped for a full roll of volunteers, and when [t]his paltry 4, 5, or 6 was all that answered to his call, he summoned us on deck and unbraiding us in the bittercup [*sic*—bitter cup] of his disappointment said "Ah," if I had known this, I would not have called for volunteers, I would have "made you come."

Looking back on that time, I do not regret my decision no[t] to volunteer, but I do see with admiration the undomitable [*sic*] pluck of our Commanding Officer, who, if the power of our men could have freed the ship, we would have stayed by her alone, hoping (as I think against reason) that sometime or another a fortunate thaw would enable him to pass with his vessel from Behring Strait to Davis Straits.[84]

Of the 33 officers and men examined, only one or two were free from "marked Evidence of Scurvy and Debility in various stages of development, with great loss of flesh and strength."[85] Surgeons Armstrong and Domville concluded that the men's "present state of health is such, as renders them utterly unfit to undergo the rigours of another winter in this climate, without entertaining the most serious apprehensions for the consequences." Armstrong's imprint was plain in remarks about the reduced allowance of provisions over the last nearly 20 months being inadequate to maintain the men's health in such a climate, and their bodies being less able to generate the necessary heat to resist the cold and keep away disease. The doctors also stated that the ship's resources were insufficient to recuperate the crew's health without disease recurring during a fourth winter.[86] That same day, McClure recorded that his "surprise and mortification at finding only four men who felt able to go through another winter were great." McClure had to finally face reality: "It was therefore decided that the 'Investigator' must be abandoned," wrote Armstrong, "and the ship's company were summoned on deck to hear the Official announcement, which appeared to be received with evident satisfaction by all, and they were ordered to be placed on full allowance of provisions." The men so fervently set upon food that their semi-starved digestive systems were unable to handle the shock, and required treatment, while others even had to be put on the sick list. Despite the rough transition, the full diet's inclusion of anti-scorbutic foods such as lime juice and vegetables resulted in rapid improvement for the Investigators.[87]

Dr. Domville and his seven Resolutes left on the evening of the 24th with Mate Henry Sainsbury (who had considerably improved, but was on the sled), and scurvy sufferers Able Seamen Thomas Morgan and Ellis Griffiths. For the benefit of the invalids, the journey was taken in easy stages, and the party arrived at *Resolute* on June 10.[88]

"In consequence of there not being a sufficiency of hands to work the ship the only alternative that remained was to abandon her," McClure somberly wrote to the Admiralty on June 1, "which it is my intention to do (reluctantly indeed) as soon as the stores and provisions have been landed to form a depot." This depot was formed of supplies sufficient to last 66 men four months, including: 1,000 lbs. of biscuit, 608 lbs. of salt beef, 1,600 lbs. of salt pork,

3,000 lbs. of preserved meat, 6,420 lbs. of flour, sugar, vegetables, tobacco, soap, clothing for 30 men for a year, 4 muskets, powder and shot, 6 fully equipped ship's boats, a chest of woodworking tools, and 100 empty casks.[89]

> This treasure trove on the northern shore of Banks Island had a significant impact upon the Copper Inuit of western Victoria Island, although it is not known how or when this material was discovered by local people. The Berkeley Point group that McClure had contacted knew that McClure and his men had come from the north, where the Investigator had wintered in 1850–1851. Possibly a group of Copper Inuit wanted to trade with McClure and so, headed north looking for him. Or perhaps a group of Inuit discovered the Mercy Bay depot while hunting.[90]

McClure was careful not to reveal the deaths of Boyle, Ames and Kerr in his dispatch. In a final farewell, on May 30 the Investigators placed headboards on all three graves, and they were put in as good a condition as allowed by the circumstances.[91]

After the ship was thoroughly cleaned from stem to stern, and everything put in flawless order, at half past five in the afternoon of June 3, the crew mustered at divisions on deck, and Captain McClure, Lieutenant Haswell, and Dr. Armstrong conducted the final inspection of the ship.[92] Ford recalled that his captain then "addressed all hands, saying that what they had done was barely their duty & that barely, as they were going to desert their ship & captain & repeated several times that all hands had barely, barely done their duty. He was happy to say all the officers came forward & volunteered except one [actually two, Carpenter Ford and Ice Mate Newton[93]] & so he had written to the Admiralty about [it] (a pretty yarn to tell people about to undertake to travel & half-starved)".[94]

The men were then piped to their assigned sleds (see Appendix 5 for the full list), which weighed between 1,200 and 1,400 lbs. each, and were provisioned for 18 days: Captain McClure—1st sled; Lieutenant Haswell and Clerk-in-Charge Paine—2nd sled; Acting Master Court—3rd sled; and Dr. Armstrong—4th sled. "The white ensign of St. George was hoisted at the peak, and the pendant [pennant] at the main, which flaunted gaily in the breeze as we stepped over the side of the ship that had so long been our home, never to visit her again. The carpenters, who remained to batten down the hatches and secure the gangways, were the last to leave—then the 'Investigator' was finally abandoned to her fate."[95]

Captain McClure walked ahead, and the officers, feeling it was their duty, lent their energy to the dragropes, and just after six in the evening, "with a fresh breeze from the southwest having set sail, we started in silence, turned our backs on the 'Investigator' for ever, and made our first step on the long wished homeward journey."[96]

# 14

# Scattered Bones and
# Frozen Memories, 1853 Onward

*Nobody ever really dies—they're just forgotten.*

—Glenn M. Stein

The Investigators reached Dealy Island on June 17,[1] and were divided between *Resolute* and *Intrepid*, but to Carpenter George Ford, things were not all right:

> On arriving on board the "Resolute" we was taken by the carpr. Mr. Dean, whose kindness I cannot recompense, but no one asked us if we wanted anything whatever. On the following day I and my mess-mates was told we must work, which I have been ever since. On asking Mr. Pim if he could please to give us a place to sit out of the way of people & put our clothes, he told me I should think myself well offf & I had better mind what I talked about, threatening me if I spoke, & I believe gave orders if any of our men was heard grumble, to report them to him. It's now 5 weeks & 3 days we have been never spoken to by any officer except on duty. We have no place to put our few things except about the lower deck, no place to sit down or wash & but for Mr. Dean's kindness no place to get our food. All that we have to sleep on is a blanket and buffalo robe we brought with us in a haversack. The men have been doing all the most servile work while the ship's company does nearly nothing & part of them officers' servants. We have never received the least extra to renew our strength, nothing but barely the ship's allowance while the travelling parties of this ship returning got preserved milk, Normandy pipins [*sic*— pippins, whole peeled and cored dried apples] etc., etc. & [blank] of our men has no place to sleep but on the chests; if they get wet they are forced to sleep in their wet cloth[e]s. Our capn. has never asked us if we are comfortable or provided for since we have been here. Our officers on board the Resolute is carousing in plenty of everything every day & never asks or cares about any one else as they all have cabins. I wish I was out of this ship. A little in comfort is better than a great quantity here.[2]

Miertsching's pen carved bold strokes of despair the day McClure returned:

> The captain had been unable to bring me my precious journal; though it would have added no more than about two pounds to the load of the sledge; but he would have been obliged to bring also the journals and records[3] of his officers, and this he could not do.... My worthy Captain McClure offered me in the friendliest way the use of his ship's journal, that with aided by memory I might reconstruct my own; he would endeavour to procure for me writing materials, which are very rare on these ships. I accepted his friendly offer with many thanks. Captain Kellett promised me twelve sheets of paper, Dr. Domville two pens, and Mr. De Bray [French naval sub-lieutenant[4]] some ink[5] [see Appendix 5].

In his June 25 dispatch, informing the Admiralty that *Investigator* had been abandoned, McClure painted a happy picture of a new life aboard Kellett's ships.[6] Though he also commented (as did Armstrong) on the men's revived health—McClure still suppressed the fact

226

that three of his men lay in graves at Mercy Bay.[7] Through this deliberate omission, and by leaving his officers' journals and records onboard the derelict *Investigator*, but saving his own, McClure continued to cunningly craft his future.

The state of the ice occupied everyone's mind, with the earnest hope that final release from the Arctic's bondage would soon be at hand—and then, England! While waiting, the Investigators volunteered their hunting skills to Captain Kellett, in order to maintain the supply of fresh meat, and the combined efforts of officers and men from both ships resulted in more than 10,000 lbs. of meat being collected.[8]

August arrived,[9] and on the 18th of the month, a northwesterly gale set the ice offshore, after which it gradually broke up around the *Resolute* and *Intrepid*, allowing the ships to set sail in a wide stretch of open water. By the 22nd, Ford recorded a familiar scene—"Ship drifting to the SE. All hands mustered with a knapsack of cloths [*sic*], ready for a start if we should get a nip."[10]

Meanwhile, the steamer HMS *Phoenix* (Commander Edward A. Inglefield) and transport *Breadalbane* (Second Master William H. Fawckner) had arrived at Beechey Island on August 8.[11] Two sailors came aboard HMS *North Star* on the 20th with news of the death of Lieutenant Bellot (a French naval officer serving in the *Phoenix*[12]). Bellot was leading four men in a sled party to deliver dispatches to Captain Belcher in Wellington Channel when he disappeared during a gale near Cape Grinnell, and was presumed to have drowned.[13] On the same day, Cresswell and Wynniatt joined the *Phoenix*.[14]

"Shortly after 4 [a.m. on the 21st], a very heavy nip came on the [*Breadalbane*] and the hands were turned up to desert the ship should it be necessary. The *Breadalbane* was not so strong as the *Phoenix*, or the pressure was heavier on her, for she was stove by the ice, and sank within 15 minutes." Fortunately, no lives were lost, and by this date nearly all of her cargo of stores for Belcher's expedition had been put ashore.[15]

Three days later, the *Phoenix* sailed for England. When she cleared Lancaster Sound, and entered Baffin Bay, Cresswell and Wynniatt became the first Europeans to travel the North-West Passage (albeit by ship and on foot), and the first people to travel around both the North and South American continents.[16]

Cresswell briefly wrote to his parents on October 4, letting them know of the *Investigator*'s rescue and his closeness to home: "We are now about 60 miles from Cape Wrath (Scotland), and as we are going about 8 knots shall be through the Pentland Firth tomorrow [on the south side of which is the town of Thurso]. Capt. Inglefield and myself will land probably at Aberdeen."[17] Sixty years later, Charles Creese, a former able seaman on the *Phoenix*, recalled a curious story about what happened next: "A great mystery was made about the finding of the North West Passage and every effort was made to guard the secret until the news had reached the Admiralty in London. On the homeward journey the Phoenix put into Thurso to land the despatches announcing the important discovery, these were hurried to Edinburgh without delay, and to check the curiosity of the visitors Mr Crees [*sic*] describes how the ship kept the Yellow flag flying [indicating the ship was under quarantine]. It was only when the Bailie [a Scottish municipal officer] came on board and demanded what was the matter that the news became known, and that M'Clure had solved the baffling problem, and that his dispatches were on their way to London."[18]

Soon Cresswell was in King's Lynn for a brief reunion with family and friends, but he then traveled to London on October 7.[19] The Admiralty reply the same day acknowledged receipt of

McClure's April 10 dispatches, "in which you report the completion of the North-West Passage"; the words that followed were the leap forward McClure had counted on the most:

> My Lords have perused the narrative of your proceedings in search of the expedition under Sir John Franklin with equal interest and satisfaction; and, as a mark of their approval of the great exertions and untiring perseverance with which that search, though unavailing, was prosecuted; have been pleased this day to promote you to the rank of Captain.
>
> My Lords desire that you will signify to the officers, seamen, and marines of the "Investigator," that their praiseworthy and exemplary conduct throughout a trying employ, entitles them to their Lordships highest commendation; and that their return to their country of officers and men who have so worthily distinguished themselves, is anxiously looked for by their Lordships.[20]

When it reached his eyes, the final portion of this dispatch played into McClure's desire to personally seek recognition for specific men under his command—a desire almost wholly linked to his obsession with the North-West Passage.

Cresswell returned to his hometown and enjoyed a hero's welcome at a civic reception, held at St. George's Guildhall near the end of the month. After being presented with a finely rendered address from the Borough of Lynn, Cresswell recounted the harrowing voyage to a considerable audience, to which his friend Sir Edward Parry responded, in part: "You have before you today about the oldest and the youngest of Arctic navigators.... I came 200 miles, and would willingly have come 2,000 to be present this day."[21]

But all was not champagne and celebration—Cresswell's artistic and career-focused mind was also set apace producing eight watercolor paintings (he always called them watercolor sketches), plus a color chart, detailing the highlights of *Investigator*'s Arctic adventures. After he showed them to Queen Victoria during a Royal audience in March 1854, nine lithographs "Dedicated by Special Permission" to Her Majesty were commissioned for publication and sale in July 1854.[22]

Cresswell was initially promoted lieutenant commander around February 21, to be sent back to the Arctic in command of the *Talbot*, under Captain Inglefield (*Phoenix*), but he did not accept the appointment, and was instead assigned to the 14-gun HMS *Archer* on March 1.[23] Just over three weeks later, Great Britain and France formally declared war against Russia: the Crimean War had begun while Cresswell was already sailing toward the Baltic Sea.[24]

And what of poor James Wynniatt? He was discharged from the *Phoenix* on October 15, and despite the absence of information in his service record, doubtless he received some sort of medical attention—although one wonders if familiar faces and a more agreeable environment did more to balance his mind. Having been promoted while still in the Arctic, Lieutenant Wynniatt eventually went back to active duty. He joined the massive 120-gun *Neptune* in February 1854, followed by the 90-gun *Prince Regent* in the first week of March, and also sailed off to the Baltic Sea.[25]

In late August 1853, *Resolute* and *Intrepid* had continued to work along the edge of the pack,[26] but for Ford, life within the *Resolute* was still unsettled: "I am forced to mix with people filled [with] jealousy & conceits and spend my time day after day in a place (for swearing, vulgarity, insults, brutishness) like a brothel." The Arctic had no intention of releasing its grasp on the ships, and they became beset by young ice off Byam Martin Island September 10. "The ship lay as motionless as a house on land," wrote a dejected Miertsching, and "we saw all our hopes dashed to the ground. As far as the eye could reach not a drop of water, but one continuous sheet of ice lay before us."[27] Drifting until early November, the ships were then frozen fast for the winter about 28 miles southwest of Cape Cockburn, Bathurst Island.[28]

"As for comfortable quarters on board [the *Resolute*], they lie beyond our sphere of knowledge: there is a desperate shortage of space; even the two captains, Kellett and McClure, must live and sleep in one cabin.... On the *Intrepid*," where Miertsching related that the temperature never rose above freezing, "our lot is even worse, for we have neither the necessary bedding nor warm cabins. Our beds consist of two woollen blankets (coverlets), one of which each man brought in his sleeping-bag from the *Investigator*, and the other issued to us here; more cannot be given us for there is no more to give."[29]

The cramped environment only added to tensions Carpenter Ford observed between McClure and Kellett's men. "The anniversary of our discovery our people kept up but no encouragement here, rather the reverse (jealousy). 2 of our men is now under punishment for it." When the ships' companies of *Resolute* and *Intrepid* paraded with effigies, masks and clowns for Guy Fawkes Night on November 5, although many of them got drunk, "no notice is taken of it, but our men are still under punishment. The 1 Lieut. told Macdonald [*sic*—McDonald] he would take care he did not keep up another 'Norwest Day' [illegible] is the 'scullions' [kitchen duty] for everybody."[30]

The strain was amplified by the "unexpected winter in the ice and the deprivation of space and comfort owning to the intrusion of us passengers does not please [Kellett's] men who had been accustomed to something better," wrote Miertsching. "One can well see here that sympathy, love, and friendship, unless kindled in our hearts by a Christian spirit, cannot endure, and may be likened to blazing straw, quickly kindled and soon extinguished." The Investigators, "owning to their good behaviour and peaceful deportment [actions], are doing nothing to provoke unpleasantness."[31]

Meanwhile, the sailor-poet Nelson cast his thoughts back to the three shipmates he left ashore in Mercy Bay:

> 'Midst the thoughts that are constantly crossing the mind
> There are few that so often take place,
> As remembrance of those we have left far behind
> Whose memory nought can efface,
> There is not a scene that we witness around
> But we said in their presence to be,
> Every Prospect is great, each Incident sad,
> Without those we're accustomed to see.[32]

The premonition of another Arctic winter had also long since made Sainsbury[33] somewhat downcast; he became withdrawn, and by his words, had lost all hope of ever reaching England. In addition to the young officer, Able Seaman Steel was in a bad way, and neither were expected to live much longer. Master George F. McDougall (*Resolute*) related how, through the kindness and humanity of Drs. Domville and Piers, Sainsbury's "path to the grave was smoothed, his heart became softened to each and all of us, and he was enabled to look forward, through faith in his Saviour's redeeming grace, to being received into the kingdom of God. Poor fellow! His body presented a dreadfully emaciated appearance. He lingered, it is hoped and believed, without much pain, until half an hour after midnight on the 14th, when he expired without a struggle." Bradbury, "that poor silly creature," wrote McClintock, spread the news of Sainsbury's passing to everyone he encountered on *Intrepid* in "the same set phrase."[34]

By month's end, the wintry mood was lightened onboard *Resolute*, when the theater curtain was raised to reveal the crewmen in Shakespeare's *The Taming of the Shrew*, followed by the officers in the comedy *The Two Bonnycastles*. During intermissions, Charles Anderson was among the singers of comic songs, "who recited a prologue composed for the occasion. Nothing could be more amusing than this negro coming on in black coat and white waistcoat to recite a piece of verse in his patois, and attempting to imitate the manners of a man of the world." More mid-winter theatrics and amusements followed when the Resolutes and Investigators went aboard *Intrepid* on December 22.[35] Throughout the month, lectures about Arctic discovery (McDougall), astronomy (Kellett), and practical chemistry (Domville) added nourishment for the brain, and one presentation on "Practical Lessons on Electricity" complemented the electric telegraph that was set up to operate between the ships.[36]

The gaiety, learned presentations, and "Arctic telegraphy" did nothing to change the reality of the Investigators' condition. According to Ford, they slept in a hold that was also the residence of a dog which often defecated beneath their hammocks; in addition, a dead dog had been stinking up the place until a few days since mid–February 1854. To top it off, they were barely afforded enough candles to sit through meals. Doubtless the gloomy and unhealthy surroundings did nothing to improve Subordinate Officers' Steward Sugden's distasteful attitude, and having faced a trial on the tenth of the month for insolence to Captain Kellett, Sugden was sentenced to walk the deck daily in three shifts, totaling 7½ hours. Two weeks later, at the intended completion of his sentence, Sugden's punishment was actually extended until further orders.[37]

Kellett detailed his proceedings up to February 10, and those intended thereafter, to Belcher; the latter included sending Court as part of a sled party to survey and arrange the stores at Port Leopold.[38] With the objective of his conserving his resources, Kellett also planned that the "officers and crew of the 'Investigator,' together with the officers of this ship, and the men who are least able to stand a further winter in this climate, will leave in three divisions for the depot at Beechey Island, in the month of April, all arriving there by the 1st of May."[39]

These plans were announced to the Investigators beforehand, and Miertsching recorded how it "was cheering news to all of us, for we are heartily sick of living on these two ships, and although we have a journey of fifty German miles on foot over the ice before us, we will rejoice on the day of our departure."[40]

However, there was unfinished business to attend to—and a sled party under the command of Master Frederick J. Krabbé (*Intrepid*)[41] departed from Cape Cockburn on April 3, and headed for *Investigator*. Krabbé was no stranger to the Arctic, having twice commanded sled parties during Austin's expedition, while second master in the *Assistance*.[42]

Krabbé commanded HM Sled *Newton* with seven men, and left in the company of his former *Assistance* shipmate, Lieutenant Mecham, commanding HM Sled *Discovery* and seven men. Mecham had orders to proceed to the Princess Royal Islands, in the Prince of Wales Strait, to gain intelligence of the *Enterprise*, or failing this, leave information for her.[43]

The orders Kellett gave Krabbé about his assignment in Mercy Bay were quite specific:

> In the cairn left there you will deposit the record which you will receive from me, as well as one of your own, describing the position you find "Investigator" in, the state of the depot, and any information that might be useful to a party visiting the bay.
>
> From the "Investigator" you will bring back the articles of medical stores mentioned in the accompanying list.

You will be most careful that those of your crew entering that ship are never out of your sight—that her hatches are closed as before, and that everything is left undisturbed; but should "Investigator" be found in such a position that the provisions on board her would be spoiled or destroyed, you will endeavour to place them, as well as the stores most useful to a retreating party, in safety on the shore.

The quantity of provisions you take away from the depot is always to be recorded on the record you deposit.

Having performed this service, you will return to your ship (touching at Dealy Island) by the 10th of June.

The zeal and ability with which you have executed all duties committed to your charge, both in the last voyage and whilst under my command, give me great pleasure in being able to place this important service under your guidance.[44]

It is understandable that Kellett ordered the items onboard *Investigator* to be left undisturbed, and (if necessary) provisions were to be cached onshore, so as to be useful to a retreating party. In addition, it seems he wished to augment his medical supplies in case his ships had to go through another winter. And though Kellett described Krabbé's mission as "important service," no such emphasis was put in Mecham's orders regarding his attempt to find traces of *Enterprise*, from which nothing had been heard since she passed through the Bering Strait in 1851.[45]

What is most interesting about Kellett's orders to Krabbé is what is *not* in them—but must have been communicated verbally. As Miertsching wrote on the day the two sleds departed: "Krabbé has orders to bring back the journals of the officers which were left on the *Investigator*." This was indeed "important service." Through a different lens, Osborn's choice of words about these sledding missions were as vague as they were contradictory: "Captain Kellett dispatched in the early spring Lieut. Mecham, supported by a party under Mr. Krabbé (master), to revisit the Bay of Mercy in Banks Land, and to place on Princess Royal Island, in Prince of Wales Strait, information of the safety of the crew of the 'Investigator.'"[46]

While Krabbé and Mecham were away, the three divisions of sleds (Haswell, Pim and McClure) left for the *North Star* at Beechey Island.[47] "Before we left the ships," recorded Miertsching on April 14, "Captain Kellett assembled us all on deck and thanked us publicly

Staff Commander Frederick John Krabbé, RN—Crimea Medal 1854–56, with Sebastopol clasp (Hunt & Roskell engraving on the edge: FRED$^{\underline{K}}$ J, KRABBÉ, MASTER H.M.S. LEANDER_); Arctic Medal 1818–55 (unnamed as issued; Second Master/*Assistance*/1850–51 & Master/*Intrepid*/1852–54); Turkish Crimea Medal (British issue/unnamed as issued) (Spencer J. Fisher, 2014; Glenn M. Stein Collection).

for the regular discipline and exceptionally good conduct which to the very last had characterized the men of the *Investigator*; he handed to our worthy Captain McClure a letter to the
Admiralty in which he gave the crew of the *Investigator* a character so good that one would
rarely find other ships worthy of it." Haswell, Pim and McClure arrived at the *North Star* on
April 23, 24 and 27 respectively, and Ford was pleased how "we have a different reception to
the Resolute as every one seems to try to assist and give us something what we stand most in
need of."[48]

In the meantime, McClintock turned up at *Resolute* and *Intrepid* on April 28, having
"brought decided orders from Sir Edward Belcher to abandon the ships, after a certain quantity
of provisions had been landed at the depot near Cape Cockburn, and for which purposes
three sledges were on their way to this ship from Beechey Island."[49] In meeting with the expedition commander, McClintock "thought Sir Edward Belcher 'looked debilitated and old,
more perhaps from want of fresh air, exercise and society than from all other causes put
together.'"[50] Belcher's skills as a surveyor were not matched by qualities of leadership—he
refused to listen to his officers, and abused his authority to "leave one or more vessels and
crews, if the safety of others demanded this." With no sign of Franklin, and four of the five
ships in his squadron still beset, Belcher was determined to sail for home in the *North Star*.[51]

The lone remaining Investigator, Able Seaman Thomas Morgan, left with a party of
invalids commanded by DeBray on May 8; he was "so sick and covered with scurvy sores that
I [DeBray] am obliged to arrange a [dog] sledge with a hanging cot for him alone." At the
same time, Lieutenant Richard V. Hamilton headed for Dealy Island with one man and five
dogs, in order to deposit a record, and also leave orders for Mecham and Krabbé to go directly
to Beechey Island with all possible speed.[52]

At 7:00 p.m. precisely, on Sunday, May 15, 1854, Her Majesty's Ships *Resolute* and *Intrepid*
were abandoned to the ice.[53]

Back on the diminutive Beechey Island, Brother Miertsching roamed around his new
surroundings,

> which is about an hour's walk in circumference, [and] lies about three hundred paces from the spot
> where the North Star is frozen in. I have twice strolled over to it; one finds the many traces of Franklin's
> expedition; it appears that here he spent his first winter. Tenting-grounds, fragments of cable, wood
> shavings, iron hoops, glass, earthenware, and the like are found in a number of places. In addition there
> are three graves, each marked by a black-painted oaken slab....[54]

Thomas Morgan took his last breath during the fourth week of May, and Carpenter Ford
set to work shaping his coffin. Captain McClure officiated the funeral service on the 24th,
while Morgan was laid to rest beside the three Franklin graves. He was the fifth—and last—
Investigator to be entombed in the Arctic.[55]

Kellett and his band joined *North Star* six days later.[56]

The middle of June saw the return of the last of Kellett's travelers, with Lieutenant
Mecham arriving on the morning of June 12, and Lieutenant Hamilton that evening. Mecham
brought the most welcome news that he found notices left by Collinson in 1851 on the Princess
Royal Islands, beside those deposited by McClure. Like *Investigator*, *Enterprise* was unable to
force her way through the strait and into Viscount Melville Sound, so turned south and eventually wintered on the southern shore of Prince Albert Land. Another notice found by Mecham
told of the *Enterprise's* sled parties visiting Point Hearne on Melville Island, and examining
the north and south shores of Prince Albert Land. Finally, beginning August 25, 1852, "Captain

Collinson's intention was to pursue the channel separating Wollaston from Prince Albert's Land [Prince Albert Sound]." A sigh of relief accompanied this intelligence, and it was felt, wrote Commander Pullen, that *Enterprise* "cannot be in very great danger."[57]

Early the next morning Krabbé returned, having spent May 5–11 onboard *Investigator*. "I soon found that the ship had leaked so much during the preceding summer, that she was full of solid ice to the level of the orlop deck forward, the tops of tanks in main hold, and within 10 inches of the orlop beams abaft. This at once decided me on clearing her of all useful stores, as per orders from Captain Kellett." On the seventh, "I sorted out thermometers to day, and overhauled for journals, for bringing back to the ship. Lieutenant Haswell's was the only one I could find." Consequently, Miertsching's comment that month was more than a little curious: "The orders of Captain Kellett—that he should bring back our journals which Captain McClure had left behind—he did not fulfil [*sic*], *because he could not find any!?*"[58] Was the discovery of Haswell's journal concealed? (see Appendix 2)

When writing his book, Dr. Armstrong referenced Krabbé's official report on the *Investigator*'s condition and state of the ice in Mercy Bay, in order to take one last jab at McClure: "The inferences to be deduced from this report are, that the 'Investigator' moved a little in the summer of 1853; that the ice never broke up in the Bay, that we consequently should have failed to liberate her had we remained; and that she will, from the accumulation of ice and water, ultimately sink at her anchors, and find repose at, or near where we left her. We had, therefore, every reason to congratulate ourselves that we abandoned her at the period we did."[59]

The Arctic—or so it seemed—would eventually claim not only *Investigator*, but *Assistance*, *Pioneer*, *Resolute* and *Intrepid* as well.

*August 26, 1854*—"We are continuing to stand off, making short tacks, waiting for the boats from *Assistance*," observed DeBray on the deck of the *North Star*, which was carrying a total of 263 souls. "Then at 1.00 p.m. just as Captain Richards came alongside with two boats, the fog cleared to the south and to our great surprise we spotted a steamer rounding Cape Riley." The *Phoenix*, towing *Talbot*, was steaming their way. "Soon a boat was heading towards us from *Phoenix* and Captain Inglefield climbed to the deck shouting: 'Great news! War with Russia! France is allied with England!'"[60]

The following day, Ford and his shipmates "started for Dear Old England in tow of the Phoenix with the Talbot, the Assistance and Resolute's crews having been distributed to the other ships,[61] leaving all of us in the N. Star & put on full allowance (of grog only)." They were treated to an address by McClure—who, Ford pointed out, spoke in a *different* tone than previously: "Our Capn. has read a letter from the Admiralty to the ship's company & added himself that he hoped they would be loyal & if he should get a ship they would join him & brave the dangers of war as they did in the past as he would give them all the first, best situations they could fill. The tune is altered now."[62] After the little convoy anchored at Greenland's Godhavn two weeks later, the *Investigator*'s commander was ordered to transfer to the *Phoenix* for an earlier arrival in England.[63]

Of the numerous official letters McClure wrote during his passage home, one in particular harked back his speech to the crew just after their discovery of the North-West Passage, wherein McClure "promised that when they returned to England he would not forget to recommend his crew to the Admiralty as favourably as he could."[64] The late Captain Kenneth J. Douglas-Morris, noted naval historian and medal collector, uncovered ample evidence that

McClure put forward "certain men specially" in a letter, and in doing so, was afterwards requested by the Admiralty to provide additional details, which produced this further response: "'Captain McClure recommends four men very strongly for a special mark of approbation.' [Admiralty decision] 'To have a Medal.'"[65]

Douglas-Morris dubbed the special decoration the "Arctic Meritorious Service Medal" (Arctic MSM),[66] and although he discovered its four recipients, all of his efforts to uncover *why* these men were recommended "have so far proved fruitless": Private 3rd Class [Corporal] James Biggs, Captain of the Forecastle John Calder, Quartermaster John Davies, and Gunroom Steward George L. Milner.[67] The present author took up the challenge—with surprising results.[68]

What *exactly* did these men do to "merit" the Arctic MSM, and what was the commonality that bound them all together? Biggs was the captain's servant, and as such probably formed a particular loyalty toward McClure; he was also given a "field promotion" to corporal on April 15, 1853. Calder had been an active sledder, including a member of the North-West Passage party, and in other sledding duties McClure described him as "a trustworthy and zealous petty officer."[69] But the mystery recipient was Milner—whose behavior early in the expedition had been anything but sterling, as a result of which he was flogged—but still somehow received a "Good" conduct rating![70]

The deciding factor for receipt of the Arctic MSM came down to a display of personal loyalty to McClure: all four men volunteered to stay onboard for a fourth winter, and beyond.[71] Davies's volunteerism stands out in particular, given that he was judged "Unfit" in the medical survey of May 23, 1853.[72]

A bravery medal—coined the "Arctic Gallantry Medal" by Douglas-Morris—was destined for the *Investigator*'s Color Sergeant John Woon.[73] Woon's sledding and hunting activities had made deep impressions on McClure and Armstrong, but in Douglas-Morris's view, Woon's bravery in rescuing Charles Anderson from certain death was the *sole reason* for the medal's award. The present author felt otherwise. The reverse of the medal boldly states that it was awarded for "EXCEPTIONAL BRAVERY AND INTREPIDITY," hence the wording relates

Quartermaster John Davies—Arctic Medal 1818–55 (unnamed as issued) and "Arctic Meritorious Service Medal" (officially engraved on the edge: JOHN DAVIS. Q.R M.R H.M.S. INVESTIGATOR.) (courtesy Captain K.J. Douglas-Morris, DL, RN).

to two separate incidents. It will be recalled that, in addition to Woon's lifesaving act, in July 1852 he killed two musk ox bulls. In his dispatches McClure wrote that Woon was "evincing the most soldier-like coolness and intrepidity during the entire transaction."[74]

While onboard the *Phoenix*, McClure set pen to paper on September 26, and acquainted his uncle (the Reverend Elgee) with the news of *Investigator*'s abandonment, and in doing so, deftly credited the entire decision making process to his superior:

**Color Sergeant John Woon "Arctic Gallantry Medal," 1853, obverse and reverse (officially named on the edge: C!R SERJ T JOHN WOON R.M.) (collection of Glenbow Museum, Calgary, Canada, R5.292).**

[M]y good friend Kellett thinking we had persevered sufficiently in our attempts to get the ship through, and fancying we were looking like denizens of the church-yard rather than honest tars, allowed the crew the privilege of volunteering for longer service or to leave the ship, it was too strong a temptation for Jack, the idea of getting home got the mastery of his patriotism & only four besides the officers stepped forward, therefore I had no alternative, it was a sad disappointment after the sacrifice made to achieve, what was the height of my ambition. Viz the bringing home of my little barque—"Man proposes, but God Disposes" is a Just maxim, and one I hope that in all humbleness I can fully feel.[75]

Two days later, the *Phoenix* dropped anchor at Cork, Ireland, and McClure was immediately on his way to London, and afterward set off for 6, St. Mary's Terrace, Hastings, East Sussex, to be with his wife Mary. However, McClure's salvation, and their reunification, evidently failed to create fond memories. According to the weary Arctic veteran, Mary's "conduct was so unpardonable after my return from the North, that I can never meet her again.... The sins of our youth visit us in our old age, most truly I can say this." From Hastings he wrote James Ross (having missed seeing him in London) that as soon as "the [returning] ships are known to be off the coast, that most excellent fellow Barrow [John Barrow Jr.] will telegraph me & I shall proceed immediately to London.... I hope to get my time antedated & that all our claims will be well considered."[76]

The *North Star*, with his Investigators onboard, let go its anchor at Sheerness on the evening of October 7, between the massive warships HMS *Waterloo* and *Royal Albert*. The next day, the Investigators were transferred to the *Waterloo*, to await the standard court-martial to inquire into the loss of their ship.[77] The court-martial took place on Tuesday, October 17,[78] with a panel of officers, and a deputy judge advocate.[79]

"The Court asked for the Orders of Captain Collinson but Captain McClure had not the Orders."[80] It seems odd that McClure did not bring his Letter and Order Book from the Admiralty to the proceedings, or at the very least, a copy of Collinson's orders could have been obtained by the court. As a result, McClure was not obligated to explain how *Investigator* came to be separated from *Enterprise*, nor his decision to enter the ice alone—or the consequences of that decision.

The key to McClure's vindication at the court-martial—and afterward his strategy regarding the North-West Passage monetary reward—was Kellett's "Order № 1" of May 5, 1853,[81] that gave the officers and men of *Investigator* the option of volunteering to stay for a fourth winter[82]: "The Court is of opinion that no blame whatever is imputable to the said Captain M^cClure his Officers or Ship's Company or any of them on the occasion of the loss of the said ship 'Investigator.' But that the said Captain M^cClure acted under the Orders of his Superior Officer and exercised a proper discretion in directing the abandonment of his Ship in pursuance of such Orders there not being a sufficient number of Volunteers from the state of their health to navigate the said Ship."[83] The crew of Her Majesty's Ship *Investigator* formally ceased to exist.

*The Times* reported a similar court's full acquittal of Kellett and his officers, and although Belcher acted with "the ample discretionary powers given to him," his sword was returned in silence—which spoke volumes. Another trial also fully acquitted Commander Richards and his officers for the loss of the *Assistance* and *Pioneer*.[84]

On October 22, the day the Admiralty received a copy of the minutes of the *Investigator* court-martial,[85] Dr. John Rae arrived in London with startling news. Having been on an expedition to survey the "last gap" in the Arctic coast, along the western shore of Boothia Peninsula, Rae had stumbled upon the fate of Franklin and his people. He encountered Eskimos with whom he traded for various relics, including pieces of telescopes, guns, watches, compasses, cross of the Royal Guelphic Order, a small silver plate engraved "Sir John Franklin, K.C.H.," and silver spoons and forks bearing the crests of Franklin and his officers. Thanks to having William Ouligbuck with him as interpreter, Rae formed a general outline of the disaster through stories about ragged survivors on King William Island and later the discovery of bodies along the Great Fish River (Back River). Although none of the Eskimos questioned had seen the white men alive or dead, "Rae had worked long enough in the north to appreciate the power and reliability of the native grapevine."[86]

In a sharp contrast to Rae's numbing revelations, two days later a humble ceremony took place at the Ship Hotel, to honor the preserver of life onboard *Investigator*. After a collection of 70 guineas[87] from her petty officers, seamen, and Marines, a delegation of ten of their number gathered to present Dr. Armstrong with an 18-carat gold chronometer and chain. The gift was handed to the doctor, and James Nelson read an address signed by each of the crew[88]: "There are few, if any of us, who have not at some time experienced your kindness at the sick bed; some who have, under Providence, to thank your skill and attention for their lives; but, above all, your constant assiduity and unwearied zeal, to those departed shipmates, whom it has pleased the Almighty to take from us, can never be forgotten."[89] Dr. Armstrong replied with words "of excellent feeling," and "then thanked the company for the handsome gift."[90]

Mr. Nelson then turned round to Lieutenant Bedford Pim, who was present,[91] as a friend of Dr. Armstrong, and said, "Were it had not been for you, sir, many of us now present would never have seen old

England again. All of us look upon you as a deliverer, and none of us will forget the joy we felt when you reached us.

Lieutenant Pim, in reply, said—"I thank you, my lads. I shall never forget our meeting. I congratulate you most heartily upon your escape from a fate similar to that of poor Sir John Franklin."[92]

McClure's further "escape"—from responsibility, that is—for the loss of his ship and the deaths of five of his men, carried a long, grim footnote. There is little doubt the Investigators' Arctic experiences and near-starvation physically weakened them. Within the coming months Wilcox and Bradbury were dead, and by 1861, Flynn, Whitefield, King, Wynniatt, and Court also passed from the scene. In the case of Wynniatt, dysentery took him in 1860, while he was on the way home from the war in China. And according to Osborn, the following year, the ever-reliable Court was the victim of "the effects of climate during this severe [Arctic] service."[93] Six years later, having nursed his father through a painful illness, Cresswell succumbed to many years of service in the Arctic and Far East. He was just six weeks shy of his 40th birthday.[94]

During the final months of 1854, McClure had made his way to Ballyleck House (Monaghan, Ireland), and was "living quietly with my [half-]Brother recruiting <u>my shattered constitution</u>" when he wrote to John

Surgeon Armstrong's testimonial gold watch, presented to him on Oct. 24, 1854. One side featured an engraved image (after Cresswell's depiction of HMS *Investigator* in a critical position during August 1851), while the other was inscribed: "Presented, October 1854, to Alexander Armstrong, M.D. (late) Surgeon H.M.S. *Investigator*, by the Petty Officers, Seamen, and Marines of that ship, as a testimony of their sincere respect and gratitude for his unwearied professional skill and humanity during the unparalleled Arctic Service, which resulted in the discovery of the North-West Passage" (*The Illustrated London News*, Oct. 28, 1854).

Barrow, Jr., on New Year's Day: "I am thinking of applying for the £20,000 having above 100 members [of the House of Commons] that will support it, if you would get Capt. [Richard Vesey] Hamilton's opinion on it will you [and] let me know, for I will not act without feel[ing out the Admiralty?]"[95]

A week and a half later, McClure again wrote his friend Barrow: "I have been paying a visit to the Lord Primate at Armagh [Ireland] where I met Adml. Eden [Second Lord of the Admiralty] and spoke of trying for the £20,000 which he approved, and since my return your kind letter has placed the affair in a very strong light, Arctic Discovery being revived so ought the reward to have also been."[96]

Armed with confidence, McClure had set about creating manifestos and sent them to members of the House of Commons in the last days of April: "Memorial of Captain Robert McClure, R.N., on behalf of Himself and the Officers and Crew of H.M. Ship 'Investigator' and 'An Abstract of the Principal Voyages Undertaken by the Different Maritime Nations of

Europe, Either Under the Orders of Their Respective Governments, or Through Private Enter-
prise, for the Purpose of Discovering a Passage Between the Atlantic & Pacific Oceans, etc.'
'It is now that the Discovery is actually completed,' ran McClure's accompanying letter, 'that
I indulge the hope of receiving your influence in Parliament to obtain for the Officers and
Crew of the Investigator that reward which although they cannot legally claim, have arduously,
equitably, and virtually earned.' These writings further included a 'Brief Statement of Captain
McClure's Services in Her Majesty's Ship "Investigator".'"[97]

McClure's "Memorial" and "Brief Statement" of services both included very specific language regarding his decision to salvage the 1850 navigable season by pushing into the ice and
*not waiting for* Collinson.[98] These sharp contradictions to McClure's past official claim were
themselves soon to be negated.

Within a few weeks—five years and 116 days after leaving the Thames—*Enterprise* arrived
at Sheerness, "of which rather more than 3 years had been spent in the ice without communication with the outside world." But her cruise had been a most unhappy one, as related by
Philip Sharpe, Mate onboard HMS *Rattlesnake*, which encountered *Enterprise* at Port Clarence
on August 21, 1854, after she emerged from the Bering Strait. Sharpe was "regaled with some
disturbing details by his fellow officers when they returned [from visiting *Enterprise*]"[99]:

> Every executive officer was under arrest. The master [Skead] had been under arrest for 2 years and 8
> months. Fancy that in such a climate. The 1st Lieut. [Phayre] had been suspended from duty for 14
> months. The 2nd Lieut. [Jago] had been lately placed under close arrest; & the 3rd [Parks] had been
> under arrest for some time. The only officers free were the surgeon [Anderson] and Assistant Surgeon
> [Adams], & those Capt. Collinson dare not arrest. The Commanding officer was an ice mate, a nobody.
> Not a soul had been out of the ship for 15 months, among the officers. Things had gone so far that all
> are determined to go to the utmost, lose their commissions, everything, to try Capt. Collinson by a
> Court Martial, for lying, drunkenness, tyranny & oppression & cowardice.[100]

Still, in spite of the troubles between Collinson and his officers, the captain wrote to John
Barrow Jr. that his "men have done their work very well & with great cheerfulness."[101] And
after *Enterprise* spent the winter of 1852–53 at Cambridge Bay, on the southern coast of Victoria Island, in the spring Collinson led three sleds along the eastern coast of the island, and
found a note left by Rae from his 1850–51 expedition. Neither Rae nor Collinson had any
way of knowing that during their sledding they were just opposite the area off the northwestern
coast of King William Island where *Erebus* and *Terror* had been beset.[102]

Not long after, McClure's campaigning had its desired effect, and the Select Committee
on Arctic Expedition was appointed in June, and convened several times during July, with the
tasks of determining "whether any and what Reward may be due" the expeditions of McClure,
Collinson and Kellett.[103]

The Committee found itself wrestling with questions that are still debated to this day:
Who discovered the North-West Passage? What constitutes "discovery"? Who had priority
over its discovery? Does a "navigable" route exist? Must the discoverer have *sailed* entirely
through the Passage? Woven within the questions and answers were still further queries revolv-
ing around the trials and tribulations that nearly cost the lives of everyone onboard
*Investigator*.[104]

First and foremost (as noted at the onset of these writings), *several* routes, or "passages,"
connect the northern Atlantic and Pacific Oceans, so there was never just one "North-West
Passage," and McClure himself found two. As ever, ice conditions could vary considerably

from year to year, and this dictated explorers' abilities to penetrate the eastern and western ends of the Arctic archipelago.

Captain John Washington, Hydrographer of the Navy, testified before the Committee that "the discovery of [McClure's] passage cannot be attributed to any one individual; it is a series of exertions which has been continued for about 30 years. Had Captain M'Clure arrived at that spot [near the end of the Prince of Wales Strait] without any one having preceded him there, he could never have attempted to cross either to Port Leopold or to Beechey Island."[105]

Over that 30-year period—and often with considerable reliance on native peoples— explorers like Kotzebue, John and James Ross, Parry, Vasilyev, Franklin, Lyon, Beechey, Back, Dease and Simpson, Richardson, and Rae all helped shape the discovery of passages; but it was Franklin's officers and Rae who actually discovered passages in the eastern Arctic. Of the various routes uncovered, only Rae's was *navigable*—Rae Strait, between King William Island and the Boothia Peninsula, which he discovered on his 1853–54 survey expedition.[106]

If the weather had cleared for *Investigator*, the possibility of her having navigated the second passage discovered by McClure (through the McClure Strait, between Banks and Melville Islands) was put to Sir George Back. He responded: "Had Captain M'Clure com-manded a steam-vessel or an auxiliary steam-vessel, perhaps it is not hazarding too much in saying that he would have got entirely through in the same season, by which means he would have brought his ship to England." Captain Kellett's opinion was also sought, but he did not feel it was "practicable for any vessel ever to go by the west through that channel with any power." But McClure's response brought to full light his (evidently) changed outlook: "Yes, I certainly am of the opinion, knowing what has been effected since by steam-vessels, that if I had steam power, I should have gone through in 1851."[107]

How McClure ended up in the Arctic alone was revealed in testimony in which he con-tradicted his manifestoes: "I was of opinion that [Collinson] had already gone on before me, and I made a signal [to Kellett] then that I could not wait upon my own responsibility, knowing the importance of the service; Captain Kellett gave me no further orders, and I proceeded." And since Collinson's testimony backed up McClure, the latter was in the clear: "I came to the conclusion that I should be up to the ice before [McClure]; I did not consider it possible that he would get there first, and so only entered in my official despatches into the question of what should happen if I proceeded without waiting for him, and told him in that contin-gency what to do.... [McClure thought] I might be ahead of him, and he took the best alter-native that could possibly have been taken. Instead of waiting, he went forward, either to succor the missing crews, or to follow me, as he might have supposed he was doing."[108]

Not all the waters during the Committee hearings were smooth sailing for McClure. When he was asked about the prospect for his escape if Kellett had not sent Lieutenant Pim, in spite of knowing all the circumstances afterward, he arrogantly rolled out: "My opinion is the same now as it was then; I consider that we should have lost four men; there were four men so weak that I thought they would have perished upon the road." And what about McClure's plan to send one of his sled parties to Beechey Island in the spring of 1853? Kellett thought "that some might have got there, but no doubt with great losses." Rear Admiral William Alexander Baillie Hamilton (who served on the Arctic Council during the search for Franklin) was of the opinion that, in devising the plan to send away sledding parties, "[McClure] did not sufficiently take into consideration the condition and circumstances of the men, attenuated and exhausted as they would have been by the uncertainty of what was before them. Although the men did a positive amount of work in proceeding to join Captain Kellett, they then had a certainty before them which kept their spirits up; and their having performed a journey with such certainty before them, was no measure of their power and capacity to perform a much longer journey with great uncertainty."[109]

With Dr. Armstrong having sailed off to the Baltic in HMS *Cornwallis* in February,[110] Dr. Domville provided compelling testimony as to the condition of the Investigators: "Of the 30 men who were taken on board [*Resolute*] during the first fortnight in May [1853], no less than 18 were under medical treatment; those were the men who arrived in the first week." When asked about the condition of McClure's remaining men, Domville was blunt: "They were in a very enfeebled state indeed. One officer among them, a lieutenant [Sainsbury], was unable to come with the first party; I brought him over; he died a few weeks afterwards.[111] They were all in a very bad condition." ... "Do you mean to infer that if the relief had not arrived, they must, most or all of them, have perished?—I do."[112]

With the Crimean War on, the government and Admiralty having faced the embarrassing situations of Belcher and Collinson—and the failure of the Franklin Search expeditions generally—McClure's discovery was a bright spot not to be spoiled. Consequently, even though for many years prior to 1818, a reward of £20,000 "was offered for the first person who should complete the North-west Passage, by actually sailing with his ship from one ocean to another," the Committee decided that McClure, his officers and crew, were "undoubtedly the first to have passed by water from sea to sea, and have returned to this country a living evidence of the existence of a North-west Passage." A blind eye was turned to the fact that the Investigators had walked through portions of the route.[113]

Given that the Act passed in 1818 also awarded £5,000 for each crossing of 110° W, 120° W and 130° W, and Parry was presented that sum sailing past the first of these longitudes, under the circumstances, the Committee recommended that £10,000 (£816,000 or $1,304,000 U.S. today)[114] be awarded to McClure and his Investigators. As a "personal tribute to his energy, bravery, and skill," half of this sum was given to Captain McClure,[115] and the Admiralty decided how the other £5,000 (£408,000 or $652,000 U.S. today)[116] was to be apportioned among the officers and crew[117]:

| | |
|---|---|
| Lieutenants (2) & Acting Master | £271–6–4 |
| Surgeon, Assistant Surgeon, Mates (2) | £174–8–4 |
| Clerk-in-Charge, Carpenter, Boatswain, Ice Mate & Eskimo Interpreter, Ship's Cook & Paymaster's Steward | £96–18–0 |
| Gunner's Mate, Boatswain's Mates (2) | £87–4–2 |
| Carpenter's Mate, Caulker, Captains of the Hold, Foretop, Forecastle & Maintop, Quartermasters (3), Captain's Coxswain, Blacksmith, Sailmaker & Sergeant, RM and Corporal, RM | £58–2–10 |
| Able Seamen (25), Carpenter's Crew, Privates, RM (6) | £29–1–5 |
| Subordinate Officers' Steward, Gunroom Steward | £19–7–7[118] |

In addition, the Committee investigated possible rewards for the claims by Captain Collinson for skillfully navigating the Arctic waters, "in pushing his ship through Dolphin and Union Straits to a point many degrees further eastward than has ever been attained by any other vessel passing from the west along the northern shores of America, and in successfully extricating her from the embarrassments of so perilous a position." It also acknowledged that without Captain Kellett's "timely assistance it may be doubted whether Captain M'Clure could have reached Beechey Island; of his crew, the remainder would have had little chance of their lives, and might have shared the fate of Sir John Franklin, in place of being now in their native land." However, its hands were essentially tied, and the members did not feel justified in extending the monetary award any further, given that McClure and his officers and men had already fulfilled the intent of the former Acts of Parliament.[119]

However, in a memorable gesture, the members of the Committee *did* feel justified in going beyond their scope of authority in one particular aspect, and recommended "that the grant of a medal to all those of every rank and class engaged in the several Arctic Expeditions, would be received with great satisfaction,"[120] thus leading to the creation of the Arctic Medal 1818–55 (see Appendix 7).

During the Committee hearings, through letter, Lady Franklin did not question McClure's claims, but she did propose that her "husband had previously, though unknown to Captain M'Clure, discovered another and a more navigable passage," and thus had priority of discovery. Lady Franklin then helped sponsor the search expedition under Captain McClintock, who sailed the steam yacht *Fox* into frigid waters from 1857 to 1859. Besides recovering numerous relics, McClintock brought back a document found in a cylindrical tin case, which Commander Gore had deposited within a large cairn on King William Island; the first entry showed Franklin was still in command and all was well in May 1847. A second entry was written around the margins of the same document on April 25, 1848, by Commander James Fitzjames (*Erebus*), which he then signed, as did the surviving senior officer, Captain Francis R.M. Crozier (*Terror*). The words told a sorrowful tale. *Erebus* and *Terror* were abandoned three days previous, having been beset in Victoria Strait since Sept. 12, 1846: "Sir John Franklin died on the 11th June 1847 and the total loss by deaths in the Expedition has been to date 9 Officers and 15 Men." In a desperate bid for safety, Captain Crozier indicated he was starting

The China Medal 1840–42 posthumously issued in 1856 to the family of Boy 1st Class/Ordinary Seaman William Gibson, HMS *Wanderer* (officially impressed on the edge: ✱✱✱WILLIAM GIBSON, H.M.S. WANDERER.✱✱✱). In 1995, the author discovered Gibson had served as the subordinate officers' steward in HMS *Terror*, and perished in the Arctic with the Franklin Expedition (courtesy DNW auctions, London, 2007; ex–Glenn M. Stein Collection).

the following day (April 26), to lead the 104 survivors toward the Great Fish River (Back River) on the North American mainland.[121]

Lady Franklin had ample ammunition to go on the offensive, and "would use every means at her disposal, especially the erecting of monuments, to influence public opinion and create the desired perception" that Sir John Franklin was the *earliest* discoverer of the North-West Passage. "Soon enough, the majority of Arctic experts stood behind Lady Franklin—experienced, credible men like Richardson, Murchison, Grinnell, McClintock, Osborn and Collinson."[122]

At one point, Captain McClure vented to John Barrow Jr., but wished to keep the controversy at arm's length:

> What is my friend Sherard Osborn doing, of one thing only I hear he is about trying to rob me of my "laurels" let the dead have as much glory as you like, only leave the living alone, let the Franklin party write as much as they like, they can never do away with the fact that the crew of the Investigator were & are the sole parties that have circumnavigated America by entering at Bherings Straits & returning to Europe by Baffins Bay, neither living or dead can contravene that fact—& upon that I rest quietly many friends have written to me to enter the arena of Debate, but I am perfectly satisfied and only laugh at all the nonsense that they write about, those who had they been alive would have had many enemies, as myself, at last of this I am only told, I really don't believe that either McClintock or Osborn would endeavour to detract any thing from our trip, as if the misery of nearly five years incarceration in an icy Sarcophagus is not enough to cool envy, hatred, malice, and all uncharitableness.[123]

And then, in writing to Ross, McClure was careful to point out, "[I]n short it was Crozier not Franklin that completed the discovery of the passage which they are so anxious to rob me of the Honor, and to which I say nothing, but all Honours be paid to the dead, of the way I think none will dispute that we actually crossed from Sea to Sea by Polar Ice." In the same letter, McClure wrote that he had heard "from a friend at Hastings [that his estranged wife Mary] is very comfortable having lately been left some addition to her income from a relative deceased near Birmingham.... I am glad to learn she is in easy circumstances."[124] It does not appear they ever divorced—nor that he held a grudge.

A knighthood came McClure's way in November 1855, and his honors eventually included the Royal Geographical Society Patron's Gold Medal, Paris Geographical Society's Gold Medal, and a testimonial statuette from fellow naval officers, of a frosted silver winged figure of Fame, standing on tiptoe on the part of the globe representing the Polar Sea, placed on an ebony pedestal.[125]

First and foremost, Captain McClure was still a serving naval officer, and in March 1856 he took command of the steam corvette *Esk*, and sailed off for a five-year commission to the East Indies and China Station. During the Second China War (1856–60), while in command of the 3rd Division ashore, he was three times MID, and later made a Companion of the Order of the Bath (CB) for the capture of Canton in 1857. Commander Cresswell, Master Court and Acting Sergeant Major Woon also shared in the taking of that city. But for all his combat honors, a shadow crept over McClure's service record: "[T]he Board [is] dissatisfied with the irregular & severe punishments inflicted by him." While in distant waters, McClure earned an unenviable reputation for awarding the maximum penalty of 48 lashes for almost every offense.[126]

The end of the *Esk*'s commission in June 1861 was also McClure's final command at sea, and he retired with a Good Service Pension in the fall of 1863.[127] Promoted to rear admiral (retired) four years later, financially comfortable—and no doubt in want of companionship—

McClure married one Constance Ada Tudor.[128] With a "young and devoted wife, and, at a small place in Hertfordshire, he amused himself with hunting and other country pursuits, and enjoyed the pleasures of a home."[129] Their union was short-lived.

After his promotion to vice admiral (retired) at the end of May 1873, McClure went abroad that summer for his health, but "when he was attacked with his last illness, he constantly begged to be taken to die in England. So his wife brought him to the lodgings in Duke Street, where he had often been before, and there he calmly breathed his last on the 17th of October, 1873, aged 66 years and 8 months."[130]

The funeral at London's Kensal Green Cemetery on the 25th was attended by Sir Bartle Frere, President of the Royal Geographical Society; Admiral Sir John Hay, his old friend and Commodore of the East Indies Station and China Station from 1861 to 1863; Mr. Ashby, the Secretary to Sir Rodney Mundy, Commander-in-Chief, Portsmouth; and the friend of all Arctic men, John Barrow Jr. A cross-section of the old Investigators came together: former arch rival Alexander Armstrong, the sturdy John Woon, and finally, the poetic James Nelson. Sherard Osborn, Richard Collinson,

TESTIMONIAL PRESENTED TO SIR ROBERT M'CLURE.

Testimonial statuette presented to McClure by Sir James C. Ross, on behalf of his fellow naval officers. It featured a frosted silver winged figure of Fame, standing tiptoe on the part of the globe representing the Polar Sea, placed on an ebony pedestal. It bore the following inscription: "Presented to Captain Sir Robert J. Le Mesurier M'CLURE, R.N., late of H.M. discovery ship *Investigator*, by the officers of the Royal Navy, in admiration of his intrepidity and perseverance in penetrating through the Polar ocean in search of Sir John Franklin, which led to the discovery of the north-west passage, and has rendered his name distinguished in the naval annals of the British Empire" (Look and Learn; *The Illustrated London News*, June 14, 1856).

George H. Richards, and Francis L. McClintock were the chief mourners, followed by fellow Arctic officers Erasmus Ommanney, Robert D. Aldrich, Robert C. Allen, Bedford C.T. Pim, John P. Cheyne, Clements R. Markham, and Allen W. Young.[131]

Lady Jane Franklin wasted no time taking pen in hand, and briskly wrote *The Times'* editor on October 27, "to dissipate the confusion which seems still to exist in some quarters as to [McClure's] claim to be considered the discoverer of the North-West Passage." Perhaps fittingly, just two years later, Lady Franklin's last resting place was also within Kensal's confines.[132]

The loss of life during the Franklin Expedition, and ensuing cost of the search expeditions, cooled British enthusiasm for Arctic exploration—but polar exploration was never far from Sherard Osborn's mind. He led a campaign over several years for the renewal of British Arctic interests, and steadily gained support. Finally, the government agreed to finance the venture, resulting in Captain George S. Nares commanding an expedition composed of HMS *Alert* and *Discovery*, which were intended to spend two winters in the Arctic. Director-General of the Medical Department of the Navy Sir Alexander Armstrong "took the most active interest in its welfare and success."[133]

Two months before the expedition's departure in the final days of May 1875, the sensitive and affable missionary turned explorer Johann Miertsching passed away in his native Saxony, worn out at age 57 from many years of service to the Moravian cause. Years before, the parting with his *Investigator* shipmates had been "distressing for them as it was for me, and several seamen, their features hardened by storm and foul weather, were not ashamed to shed tears."

Though he very soon received two "most advantageous" offers from the Admiralty to join a search for the Franklin relics described by Rae, Miertsching's mind was made up, and he turned his back on the Arctic forever.[134]

Upon returning home, at a court reception in Dresden, Miertsching conversed with the King of Saxony, as well as the well known doctor, naturalist, scientist, psychologist, and landscape painter Carl Gustav Carus. He went on to marry Clementine Auguste Erxleben in Herrnhut in 1856, and although the couple had five or six children, only two daughters survived. The missionary was not sent back to his beloved Eskimos in Labrador, but instead to be among the Hottentots of Elim, and later Gnadenthal, South Africa. Apparently he met his old commander just one more time, during McClure's stay in Cape Town; McClure arranged for Miertsching's transportation by carriage to that place, and was excited to see his Arctic companion. After 12 years in South Africa, Miertsching and Clementine returned to settle down in Kleinwelka in April 1869, but she died there that December.[135]

**Sir Robert McClure, c. 1870 (courtesy Douglas Wamsley).**

In 1876, Nares's Arctic Expedition sent

out three major sled parties, one of which reached further north than any white man had ever been before, but all suffered severely from scurvy, resulting in the loss of three sledders. Altogether, 40 men in *Alert* and 20 in *Discovery* suffered from the disease, and Nares reluctantly brought his men home by early November. "It is well known that had his directions been carefully followed the disaster and failure which attended that expedition would not have occurred," deceptively wrote one of Armstrong's obituarists after the medical man passed away at 84, on the anniversary of American Independence in 1899. "He forced the Government to institute an inquiry into the matter, the results of which completely exonerated him from all blame."[136]

Carpenter 1st Class George Ford, who earned McClure's disdain by refusing to volunteer for a fourth Arctic winter, had been on half pay since 1870. Ford's circumstance was partly the product of "long and hard previous sea service in all parts of the world including 4½ years in the North Pole," and he lived just long enough to see Nares's return, before passing away in January 1877. Two months later, the English winter did what its Arctic counterpart could not, and the valiant John Woon was also gone. Woon rose to the rank of quartermaster lieutenant in 1867, and in addition to his gallantry medal for the Arctic, he earned a MID and the Royal Marines Meritorious Service Medal for "having saved the life of a wounded comrade under a heavy fire" during the unsuccessful attack on the Peiho Forts, June 25, 1859.[137]

When the 19th century began to draw to a close, McClure and his people were not forgotten. Predictably, the main panorama at the Royal Naval Exhibition of 1891 was *The Battle of Trafalgar*, but a large spread of canvas in the Arctic pavilion featured the voyage of HMS *Investigator*[138]:

> An Illustration of the Voyage of H.M.S. "Investigator," under Commander M'CIure, during the discovery of the North-West Passage, 1850–3. The scene reproduced represents the ship "Investigator" nipped in the ice-pack on October 8th, 1850; and the sledge parties, under Lieutenant S. Gurney Cresswell, prepared to leave the ship on their attempt to reach the mainland over the ice floes. The representation of ice and snow, and the effects of luminous colour being an amalgamation of natural tints giving a facsimile of the Aurora Borealis, are produced by an elaborate arrangement of mechanism specially designed by Messrs. J. Lyons & Co., Limited, for the Royal Naval Exhibition. On view each day from 10 a.m. till 10 p.m.[139]

"This pavilion was one of the centerpieces of the exhibition, being described as 'like an iceberg in aspect' by *The Illustrated London News* and rather more prosaically by *The Times* as 'an ice hummock.' This attraction was visited by Queen Victoria. The Queen 'alighted [from a horse-drawn carriage which was taking her around], passing within the iceberg, in order to see the pictures of the Arctic exploration ships nipped in the ice.'" Perhaps among the many relics in the Franklin Gallery, Her Majesty even caught a glimpse of the Union Jack carried home through the North-West Passage by the Investigators, which Stephen Court's widow had so generously lent to the exhibition.[140]

May 19, 1895, marked the 50th anniversary of Franklin's departure—but changes were in the air. When the International Geographical Congress met in London that July, it was decided that the southernmost continent would become the primary focus of new exploration. Up until that time, the vast majority of its coastline was still unknown, and no one had explored the hinterland of the frozen continent. The meeting touched off a wave of activity, and national expeditions and private ventures started organizing: the Heroic Age of Antarctic Exploration had begun.[141]

At the end of July, the *Norfolk Daily Standard* published writings stating that Sir Joseph Hooker was the sole remaining survivor of Sir James Ross's 1839–43 Antarctic Expedition. This moved one old Investigator to set pen to paper for the eyes of the *Standard*'s editor:

> I wish to point out that Sir Joseph is not the last or only survivor, as I was on that Expedition as captain of the forecastle of the Erebus, and was always of Dr. M'Cormick's party when he was ashore botanising. And I was with Sir James on the first Franklin Search Expedition, and accompanied that Commander on his land journeys; was boatswain's mate in the Investigator, with Captain M'Cluer [*sic*], and made the North-west passage. I am now in my eighty-third year of age, hale and hearty, except a little shaky on my "pins."
>
> I am, Sir, your obedient servant,
>
> EDWARD FAWCETT, Pensioner, R.N.
>
> Winterton, Norfolk, August 2.[142]

As it happened, another former Investigator also lived in Winterton parish—James Williams—who was Fawcett's son-in-law! The two men were only six years apart in age, and had become such good friends during their time under McClure's command, that Edward introduced James to his daughter Priscilla. The couple were married only three weeks after the Investigators returned to England.[143]

Priscilla lost her father within two years of his declaration of being "hale and hearty," and then her husband James during the first month of 1901. He died January 20—just two days after retired Vice Admiral William H. Haswell. Williams was born only nine days before the Queen, and passed away two days before her reign ceased. By the end of 1901, while in his 81st year, time had also run out for Deputy Inspector General Henry Piers.[144]

In the years following their return from the frozen north, at least two Investigators gambled on a distant land called America.

John Calder had decided he had enough of a sailor's life, and after marrying Somerset girl Fanny Cattle in February 1855, they left for the United States. After arriving in Chicago, Illinois, Calder took up the training of his youth, and was "engaged in butchering, feeding cattle and speculating, until 1863, when on account of failing health he was compelled to leave the city." Calder and his family settled in Kelly Township (Warren County), where over time, he developed a 640-acre farm and ranch. The Calders had several children, some of whom did not survive infancy.[145]

Although far away from his native land, Calder found ties to his polar past were closer than he imagined: "Early in the sixties I met a man in Chicago who was a member of the crew. Since that time I have not heard anything from any of the party except Capt. McClure whose death I saw chronicled in a Chicago paper. For all I know I am the only member of the *Investigator*'s crew who is now living."[146]

Edward Fawcett, c. 1894 (courtesy Jane Inglesby).

Nearly three decades after meeting up with a former shipmate, the old sailor's Arctic adventures brought a *Chicago Tribune* reporter to his doorstep. During the ensuing interview, "Mrs. Calder, who is a well-preserved, motherly little woman of 60 years, tripped into an adjoining room, and in a bureau drawer where a number of sacred souvenirs are kept found a couple of medals, of which both are justly proud. One was given Mr. Calder by the English Government as a special recognition of his services, while each member of the crew received one similar to the other one. The inscription on the first is as follows: MERITORIOUS SERVICE AR[C]TIC EXPLORATIONS [*sic*] 1854. Capt. Calder, as he is always called, is 70 years old, but is still rugged as ever."[147]

Captain McClure's "trusty and zealous petty officer" John Calder—probably the last survivor of HMS *Investigator*—slipped his Earthly bonds on January 7, 1905. That December, from Eagle City, Alaska, Norwegian Roald Amundsen telegraphed to the world his success of a three-year voyage in the tiny 47-ton sloop *Gjøa*—the first European expedition to sail the entire length of a North-West Passage between great oceans.[148]

Epilogue

# Found Beneath the Ice, 2010–11

---

*Within three minutes, anomalies began to show up on the sea floor....*
—Ryan Harris, Senior Marine Archeologist
Underwater Archaeology Service, Parks Canada

---

The first recorded time that Mercy Bay, in Aulavik National Park, was ice-free was the summer of 2007.[1]

But three summers later, the search window for Parks Canada's Ryan Harris and his team was down to less than a week—and then fate smiled upon them ... or so they thought. Word that the ice pack was breaking up sent Harris and his Underwater Archaeology Service colleagues scrambling to the bay, only to find it "still clogged with massive chunks of ice. It was

Diver on bow of *Investigator* (Brett Seymour, Parks Canada).

a crushing blow. 'What could we do? We set up camp and settled in to watch the ice,' says Harris, 'just as the crew of the *Investigator* undoubtedly did in 1853.'"[2]

Worse was ahead. An Arctic gale descended on their tent camp, and sand was blown into the remote sensing equipment; the vital sonar module intended to scan the ocean floor for signs of the wreck was out of commission. Harris disassembled and carefully cleaned the equipment, but it would have to be tested. A patch of open water tempted him and two others, so they cautiously shoved off in their inflatable Zodiac boat. "Within three minutes, anomalies began to show up on the sea floor, which were inconclusive but certainly caught my attention," recalls Harris. "Within two hours, as more ice cleared, we started getting really good images of the wreck site. It all happened so quickly, we were just in disbelief."[3]

On July 25, 2010, HMS *Investigator* had been found just 26 feet (eight meters) below the surface of Mercy Bay. For Harris, it was "a bit like finding a Columbus ship." Though encased in silt and missing her masts (probably the result of ice), the ship was sitting upright, and largely intact, thanks to the very cold water.[4]

Parks Canada archeologist Henry Cary and his team documented the remains of the cache of *Investigator's* provisions, stores and boats that were landed nearby. A magnetometer (which measures magnetic fields) aided in the location of the graves of Boyle, Ames, and Kerr, and was also used to find small iron artifacts beneath the topsoil. Miertsching's writings allowed Cary to locate the remnants of whalebone from a 2500-year-old Paleoeskimo campsite.[5]

The soil around the graves was still raised—an effect of the permafrost—as if they had

Copper sheeted sternpost of *Investigator* (Brett Seymour, Parks Canada).

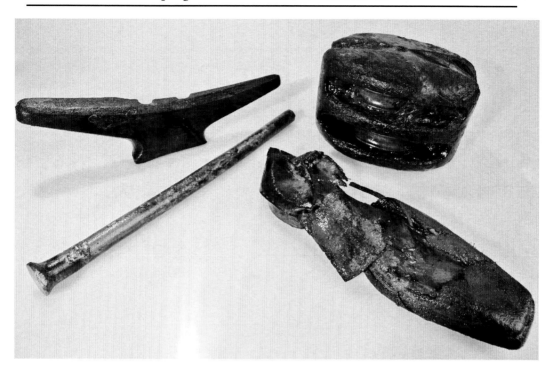

**Relics recovered from *Investigator*: horn cleat, double pulley, copper bolt and shoe (Louis Barnes, Parks Canada).**

only "been dug and filled in yesterday, Cary says, underlining for him the power and permanence of the *Investigator* story. 'It hasn't changed in 150 years. When you're standing at McClure's cache, the landscape that the men of *Investigator* would have looked out at from the ship and from the shore is exactly the same. There's been absolutely no change whatsoever,' he says. 'And when you're at the Paleoeskimo site, you realize there's been no change for 2,500 years.'"[6]

Harris returned to dive on the wreck in 2011, and became the first human being to touch *Investigator* after nearly 160 years.[7]

# Appendix 1.
# Weights and Measurements

long hundredweight = 112 lbs. (used in the British Imperial System)

1 meter = 3 feet 3.37 inches

1 fathom = 6 feet

100 fathoms = 1 cable's length (ordinary) = 608 ft. or about 200 yards

10 cables' lengths = 1 nautical mile

1 nautical/geographical/sea mile = 1.1515 statute miles

3 nautical miles = 1 league

The nautical/geographical/sea mile (called *Admiralty mile* in Great Britain) is the length of a minute of longitude, or $1/21600$ of a great circle of the Earth.

Temperatures are expressed in Fahrenheit, and negative readings are below zero.

1 imperial gill = 1.2 U.S. gills or 4.8 U.S. fl. oz. (1 U.S. gill = 4 U.S. fl. oz.)

# Appendix 2.
# Notes on Sources

## General Comments

While researching the journals and other writings of the Investigators 160 years on, a virtual Pandora's Box of mystery and intrigue spilled forth from them.

> *Through a written order of the captain's it has been announced:*
> *That all journals, sketches, charts, and other documents, written,*
> *drawn up, or prepared in connection with our expedition must, by*
> *the 5th of this month, be sealed, marked with the proper address,*
> *and delivered to the captain, who will turn them over to the Admi-*
> *ralty whence we may recover them.*[1]
>
> —Johann Miertsching, April 1853

Of the 66 souls onboard *Investigator* when she entered the ice in 1850, 13 were officers—including three warrant officers (boatswain, carpenter, and ice mate—a civilian) and the civilian interpreter. The balance of the 53 men were sailors and Marines. Currently, only the writings of six officers (Commander Robert McClure, Lieutenant Samuel Cresswell, Surgeon Alexander Armstrong, Assistant Surgeon Henry Piers, Carpenter George Ford and Interpreter Johann Miertsching) and two sailors (Able Seaman James Nelson and Quartermaster George Brown), are known to exist. One other journal, that of Lieutenant William Haswell, was known in 1854, having been salvaged from the abandoned *Investigator* in the spring of that year.

Along with McClure's dubious handling of the writings of his officers and men, it is critical to understand the overall content—and lack thereof—of three important primary sources, that of McClure, Piers and Ford. Large portions of McClure's and Piers's journals have gone "missing," and there is a sizeable "gap" in Ford's writings. In each case, the absentee portions include the most difficult period of the expedition, and as such, it is difficult to believe that mere coincidence was at play.

McClure's general order regarding record keeping during Haswell, Cresswell and Wynniatt's spring 1851 journeys read: "NOTE.—You are to keep a Diary, from which, upon your return, you will be required to draw up a detailed account of your proceedings for my information.—R.M'C." There is every reason to believe these diaries were kept and the accounts written, and handed over to McClure. It appears McClure disposed of them, as they have not surfaced in any public or private archives.[2]

To ease referencing, I created name indexes for the unpublished journals of Piers and Ford, the surviving first volume of McClure's journal, and volume one of Nelson's draft manuscript. In the case of Armstrong's handwritten journal, where necessary, any such references were noted on a printed out version from images taken of the its pages. No index was created for Brown's autobiographical writings, as they only run 10 transcribed pages. Name indexes were also created for the published works of McClure and Armstrong. Finally, Neatby's translation of Miertsching's writings required a much-needed supplemental name index.

## *Journal of Commander Robert John Le Mesurier McClure*

Before dealing with McClure's journal, it is convenient to briefly consider the related Letter & Order Book and Log Book.

The Letter & Order Book is held by the Royal Geographical Society (RGS), but this single volume only spans December 29, 1849–October 1, 1851, although entries were sparse between the last half of 1850 and October 1851. It is not annotated or date-stamped as received by the Admiralty, but does have plates stuck in the front and back with the RGS stamp, the former having the date June 6, 1910, evidently when it was accessioned.[3]

The Log Book of *Investigator* (and that of *Enterprise*) are held at The National Archives (NA). The *Investigator*'s log relates to both her first and second Arctic voyages, whereas the *Enterprise*'s log only deals with her second voyage. Although catalogued as "supplementary logs," they are marked as "logs" on the actual documents, and have every appearance of being regular logs. The single volume log for *Investigator* covers December 17, 1849–June 30, 1850, while the *Enterprise*'s single volume log runs from December 14, 1849 to August 7, 1851.[4]

McClure's journal must have been a multi-volume work, but the single volume held by the RGS only covers January 20–September 30, 1850. Like the Letter & Order Book, it is not annotated or date-stamped as received by the Admiralty, but does have plates stuck in the front and back with the RGS stamp, the former having the date June 6, 1910, evidently when it was accessioned.[5]

The task of carefully tracking McClure's writings through time produced some noteworthy insights to this primary source.

In October 1850, according to Miertsching: "The captain is very busy writing: he is making a good copy of his daily journal."[6] The questions spawned by this statement include: Why make a copy? And was it a *faithful* copy? But those queries represent just the beginning of a long and winding road for McClure's "journals," and although it must be assumed that both an original journal *and* a copy journal existed in October 1850, the fates of all but one of the volumes are uncertain at best.

The first time McClure traveled to *Resolute* from *Investigator* was on April 19, 1853, and he left to return to his ship on May 5.[7] The events during this period demonstrate he had his journal with him, and it seems entirely plausible that McClure conferred with Kellett and/or McClintock regarding its publication, and Lieutenant Sherard Osborn (commanding HMS *Pioneer* in the eastern Arctic) then became a prime candidate for the editorship. It is not known if McClure knew Osborn before *Investigator* departed in 1850. Osborn appears to have only started building his reputation as a writer in the 1850s, and published *Stray Leaves of an Arctic Journal*[8] prior to the departure of Belcher's squadron from England in April 1852, a fact no doubt well known among its officers.

McClure had his journal sent to Osborn, through Lieutenant Vesey Hamilton (*Resolute*), who began a sled journey from Dealy Island overland to Hecla and Griper Bay, and around Sabine Peninsula, on April 27, 1853. Although Kellet's orders to Hamilton did not specify the journal's delivery to Osborn, this was obviously one of his tasks.[9] Since at this point McClure still assumed he would return to *Investigator* and continue his command, he wanted to make sure his version of the voyage was set on the path to publication as soon as possible, and Osborn would have the opportunity to look over the journal before it was forwarded to the Admiralty.

On May 18, Hamilton met up with Commander George H. Richards (*Assistance*) on the sledding trail, and the commander was "desiring him to endeavour to overtake Lieutenant Osborn, and deliver to him Commander M'Clure's journal." Consequently, on May 21 Hamilton wrote, "I delivered up to Osborn the charts with which I had been supplied and the journal of proceedings of H.M.S. 'Investigator.'" Hamilton eventually returned to *Resolute* on June 21.[10]

On May 5—the very day McClure departed *Resolute* to return to *Investigator*—Cresswell left *Resolute* with McClure's dispatches, and headed for the *North Star* at Beechey Island. Arriving June 2, he waited for the expected supply ship from England. HMS *Phoenix* (Commander Edward A. Inglefield) and the transport *Breadalbane* arrived at Beechey Island on August 8. The *Phoenix* sailed for England on August 24, but without *Breadalbane*, which had been crushed and sunk by the ice three days before. Onboard the *Phoenix* off Thurso, Scotland, Inglefield wrote in his October 4 dispatch, "Lieutenant

Cresswell of the 'Investigator,' whom I appointed from the 'North Star' as supernumerary to this ship [*Phoenix*], is charged with the letters and journals of Commander M'Clure." Inglefield and Cresswell landed at Thurso, and within days Cresswell was back in King's Lynn for a brief reunion with family and friends; he then traveled to London and delivered McClure's dispatches and journal on October 7.[11]

In a reply to McClure that same day, Second Secretary of the Admiralty Captain W.A.B. Hamilton wrote: "My Lords have perused the narrative of your proceedings in search of the expedition under Sir John Franklin with equal interest and satisfaction; and, as a mark of their approval of the great exertions and untiring perseverance with which that search, though unavailing, was prosecuted; have been pleased this day to promote you to the rank of Captain."[12] The journal would have been returned to McClure after his arrival home in October 1854.

Osborn was now a commander, and as a result of his Arctic service, his "health had been somewhat shaken, and for a few months he held the appointment of Commander of the Norfolk District Coast Guard, to recruit," wrote Clements Markham. "During this interval he undertook the difficult and delicate work of preparing and editing Sir Robert M'Clure's logs and journals for the press; which he performed with admirable tact and literary skill."[13] In the finished work, Osborn tellingly wrote, "in reading over the journals of the officers"... but *which* ones?[14] Also, Osborn wrote: "For information on various points, and for assistance ... the Editor has been indebted to Captain (now Sir Robert) M'Clure, [and] Commander Gurney Cresswell (whose sketches enliven the letter-press)." This falls in line with a statement by Cresswell's descendant the late Dominick Harrod, who wrote that in addition to using the journals of McClure and Cresswell (the latter for April 6–October 6, 1853), Osborn had many conversations with them to aid his writing.[15] Any such conversations with Cresswell must have taken place before he left the Arctic, as it does not appear their naval assignments allowed the two to cross paths before the book's publication. The situation with McClure was quite different, as he and Osborn could easily have had a good deal of contact on the way home from the Arctic.

In early 1855, Osborn sailed to the Black Sea (the main Crimean theater of war), in command of HMS *Vesuvius*, and was eventually promoted to post captain and appointed to the *Medusa*. *The Discovery of the North-West Passage by H.M.S. "Investigator" Capt. R. M'Clure 1850, 1851, 1852, 1853, 1854, Edited by Commander Sherard Osborn From The Logs and Journals of Capt. Robert Le M. M'Clure* was published in 1856.[16] Osborn noted within the Preface that the "delay in the production of this work has arisen from the Editor having been obliged to leave England upon active service." And in fact, the place and date at the end of the Preface is "H.M.S. 'Medusa,' Sea of Azov, April 1856." The book went through four editions.[17]

Sir Robert McClure died on October 17, 1873, and his second wife, Lady Constance A. McClure, passed away on October 13, 1909. The following month, Henry F. McClintock (eldest son of Admiral Francis L. McClintock) was in the London law office of Pollock & Co., and saw some of McClure's Arctic journals, so he "suggested that the RGS might be glad to have them as relics." Pollock & Co. was the executor of Lady McClure's estate, and in December informed the RGS Secretary, John Scott-Keltie, that she bequeathed her husband's RGS Patron's Gold Medal and the Paris Geographical Society's Gold Medal to the RGS. Pollock further wrote to Scott-Keltie on December 20: "Referring to our interview with you on the 15th instant we send herewith as arranged the manuscript books & letter books relating to the late Sir Robert McClure's expeditions which we should be glad if, at your convenience, you would kindly go through, and afterwards let us know whether your Society would care to purchase them & if so at what price."[18]

Of the several manuscript volumes offered, the RGS wished to acquire three of them—but had a question. "One of them is a diary kept by Sir Robert M'Clure during the expedition in the 'Investigator.' This diary is continued in another volume which is not among those that you sent us. Perhaps you might be able to find it, and if so, you might be good enough to send it to me. The diary begins on January 20, 1850, and the portion which we have, ends on September 30," wrote Scott-Keltie. Pollock's reply: "We saw Mr Atkinson [the trustee] yesterday who informed us that there were no other manuscript volumes beyond those forwarded to you." Scott-Keltie therefore presumed there was a "second volume" that he understood "cannot be found" and "may possibly be lost."[19]

Henry McClintock was also offered the manuscripts, and eventually secured four of them for £3, and afterward sold them to the RGS for the same amount: 1) journal of HMS *Terror*, 1836–37; 2) journal of HMS *Investigator*, 1850 (one volume); 3) Letter and Order Book of HMS *Investigator*, 1850–51 (one volume); and 4) a signed copy of McClure's dispatches to the Admiralty, 1850–53. McClintock wrote that the "fourth book was found later & "thrown in" with the others." "They [Pollock & Co.] tell me that these books, and those you [Scott-Keltie] have already seen, are all the journals or manuscript left by Lady McClure. The other volume of the "Investigator" journal must therefore be lost," concluded McClintock.[20]

When one considers the signed copy of McClure's dispatches was "found later & "thrown in" with the others," the temptation might be to believe that the other volume(s) of his *Investigator* journal may actually have been lost. However, given McClure's penchant for political intrigue, this would be too easy of an explanation. A much more likely scenario is that McClure either disposed of the additional journal (and Letter & Order Book) volumes before his death, or left instructions for his widow to do the same. Indeed, perhaps Lady McClure even destroyed them on her own, so in the future their contents would not in some way tarnish her husband's memory.

## Journal, Letters and Artwork of Lieutenant Samuel Gurney Cresswell

Biographical notes and copies of Cresswell's letters were compiled by his mother c. 1870, and are bound with McClure's *The Discovery of the North West Passage* (4th edition, 1865) at the National Maritime Museum (NMM).[21] Dominick Harrod, Cresswell's great-great-great-nephew, drew upon the hundreds of letters Cresswell wrote to his family during his time in the Royal Navy (including both the 1848–49 and 1850–54 Arctic expeditions), and in 2000 published *War, Ice & Piracy: The Remarkable Career of a Victorian Sailor—The Journals and Letters of Samuel Gurney Cresswell*.[22]

The last letter Cresswell wrote home (to his parents), before *Investigator* headed from the North American coast into unknown seas, was dated August 30, 1850. The next letter to his parents was dated October 4, 1853, as he neared the Scottish coast in HMS *Phoenix*. It is presumed that Cresswell kept a journal up until the first week of April 1853, turned it in to the captain as ordered, and then McClure disposed of it in the Arctic. Consequently, his only surviving journal covers the time from Pim's arrival at *Investigator* on April 6, until when Cresswell reached Scotland on October 6, 1853.[23]

Cresswell's writings offer some insights into his captain's personality and actions during the early stages of the expedition, and touched on the interrelationships of the ship's officers. Of particular assistance in understanding the relationship between McClure and Haswell are Cresswell's writings on the interactions of these two men before the ship departed England.[24]

Cresswell was also a very talented artist, and the resulting lithographs of his superb watercolors from the 1850–54 expedition are indispensable in preserving the highpoints and drama of *Investigator*'s journey, and certainly complement his and others' writings.[25] Harrod and his brother owned several of Cresswell's original sketches and paintings, and the former also possessed his ancestor's Baltic Medal 1854–55, China Medal 1856–60 with clasps Canton 1857 and Taku Forts 1858, and Arctic Medal 1818–55 (all unnamed as issued).[26]

## Journal of Surgeon Alexander Armstrong

*A Personal Narrative of the Discovery of the North-West Passage; with Numerous Incidents of Travel and Adventure During Nearly Five Years' Continuous Service in the Arctic Regions While in Search of the Expedition Under Sir John Franklin*, by Alexander Armstrong, was published in 1857.[27] In his published journal, Armstrong wrote that "It possesses the advantage of having been compiled from a Journal in which I daily noted events precisely as they occurred, and now publish at the request of my former shipmates."[28] Armstrong's journal is held in the NA, and written in his hand in three separate places therein, it is stated that it covers January 1, 1850–June 3, 1853 (the day of the final abandonment of *Investigator*). However, the writings also contain very brief notations of events up to April 26, 1854.[29] Given the dates concerned, *this* particular journal was obviously not handed over to McClure, as ordered on April 5, 1853.

In three places listed above, the manuscript is also stamped *and* annotated (in a different hand) as received on October 12, 1854, by the Director General of the Medical Department—this being immediately after the return home of *Investigator*'s officers and men and the survivors of Belcher's expedition.

Below is a breakdown of the journal, which has noncontinuous pagination, and copy documents (all written in Armstrong's hand) contained therein[30]:

(1) "Copy of the Daily Sick List of H.M.S. Investigator. From the 1st day of January 1850 To the 3rd day of June 1853" [handwritten title; pp. 2–10].

(2) "General Remarks" [printed title; pp. 34–38].

(3) "Report of Survey. Held on the Crew of H.M.S. Investigator. in the year 1853. prior to her abandonment, and correspondence connected therewith" [handwritten title; pp. 55–61].

 (a) Dr. Domville's medical survey of Cresswell's party (undated *copy*, c. May 2, 1853).

 (b) "Report of the State of health of the Officers & Crew of Her Majesty's Discovery Ship Investigator, Rob.[t] M.[c]Clure Esq. Commander.—as found on Survey held on board the said ship in the Bay of Mercy, Baring Island this 23rd day of May 1853. in accordance with the orders of Captain Henry Kellett C.B. of Her Majesty's ship Resolute" (*copy*).

 (c) "Order N.[o] 1" (missing)—Kellett to McClure (May 5, 1853)—The option for the officers and men of *Investigator* to volunteer to stay for a fourth winter. [A *copy* of this order is contained in the court-martial proceedings of October 17, 1854 (ADM 1/5645).]

 (d) "Order N.[o] 2"—Kellett to McClure, Domville & Armstrong (May 5, 1853)—A medical survey of the officers, seamen and Marines remaining on *Investigator* (*copy*).

 (e) Armstrong & Domville to Kellett (May 23, 1853)—Letter respecting the state of health of those remaining onboard *Investigator* (*copy*).

 (f) "General Remarks" [printed title; pp. 69–73].

 (g) "A NOSOLOGICAL SYNOPSIS of the Sick Book kept during the Period of this Journal, in conformity with the 30th Article of the Surgeons' Instructions" [printed title; p. 90].

 (h) "A LIST of Men who have received Wounds or Hurts, during the Period of the Journal" [printed title; p. 90].

 (i) "General Remarks" [printed title; pp. 91–95].

 (j) "Copy of Meteorological Journal kept on board. H.M.S. Investigator. From the 1st day of January 1850. To the 31st of March 1853" [handwritten title; pp. 96–119].

 (j–1) "Abstract of Meteorological Journal for the year 1850."

 (j–2) "Abstract of Meteorological Journal for Jan.[y] 1851."

 (j–3) "September 1852."

 (j–4) "Summary of Meteorological Abstracts for the years 1850–51–52–53."

 (k) "Appendix to Medical Journal" [handwritten title; p. 120].

 (l) "Remarks on the Physical characteristics and Natural History of the lands discovered in H.M.S. Investigator in the Polar Sea, during the years 1850–51–52–53 and 54" [handwritten title; pp. 121–37].

 (m) "A List of Game and animals Killed by the Officers and men of H.M. Ship 'Investigator,' during the years 1850–51–52–53. In the Strait of Princes of Wales and Bay of Mercy. in the Polar Sea" [handwritten title; p. 138].

 (n) "Observation on the Esquimaux. Of the Northern Coast of America" [handwritten title; pp. 139–141].

 (o) "Medical & Surgical Journal of H.M. Ship. Investigator. continued from, Journal N.[o] 3" [handwritten title; pp. 143–76].

Although many of the manuscript entries match the published version, Armstrong's claim of having "daily noted events precisely as they occurred" does not entirely ring true, given that several entries were written in *retrospect*. Examples of such writing are *italicized* in the following excerpts:

(a) *November 1850 (p. 73)*—"The quantity [of provisions] issued did not exceed the usual Service allowance, but the preserved meat was issued every alternate day with four ounces of vegetables, either Scotch barley or potatoes, *we likewise during the first year had once a month....*"

(b) *September 24, 1851 (p. 126)*—"This bay, *subsequently* called the 'Bay of Mercy' has from the circumstance of its being *the region of our dreary abode for nearly two years.*"

(c) *February 1852 (p. 94)*—"[A]lthough the prospective loss of flesh and strength, with a general
improvement of the physical powers which I anticipated, could not but strongly predispose them
to other attacks of that disease [scurvy], *which in a few months subsequently....*"

Consequently, nearly the *entire* handwritten journal in the archives has every appearance of being
a copy.

Perhaps the best explanation for its existence could be that Armstrong—with his deep mistrust
of McClure—made the copy of his original journal before turning the latter over to McClure in early
April 1853 (who then disposed of it). Historian Leslie Neatby made the following comment regarding the survival of Armstrong's writings: "It appears that Dr. Armstrong *did* salvage his journal, but for
this, no doubt, he was indebted to the good offices of his colleague, Dr. Domville, who bore written
orders from Kellett and was exempt from McClure's control." If Armstrong made a copy journal, he
may have felt free from McClure's suspicions, and carried it himself over to Dealy Island (making
Neatby's assertion false)—or he may have given it to Domville to carry for safekeeping (making Neatby's
assertion true).[31]

"With our arrival on board the 'Resolute' I consider the Narrative of the 'Investigator's voyage
ceases," wrote Armstrong in his book, "although I have before me copious notes of our daily proceedings
until we reached England; their publication is not within the limits of this work. Indeed, I have neither
wish nor inclination to narrate them." These "copious notes," assuming they still exist, have yet to be
found.[32]

## *Journal of Assistant Surgeon Henry Piers*

"A Journal of the voyage of H.M.S. 'Investigator'; 1849, '50, '51. '52 and '53_" was written by Piers
at the beginning of the document. The full stop after "'51" is notable, since "'52 and '53_" was added
at a later time, having been written in a thinner line. Plainly Piers kept the journal through the years
1852 and 1853. The manuscript is held at the NMM, and is bound up in sailcloth. Its only markings
are "H.M.S. Investigator Dec. 1849" (written in Piers's hand) on the first page, with the owner's name
above, "H. Piers." (stamped in Old English lettering), and the same name stamp on an otherwise blank
second page. There are no stamps or annotations that would indicate when it was handed in to the
Admiralty.[33] The path of Piers's journal back to England is unknown.

The journal starts on December 2, 1849—but abruptly ends in the midst of the March 31, 1852
entry. This of course was just prior to the most difficult period of the expedition.[34] The NMM accession
document kept with the manuscript states, "Journal of H.M.S. Investigator Dec. 1849—March 1853,
keeper unknown," with the following just below: "[also map to N.A. & 2 books to L]." It was presented
to the museum on February 20, 1967, by a certain J. Paine, 39 Dixon Road, Bangor, County Down,
Northern Ireland.[35] As the journal was examined on microfilm, handwriting can plainly be seen beyond
the right and bottom edges of the page containing the March 29, 30, and (partial) 31, 1852, entries, but
the frame that follows is blank on the film (except for writing from the previous page appearing along
the left-hand margin). I asked the NMM archives manager about this, and he replied, "I have checked
the original manuscript for JOD/102 and this volume covers 2 December 1849 to 31 March 1852.
Therefore, the microfilm reel entry [accession document] is a mistake—the extent of the material with
the volume is 1852. The volume does end abruptly, which you noticed whilst viewing the microfilm
reel."[36]

Notations written post–March 1852 prove there was at least a second volume:

(a) Between the entries for December 31, 1850, and January 1, 1851, is a page with a vertical line forming
a left-hand margin (as in all the other pages of the journal), but with two closely drawn horizontal
lines across the upper third of the page, and having the following written above:

P.S.—Notes—

Drawn out by Court for Capt. M^cClintock—
Land discovered & searched by "Investigator"—

| | Miles | | | Miles | |
|---|---|---|---|---|---|
| Baring | — | 790 | Baring | — | 456} Ship |
| Albert | — | 750 | Other id^{ds} | — | 21} |
| Norway | — | 14 | | | 1114 Foot |
| Robilliard | — | 7 | | | 1591 |
| Other | — | 30 | | | |
| | | 1591 | | | |

These notes were clearly written *well after* March 31, 1852, and in no way appear to be tipped in. Their location within the journal is strange, since Norway and Robilliard Islands were not discovered and named by McClure until mid–August 1851,[37] and McClintock commanded HMS *Intrepid* during Belcher's 1852–54 expedition, so would have met the survivors of *Investigator* only *after* she was abandoned in June 1853.

(b) *Part of the June 13, 1851 entry*: "Several on board, and myself amongst them, are of opinion that the ships ("Erebus" & "Terror") never got further than Baffin's bay,^X but were both together suddenly overwhelmed by some fearful accident—such as the upsetting of an ice-berg on them." A later footnote: "^X Proved by discoveries at Beechey Is^d Aug. 1854."

(c) *Part of the October 15, 1851 entry*: "With deer also I think we may look for Musk Oxen^X..." And a later footnote: "^X Musk oxen & Reindeer have not been seen together in any numbers, seen in Melville Is. where both are plentiful—Aug. 1854."

At least two other journals kept by Piers have survived. One as assistant surgeon onboard HMS *Cleopatra*, on anti-slavery patrols on the East African coast (1844–47), and the other as surgeon on board HMS *Satellite*, on a voyage to Vancouver Island (1856–57). Piers was based at Vancouver Island during the governorship of Sir James Douglas, when British Columbia was declared a British Colony. Both journals are held by the Wellcome Library in London.[38]

## Diary of Carpenter George James Ford

The diary of George James Ford, HMS *Investigator*, which covers January 10, 1850–June 8, 1852, and May 26, 1853–September 21, 1854, is held at the Karpeles Manuscript Library (Santa Barbara, California). It was transcribed by Professor William "Bill" Barr in 1994, during research work at Karpeles.[39]

Up until June 8, 1852, Ford's writings take the form of a series of letters to his wife, with daily entries, and as such, it is presumed he was allowed to keep them, rather than turn them over to McClure. These were written on loose sheets of paper, and then cross written,[40] which made them extremely difficult to read for Barr, especially since the ink bled through in several places. The entries from May 26, 1853 to September 21, 1854, were kept in a small notebook, and deciphering these for transcription was comparatively easy.[41] Since Ford's diary was never turned in to McClure or the Admiralty, it was not consulted by Osborn.

After only a handful of his crew volunteered to remain onboard *Investigator*, McClure's attitude toward the men was hinted at by Armstrong in his book, just before the final abandonment: "[A] few words, not complimentary, were addressed [by the captain] to the men." Ford expounded on McClure's disposition regarding the lack of volunteers, and was also blunt about the unwelcome reception the Investigators received onboard *Resolute*. The latter was amplified by Miertsching, when he wrote that an "unexpected winter in the ice and the deprivation of space and comfort owing to the intrusion of us passengers does not please [Kellett's] men who had been accustomed to something better. One can well see here that sympathy, love, and friendship, unless kindled in our hearts by a Christian spirit, cannot endure, and may be likened to blazing straw, quickly kindled and soon extinguished."[42]

## Journal of Interpreter Johann August Miertsching

Miertsching's journal is the "Travel Narrative of a North Pole Expedition in Search of Sir John Franklin and for the Discovery of the Northwest Passage in the Years 1850–1854," and is held by Barbara Jannasch, Nova Scotia, Canada (widow of Niels Windekilde Jannasch, Miertsching's descendant). In addition, she also has Miertsching's handwritten notes. The entries for April 7, 1853–November 10, 1854, are the journal's only original day-by-day record, as everything prior was *reconstructed* by Miertsching.[43]

As Miertsching was preparing to leave *Investigator* on April 11, 1853, he lamented: "It grieves me bitterly to be obliged to leave behind my journals which have cost me so much effort and are worth more to me than everything else." However, on May 4 he wrote: "My good Captain McClure has promised to send me my journal which he has had in his keeping since April 4, with Dr. Domville when he comes back, or, in event of the ship being abandoned, to bring it himself." But on June 17 he wrote, "The captain had been unable to bring me my precious journal; though it would have added no more than about two pounds to the load of the sledge; but he would have been obliged to bring also the journals and records of his officers, and this he could not do.... My worthy Captain McClure offered me in the friendliest way the use of his ship's journal, that with aided by memory [and penciled notes,[44]] I might reconstruct my own; he would endeavour to procure for me writing materials, which are very rare on these ships. I accepted his friendly offer with many thanks."[45] But was it McClure's *original* journal—or the copy? It is doubtful Osborn had any access to this reconstructed journal, and given it was written in German, it probably would have been difficult to utilize.

As would be expected, variances exist between Miertsching's reconstructed journal and its published versions.

Two editions were published in German, in 1855 and 1856, as *Reise-tagebuch des missonars Joh. Aug. Miertsching, welcher als dolmetscher die Nordpol-expedition zur aussuchung Sir John Franklin auf dem schiff Investigator begleitete in dem jahren 1850 bis 1854*.[46] For the 1855 edition, it is possible that either Miertsching, or a German Moravian editor, adapted the text to meet the expectations of Moravian religious principles and views. However, there is no doubt that the 1856 edition was revised by a Moravian editor to conform to the church's "official" view.[47]

In 1854, Daniel Benham used the journal as a source in *Sketch of the Life of Jan August Miertsching, Interpreter of the Esquimaux Language to the Arctic Expedition On Board H.M.S. "Investigator," Captain M'Clure, 1850, 1851, 1852, 1853*. The journal appeared in French in 1857 as *Journal de M. Miertsching interprète du capitaine Mac Clure dans son voyage au Pôle Nord*, and four years later, a serialized English version appeared as "Notes from an Arctic Diary." But it was not until 1967, when Leslie H. Neatby translated the manuscript, that the journal was published in English in book form as *Frozen Ships: The Arctic Diary of Johann Miertsching 1850–1854*.[48]

Neatby omitted a fair bit of text in places, and these appear as "..." in *Frozen Ships*. In most cases, Neatby evidently felt the omitted material was not too important, and dealt with personal subjects, such as reading books, his health, moods and feelings, or religious topics. In a very few cases, Neatby's translation was somewhat imprecise, but for the most part these were nuances. Though Neatby probably had a typed script *and* photocopy of Miertsching's manuscript, he did not always double-check, and some typos made it into his translation. For example, Miertsching used a more correct spelling of Inuktitut (Eskimo) words, which were misinterpreted by whoever created the typed script; Neatby did not recognize these errors, and so most Inuktitut words and names in his translation are incorrect.[49]

"Miertsching often appears casual and imprecise in his treatment of details," declared Neatby.[50] To be fair, being an almost entirely reconstructed journal, consideration must be given for disagreements in dates, times and details compared to other sources.

## Writings of Able Seaman James H. Nelson

The introduction to "The Last Voyage of HMS Investigator, 1850–53, and the Discovery of the North West Passage," in a 1967 issue of the *Polar Record*, reads in part: "Recently J.W. Nelson [of 5 Victoria Avenue, Leicester], a descendant of Nelson's, brought to the Institute two copy-books[51] containing accounts by him of the last voyage of *Investigator*." A long transcribed section from volume one follows, covering July 26, 1850 (when *Investigator* entered the Bering Strait), to October 31 (when McClure returned from verifying a North-West Passage).[52]

The two volumes donated to the Scott Polar Research Institute (SPRI) were *photocopies* of copy-books. Although catalogued as James Nelson's "journals," they are book drafts written in a journal style, and there are specific indicators that these are book drafts: Volume 1—the first 15 pages comprise a short history of Arctic exploration; numerous corrections (up to p. 28); and occasional references to "THE READERS." Volume 2—this is essentially a much shorter draft of the first volume, and also contains a few sketches of landscapes, the *Investigator* and people.[53]

James Nelson and William Mumford (Carpenter's Crew and Mate in *Resolute*) became friends in the Arctic, and several of Nelson's poems are preserved within Mumford's journal, having been sent with a letter from Nelson[54]:

> For whenever I look on the old manuscript, & pencillings I cannot help even now casting my thoughts back to those bleak [instances] of many a cold hand & hungry stomachs [in] the Arctic Regions. Are you quite well, I was not prepared to hear of your being in the land of coal mines. I have written a Manuscript "Narrative of the Voyage of the Investigator." & so well was it liked that many requested publishing. However I have no desire to become the target of critics, so have forborne [declined], but when you come to London, it shall be for your perusal.[55]

By the drafts' contents, they must have been based on a journal, or notes at the very least. Did Nelson turn in his original journal to McClure, but keep notes—or did he conceal his original writings altogether? When Nelson wrote of his manuscript that "so well was it liked that many requested publishing. However I have no desire to become the target of critics"—who was he concerned about—ex-shipmates, laymen, or both? The whereabouts of the original manuscripts is unknown.

## Reminiscences of Quartermaster George Brown

"The Manuscript of My Grandfather the Late Mr. George Brown of His Naval Service from 1841 to His Retirement in 1876" is the title of a 1968 photocopy of a typewritten manuscript of a transcription by Brown's grandson (undated, c. 1876).[56] As might be imagined with recollections written so long after the period concerned, there are many inaccuracies in respect to names, dates and events, so this source was used to a lesser extent and treated with due caution.

## Journal of Lieutenant William Henry Haswell

The *Intrepid*'s Master Frederick J. Krabbé was ordered to sled over to the abandoned *Investigator* in the spring of 1854. On May 7, Krabbé recorded in his sled journal that he "overhauled for journals, for bringing back to the ships. Lieutenant Haswell's was the only one I could find."[57] Unfortunately, Krabbé did not leave any information as to where the journal was found. This was odd—if Haswell turned his journal over to the captain, it seems that McClure would have made it "disappear," rather than simply leave it someplace onboard where it could be found at a later time.

After all, Cresswell, Court, Paine, Sainsbury and Wynniatt would have all kept journals—which were presumably turned over to McClure in April 1853 and (supposedly) left onboard. And we know that McClure told Miertsching he was unable to bring his journal away, because "he would have been obliged to bring also the journals and records of his officers."[58] But they all "disappeared"; and of course, Armstrong and Piers's journals are mysteries within themselves.

The material sent to the Admiralty by Kellett was examined, which included the original sled journals of his officers, a copy of the orders he gave to Krabbé, and the summary of the latter's journey. Except for Krabbé noting in his sled journal that he found Haswell's journal, there is no mention of it in the summary, and the only statement Krabbé gave is that he left the *Investigator* in the same state that he found it, along with a document that described his visit and activities. Consequently, Miertsching's comment that month was more than a little curious: "The orders of Captain Kellett—that he should bring back our journals which Captain McClure had left behind—he did not fulfil [*sic*], *because he could not find any!?*" Was the discovery of Haswell's journal concealed?[59]

It occurred to me that just because Krabbé salvaged Haswell's journal, this did not *necessarily* mean it made it out of the Arctic. Since *Resolute* and *Intrepid* were already abandoned, Krabbé had orders to return to the *North Star*.[60] Although McClure undoubtedly made it his business to know what was brought back from *Investigator*, Krabbé would have turned the journal over to Kellett—but what happened next? Kellett was certainly keenly aware of McClure's political maneuverings, and as his superior officer, could have easily kept Haswell's journal, with the intention of handing it over the Admiralty himself. Alternately, he could have handed it back to Haswell, but then McClure could have rightly demanded the journal be turned over to him. It was, after all, McClure's "responsibility" to see all journals and documents were turned in to the Admiralty. Supposing McClure did get possession of it again, maybe the journal "disappeared" before ever reaching England.

Over the years I had searched for Haswell's original manuscript and/or a published version in places such as the Scott Polar Research Institute, Royal Geographical Society, National Maritime Museum, Royal Naval Museum, Imperial War Museum, The National Archives, and the British Library, but found nothing. I also searched the Archives Hub online, which represents over 220 institutions across the UK, again without any results (and kept in mind there can be no accounting for items that have not been catalogued, are misidentified, or are unknown or lost within institutions' collections).[61]

The question of the journal's existence in any form was posed to Haswell family genealogist Dr. Todd Farmerie, who replied to me that he has periodically looked into the matter, but not in any systematic manner, and without success. Farmerie suggested it was possible that Haswell's will directed that his papers be left to a particular individual or institution, or they could have simply passed with the body of the estate, distributed by the executor. Farmerie then generously provided guidance to finding and examining Haswell's will for clues, as well as information on his unmarried sisters and other relatives.[62]

Haswell's will equally divided his estate between two unmarried sisters: Elizabeth Ann Gray Haswell (died 1903) and Clara Standbridge Haswell (died 1915, and was living with Admiral Haswell at the time of his death), but provides no details of items within the estate. Along with a nephew, Commander George Gray Haswell, RN (died 1933), all three individuals were executors of Haswell's will. I sent a message via Facebook to Commander G.G. Haswell's descendant, Drummond Mcleod Irvine-Fortescue (Stellenbosch, Western Cape, South Africa), but never received a reply.[63]

The wording of Haswell's will speaks of someone who was not at all concerned about being honored or remembered: "I wish to be buried in the Church yard or Burial ground nearest to the place of my decease without pomp or ceremony." Consequently, one wonders if Haswell, and/or his descendants, ever entertained the idea of publishing the manuscript and/or donating it to an institution. Considering Haswell's very contentious relationship with McClure, publishing an account of the voyage probably would not have been a good career move. He went on to retire as a captain from the Navy in 1872, and eventually became a retired vice admiral in 1881, passing away in 1900.[64]

Nonetheless, I wondered if there was any *need* for Haswell (and his descendants) to put his words in print or make anything public. In this regard, perhaps the preface of Armstrong's book provided a tantalizing clue: "I daily noted events precisely as they occurred, and now publish at the request of my former shipmates. My principal object in writing this Work, has been to do justice *to every one* engaged in the voyage which, for its duration and privations, is, I believe, unparalleled in Maritime annals."[65] Haswell could easily have been one to whom Armstrong made reference.

Copies of the wills for Haswell's executors were obtained and examined, but there was no hint of Haswell's journal. The will for Clara Haswell seemed to missing one page, but was received as such from HM Courts and Tribunals, and there is no indication as to the placement of her possessions with individuals. At the time of Haswell's death in 1900, Elizabeth Haswell was living at the Morwenstow Vicarage, Cornwall (now The Old Vicarage B&B), and (then) Lieutenant George G. Haswell was living in Tenby, Pembrokeshire.[66]

I contacted The Old Vicarage B&B, as well as the Tenby Museum & Art Gallery, and individuals knowledgeable of the area's history, with the hope of tracking down some of the Haswell family papers. Although the museum does not have any papers relating to the Haswell family, within a list of monumental inscriptions for the Tenby cemetery is recorded the death of a certain Frances Haswell, who died on May 17, 1898, at only five days old.[67]

# Appendix 3.
# HMS *Investigator* Crew List

## Information Used to Compile HMS Investigator *Crew List*

1861 England Census, ancestry.co.uk; 1881 British Isles Census, www.familysearch.org; Arctic Medal 1818–55 Roll, Baltic Medal 1854–55 Roll, Crimea Medal 1854–56 Roll, and St. Jean d'Acre Medal 1840 Roll, NA, ADM 171/9, ADM 171/19–22, ADM 171/26–28 (Royal Navy), ADM 171/14; Armstrong's journal & Sick List, NA, ADM 101/250; Armstrong (1857); Asplin (2004); Court-Martial Proceedings of Capt. Robt. J. Le M. McClure and Officers and Crew of HMS Investigator, NA, ADM 1/5645; McClure (1856); Claims by Executors and Next-of-Kin for Back Pay for Ratings, NA, ADM 141, Series AF and Series EC, NA, ADM 44; Claims by Executors and Next-of-Kin for Back Pay for Officers, NA, ADM 141, Series ED, ADM 45; Clydesite & TugTalk, www.clydesite.co.uk; Continuous Service engagement books, NA, ADM 139; Coastguard Service Records, NA, ADM 175; Douglas-Morris (1982, 1987, 1991 & 1994); Ford's diary, KML, 18500119Arctic1xx; *The Geographical Magazine*; *The Geographical Review*; Glendining's; Great Britain (1854a); Guildhall Museum (Rochester); *Guy's Hospital Gazette*; Harrod (2000); Hunterian Museum (Glasgow); *The Illustrated London News*; Just Plain Folks, http://just-plain-folks.co.uk; Labrador Retriever, http://en.wikipedia.org; *The London Gazette*, www.thegazette.co.uk; McDougall (1857); *Modern English Biography*; Museum of Science and Industry (London); Naval Officers' Service Records, NA, ADM 104, ADM 107, ADM 196; McClure, NMM, MCCLU/14; *The Navy List*; *The New Army List*; Neatby (1967); O'Byrne (1849); Piers's journal, NMM, JOD/102; *Portrait and Biographical Album of Warren County, Illinois, Containing Full Page Portraits and Biographical Sketches of Prominent and Representative Citizens of the County*, etc. (1886); Poulsom & Myres (2000); Register of Mates, NA, ADM 11/22; Registers of Seamen's Effects, NA, ADM 44 & ADM 141; Registers of Officers' Effects, NA, ADM 45; Registers of Deceased Ratings, NA, ADM 154; Registers of Seamen's Services, NA, ADM 29 & ADM 188; Registry of Shipping and Seamen: Register of Seamen's Tickets, NA, BT 113; Royal Geographical Society; Royal Marines' Attestation Forms, NA, ADM 157; Royal Marines' Description Books, NA, ADM 158; Savours (1999); Sotheby's; Succession Book of Mates, Midshipmen, Admiralty Midshipmen, etc., NA, ADM 11/29; Warrant Officers' Service Records, NA, ADM 29; Various Royal Navy ships' musters and description books.

## Officers

McCLURE, Robert John Le Mesurier (1807–73)—Commander

*Previous Polar Experience*: Mate, *Terror* (1836–37) & Lieutenant, *Enterprise* (1848–49)

*Honors & Awards*: Knighthood (Kt/1855); Companion of the Order of the Bath (CB/military/1859/ capture of Canton, 1857); China Medal 1856–60/Canton 1857 (Captain/*Esk*), MID (LG, Feb. 16, 1858)—in command of the 3rd Division ashore & (LG, Feb. 26, 1858)—made a sortie against the North

Gate & Major General Straubenzee expressed his admiration; Arctic Medal 1818–55; RGS Patron's Gold Medal (1854); Paris Geographical Society's Gold Medal (1855)—Lady Constance A. McClure bequeathed the latter two medals to the RGS upon her death in 1909; Address from the Grand Jury of the County Wexford (1855); Testimonial statuette from fellow naval officers (1856); Diploma as an Honorary Member of the Society of Arts and Sciences of Mauritius (1861). Among McClure's papers at the Royal United Services Institution was/is a "White cardboard box labeled 'China medal' containing a red silk ribbon with a medallic crescent moon enclosing a floret, n.d." McClure wanted the testimonial statuette given to the museum at Wexford after his death.

*Notes*: North-West Passage Sled Party. Promoted to Captain Oct. 7, 1853, with seniority from Dec. 18, 1850. Died in London a retired Vice Admiral, Oct. 17, 1873. Journal of Captain Robert McClure, RGS; *The Discovery of the North-West Passage by H.M.S. "Investigator" Capt. R. M'Clure 1850, 1851, 1852, 1853, 1854, Edited by Commander Sherard Osborn from the Logs and Journals of Capt. Robert Le M. M'Clure* (1856).

### HASWELL, William Henry (1818–1900)—Lieutenant

*Previous Polar Experience*: none

*Honors & Awards*: Naval General Service Medal 1793–1840/Syria (Mate/*Talbot*—renamed: "W.H. HASWELL, "TALBOT," 1840"); Arctic Medal 1818–55, MID (privately engraved: "W.H. HASWELL, 'INVESTIGATOR'"); Turkish St. Jean d'Acre Medal 1840 (silver issue, privately engraved: "W.H. HASWELL, "TALBOT" 1840"), plus a pewter Boulton's Trafalgar Medal (in a copper frame, glass missing), attributed to Haswell's father [Midshipman/*Phoebe*], and a copy of *The White Ribbon*, by Neville Poulsom, Glendining's, September 1985, lot 187, VF. The group was split up after this time. "Captain Kellett, of the *Herald*, strongly recommending him for his services in the Arctic Seas:= See Memorial stating his services 29 October 1853" (Oct. 17, 1851).

*Notes*: Specially promoted to Commander May 5, 1854, with seniority from Oct. 26, 1850, but time as Commander not allowed from this date. Died in London a retired Vice Admiral, Jan. 18, 1900.

### CRESSWELL, Samuel Gurney (1827–67)—Lieutenant

*Previous Polar Experience*: Mate, *Investigator* (1848–49)

*Honors & Awards*: MID (LG, Sept. 29, 1846)—service against Borneo pirates, while part of Rear Admiral Cochran's personal staff; Baltic Medal 1854–55 (Lieutenant/*Archer*); Arctic Medal 1818–55, MID; China Medal 1856–60/Canton 1857 & Taku Forts 1858 (Commander/*Surprise*), MID (LG, Feb. 28, 1858)—capture of Canton—"The fire from his heavy guns materially assisted in disconcerting the enemy on the distant part of the wall"; MID (LG, July 28, 1858)—employed onshore at capture of Taku Forts; MID (LG, Nov. 2, 1858)—destruction of a Chinese piratical fleet. Received a written testimonial and civic reception at St. George's Guildhall by the people of King's Lynn, Norfolk (Oct. 26, 1853). All three medals are held by a direct descendant, and are unnamed as issued.

*Notes*: Delivered the North-West Passage dispatches to the Admiralty (Oct. 7, 1853). Promoted to Commander for the Arctic expedition on Oct. 21, 1854, but not backdated. Captain Sept. 17, 1858, and retired Feb. 25, 1867. Died Aug. 14, 1867, at Lynn's Bank House; his health was shaken by long years of service in China and the Arctic, and helping to nurse his father through a painful illness. Biographical notes and copies of letters of Captain Samuel Gurney Cresswell, compiled by Mrs. Cresswell, c. 1870, NMM. *War, Ice & Piracy: The Remarkable Career of a Victorian Sailor—The Journals and Letters of Samuel Gurney Cresswell* (2000).

### SAINSBURY, Henry Hubert (c. 1828–53)—Mate

*Previous Polar Experience*: none

*Honors & Awards*: Arctic Medal 1818–55, MID—"12/5/57 [illegible signature] for Goode"

*Notes*: Promoted to Lieutenant Dec. 10, 1852, with seniority from Oct. 26, 1850. Discharged Dead

Nov. 14, 1853, of tuberculosis and scurvy, *Resolute*, off Cape Cockburn, Barrow Straits. Remembered on the Beechey Island Cenotaph, along with the following inscription: "Relieved from earthly sorrow, which on my heart hath press'd, I thank the gentle hand Divine which lays this heart to rest."

WYNNIATT, Robert James (1830–60)—Mate

*Previous Polar Experience*: none

*Honors & Awards*: Baltic Medal 1854–55 (Lieut./*Exmouth*), MID (LG, Aug. 20, 1855)—in rocket boats at Sveaborg; Arctic Medal 1818–55, MID; China Medal 1856–60/Fatshan 1857 & Canton 1857 (Lieutenant/*Calcutta*) MID (LG, Aug. 1, 1857)—*Calcutta*'s first pinnace at Fatshan; MID (LG, Nov. 2, 1858)—"high praise for his conduct at the destruction of a Chinese piratical fleet, and also in an action with a pirate action a few days afterwards"; MID (LG, Sept. 16, 1859)—while commanding the *Nimrod* on June 25, 1859, "praise for his conduct at the unsuccessful attack on the forts in Pey-ho River"; "Captain Vansittart [*Magicienne*] speaks highly of Acting-Commander R.J. Wynniatt of the *Nimrod*." All three medals are known to exist.

*Notes*: Promoted to Lieutenant Feb. 25, 1852, with seniority from Oct. 26, 1850, but time as Lieutenant not allowed from this date. Discharged Dead Nov. 29, 1860, of dysentery, while on passage home from China, and buried with military honors on Dec. 1, 1860, in Galle, Ceylon.

ARMSTRONG, Alexander (1818–99)—Surgeon & Naturalist

*Previous Polar Experience*: none

*Honors & Awards*: Knight Commander of the Order of the Bath (KCB/military/June 17, 1871); Baltic Medal 1854–55 (Surgeon/*Cornwallis*)—MID for Aug. 9, 1855, attack of rocket boats on a Russian frigate moored in the Kung Sund, under the batteries of Storholm? (not in the LG); Arctic Medal 1818–55, MID; Jubilee Medal 1897 (silver issue); the Sir Gilbert Blane Medal for the best journal kept by a RN surgeon (1857); in October 1854, presented a testimonial 18ct. gold watch and chain (by Bennett, London, valued at 70 guineas), as a gift from the *Investigator*'s petty officers, seamen and marines.

KCB, medals (minus the Blane Medal), miniatures of the Baltic and Arctic, and gold watch and chain, were sold at Sotheby's, Feb. 2, 1905, and appeared at Glendining's, July 26, 1906. Baltic, Arctic and Blane Medal (all named) were in the Payne Collection, 1911; Murray Brothers Collection at Sotheby's, May 10–14, 1926, lot 191; and Ron Penhall Collection at Dix Noonan Webb, Sept. 22, 2006, lot 3. A single Arctic Medal named "ALEX. ARMSTRONG. M.D. R.N." was sold in Stevens's Auction Rooms, London, 1930, lot 478, and was acquired by the Museum of Science & Industry (London); when catalogued on Dec. 22, 1981, noted with "punched" naming; Accession No. A87804.

*Notes*: MD (Edinburgh), 1841; F and MRCP (London), 1860; LRCS (Edinburgh), 1841; FRGS, 1857; Promoted to Staff Surgeon April 21, 1857; Hon. Physician to HRH the Prince of Wales, Feb. 16, 1863, to death; Hon. Surgeon to the Queen, Oct. 9, 1866, and Hon. Physician, Feb. 3, 1870, to death; LLD (Trinity College, Dublin), 1872; FRS, June 12, 1873; Justice of the Peace for Middlesex, City and Liberties of Westminster and County of London; Director-General of the Medical Department of the Navy 1869–80, when the 1875–76 Arctic Expedition was fitted out, and took an active interest in its welfare and success. Attended McClure's funeral in 1873. Retired February 1880. Died July 4, 1899, at Sutton Bonington, Loughborough, Leicestershire. Journal of Dr. Alexander Armstrong, NA; *A Personal Narrative of the Discovery of the North-West Passage; with Numerous Incidents of Travel and Adventure During Nearly Five Years' Continuous Service in the Arctic Regions While in Search of the Expedition Under Sir John Franklin* (1857).

PAINE, Joseph Cave (1820–93)—Clerk-in-Charge

*Previous Polar Experience*: none

*Honors & Awards*: Arctic Medal 1818–55, MID

*Notes*: Promoted to Paymaster Oct. 2, 1850, with time as Paymaster allowed from this date. Retired as

Paymaster-in-Chief in February 1871. There was a Purser William Paine, RN (born 1794, Cobham, Surrey) and Joseph was possibly his son. Around September–October 1828, the new position of Cashier of Greenwich Hospital was created, and William Paine became the first to hold this position. He disappeared from *The Navy List* (half-pay) in 1863, and when he died, Joseph C. Paine assumed the position. Died in October 1893, in East Preston, Sussex.

PIERS, Henry (1818–1901)—Assistant Surgeon

*Previous Polar Experience*: none

*Honors & Awards*: Arctic Medal 1818–55, MID

*Notes*: MD (London), 1840; Promoted to Surgeon, with seniority from Oct. 26, 1850, and time allowed as Surgeon from this date. Retired June 12, 1873, and "allowed to assume the honorary rank of Deputy Inspector General of Hospitals and Fleets." Died Nov. 30, 1901, in Burnham, Somerset. Journal of Assistant Surgeon Henry Piers, NMM.

COURT, Stephen (1826–61)—Second Master/Acting Master (April 19, 1853)

*Previous Polar Experience*: Second Master, *Enterprise* (1848–49)

*Honors & Awards*: Crimea Medal/Sebastopol (Master/*Odin*); Arctic Medal 1818–55, MID; China Medal 1856–60/Canton 1857 & Taku Forts 1858 (Master/*Furious*); Royal Humane Society Medal (silver/Peiho River, May 1858/date of award 1861); Turkish Crimea Medal (Master/*Odin*); all medals named and in the NMM, except the last, which may be held, but unnamed and unattributed.

*Notes*: North-West Passage Sled Party. Promoted Master, with date of seniority Oct. 26, 1850. Harbor Master at Shanghai 1859–61. Died April 11, 1861, due to effects from his Arctic service, while on half-pay in Folkestone, Kent.

MIERTSCHING, Johann August (1817–75)—Interpreter of the Eskimo Language (civilian)

*Previous Polar Experience*: Moravian Missionary, Labrador (1844–49)

*Honors & Awards*: Arctic Medal 1818–55, MID—"our invaluable interpreter"; unnamed as issued, with a long length of original ribbon, and in family hands.

*Notes*: Miertsching was not sent back to Labrador, but after his marriage in Saxony, he was ordered to practice among the Hottentots, near Cape Town, South Africa. In 1868, he retired to Kleinwelka, Saxony, and died there seven years later. Reconstructed journal of Johann Miertsching in family hands. *Frozen Ships: The Arctic Diary of Johann Miertsching 1850–1854* (1967).

## *Warrant Officers*

FORD, George James (1821–77)—Carpenter 3rd Class

*Previous Polar Experience*: none

*Honors & Awards*: Baltic Medal 1854–54 (Carpenter 1st Class/*Hogue*) & Arctic Medal 1818–55, MID— "Mr. Ford, the carpenter, who is always ready to meet any emergency."

*Notes*: Promoted to Carpenter 2nd Class June 5, 1853, and 1st Class Oct. 18, 1854. In December 1870, Ford wrote to the Secretary of the Admiralty, and requested some medical compensation after suffering from "defective vision and general shock to my system" in relation to exposure to the elements during the trial of Steam Launch No. 7 in the fall of 1868, "and as that circumstance combined with long and hard previous sea service in all parts of the world including 4½ years in the North Pole under Sir R. MacClure [sic] has according to medical testimony been the chief cause of my present helpless condition." Half-pay in May 1870, and died Jan. 14, 1877 in Southsea, Hampshire. Diary of Carpenter [George] James Ford, Karpeles Manuscript Library, Santa Barbara, California.

KENNEDY, George (1808/16-alive in May 1884)—Acting Boatswain 3rd Class

*Previous Polar Experience*: none

*Honors & Awards*: Baltic Medal 1854–55 (Boatswain 2nd Class/*Arrogant*); Arctic Medal 1818–55, MID

*Notes*:—Promoted Acting Boatswain 3rd Class on *Investigator* April 18, 1850, formerly Boatswain's Mate, HMS *Gorgon*. Promoted Boatswain 2nd Class Oct. 21, 1854, and 1st Class July 20, 1859; Permanent Harbor Duty Oct. 24, 1862; Superannuated Aug. 12, 1869.

NEWTON, William (born c. 1803)—Ice Mate (civilian)

*Previous Polar Experience*: Arctic whaling/sealing

*Honors & Awards*: Arctic Medal 1818–55, MID

*Notes*: Judging by his name and position, Newton was surely a Yorkshireman or Scot with experience in the whaling and sealing trade. There was a William Newton (seaman's register ticket no. 65776), born Nov. 3, 1804, in Hexthorpe, Yorkshire, who in December 1844 was a mate in the merchant service. This could be the same man.

## *Petty Officers*

BLUFF, Henry (born 1822)—Boatswain's Mate

*Previous Polar Experience*: none known

*Honors & Awards*: Crimea Medal 1854–56/Sebastopol (Ship's Corporal/Quartermaster/*Diamond*); Arctic Medal 1818–55; Turkish Crimea Medal

*Notes*: Entered the Coastguard as a Boatman Feb. 19, 1857. Invalided April 30, 1863, after 21 years of RN/Coastguard service.

BROWN, George (1826–80)—Able Seaman/Acting Captain of the Foretop/Quartermaster (Dec. 25, 1850)

*Previous Polar Experience*: none known

*Honors & Awards*: Arctic Medal 1818–55, MID—claimed to have been presented by the family to the "Rochester Museum, Kent" (Guildhall Museum, Rochester), but not held by the museum or listed in its records.

*Notes*: North-West Passage Sled Party. Brown left the RN in January 1862, and afterwards joined the Coastguard. Pensioned in 1876, after 31 years of RN/Coastguard service.

CALDER, John (1819–1905)—Captain of the Forecastle

*Previous Polar Experience*: Able Seaman, *Investigator* (1848–49)

*Honors & Awards*: "Arctic Meritorious Service Medal" (officially engraved)—held by a family member; Arctic Medal 1818–55, MID—"a trusty and zealous petty officer"—held by a different family member, unnamed as issued, with a long length of (distressed) original ribbon.

*Notes*: North-West Passage Sled Party. In May 1853, Calder was one of only four men of *Investigator*'s crew who volunteered to stay onboard with McClure. Emigrated to Chicago, Illinois, USA, where he worked as a butcher, until he and his family eventually settled in Kelly Township (Warren County), where Calder developed a 640-acre farm and ranch. About two years before his death, Calder moved to the village of Alexis (Warren County). Died Jan. 7, 1905—probably the last survivor of HMS *Investigator*.

DAVIES/DAVIS, John/Jonathan (born 1821)—Able Seaman/Quartermaster (April 15, 1853)

*Previous Polar Experience*: Able Seaman, *Herald* (1848—briefly in Alaska)

*Honors & Awards*: "Arctic Meritorious Service Medal" (officially engraved: "JOHN DAVIS. Q$^R$ M$^R$ H.M.S. INVESTIGATOR."); Arctic Medal 1818–55, MID—unnamed as issued; Douglas-Morris Collection (c. 1960s-1990s), and now in a private collection.

*Notes*: In May 1853, Davies was one of only four men of *Investigator*'s crew who volunteered to stay onboard with McClure.


EVANS, James (born 1822)—Caulker

*Previous Polar Experience*: Caulker, *Enterprise* (1848–49)

*Honors & Awards*: Arctic Medal 1818–55


FACEY, Jospeh (born c. 1820)—Sailmaker

*Previous Polar Experience*: none known

*Honors & Awards*: Baltic Medal 1854–55 (Sailmaker/*Cornwallis*); Arctic Medal 1818–55

*Notes*: Served in the Baltic and North America and West Indies Station onboard the *Cornwallis*, with Dr. Alexander Armstrong and Henry May. Due to severe frostbite, Armstrong wrote that Facey "never entirely recovered the use of his hands and feet, [they] were particularly influenced by the state of the weather—changes he could foretell with the greatest accuracy from the pain and uneasiness he experienced in them."


FAWCETT, Edward Henry (1813–97)—Boatswain's Mate

*Previous Polar Experience*: Able Seaman, *Erebus* (Antarctic Expedition 1839–43) & Boatswain's Mate, *Investigator* (1848–49)

*Honors & Awards*: Arctic Medal 1818–55—An example of this medal (minus claw and suspender) exists with a descendant, set as a pendant in an octagonal frame, but it is not known if it belonged to Edward Fawcett or his son-in-law, former shipmate James Williams.

*Notes*: Pensioned from the RN, and evidently returned to his father's trade as a fisherman, but memories of his polar adventures remained strong until the end of his life: "To the Editor of the Standard" from Edward Fawcett, Pensioner RN, Winterton, Norfolk. Sir—Seeing the statement in *The Standard* of July 30 [1895] that Sir Joseph Hooker was the only survivor of Sir James Ross's Antarctic Expedition, I wish to point out that Sir Joseph is not the last or only survivor, as I was on that Expedition as captain of the forecastle of the Erebus, and was always of Dr. McCormick's party when he was ashore botanising. And I was with Sir James on the 1st Franklin Search Expedition, and accompanied that Commander on his land journeys; was boatswain's mate in the Investigator, with Captain McClure, and made the NW passage. I am now in my 83rd year of age, hale and hearty, except a little shaky on my 'pins.' I am, Sir, your obedient servant...." Died 1897.


FLYNN/FLINN, Michael (1818-c. 1854–57)—Quartermaster

*Previous Polar Experience*: Able Seaman, *Enterprise* (1848–49)

*Honors & Awards*: Arctic Medal 1818–55, MID—"Sent Widow 3/6/57"

*Notes*: North-West Passage Sled Party.


GAUEN/GAWN/GAVEN/DAWN, Henry (born 1824)—Carpenter's Mate

*Previous Polar Experience*: none known

*Honors & Awards*: Arctic Medal 1818–55

HULOTT/HULLOTT/HULETT/HULLETT/HEWLETT, Cornelius/James Cornelius/George
(c. 1831–99)—Able Seaman/Capt.'s Coxswain (Jan. 11, 1850)

*Previous Polar Experience*: none known

*Honors & Awards*: Arctic Medal 1818–55, MID

*Notes*: Pensioned from the RN November 1854, due to the amputations of several toes in the Arctic. Afterwards employed as a Rigger at Sheerness Yard, along with Mark Griffiths, until at least the spring of 1857; later at Woolwich Yard, and then Chatham Yard in 1881. Died March 1899.


KERR, John (c. 1819–53)—Gunner's Mate

*Previous Polar Experience*: none known

*Honors & Awards*: Arctic Medal 1818–55, MID—ice blasting under very difficult circumstances—"DD. [discharged dead] 13th [*sic*] April 1853 Bay of Mercy Sent 16/5/57 Widow."

*Notes*: Discharged dead April 12, 1853, of ascites, dysentery and debility, Bay of Mercy, Banks Island. Remembered on the Beechey Island Cenotaph.


MAY, Henry (born 1800)—Able Seaman/Quartermaster (April 18, 1850)

*Previous Polar Experience*: Quartermaster, *Enterprise* (1848–49)

*Honors & Awards*: Baltic Medal (QM/*Cornwallis*); Arctic 1818–55, MID

*Notes*: Served in the Baltic and North America and West Indies Station onboard the *Cornwallis*, with Dr. Alexander Armstrong and Joseph Facey. Pensioned from RN Aug. 24, 1857, after 21 years of service.


STONE, Henry (born 1824)—Blacksmith (& Armorer)

*Previous Polar Experience*: none known

*Honors & Awards*: Arctic Medal 1818–55

*Notes*: Nicknamed "the Jolly Tinker." *Survivors' Tales of Famous Shipwrecks* (1932), features an account of Stone's time on *Investigator*, evidently taken from an interview in the late 19th century. Therein, Stone related, "I had never been to sea before—and never went afterwards."


STUBBERFIELD, Isaac (born 1823)—Quartermaster/Ship's Cook (April 18, 1850)

*Previous Polar Experience*: none known

*Honors & Awards*: Arctic Medal 1818–55; Naval Long Service and Good Conduct Medal, Wide Suspension (Quartermaster/*Formidable*/20 Years)—Stubberfield deserted from HMS *Ocean* in September 1846, but 19 years later, per Admiralty order, "Run" was removed from his service record, and he was allowed the 1 year and 126 days of service on that vessel to count toward his pension. Most unusually for this circumstance (after earning a third Good Conduct Badge *just* two years after his second one), he was awarded the Long Service and Good Conduct Medal and gratuity, and then pensioned on Dec. 12, 1868.

*Notes*: Nicknamed "Old Stubber." Pensioned from the RN Dec. 12, 1868, after 20 years of service. Greenwich Pensioner in 1881, living in Minster, Isle of Sheppey, Kent.


THOMPSON/THOMSON, Peter (born 1823)—Able Seaman/Captain of the Foretop (after June 30, 1850)

*Previous Polar Experience*: Able Seaman, *Investigator* (1848–49)

*Honors & Awards*: Arctic Medal 1818–55, MID

*Notes*: North-West Passage Sled Party.

TIFFENY/TIFFNEY/TIFFENEY, Robert (born 1824)—Able Seaman/Captain of the Maintop (promoted April/May 1850)

*Previous Polar Experience*: none known

*Honors & Awards*: Arctic Medal 1818–55, MID

*Notes*: North-West Passage Sled Party.


WILLIAMS, James (1819–1901)—Able Seaman/Capt. of the Hold (April 18, 1850)

*Previous Polar Experience*: none known

*Honors & Awards*: Arctic Medal 1818–55—An example of this medal (minus claw and suspender) exists with a descendant, set as a pendant in an octagonal frame, but it is not known if it belonged to James Williams or his father-in-law, former shipmate Edward Fawcett.

*Notes*: In the early 1840s, Williams was an able seaman in the *Vindictive*, and "went by the name of James Anderson," but his seaman's register ticket (no. 28635, issued June 20, 1845) features his real name. Williams and Edward Fawcett were only seven years apart in age, and on *Investigator*, their solid friendship led to the subsequent marriage of James to Edward's daughter, Priscilla, shortly their return in October 1854. Williams left the RN around this time, but joined the Coastguard as a Boatman in March 1857, and retired in July 1869. Williams was born May 15, 1819—only nine days before the birth of Queen Victoria—and died Jan. 20, 1901—only two days before the Queen's death.


## Seamen & Other Ratings

AMES/EAMES, John (1820–53)—Able Seaman & Sick Bay Attendant (from at least January 1851)

*Previous Polar Experience*: none known

*Honors & Awards*: Arctic Medal 1818–55—"DD [discharged dead] 11 [*sic*] April 53 Sent 14/10/57"

*Notes*: Real name was "Moses Ames." Discharged dead April 9, 1853, of dropsy and scurvy, Mercy Bay, Banks Island. Remembered on the Beechey Island Cenotaph.


ANDERSON, Charles (born 1825)—Able Seaman/Gunroom Cook

*Previous Polar Experience*: none known

*Honors & Awards*: Arctic Medal 1818–55

*Notes*: Claimed to have been born in Port Robinson, British North America (Canada), and lived as an outdoorsman, having also worked for two years as a cook on a vessel carrying German emigrants to America.


BATTEN, William (born c. 1812)—Able Seaman

*Previous Polar Experience*: none known

*Honors & Awards*: Arctic Medal 1818–55


BOUNSALL/BONNSALL/BOUNSELL, Samuel; BOUNSELL/George (born c. 1822)—Able Seaman

*Previous Polar Experience*: none known

*Honors & Awards*: Arctic Medal 1818–55


BOYLE, John (born c. 1824)—Able Seaman/extra Sick Bay Attendant (April 4, 1853)

*Previous Polar Experience*: none known

*Honors & Awards*: Arctic Medal 1818–55—evidently not issued

*Notes*: Discharged dead April 5, 1853, officially from dysentery and scurvy, but evidently an accidental death, Mercy Bay, Banks Island. Remembered on the Beechey Island Cenotaph.


BRADBURY, Mark (1822–55)—Captain's Steward/Ordinary (April 18, 1850)/Able Seaman (and ship's fiddler)

*Previous Polar Experience*: Subordinate Officers' Steward, *Enterprise* (1848–49)

*Honors & Awards*: Arctic Medal 1818–55—"Rachel B Penney"—signature, no date, a married sister.

*Notes*: Real name was "Mark Sunday Bradbury." Private Biggs evidently took over Bradbury's domestic duties in April 1850. Bradbury suffered from epilepsy, and at the *Investigator*'s court-martial (Oct. 17, 1854), was listed as "Sick in Hospital." Died April 16, 1855.


CARMICHAEL, Thomas S. (born 1825)—Able Seaman

*Previous Polar Experience*: none known

*Honors & Awards*: Arctic Medal 1818–55


CARROLL, William (born 1823)—Able Seaman

*Previous Polar Experience*: Able Seaman, *Investigator* (1848–49)

*Honors & Awards*: Arctic Medal 1818–55

*Notes*: Volunteered for Continuous Service March 1, 1858, and invalided from the RN Oct. 6, 1866, with 22 years of service.


GIBBS, George (born c. 1820)—Able Seaman

*Previous Polar Experience*: none known

*Honors & Awards*: Arctic Medal 1818–55


GRIFFITHS, Ellis (born 1826)—Able Seaman

*Previous Polar Experience*: none known

*Honors & Awards*: Arctic Medal 1818–55


GRIFFITHS, Mark (born c. 1825)—Able Seaman

*Previous Polar Experience*: Able Seaman, *Herald* (1848–50)

*Honors & Awards*: Arctic Medal 1818–55

*Notes*: Afterwards employed as a Rigger at Sheerness Yard, along with Cornelius Hulott, until at least the spring of 1857.


HARRIS/HARRIES, David (born 1821)—Able Seaman

*Previous Polar Experience*: none known

*Honors & Awards*: Arctic Medal 1818–55


KEEFE/O'KEEFE, John (born c. 1827)—Able Seaman

*Previous Polar Experience*: none known

*Honors & Awards*: Arctic Medal 1818–55

MACKENZIE/MacKENZIE/McKENZIE, Samuel (born 1826)—Able Seaman

*Previous Polar Experience*: none known

*Honors & Awards*: Arctic Medal 1818–55

McDONALD, James (born 1813)—Able Seaman

*Previous Polar Experience*: none known

*Honors & Awards*: Baltic Medal 1854–55 (Quartermaster/Captain of the Hold/*Cossack*); Arctic Medal 1818–55

*Notes*: Volunteered for Continuous Service Dec. 2, 1854, and pensioned from the RN Sept. 15, 1863, with 21 years of service.

MILNER, George Luke (born 1819)—Gunroom Steward

*Previous Polar Experience*: none known

*Honors & Awards*: "Arctic Meritorious Service Medal" (officially engraved: "GEORGE MILNER. GUN$^M$ ST$^D$ H.M.S. INVESTIGATOR."); China Medal 1840–42 (officially *renamed*: "GEORGE F.L. MILNER, H.M.S. APOLLO" [Wardroom Steward]); Baltic Medal 1854–55 (Gunroom Cook/*Pylades*); Arctic Medal 1818–55 (privately engraved with name and ship), MID; J. Lawson Walley Collection (1877/ minus Baltic Medal); Captain A.E. Whitaker Collection (1890s/minus Baltic Medal); Douglas-Morris Collection (c. 1960s-1990s/minus China and Baltic Medals); Arctic pair held in the Royal Naval Museum (Portsmouth).

*Notes*: Real name was "George Frederick Luke," and began using the alias "Milner" in January 1850. In May 1853, Milner was one of only four men of *Investigator*'s crew who volunteered to stay onboard with McClure. Discharged Sept. 19, 1861, on a disability pension, having served close to 19 years in the RN.

MORGAN, Thomas (1817–54)—Able Seaman

*Previous Polar Experience*: none known

*Honors & Awards*: Arctic Medal 1818–55, MID

*Notes*: Discharged dead May 22, 1854, of scurvy, *North Star*, Beechey Island. Remembered on the Beechey Island Cenotaph, and a headboard placed over his remains included the following inscription: "By grace are ye saved through faith, and that not of yourselves, it is the gift of God. Eph. chap. ii. Verse 8."

NELSON, James H. (born 1828-alive in October 1873)—Able Seaman

*Previous Polar Experience*: none known

*Honors & Awards*: Arctic Medal 1818–55

*Notes*: In October 1854, Nelson read an address during a gathering of the Investigators, to present Dr. Armstrong with a testimonial gold watch and chain, and he also thanked Lieutenant Pim for rescuing them. Nelson left the Navy and later became a customs officer in Gravesend (just outside London), and attended McClure's funeral in 1873. "Voyage H.M.S. Investigator In Search of Sir J. Franklin and Resulting in the Discovery of the North West Passage" (2 volumes, draft manuscripts), SPRI.

OLLEY/AULEY, George (born 1826)—Able Seaman

*Previous Polar Experience*: Able Seaman, *Investigator* (1848–49)

*Honors & Awards*: Arctic Medal 1818–55

RAMSAY, John (born 1819)—Able Seaman

*Previous Polar Experience*: none known

*Honors & Awards*: Arctic Medal 1818–55—held by the Hunterian Museum (Glasgow), ex–Coats Collection (Coats 4769), and privately named "JOHN RAMSAY" on the reverse, above the ship.

RELFE/ROLFE/RALPH, Samuel (born c. 1825)—Able Seaman
*Previous Polar Experience*: none known
*Honors & Awards*: Arctic Medal 1818–55
*Notes*: Alias "Relfe" as of December 1849.

ROSS, Richard A. (born c. 1811)—Quartermaster/disrated to Able Seaman (Dec. 25, 1850)
*Previous Polar Experience*: none known
*Honors & Awards*: Arctic 1818–55
*Notes*: Discharged October 1854 as "Unfit for the Service." On July 20, 1855, Ross appears to have sailed as boatswain ("Bn"?) on the screw steamer SS *Zebra*, passenger/cargo vessel chartered for government service. She was lost in 1856, having stranded at the Lizard, a peninsula in southern Cornwall.

STEEL/STEELE, Charles (born 1823)—Able Seaman
*Previous Polar Experience*: none known
*Honors & Awards*: Arctic Medal 1818–55

SUGDEN, Henry H. (born 1824)—Subordinate Officers' Steward/Gunroom Cook
*Previous Polar Experience*: none known
*Honors & Awards*: Arctic Medal 1818–55
*Notes*: "Shore. Services no longer required," Dec. 31, 1877, and pensioned Jan. 1, 1878; Pensioner RN, married and living in Stoke Damerel, Devon, in 1881; briefly served as a Domestic/2nd Cl. on HMS *Hotspur* (May-Aug. 1885), before being paid off to shore; "N.P. 399 8/06 Statement of Services to Royal Patriotic Fund."

TAYLOR, Frederick (born c. 1818)—Able Seaman
*Previous Polar Experience*: none known
*Honors & Awards*: Arctic Medal 1818–55

TOY, Thomas (born c. 1825)—Able Seaman
*Previous Polar Experience*: none known
*Honors & Awards*: Arctic Medal 1818–55

WHITEFIELD/WHITFIELD, William (1824-c. 1854–57)—Carpenter's Crew
*Previous Polar Experience*: none known
*Honors & Awards*: Arctic Medal 1818–55—"D.D. [discharged dead] Sabina Whitefield Her × mark 12/10/57."
*Notes*: The crew's medical report of May 23, 1853, stated that Whitefield "has lost strength, had Dysentery in a severe form during the last winter." The medical exam of the Investigators between May 20 and 29, 1854, showed his condition as "Indifferent."

WILCOX, John (c. 1825–1855)—Paymaster & Purser's Steward
*Previous Polar Experience*: none known
*Honors & Awards*: Arctic Medal 1818–55—"DD [discharged dead] 7139 Sent 15/7/57."

*Notes*: Real name was "John Willcocks," and began using the alias "Wilcox" in January 1850. The crew's medical report of May 23, 1853, stated that Wilcox was "Stout & healthy looking—but has lividity and tumidity of the gums." The medical exam of the Investigators between May 20 and 29, 1854, showed his condition as "Good" and "Fit" for long service. Died on or about Feb. 24, 1855.

## Royal Marines

WOON, John (1824–77)—Sergeant/Color Sergeant (Feb. 17, 1854)

*Previous Polar Experience*: none

*Honors & Awards*: "Arctic Gallantry Medal" of Color Sergeant John Woon, RM (officially named on the edge: C.$^{LR}$ SERJ$^T$ JOHN WOON R.M.)—lifesaving and hunting prowess; Royal Marines Meritorious Service Medal (RM MSM; with an annuity of £10)—"having saved the life of a wounded comrade under a heavy fire" during the unsuccessful attack on the Peiho Forts, June 25, 1859; Arctic Medal 1818–55 (privately named: COL-SERJT JOHN WOON H.M.S. INVESTIGATOR.), MID—hunting prowess; China Medal 1856–60/Canton 1857 (Acting Sergeant Major, 4 Company, RM Battalion), MID (LG, Sept. 16, 1859)—Hope's Dispatch, per lifesaving actions resulting in the RM MSM; the Glenbow Museum (Calgary) holds the two Arctic awards.

*Notes*: Appointed Color Sergeant Feb. 17, 1854; (appointed) Acting Sergeant Major Aug. 12, 1857; Sergeant Major Nov. 5, 1861; Quartermaster Lieutenant 1867; attended McClure's funeral in 1873; Died March 8, 1877, as a serving officer, after 33 years of service, of acute rheumatism and cardiac disease.

FARQUHARSON, John Bouchard (born 1822)—Corporal 3rd Class

*Previous Polar Experience*: none

*Honors & Awards*: Arctic Medal 1818–55

*Notes*: Miertsching's servant. Sergeant Dec. 8, 1854 (Corporal for only six months before joining *Investigator*); appointed Color Sergeant June 16, 1860; divested of Color Sergeant Oct. 23, 1860; Discharged May 10, 1862, after 21 years—"Length of Service and under the provisions of the Order in Council dated 4 April 1856, respecting Pensions, at his own request." Farquharson received "a private Certificate from Dr. Armstrong D.I.H. [Deputy Inspector of Hospitals] of his "excellence of character"—Sergeant Farquharson is entitled to reckon five Good Conduct Badges or 5d per day towards increase of Pension." A certain "Mr. Farquharson" was one of the vocalists at the party held at the Lord Mayor of London's home for returning crews of the 1875–76 Arctic Expedition. Since the event featured "Old Arctics" as guests, this may have been the same former Royal Marine.

BANCROFT, Thomas (born 1820)—Private 3rd Class/Corporal (Oct. 19, 1853)

*Previous Polar Experience*: none

*Honors & Awards*: Arctic Medal 1818–55

*Notes*: Rank of Corporal confirmed on return to England, but reduced to Private Dec. 2, 1856; Discharged Oct. 8, 1863, after 21 years—"Length of Service and under the provisions of the Order in Council respecting Pensions at his own request"; four Good Conduct Badges.

BIGGS, James (born 1822)—Private 3rd Class/Corporal (April 15, 1853)

*Previous Polar Experience*: none

*Honors & Awards*: "Arctic Meritorious Service Medal"; Arctic Medal 1818–55, MID

*Notes*: McClure's steward; rank of Corporal not confirmed on return to England. In May 1853, Biggs was one of only four men of *Investigator*'s crew who volunteered to stay onboard with McClure. Discharged Oct. 27, 1854, after 13 years—"Having relinquished all claim to Pension on Discharge and allowances for past Services, & agreeably to Admiralty Order dated 24 Oct$^r$ 1854"; two Good Conduct Badges.

BOW, Elias (born c. 1817)—Private

*Previous Polar Experience*: none

*Honors & Awards*: Naval General Service Medal 1793–1840/Syria (Private, RM/*Bellerophon*); Arctic Medal 1818–55 (privately engraved: ELIAS BOW RM)—private collection; Turkish St. Jean d'Acre Medal 1840 (bronze issue)

*Notes*: Servant to Sainsbury and Piers. Discharged June 22, 1858—"Length of Service and at his own request he having served upwards of Twenty one years," with four Good Conduct Badges, and "produces several Certificates of <u>Very</u> <u>Good</u> Character."

KING, Thomas (1824–59)—Private 3rd Class

*Previous Polar Experience*: none

*Honors & Awards*: Arctic Medal 1818–55

*Notes*: The medical exam of the Investigators between May 20–29, 1854, showed his condition as "Very Indifferent." Discharged dead April 1, 1859, in the infirmary (presumably at Woolwich), nearly 17 years to the day after joining the Royal Marines. A W.R. Rayner, of Bury St. Edmunds, Suffolk, wrote a letter to the editor of *The Listener* (May 6, 1954), in response to Murray Parks's article, "The Discovery of the North-west Passage" (April 8, 1954). Rayner's last line: "Like Mr. Murray Parks my interest in the discovery of the North-west Passage was aroused by the fact that a great-uncle of mine was a member of the crew of H.M.S. *Investigator*." Given that Private King was (as far as is known) the only member of the crew from Bury St. edmunds, it seems quite likely he was Rayner's great-uncle.

PARFITT, George (born 1818)—Private 1st Class

*Previous Polar Experience*: none

*Honors & Awards*: Naval General Service Medal 1793–1840/Syria (Private, RM/*Powerful*—officially impressed: GEORGE PARFITT.)—author's collection; Arctic Medal 1818–55; Turkish St. Jean d'Acre Medal 1840 (bronze issue)

*Notes*: Promoted Corporal, Oct. 25, 1854. Discharged Sept. 28, 1856, after 18 years—"Invalided for Paralysis Contracted in and by the Service unserviceable." "This man served on 5 of HM Ships. He possesses 'very good' discharge certificates—and an excellent certificate from Captain M$^c$Clure for nearly 5 years Service in HMS Investigator. He is in possession of the Syrian Medals having been landed for that Campaign. He was once tried by Court Martial [in] consider[ation] of absence in 1838. He is in possession of 4 good conduct Badges. Since 1838 he has not been entered in defaulters book."

SAUNDERS, James (born 1825)—Private 3rd Class

*Previous Polar Experience*: none

*Honors & Awards*: Baltic (Private, RM/*Orion*); Arctic Medal 1818–55, MID

*Notes*: North-West Passage Sled Party. As of Nov. 20, 1850, in possession of one Good Conduct Badge. Transferred to RMA Dec. 26, 1855; Discharged Nov. 27, 1866, after 21 years—length of service.

## *Mascot Dog*

MONGO/MICKY/VESTY—Miertsching called the dog Mongo, but Piers used the name Micky, and more often afterward, Vesty (the ship's nickname). According to Armstrong, the mascot was a little female Eskimo dog taken onboard along the coast of North America, but Piers referred to the dog as a female and a male. Miertsching noted that the dogs of the people at Cape Bathurst are the same breed as those in Labrador. They originated on the island of Newfoundland, and the founding breed of the Labrador was the St. John's water dog, which emerged through special breeding by the 16th century settlers of Newfoundland. The ancestors of the St. John's dog are unknown, but were probably a random-bred mix of English, Irish, and Portuguese working breeds.

# Appendix 4.
# Extracts from Admiralty Orders to Captain Richard Collinson, CB, RN

*Information Used to Compile Admiralty Orders to Captain Collinson*

Great Britain (1850a); Collinson (1889)

By the Commissioners for executing the Office of Lord High Admiral of the United Kingdom of Great Britain and Ireland, &c.

1. Whereas the efforts that have been made during the two last years to relieve the *Erebus* and *Terror* have failed, and all access to the Parry Islands has been prevented by the accumulation of ice in the upper part of Barrow Straits; and whereas it is possible that the same severity of weather may not prevail at the same time in both the eastern and western entrances to the Arctic Sea; we have now determined, in a matter of such moment, to send an expedition into the Polar Sea from the westward; and having a full confidence in your zeal and skill, we have thought proper to appoint you to the command of Her Majesty's ship *Enterprise*, and also to place under your orders Her Majesty's ship *Investigator*, both of which vessels having been duly fortified against collision with the ice, equipped for the Polar climate, by warm-air apparatus, and furnished with provisions for three years, as well as a large supply of extra stores; you are now required and directed, so soon as they are in all respects ready for sea, to proceed to make the best of your way to Cape Virgins, in order to arrive at Behring's Straits in July.

2. At Cape Virgins, the Commander-in-Chief in the Pacific has been desired to have a steam vessel waiting for you, and by her you will be towed through the Strait of Magellan and the Wellington Channel, and on to Valparaiso.

3. At that port, you will use the utmost dispatch in watering and refreshing your crews, and in fully replenishing your bread and other provisions and stores; and having so done, you will again use your best exertions to press forward to the Sandwich Islands.

4. There is only a bare possibility of your reaching those Islands in time to meet with Her Majesty's ship *Herald*, under the command of Captain Henry Kellett, but if that should be the case you will receive from him not only every assistance, but much useful information touching your passage to the Strait, and your further proceedings to the northward. It is still more improbable that Her Majesty's ship *Plover* should be there; but wherever you fall in with her, you are hereby directed to take her and Commander Moore under your orders.

5. At the Sandwich Islands you will find additional orders from us for your guidance, which we propose to forward from hence by the Panama Mail of next March; but if none should arrive, or if they do not in any way modify these directions, you will enforce the greatest diligence in revictualling your two vessels, in procuring if possible the necessary Esquimaux interpreters, and in making all requisite preparations for at once proceeding to Behring's Straits, in order to reach the ice before the 1st of August.

6. An examination of several orders issued to Captain Kellett will show that it is uncertain where he may be fallen in with. You may probably find the "Herald" and "Plover" together.

7. We consider it essential that after entering the ice there should be a depôt or point of succour for any party to fall back upon. For this purpose, the *Plover* is to be secured in the most favourable quarter, as far in advance as can be found, such as Wainwright Inlet or the Creek at Hope Point, but if they be unsafe, and none other discovered nearer to Barrow's Point, then at Chamisso Island or any part of Kotzebue Sound which may afford the necessary shelter.

8. Considering, however, the nature of the service in which the "Plover" will already have been employed, and that a portion of her crew may be unfit to contend with the rigours of a further stay in those latitudes, you will call for volunteers from that ship, and from the "Herald" if in company, sufficient to form a crew for the "Plover"; taking care that the men to be selected are men of good character, and that they do not exceed in number what is actually required for the care of the ship, and for defence and security against any treacherous attack on the part of the natives of Norton Sound.

9. The petty officers' ratings may be vacated by men invalided are to be filled by men volunteering to remain; such volunteers are to be subjected to strict and careful survey by the medical officers of the several ships; and those only are to be retained who would seem to be in all respects fit to encounter this extended service; and the remainder necessary to complete the crew is to be made up from the "Enterprise" and "Investigator."

10. Such crew having been formed (to continue under the command of Commander Moore, and with the officers now in the "Plover," or with those who may volunteer for the service), the "Plover," if the "Herald" should be in company, is to be filled up by Captain Kellett with all the provisions, fuel and stores that can possibly be spared by Captain Kellett, who will bear in mind not only what may be required not only for the use of the "Plover's" crew until the autumn of 1853, and the contingency of parties arriving onboard from Sir John Franklin's Expedition, but also the possibility of any party from the "Enterprise" and "Investigator" having to fall back on the "Plover."

11. In providing this necessary equipment for the "Plover," attention will be paid to the numbers left in the "Herald," and the supplies necessary to carry that vessel to Whoahoo; having received from Captain Kellett any baiders, or light boats, that he may be able to spare, and which may be likely to form a useful addition to your own boats, or those of the "Investigator," when searching parties may be detached from the ships in the spring, the "Herald" will return to the Sandwich Islands, there to fill up provisions, and from thence to proceed to Hong Kong on her way to England, in pursuance of our orders of the 14th December last.

12. On detaching the "Plover" to take up her winter quarters, you will direct Commander Moore to remain there until you join him, or, failing your return to him, until the end of the summer of 1853; when, but not till it is absolutely necessary for securing the "Plover's" passage through the Aleutian group of Islands, he is to quit Behring's Straits.

13. If the "Herald" and "Plover" should be fallen in with to the northward and eastward of Behring's Straits, or in the Polar Sea, Captain Kellett, on detaching himself from your company, should consort with the "Plover" as far as her winter quarters, and if time and circumstances admitted of it, he should assist in securing her there.

14. In the event of your having to winter your ships on the continent or Esquimaux shores, you will probably meet with some of the wandering tribes, or with Indians. With these you will cultivate a friendly feeling, by making them presents of those articles to which they are apt to attach a value; but you will take care not to suffer yourself to be surprised by them, but use every precaution, and be constantly on your guard against any treacherous attack. You will also, by offering rewards, to be paid in such a manner as you may be able to arrange, endeavour to prevail on them to carry to any of the settlements of the Hudson Bay Company an account of your proceedings, with an urgent request that it may be forwarded to England with the utmost possible dispatch.

15. In whatever place you may have to establish your winter quarters, you will devote every resource in your power to the preservation of the health, the comfort and the cheerfulness of the people committed to your care.

16. We leave it to your judgment and discretion as to the course to be pursued after passing Point Barrow, and on entering the ice; and you will be materially assisted in this respect by what you will learn from Captain Kellett, if he should be fallen in with at the Sandwich Islands, as well as from the obser-

vations of Sir Edward Parry and Captain Beechey, contained in the Memoranda of which we send you copies.

17. You will further be supplied with all the printed Voyages and Travels in those Northern Regions; and the Memorandum and Instructions drawn up by Sir John Richardson as to the manners and habits of the Esquimaux, and the best mode of dealing with that people (a copy of which is also sent), will afford a valuable addition to the information now supplied to you.

18. We deem it right to caution you against suffering the two vessels under your orders to separate, except in the event of accident or unavoidable necessity; and we desire that you keep up the most unreserved communications with the commander of the "Investigator," placing in him every proper confidence, and acquainting him with the general tenor of your orders, and with your views and intentions from time to time, so that the service may have the full benefit of your united efforts in the prosecution of such a service; and that in the event of any unavoidable separation, or of any accident to yourself, Commander M'Clure may have the advantage of knowing up to the latest period all your ideas and designs relative to the satisfactory completion of this undertaking.

19. We also recommend that as frequent an exchange may take place as conveniently may be of the observations made in the two ships; that any information obtained by the one be as quickly as possible communicated for the advantage and guidance of the other.

20. In case of any irreparable accident happening to the "Enterprise," you are hereby authorised to take the command of the "Investigator," and to make such arrangements for the officers and crews as may be most consonant to the rules of the service, and most conducive to the objects of the Expedition.

21. In the event of Great Britain being involved in hostilities with any foreign power during your absence, you are to abstain from the smallest act of aggression towards any vessel belonging to such nation, it being the practice of all civilized countries to consider vessels engaged in service of this kind as exempt from the rules and operations of war.

22. On your reaching England, you will call on every person, in both vessels, to deliver up to you all their logs, journals, charts, and drawings, but which, they may be informed, will be returned to them in due time.

23. With respect to your search proving fruitless, and your finally quitting the Polar Seas, as well as your securing your winter quarters towards the close of any one season, we cannot too strongly impress upon you the necessity of the utmost care and precaution being exercised in withdrawing in time; so as in no case to hazard the safety of the ships, and the lives of those entrusted to your care, by your being shut up in a position which might render a failure of provisions possible.

We feel it unnecessary to give you more detailed Instructions, which might possibly embarrass you in a service of this description; and we have therefore only to repeat our perfect reliance on your judgment and resolution, both in doing all that is possible to relieve the missing ships, and in withdrawing in time, when you come to the painful conclusion that your efforts are unavailing.

24. You will bear in mind that the object of the Expedition is to obtain intelligence, and to render assistance to Sir John Franklin and his companions, and not for the purpose of geographical or scientific research; and we conclude these orders with an earnest hope that Providence may crown your efforts with success, and that they may be the means of dispelling the gloom and uncertainty which now prevail respecting the missing Expedition.

Given under our hands, this 15th day of January 1850.

(signed)     F.T. Baring.
             J.W.D. Dundas.

By command of their Lordships,
(signed)     J. Parker

Richard Collinson, Esq., C.B.
Captain of H.M.S. "Enterprize," at Devonport.

# Appendix 5.
# Notable Sled Parties of the Investigators

## Information Used to Compile Notable Sled Parties of the Investigators

Armstrong's journal & Sick List, NA, ADM 101/250; Armstrong (1857); Barr (1992); Brown manuscript, GM, M-141; Ford's diary, KML, 18500119Arctic1xx; Harrod (2000); Krabbé (1855a); McClure's journal, RGS, SSC/10; Inglefield's Chart (1853); *Investigator's* Letter & Order Book, RGS, SSC/106; McClure (1854a & 1855a); McClure (1856); Neatby (1967); McClintock (1852–54), SPRI, MS1; McDougall (1857); Nelson, SPRI, MS 748/1; Photographs and transcriptions of two letters to McClure's uncle, LAC, R6790–0–8-E; Piers' journal, NMM, JOD/102; Pim (1855a); Registers of Seamen's Services, NA, ADM 29 & ADM 188; Royal Marines' Attestation Forms, NA, ADM 157

## Notable Sled Parties of the Investigators

Captain McClure
Lieutenant Cresswell
Dr. Armstrong
Mr. Miertsching, Interpreter
4 men
*Ship Location*: Prince of Wales Strait
*Departure*: Oct. 10, 1850
*Destination*: Prince Albert's Land
*Return*: Oct. 11, 1850
*Notes*: Took possession of Prince Albert's Land.

---

Captain McClure
Second Master Court
Dr. Armstrong
Mr. Miertsching, Interpreter
2 men
*Ship Location*: Prince of Wales Strait
*Departure*: Oct. 18, 1850
*Destination*: Princess Royal Islands (the larger one)
*Return*: Oct. 18, 1850 (presumed)
*Notes*: Took possession of the Princess Royal Islands

---

Captain McClure
Second Master Court (to take observations)

John Calder, Captain Forecastle; Robert Tiffeny, Captain of the Maintop; Michael Flynn, Quarter-master; Peter Thompson, Captain of the Foretop; George Brown, Able Seaman; Private 3rd Cl. James Saunders, RM

*Ship Location*: Prince of Wales Strait
*Departure*: Oct. 21, 1850
*Destination*: northern point of Prince Albert's Land (North-West Passage discovery, Oct. 26, 1850)
*Return*: Oct. 31, 1850
*Notes*: By no coincidence, Court had been under McClure in *Enterprise* (1848–49), as had Flynn (an Irishman), while Calder and Thompson served together for nearly five of the previous years, including the 1848–49 voyage. Also, four of the six men were first class petty officers—McClure picked tried-and-true men—and Brown was promoted to quartermaster on December 24. Brown stated he was pro-moted to quartermaster from acting captain of the foretop; the latter rating went to Thompson at an earlier time. Did Brown earn McClure's respect during the North-West Passage sled journey? McClure had written (on May 31, 1850) that he was "much pleased with the conduct of the Petty Officers, they evince every desire to perform their duty in which I give them every support."
A fatigue party (Mate Wynniatt, Dr. Armstrong and eight men) accompanied the party about 15 miles from the ship. Was Able Seaman Samuel Mackenzie frostbitten on fatigue party? A broken sled caused Mr. Court and one man to return to the ship the same night and obtain a new one, and then set off October 22 (with Mr. Wynniatt leading a fatigue party). McClure constructed a large cairn with a record of party.

Mate Wynniatt
Carpenter Ford
6 men
*Ship Location*: Prince of Wales Strait
*Departure*: Oct. 22, 1850
*Destination*: direction of McClure's party
*Return*: Oct. 23, 1850
*Notes*: This was a fatigue party to accompany Court, Thompson, and another man, as they headed to rejoin McClure's party. The snowdrift wiped out the sled tracks, so Wynniatt's party lost its way going back to the ship, and spent the night out in the open; arrived back onboard the following day, with only a few frostbites.

Boatswain Kennedy
(number and names of men unknown)
*Ship Location*: Prince of Wales Strait
*Departure*: Oct. 24, 1850
*Destination*: Princess Royal Islands (larger island).
*Return*: Oct. 26, 1850
*Notes*: Kennedy erected a large cairn on the summit of the larger island as a landmark.

Lieutenant Haswell
6 men (including George Brown, Quartermaster and Mark Griffiths, Able Seaman)
*Ship Location*: Prince of Wales Strait
*Departure*: April 18, 1851 (Good Friday)
*Destination*: southwestern coast of Prince Albert's Land
*Return*: May 29, 1851
*Notes*: Provisioned for 40 days and accompanied by a fatigue party. In good health on return.

Lieut. Cresswell
John Calder, Captain of the Forecastle (sled captain); Joseph Facey, Sailmaker; Ellis Griffiths, Able Sea-man; and 3 additional men
*Ship Location*: Prince of Wales Strait

*Departure*: April 18, 1851 (Good Friday)
*Destination*: northeastern coast of Banks Land [Island]
*Return*: May 20, 1851
*Notes*: Provisioned for 40 days, and accompanied by a fatigue party led by Dr. Armstrong. Notice left at Russell Point. Calder was Cresswell's "chief man" (i.e.—sled captain), and superintended the construction of the cairn at the furthest point. Joseph Facey and Ellis Griffiths returned on the sled as invalids, with severe frostbite that resulted in gangrene, and amputation of portions of fingers and toes.

Mate Wynniatt
6 men
*Ship Location*: Prince of Wales Strait
*Departure*: April 18, 1851 (Good Friday)
*Destination*: northwestern shore of Prince Albert's Land to search the southern shores of Barrow's Strait towards Cape Walker
*Return*: May 6 (due to a broken chronometer); redeployed same day with 30 days' provisions, and returned June 7
*Notes*: Provisioned for 40 days, and accompanied by a fatigue party. Wynniatt reached Reynolds Point (which no longer appears on charts), located at the tip of the eastern side of Glenelg Bay/Beaufort Bay, which is now called Wynniatt Bay. According to Armstrong's book and Inglefield's 1853 chart, this furthest point was reached on May 24; on the previous day, a sled party under Lieutenant Osborn (Austin's expedition) came within about 60 miles of Wynniatt's turnaround point. The chart in McClure's book indicates Wynniatt's farthest was reached on May 26, but this must be incorrect.

Lieutenant Cresswell
John Calder, Captain of the Forecastle (presumed sled captain) and Private 3rd Cl. Thomas King, RM, and 4 additional men (4 men from Cresswell's previous team, plus 2 fresh men)
*Ship Location*: Prince of Wales Strait
*Departure*: May 22, 1851
*Destination*: southeast coast of Baring Island, in an attempt to find *Enterprise*
*Return*: June 8, 1851
*Notes*: Provisioned for 20 days, and accompanied by a fatigue party led by Captain McClure and Dr. Armstrong. No trace was found of *Enterprise*. A few men were afterward placed on the sick list.

Captain McClure
Mr. Miertsching, Interpreter
Cornelius Hulott, Captain's Coxswain; Henry Gauen, Carpenter's Mate 1st Class; William Carroll, Able Seaman; William Whitefield, Carpenter's Crew; and 2 additional men
*Ship Location*: Prince of Wales Strait
*Departure*: May 29, 1851
*Destination*: seek out an Eskimo encampment on the ice, near Berkeley Point
*Return*: June 5, 1851
*Notes*: Provisioned for 12 days. Hulott was severely frostbitten, and was on the sick list from June 5 to November 2, while Whitefield suffered from exhaustion and was in sick bay for five days. Miertsching wrote on June 7: "The captain caught a severe cold on his last journey, and now lies confined to his bed; also two of our travelling sailors, Dawn [Gauen?] and Caroll, are quite ill." The latter is difficult to understand, as neither man appears on the sick list.

Second Master Court
Ice Mate Newton
(number and names of men unknown)
*Ship Location*: Mercy Bay, Banks Island
*Departure*: Sept. 15, 1851
*Destination*: scout land for about 14 miles eastward down the coast

*Return*: Sept. 15, 1851

*Notes*: Ford wrote on September 16 that the party "found the land going in the direction of as we expected, leading into Barrows Strait (*sic*—Banks Strait) between Cape Dundas & Banks Land."

Second Master Court
John Calder, Captain of the Forecastle, and 5 additional men
*Ship Location*: Mercy Bay, Banks Island
*Departure*: Oct. 4, 1851
*Destination*: Cape Hamilton, northeast coast of Banks Island, to connect with Cresswell's furthest
*Return*: Oct. 7, 1851
*Notes*: Provisioned for six days. Piers wrote that Court needed "to determine the position of [Cresswell's cairn], as, from some error in [Cresswell's] chronometer, there appears to be a mistake in the longitude." Perhaps for this reason, sources disagree as to the cairn's distance from the ship (Chapter 11 of this book). Court reached the area concerned, but was unable to locate the cairn; he also viewed an open expanse of water toward Melville Island. Armstrong, Piers and Miertsching suggested that evidence of recent landslides may have accounted for the cairn's disappearance. A sled party commanded by Master Krabbé (*Intrepid*) also failed to locate the cairn in May 1854.

Mate Sainsbury
(number and names of men unknown)
*Ship Location*: Mercy Bay, Banks Island
*Departure*: Oct. 10, 1851
*Destination*: examine an inlet at the south end of the bay
*Return*: Oct. 11, 1851
*Notes*: Armstrong wrote that the inlet Sainsbury was sent to examine "appeared to extend inland for some distance; but he returned the following day after having explored it for twelve miles, when it ended in a marsh. Instead of its proving an inlet, as was supposed, it was merely a river bed, into which the sea-water extended for a short distance." In the Letter & Order Book appears an undated transcription of a cairn note most likely attributable to Sainsbury's party (mention of the cairn is only found in this source):

> This Cairn was erected by a travelling Party from HM's DShip Investigator which is Anchored in this place having taken up this position for the Winter on the 25th September 1851 after having circumnavigated this Land which is called "Baring's Island"
> No mark or Intelligence whatever has been found which could throw the least light upon the fate of the missing expedition under Sir John Franklin
> Crew all in Excellent health & Spirits
> Dated onboard HM's DShip Investigator
> 10th October 1851. Lat: 74°6'N Lon: 117°54'W
> /sig^d Rob^t M^cClure Comm^r

Captain McClure
Second Master Court
John Calder, Captain of the Forecastle; Peter Thompson, Captain of the Foretop; Sergeant John Woon, RM; George Gibbs, Able Seaman; Samuel Bounsall, Able Seaman; John Davies, Able Seaman
*Ship Location*: Mercy Bay, Banks Island
*Departure*: April 11, 1852
*Destination*: Winter Harbour, Melville Island
*Return*: May 9, 1852?
*Notes*: Armstrong stated the party was provisioned for 28 days, but Ford indicated 30, and Miertsching 32 days. McClintock's message dated June 6, 1851, was found in a cairn atop Parry's Rock; McClure deposited a record in the same. McClure's dispatch, Ford and Armstrong's journals indicated the return date was May 9, but Armstrong's book has May 7, and McClure's book, May 11.

Captain McClure
Second Master Court
James Nelson, Able Seaman and Peter Thompson, Captain of the Foretop, and 4 additional men
*Ship Location*: Mercy Bay, Banks Island
*Departure*: April 8, 1853
*Destination*: Dealy Island (*Resolute* and *Intrepid*)
*Arrival*: April 19, 1853
*Notes*: Nelson suffered a crippling leg injury when the sled capsized two days out, and according to Nelson, McClure and Thompson were "taken very unwell" during the journey.

---

Lieutenant Cresswell
Assistant Surgeon Piers
Mate Wynniatt (insane)
Mr. Miertsching, Interpreter
Henry May, Quartermaster; Robert Tiffeny, Captain of the Maintop; Edward Fawcett, Boatswain's Mate; Jospeh Facey, Sailmaker; James Evans, Caulker; Henry Gauen, Carpenter's Mate; Charles Anderson, Able Seaman; John Keefe, Able Seaman; John Ramsay, Able Seaman; Charles Steel, Able Seaman; Mark Griffiths, Able Seaman; Frederick Taylor, Able Seaman; George Gibbs, Able Seaman; William Batten, Able Seaman; James McDonald, Able Seaman Thomas Toy, Able Seaman; David Harris, Able Seaman; Samuel Relfe, Able Seaman; Richard A. Ross, Able Seaman; Mark Bradbury, Able Seaman (deranged); Corporal John B. Farquharson, RM; Private 1st Class George Parfitt, RM; Private 3rd Class James Saunders, RM; Private 3rd Class Thomas King, RM
*Ship Location*: Mercy Bay, Banks Island
*Departure*: April 15, 1853
*Destination*: Dealy Island (*Resolute* and *Intrepid*)
*Arrival*: May 2, 1853
*Notes*: Three sleds were provisioned for 24 days, and the fatigue party was away four days. "The second Lieutenant in command of the party, Assistant Surgeon and Interpreter were not examined [by Dr. Domville]. I may here state, the three first [Cresswell, Piers and Wynniatt] were most debilitated on leaving "Investigator" and the mate was also insane. The Interpreter was in fair health but had lost flesh, <u>A.A.</u>" Armstrong stated 24 sailors and marines were in this party, but 26 are shown on Domville's medical survey. Captain McClure and Assistant Surgeon Piers returned on May 19.

---

Captain McClure
Acting Master Court
Dr. Domville (*Resolute*)
James Nelson, Able Seaman, and 4 other *Investigator* men
7 *Resolute* men
*Location of Resolute and Intrepid*: Dealy Island
*Departure*: May 5, 1853
*Destination*: *Investigator* (Mercy Bay, Banks Island)
*Arrival*: May 19, 1853
*Notes*: Two sleds. Nelson made the return trip, despite objections from Dr. Domville, who was concerned his leg injury was not properly healed. Nelson was afterward on the sick list for seven days (May 24–30) with snow blindness.

---

Lieutenant Cresswell
Mate Wynniatt
Mate Roche (*Resolute*)
Boatswain Chandler (*Resolute*)
10 *Resolute* and *Intrepid* men unfit for further service
*Location of Resolute and Intrepid*: Dealy Island

*Departure*: May 5, 1853
*Destination*: Beechey Island (*North Star*)
*Arrival*: June 2, 1853
*Notes*: One sled.

---

Dr. Domville
7 *Resolute* men
Mate Henry H. Sainsbury (invalid on sled); Ellis Griffiths, Able Seaman (invalid); Thomas Morgan, Able Seaman (invalid)
*Ship Location*: Mercy Bay, Banks Island
*Departure*: May 24, 1853
*Destination*: Dealy Island (*Resolute* and *Intrepid*)
*Arrival*: June 10, 1853
*Notes*: Presumably one sled.

---

Captain McClure—commanding 1st sled
Lieutenant Haswell—commanding 2nd sled
Clerk-in-Charge Paine—attached to Haswell's sled
Acting Master Court—commanding 3rd sled
Dr. Armstrong—commanding 4th sled
Boatswain Kennedy
Carpenter Ford
Ice Mate Newton
Cornelius Hulott, Captain's Coxswain; Michael Flynn, Quartermaster; George Brown, Quartermaster; John Davies, Quartermaster; John Calder, Captain of the Forecastle; Peter Thompson, Captain of the Foretop; Henry Stone, Blacksmith; Henry Bluff, Boatswain's Mate; James Williams, Captain of the Hold; Isaac Stubberfield, Ship's Cook; James Nelson, Able Seaman; William Carroll, Able Seaman; George Olley, Able Seaman; Samuel Mackenzie, Able Seaman; William Whitefield, Carpenter's Crew; George L. Milner, Gunroom Steward; Henry Sugden, Subordinate Officers' Steward; John Wilcox, Paymaster & Purser's Steward; Sergeant John Woon, RM; Corporal James Biggs, RM; Private Elias Bow, RM; Private 3rd Class Thomas Bancroft, RM
*Ship Location*: Mercy Bay, Banks Island
*Departure*: June 3, 1853
*Destination*: Dealy Island (*Resolute* and *Intrepid*)
*Arrival*: June 17, 1853
*Notes*: Provisioned for 18 days.

---

Lieutenant Haswell
Clerk-in-Charge Paine
Carpenter Ford
Ice Mate Newton
19 men
*Location of Resolute and Intrepid*: Southwest of Cape Cockburn, Barrow Strait
*Departure*: April 10, 1854
*Destination*: Beechey Island (*North Star*)
*Arrival*: April 23, 1854
*Notes*: Two sleds, provisioned for 15 days. A detailed account of this journey is in Nelson, 1850–54.

---

Dr. Armstrong
Lieutenant Pim
James Nelson, Able Seaman, and 11 other Investigator men
5 *Resolute* men
*Location of Resolute and Intrepid*: Southwest of Cape Cockburn, Barrow Strait

*Departure*: April 11, 1854
*Destination*: Beechey Island (*North Star*)
*Arrival*: on or about April 23, 1854
*Notes*: Two sleds (presumably provisioned for 15 days). Nelson wrote a detailed account of this party.

Captain McClure
Assistant Surgeon Piers
Mr. Miertsching, Interpreter
17 men
*Location of Resolute and Intrepid*: Southwest of Cape Cockburn, Barrow Strait
*Departure*: April 14, 1854
*Destination*: Beechey Island (*North Star*)
*Arrival*: April 28, 1854
*Notes*: Provisioned for 15 days. Miertsching indicated three sleds were used, but De Bray wrote only two. This party included all the *Investigator* survivors who remained onboard, except for Morgan, who was still too ill to travel.

# Appendix 6.
# Notes on Map Features

## Information Used to Compile Notes on Map Features

Armstrong, Alexander. *Chart Illustrating the Discovery of The North West Passage by H.M. Ship Investigator* (1857).

Armstrong's journal, NA, ADM 101/250.

Armstrong, Alexander. *A Personal Narrative of the Discovery of the North-West Passage* (1857).

Barr, William. *Arctic Hell-Ship: The Voyage of HMS Enterprise 1850–1855* (2007).

Canadian Topographic Map Source, www.canmaps.com.

"Captain M'Clure, R.N." DUM (March 1854).

Cyriax, Richard J. *Sir John Franklin's Last Arctic Expedition* (1939).

*Discoveries in the Arctic Sea by the Squadrons Under the Orders of Capt$^n$ Sir Edw$^d$ Belcher C.B. H.M.S. Assistance, Capt$^n$ Kellett C.B. H.M.S. Resolute, Capt$^n$ Collinson C.B. H.M.S. Enterprise and Capt$^n$ McClure H.M.S. Investigator up to MDCCCLIV* (1855a).

Harrod, Dominick (editor). *War, Ice & Piracy: The Remarkable Career of a Victorian Sailor—The Journals and Letters of Samuel Gurney Cresswell* (2000).

Inglefield, Edward A. *Chart Shewing the North West Passage Discovered by Capt. R. Le M$^c$Clure, H.M. Ship. Investigator*, etc. (1853).

Manning, Thomas H. "Narrative of a Second Defence Research Board Expedition to Banks Island, With Notes on the Country and Its History" (1956).

*Map of Banks Island* (1956).

*Map of Central Arctic America showing the track of H.M.S. Enterprise and Investigator in 1850–54* (1889).

Markham, Clements R. *The Arctic Navy List* (1875).

McClure, Robert J. Correspondence and papers, NA, BJ2/10.

_____. "Proceedings of Captain M'Clure, of Her Majesty's Discovery Ship "Investigator," in search of the Expedition under Sir John Franklin, from August 1850 to April 1853, and reporting the Discovery of the North-West Passage" (1854a).

McClure, Robert J., and Sherard Osborn (editor). *The Discovery of the North-West Passage by H.M.S. "Investigator" Capt. R. M'Clure 1850, 1851, 1852, 1853, 1854, Edited by Commander Sherard Osborn From The Logs and Journals of Capt. Robert Le M. M'Clure* (1856).

Morse, Charles W. *Chart Showing the Recent Search for a North-West Passage. Also the Coast Explored in Search of Sir John Franklin between the Years 1848 and 1854* (1856).

Naval Correspondence, Indexes and Digests for 1793–1913, NA, ADM 12

Naval Officers' Service Records, NA, ADM 196.

Neatby, Leslie H. (translator and editor). *Frozen Ships: The Arctic Diary of Johann Miertsching 1850–1854* (1967).

Osborn, Captain Sherard. *Chart to Illustrate the Narrative of the Accomplishment of the North West Passage by H.M. Ship "Investigator"* (1856).

Wrottesley, John, 2nd Baron Wrottesley, http://en.wikipedia.org.

*Note*: Some features were originally referred to as "points," but were afterward changed to "capes."

*Armstrong Point*—west coast of Prince Albert Land; noted by McClure in his dispatch and in his book, but not on Osborn (1856); noted in text of Miertsching and Armstrong; shown on the charts of Inglefield (1853), Morse (1856), and Armstrong (1857), and appears in Markham (1875).

*Banks Strait/McClure/M'Clure Strait*—between Banks Island and Prince Patrick and Melville Islands; Banks Strait on Inglefield (1853), *Discoveries in the Arctic Sea* (1855a), Osborn (1856), and Armstrong (1857); McClure Strait on *Map of Central Arctic America* (1889) and M'Clure Strait on *Map of Banks Island* (1956).

*Cape Austin/Cape M'Clure/McClure*—north coast of Banks Island, just to the northwest of Cape Crozier; originally named Cape Austin in McClure's official dispatch (to honor Captain Horatio Austin), and name retained on Armstrong (1857), but afterwards changed to Cape M'Clure/McClure; Cape M'Clure on Osborn (1856), and as such today.

*Cape Collins*—located today on Bernard Island (across from Norway Island), northwest coast of Banks Island, lat. 73° 39' N. and long. 124° 20' W.; on *Discoveries in the Arctic Sea* (1855a) and *Map of Central Arctic America* (1889), the cape juts out from Banks Island, but is not mentioned in McClure or Armstrong's writings; probably in memory of Second Master Henry Foster Collins, HMS *Erebus*.

*Cape Crozier*—north coast of Banks Island; on Inglefield (1853), but does not appear on Osborn (1856) or Armstrong (1857), but is found in McClure's and Armstrong's books.

*Cape Kellett*—southwest coast of Banks Island.

*Cape Lambton*—southeast coast of Banks Island; referred to as Cape Hamilton by McClure, and shown on Osborn (1856) as "C. Lambton or Hamilton." Manning attributes the error to a probable slip in McClure's notes. There is a Cape Vesey Hamilton on the northeastern coast of Banks Island, and Manning confuses this place and Cape Lambton.

*Cape Sandom*—Cresswell's sled journey (Cresswell's sled journey (May 22–June 8, 1851) and/or Court's sled journey (Oct. 4–7, 1851) along the north-northeastern portion of Banks Island evidently resulted in McClure's naming Cape Sandom on the northern coast, most probably after his former commander, Captain Williams Sandom (HMS *Niagara*, 1838–39).

*Cape Vesey Hamilton*—north coast of Banks Island; in Manning, and as Cape Hamilton on Morse (1856); not in Markham (1875).

*Cape Wrottesley*—north coast of Banks Island; named for English astronomer John Wrottesley, 2nd Baron Wrottesley, FRS, FRAS (1798–1867); its earliest appearance is on the Admiralty chart (1854); on Osborn (1856).

*Court Point*—on the coast of Banks Island in Markham (1875), but without specific details; cannot be located on contemporary or modern maps.

*Gore Island(s)*—Mate Graham Gore was with McClure in the *Terror* (1836–37), and was Franklin's first lieutenant on *Erebus*; Inglefield (1853) noted the singular "island"; Armstrong wrote "islands" in his handwritten journal, but "island" in his book; "islands" on *Discoveries in the Arctic Sea* (1855a), Osborn (1856) and Collinson (1889), and in Manning; not on modern maps

*Haswell Point*—southwest coast of Banks Island, lat. 72° 41' 2" N. and long. 125° 7' 11" W.; According to Manning, the earliest map to show it is on *Discoveries in the Arctic Sea* (1855a); on *Map of Central Arctic America* (1889) and in Markham (1875), but not in McClure or Armstrong's books, or on Osborn (1856), or Morse (1856); still exists today—lat. 72° 41' 2" N. and long. 125° 7' 11" W. The naming may have been partly the result of a recommendation in Haswell's service record: "17 October 1851, Captain Kellett, of the *Herald*, strongly recommending him for his services in the Arctic Seas:= See Memorial stating his services 29 October 1853:="

*McClure Bay*—in Markham (1875).

*McClure Strait*—Banks Strait on the map accompanying Pim's sled expedition to *Investigator* and on Morse (1856), but McClure Strait in Markham (1875); in 1860, McClure wrote to James Ross that "[the Hydrographer of the Navy, Captain] Washington has very kindly I observe by the new chart he has sent me restored my name to the Strait which divides Baring and Melville Island that poor Sir Francis [Beaufort] erased and gave to his friend Sir Joseph Banks."

*Point Lady Ross*—located about 25 miles northeast of Armstrong Point, along the eastern shore of Prince of Wales Strait; mentioned by McClure in dispatches and in a letter to Sir James C. Ross: "I have taken a great license by naming a Point in the Straits after Lady Ross," but does not appear in his book, or on Osborn (1856); noted in Piers' and Armstrong's writings, and on Armstrong (1857); not on Inglefield (1853) or in Collinson (1889).

*Russell Point*—Manning: "The Russell Point region is poorly delineated on both the *Investigator* MS. charts and on later published charts. The MS. charts are also distinctly variable. Chart 1854 and subsequent charts appear to agree with the track chart accompanying Mecham (1855b) [Great Britain, Parliament], and were probably derived from his observations. This means that the position of the actual point that should be called Russell is in doubt. The decision to place it as on the present map is based primarily on MS. Chart L9304, which clearly shows M'Clure's beacon well to the south of Russell Point, and, therefore, close to the point now called Passage. It appears also that Storkerson and Stefansson (1921a, p. 636; Montgomery, 1932, p. 212) placed Russell Point close to Knight Harbour, and when we came along the coast from the northwest it was there that ice conditions altered and we considered that we had entered Prince of Wales Strait."

*Wynniatt Bay*—as Beaufort Bay on Inglefield (1853); Collinson sledded there in May 1851, and named it Glenelg Bay, and this name appears in McClure's book, and on Osborn (1856); though sometimes known as Glenelg Bay through recent times, it is properly Wynniatt Bay.

# Appendix 7.
# Polar Crumbs: Creation
# of the Arctic Medal 1818–55

The design of the Arctic Medal 1818–55 was so dramatically different from the standard British military and naval campaign medals before and after it, that its star-capped octagonal form raises the question—"Why?"

The answer bloomed from of the culmination of a 350-year search for the North-West Passage ... and the curious mind of a starry-eyed princess, whose youthful mind embraced the exploration of far-off lands[1]:

> Let us fancy ourselves in a room in Kensington Palace in the winter of 1833. There is the Duchess of Kent with the young Princess Victoria, then in her fourteenth year. Maps are spread out before them, and the Secretary of the Geographical Society is in attendance. With him are two great arctic explorers, Captains Beechey and Back. They are there to explain to the young Princess the geography of the region in which [John and James Ross, of the private ship Victory] were lost, and the route Captain Back intended to take in searching for them; and the Princess Victoria took a lively interest in following the intended track on the chart. Nor did her interest end with the interview. When her mother subscribed £100 towards the expenses of the expedition, the young Princess sent Captain Back a present of a case of mathematical instruments and a pocket-compass as her contribution to the equipment.

The pocket tortoise-shell case of instruments and silver-mounted pocket compass were received in two small packages by Back, through Sir George Cockburn, a few days after the interview with the princesses. Each was inscribed: "CAPTAIN BACK, R.N.,/February 1833,/ VICTORIA." "On my return from America, I was honoured by another private audience at Kensington Palace and after a brief explanation of my Journey &c I did not fail to inform their R. H^{sses} how much interest, the Compass had created at New York among the ladies and the use I had really found it in one or two difficult positions."[2]

Arctic Medal 1818–55, obverse and reverse (Spencer J. Fisher, 2014).

292

One of the first acts of Her Majesty's reign was to intimate her gracious intention to succeed her uncle, our Founder, as Patron of the [Royal Geographical] Society, and to bestow upon us her royal premium for the encouragement of geographical science and discovery. Since Her Majesty's accession this royal premium has taken the form of two gold medals granted annually—the Founder's Medal and the Patron's Medal.[3]

## The Notion of a Special Medal

On April 6, 1853, when Lieutenant Bedford Pim's sled party from HMS *Resolute* arrived in Mercy Bay, Banks Island, he found the trapped *Investigator*, her people having endured much suffering—and staring Death in the face. The western division of Sir Edward Belcher's five-ship Arctic squadron, HMS *Resolute* (Captain Henry Kellett) and *Intrepid* (Commander Francis L. McClintock), were frozen in at Dealy Island.

The week after Pim arrived at *Investigator*, Captain Kellett himself returned to *Resolute* from a 10-day journey, with a crew of seven men pulling HM Sled *Erin*.[4] He then wrote movingly in a private dispatch to John Barrow, Jr., Keeper of the Records at the Admiralty, calling attention to the toil of man-hauling heavily laden sledges, and pondered the idea of an honor for sled travelers:

> I have been a long time at Sea, and seen various trying circumstances but never have I seen (for Men) such labour and such misery after. No amount of Money is an equivalent. The travelling Parties ought to have some honorary and distinctive mark, the Captain of the Sledge something better than the others. Men require much more heart and Stamina to undertake an extended travelling Party than to go into Action. The Travellers have their enemy chilling them to the very Heart and Paralyzing their limbs, the others the very contrary. I should like to see the Travelling Men get an Arctic Medal and I would gladly give £50 towards it and I am sure every Arctic Officer would be anxious to subscribe but to be of value it ought to be presented by the Authority of Her Majesty.[5]

Kellett's suggestion was perhaps the earliest of its kind for the institution a special Arctic service medal, and given that the Naval General Service Medal 1793–1840 (NGS) and Military General Service Medal 1793–1814 (MGS) were issued only a handful of years prior to Kellett's words, the timing was ideal to sprout an Arctic equivalent of these two retroactive campaign awards.

Kellett specifically pointed to members of traveling parties as the intended recipients of any such medal, and further suggested that "the Captain of the Sledge [should have] something better than the others." This triggered the author's wandering eye, and he spied an unpublished Arctic numismatic oddity among the collections at the Scott Polar Research Institute (SPRI). The piece concerned features the same obverse design as a 28 mm, pewter Franklin portrait medal from London's Royal Polytechnic Institution series to great men, by painter, illustrator and engraver Thomas Stothard (1755–1834): a bust of Franklin facing right, surrounded by the words, "SIR JOHN FRANKLIN. R.N." The SPRI medal appears to be silver, and the reverse has the word "TO" in the upper center of a plain field, encircled by the following along the outer edge: ".ARCTIC SEARCH.TESTIMONY OF GOOD CONDUCT." As far as the author knows this medal was never issued, but dubbed it the "Arctic Search Good Conduct Medal."[6]

## The Gathering Arctic Steam

News of the North-West Passage's discovery by McClure reached England in October 1853, via her third in command, Lieutenant Samuel G. Cresswell. Nearly all the rest of the Investigators arrived back home the following October, along with the survivors of Belcher's expedition.[7]

*The Times* reported on March 22, 1854, that Queen Victoria had commanded Cresswell to attend an audience at Buckingham Palace, where he

> submitted [watercolor] sketches made by him during his service in the Investigator, and exhibiting some of the most interesting scenes brought under his notice during the discovery of the North-West

Passage by Captain M'Clure. Her Majesty examined the drawings minutely, and put numerous questions to Lieutenant Cresswell relative to the long and hazardous voyage of the Investigator which he answered to the entire satisfaction of the Queen. The Sketches are to be, by special permission, dedicated to Her Majesty.[8]

Enter one Richard Sainthill. Born in 1801 in Topsham, Devonshire, Sainthill went to Cork to join his father (Captain Richard Sainthill, RN (1739–1829), Agent for Transports afloat at Cork), and became a wine merchant, and the Commons Speaker of Cork Corporation. Both father and son were coin and medal collectors, and the junior Sainthill had friends in medalist Leonard C. Wyon, and Sir Thomas Dyke Acland, Bart. (Member of Parliament for North Devonshire 1837–57)—"one of the most zealous promoters of the [Franklin] search, in and out of the House of Commons."[9] In the wake of the Investigators' return, the trio were to become actors on a snowy medallic stage.[10]

Sainthill published his "Suggestions for a Medal to Record 'The Discovery of the Passage by the North Pole'" on February 3, 1855, and wrote: "I venture humbly to trust that every surviving individual of all the attempts, from Sir Edward Parry and Franklin to the last, may receive this mark of their Sovereign's approbation of the service which they have rendered to our geographical knowledge." By writing "every surviving individual," Sainthill evidently did not consider posthumous awards, and was likely acquainted with the government's general policy of not posthumously awarding the NGS and MGS.[11]

But the avid numismatist also had some (naïve) proposals regarding the "Passage" medal's design—which conveniently brushed aside the reality that *Investigator* was nowhere near the North Pole, *and* she had not sailed the Passage:

> We have to record a discovery, which has occupied the thoughts and exertions of Europe for centuries, and England has now determined the geography of our globe.
>
> The medal should therefore communicate this splendid achievement to the world (present and to come,) in the most perspicuous [clearest] manner possible, and this I submit will be best accomplished by giving a map of the North Pole, and shewing on it the line of communication from one sea to the other, distinguishing "The Passage," either by a line of arrows (as usual to denote the flow of a river,) or by ships sailing on it, or by combining both, which perhaps would be still more decisive.
>
> I think that the maritime nature of the medal might also be indicated, by changing the uppermost line of the Tiara worn by Her Majesty, and rendering it a naval crown, by substituting the hull for the cross pattee, and the sail for the intermediate floral ornaments.
>
> Clasps, with the names of Her Majesty's ships, and the years of their respective services, would classify the different expeditions.[12]

## Parliamentary Twist

When Parliament set up a Select Committee on June 19, 1855, to examine Robert McClure's monetary claim for the discovery of the North-West Passage, one of its members just happened to be none other than Sir Thomas Acland. The Select Committee issued its Report on July 20. Though Parliamentary Acts awarding various sums of money for passing certain degrees of longitude in the Arctic, and the actual sailing of a ship through a Passage, had been repealed in 1828, under the circumstances, the Committee awarded McClure and the officers and crew of *Investigator* £10,000. The sum was split in half, with £5,000 pounds going to McClure, and the balance being divided among the officers and men based on rank.[13]

The Committee investigated possible rewards for the claim by Captain Collinson for skillfully navigating the Arctic waters, and safely bringing *Enterprise* home again, and that of Captain Kellett for saving McClure and his Investigators. However, the Committee's hands were essentially tied, and it did not feel justified in extending the monetary award any further, given that McClure and his officers and men had already fulfilled the intent of the former Acts of Parliament.[14]

In spite of that decision, the Committee members still felt themselves in a quandary—and therefore seized the opportunity to go beyond their scope of authority:

[The Committee] cannot but consider it their duty to suggest that the country at large would hail with satisfaction any distinctions which might be conferred, not only upon the officers whose names have been referred to Your Committee, but upon others who are no less honourably connected with the perils and the exertions that have attended the exploration of the Arctic Seas.

For the last 30 years, and also since the loss of the gallant and lamented Sir John Franklin, some of the most distinguished officers of the British Navy have been commissioned to explore the Arctic regions, and in so doing have encountered great dangers, hardships, and privations of every description, much more severe and less endurable than those usually met with in ordinary maritime warfare.

(This line was curiously reminiscent of Kellett's words from two years before: "Men require much more heart and Stamina to undertake an extended travelling Party than to go into Action."[15])

It is customary to award Clasps to [recognize] military prowess in the field. Service in the Arctic regions may well be deemed worthy of similar distinction. Her Majesty's gracious recommendation has invited Your Committee to consider the proper mode of rewarding the officers and whose names have been specially referred to them. Your Committee therefore venture to suggest that there are marks of honour and distinction which, by brave and high-spirited men, would be valued even more highly than that reward which Your Committee have felt compelled to confine to those within the spirit, if not the letter, of the legislature enactment which originally offered it.

In connexion with this subject, Your Committee beg to direct attention to the evidence, which establishes that the grant of a medal to all those of every rank and class engaged in the several Arctic Expeditions, would be received with great satisfaction. Your Committee feel persuaded that such a medal would honour deeds of heroism, which, though not accompanied by the excitement and the glory of the battle-field, yet rival in bravery and devotion to duty the highest and most successful achievements of war.[16]

Since the names of no other officers had been referred to the Committee, its members were further of the opinion that it might be unfairly discriminatory to mention individuals, "where all have not only performed their duty but earned distinction." The Report went on to state that, in addition to the officers and men of the Royal Navy, individuals of the Hudson's Bay Company and the merchant navy, as well as persons from France and the United States, contributed their energy and enthusiasm for Arctic discovery and the search for Franklin.[17]

But the medal's future was far from assured, as Richard Sainthill pointedly recorded:

The recommendation for the Medal, however, found no favor with Her Majesty's Ministers, and an ominous, but clearly understood silence, was observed respecting it on the Treasury Bench. In consequence Colonel Freestun on the* 9th August, enquired of the First Lord of the Admiralty, whether the Decoration would be given? Sir Charles Wood evaded the question, by replying, "that he had not read the "Report." On the# 13th August, the Colonel attacked the Prime Minister, with the same question, and met a similar evasion. "[Prime Minister] Lord Palmerston said, he would communicate with the Admiralty upon the subject," and as Parliament broke up on the same day, no doubt remained, but, as in so many other instances, the recommendation in this Blue Book so far as the Medal was concerned, was intended, to take an eternal sleep, in the Parliamentary Limbo.[18]

*Times, Aug. 10, 1855.
#Standard, Aug. 14, 1855.

Wood did come to write Queen Victoria on October 20, with the Committee's suggestion for an Arctic Medal,[19] and the Queen, in her response two weeks later, remarked on the way

in which the proposal has originated has struck her as not quite correct & that it will open a new first for honours not hitherto conferred.[20] [Prime Minister Lord] Palmerston will speak to Sir Ch[arles] on the subject: It will probably have to be granted & should in that case be so carried out, as to make the distinction between this Medal & those granted for Victories apparent. The conduct of those who went through trials of Arctic regions cannot be too much praised, and there have been many other expeditions which have called forth qualities no less prominent.[21]

So from the very start, the Arctic Medal was intended to be distinct (in some way) from war medals. In addition, although it was recognized that others had served in an equally fine manner on expeditions in different parts of the globe, no tangible mark of distinction would find its way to these explorers.

By early February 1856, Rear Admiral John E. Walcott (formerly of the Select Committee) questioned the First Lord of the Admiralty in Parliament about the entitlement of the Arctic officers and men "to a recommendation to their Sovereign for a special medal in acknowledgement of their services," and "whether it was the intention of the Government to grant a medal," conforming with the Committee's recommendation. In his response, Sir Charles Wood indicated the Queen intended to confer a medal, "and measures were being taken to carry that intention into effect. There was, however, great pressure at present in preparing the Crimean medals, and it would be some time before the Arctic medal could be prepared."[22]

The following month, Captain James C. Ross wrote to the Admiralty, asking that his Antarctic officers and men in HMS *Erebus* and *Terror* during 1839–43 receive the Arctic Medal. But a few days later he was tersely turned down: "I am commanded to acquaint you that my Lords do not consider this Service comprised within those for which Her Majesty has signified Her Gracious Intention of conferring a Medal."[23] As it happened, during the Select Committee discussions, the First Lord "had asked whether those officers and men who had been in the Antarctic and the [1841–42] Niger Expeditions were not to be included in the grant [of medals, along with the Arctic Medal]?" The subject does not appear to have been discussed at the time, or arisen thereafter, and it is assumed nothing further was done on this matter.[24]

## *The Reverse Design*

Leonard Wyon wrote in his diary on December 14, 1855: "Received a letter and sketches for the Arctic medal from Sir Geo. Back" (one of which showed *Investigator* sailing along the northern coast of Banks Island, before reaching Mercy Bay—see below).[25] Wyon worked up various designs based on these sketches, but Sir Charles Wood did not like them, as Wyon explained in his March 15, 1856, diary entry: "I went to the Admiralty and was informed that Lieut. [*sic*—Commander] Cresswell is making a sketch for the Arctic Medal, as Sir George Back's and mine are not liked." Four days later he added: "To the Admiralty. Sir C Wood gave me a sketch by Commander Cresswell for the Arctic medal which I am to carry out."[26] Not to be forgotten is Cresswell's audience with Queen Victoria in March 1854, where "Her Majesty examined [his] drawings minutely," and by special permission they were dedicated to the Queen; consequently, one can assume he may have enjoyed some favoritism in this situation. And according to the late Dominick Harrod (Cresswell's descendant), the artist always understated his

"Position of HMS *Investigator* Sep 19, 1851," by S.G. Cresswell (detail—note the two ridges of ice in the center and parallel arrangement of the spars in comparison to the medal); "Position of HMS *Investigator* after heavy pressure, 1852" (detail), by S.G. Cresswell (courtesy Norfolk Record Office, WMH 3/1/DA/1); Arctic Medal 1818–55, reverse detail (Spencer J. Fisher, 2014).

watercolor paintings by referring to them as "water-colour sketches," so it can be fairly assumed the submitted "sketch" contained a fair bit of detail.[27]

In 1994 and 1995, the author published writings on the design origins of the both the Arctic Medal 1818–55, and a second Arctic exploration medal in the 1870s.[28] At the time, he held the belief that Cresswell could have sought inspiration from another artist and naval officer—William Smyth—who served as Captain Back's first lieutenant (and McClure's superior) onboard the *Terror* during 1836–37. In spite of the long-held belief that Smyth's renditions of the *Terror* were the source of the design,[29] further research has since caused the author to alter his views.

The sketch Cresswell submitted to the Admiralty was not found in The National Archives; however, in studying three watercolor sketches from Cresswell's artwork collection held in the Norfolk Record Office, the author formed the opinion that the submitted sketch was most likely a composite drawing of these images: (1) "Position of HMS Investigator Sep 19, 1851" [near Cape Wrottesley, north coast of Banks Island]; (2) "Position of HMS Investigator after heavy pressure, 1852" [in Mercy Bay]; and (3) "Cliff at North West Extremity [*sic*] of Banks Land & Cape Hamilton May 8th 1851." The last is especially notable, since it represents Cresswell's sled party.[30]

On the medal's reverse, an iceberg occupies the middle ground on the left, while another is in the background on the right—but as Captain Back pointed out below, icebergs were not found at the latitude concerned. The author therefore believes their inclusion was most likely the result of Wyon's innocently transforming large hummocks into icebergs. In the space above the ship is written "FOR ARCTIC DISCOVERIES." in sans serif capital letters, while the dates "1818–1855" appear in the exergue.

"Cliff at North West Extremity [*sic*] of Banks Land & Cape Hamilton May 8th 1851" (detail). This was Cresswell's sled party and his farthest was lat. 74° 16' N. and long. 117° 30' W., being the eastern entrance of the later named Mercy Bay. Cresswell's party was the model for the sled party which appeared on the Arctic Medal's reverse (courtesy Norfolk Record Office, WMH 3/1/DA/1).

Back corresponded with Sainthill late in 1856 about details of the design:

> I am glad to hear on examination, you approve of the Arctic Medal, though so keen a critic as the author of the 'Olla' [*An Olla Podrida*, 1844], cannot fail to discover the anomaly of making the Sledge (in the original) going to the East instead of the West, in search of Franklin.
>
> However, that is of no consequence in a Medal for Polar services: except that some reason ought to be assigned for the sledge being placed there at all.
>
> It might look as if the Crew was deserting the Ship if not accounted for in some other way. [A drawing of the four compass directions follows.]
>
> But, as there may have been large 'hummocks' of ice to prevent the party going directly west, it may fairly be conjectured, they are making a circuitous route to go in that direction.
>
> After all who cares which way they are going.[31]

And further in the letter, Back remarked how he "always intended [Sainthill to have] the original sketch now in Wyon's possession of the 'Investigator' making the NW. passage—before she was laid up in Mercy Bay. There, you will have truth as regards the ice, in the summer—though the Bergs are not found in that latitude."[32]

And yet, Sainthill's historical eye was not wholly pleased with the *factual* representation of the design. With a fully active sled party in the foreground, and "the Ship embedded in ice, dismantled, literally a lifeless log" in the background, he argued that this implied that geographic discoveries were primarily made by sledding, while ships were merely secondary, and simply used for transportation. In an "estimate of the relative value of the Sea and Land Discoveries, we should reverse the Admiralty design, and present a Ship under full Sail at Sea," he concluded. While one can understand Sainthill's point of view, to have relegated the sledding party to the background would have largely removed the human element from the scene, and given the confined space, made it very difficult to appreciate at all.[33]

## An Unsatisfied Numismatist

Though Richard Sainthill knew about the forthcoming Arctic Medal, in March 1856 he wrote, "[W]hile this arrangement must be the most gratifying to the Northern Navigators, it is necessarily incomplete, as a Record for future Ages." Sainthill suggested the Royal Geographical Society bring out a medal that was

> a larger area than that of the War Medals ... at least two inches and a quarter in diameter. The Obverse, giving a Map of the North Pole, showing on it, the line of communication, from one Sea to the other, distinguishing this clearly, by Ships at intervals, entering from one Sea, and passing out into the other; with lines of arrows, (as usual to indicate the flow of a current, on Maps,) from each Ship to the next in advance.
>
> The Reverse, I would suggest, should be an actual representation of the difficulties of the service, and the manner in which they were overcome—no allegory, but the real Scenery of the dread North, and the real ship herself, ploughing her way, and daring all opposition....
>
> The Inscription, I should suggest, would be carried on, from the Obverse to the Reverse—thus:–
> OBVERSE—{ The Passage by the North Pole, ascertained by the Royal Navy, of—
> REVERSE—{ Her Majesty, Victoria, Queen of Great Britain and Ireland, A.D., 1854.
> A Medal of this nature would be a complete Record in itself, combining, the fact of discovery, its Geography, and the mode and means, by which the achievement had been accomplished.[34]

Sainthill went on to suggest that such a medal could be carried out by Leonard Wyon, and made a comparison with a medal of the same size that the medalist recently delivered to a party, at a cost of £180 for 300 bronze medals and dies.[35] For reasons unknown—but probably due to the forthcoming Arctic Medal—Sainthill's "Record for future Ages" never came to pass.

## Approving a Design

On May 23, 1856, the Queen received a letter from the Admiralty, explaining the "great delay in preparing a design for [the Arctic] medal, but Sir Charles Wood begs to submit one to Your Majesty in a few days." Four days later, Wood was able to "submit to Your Majesty the design of a medal for the Arctic Discoveries. It has been adapted by Mr Wyon by a sketch from one of the officers engaged in the Arctic Service who is a very clever artist. The object has been to combine in some way the land operations by representing a party of men harnessed to a sledge, with the greater feature of a ship inbedded [*sic*] in ice & surrounded by ice bergs."[36]

Presumably, Queen Victoria examined one or both of the following patterns:

*Prototype 1*—Circular pattern, silver, clip and straight bar suspender (like that for the Candahar, Ghuznee and Cabul Medals 1841–42), 33 mm in diameter, but as the late Alec Purves wrote, "appreciably thicker than the issued medal." Based solely on visual evidence of a b/w photograph, it had a contemporary 40 mm plain white ribbon, with corded edges.[37]

*Prototype 2*—Circular pattern, silver, foliated suspender (similar to that of the Crimea Medal 1854–56—to take clasps?), 33 mm in diameter, and 3.175 mm thick. The only example seen by the author had a modern manufacture 32 mm plain white ribbon (as found on the Arctic Medal 1875–76 and Polar Medal 1904).[38]

On May 30, the Queen wrote to Wood that she approved of the design, "but wishes it be entirely *different* to the Military & Naval Medals. Why might it not be triangular? [followed by a rough sketch of a triangular-shaped medal on a ribbon]."[39] In his reply on June 10, Wood explained that he discussed the shape with Wyon, and although the medalist looked at some collections to find any medals with triangular or other shapes, he

has not found any of a shape deviating much from the circular shape, which is almost universal. A triangular shape would not suit the design, & although it may be desirable to have a marked distinction

Round "Prototype 2" of the Arctic Medal 1818–55 (private collection).

between the arctic & other medals, Sir Charles Wood would humbly submit to Your Majesty that a tri-angular shape could perhaps too much recall a sort of badge worn by freemasons, & that it would be objectionable that the shape of the medal should be the object of much remark.

A smaller medal is frequently given by the Secretary of State for service rendered to British subjects by foreigners, & this was given to the American arctic expeditions. This however is circular, & Sir Charles Wood encloses one for Your Majesty's inspection.[40]

Sir Charles Wood also submits to Your Majesty two medals which Mr Wyon has brought here this morning, both octagonal, but of different shapes. The nearer the circular form, provided the distinction is as marked, as Your Majesty would wish, the better for the design, & the effect of the medal is the purport of Mr Wyon's representations on this subject, & with this view the medal of Louis XVIII might perhaps answer Your Majesty's purpose. Sir Charles Wood sends an ordinary medal that Your Majesty may compare the size, and perhaps it would be better to make the arctic medal somewhat smaller. If it were reduced to the size of the lesser medal, the design would be too much cramped.

The other piece representing the night mare, is hardly a medal, but might not be an inconvenient form for the design.[41]

The following day, the Queen wrote that she "returns three Medals. She thinks the Shape of the Octagon [of] one of Louis XVIII Sh$\underline{d}$ [should] be adopted & the size of the Crimean Medal—with the difference taken off it, (not added to it) to make it octagon[al]."[42]

## Portrait of a Queen

Turning to the obverse design, Wood wrote to the Queen about her portrait on June 16: "It varies slightly from what appears on the existing medals & Sir Charles Wood wishes to receive from Your Majesty, directions as to whether any change is to be made for this medal." The reply came four days later: "The Queen approves of this Design for the Arctic Medal—tho' She thinks M$\underline{r}$ Wyon Sh$\underline{d}$ [should] correct the likeness from the original one."[43]

Wyon sculpted a new "Young Head," which was evidently only used on this medal. The Queen's hair is in a chignon (a knot of hair that is worn at the back of the head and especially at the nape of the neck), with a diadem (jeweled headband).[44]

The legend "VICTORIA REGINA" is in sans serif capitals, and of the 19 obverse portraits of Queen Victoria on official medals (1842–99),[45] the author noted that this was the only instance of sans serif lettering (and probably the same case on any reverse design as well). But the traditional *serif* capitals lettering was originally chosen for the obverse legend on Prototype 1.[46] However, the lettering on the reverse has evidently always been sans serif.

## Enter the Octagon

The Master of the Royal Mint, Thomas Graham,[47] sent Wood "a pattern Arctic Medal for the purpose of being submitted to Her Majesty's approval" on October 17. Three days later, she returned the specimen medal, which she approved, "but only thinks it rather too thick & massive." Afterward, in writing to Graham, Wood indicated that the "Queen approves of the design & execution of the Medal but thinks it too heavy & massy [massive]."[48]

Further specimens were struck, and on November 8, Wyon wrote to Sir Thomas Acland, offering him "a 'bronze Arctic medal' as approved by the Queen."[49] By mid–November, Queen Victoria "returned the Medals to Sir C. Wood & s$\underline{hd}$ [should] wish the smaller Medal to be adopted as the Arctic Medal."[50]

Graham wrote to Wood on December 12 that a specimen of the Arctic Medal was being mounted "with a Small Silver Star, symbolized of The 'North Polar Star,' which was thought not inappropriate," and he requested guidance on the following point: "In regard to the 'Arctic' Medal no Official information has been received by me, on The number, nor have any nominal lists been received. The form of This medal will require The engraving of The names to be executed by hand."[51]

Wood submitted the star-topped octagon to the Queen for her consideration on December 13, and although the First Lord wrote that the "Master of the Mint has added a star above the Arctic Medal," Graham's writings to Wood do not specifically indicate the star was his (Graham's) idea—although one assumes he must have approved it.[52]

Wood wrote to Graham on December 18 with the final result: "The Queen approves of the Baltic & Arctic Medals and ribbands as you have sent them to me. She wishes to have one of each to keep so perhaps you will be good enough to have two properly fitted boxes prepared, to contain them."[53]

There are two *possible* octagonal prototypes known to the author:

*Prototype 3*—Octagonal pattern, with beaded inner rim on both sides, silver, 33 mm in diameter, ring suspender and foliated claw and pin (described as a "contemporary replacement suspension claw" at auction), thickness unknown. A bowl-shaped connection between the star and ring is considerably more substantial than in the adopted pattern. The modern 32 mm, plain white ribbon is incorrect, being that found on the Arctic Medal 1875–76 and Polar Medal 1904.[54]

*Prototype 4*—Octagonal pattern, with beaded inner rim on both sides, 33 mm in diameter, silver, ring suspender and foliated claw and pin (nearly identical to that of Prototype 3), 3.4 mm thick. Although the connection between the star and ring is also more substantial than in the adopted pattern, it is a slight V-shape, possibly from a repair. The medal was acquired in a box marked "Arctic Medal," but the ribbon appeared to be that for the adopted issue, though not a contemporary piece.[55]

What was finally adopted to join the ball at the bottom of the star to the 12 o'clock edge of the medal was a three-toed claw, as opposed to the two-toed claw commonly found on campaign medals. The three-toed claw appears to be a refined version of the foliated claw found on the (possible) Prototypes 3 and 4.

## Die Problems

In examining several examples of the adopted octagonal pattern over the years, the author often noted how the edges were uneven, and ranged from 2–3 mm in thickness. Looking at the obverse facing up, the extremes of these variances often occur on the 12 o'clock edge (2 mm), and along the area where the three and five o'clock edges meet (3 mm).

Some understanding as to the origin of this unevenness *might* be gleaned in a letter from Thomas Graham to Sir Charles E. Trevelyan, Assistant Secretary to Her Majesty's Treasury, which involved a disagreement over Wyon's fee for his work on the medal:

From a representation which he [Wyon] has made to me of the unusual trouble he has had in the execution of that Medal, caused by alterations in the details of the design made by Order during the progress of the Work, and of an un[u]sual expenditure of 14 Guineas which he incurred in preparing a puncheon [matrix die] and multiplying dies of the Medal, I am led to consider this reduced charge as reasonable in the circumstances of the case, and beg to submit accordingly that the payment of 150 Guineas now applied for by M[r] L. Wyon for the Arctic Medal should be allowed.[56]

There is suspicion that the original dies failed sometime after the initial batch of medals were struck in the late 1850s, and new dies evidently resulted in thicker medals.

The medal roll shows that "Issue No. 1835" was sent to retired Hudson's Bay Company Superintendent for the Mackenzie District Roderick MacFarlane on May 6, *1902*.[57] On June 14 of that year, a *Manitoba Morning Free Press* headline ran, "Arctic Medal for Winnipeg Resident," along with an image of the award. "The medal is *exceptionally thick* [author's emphasis], made of silver, and has inscribed along the edge 'Mr. R. Macfarlane, Hudson's Bay Co.'" One wonders if it was officially inscribed before being sent to MacFarlane?[58]

A notation on the first page of the medal roll provides insight to another late issue four decades later—along with a reference as to the condition of the dies: "Letter from Royal Mint dated 18/5/42 states dies no longer available for further medals to be struck. (3 A/M.22901). Duplicate case 9592."

(This case number does not refer to the total issue of Arctic Medals.) This duplicate medal was issued through the American Consul, West Indies, on May 25, 1942, presumably for a descendant of First Assistant Engineer Harman Newell, USN. Newell was onboard the USS *Arctic* during Lieutenant Henry J. Harstene's 1855 expedition in search of Dr. Elisha Kent Kane; he attained the rank of chief engineer in 1859, and died March 24, 1880.[59]

Consequently, the Arctic Medal struck for Donald Bray (descendant of John Hartnell, Able Seaman, HMS *Erebus*) in late 1985, and presented to him on January 8, 1986, was evidently struck from yet another set of new dies. This medal was about 3.2 mm thick.[60]

## *Preparations for Distribution*

On December 18, 1856, the First Lord issued orders to the Accountant General of the Navy, Richard M. Bromley, to begin preparing lists of those employed on Arctic service since 1818. Five days later, Clerk 1st Class William Kenrick wrote:

> In making out the lists I do not think it will be necessary to abstract the names in alphabetical order as the complements of the ships are small.
> As in all probability the names will be inscribed on the Medals from the lists it is desirable that the names should be taken out accurately and written very legibly. With a little exertion I think we may complete the list by tomorrow evening provided the Books can be obtained. All other business can be set aside for the present.[61]

So at this point, in the Accountant General's office—along with Graham at the Royal Mint—there was still an assumption that the medals would be issued with official naming. This did not come to pass, and the most likely reason for the medals remaining plain-edged is the extra expense of hand engraving—thus, many were forever consigned to anonymity.

By New Year's Eve 1856, Clerk 3rd Class W. Edward P. Hooper indicated: "[T]he whole staff of the [Service & Pension] Branch (except one) were employed in the preparation of the lists which were completely copied by the evening of the 24th, but from the fact that many of the officers and crews were employed in two or three different expeditions it was found desirable to arrange them in alphabetical order. Four of the gentlemen of the Branch have been thus employed and the lists are now complete."[62] The Accountant General forwarded the lists to the Admiralty on January 12, 1857. Two days before, Wood received the Baltic and Arctic Medals the Queen asked to be prepared for her, and he sent them to Her Majesty the same day.[63]

Also on January 12, the Accountant General sent the lists to the Secretary of the Admiralty, Ralph R. Osborne, which totaled 2, 206 possible recipients, representing the officers and men of the Royal Navy and Royal Marines, and included those onboard the private ship *Victory* (1829–33), and HMS *Lady Franklin* and HMS *Sophia* (1850–51). The latter two ships originally composed a private expedition organized by Lady Franklin, but prior to sailing it was taken up and fitted out by the Admiralty. Captain John Washington, Hydrographer of the Navy, made the following addition to the total on January 14: "United States, Private and Land Arctic Expeditions, say 250/Grand Total 2456." Washington further wrote: "Taking into consideration the uncertainty of life and that the period embraces 40 years I submit that 1500 medals would probably be found sufficient to meet all demands for the present."[64]

On the other side of the same page is another notation, written vertically, but not in Washington's hand: "The 'Cove' which went in search of the Missing Whale Ships in the winter of 1835 has been accidentally omitted in this list." A further notation was made just below in the same hand, and afterwards scratched through, so as to be unreadable.[65]

During the depth of the 1835–36 winter, HMS *Cove* was sent to relieve whale ships reported to be trapped in the ice in the Davis Strait. Captain James C. Ross was in command, while two of his lieutenants were the future Arctic captain Erasmus Ommanney, and Arctic veteran Francis R.M. Crozier (who met his end on the Franklin Expedition). Mate Alexander J. Smith also served as a mate and lieutenant on the *Erebus* with Ross in the Antarctic, and Quartermaster James Sefton had already served on four Arctic expeditions. At some point, it must have been decided that the *Cove* was not eligible, since the medal was never officially authorized for this ship.[66]

The Accountant General then indicated to the Financial Secretary to the Treasury, James Wilson, "that the number of Persons Entitled to the Medal proposed to be awarded for Arctic Services, may be estimated at 1500," and to make arrangements for this number of medals to be delivered to the Accountant General.[67]

By February 6, the medals had been struck, and were in the "course of being mounted by Mess^rs Hunt & Roskell." In a draft letter to the Accountant General on the 25th, the Mint wrote: "Forwarding 10 'Arctic' Medals as the first installment of 1500."[68]

## The Announcement and Distribution

On January 14, 1857, "a fortnight before the first general publication was made concerning the institution of this medal—the Admiralty Board approved the award of this Arctic Medal posthumously, once it had been minted, to Miss Jane M. Little, sister of the late Commander E. Little R.N. who had served aboard H.M. Discovery Ship *TERROR* in Sir John Franklin's ill-fated Expedition during the seasons of 1845–1848."[69]

FROM *THE LONDON GAZETTE* OF FRIDAY, JAN. 30, 1857.

Admiralty, January 30, 1857.

HER Majesty having been graciously pleased to signify Her commands that a Medal be granted to all persons, of every rank and class, who have been engaged in the several expeditions to the Arctic Regions, whether of discovery or search, between the years 1818 and 1855, both inclusive, the Lords Commissioners of the Admiralty hereby give notice of the same.

The Medal will accordingly be awarded as follows:

1st. To the Officers, Seamen, and Marines of Her Majesty's ships and vessels employed on the several voyages to the Arctic Seas during the specified period, and also to the Officers of the French Navy, and to such Volunteers as accompanied those expeditions:

2ndly. To the Officers, Seamen, and others who were engaged in the expeditions to the Arctic Seas, equipped by the Government and Citizens of the United States.

3rdly. To the Commanders and Crews of the several expeditions which originated in the zeal and humanity of Her Majesty's subjects.

4thly. To persons who have served in the several land expeditions, whether equipped by Her Majesty's Government, by the Hudson's Bay Company, or from private resources.

As a short period must necessarily elapse before the Medals will be ready for distribution, no application should be made for a Medal, until further notice shall have been published in *The London Gazette*.[70]

A further *London Gazette* notice during the first week of May indicated the medal was ready to be issued: "Every applicant must state his rank or rating, and the name of the ship or ships on board which he served; also, in the case of every petty officer, seaman, or marine, it is indispensible that his application should be accompanied by a certificate of service, except in the case of his being on board one of Her Majesty's ships, and the application be made through his commanding officer, in which case the certificate will not be required." A list of ships entitled to the medal, and the year the expeditions officially commenced, was also published.[71]

Various Admiralty Orders afterward extended the award to American expeditions that searched for Franklin, certain Hudson's Bay Company personnel, and to the officers and men who sailed with Captain Leopold McClintock onboard the yacht *Fox* (1857–59), hired by Lady Franklin. On September 23, 1859, McClintock took receipt of 11 Arctic Medals, which four days later he personally presented to members of his crew who had not previously received the award.[72] Several entitled land and sea expeditions between 1821 and 1853 were not listed in the *London Gazette*, and their entitlements only appear within the medal roll.

## Ribbon

On May 23, 1856, Wood asked the Queen to approve "a simple white ribband for the Arctic Medal," which she did seven days later.[73] Graham wrote to Wood on October 17 that he was

> not aware that anything has been decided respecting the Ribbon for this medal. But a White ribbon having been suggested by the Artist Mr. L. Wyon & also by a distinguished Arctic officer [who?], I have had a specimen of the proper width manufactured for your inspection. You will find it in two conditions, plain & watered. The watering is general with decoration ribbons abroad, & was applied to the Caffir [*sic*—Kaffir, the South Africa Medal 1834–53] medal ribbon. It appears an improvement.[74]

The following notation is written diagonally upside down on the second page: "I know that the Queen has already approved a white ribbon for one another medal. Is this okay? G"[75] Although it was not founded by Queen Victoria until 1862, it appears Professor Graham was referring to the Royal Order of Victoria and Albert, the ribbon of which is a 38 mm wide, white moiré[76]—in other words, having a rippled or "watered" appearance—and thus identical every respect to the ribbon chosen for the Arctic Medal.

On February 5, 1857, the Admiralty inquired with the Mint "whether The Ribbon for the 'Arctic' Medal has been provided—to be White, Silk & Watered." The reply the following day indicated the ribbon had been ordered.[77]

Since the Arctic ribbon was six millimeters (or more) wider than those for the NGS, MGS, and other war medals of the period, and the medal's octagonal shape was intended to make it distinct from military and naval campaign awards, it could well be the Arctic Medal was *intentionally* fitted with a wider ribbon as a matter of further distinction. However, lest simple aesthetics be forgotten, in the author's opinion, the wider ribbon is more complimentary to the octagonal shape than a narrower width, so perhaps this was also the prevailing thought at the time.

The snowy ribbon easily catches the viewer's eye in contemporary images of recipients wearing their medals. Of course, such a light color easily became soiled, and was apt to be replaced with a narrower watered or unwatered length of ribbon, so that the Arctic Medal often encountered by collectors, and depicted in illustrations, paintings, and photographs, hangs from an unwatered or watered ribbon of an incorrect width. In fact, the author spied one contemporary replacement candidate on eBay: a 30 mm, watered white ribbon (aged to an ivory color), with corded edges. This ribbon was (incorrectly) used for a post–1867 medal of the Soldiers' Total Abstinence Association, but would have been ideal for Prototype 2 above.[78]

Even military tailors did not always get it right. A photograph of Vice Admiral Sir George S. Nares shows him wearing his Arctic Medal 1818–55 (Mate/*Resolute*/1852–54) and Arctic Medal 1875–76 (Captain & Commanding Expedition/*Alert*) mounted together—but with the ribbons *reversed*—so that the former was fitted with the latter's 32 mm ribbon.[79]

## A Question of Clasps

A sailor or Marine may not have wintered-over in the north, but received the medal, whereas a man with Franklin's expedition spent four (or more) winters suffering untold privations before his death, and his next-of-kin was issued with the same award. Had the Arctic Medal be designed to take clasps, date clasps would have made important distinctions between the service of such recipients.

As mentioned previously, in February 1855, as part of his suggestion for a medal to record the North-West Passage discovery, the numismatist Richard Sainthill put forth his thoughts along these lines: "Clasps, with the names of Her Majesty's ships, and the years of their respective services, would classify the different expeditions."[80] Thus, early on Sainthill recommended clasps to individualize each medal, and in doing so, was no doubt drawing a parallel with the battle clasps on the NGS and MGS.

And again, while members of the Select Committee discussed the subject of establishing an Arctic Medal that summer, they touched on the subject of clasps: "It is customary to award Clasps to [recognize] military prowess in the field. Service in the Arctic Regions may well be deemed worthy of similar distinction."[81]

And following the official announcement of the Arctic Medal in January 1857, Sainthill wrote (in part) to the editor of *The Times* on February 12:

> In the many Grants of Medals, made by Her Majesty for Navy and Military achievements, it has hitherto been the Rule, that the Medal has been accompanied by Clasp, specifying the particular Service, for which it was conferred: and when the individual had been in more than one, then additional Clasps were added, so, that we frequently observe many Clasps to the same Medal. I myself have noticed Five, and I have heard of as many as ten and twelve [in reference to the NGS and MGS].
>
> From the wording of the Admiralty notice, I infer, that a Medal will be given to each Arctic Investigator, without any Clasp specifying the time of his Service, and still less, Clasps distinguishing those who have been engaged in several of the Twenty Expeditions, sent out by the British Government since 1818.
>
> Now it is a matter of common notoriety, that many distinguished Arctic Officers, made their first acquaintance with the Northern Regions, as Midshipmen, and in that service, have passed through the successive Grades of Lieutenants, Commanders, Captains. I think, therefore, that if, (as I suppose,) the Admiralty have not ordered Clasps, signifying the distinct, and where there has been the different Services of each Individual, they will not carry out Her Majesty's Maternal and Beneficient [sic] intentions, to her meritorious, and severely tried servants, through whom, (to use the words of "the Select Committee of the House of Commons, on Arctic Expedition.") "The long sought for Problem has at length been solved by this Country, and another ray has been added to the Maritime Glory of the British Empire."[82]

Just two weeks later, Admiral Walcott queried First Lord Sir Charles Wood in Parliament, "whether, as it was believed some objection seemed to be made to granting clasps to those who were to receive the Arctic Expedition Medals according to the number of times they had served in the Polar Regions, [would he] have any objection to having the number of times stamped on the bar of the medal in lieu of clasps?"

It was said,

> that the question whether medals should be given for each Arctic voyage had been considered soon after the question had arisen relative to the granting of medals, and subsequently [Wood] had asked whether those officers and men who had been in the Antarctic and the Niger Expeditions were not to be included in the grant? One of the officers engaged in the Arctic Expeditions had also inquired whether it was intended to grant a medal for each year in which the claimants had been in the Arctic Expeditions, and a clasp for each voyage, because in that case he would be entitled to nine medals and twenty clasps. He thought that we had gone far enough in discrediting medals by the profusion with which they had been already granted—and the case put by

Dr. John Rae's Arctic Medal with unofficial date clasps (on loan from the University of Edinburgh; Photography ©National Museums Scotland).

the hon. and gallant Member for Christchurch [Walcott] had reduced the argument against that profusion ad absurdum. In the case of the officers engaged in the late war forty years ago, one simple medal was granted for all the services performed; and he thought the best course, to pursue in the present case was to issue one simple medal for the Arctic voyages. The medal was ready to be issued. There was no bar on which the number of voyages could be engraved, and if that addition was to be made to them, it would require the issue of 48,000 circulars, and the reconstruction of the medal.[83]

Arctic Medal 1818–55 with an unofficial "ARCTIC" clasp (courtesy Tim Popp).

This was hardly the end of the "clasps" question for the Arctic Medal.

Though he did not have the edge engraved with his details, the much-traveled Dr. John Rae had the upper point of the star on his award reinforced, and with the addition of a straight suspender, five specially made-up date clasps were added to the medal: "1846–47," "1848," "1849," "1850–51," and "1853–54."[84]

Another unnamed—but unattributed—Arctic Medal exists, also with the upper point of the star reinforced, and fitted with an unofficial suspender to accept a clasp boldly engraved "ARCTIC" in thick sans serif capitals.[85] The styling of the clasp is similar to those seen on the Indian General Service Medal 1849–95, and is complete with finely engraved five-petal flowers on each end. Such elaborate and costly modifications point to an officer's medal.[86]

## Future Influence

The *Investigator*'s voyage had wide-ranging and tangible consequences for many future Arctic *and* Antarctic explorers, since the Arctic Medal 1818–55 set a precedent for the creation of the Arctic Medal 1875–76 and Polar Medal 1904.

Although the circular pattern was adopted for the Arctic Medal 1875–76, Leonard Wyon initially suggested the 1818–55 medal's reverse design could be used for this award by altering the dates.[87] A similar design (adapted from a photograph) was ultimately chosen, which "gives one a feel of the vast polar landscape, punctuated by broken ice. More importantly, the scene is devoid of human beings, further adding to the reality of isolation and starkness in a white ocean."[88]

Reverting to an octagonal shape for the Polar Medal 1904, the choice of the reverse design of Scott's *Discovery* in winter quarters, with a sledding party in the foreground (also adapted from a photograph),[89] may have very well been influenced by its predecessor a half-century before. The fitting of a scroll suspender meant the medal could take clasps, indicating the Arctic or Antarctic and date(s) of the recipient's service. The Polar Medal is still being awarded to this day.

"In qualifying for these white-ribboned awards, generations of men have pitted their wits and their strength against the mighty forces of nature, and more often than not nature has been the victor."— Alec Purves[90]

# Chapter Notes

## Chapter 1

1. A description of Shackleton's *Endurance* in the ice in January 1915, by Thomas H. Orde-Lees, Imperial Trans-Antarctic Expedition, 1914–17 (Lansing, p. 30).

2. Armstrong (1857), p. 559; Neatby (1967), p. 34.

3. Armstrong (1857), p. 560; McClure (1856), p. 272.

4. McClure to Barrow, Jr. (January 11, 1855), BL, Add.35308.

5. Robert McClure was born c. 1775 (Dunlop [1972], p. 13); "Captain M'Clure, R.N." (March 1854), p. 334. In writing to John Barrow, Jr., McClure stated he had "a scrap-book containing a very good sketch of my Birth parentage and education written by my Brother for one of the papers" (McClure to John to Barrow, Jr. [January 11, 1855], BL, Add.35308). The publication referred to was quite likely *The Dublin University Magazine*, while his "Brother" was surely a half-brother, as his mother had remarried.

6. "Captain M'Clure, R.N." (March 1854), p. 334.

7. Le Mesurier-Foster, www.guernsey-society.org.uk, p. 163; "Captain M'Clure, R.N." (March 1854), p. 334.

8. Lieutenant-General John Le Mesurier (1781–1843); *The Military Annual for 1844*, pp. 444–45; Le Mesurier-Foster, www.guernsey-society.org.uk, p. 163.

9. "Captain M'Clure, R.N." (March 1854), p. 334; Le Mesurier-Foster, www.guernsey-society.org.uk, p. 163. The latter states three sons were born to the Le Mesuriers in three successive years, but one may have died in infancy, as I can only trace Peter Perchard Le Mesurier (1817–34) and John Le Mesurier (1818–1903) (Hughes-Hughes [1893], p. 41).

10. "Captain M'Clure, R.N." (March 1854), p. 334. McClure first served as a supernumerary (extra) aboard HMS *Britannia* (April–May 1824) and *Primrose* (May–June 1824) before appearing as a volunteer onboard *Windsor Castle*

from June 2 to 24, 1824, and then as a volunteer/midshipman on *Primrose* until August 1827 (McClure's service record, NA, ADM 107/62).

11. Lewis (1965), pp. 155–56.

12. Ibid., p. 194.

13. Ibid., p. 198; Winton, p. 30.

14. Librarian & Keeper of the Papers, *British and Foreign State Papers, 1824–1825* (vol. 12), pp. 344–50.

15. Mary was the daughter of George and Elizabeth Mallors, and she was baptized at St. Mary's Church on January 24, 1808 (IGI); Lewis (1965), pp. 87, 90; McClure's service record, NA, ADM 107/62; McClure's service details, NMM, MCCLU/1.

16. McClure's private journal onboard HMS *Terror*, RGS, MG387B.

17. Ibid. A notation on a copy of a letter McClure wrote to Back in 1853 states that McClure "served as Admiralty Mate in H.M.S. 'Terror.'" An 1833 Admiralty notice stated that "Mates and Midshipmen are in future to be considered qualified to be entered as Admiralty Mates or Midshipmen, after having passed for seamanship abroad, or both examinations, if at home, one complete year, and not as heretofore, only those passed prior to 1830" (McClure to Back [April {day not written} 1853], RGS, JMS/17/28; Late 18th, 19th and early 20th Century Naval and Naval Social History Index, www.pbenyon.plus.com/Naval.html). A letter McClure wrote to his "sister" (actually half-sister) in April 1853 was published, and she was noted as "Mrs. Thomas E. Wright, of Dublin." Her first name may have been Jane, as someone by this name was mentioned as giving McClure an account of his mother's passing (McClure, "The North-West Passage, etc." [1853], pp. 670–75; McClure to his uncle [the Rev. Richard W. Elgee] [April {no day written} 1853] LCA, R6790–0-8-E).

18. An unnamed Arctic Medal 1818–55, with a silver ribbon buckle, and in a fitted Hunt & Roskell case, sold at auction in 1996, and was accompa-

nied by a brass medallion: "31mm. diameter. Obverse: seated Britannia, her right arm outstretched holding an olive branch; reverse: a crown surmounting the legend 'H.M.S. Terror/ Captn. Back/1836.' *Provenance*: Admiral Sir George Back." "The Back Collection," Christie's Exploration and Travel, lot 133, September 27, 1996.

19. Holland, pp. 212–13.

20. Mills (vol. 2), pp. 474–75.

21. Cyriax (1939), pp. 3–4; Haydn, p. 490.

22. Cyriax (1939), p. 10.

23. www.measuringworth.com.

24. Mills (vol. 1), pp. 66–67.

25. Cyriax (1939), p. 5; Ross (1994), p. 29.

26. Ross (1994), p. 29.

27. Mills (vol. 1), p. 66; Levere, p. 75.

28. Levere, pp. 43–44. Notably, changes in the Arctic Ocean "play a major role in determining the characteristics of the global overturning circulation which regulates global climate" (Lenn, p. 28).

29. A group of Parry family medals sold at auction in 1971: Naval General Service Medal 1793–1840, with clasp 8 April Boat Service 1814 (Lt. W.E. Parry); China Medal 1856–60, with clasps Canton 1857 & Taku Forts 1858 (Lt. C. Parry, "Surprise"); and Arctic Medal 1818–55 (Lt. W.E. Parry, H.M.S. *Alexander*, 1818), with miniatures for the first and second (Glendining's, lot 113, April 21, 1971).

30. Holland, pp. 185–86; Parry (1821), pp. 96–97; Savours (1999), p. 210.

31. Parry (1821), p. ii.

32. Riffenburgh, pp. 11–14.

33. Ibid., p. 6.

34. Ibid.

35. The Arctic Medal 1818–55 Roll does not show the issue of Gore's Arctic Medal. Though he was a midshipman onboard HMS *Albion* during the Battle of Navarino, no one claimed his Naval General Service Medal 1793–1840, with Navarino clasp, on his behalf. Gore served on the *Volage* as first lieutenant

from January 1838 to October 1840, at the capture of Bogue Forts and Chusan—actions which did not qualify for the China Medal 1840–42 (Arctic Medal 1818–1855 Roll, NA, ADM 171/9, p. 34; O'Byrne [1849], p. 413; Clowes [vol. 6, 1901], pp. 281–83; Douglas-Morris [1987], p. 240). He was then posted to the *Herald* in Australia, but when he arrived in Sydney, the ship could not be located; however, Gore found the *Beagle*, and sailed in her from November 1840 to October 1843 (Battersby, http://hidden-tracks-book.blogspot.com).

36. Battersby, http://hidden-tracks-book.blogspot.com.

37. Back, pp. 105–08.

38. Ibid., pp. 160–61.

39. Hypothermia, www.wikipedia.org.

40. Back, pp. 407–43.

41. McClure's service details, NMM, MCCLU/1; McClure's service record, NA, ADM 107/62; Clowes (vol. 6), p. 277.

42. Rebellions of 1837, http://en.wikipedia.org.

43. Clowes (vol. 6), p. 277; Williams Sandom, www.biographi.ca. McClure "became the hero of a most daring and successful adventure," being the captor of a rebel named Kelly. Supposedly, McClure was cheated out of the £5,000 reward offered by the British government for Kelly's apprehension, and Captain Sandom showed his appreciation by appointing his lieutenant to "the superintendence of the dock-yard, and subsequently he was placed in command of the Romney receiving-ship at the Havanna." Only the latter part of this story has been confirmed, and the command did not commence until August 1842 ("Captain M'Clure, R.N." [March 1854], p. 345; McClure's service record, NA, ADM 196/1/395).

44. Royal Navy Hulks Overseas, 1800–1976.

45. Ross' Arctic Medal 1818–55, RGS Founder's Gold Medal, and Paris Geographical Society's Gold Medal, are held at SPRI (Yelverton, "Sir James Clark Ross [1800–1862]," p. 235).

46. Ross (1994), p. 248.

47. Ross (1982), p. 254.

48. Beechey, p. 206–07.

49. Church, "John Ericsson, The Engineer—July 31, 1803–March 8, 1889," pp. 336–37; John Ericsson, https://en.wikipedia.org.

50. Ross (1994), pp. 121–29, 140–41, 188–89.

51. Cyriax (1939), pp. 17–18.

52. Neatby (1958), pp. 87–89; Mills (vol. 1, Beaufort Sea [Arctic Ocean]), p. 71.

53. Cyriax (1939), p. 19.

54. Franklin's Naval General Service Medal 1793–1840, with clasps Copenhagen 1801, Trafalgar and 14 December

Boat Service 1814, was sold at auction in 1980 to the Canadian War Museum, and is officially impressed on the edge: SIR JOHN FRANKLIN, LIEUT. R.N. The whereabouts of Franklin's Arctic Medal 1818–55 are unknown, but it was issued, "[signed] Edward Sabine 7/5/57 for Lady Franklin." Edward Sabine (1788–1883) was a Royal Army officer and scientist who participated in three Arctic expeditions between 1818 and 1823. However, displayed in a case with Franklin's medal is another Arctic Medal, privately engraved on the edge: JOHN H. BUCHAN. MIDSHIPMAN. H.M.S. DOROTHEA. Buchan's medal was issued (Sotheby's, November 26, 1980; Stein to Oliver, personal communication, February 6, 2005; Pulsifer to Stein, personal communication, February 7, 2005; Arctic Medal 1818–55 Roll, NA, ADM 171/9, pp. 6, 29).

55. Cyriax (1939), p. 27.

56. Franklin to Barrow (January 24, 1845), Cyriax (1939), p. 24. Franklin had earlier proposed, as a result of tracing the North American coast during 1819–22 and 1825–27, that favorable northwest winds during the navigable season made a Bering Strait attempt by ship a better option than Parry's opinion of an Atlantic approach. "It is also well known, that the coast westward of the Mackenzie is almost unapproachable by ships, and it would therefore, be very desirable to get over that part of the voyage in the first season" (Franklin [1823], p. 388; Franklin [1828], pp. 316–18).

57. Mills (vol. 2), pp. 483–85.

58. Ross stated "King William Island," but at this time was King William Land, believed to be connected to the North American mainland, and remained so until McClintock and his officers completed a circuit of the King William during the *Fox*'s 1857–59 expedition (Ross [1994], p. 280); (*Discoveries in the Arctic Sea by the Squadrons Under the Orders of Capt^n Sir Edw^d Belcher C.B. H.M.S. Assistance, etc.* [1855a]); Arrowsmith, *Map of a Portion of the Arctic Shores of America to Accompany Capt^n Mc Clintock's Narrative* (1859).

59. Ibid., p. 275.

60. Cyriax (1939), p. 25; see Bourne (1855).

61. Cyriax (1939), p. 39–40.

62. The Arctic Medal 1818–55 Roll does not show the issue of Crozier's medal, but it was claimed by Mr. Rawdon Crozier, his great-great-nephew, and presented to him on August 5, 1988 (Arctic Medal 1818–55 Roll, NA, ADM 171/9, p. 15; Poulsom and Myres, p. 150).

63. Fitzjames's medal group sold at auction in 1927. The author has not been able to find any trace of the group after this date, and it may be held by a

private or public institution: Naval General Service Medal 1793–1840 with Syria clasp (Lieutenant/*Ganges*); China Medal 1840–1842 (Lieutenant/*Cornwallis*); Royal Humane Society's silver medal (Midshipman/*Euphrates*/ Liverpool Dock/January 1835; the catalogue description states 1836); Turkish St. Jean d'Acre Medal (silver). It seems likely his agent claimed his Naval General Service Medal while Fitzjames was on the Arctic expedition. The China Medal 1840–1842 was evidently also claimed by an agent, being issued March 6, 1851. The Arctic Medal 1818–55 Roll does not show the issue of this medal (Glendining's, December 20–21, 1927, lot 367; China Medal 1840–42 Roll, NA, ADM 171/12, p. 67; Arctic Medal 1818–55 Roll, NA, ADM 171/9, p. 30).

64. Cyriax (1939), p. 208; Battersby, "The remarkable background of Lt. Graham Gore."

65. Report from the Comptroller of Victualling for Arctic Expeditions, 1845–48 (Cyriax [1939], pp. 41–42 & 64). At the Whalefish Islands, near Disco Island (off Greenland's west coast), Franklin wrote to the Admiralty on July 12, 1845: "the ships are now complete with supplies of every kind for three years" (Franklin to Admiralty [*copy*; July 12, 1845], Great Britain [1848a], p. 50). Franklin was stopped by ice in the upper part of Baffin Bay, and while waiting for it to clear, encountered two whale ships on July 25, *Enterprise* (Captain Martin) and *Prince of Wales* (Captain Dannet). According to "Captain Martin's detailed statement made about *six and half years later, in December 1851* [author's emphasis], his ship was close to the *Erebus* and *Terror* for about a quarter of an hour, and he spoke with Sir John Franklin and with James Reid, the Ice-Master of the *Erebus*. He asked for how long the expedition had been provisioned, and Sir John Franklin answered that he had enough food for five years, and that it could be made to last for seven, adding that he would seize every chance of killing game." A few days afterward, "several of Sir John Franklin's officers visited Captain Martin, and told him that they would probably be away for several years—possibly six." "Captain Martin swore to the truth of his statement, and it was corroborated in all important respects by the affidavit of his second in command." (Cyriax [1939], pp. 64–65); Cyriax (1939), pp. 43–44.

66. Ross (1994), p. 281; Cyriax (1939), pp. 51–53.

67. Cyriax (1939), p. 32; List of ship names of the Royal Navy (I–L), https://en.wikipedia.org.

68. Cyriax (1939), p. 64.

## Chapter 2

1. Beattie and Geiger, image between pp. 52 and 53. Bearing a departed comrade to a grave on a flag-draped sled was a traditional Arctic ceremony.

2. Beattie and Geiger, p. 23. John Hartnell previously served in the frigate *Volage* (September 18, 1841–February 1, 1845), as did his younger brother Thomas (January 1838–May 1841), along with Franklin Expedition members Lieutenant Graham Gore (January 23, 1838–October 28, 1840), and Boy 1st Class John Strickland (1838–41) (*Erebus*'s Muster, NA, ADM 38/672; Lloyd-Jones [2005], pp. 315–16; O'Byrne [1849], p. 413).

3. Beattie and Geiger, p. 23. The Arctic Medal 1818–55 Roll states John Hartnell was discharged dead (DD) on January 4, 1846, but does not show the issue of his medal, even though the medal to his brother Thomas was sent on May 29, 1857. Their descendants are in possession of several documents and letters, including one from the Department of the Accountant General, dated May 1, 1854, which states that John Hartnell "died on the 4th January 1846 in debt to the Crown £117.4.8." Most likely both medals were claimed, but John's was refused on account of his debt. However, an Arctic Medal was issued on January 8, 1986, to John's great-great-nephew, Mr. Donald Bray (Arctic Medal 1818–55 Roll, NA, ADM 171/9, p. 40; Myres [1986], pp. 148–49).

4. Ibid.; *Erebus*'s Muster (1845), NA, ADM 38/672. This was 32-year-old Private William Braine, 8th Company, Woolwich Division, Royal Marines, who died on April 3, 1846.

5. McClure's service record, NA, ADM 107/62.

6. Great Britain (1846), p. 116.

7. McClure's service record, NA, ADM 107/62.

8. Great Britain (1847), pp. 109, 117.

9. Great Havana Hurricane of 1846, www.wikipedia.org.

10. Collins, p. 228.

11. Index to Coast Guard Appointments (No. 1541), NA, ADM 175/98.

12. McGoogan (2005), pp. 276–77.

13. Cyriax (1939), pp. 72–74.

14. Armstrong (1857), p. 285 and fn; Savours (1999), pp. 23, 186.

15. On February 21, 1859, 187 Arctic Medals were sent to the Hudson's Bay Company for distribution. Many men could not be found, so at least 40 medals went unissued, and although they were supposed to have been returned to the Admiralty, this was not done. Rae issued a medal to himself at the Red River Settlement in June 1859 (see Appendix 7) (Arctic Medal 1818–55 Roll, NA, ADM 171/9, p. 125; Poulsom and Myres, pp. 278, 348).

16. Savours (1999), p. 186; McGoogan (2002), pp. 27, 33–39.

17. Inuit, http://en.wikipedia.org; Oxford Dictionaries, http://oxforddictionaries.com; Armstrong (1857); pp. 191–92.

18. McGoogan (2002), pp. 82–92. *Voyageur* is French for "traveler," and such a person was engaged in the transportation of furs by canoe during the fur trade era.

19. Ross (1994), p. 298; Great Britain (1850a), p. 83; Neatby, "Sir Henry Kellett," www.biographi.ca.

20. Cyriax (1939), p. 74; "I am fortunate that the University of Glasgow holds the archives for all Scottish shipbuilding on the River Clyde (1700 onwards) where, as you know, the *Investigator* was built prior to delivery to R&H Green at Blackwall, Woolwich, for final fitting for the ice. I discovered in the correspondence concerning *Investigator* that the original intention was to name her *Sir Edward Parry*, but this was changed to *Investigator* midway through construction. I assume that the change was made on discovering that a British ship was already named *Sir Edward Parry* (it appears to have operated on the route between UK and Australia)." (Millar to Stein, personal communication, May 31, 2015; McClure's service record, NA, ADM 196/1/395).

21. Ross (1994), p. 303.

22. Lewis, pp. 131–93; Douglas-Morris (1990), pp. 271–73.

23. Merchant Seamen Research—General, www.poheritage.com; Properly called a Mariner's Register Ticket, it contained the ticket number, sailor's name, place, county and date of birth, capacity (position), height, complexion, color of hair and eyes, marks or scars on his body, his capacity when he first went to sea and in what year, whether or not he had RN service, whether or not he had been in a foreign service, residence when unemployed, and place and date of issue (Registry of Shipping and Seamen: Register of Seamen's Tickets, NA, BT 113).

24. Douglas-Morris (1991), p. 204.

25. Court's service record, NA, ADM 196/77; ADM 73; *The Arctic Navy List*, p. 12. Up until 1843, Master was also a warrant rank, but then became a commissioned rank (Lewis, p. 139).

26. May's seaman's register ticket no. 304.335, NA, BT 113/153. May's service record, NA, ADM 139/219/21814; *Enterprise*'s Description Book (1848–49), NA, ADM 38/8041; Seamen's Effects, NA, ADM 44/B37. Flynn first went to sea as a boy in 1830. Two of Flynn's shipmates (Quartermaster Thomas Dawe and Boatswain's Mate Henry Mitchell) received Naval Long

Service and Good Conduct Medals (Anchor) in 1847. Still another shipmate, Ordinary/Able Seaman Henry Curtis, was later awarded the Victoria Cross while a boatswain's mate (HMS *Rodney*) in the naval brigade, for combat lifesaving before Sebastopol during the Crimean War (seaman's registry ticket no. 322.402, NA, BT 113/162; Douglas-Morris (1991), p. 60; Curtis's service record, NA, ADM/139/169/16 817; Wilkins, p. 41). Bradbury first went to sea as a boy in 1836 (seaman's registry ticket no. 387.384, NA, BT 113/194).

27. Ross (1994), p. 303.

28. Cresswell's service record, NA, ADM 196/36; Harrod (2000), pp. 21–48; LG, September 29, 1846, no. 20645, p. 3442. A Mention in Dispatches (MID) requires some historical perspective. There was a long tradition of British commanders on land and sea of mentioning subordinates in official dispatches, so that praiseworthy officers were brought to the notice of higher powers. It appears the first enlisted men were mentioned in the early 1840s. "The actual form of mention varied from a mere listing of names to a description of the individual services performed. Where the latter was the basis for an award, or of promotion in rank, it sometimes took the form of what now would be regarded as a citation." A promotion in rank is a "device frequently used in the Royal Navy" (Abbott and Tamplin, p. 296 and fn).

29. Harrod (2000), p. 49; see Cresswell's watercolor sketches of the expedition (Harrod, between pp. 96 and 97).

30. *Investigator*'s Description Book (1848–49), NA, ADM 38/8387; "*March 18th* [1845].—I met Captain Crozier in the Strand, from whom I learnt that Fawcett, one of my boat's crew at Kerguelen's Land, and old Wall of the *Erebus* were both going out with Sir John Franklin" (McCormick, vol. 2, p. 284); *Erebus*'s Musters (1839–43 and 1845), NA, ADM 38/8045 and 38/672 and *Terror*'s Musters (1839–43 and 1845), NA, ADM 38/9162 and 38/1962. Fawcett's anchor tattoo could also have been a Masonic symbol representing hope.

31. *Investigator*'s Description Book (1848–49), NA, ADM 38/8387; *Portrait and Biographical Album of Warren County, Illinois*, p. 571.

32. Carroll's service record, NA, ADM 38/139/37344; *Investigator*'s Description Book (1848–49), NA, ADM 38/8387. Olley was probably the son of George Holley/Holly, AB on Arctic expeditions in the *Griper* (1823) and *Hecla* (1824–25), and nephew of William Holley/Holly, AB on the same voyages (Poulsom and Myres, pp. 200, 262). Some records also show Thomp-

son's surname as "Thomson," but the former spelling is the one most often encountered.

33. HMS *Enterprise* (1848) and HMS *Investigator* (1848), http://en.wikipedia.org; Jones (1971), p. 165; Collinson (1889), p. 35; Armstrong, p. 606 (*Investigator* only); Admiralty plans of *Investigator*, NMM, S.6837; and Allen (1854), pp. 231, 237. After a careful study of these references, the author believes the figures he has quoted in the text are accurate. Builder's Old Measurement (BOM) is the method of calculating the size or cargo capacity of a ship used in England from approximately 1720 to 1849. The BOM estimated the tonnage of a ship based on length and maximum beam.

34. Cyriax (1942), p. 533. The barque rigging can be seen in an 1848 watercolor sketch by Cresswell of the ships under sail off Greenland (Harrod [2000], between pp. 96 and 97), and in W.H. Browne's painting, *The Devil's Thumb, Ships Boring and Warping in the Pack* (NMM, PAD6191).

35. Lavery, pp. 75–80, 157.

36. Bolster, pp. 78–79; Lavery, pp. 133–34, 157–66.

37. Cyriax (1942), p. 533; Armstrong (1857), pp. 606–08; Admiralty plans of HMS *Investigator*, NMM (S.6837).

38. Osborn (1852), pp. 32–3.

39. Armstrong (1857), pp. 606–08. Though this description of strengthening by the Master Shipwright of Woolwich Dockyard in Armstrong's appendix concerns only *Investigator*, it can be assumed that identical work was carried out on *Enterprise*. An anonymous reporter incorrectly described the heating systems of the ships in a November 24, 1849, article in *The Times* as a "hot water apparatus, which was carried round the interior of the ship to keep up such a temperature below as was constant with existence." This description is suggestive of a Perkins high-pressure hot water system for heating (Battersby and Carney, p. 163, 169, 179).

40. McClure (1856), p. 21.

41. Cresswell to parents (May 28, 1848), Harrod, p. 53.

42. McClintock signed for his original Arctic Medal 1818–55 on May 13, 1857, and a duplicate medal was issued December 16, 1891. Group known in the County Museum Dundalk: Knight Commander of the Bath (KCB/military/1891/cased), two full-sized and one miniature Arctic Medals. The full-sized Arctic Medals are privately engraved: LIEUT F L McCLINTOCK HMS ENTERPRISE and F. LEOPOLD McCLINTOCK CAPTAIN R.N.; the latter is believed to be the duplicate issue. A third Arctic to McClintock was sold at auction in 2010 (Dix Noonan Webb,

September 16, 2010, lot 617). (County Museum Dundalk, www.dundalkmuseum.ie; Arctic Medal 1818–55 Roll, NA, ADM 171/9, p. 58.)

43. McClintock's journal, NMM, MCL/9. Of the 69 persons onboard *Enterprise*, the four individuals were: Ross, Surgeon John Robertson, McClure, and Gunner 1st Class Thomas Abernathy (acting as ice master) (Markham [1875], pp. 31–32, 45, 46; Holland [1994], p. 575).

44. Ross (1994), pp. 303–04; Murphy, p. 32; McClintock's journal, NMM, MCL/9.

45. Cyriax (1942), pp. 535–38.

46. Ross (1994), pp. 305–06.

47. Ross (1994), pp. 303–06; Jones (1971), p. 166; McClure to Ross (July 20, 1850), SPRI, MS 1226/18/3.

48. Ibid. (November 30, 1848). Passed Clerk Edward Whitehead was officiating, while the master's assistant was either Robert H. Gransell or William B. Shellabear (Poulsom and Myres, pp. 183, 297, 334).

49. McClintock's journal (November 25, 1848), NMM, MCL/9.

50. *The English Cyclopædia*, pp. 531–32.

51. *Terror's* Muster (1845), NA, ADM 38/9162; Baynham, pp. 57, 62–63.

52. White (1850), p. 95.

53. Jones (1971), pp. 171–75; Cyriax (1942), p. 539. Cresswell Bay was named by Parry during his 1824–25 expedition, so was not after Mate Samuel G. Cresswell. Contemporary sources spell the bay "Cresswell," whereas modern references spell it "Creswell."

54. Ross (1994), p. 310.

55. Taylor (1981), pp. 106, 108.

56. Scurvy—Symptoms, www.nhs.uk.

57. Ross (1994), p. 310; see also McClure's journal (April 29 and May 7, 1850), RGS, SSC/106.

58. Ross (1994), p. 311.

59. Jones (1971), pp. 177–78.

60. Ross (1994), p. 314.

61. ILN, October 13, 1849.

62. Harrod (2000), p. 60. Undated letter written in the autumn of 1849.

63. McGoogan (2005), pp. 283, 289.

64. Jones (1971), p. 168; McClure's service record, NA, ADM 107/62; Ross (1994), pp. 105–06.

65. McClure's service record, NA, ADM 107/62; Lewis (1965), pp. 212–13.

66. Cyriax (1942), p. 540.

67. Ross (1994), pp. 319–23.

68. Cyriax (1942), p. 540; Ross (1994), p. 319.

69. Collinson (1889), p. 34.

70. Lavery, p. 73.

71. Collinson (1889), p. 34. In the supplementary log for the period of fit-

ting out, there is no specific mention of the addition of horizontal yards to the mizzenmast (*Enterprise's* Log [December 14, 1849–January 1, 1850], NA, ADM 55/45, pp. 9–13). However, the images of *Enterprise* by Bedwell (1889) and Adams (c. 1854) clearly show two large yards on her mizzenmast. The former depicts the ship under sail, and the upper gaff is not present.

72. See the images, *First Discovery of Land by H.M.S. Investigator* (September 6, 1850) and *Bold Headland on Baring Island* (September 7, 1850) (Cresswell [1854]).

73. Collinson (1889), p. 36. In his testimony to the Parliamentary Select Committee on July 6, 1855, Collinson also noted, "[O]n examining our coals, we found we were 18 tons short" (Great Britain [1855d], p. 28).

74. Collinson (1889), pp. 447–58; Ross (1994), p. 322.

75. Collinson (1889), pp. 447–93. With Austin's squadron would be a certain Lieutenant Sherard Osborn, on his first Arctic voyage, who later edited McClure's *Investigator* journal for publication.

76. McClure's service details, NMM, MCCLU/1; McClure's service record, NA, ADM 107/62; Lewis, p. 120.

77. McClure's service details, NMM, MCCLU/1; *Sir Robert McClure*, portrait by Stephen Pearce (1855); ILN, November 5, 1853.

78. Barr (2007), pp. 11–12.

79. Skead's journal (January 1850), private collection.

80. Collinson (1889), p. 38.

81. Great Britain (1850a), pp. 82–85; Great Britain (1855d), p. 29.

82. Great Britain (1850a), pp. 82–83.

83. Ibid., p. 83.

84. Ibid., pp. 84–85.

85. Letter & Order Book, RGS, SSC/106; Armstrong's service record, NA, ADM 104/23 (recommendation by explorer-naturalist Sir John Richardson); Collinson (1889), pp. 39–40 and fn.

86. Collinson (1889), p. 377; Ford's diary (March 6 and 12, 1851), KML, 18500119Arctic1xx.

87. Lehane (1981), pp. 146–47; "Captain Austin's Arctic Expedition." ILN (May 11, 1850), p. 333; Collinson (1889), pp. 145, 315; Watt to Stein, personal communications, May 1, 2009; Osborn (1852), pp. 134–36; Barr (2007), p. 90. When Austin's expedition stopped at Disco Island, Greenland, in May 1850, Lieutenant Osborn presented one of the dolls to a youthful seamstress, "who was very busy making shoes for her brothers out of cured skin" (Osborn [1852], p. 23).

88. The following evidence shows both assertions to be false: (a) Privates 3rd Class James Langley and William

Wilson, while aboard HMS *Winchester*, volunteered for the Antarctic expedition of HMS *Pagoda* (1844–45), and received double pay (*Winchester's* Muster (1845), NA, ADM 38/2278); (b) Private William Hull (*Plover*) received double pay when it commenced on May 22, 1848 (attestation form, NA, ADM 157/31 and *Plover's* C,D,O (1847–55), NA, ADM 38/8740); (c) On April 19, 1850, Collinson, "exchanged a bombardier of the Marine Artillery (who it appeared had not volunteered for the expedition) for a corporal of the same corps" (Collinson [1889], p. 51); (d) Corporal 3rd Class John B. Farquharson (*Investigator*) "received the Second Class Gratuity for [Arctic] Service" (attestation form, NA, ADM 157/56); (e) When Captain Scobell, a member of the Select Committee of Parliament, asked McClure: "And the men had double pay?", McClure replied, "They had double pay the whole time" (Great Britain [1855d], p. 17).

89. McClure (1856), pp. xxxiv-xxxv; Collinson (1889), p. 33; Lewis, p. 137.

90. Collinson (1889), p. 35; Neatby (1967), pp. 7–8. Ford and Piers mentioned the mortar (Ford's diary [February 4, 1852], KML, 18500119Arctic1xx; Piers's journal (February 4 and March 18, 1852), NMM, JOD/102).

91. Lavery, pp. 145–46.

92. Neatby (1967), p. 7; Admiralty memoranda, June 12, 1832: "As some doubts appear to exist of the propriety of allowing private Marines to do the duty of officers' servants on board HM Ships, my Lords Commissioners of the Admiralty are pleased to direct that, in addition to the servants of the Officers of the Royal Marines, this indulgence may be carried to the extent, in each rate, of the following numbers, viz.: 1st rates—5 men; 2nd rates—4 men; 3rd and 4th rates—3 men; 5th rates and sloops commanded by commanders—2 men, provided the men do it with their own free will, and that they only attend on the Captain or Officers of the Ward or Gun-room (according to the rate of ship); but their so serving is not in any way to interfere with the necessary attendance at drill, inspection, or exercise of the great guns at quarters" ("Marine Servants to Officers," *The Navy List*, 1835).

93. Woon's attestation papers, NA, ADM 157/40 and 157/1114; Farquharson's attestation papers, NA, ADM 157/35.

94. McClure (1856), pp. xxxiii-xxxiv; Collinson (1889), pp. 30–33; officers' and sailors' service records.

95. *Enterprise* may have had one more person with Arctic experience. The blacksmith was Thomas Bugbee, and a person of the same name was with the 1848 overland search expedition.

Though the latter's position within the expedition was not recorded, it is an unusual name, and the two men may be one and the same (Poulsom and Myres, p. 130); Armstrong's journal (Sick List), NA, ADM 101/250, p. 4.

96. The figure of 39 was arrived at by cross-referencing the records in NA, ADM 29, 38, 104, 107, 139, 157, 158, 188 and 196; Neatby (1967), p. 8.

97. Lavery, pp. 195, 202–03; *Traditional Watch System*, http://en.wikipedia.org.

98. Cresswell to parents (Sunday, January [13], 1850), Harrod, pp. 61–62; www.timeanddate.com.

99. Farmerie to O'Connell, October 14, 2010 (Haswell family, London [Middlesex], http://genforum.genealogy.com/haswell/messages/232.html); Marshall (vol. 4, part 2, p. 359); Haswell's service record, NA, ADM 196/1/548; obituary, *The Annual Register* (1901), p. 101.

100. Haswell's service record, NA, ADM 196/1/548; obituary, *The Annual Register* (1901), p. 101; Mennell, p. 240; "*Sketches from my Life. By the late Hobart Pasha*. London: 1886" (review), ER, January 1887; Sulivan, p. 65; William Loney RN—Victorian naval surgeon, http://home.wxs.nl/~pdavis/Loney.htm.

101. Jacob, pp. 124–26; Kingston, p. 36; Ingram, pp. 33–35.

102. Haswell's service record, NA, ADM 196/1/548; Lloyd, p. 119.

103. Haswell's service record, NA, ADM 196/1/548.

104. Winton, pp. 243–44; Haswell's service record, NA, ADM 196/1/548; McClure to Ross (July 20, 1850), SPRI, MS 1226/18/3.

105. Cresswell to Joseph Cresswell (January 16–17, 1850), Harrod (2000), p. 62; www.timeanddate.com.

106. Cresswell to parents (January 18, 1850), Harrod (2000), p. 63.

107. Farmerie to Stein, personal communication, August 10, 2013 (Dr. Todd Farmerie, Haswell family genealogist).

108. Cresswell to parents (January, 18, 1850), Harrod (2000), p. 63. Pay clerks had come onboard January 11 and the crew were paid a six-month advance (McClure, Supplementary Log of HMS *Investigator* [January 11, 1850], NA, ADM 55/80, p. 164). The boatswain ran on January 18, but *Investigator's* Musters show different dates of desertion for two of the three sailors (*Investigator's* Musters [1849–50], NA, ADM 38/1026).

109. Lewis, p. 150.

110. Cresswell to parents (January, 19, 1850), Harrod (2000), p. 64.

111. Ibid. (January 20, 1850), Harrod (2000), p. 65; Neatby (1967), p. 8.; Armstrong (1858), p. 14.

112. Lewis, p. 267–68.

113. McClure (1856), fn, p. 67.

114. Collinson (1889), p. 38.

115. Neatby (1967), p. 5.

116. Benham, p. 6.

117. Moravian Church, www.wikipedia.org.

118. Benham, pp. 2–6; Church book, Gröditz, Baruth Parish, Upper Lusatia.

119. Okak Diary, northern Labrador (R 15 kb 5e, MAH); Inuktitut, www.wikipedia.org.

120. Great Britain (1850a), pp. 83–89—Collinson' Admiralty orders were dated January 15 (the day La Trobe's letter was received by Hamilton), and included directions to procure "if possible the necessary Esquimaux interpreters" while in the Sandwich Islands (Hawaii). It therefore appears their Lordships were unsure of Miertsching's timely arrival, and/or wanted Collinson to have, if possible, an additional interpreter (i.e., one for each ship); Miertsching (1861), p. 65; UAC Protocol, 1850 (MAH); Neatby, p. 7. It's not without interest that Captain John Washington, RN, compiled the *Eskimaux and English Vocabulary, For the Use of the Arctic Expeditions*, which was published by order of the Admiralty in early 1850. This was followed up the supplemental *Greenland-Eskimo Vocabulary, For the Use of the Arctic Expeditions* in 1853.

121. Inuktitut, www.wikipedia.org; Inuvialuktun, www.wikipedia.org; Neatby (1967), pp. 42, 45, 56, 58, 61, 63, 115.

122. Neatby (1967), pp. 5–6; Benham writes that, on a London stopover, Miertsching "was liberally supplied with everything necessary for his outfit," and then he proceeded to Plymouth (Benham, p. 7).

123. Neatby (1967), p. 6; McClure (1856), p. 22.

124. Neatby (1967), pp. 6–8, 34, 44. It appears La Trobe was misinformed about Miertsching's grasp of the English language, since in writing to the Secretary of the Admiralty, he indicated, "I am instructed to further inform their Lordships, that Mr. Miertsching, who is not unacquainted with the English language" (La Trobe to Hamilton [January 14, 1850], Great Britain [1850a], pp. 86–87); Farquharson's attestation papers, NA, ADM 157/35).

125. Neatby (1967), p. 6.

126. Neatby (1967), p. 6.

## Chapter 3

1. Collinson (1889), p. 38; McClure's journal (January 24, 1850), RGS, SSC/106; Lieutenant Cresswell was officer of the watch at the time of this

incident (McClure to The Senior Officer of HM Ships & Vessels at the Sandwich Islands [June 24, 1850], Letter & Order Book, RGS, SCC/106).

2. Collinson (1889), p. 38. In fact, Collinson later testified before the Parliamentary Select Committee that "until we [*Enterprise*] arrived at the ice I thought it more likely we should make a quicker passage, as one vessel might have the advantage in sailing in light winds [*Investigator*], and the other in strong winds" (Great Britain [1855d], p. 29).

3. Nelson (vol. 1, January 20, 1850 and following), SPRI, MS 748/1.

4. Seaman's register ticket no. 367.708, NA, BT 113/184; certificate of service, SPRI, MS 748/3; Paine's service record, NA, ADM ADM 196/11; Nelson (1967), p. 753; Index of 19th Century Naval Vessels and a few of their movements, http://freepages.genealogy.rootsweb.ancestry.com; O'Byrne (1849), pp. 256–57; Armstrong (1857), pp. 549–50, fn. A reference to Nelson's application to join *Investigator* is preserved in the records. Clerk in Charge Joseph Paine wrote to a Lieutenant Keary (HMS *Clyde*, in Ordinary at Sheerness): "I am desired by Commander McClure to acknowledge the receipt of your letter of the 28th Inst respecting, James Nelson (AB) who has volunteered for this Ship and to inform you that a vacancy will be kept open for this man provided he passes a very strict examination before a Doctor which it is necessary for every one to do before he is shipped for this expedition, and also that he presents himself here as soon as possible" (Letter & Order Book [December 30–31, 1849], RGS, SCC/106).

5. Piers's journal (January 24, 1850), NMM, JOD/102. The words "and perhaps a laugh" are struck through, so maybe Piers did not wish to raise the eyebrows of superiors at a later date; RootsWeb.com, www.rootsweb.ancestry.com; Obituary. "Henry Piers, M.R.C.S. ENG., L.S.A., Deputy Inspector-General of Hospitals and Fleets (Retired)" (December 14, 1901), p. 1706; Piers's service record, NA, ADM 104/29; Lloyd (1949), pp. 221–23.

6. McClure's journal (January 24, 1850), RGS, SSC/106.

7. Neatby (1967), p. 9.

8. Neatby (1967), p. 9; Armstrong, p. 5.

9. McClure's journal (January 25, 1850), RGS, SSC/106; Ford's diary (January 25, 1850 and following), KML, 18500119Arctic1xx.

10. McClure's journal (January 25, 1850), RGS, SSC/106; Neatby (1967), p. 9.

11. McClure's journal (January 24–28, 1850), RGS, SSC/106.

12. Piers's journal (January 31, 1850), NMM, MS 67/013.

13. Neatby (1967), p. 9; Nelson (vol. 1, May 2, 1853), SPRI, MS 748/1; *Investigator*'s Musters (1849–50), NA, ADM 38/1026; Biggs's attestation form, NA, ADM 157/945. Piers identifies Biggs as McClure's steward on August 29, 1851. The official rating of musician was introduced in the RN in 1842 (Proctor, p. 37). The *Enterprise*'s fiddler can be tentatively identified as Able Seaman John E. Davidson, whose fiddle was stored in a depot on the Princess Royal Islands, and while there, broken by a bear who took a fancy to it (Collinson [1889], pp. 200–01). Other Arctic fiddlers include William Simmonds, a musician on the *Assistance* until April 28, 1850 (then becoming a ship's cook), and on the same ship, Gunroom Steward James Gore was rated a musician on July 1, 1850 (Douglas-Morris [1991], p. 273; Poulsom and Myres, p. 66).

14. Lavery, pp. 208–09; Navy Song, "Working Song," http://myweb.tiscali.co.uk; Proctor, pp. 65–66.

15. "Good News for the Navy" (July–December 1861), p. 236. A common nickname for a sailor was Jack Tar, or simply tar.

16. Piers's journal (February 1, 1850), NMM, JOD/102; Armstrong (1857), p. 5.

17. Armstrong (1857), pp. 5–6; Neatby (1967), pp. 9–10.

18. Armstrong (1857), p. 6; McClure's journal (February 23, 1850), RGS, SSC/106; *Enterprise*'s Description Book (1848–49), NA, ADM 38/8041; Haswell's service record, NA, ADM 104/23.

19. Neatby (1967), p. 10.

20. Ibid., pp. 10–11.

21. Ibid., p. 11.

22. Piers's journal (February 10, 1850), NMM, JOD/102; Campbell (Part 3, Appendix 6), pp. 163–69).

23. Armstrong's service record, NA, ADM 104/23; Neatby, Leslie H., "Sir Alexander Armstrong," www.biographi.ca.

24. Armstrong's service record, NA, ADM 104/23; Urban, "The Xanthian Expedition," p. 191; Vaux, pp. 143–63.

25. Armstrong's service record, NA, ADM 104/23.

26. Ibid., Irish Potato Famine, www.historyplace.com.

27. Armstrong's service record, NA, ADM 104/23. He is also stated as being "appointed as surgeon and naturalist to the *Investigator*" in the following: Armstrong (1857), title page; Lee (vol. 22, Supplement, 1909), p. 61.

28. "Obituary. Sir Alexander Armstrong, KCB, RN, FRS, Sometime Director-General of the Royal Navy Medical Department" (July 15, 1899), p. 181.

29. Armstrong (1857), pp. 6–7

30. Millar to Stein, personal communication, May 31, 2015, in reference to Millar, Bowman, Battersby and Welbury (submitted for publication 2015).

31. Neatby (1967), p. 11.

32. Nelson (vol. 1, February 1852), SPRI, MS 748/1; Armstrong (1857), pp. 9–12; Piers's journal (February 19, 20, 26, 1850), NMM, JOD/102.

33. McClure's journal (February 25, 1850), RGS, SSC/106.

34. Ibid. (February 23, 1850).

35. Neatby (1967), pp. 11–12; Piers's journal (March 6, 1850), NMM, JOD/102—comments in reference to dinner with the captain on February 28.

36. Armstrong (1857), pp. 12–13.

37. Armstrong (1857), p. 500, fn; *Snake*'s Description Book (1846–48), NA, ADM 58/9047.

38. Armstrong (1857), p. 500, fn; Neatby (1967), p. 15. The Confederation of Canada did not come in existence until 1867, with Ontario being one of the original four provinces to enter the union (Canadian Confederation, http://en.wikipedia.org).

39. Myres (1996), pp. 70–71.

40. Crispus Attucks, www.africawithin.com; Bolster, p. 102.

41. "A Kings County Hero" (September 14, 1938), p. 4; Melville, p. 2.

42. "Hulott," as spelled in the *Investigator*'s Muster, Armstrong (1857), McClure (1856) and the 1861 Census. However, he is shown as "Cornelius Hewlett/Hulett/Hullett/Hullott," "George Hullott," "James Hullott," and "James Cornelius Hulott" in various other musters and description books on ships in which he served, the *Investigator*'s sick list, and court-martial, census records, etc. "In keeping with African Americans' theatrical tastes, a black West Indian named James Hewlett opened the African Grove Theater on the corner of Bleeker and Grove Streets in New York City shortly after the War of 1812. Hewlett led his repertoire company in several Shakespearean productions, dominated by *Richard III*, until white hoodlums wrecked the theater" (Bolster, p. 121).

43. Neatby (1967), p. 113; *Snake*'s Description Book (1846–48), NA, ADM 58/9047; Hulott's service record, NA, ADM 29/52; Piers's journal (May 5, 1851), NMM, JOD/102. The author spoke to a Robert Hulott (of Bexley, Kent) on February 14, 2010, who said he was probably related to Cornelius Hulott, as his family roots go back to the Isle of Sheppey. On the same day, Robert's brother, Colin Hulott, wrote in a Facebook message to the author that the family name is quite unusual, the spelling being exact, and during the 19th century this surname related to only a limited number of families in Kent and the Midlands.

44. Pineau, p. 98.

45. Letter & Order Book and McClure's journal (March 4, 1850), RGS, SSC/106.

46. Ford's diary (March 22, 1850), KML, 18500119Arctic1xx.

47. remedianetwork, "Specimen: Memento Mori."

48. Ford's diary (March 5, 1850), KML, 18500119Arctic1xx.

49. Line-crossing ceremony, http://en.wikipedia.org.

50. McClure's journal (March 6, 1850), RGS, SSC/106; Brazilian brig *Atalante*—Piers's journal (March 6, 1850), NMM, JOD/102.

51. Neatby (1967), p. 13.

52. Ibid.; Piers's journal (February 26, 1850), NMM, JOD/102.

53. McClure's journal (March 10, 1850), RGS, SSC/106; Neatby (1967), p. 14.

54. Neatby (1967), pp. 14–15.

55. Brown manuscript, GM, M-141, p. 9; *Calypso*'s Description Book (1845–49), NA, ADM 38/7736; Pitcairn Island Encyclopedia, http://library.puc.edu/pitcairn. Teraura passed away on July 15, 1850; Brown again sailed aboard the *Calypso* to Pitcairn Island in 1860 (Brown manuscript, GM, M-141, pp. 2, 20).

56. Collinson (1889), pp. 38, 48.

57. Piers's journal (March 31, 1850), NMM, JOD/102; Ford's, diary (April 2, 5, 6, 1850), KML, 18500119Arctic1xx; Armstrong (1857), p. 18–19. Armstrong identifies the whales as *Physeter macrocephalus* (sperm whale), but the "huge cawdal [dorsal] fin" leads one to believe they were high-finned sperm whales, the existence of which are still unconfirmed by science.

58. Piers's journal (May 1 and June 1, 1851), NMM, JOD/102—"our steward—a strong, wiry fellow," and afterward, "Sugden, our steward"; Sugden is shown as the subordinate officers' steward (i.e., steward for the warrant officers—boatswain, carpenter and ice mate) on his service record and in the crew list in McClure's book, but as the officers' [gunroom] cook in the crew list in Armstrong's book. Ford and Piers's writings suggest Anderson took over Sugden's cooking chores at some point, and Nelson wrote that Anderson cooked for the warrant officers as well. George Milner was rated the gunroom steward, but requirements onboard no doubt resulted in a fair bit of changeability in the domestic department (Sugden's service record, NA, ADM 29/73 and 188/9/42634; McClure [1856], p. xxxiv; Armstrong [1857], Introduction; Ford's diary [February 4, 1852], KML, 18500119Arctic1xx; Piers's journal [February 4, 1852], NMM, JOD/102; Nelson [vol. 1, February 1852], SPRI, MS 748/1). On Sugden's service record, McClure marked his

conduct as only "Fair" for *Investigator* (January 11, 1850–June 4, 1853); McClure's journal (April, 8, 1850), RGS, SSC/106; Piers's journal (April 8, 1850), NMM, JOD/102; Neatby (1967), p. 16, Miertsching wrote April 6.

59. The Royal Navy & Marine Customs and Traditions, www.hmsrichmond.org & Winton, pp. 68–70.

60. McClure wrote from the Straits of Magellan, "I have the honor to report to you for the information of my L.C.A. [Lords Commissioners of the Admiralty] that HM's Ship under my command passed to the Westward of the Longitude of Cape Horn on Sunday last the 14$\underline{\text{th}}$ Inst. from which date we are entitled to Double Pay agreeably with their Lordships order" (McClure to the Secretary of the Admiralty and the Accountant General [April 18, 1850], Letter & Order Book, RGS, SCC/106).

61. Armstrong (1857), pp. 21–22.

62. Gorgon, https://en.wikipedia.org; Collinson (1889), pp. 44–54; Armstrong (1857), pp. 23–24.

63. Collinson to Admiralty (April 10, 1850), Great Britain, Parliament, *Papers relating to the Arctic Relief Expeditions* (1851a), p. 5.

64. Collinson (1889), p. 44.

65. Piers's journal (April 17, 1850) NMM, JOD/102; Armstrong (1857), pp. 26–28.

66. Skead's transcribed journal, private collection, April 1850.

67. Armstrong (1857), pp. 27–29.

68. Ibid., pp. 29–31.

69. On April 18, Captain of the Hold George Long, Able Seaman Henry Long—who were probably brothers, as both came from Mistley, Essex, and were about three years apart in age—and Ship's Cook Thomas Playfair, were all invalided to the *Gorgon* for passage back to England. George Long was discharged dead from HMS *Asia* on July 15, having died at the naval hospital, Valparaiso. On the same day, Able Seaman James Williams was promoted to captain of the hold, and Quartermaster Isaac Stubberfield was made the ship's cook (*Gorgon*'s Description Book [1848–1852], NA, ADM 38/8198; *Prometheus*'s Description Book [1844–47], NA, ADM 38/8783; McClure's journal [April 19, 1850], RGS, SSC/106; Collinson [1889], p. 51; Hornby's Journal, NA, ADM 50/253, p. 625; *Investigator*'s Musters [1849–50], NA, ADM 38/1026).

70. Neatby (1967), p. 18.

71. Armstrong (1857), p. 34; McClure's journal (April, 19 1850), RGS, SSC/106; Collinson (1889), p. 51; Kennedy's service record, NA, ADM 29/23/486.

72. Armstrong (1857), pp. 34–35.

73. Armstrong (1857), p. 35; Piers's journal (April 20, 1850), NMM,

JOD/102. Later on, McClure gave a rare nod to steam when he wrote to James Ross, "Without the aid of steam we might have remained [in the Strait] until this time" (McClure to Ross [July 20, 1850], SPRI, MS 1126/18/3).

74. McClure's journal (April 25, 1850), RGS, SSC/106.

75. Ibid. (April 29, 1850).

76. Ibid. (May 7, 1850).

77. Cyriax (1939), pp. 109–12. The quality of the provisions supplied to the Franklin Expedition, and their possible adverse affects on Franklin and his men, have been the subject of a long and ongoing debate among historians.

78. Armstrong (1858), p. 13.

79. Armstrong's journal, NA, ADM 101/250, p. 70.

80. Armstrong's journal (sick list), NA, ADM 101/250, p. 3.

81. Nelson (vol. 1, April 29, 1850), SPRI, MS 748/1.

82. Ibid. (vol. 1, May 15, 1850 and following); Armstrong (1857), p. 42.

83. Neatby (1967), pp. 20–21.

84. McClure's journal (May 8 and12, 1850), RGS, SSC/106.

85. Piers's journal (April 30, 1850) NMM, JOD/102.

86. Neatby (1967), p. 21; Armstrong (1857), p. 38.

87. Neatby (1967), p. 22.

88. Ibid.

89. Armstrong (1857), p. 39.

90. Ibid., pp. 39–40; Ford's diary (May 15, 1850), KML, 18500119Arctic1xx.

91. Neatby (1967), p. 22.

92. Ibid.

93. McClure's journal (May 15, 1850), RGS, SSC/106.

94. Armstrong (1857), p. 40.

95. McClure to Haswell (May 15, 1850), Letter & Order Book, RGS, SCC/106.

96. Ford's diary (May 16, 1850), KML, 18500119Arctic1xx & McClure's journal (May 16, 1850), RGS, SCC/106.

97. McClure's journal (May 16, 1850), RGS, SCC/106.

98. Haswell to McClure (May 16, 1850), Letter & Order Book, RGS, SCC/106.

99. Ibid.

100. Ibid.

101. Ibid. Cresswell was in charge of the deck during the accident of January 24 (McClure to The Senior Officer of HM Ships & Vessels at the Sandwich Islands [June 24, 1850], Letter & Order Book, RGS, SCC/106).

102. Haswell to McClure (May 16, 1850), Letter & Order Book, RGS, SCC/106.

103. Neatby (1967), p. 22. Although Miertching's entry is dated May 16, the inquiry was evidently held the following day, after which Haswell was arrested.

104. "Investigation gone into"

(undated, but assumed to be May 17, 1850), Letter & Order Book, RGS, SCC/106; Bluff's service record, NA, ADM 139/271/27023. Seamen gunners were allowed 20% of the time served in this position to count as "bonus time" toward their pensions. (Douglas-Morris [1987], p. 453). Bluff served with the following Franklin Expedition officers on the *Excellent*: Lieutenant James Walter Fairholme (*Erebus*), Lieutenant George Henry Hodgson (*Terror*), Lieutenant John Irving (*Terror*), Mate Robert Orme Sargent (*Erebus*), and Mate Charles Frederick Des Vœux (*Erebus*) (O'Byrne [1849]), pp. 282, 345, 525, 569; *Erebus*'s Muster (1845), NA, ADM 38/672).

105. "Investigation gone into" (undated, but assumed to be May 17, 1850), Letter & Order Book, RGS, SCC/106.

106. Ibid.

107. Ibid.

108. Ibid.

109. Ibid.

110. Great Britain (1851a), pp. 5–6; Barr (2007), p. 20.

111. Neatby (1967), p. 22. It is worth keeping in mind that up until the first days of April 1853, Miertsching had to recreate his journal from his memory, with the aid of notes and McClure's journal (see Appendix 1).

112. McClure's journal (May 17, 1850), RGS, SCC/106; Admiralty lower deck plans of HMS *Investigator*, NMM, S.6837. On June 6, Kennedy and Ford "took possession of our mess berth: that was kindly given to us by our Captain" (Ford's diary [June 6, 1850], KML, 18500119Arctic1xx). "Placed Lieut Haswell under an arrest (as prisoner at large) for making improper remarks upon the conduct of his commanding officer in a letter addressed to him detailing the loss of spars upon the morning of the 15th Inst. RMc" (*Investigator*'s Log [May 17, 1850], NA, ADM 55/80, p. 194).

113. McClure to Collinson (April 20, 1850), Letter & Order Book, RGS, SCC/106—McClure was also displeased when his officers again raised the subject of the gunroom alterations after his announced plan, having presented their feelings to him through the writings of Assistant Surgeon Piers, a junior officer.

114. McClure to Ross (April [no day written] 1853), NA, BJ2/10.

115. McClure to the Secretary of the Admiralty (May 22, 1850), Letter & Order Book, RGS, SCC/106.

116. McClure to Admiralty (May 22, 1850), Letter & Order Book, RGS, SCC/106.

117. Neatby (1967), p. 23.

118. Ibid.

119. Ibid.

120. McClure's journal (May 19 and 23, June 4, 5, 10, 14, 22, 1850), RGS, SSC/106.

121. Ibid. (May 28, 1850); Armstrong states "no less a quantity than 986 lbs. was condemned as unfit for use, and thrown overboard" (Armstrong [1857], p. 43).

122. McClure's journal (May 31, 1850), RGS, SSC/106. It would appear McClure had taken a shine to Tiffeny, since while in the Magellan Straits, he wrote to the Admiralty that Able Seaman Tiffeny had left his Register Ticket and Certificate onboard HMS *Indefatigable* (Captain Smart), and "I have the honor to request that you will be pleased to move my L.C.A. [Lord Commissioners of the Admiralty] to take such measures to obtain them that their Loss may not be to his prejudice, as I had obtained permission from Captain Smart to enter him" (McClure to the Secretary of the Admiralty [April 17, 1850], Letter & Order Book, RGS, SSC/106).

123. McClure's journal (May 31, 1850), RGS, SSC/106.

124. McClure's journal (June 9, 1850), RGS, SSC/106.

125. Ibid. (June 2, 1850).

126. Armstrong (1857), p. 45. McClure states the longest run yet accomplished was on June 24 (McClure [1856], p. 33).

## Chapter 4

1. Neatby (1967), p. 24.

2. McClure's journal (June 12, 1850), RGS, SSC/106.

3. Ibid. (June 11, 1850).

4. Ibid. (June 13, 1850).

5. Ibid. (June 14, 1850). Just over a week later, "a couple of Goldner's [2-lb.] cases of Beef, and [a 6-lb. case of] Roast Mutton condemned" (McClure's journal [June 22, 1850], RGS, SSC/106; McClure, Supplementary Log of HMS *Investigator* [December 17, 1849–June 30, 1850], NA, ADM 55/80).

6. Studding sails, Ford's diary (June 15, 1850), KML, 18500119Arctic1xx; Neatby (1967), p. 25.

7. Piers's journal (June 15, 1850), NMM, JOD/102. Court was suffering from dyspepsia (indigestion), Armstrong's journal (sick list), NA, ADM 101/250, p. 4.

8. Neatby, p. 25. McClure's journal (June 29, 1850), RGS, SSC/106; McClure (1856), p. 33; Armstrong (1857), p. 47.

9. Armstrong (1857), p. 49. Also see Wyllie to Barclay (June 27, 1850), Great Britain (1851a), p. 7.

10. Collinson (1889), p. 57.

11. Ibid., p. 26.

12. Armstrong (1857), p. 48; Mc-

Clure to the Senior Officer of HM Ships & Vessels at Wahou (July 1, 1850), Letter & Order Book, RGS, SSC/106; Court's service record, NA, ADM 196/77; McClure to Ross (July 27, 1850), SPRI, MS 1226/18/3. McClure wrote to Rear Admiral Hornby, Commander-in-Chief of the Pacific Station, publicly expressing his thanks to Aldham (McClure to Hornby [July 4, 1850], Letter & Order Book, RGS, SSC/106). McClure forwarded the meteorological observations of January 20–June 30 to the Hydrographic Department, Court having taken the azimuths and summed up the meteorological observations. McClure favorably mentioned Court, "whose readiness at all times to make himself useful is most gratifying, and I sincerely hope that you will bring the same under the Notice of their Lordships" (McClure to the Secretary of the Admiralty [July 3, 1850], Letter & Order Book, RGS, SSC/106).

13. Great Britain (1855d), p. 29. There is some geographical confusion here. At Honolulu, Captain Kellett left Collinson charts and sailing directions for safe passage through the "Straits of Seguan [Seguam Pass] (Amouchta)" in a private letter dated May 20, 1850, but Seguam Pass is between Seguam and Amlia Islands, whereas Amukta Pass is between Seguam and Amukta Islands (Skead referred to it as the "Amouchta Channel"). Armstrong wrote that Amila Island was sighted on July 20 off the port bow, distant about 10 miles; consequently the impression is that *Investigator* sailed through the Seguam Pass (Collinson [1889], pp. 54–55; Seguam Pass, https://en.wikipedia.org; Amukta Pass, https://en.wikipedia.org; Skead's transcribed journal [June-July 1850], private collection; Armstrong [1857], p. 66).

14. Great Britain (1851a), p. 10. McClure told Miertsching he would remain on *Investigator* until she reached the Bering Strait (Neatby [1967], p. 28).

15. Armstrong (1857), p. 59.

16. Ibid.; McClure (1856), pp. 36–37; Collinson (1889), p. 25.

17. Piers's journal (July 1, 1850), NMM, JOD/102.

18. Nelson (vol. 1, July 2, 1850), SPRI, MS 748/1.

19. McClure to Ross (July 20, 1850), SPRI, MS 1226/18/3. Ford also referenced this in his diary: "After breakfast I went on shore to select some spars to make masts & yards that we were deficient through our accidents" (Ford's diary [July 2, 1850], KML, 18500119Arctic1xx).

20. Piers's journal (July 2, 1850), NMM, JOD/102.

21. Barr (2007), p. 24. Dr. Armstrong mentions Wyllie in his writings (Armstrong [1857], p. 51); details

related to Rae's letter are in Rae to Secretary of the Admiralty, September 1, 1849 (Great Britain [1851a], pp. 45–50), and McClure wrote in an official dispatch, "I certainly should have considered it my duty to endeavour deciding this point by detaching a boat through the Dolphin and Union Straits; but I feel assured that service has been accomplished by Dr. Rae last year, as he evidently was not in this direction" (McClure [1854a], p. 41); McGoogan (2001), p. 114; McClure (1856), p. 185.

22. Armstrong (1857), p. 59; HMS *Cockatrice* was the tender to HMS *Asia*, the second rate ship-of-the-line *Asia* in Valparaiso harbor, which flew the flag of Rear Admiral Sir Phipps Hornby, Commander-in-Chief of the Pacific Station, 1847–51 (Late 18th, 19th and early 20th Century Naval and Naval Social History Index, www.pbenyon. plus.com/Naval.html; Egerton, pp. 27, 36).

23. Neatby (1967), p. 28.

24. Ford's diary (July 3, 1850), KML, 18500119Arctic1xx.

25. The official and unofficial sources conflict as to the arrivals and departures of these men; *Amphitrite*'s Log (February 12–September 27, 1849), NA, ADM 53/2094; Armstrong's journal (sick list), NA, ADM 101/250; Armstrong (1857), p. 64; *Asia* Muster & Description Book and *Cockatrice*'s Muster (tender to *Asia*) (1850), NA, ADM 38/2531; Bow's attestation form, NA, ADM 157/56; Ford's diary (July 4, 1850), KML, 18500119Arctic1xx; *Investigator*'s Letter & Order Book (July 2, 1850), RGS, SSC/106; *Investigator*'s Musters (1849–50), NA, ADM 38/1026; Jackson's service record, NA, ADM 139/425/2430A; Piers's journal (July 3 & 4, 1850), NMM, JOD/102; *Swift* C,D,O (1849–53), NA, ADM 38/9133. There are several men with the name John Boyle in the Board of Trade records, but only two named Thomas Toy, both of whom were born in Dublin, and holding ticket numbers 20.010 and 375.319 (Registry of Shipping and Seamen: Alphabetical Index to Registers of Seamen's Tickets, NA, BT 114).

26. McClure to the Senior Officer of HM Ships & Vessels at the Sandwich Islands (May 27, 1850), Letter & Order Book, RGS, SSC/106.

27. Ibid., May 29, 1850.

28. Ibid., June 24, 1850 (1).

29. Ibid., June 24, 1850 (2).

30. Ibid., July 3, 1850.

31. Egerton, pp. 27, 36; in-letters and papers from Admirals (ADM 1/5602), letters from Admirals Pacific (1/5609), and Promiscuous (1/5606), and Rear Admiral Hornby's journal (ADM 50/253); Armstrong (1857), p. 62.

32. Neatby (1967), p. 30.

33. Armstrong (1857), p. 62. This

contradicts what McClure wrote to the Admiralty on July 20, 1850: "It gives me great pleasure to say that the good effects of the fruit and vegetables (a large quantity of which we took on board at Oahu) are very perceptible" (McClure [1856], p. 46).

34. Neatby (1967), pp. 32–33.

35. Ibid., p. 33–34; Samuel C. Damon, https://en.wikipedia.org.

36. Neatby (1967), p. 34.

37. McClure to Paine (July 15, 1850), Letter & Order Book, RGS, SSC/106.

38. Neatby (1967), p. 34.

39. Armstrong (1857), p. 66.

40. Collinson (1889), pp. 26.

41. Dickerson (1992), p. 17; Ross (1994), p. 306.

42. McClure (1856), pp. 42–47; Great Britain (1851a), pp. 12–13. Both of these are *copies* of the letter McClure sent to the Admiralty.

43. Neatby (1967), p. 35.

44. Ibid.

45. Armstrong (1857), p. 69.

46. McClure to Ross (July 27, 1850), SPRI, MS 126/18/3; Great Britain (1855d), p. 29; McClure (1856), p. 36; McClure was wrong when he wrote that Haswell "served all his time in the Penelope & positively is as ignorant of sails and their utility as if he had never seen them." Between 1838 and 1846, Haswell served as a midshipman/mate/acting lieutenant/lieutenant onboard seven sailing vessels, before joining the *Devastation* (steam) in 1846, and then *Penelope* (steam) in 1847 (Haswell's service record, NA, ADM 196/1/548).

47. McClure to Cresswell (copy; July 28, 1850), NMM, BGR15.

48. McClure to Secretary of the Admiralty (July 28, 1850), "off Kotzebue Sound" and "sent Per Plover 29$^{th}$ July 1850," Letter & Order Book, RGS, SSC/106.

49. Ibid.

50. Armstrong (1857), pp. 69–70.

## *Chapter 5*

1. Armstrong (1857), p. 70; Brown manuscript, GM, M-141, p. 11. In a memo to Paine, McClure notes: "There are no Mittens amongst the Presents of Warm Clothing supplied for the Crew," and has two pairs issued to each man, having them charged against the slop account (McClure to Paine [July 29, 1850], Letter & Order Book, RGS, SSC/106. The cold weather clothes supplied to Collinson's command were surely identical, but his opinion of them differed sharply: he stated they were "not very satisfactory; not good enough material, and badly made" (Collinson [1889], p. 38 fn).

2. Ibid., p. 71; McClure (1856), p.

48; Ford's diary (July 31, 1850), KML, 18500119Arctic1xx; Brown manuscript, GM, M-141, p. 10; Neatby (1967), p. 145.

3. Letter & Order Book (July 29, 1850), RGS, SSC/106.

4. Ibid.; Armstrong (1857), p. 86; Neatby (1967), p. 36; Farmerie to Stein, personal communication, August 10, 2013; Pullen, "William John Samuel Pullen," www.biographi.ca; McClure (1856), pp. 40–41.

5. Nelson (vol. 1, July 30, 1850), SPRI, MS 748/1.

6. Neatby (1967), p. 36. The words "she dwells in his cabin" are not present in the 1855 German edition of Miertsching's journal (M. Opel to Stein, personal communication, August 12, 2010). Although not included in the roll for the Arctic Medal 1818–55, Mary Natalia was the only woman ever entitled to this honor. Two others were taken onboard *Plover* as interpreters: Taleshuk Nekeevar/Nakevar was probably an Eskimo, and joined the ship at Michaelovski the same day as Natalia (April 7, 1850), and left at Gariska on March 3, 1851, "claimed by the Russian authorities." He also served on *Enterprise* (evidently in the same capacity), from September 14 to October 4, 1850. Parvieul/Paviral Oclayook/Oclagook joined the ship as an interpreter at Petropavlovsk on June 24, 1849, and was landed (sick) at Michaelovski, on April 6, 1850. Neither was included on the medal roll and they were not issued Arctic Medals (Poulsom and Myres, pp. 258, 261).

7. Neatby (1967), pp. 36–37.

8. Bockstoce (vol. 1), p. 2.

9. Brown manuscript, GM, M-141, p. 10; Sir Henry Kellett, www. biographi.ca; Nelson (vol. 1, July 31, 1850), SPRI, MS 748/1–2; Armstrong (1857), pp. 72–73; Urban (July 1860), p. 97; Poulsom and Myres, pp. 51, 53. On September 21, 1851, Pim wrote to the Admiralty, and proposed mounting an overland search for Franklin along the northeastern shores of Siberia. "It is particularly ironic, in view of Pim's prediction in his first letter to the Admiralty (27 September 1851), that the expeditions then in the field (including McClure's) 'can only follow in the path and consequently incur a similar risk as Sir John Franklin' (Great Britain, 1852), that the following spring [of 1853] Pim played a key role in averting what came very close to a second major disaster" (Barr [1992], pp. 37, 44–45).

10. McClure (1856), p. 55.

11. Armstrong (1857), pp. 73–74.

12. Ibid.

13. Armstrong to Richardson (August 22, 1850), SPRI, MS 1503/42/3. This letter was written off the Mackenzie River, and addressed to

Richardson as the "Medical Inspector/Haslar Hospital/Gosport." The letter was given to the Inuit to pass along to an HBC outpost, but its delivery was delayed for over 12 years, as the envelope carries the following notation: "Received 13 May 1863 through the Officer in charge of Fort Anderson on the Beghulatessy who got it from the Eskimos."

14. Ford's diary (August 2, 1850), KML, 18500119Arctic1xx.

15. Piers's journal (July 31, 1850), NMM, JOD/102.

16. Cresswell to parents (August 21, 1850), Harrod, p. 67.

17. *Herald*'s Description Book (1845–1851), NA, ADM 38/8269.

18. Armstrong (1857), pp. 75–77.

19. Haswell's service record, NA, ADM 196/1/548; see Haswell Point (Appendix 6).

20. McClure (1854a), p. 57; Nelson (vol. 1, August 2, 1850), SPRI, MS 748/1; Neatby (1967), p. 39.

21. Nelson (vol. 1, August 2, 1850), SPRI, MS 748/1.

22. Armstrong (1857), pp. 84–85; Ford's diary (August 2, 1850), KML, 18500119Arctic1xx; McClure (1856), p. 57; Nelson (vol. 1, August 2, 1850), SPRI, MS 748/1; Piers's journal (August 2, 1850), NMM, MS 67/013.

23. Armstrong (1857), pp. 84–85.

24. Ibid., pp. 85–86; Neatby (1967), p. 39; Piers's journal (August 5, 1850), NMM, MS 67/013.

25. Armstrong (1857), p. 87.

26. Nelson (vol. 1, August 8, 1850), SPRI, MS 748/1; Armstrong (1857), p. 85; Neatby (1967), p. 39.

27. Piers's journal (August 3, 1850), NMM, JOD/102.

28. Cresswell to parents (August 21, 1850), Harrod (2000), p. 67; Ford's diary (August 6, 1850), KML, 18500119Arctic1xx. The first European to reach Point Barrow was Master Thomas Elson, on August 23, 1826, in the barge of HMS *Blossom* (Captain F.W. Beechey), his farthest point (Gough, p. 161). Captain John Franklin, leading a portion of his 1825–27 Arctic expedition, was traveling westward along the coast, attempting to rendezvous with Beechey at Icy Cape. Due to poor weather and ice conditions, Franklin turned back at the Return Islands; Elson and Franklin had come within 186 miles (300 km) of one another (Holland [1994], pp. 197–98).

29. Piers's journal (August 6, 1850), NMM, JOD/102.

30. McClure (1856), p. 60.

31. Piers's journal (August 7, 1850), NMM, JOD/102; Neatby (1967), p. 40.

32. Armstrong (1857), p. 93.

33. Piers's journal (August 7, 1850), NMM, JOD/102.

34. Armstrong (1857), p. 93; Neatby (1967), p. 40.

35. Neatby (1967), p. 41.

36. McClure (1854a), p. 57; Armstrong (1857), p. 94; Piers's journal (August 8, 1850), NMM, JOD/102; Neatby, pp. xii, 41.

37. Armstrong (1857), p. 95.

38. Armstrong (1857), pp. 95–96; Neatby (1967), p. 41.

39. Piers's journal (August 8, 1850), NMM, JOD/102.

40. Armstrong (1857), p. 96.

41. Ibid.; McClure (1854a), p. 27.

42. Iñupiat people, http://en.wikipedia.org/wiki/Inupiat.

43. McClure (1856), p. 62; Armstrong (1857), p. 96.

44. McClure to Admiralty (August 24, 1850) (1854a), p. 25.

45. Burying a bottle in this position relative to a cairn appears to have been a standard practice, in order to frustrate the Eskimos from finding it. Miertsching writes that the bottle was buried "ten feet east," and this equates to the general direction of the North Magnetic Pole from the *Investigator*'s position during this time period (Neatby [1967], p. 42; Magnetic North Pole Positions, https://en.wikipedia.org); Piers's journal (August 8, 1850), NMM, JOD/102; Armstrong (1857), p. 97; Neatby (1967), pp. 41–42.

46. Piers's journal (August 8, 1850), NMM, JOD/102; Armstrong (1857), p. 98; Bruemmer (1992); Umiak, http://en.wikipedia.org.

47. Piers's journal (August 8, 1850), NMM, JOD/102.

48. Armstrong (1857), pp. 98–99, 111. In a memorandum to Paine the same day, McClure set forth that the "Esquimaux along the Coast being partial to Tobacco and it being more convenient as an Article of barter than the presents onboard; It is my direction that you supply such quantities as may be required for the above purposes from the Tobacco in your charge" (Letter & Order Book [August 8, 1850], RGS, SSC/106).

49. Ibid., pp. 111–12. At least one such memento arose from the *Enterprise* as well. On October 16, 1850, when her ship's company was saying goodbye to a group of departing natives, west of Cape Nome (on the northern coast of Kotzebue Sound), a young lady was "decorated with a copper medal on which was stamped the date and place where they were picked up" (Collinson [1889], p. 85). The distribution of official and unofficial medals to native peoples by European explorers was a common practice going back at least 50 years. Another Arctic example occurred during Parry's 1821–23 North-West Passage expedition of HMS *Fury* and *Hecla*. Commander George F. Lyon (*Hecla*) wrote on February 14, 1822, that one of the Eskimos "wore a medal of copper,

which had been given him by Pā-ri, with the ships' names stamped on it; and other medals were afterwards distributed, in the hope that owning to the wandering life of the Esquimaux, some of these ornaments might, through our factories, reach England before our return" (Lyon [1824], p. 140).

50. Ibid., pp. 98, 111–12; McClure (1856), pp. 71–72.

51. Oswalt, pp. 209–10.

52. Piers's journal (August 8, 1850), NMM, JOD/102.

53. Bockstoce (vol. 2), pp. 516–17, Appendix 7—"Dr. John Simpson's essay on the Eskimos of northwestern Alaska."

54. Armstrong (1857), pp. 102–03; McClure (1856), p. 69. Piers wrote the grounding was "by a mistake, I believe of the leadsman" (Piers's journal [August 8, 1850], NMM, JOD/102).

55. Armstrong (1857), pp. 103–04; Piers's journal (August 8, 1850), NMM, JOD/102; Piers states Point Halkett (Cape Halkett), while Armstrong identifies it as Pitt Point.

56. Armstrong (1857), p. 104.

57. Neatby (1967), p. 44.

58. Ibid.

59. Piers's journal (August 8, 1850), NMM, JOD/102.

60. Armstrong states the ship "seldom averaged more than twenty or thirty miles a day" (Armstrong [1857], p. 112), but in McClure's narrative, *Investigator* was able "to work to windward between thirty and forty miles a day" (McClure [1856], p. 71).

61. McClure (1856), p. 72.

62. Armstrong (1857), pp. 105–06; Neatby (1967), p. 44.

63. Neatby (1967), fn 1, p. 65.

64. Armstrong (1857), between xxii and p. 1; McClure (1856), p. xxxv; McClure (1857), p. xxv; McClure (1865), p. xix.

65. McClure to Ross (April [no day written] 1853), NA, BJ2/10; Armstrong (1857), p. 198; Neatby (1967), p. 166. Miertsching wrote on July 9, 1852: "I have up till now gathered and dried 3,785 specimens of plants, grasses and moss from various lands, and this month I will reap a good harvest." The Royal Botanic Gardens, Kew holds botanical specimens collected during the expedition: by McClure—K000692986, *Ranunculus nivalis*, north shore of Baring Island, August 1851, and by Miertsching—K000907126, *Salix arbusculoides Andersson*, Prince Albert Sound, 1852–53 [*sic*] and K000692986, *Ranunculus nivalis*, Mercy Bay, August 1852 (Kew, Royal Botanic Gardens, www.kew.org; Mechtild Opel to Stein, personal communication, March 13, 2011).

66. Neatby (1967), p. 41.

67. *Investigator*'s Musters, NA,

ADM 38/1026; Cresswell to Joseph Cresswell (January 16/17, 1850), Harrod, p. 62; www.timeanddate.com.

68. McClure (1856), pp. xxxiii–xxxv, 57, 85, 240; McClure (1857), pp. xxiii–xxv; McClure (1865), pp. xviii–xix; Armstrong (1857), between xxii and p. 1.

69. Armstrong (1857), p. 107.

70. Armstrong (1857), pp. 107–08; McClure (1856), p. 74.

71. Armstrong (1857), p. 108.

72. Armstrong (1857), pp. 108–09; Neatby (1967), p. 45; Piers entered the date in his journal as August 12 (Piers's journal [August 12, 1850], NMM, JOD/102).

73. McClure (1854a), p. 57; Armstrong (1857), p. 109.

74. Armstrong (1857), p. 109; McClure to the Chief Trader of the Russian Fur Company and McClure to the Admiralty (August 11, 1850) (Letter & Order Book, RGS, SSC/106).

75. Neatby (1967), pp. 45–46.

76. Ford's diary (August 12, 1850), KML, 18500119Arctic1xx; McClure (1856), pp. 75–76; Armstrong (1857), pp. 110–11; Neatby (1967), p. 46.

77. Ford's diary (August 13, 1850), KML, 18500119Arctic1xx; Armstrong (1857), p. 114; Neatby (1967), p. 47.

78. Piers's journal (August 14, 1850), NMM, JOD/102.

79. Cresswell to parents (August 21, 1850), Harrod (2000), p. 67.

80. Piers's journal (August 14, 1850), NMM, JOD/102; Armstrong (1857), pp. 116–17.

## Chapter 6

1. Armstrong (1857), p. 117.

2. Ibid.

3. Piers's journal (August 14, 1850), NMM, JOD/102.

4. Armstrong (1857), pp. 117–18; McClure (1854a), p. 28; Piers's journal (August 14, 1850), NMM, JOD/102; Neatby (1967), p. 47; McClure (1856), p. 78.

5. Armstrong (1857), p. 118; McClure differs from Armstrong regarding the water, stating that "some tons of fresh water were started from the tanks in her hold" (McClure [1856], p. 78).

6. Armstrong (1857), p. 119; McClure (1854a), p. 28. However, if each cask was full, the total loss would have equaled nearly 3,700 lbs.

7. Piers's journal (August 14, 1850), NMM, JOD/102.

8. Nelson (vol. 1, August 14, 1850), SPRI, MS 748/1; McClure later refers to this place as Point Manning (McClure [1856], p. 121), but such a place cannot be located on contemporary or modern maps.

9. Piers's journal (August 14, 1850), NMM, JOD/102.

10. Letter & Order Book (September 1, 1850), RGS, SSC/106.

11. Nelson (vol. 1, August 14, 1850), SPRI, MS 748/1.

12. Neatby (1967), p. 48.

13. McClure (1856), pp. 80–81.

14. McClure (1856), p. 81.

15. Armstrong (1857), pp. 123–24; Piers's journal (August 16, 1850), NMM, JOD/102.

16. Ibid.

17. Ford's diary (August 17, 1850), KML, 18500119Arctic1xx.

18. McClure (1856), pp. 81–82.

19. Piers's journal (August 18, 1850), NMM, JOD/102; Armstrong (1857), p. 147 (Note: Armstrong's pagination is flawed as follows: 1–128, 145–160, 145–616); McClure (1856), p. 82; Neatby (1967), p. 49.

20. McClure (1856), p. 83.

21. Piers's journal (August 19, 1850), NMM, JOD/102.

22. Neatby (1967), p. 50; Armstrong (1857), p. 151; Piers's journal (August 19, 1850), NMM, JOD/102; Cresswell to parents (August 21, 1850), Harrod (2000), p. 68.

23. The line of demarcation between Russian America and British North America was long. 141° W., United States Department of State, p. 6.

24. Piers's journal (August 20–21, 1850), NMM, JOD/102.

25. Ibid. (August 22, 1850).

26. Nelson (vol. 1, August 22, 1850), SPRI, MS 748/1.

27. McClure (1854a), p. 28; McClure (1856), p. 42; Great Britain (1851a), p. 12.

28. McClure to Ross (April [no day written] 1853), NA, BJ2/10.

29. Recordings of the ship's positions during this time period are cause for some confusion. Cresswell's letter was written August 21, and is headed "off Flaxman Is." [long. 146°], but therein states the ship is presently off Cape Warren [also called Point Warren, long. 132°]. Miertsching states Flaxman Island was passed on August 18, long. 148°. Miertsching again states Flaxman Island was passed on August 21, but now gives long. 136°. Piers states Flaxman Island was passed on August 18, long. 145°. Ford states long. 148° on August 18, and long. 136° on August 21. Armstrong records the sighting of Garry Island on August 21 (at the mouth of the Mackenzie River, long. 135°). Piers states the ship is off the mouth of the Mackenzie River on August 21, long. 136°.

30. Cresswell to parents (August 21, 1850), Harrod (2000), p. 68. This letter was sent at Liverpool Bay, just southwest of Cape Bathurst (Harrod [2000], fn, p. 67).

31. McClure (1856), p. 84; Armstrong (1857), p. 157.

32. Armstrong (1857), pp. 159–60, 145–56 (see endnote 19 above regarding pagination); Ford's diary (August 24, 1850), KML, 18500119Arctic1xx; McClure (1856), pp. 85–88; Neatby (1967), pp. 51–54; Nelson (vol. 1, August 24, 1850), SPRI, MS 748/1; Piers's journal (August 24, 1850), NMM, JOD/102.

33. Piers's journal (August 24, 1850), NMM, JOD/102.

34. Armstrong (1857), p. 160.

35. Ibid., p. 152.

36. Ibid., p. 154; Holland (1994), p. 225.

37. Neatby (1967), p. 54.

38. Ibid., p. 55; Armstrong (1857), pp. 158–59; McClure (1856), pp. 89–90; Ford's diary (August 28, 1850), KML, 18500119Arctic1xx.

39. Armstrong (1857), p. 159; McClure (1856), p. 90.

40. Cresswell to parents (August 30, 1850), Harrod (2000), p. 69.

41. Armstrong (1857), pp. 159–62.

42. Ibid., p. 160; Piers's journal (August 30, 1850), NMM, JOD/102.

43. Ford's diary (August 30, 1850), KML, 18500119Arctic1xx; Armstrong (1857), p. 162.

44. "Kenalik" is correct, instead of "Renalik" by Neatby (Neatby [1967], p. 56; M. Opel to Stein, personal communication, August 11, 2014); Armstrong (1857), pp. 162–63.

45. Armstrong (1857), pp. 168–69.

46. Armstrong (1857), pp. 170–71; Nelson (vol. 1, August 31, 1850), SPRI, MS 748/1; Neatby (1967), pp. 56–57; Ford's diary (August 31, 1850), KML, 18500119Arctic1xx.

47. Piers's journal (August 31, 1850), NMM, JOD/102.

48. Armstrong (1857), p. 171.

49. Ibid., p. 172.

50. Ibid.; Neatby (1967), p. 58; McClure (1854a), p. 31

51. Armstrong (1857), p. 173; Nelson recollected only two men were left to guard the boat, and that he carried a Union Jack, rather than a White Ensign, on a boarding pike (Nelson [vol. 1, August 31, 1850], SPRI, MS 748/1–2).

52. Armstrong (1857), pp. 173–74.

53. Neatby (1967), p. 58.

54. "The interpreter told them that our visit was friendly, and that they should put away their knives. "Yes," said they, "when you do your guns." To be allowed to carry the musket appeared a great favour, for which they presented you with their knife as a token of friendship." (McClure [1854a], pp. 31–32).

55. Neatby (1967), p. 58.

56. Ibid., p. 59; McClure (1856), p. 97; Piers's journal (August 31, 1850),

NMM, JOD/102; McClure (1856), p. 96.

57. Piers's journal (August 31, 1850), NMM, JOD/102.

58. McClure (1854a), p. 32; Neatby (1967), p. 61.

59. Armstrong (1857), pp. 178–79; Piers's journal (August 31, 1850), NMM, JOD/102.

60. "On inquiring as to the value of a silver fox-skin, and the amount it realized in barter, they confirmed a story we had heard from the women the day previous, that for three of those precious skins they had got from traders cooking utensils, which we estimated at eight shillings and sixpence. I may mention that the skin of the silver fox is one of the most valuable furs, and at the annual sale of the Hudson's Bay Company varies in price, sometimes being as high as twenty-five or thirty guineas, so that an idea of their profits may be formed when we consider the amount of the original cost" (Armstrong [1857], p. 177).

61. Piers's journal (August 31, 1850), NMM, JOD/102.

62. McClure (1854a), p. 32.

63. McClure (1856), p. 97.

64. Roderick Ross MacFarlane, www.clanmacfarlanegenealogy.info; Roderick MacFarlane, www.collectionscanada.gc.ca, 2008. For his efforts, MacFarlane was awarded the Arctic Medal 1818–55, which was not issued to him until 1902 (see Appendix 7).

65. MacFarlane to Richardson (July 14, 1862), SPRI, MS 1503/65/9. MacFarlane collected ethnographic objects—clothing, tools, ornaments and other items made by Inuvialuit (Western Canadian Inuit)—for the Smithsonian Institution while he was in charge of Fort Anderson. One of the items was a pipe, of which the uppermost portion of the bowl was formed from one of the "rescue buttons" given to native peoples by Sir Edward Belcher's 1852–54 Franklin Search expedition (see Chapter 2) (Inuvialuit Pitqusiit Inuuniarutait: Inuvialuit Living History, The MacFarlane Collection, E2156-0, www.inuvialuitlivinghistory.ca).

66. Armstrong (1857), pp. 175–76, 178.

67. Ibid., pp. 175, 177, 180; McClure to wife Mary (April 15, 1853), PBA Galleries, April 30, 2009.

68. McClure (1856), pp. 94–95.

69. Neatby (1967), pp. 61, 102; Labrador retriever, http://en.wikipedia.org; Armstrong (1857), p. 292. Captain Collinson kept a pet Newfoundland dog named Neptune onboard *Enterprise* (Collinson [1889], p. 94). "The Newfoundland breed originated in Newfoundland, and is descended from a breed indigenous to the island known as the lesser New-foundland, or St. John's Dog [Newfoundland dog]" (https://en.wikipedia.org); Piers's journal (January 14, 1851), NMM, JOD/102. In Piers's November 21, 1850 entry, the dog is referred to as "he," but as "her" and "she" in his entry for February 7, 1851, and Armstrong refers to the dog as "her" (Armstrong [1857], p. 301). In Piers's latter entry, for the first time he names the dog—Micky. Then, in his March 15, 1851, entry, Piers began referring to the dog as "Vesty"—the ship's nickname—which was also used by McClure (McClure to Ross [September 15, 1854], NA, BJ 2/10).

70. Neatby (1967), p. 59.

71. Ibid., pp. 59–60.

72. Armstrong (1857), p. 180; Nelson (vol. 1, August 31, 1850), SPRI, MS 748/1–2; Armstrong writes of a different fate for the boarding pike and flag, indicating that it was given to an Eskimo just before going onboard *Investigator*, the cutter having picked up the native and his kayak on the way back to the ship (Armstrong [1857], p. 184).

73. McClure (1854a), p. 32; Armstrong (1857), p. 180.

74. McClure (1854a), p. 32.

75. Armstrong (1857), pp. 182–84; McClure (1854a), p. 32.

76. Armstrong's writings lead one to believe it was Corporal Farquharson's coat (Armstrong [1857], pp. 184–85, 187), but Nelson indicates it was Sergeant Woon's coat (Nelson [1967], p. 762); Piers's journal (August 31, 1850), NMM, JOD/102.

77. Armstrong (1857), p. 185; McClure (1854a), p. 33.

78. Skead's journal (August 1850), private collection; Collinson (1889), p. 67–68; Barr (2007), pp. 29–36; "I am indebted to Dr. J.D. Hooker, F.R.S., of Kew, for the information, that he had described and published an account of the plants collected by my late friend, Robert Anderson, Esq., Surgeon of H.M.S. 'Enterprize,' (by whose death the Navy lost one of its ablest and most accomplished Medical Officers). As these specimens were obtained on the same lands as my own, and as they are identical with them, I have placed a list of them in the Appendix [pp. 604–05]" (Armstrong [1857], p. vii). Dr. Anderson was also Cresswell's former shipmate on two occasions, HMS *Agincourt* (assistant surgeon) in the Far East (1842–44), and at the same rank in HMS *Investigator* (1848–49) for Ross's expedition (Anderson's service record, ADM 104/22, Harrod, p. 21, and Cresswell's service record, NA, ADM 196/36).

79. Skead's journal (September 1850), private collection.

80. Collinson (1889), pp. 72, 76.

81. Ford's diary (September 1, 1850), KML, 18500119Arctic1xx; Mc-Clure (1854a), p. 33; Armstrong (1857), p. 201.

82. Armstrong (1857), pp. 201–02; Neatby (1967), p. 63; Piers's journal (September 2–4, 1850), NMM, JOD/102.

83. Armstrong (1857), p. 202.

84. Ibid., pp. 203–04; Piers states "the Captain, Miertsching & two other officers landed where the smoke was still observed ascending" (Piers's journal [September 5, 1850], NMM, JOD/102).

85. Neatby (1967), pp. 64–65.

86. Ibid., p. 67; Nelson (vol. 1, September 5, 1850), SPRI, MS 748/1–2. According to Miertsching, "a large part of the ship's new tackle had been ruined" by the fire, but Armstrong writes that it was "extinguished without much damage or destruction of stores" (Neatby [1967], p. 67; Armstrong [1857], p. 206).

87. Neatby (1967), p. 65.

88. Armstrong (1857), p. 204.

89. Neatby (1967), p. 65.

90. Neatby writes that Newton has "hallucinations" or "visions," but such a characterization is inappropriate in the absence of more substantial evidence (Neatby [1967], pp. xviii & 64).

91. Ibid. and footnote.

92. Armstrong (1857), p. 206; McClure (1854a), p. 34.

93. Armstrong (1857), p. 207; Piers's journal (September 6, 1850), NMM, JOD/102; Neatby (1967), pp. 66–67; Nelson (vol. 1, September 6, 1850), SPRI, MS 748/1–2.

94. Armstrong (1857), p. 207; Sometime afterward, Piers described "our accidently sighting Baring's Land—or Banks' Land which it appears to be—(for the Captain, I believe, says that, after what he had seen of the ice, and experienced in standing off to seaward, he intended keeping the shore from Cape Parry till he reached the known part of Dolphin & Union Straits, then to endeavour to cross and sail along the coast of Wollaston Land to the westward with the hope of getting to the northward by the west coast of Banks' Land, but the wind caused him to reach further off shore, which the state of the loose sailing ice did not prevent)—from the southward of the line there" (Piers's journal [November 6, 1850], NMM, JOD/102).

## Chapter 7

1. Neatby (1967), p. 68; Armstrong (1857), p. 208.

2. Ibid.

3. Cresswell's watercolor sketches of *Investigator* in sight of Banks Land (September 6, 1850), Lord Nelson's Head, and Moonlit seascape (Harrod [2000], between pp. 96, 97).

4. Piers's journal (September 7, 1850), NMM, JOD/102.

5. "Until 1864, the Red Ensign was also the principal ensign of the Royal Navy, and as such it was worn by ships of the Red Squadron of the navy, as well as by those warships that were not assigned to any squadron (i.e., those sailing under independent command). The white ensign and the blue ensign were also used by the Royal Navy" (Red Ensign, http://en.wikipedia.org).

6. Armstrong (1857), pp. 208–09. "A pole erected with a large painted ball upon it, near a cask ... latitude 71° 6' N., longitude 123° 0' W." (McClure [1854a], p. 34).

7. Miertsching writes that the cliff is "780 feet," and the peak "was estimated at over two thousand feet" (Neatby [1967], p. 68), while Armstrong writes "the headland itself we estimated at 850 feet," and the higher land "not less than 1000 feet" (Armstrong [1857], p. 211), and "Court found, by his observation, the cliff near there to be between 800 and 900 feet high, but from the Ship the land was seen to reach a considerably greater altitude" and "the highest part of the land, which was close to the cliff, appeared to be about 1000 or 1200 feet high" (Piers's journal [September 7, 1850], NMM, JOD/102).

8. McClure (1854a), p. 34.

9. Armstrong (1857), p. 211. Armstrong incorrectly states that Horatio Nelson was "not hitherto honoured by Arctic discoverers in the bestowal of their favours." In fact, Nelson Island, in Spitsbergen (Nelsonøya, Svalbard) was named after Midshipman Horatio Nelson (HMS *Carcass*), who was part of Captain Constantine John Phipps's expedition to that archipelago in 1773 (Nelsonøya, https://en.wikipedia.org).

10. Piers's journal (September 7, 1850), NMM, JOD/102; Armstrong (1857), p. 213.

11. Piers's journal (September 7, 1850), NMM, JOD/102.

12. Traditional Nautical Terms & Sayings, www.goatlocker.org; Fix (position), https://en.wikipedia.org; Burridge (does not contain page numbers).

13. Friendly society (https://en.wikipedia.org).

14. Piers's journal (September 9, 1850), NMM, JOD/102.

15. McClure (1854a), p. 35; McClure (1856), p. 105.

16. Ibid.; Armstrong (1857), p. 266.

17. McClure (1856), p. 106.

18. Ibid., p. 108; Piers's journal (September 11, 1850), NMM, JOD/102.

19. Piers's journal (June 13, 1851), NMM, JOD/102.

20. McClure (1856), pp. 108–09; Holland (1994), pp. 231–34.

21. McClure (1856), pp. 110–12; Armstrong (1857), pp. 217–23; Piers's journal (September 17, 1850), NMM, JOD/102; Neatby (1967), p. 71.

22. Piers's journal (September 15, 1850), NMM, JOD/102.

23. Parry (1824), p. 117.

24. Armstrong (1857), p. 230.

25. Piers's journal (September 13, 1850), NMM, JOD/102.

26. Neatby (1967), p. 70; Armstrong (1857), pp. 227–28; Neatby (1967), p. 71; McClure (1856), pp. 109, 113, 115.

27. McClure (1856), p. 113.

28. Armstrong (1857), p. 232.

29. McClure (1856), p. 113.

30. McClure (1854a), p. 36.

31. Ibid.

32. Piers's journal (September 19, 1850), NMM, JOD/102.

33. Ibid. (September 18, 1850).

34. Piers's journal (September 23, 1850), NMM, JOD/102.

35. Neatby (1967), p. 70; Milner's service record, NA, ADM 29/64; *Investigator*'s Musters (1849–50), NA, ADM 38/1026; Paine's service record, NA, ADM 196/11; Milner's seaman's register ticket no. 313.182 was issued under the name "George Luke," on April 2, 1846, while at Devonport, onboard HMS *Belleisle* (Registry of Shipping and Seamen: Register of Seamen's Tickets, NA, BT 113/157).

36. Piers's journal (September 24, 1850), NMM, JOD/102.

37. Neatby (1967), pp. 72–73.

38. Ibid., p. 73.

39. McClure (1854a), p. 36; McClure (1856), p. 118; Armstrong (1857), pp. 238, 241.

40. Neatby (1967), pp. 73–75.

41. Neatby (1967), p. 77; Ford's diary (September 27, 28 & 30, 1850), KML, 18500119Arctic1xx.

42. As "Steel" on the seaman's register ticket no. 317.573, NA, BT 113/159; *Investigator*'s Musters (1849–50), NA, ADM 38/1026; Arctic Medal 1818–1855 Roll (signature), NA, ADM 171/9, McClure (1856), xxxiii, and Armstrong (1857), between p. xxii and p. 1, but "Steele" on the sick list (Armstrong's journal [sick list], NA, ADM 101/250, p. 4).

43. Armstrong's journal (sick list), NA, ADM 101/250, p. 4.

44. Neatby (1967), pp. 77–78. Neither the breaking into of the spirit room or the punishments are mentioned by McClure, Armstrong, Piers, Ford or Nelson in their writings.

45. Armstrong (1857), pp. 237, 242; Neatby (1967), p. 79; McClure (1854a), p. 36; Piers's journal (October 5, 1850), NMM, JOD/102.

46. Armstrong (1858), p. 12.

47. Nelson (vol. 1, September 29, 1850), SPRI, MS 748/1; Piers's journal (September 30, 1850), NMM, JOD/102; Armstrong (1857), pp. 242 & 290 & fn—"...and early in the spring [of 1851], when visiting the Western Land, found the wing feathers of our missing friend, which had, no doubt, become the prey of a Fox"; McClure (1856), p. 158; "Ralph Ravens (c. 1553–1615) was an English clergyman and academic. He was nominated in 1604 as one of the translators for the Authorised King James Version [of the Bible], in the Second Oxford Company, but his status is unclear. It is said that he was substituted, for reasons unknown, and did not actually take part in the project. It has been suggested that the Second Oxford Company, in which Richard Edes had died, had two substitutes, namely Leonard Hutten and John Aglionby. On the other hand Ravens may have taken part in early meetings as a Greek scholar" (Ralph Ravens, http://en.wikipedia.org).

48. Letter & Order Book (October 1, 1850), RGS, SSC/106 (similar to the order issued to Haswell, Cresswell and Court on March 4); McClure (1856), pp. 121–22.

49. Armstrong (1857), p. 243; Piers's journal (October 4, 1850), NMM, JOD/102.

50. Armstrong (1857), p. 243.

51. Piers's journal (October 4, 1850), NMM, JOD/102.

52. Armstrong (1857), pp. viii, 423, 606–608.

53. Armstrong (1857), p. 245; Piers's journal (October 4, 7, 1850), NMM, JOD/102.

54. Armstrong (1857), p. 245.

55. *Investigator*'s Musters (1849–50), NA, ADM 38/1026; Register for Mates, NA, ADM 11/22; A contemporarily framed 19th century watercolor portrait (c. 1845) of Wynniatt in a naval cadet's uniform exists, with a brief manuscript biography (evidently written by a relative), and visiting card (Commander Wynniatt, R.N., H.M.S. *Nimrod*) mounted on reverse, together with a black velour bicorn hat attributed to Wynniatt, trimmed with golden braid on the upper edges, and golden wire cockade with RN button (The Wayfarer's Bookshop, www.wayfarersbookshop.com); Kerr's service record, NA, ADM 29/59/345; *Winchester*'s Muster, July 1–September 30, 1845, NA, ADM 38/2278; Kerr's service record, NA, ADM 29/59/345; Cowan, pp. 121, 138, 140–41; Clowes (vol. 6, 1901), p. 353. Twenty of the *Inflexible*'s sailors and Marines received the campaign medal for the First New Zealand War (1845–47), which was not instituted until 1869, and only granted to survivors who actually took part in operations against the Maoris. Kerr was not one of the recipients (Douglas-Morris [1987], pp. 280, 284).

56. Obituary. Major-General Richard Hugh Stotherd, *Minutes of the Proceed-*

*ings of the Institution of Civil Engineers,* 1895. 121: pp. 343–44. The rank of captain is incorrectly attributed to Lieutenant Stotherd in Collinson (1889), p. 431; McClintock, Notes on Blasting Thin Ice (Collinson [1889], pp. 430–31; Piers's journal (September 14, 1850), NMM, JOD/102.

57. McClintock, "Notes on Blasting Thin Ice" (Collinson 1889), pp. 430–31.

58. Piers's journal (October 5–8, 1850), NMM, JOD/102; McClure (1856), p. 122; Neatby (1967), p. 79.

59. Neatby (1967), p. 79; Rao, "The Myth of Arctic Daylight and Darkness Exposed"; *Twilight,* www.wikipedia.org.

60. Armstrong (1857), pp. 250–52; Piers's journal (October 10, 1850), NMM, JOD/102.

61. Neatby (1967), p. 80; McClure (1856), p. 124; Armstrong (1857), p. 254.

62. Armstrong (1857), p. 255.

63. Sources disagree on the width of the water—20 yards (Armstrong [1857], p. 255); 100 feet [33 yards] (Neatby [1967], p. 81); and 50 yards (McClure [1856], p. 126).

64. Armstrong (1857), pp. 256–57; Neatby (1967), p. 81.

65. Piers's journal (October 10, 1850), NMM, JOD/102; Jones (1958), pp. 155–56; Ford's diary (October 10, 1850), KML, 18500119Arctic1xx—Collinson stated the Halkett's portable boats "were 46 lbs. weight, and held four persons" (Collinson [1889], p. 416).

66. McClure (1856), p. 128; Armstrong (1857), pp. 258–59.

67. Piers's journal (October 11, 1850), NMM, JOD/102.

68. Sick list, Armstrong's journal (sick list), NA, ADM 101/250, p. 4. The sick list shows both men were admitted on October 10, which means night of the 10th/morning of the 11th, as Piers's writings indicate the first party did not return to the ship until 1:45 a.m. on October 11 (Piers's journal [October 11, 1850], NMM, JOD/102).

69. Attestation form, NA, ADM 157/56; *Columbia*'s Description Book (1842–48), NA, ADM 38/7820; William Fitzwilliam Owen (1774–1857), p. 218; William John Samuel Pullen, www.biographi.ca; Markham (1875), p. 9; Douglas-Morris (1994), p. 214; Private George Parfitt's Naval General Service Medal 1793–1840, with Syria clasp (Private/*Powerful*) exists in the author's collection. In addition to medals from Franklin Expedition members being recovered in the Arctic, the Naval General Service Medal 1793–1840, with Syria clasp, to Jeremiah Galavan (Boy/*Castor*) was used in a Christmas chandelier decoration onboard Belcher's ship HMS *Assistance*

in 1853 ("List of Objects Shown at the Franklin Commemoration Meeting, Edinburgh, On 4th June 1895, and on Subsequent Days," pp. 410, 414; Belcher [vol. 2], p. 82).

70. Piers's journal (October 12, 1850), NMM, JOD/102.

71. Ford's diary (October 14, 1850), KML, 18500119Arctic1xx; Neatby (1967), p. 82.

72. Neatby (1967), pp. 82–83; Piers's journal (October 15, 1850), NMM, JOD/102; McClure (1856), pp. 130–31.

73. Armstrong (1857), pp. 265, 284. Though stated that McClure would try to reach "Barrow's Strait" (McClure [1856], p. 129), this was actually Viscount Melville Sound, the westward expansion of Barrow Strait (Neatby [1960], p. 31).

74. Armstrong (1857), p. 266.

75. Armstrong (1857), p. 273.

76. McClure (1856), pp. 131–32; McClure (1854a), p. 37. At some point, Brown, who had been the acting captain of the foretop, reverted back to an able seaman, and Able Seaman Thompson was promoted to this first class petty officer rating sometime after June 30, 1850 ("Thomson" in *Investigator*'s Muster [1849–50], NA, ADM 38/1026 and McClure [1854a], p. 37); *Investigator*'s Description Book (1848–49), NA, ADM 38/8387; *Enterprise*'s Description Book (1848–49), NA, ADM 38/8041; Armstrong (1857), p. 273; McClure's journal (May 31, 1850), RGS, SSC/106. Sources do not bear out the identity of the sixth man (Armstrong [1857], p. 274. Piers's journal [October 22, 1850], NMM, JOD/102).

77. Letter & Order Book (October 20, 1850), RGS, SCC/106 (a detailed list of provisions in the margin runs nearly the length of one page, and into part of a second); Ross (1994), p. 306.

78. Brown manuscript, GM, M-141, pp. 11–12; "Expedition in Search of Sir John Franklin"; McClure (1856), p. 135; McDougall, p. 494.

79. Armstrong (1857), p. 272.

80. Piers's journal (October 21, 1850), NMM, JOD/102.

81. Ibid.

82. This weight is based on Piers's stating the sled was "between 6 and 7 Cwt"—hundredweight, or 672–784 lbs. (Piers's journal [October 31, 1850], NMM, JOD/102), and McClure indicating its weight upon return was "793 pounds, being an *increase,* upon what we started with, of upwards of 100 pounds" (McClure [1856], p. 144).

83. The list of stores is compilation from the following sources: Collinson (1889), pp. 183–84, McClintock (1875), p. 465; Neatby (1960), p. 43, Piers's journal (October 31, 1850), NMM, JOD/102; McClure (1856), p. 144; Collinson (1889), p. 374.

84. Neatby (1960), p. 43.

85. McClure (1856), p. 132–33; Since Collinson indicated *Enterprise* had only two sleds fitted at Woolwich, it seems likely *Investigator* also left with only two as well (Collinson [1889], p. 262); Jones (1971), p 175. In discussion about "On Arctic Sledge-travelling," which McClintock presented before the June 14, 1875, RGS meeting, Collinson remarked, "When the expedition in which he was engaged left England in 1850 they had the advantage of the experience gained up to 1849; but as they did not return until 1855 they could not profit by the improvements made in the intervening years, and were thrown upon their own resources" (McClintock [1875], p. 476); McClure had already passed from the scene in October 1873).

86. Cyriax (1963), pp. 127–35; Barr (2008), p. 271. "If one excludes the extremely short trips for which dog sledges were used, e.g., for hauling gravel or for short hunting or surveying trips, the total length of the major dog-sledge trips was conservatively 11,576 km [7,193 miles]" (Barr [2008], p. 269). Although McClure did not acquire any dogs for sledding, Collinson bought three dogs from the Yupik Eskimos in the area of the Bering Strait, and his third lieutenant (Lieutenant Charles Jago) purchased an undetermined number of dogs for a team in the spring of 1852, from the Eskimos around Walker Bay (western Victoria Island) (Barr [2008], p. 259).

87. Mills (vol. 2), p. 400.

88. Mackinnon, p. 132. Mackinnon went on to write, "Gradually during the Franklin search, the quest for survivors to be rescued gave way to the mundane activity of charting new discoveries. This work of precision was part of the worldwide self-imposed task of compiling the Admiralty Chart.... The shift in emphasis from search-and-rescue to exploration actually reinforced the decision to use man-hauled sledging. A slow-moving (18 kilometers per day [11+ miles]) man-hauled sledge, with an accompanying officer, was a very suitable way of surveying a coastline in detail. For these reasons, the Britishers' choice of man-hauling sledging, from 1849 to 1859, makes some sense.... In summary, the British choice of man-hauled sledging was a rational one, given the circumstances of the 1850s. Thereafter it became increasingly inappropriate, but tradition overruled common sense" (Mackinnon, pp. 132, 137). "The total distance traveled by man-hauled sledges [in the British search for Franklin during 1848–59] amounted, conservatively, to 41,555 km [25,821 miles] (Barr [2008], p. 269)."

89. Cyriax (1963), pp. 135–36.

Collinson had a sled named the *Royal Albert* made aboard *Enterprise*, "and having sacrificed one of our large ice saws in order to make runners (as the *Resolution* being shod with iron hoops was found to run heavy), we had the satisfaction of finding she answered very well, although not equal to the two fitted at Woolwich" (Collinson [1889], p. 262).

90. McClintock (1875), pp. 465–66.

91. Tomlinson, pp. 215–17; Carr, pp. 5–9; Collinson (1889), p. 376. In 1869, when American explorer Charles Francis Hall was interviewing Eskimos about their memories of Franklin survivors, one man said he "saw something in the distance on the smooth ice that looked white & thought it was a bear," and on telling his companions, "they watched, the white object grew larger, for it was coming down towards them. They saw the white thing moving along in the direction of the coast, turning in a kind of a circling way, just as the little bay turned. At length they began to see many black objects moving along with what they had first espied as white in the distance. The object that they 1st had seen as white proved to be a sail raised on the boat & as this got nearer saw this sail shake in the wind. On seeing what they did, the object grew plainer and they thought of white men and began to be afraid" (Woodman, pp. 124–25). This was obviously a ship's boat mounted on a sled.

92. Collinson (1889), pp. 184, 263. None of the Parliamentary Papers containing McClure's reports have any sketches of sled flags, and the junior officers' sled journals (which would most likely have contained illustrations of sled flags) are not known to have survived. However, examples of sled flags from *Investigator* may survive in family hands, but will be difficult to trace until they are offered to museums, churches or at auction (Tomlinson to Stein, personal communication, May 11, 2010).

93. Armstrong (1857), pp. 274–75; Piers's journal (October 22, 1850), NMM, JOD/102; Ford's diary (October 22, 1850), KML, 18500119Arctic1 xx. Due to the snowdrift wiping out the sled tracks, Wynniatt's party lost its way going back to the ship, and spent the night out in the open, arriving back onboard the following day, fortunately with only a few frostbites (Armstrong [1857], pp. 274–75).

94. Neatby (1967), p. 85.

95. Ford's diary (October 24–26, 1850), KML, 18500119Arctic1xx. The Royal Navy & Marine Customs and Traditions, www.hmsrichmond.org. "From tonight [June 22, 2013], for the first time in 200 years, Royal Navy officers aboard ship will no longer utter the traditional Saturday night toast to 'Our

Wives and Sweethearts.' The toast, which elicits the unofficial response: 'May they never meet!' has been changed because there are so many women officers at sea. The instruction changing the toast to 'Our Families' was issued this week by the new Second Sea Lord, Vice-Admiral David Steel" (Coghlan, "Navy bans historic toast to the wives and sweethearts").

96. Armstrong (1857), p. 275.

97. According to Armstrong, a Marine was also with the party (Armstrong [1857], p. 276); Neatby (1967), p. 85.

98. Neatby (1967), pp. 85–86.

99. Ibid., pp. 86–87.

100. Ibid., pp. 87–88. "Messrs. Sainsbury and Newton, who had both frozen their fingers completely, went back to the ship; we two, Paine and I, remained to guard our booty (Neatby [1967], p. 87)." Newton's frostbite injuries were so severe, he spent 14 days on the sick list; Able Seaman Samuel MacKenzie (Ford's fatigue party) was also frostbitten and spent six days on the sick list (Armstrong's journal [Sick List], NA, ADM 101/250, p. 4; Ford's diary [October 31, 1850], KML, 18500 119Arctic1xx ).

101. Armstrong (1857), p. 276; Neatby (1967), p. 88; Neatby omitted the final portion of Miertsching's entry for October 30: "Although these animals did not have much fat (or tallow), the meat, especially of the young animals, was marbled with fat and, given the absence of European beef, was also good tasting; the heavy frost in winter has taken away the musk flavor, therefore one could not taste it anymore; whereas, the whole head, with tongue, and the kidneys, are all inedible because of the strong musk flavor.—The largest hide weighed 147 pounds" (M. Opel to Stein, personal communication, August 11, 2014).

102. Armstrong (1857), pp. 277–78. The "blue lights" referred to were Bengal blue lights, used for signaling and illumination. Miertsching's April 17, 1851, entry made reference to them in his catalogue of traveling equipment, but the detailed list of items in this catalogue were omitted in Neatby's translation (M. Opel to Stein, personal communication, October 4, 2014).

## *Chapter 8*

1. McClure (1856), p. 141; McClure, "The North-West Passage, etc." (1853), p. 671.

2. Piers's journal (October 31, 1850), NMM, JOD/102.

3. Armstrong (1857), p. 283.

4. Piers's journal (October 31, 1850), NMM, JOD/102.

5. Ibid.

6. McClure (1856), pp. 140–41, at the coordinates lat. 73° 31' 39" N. and long. 114° 39' W. Sir Robert Peel was a former prime minister, who died only four months before, on July 2 (Piers's journal [October 31, 1850], NMM, JOD/102; Armstrong [1857], pp. 281–82; McClure [1854a], p. 38).

7. McClure (1854a), p. 38; Piers's journal (October 31, 1850, marginal notation), NMM, JOD/102. Cresswell's painting, *Melville Island from Banks' Land. May 1852* (Cresswell [1854], Plate VI), demonstrates Melville Island was plainly visible during the favorable spring weather. Also, written on Cresswell's chart of the *Investigator*'s route is "Bank's Land was seen by Sir E^d Parry from Mellville [*sic*] Island. Melville Island could also be distinctly seen from Banks' Land" (Cresswell [1854], Plate IX).

8. McClure (1856), p. 133.

9. Armstrong (1857) pp. 284–85. "The period of travelling was nine days three hours" (McClure [1856], p. 145; Piers's journal [October 31, 1850], NMM, JOD/102).

10. Piers's journal (October 31, 1850), NMM, JOD/102.

11. Ibid.

12. Ibid.

13. Ward, p. 216; Giesbrecht and Wilkerson, p. 120; Forgey, p. 44.

14. Piers's journal (October 31, 1850), NMM, JOD/102.

15. McClure (1856), pp. 133–41; Armstrong (1857), p. 284–85; Piers's journal (October 31, 1850), NMM, JOD/102.

16. Piers's journal (October 31, 1850), NMM, JOD/102.

17. McClure (1856), p. 144; Armstrong (1857), p. 286.

18. Armstrong (1857), p. 286; McClure (1856), p. 147; Ford's diary (November 1, 1850), KML, 18500119 Arctic1xx; Neatby (1967), p. 93.

19. Armstrong (1857), pp. 286–87; Neatby (1967), p. 92.

20. Armstrong (1857), p. 287. "But on this principle of ventilation, should ships be prepared for wintering in the Arctic Regions; it admits, however, of very considerable improvement, and would have been rendered much more perfect with a larger allowance of coals, and an additional stove on the lower deck, which would not only prevent a great degree the condensation of vapour and consequent humidity of atmosphere, but facilitate the escape of impure air, and contribute to the general warmth, dryness and salubrity [well-being] of the ship" (Armstrong [1857], pp. 287–88).

21. Neatby (1967), p. 90.

22. Ford's diary (November 1, 1850), KML, 18500119Arctic1xx.

23. Piers's journal (November 6, 1850), NMM, JOD/102.

24. Armstrong (1857), pp. 289–90.

25. Armstrong (1857), p. 290; McClure (1856), p. 149; Piers's journal (November 21, 23, 1850), NMM, JOD/102; In December, Mongo did not show the same timidity towards another captured fox, when the Investigators "formed a circle some 200 or 300 yards in diameter, to prevent [the fox's] escape," and Mongo's "chase invariably proved amusing, and never failed to afford us a pleasing degree of excitement, as long as the cold enabled us to remain spectators" (Armstrong [1857], p. 292). The captures of other foxes followed, until six were taken by December 21 (Piers's journal [December 21, 1850], NMM, JOD/102).

26. Armstrong's journal, NA, ADM 101/250, p. 73. On a level piece of ice, about 150–200 yards from the ship, "the men, by constantly walking round it, have made a circle exactly like a riding ground: here too they frequently play rounders and pot-ball—I call this place 'the Circus'" (Piers's journal [December 2, 1850], NMM, JOD/102). Nelson (vol. 1, November 12, 1850), SPRI, MS 748/1–2; Armstrong (1858), pp. 14 & 17; see "A Historic Enquiry into the Efficacy of Lime Juice for the Prevention and Cure of Scurvy," by Alice Henderson Smith, *Journal of the Royal Army Medical Corps* (February 1919), 32(2): pp. 93–116 and (March 1919), 32(3): pp. 188–208.

27. Savours and Deacon, p. 151; Armstrong (1858), pp. 14 and 92.

28. Armstrong's journal, NA, ADM 101/250, p. 73; Neatby (1967), pp. 100–101.

29. Ford's diary (November 17, 1850), KML, 18500119Arctic1xx; Neatby (1967), p. 93.

30. Piers's journal (December 9, 1850), NMM, JOD/102.

31. Armstrong (1857), p. 291.

32. Nelson (vol. 1, November 1850), SPRI, MS 748/1; Armstrong (1857) p. 293 and fn, wherein Armstrong describes the hole as "about two feet square" and wrote, "On the 28th [of December], we were favored with a hasty visit from a Seal, which made his appearance in the fire-hole."

33. Ibid., pp. 288–89; Nelson (vol. 1, November 12, 1850), SPRI, MS 748/1–2.

34. Piers's journal (November 30, 1850), NMM, JOD/102.

35. McClure (1856), p. 147; Nelson (Vol. 1, December 1850), SPRI, MS 748/1; Piers's journal (December 9, 1850), NMM, JOD/102.

36. Piers's journal (December 9, 1850), NMM, JOD/102.

37. Letter & Order Book (December 3, 1850), RGS, SCC/106. Shipmate

James Nelson wrote a poem titled "A Old Worn Out Lanthorn in possession of James Williams, Captain of the Hold, 1851–2–3" (Nelson, SPRI, MS 748/1). "In it he [Nelson] gently mocks the attempts of the Captain [of the Hold] to protect his battered light from the blows it received from casks rolling about below deck," wrote Jane Inglesby, Williams's great-great-granddaughter (Just Plain Folks, http://just-plain-folks.co.uk).

38. Certificate of service and seaman's register ticket (Jane Inglesby); service record, NA, ADM 29/70; O'Byrne (1849), p. 662; "Fete On Board H.M.S. 'Vindictive'"; Cyriax (1939), pp. 212–13.

39. Service record, NA, ADM 29/70; Robertson-Lorant, pp. 117–20, 122, 129; Hodak, p. 72.

40. *Investigator's* Musters (1849–50), NA, ADM 38/1026.

41. Piers's journal (December 18, 1850), NMM, JOD/102; also see Neatby (1967) fn, p. 96; "Gauen" in musters for *Investigator* and *North Star*, McClure (1856), xxxiv, Armstrong (1857), between p. xxii and p. 1, and seaman's register ticket no. 239.524, NA, BT 113/120, but "Gawn" in the sick list, "Gaven" in the Arctic Medal 1818–55 Roll, and "Dawn" in Neatby (1967), p. 120; "Whitefield" in *Investigator's* Muster, McClure (1856) and Neatby (1967), but "Whitfield" in sick list.

42. Neatby (1967) pp. 96–97.

43. Piers's journal (December 25, 1850), NMM, JOD/102.

44. Ibid.

45. *Investigator's* Musters (1849–50), NA, ADM 38/1026; Ross's service record, NA, ADM 29/65; Ross's illiteracy was determined from the fact that he signed for his Arctic Medal on August 5, 1857, with "his × Mark" (Arctic Medal 1818–55 Roll, NA, ADM 171/9). His conduct on the *Phoenix* and *Investigator* was "Good," but that for the *North Star* (April 16, 1853–October 17, 1854) was only "Indifferent," and he was then discharged as "Unfit for this Service" (service record, NA, ADM 29/65). Franklin's officers, Boatswain 3rd Class John Lane and Acting Surgeon John Smart Peddie, HMS *Terror*, both left the *William & Mary* on March 11, 1845, so may have served onboard when Ross was present (*Terror's* Muster [1845], NA, ADM 38/1962 & Cyriax [1939], p. 213).

46. Brown manuscript, GM, M-141, p. 14.

47. Barr (1999), p. 103; Ford's diary (December 26, 1850), KML, 18500119 Arctic1xx.

48. Armstrong (1857), p. 294; McClure (1856), p. 150; McClure (1854a), p. 38.

49. Neatby (1967), p. 99. "Christmas pudding is a type of pudding tradi-

tionally served on Christmas Day (December 25) as part of the Christmas dinner. It has its origins in medieval England, and is sometimes known as plum pudding or Christmas Pudding or just "pud," though this can also refer to other kinds of boiled pudding involving dried fruit. Despite the name "plum pudding," the pudding contains no actual plums due to the pre–Victorian use of the word "plums" as a term for raisins. The pudding is composed of many dried fruits held together by egg and suet, sometimes moistened by treacle or molasses and flavored with cinnamon, nutmeg, cloves, ginger, and other spices. The pudding is aged for a month or even a year; the high alcohol content of the pudding prevents it from spoiling during this time" (Christmas pudding, http://en.wikipedia.org).

50. Piers's journal (January 1, 1851), NMM, JOD/102.

51. This is a part of Miertsching's January 1, 1853, entry, the entry having been omitted in Neatby's translation (M. Opel to Stein, personal communication, September 11, 2014).

52. In the late 1820s, there was a Peter Green in Weymouth, who was a well-known proprietor of boats, etc., and since Milner was almost 19 when he entered the Navy on September 10, 1838, he could have conceivably worked for several years prior to this time (Barrett, p. 18; Milner's service record for Luke/Milner's, NA, ADM 29/64).

53. Armstrong (1857), p. 298. In 1833, "a directive was issued to all captains of ships to organize a "Sick-Berth-Attendant" category or rating.... One thing, however, is reasonably certain. Up to the time of the Crimean War [1854–56] the standards of the Sick-berth-attendants were decidedly low" (Lewis [1965], p. 260). According to Piers, searches were carried out for any signs of the deer on January 6 and 7, "so as to establish the fact of these animals wintering so far north as these Islands," but no traces could be found (Piers's journal [January 6, 7, 8, 1851], NMM, JOD/102).

54. Descendants of Thomas Ames, www.fadedgenes.co.uk/ThomasAMES Descendants.html; Armstrong (1858), p. 62; *Castor's* Description Book (1843–47), NA, ADM 38/7771; William Loney RN—Victorian naval surgeon, http://home.wxs.nl/~pdavis/Loney.htm. For the First New Zealand Medal 1845–47, 54 RN and 8 RM medals (dated 1845–46) were issued to the *Castor* (Douglas-Morris [1987], p. 284); Registers of Deceased Ratings, NA, ADM 154; Registers of Seamen's Effects, NA, ADM 44, A/2361; Ames (surname), http://en.wikipedia.org; Ames in *Investigator's* Muster, ADM 44, Armstrong (1857), but Eames in

the sick list, McClure (1856), and Piers.

55. Neatby (1967), pp. 101–02; Armstrong (1857), pp. 298–99.

56. Understanding Pleurisy—the Basics, www.webmd.com.

57. Nelson (vol. 1, January 1851), SPRI, MS 748/1; Armstrong's journal (sick list), NA, ADM 101/250, p. 5; Piers's journal (January 23, 1851), NMM, JOD/102.

58. Piers's journal (January 28, 1851), NMM, JOD/102; Miertsching: "Yesterday, after a long time, together with the captain we went—or better to say stumbled—finally yet again to Princess Royal Island, but came back with frostbites in the faces. Today is the captain's birthday (46 years old), but like me he has to stay inside, because the doctor has bandaged our frostbitten faces, and so, in the mishap, we are consoling each other." This is a part of Miertsching's January 28, 1853 entry, this entry having been omitted in Neatby's translation (M. Opel to Stein, personal communication, September 11, 2014).

59. McClure (1854a), p. 38.

60. Armstrong (1857), p. 299.

61. Nelson (vol. 1, February 1851), SPRI, MS 748/1.

62. Nelson (vol. 1, February 1851), SPRI, MS 748/1; Piers's journal (February 3, 1851), NMM, JOD/102; White, p. 466; Registers of Officers' Effects, NA, ADM 45/33; *Investigator*'s Musters (1849–50), NA, ADM 38/1026; Sainsbury's service record, NA, ADM 196/37.

63. Piers's journal (February 3, 1851), NMM, JOD/102; Bow's attestation form, NA, ADM 157/56; Cresswell's service record, NA, ADM 196/36; Elias Bow also possessed, or went by, the name "Robert" ("Bob"), as this is how he's referred to by his family during the conversation with Piers. One year he's Piers's servant, and referred to as "'Bob Bow,' R.M. my servant" (Piers's journal [February 5, 1852], NMM, JOD/102).

64. Piers's journal (February 3, 1851), NMM, JOD/102.

65. Armstrong (1857) p. 300; Piers's journal (February 7, 1851), NMM, JOD/102.

66. Piers's journal (February 8, 10, 1851), NMM, JOD/102.

67. Piers's journal (February 13, 14, 17, 1851), NMM, JOD/102.

68. Armstrong (1857), p. 302.

69. Neatby's original translation: "Dr. Armstrong, who is not the best of comrades, was properly humiliated by the other officers today. The captain was informed of the whole affair, but took not the least notice of it" (Neatby [1967], p. 103 & fn). Mechtild Opel's more nuanced translation of the passage within the text, and the inclusion of the omitted final sentence puts the situation in better context (M. Opel to Stein, personal communication, September 11, 2014).

70. *Asia*'s Description Book (1847–51), NA, ADM 38/7567; Griffiths' seaman's register ticket no. 358.503, NA, BT 113/180; Late 18th, 19th and early 20th Century Naval and Naval Social History Index, www.pbenyon.plus.com/Naval.html; Registers of Seamen's Effects, NA, ADM 44/7139; *Superb*'s Description Book (1844–48), NA, ADM 38/9119; Le Vesconte Family Tree, http://jamcnairn.com/Genealogy/LeVesconteFamilyTree.htm.

71. Piers's journal (February 28 and March 1, 1851), NMM, JOD/102.

72. Neatby (1967), p. 103, with additional details from McClure (1854a), p. 38; March 8, 1851: Regarding the daily sledding of supplies to the island, the following was omitted in Neatby's translation: "They were wheat flour, peas, dried potatoes, salted beef and pork, preserved meat, hardtack, cocoa, tea, sugar, a barrel of strong spirits, a case with gunpowder, lead shot and bullets, and a case of medicine, along with some barrels of thick clothes" (M. Opel to Stein, personal communication, October 4, 2014).

73. Piers's journal (March 3, 1851), NMM, JOD/102; Ford's diary (March 11, 1851), KML, 18500119Arctic1xx; Neatby (1967) p. 104.

74. Piers's journal (March 8, 1851), NMM, JOD/102; Ford's diary (March 6, 1851), KML, 18500119Arctic1xx; McClure (1854a), p. 38; Armstrong (1857), p. 303. Armstrong's lack of Arctic experience was evident when he related McClure's precautions, and commented on "the very remote probability of a sudden disruption of the ice, and injury or loss of the ship" (Armstrong [1857], pp. 302–03).

75. Piers's journal (March 15, 20, 21, 1851), NMM, JOD/102; Armstrong (1857), pp. 303–04. Armstrong found the stomachs of the foxes either empty or barely containing any contents, and attributed the tameness to their famished condition; Armstrong (1857), p. 303; Piers's journal (March 15, 1851), NMM, JOD/102; Nelson (vol. 1, March 1851), SPRI, MS 748/1–2; Reynard the Fox, www.britannica.com.

76. Armstrong (1857), p. 304; Neatby (1967), p. 104 and fn; McClure (1856), pp. 101–03; McClure (1854a), p. 34; Armstrong (1857), pp. 208–09; Piers's journal (September 7, 1850), NMM, JOD/102; Ford's diary (September 7, 1850), KML, 18500119Arctic1xx; Armstrong (1857), p. 305.

77. Neatby (1967), p. 105; Piers's journal (March 22, 1851), NMM, JOD/102; Armstrong (1857), fn, p. 506. A tinker was a person who in the past traveled to different places and made money by selling or repairing small items (such as pots and pans), and "The Jolly Tinker" is a traditional Irish folk song (Traditional Music Library, www.tradionalmusic.co.uk).

78. *Cornwallis*'s Description Book (1855–56), NA, ADM 38/7855; Wood, p. 72; St. Mary Magdalen Church, Woolwich (1813–37 baptisms); Edward Stone's service record, NMM, ADM 359/51A/223; Wood, p. 71; Clowes (vol. 4), p. 333.

## Chapter 9

1. Bruin, http://en.wikipedia.org.

2. Armstrong (1857), p. 304.

3. Piers's journal (March 29, 1851), NMM, JOD/102.

4. Armstrong (1857), p. 305; Piers's journal (March 29, 1851), NMM, JOD/102.

5. Piers's journal (April 1, 1851), NMM, JOD/102.

6. Piers's journal (April 1, 1851), NMM, JOD/102; Ford's diary (April 1 and 2, 1851), KML, 18500119Arctic1xx; Armstrong (1857), pp. 307–08.

7. Piers's journal (April 13, 1851), NMM, JOD/102; Neatby (1967); p. 107.

8. Armstrong (1857), p. 308; Piers's journal (April 9, 1851), NMM, JOD/102. Part of Miertsching's April, 12, 1851 entry was omitted in Neatby's translation: "[T]he result is, that our food, combustible materials and other supplies and things which are necessary for living will be sufficient for the next 2 years; but the lighting material, tallow candles and oil for the dark winter time will not last for 2 winters. Hopefully, we will not need it, because everybody, especially the captain, is predicting that we will enjoy our roast beef and plum pudding of next winter in Old England" (M. Opel to Stein, personal communication, October 4, 2014).

9. Piers's journal (April 15 and 16, 1851), NMM, JOD/102; *Investigator*'s Musters (1849–50), NA, ADM 38/1026.

10. *Enterprise*'s Description Book (1848–49), NA, ADM 38/8041; Arctic Medal 1818–55 Roll, NA, ADM 171/9; *Investigator*'s Description Book (1848–49), NA, ADM 38/8387; Attestation form, NA, ADM 157/56; *Investigator*'s Musters (1849–50), NA, ADM 38/1026; Gauen's seaman's register ticket no. 239.524, NA, BT 113/120; *Carysfort*'s Description Book (1841–45), NA, ADM 38/7769.

11. Piers's journal (April 17, 1851), NMM, JOD/102; McClure (1856), p. 163.

12. Neatby (1967), p. 108. Miertsching wrote about the "equipment of a travelling party," and Neatby referred to a "detailed catalogue" of the same, but

omitted the specific list of items: "together with 4 tent poles with iron pike, weighing altogether 60 pounds; 2 tent sheets from buffalo hide, one as bottom layer, the other as duvet [a soft flat bag filled with down, feathers, wool, silk], weighing 40 pounds; 9 thick woollen sleeping bags weighing 42 pounds; a shovel and a pickax weighing 5 and a half pounds; a cooking device for melting ice and snow and cooking cocoa, consisting of kettle, lamp etc. weighing 12 pounds; a bag with 9 tin mugs and spoons weighing 5 pounds; a sextant, double-barreled shotgun with ammunition, weighing 12 pounds; a tin can containing pepper, salt, lighter, cotton and flannel bandage, plaster, lint, liniment, eyewash, pills etc., lancet, opium tincture, scissors, needles and twine, weighing 16 pounds; a bag with a big strong brush to remove snow from tent and clothing, boot soles, wax, bristles, shoemaking wire, nails, awl, wicks, rockets (bengal [Bengal]), blue lights, copper tubes for leaving messages at the coast, and other things, weighing altogether 16 pounds; gunpowder, grist and rifle 15 pounds; a bag with reserve stockings, boots etc., and soap, towels, combs etc.—10 and a half pounds; altogether 258 pounds" (M. Opel to Stein, personal communication, October 4, 2014).

13. McClure (1856), p. 163. "Each party consisted of one officer and six men, with a sledge provided with food, fuel, and clothing for forty days; the aggregate weight of which amounted to 1028 pounds (Armstrong [1857], p. 310); "an Officer & six men to each sledge, with fifty days of provisions &c." (Piers's journal (April 18, 1851), NMM, JOD/102). However, Miertsching wrote: "Each officer has eight men to draw the sledge.... The total weight of such a sledge load for forty-two days exceeds a thousand pounds" (Neatby [1967], pp. 107–08).

14. Holland (1994), p. 232; Markham (1908), p. 5.

15. Ross (1994), pp. 309, 322; Markham (1908), p. 3; Holland (1994), pp. 231–32; Neatby (1960), p. 42. Rev. Samuel Haughton was a professor of geology at the University of Dublin, and president of the Geological Society of Dublin (Levere, p. 213).

16. Ross (1994), p. 332.

17. Bradford's medal group is held by the Glenbow Museum, Calgary, Canada: Naval General Service Medal 1793–1840, with Syria clasp, for service on HMS *Hazard* in 1840 (officially impressed on the edge: A.R. BRADFORD, SURGEON R.N.); Baltic Medal 1854–55 (unnamed/Surgeon/*Hogue*); Arctic Medal 1818–55 (unnamed/Surgeon/*Resolute*/1850–51); Turkish St. Jean d'Acre Medal (silver issue/unnamed/

Surgeon/*Hazard*). Since three of the four medals are unnamed, they were stored in different areas of the museum, until the group was reunited in 2007 by Captain Michael W. Clare, CD, a member of the British Medals Forum (Roback to Stein, personal communication, March 3, 1995); British Medals Forum, www.britishmedalforum.com; Free Settler or Felon? www.jenwilletts.com; Douglas-Morris (1982), p. 322; Baltic Medal 1854–55 Roll, NA, ADM 171/19–22; Arctic Medal 1818–55 Roll, NA, ADM 171/9; St. Jean d'Acre Medal Roll, NA, ADM 171/14.

18. Osborn (1852), p. 156.

19. McClintock and Haughton, pp. 206–07.

20. McClure (1856), pp. 163–64; Brown manuscript, GM, M-141, p. 15; Piers's journal (May 20, 1851), NMM, JOD/102, described Calder as Cresswell's "chief man." Armstrong (1857), pp. 310, 335, 472: Armstrong confused the *direction* of Haswell's party (southeast) with the *coastal area* of Prince Albert's Land to be searched (western and southern), and McClure recorded the same error (McClure [1854a], p. 56). Armstrong also made the error regarding Cresswell's party, which headed in a northwesterly direction to examine the northeastern coast of Banks Land (Armstrong [1857], pp. 310). Every attempt was made to discover the names of the sledders and anything about their journeys from available sources. Since Joseph Facey and Ellis Griffiths were admitted to sick bay on the day of Cresswell's return (May 20) with severe frostbite, resulting in gangrene and amputation of portions of fingers and toes, the assumption has been made that they were sledders (Armstrong's journal [sick list], NA, ADM 101/250, p. 5).

21. "A slow-moving (11 miles/18 kilometer per day) man-hauled sledge, with an accompanying officer, was a very suitable way of surveying a coastline in detail. For these reasons, the Britishers' choice of man-hauled sledging, from 1849 to 1859, makes some sense" (Mackinnon, p. 132).

22. Letter & Order Book (April *21*, 1851), RGS, SSC/106; McClure (1854a), pp. 56–57; however, this is dated April *18*, 1851, the day the sled parties departed.

23. Ross (1994), p. 311.

24. Letter & Order Book (April 21, 1851), RGS, SSC/106 & McClure (1854a), p. 57.

25. Cyriax (1939), pp. 19 & 24.

26. Rae to the Secretary of the Admiralty, September 1, 1849, Great Britain, Parliament, *Papers relating to the Arctic Relief Expeditions* (1851a), pp. 45–50; Armstrong (1857), p. 313.

27. Armstrong (1857), pp. 312–13.

Two months later, Piers wrote that he considered *Investigator* might get through and search Melville Island, but also wondered if it was considered Austin's sphere. If the ship could navigate the middle ice of Viscount Melville Sound before going too far east, or early enough in the season to escape the ice, "I have no doubt we shall visit it in the ship. Lastly; although, from the fact of Melville Is. having been seen by Cresswell, it might now be wished that a sledge party had been sent there, still situated so far down this strait as we are, and unacquainted thence with the state of Barrow's Str. [Viscount Melville Sound], together with the uncertainty of the breaking up of the ice, such a journey might have been considered hazardous; and had any casualty occurred in attempting its performance, it might have been condemned as rash" (Piers's journal [June 13, 1851], NMM, JOD/102).

28. Armstrong (1857), p. 311. McClure was certainly aware of Austin's mission, as Piers noted: "Capt. Austin's ships, the fitting out of which we were unacquainted with till our arrival in 'the Pacific [evidently from HMS *Gorgon*]'" (Piers's journal [June 13, 1851], NMM, JOD/102).

29. McClure (1856), pp. 234–36; Armstrong (1857), pp. 515–20. Armstrong wrote that McClure reached Winter Harbour on "the morning of the 20th," but this is an error or misprint, as it should read the 28th; Ford's diary (April 2 and May 9, 1852), KML, 18500119Arctic1xx; Neatby (1967), pp. 162–63. There are slight variations of dates and the number of days between these sources; McClintock and Haughton (1858), p. 204. McClintock left his own message, dated June 6, 1851 (McClure [1856], p. 234).

30. Collinson (1889), p. 111. Also formerly known as Rasa Island, its current name is Oki Daitō Island (Okidaitōjima, www. http://en.wikipedia.org).

31. Neatby (1967), p. 108. "A pocket knife was issued, as a present, to each of the ship's company in the forenoon" (Piers's journal [April 18, 1851], NMM, JOD/102).

32. Nelson (vol. 1, April 18, 1851), SPRI, MS 748/1. Ford wrote, "Our Captain addressed them with a few words concerning the service they were going on, concluding with an admirable sentence, which was that he commended them to *Him* who watches over us everywhere" (Ford's diary [April 18, 1851], KML, 18500119Arctic1xx).

33. Piers's journal (April 18, 1851), NMM, JOD/102; Neatby (1967), p. 108; Armstrong (1857), p. 310; Ford's diary (April 18, 1851), KML, 18500119Arctic1xx. Piers states the parties left at 7:00 p.m. Armstrong wrote 7:30 p.m. and Ford wrote "the evening."

34. Piers's journal (April 24, 1851), NMM, JOD/102.

35. Armstrong (1857), p. 313.

36. Piers's journal (April 23, 1851), NMM, JOD/102; Armstrong (1857), p. 314; Piers's journal (April 29, 1851), NMM, JOD/102.

37. Ford's diary (April 20, 1851), KML, 18500119Arctic1xx; Neatby (1967), p. 109.

38. Armstrong (1857), p. 315; Piers's journal (May 1, 1851), NMM, JOD/102; Stubberfield's service record, NA, ADM 139/348, CS 34759; Relfe's service record, NA, ADM 29/57. Stubberfield joined the RN on May 21, 1845, as an ordinary seaman, and the *Ocean* was his first ship. He deserted on September 23, 1846, but rejoined the ship December 8, and was discharged June 22, 1847, with "Fair" conduct. Acting Carpenter 3rd Class George J. Ford also briefly served on the *Ocean* from May 22–June 22, 1846 (Ford's service record, NA, ADM 29/23/531).

39. Piers's journal (May 1, 1851), NMM, JOD/102.

40. Ibid.

41. Armstrong (1857), p. 315; Piers's journal (May 1, 1851), NMM, JOD/102; Ford's diary (May 2, 1851), KML, 18500119Arctic1xx.

42. Piers's journal (May 5, 1851), NMM, JOD/102. One wonders how the 25-year-old Cheshire Marine got along during and after the arduous time with McClure's sled party the previous October (Saunders's service record, NA, ADM157/2885).

43. Wynniatt "reached about Lat. 73° 16. Long. 112°" (Piers's journal [May 6, 1851], NMM, JOD/102).

44. Letter & Order Book (Spring, 1851), RGS, SSC/106. The words "I was much surprised to see" and "injudiciously" do not appear in the published dispatch (McClure [1854a], p. 38).

45. Neatby (1967), pp. 109–10.

46. Piers's journal (May 6, 1851), NMM, JOD/102.

47. Neatby, p. 109, fn; Piers's journal (May 6, 1851), NMM, JOD/102.

48. Letter & Order Book (Spring, 1851), RGS, SSC/106; Armstrong (1857), p. 317; Neatby (1967), p. 110; Ford's diary (May 6, 1851), KML, 18500119Arctic1xx; Piers's journal (May 6, 1851), NMM, JOD/102.

49. Piers's journal (May 6, 7, 1851), NMM, JOD/102. Piers incorrectly states that Miertsching's party went to the eastern shore, whereas McClure, Armstrong, Ford and Miertsching all indicated the western shore (McClure [1856], p. 178; Armstrong [1857], p. 317; Ford's diary [May 7, 1851], KML, 18500119Arctic1xx; Neatby [1967], p. 110).

50. Piers's journal (May 8, 1851), NMM, JOD/102; Armstrong (1857), pp. 319–20.

51. Armstrong (1857), pp. 320–21; Piers's journal (May 8, 1851), NMM, JOD/102.

52. Piers's journal (May 8, 1851), NMM, JOD/102; Armstrong (1857), p. 321; Whitefield spent nine days on the sick list (Armstrong's journal [sick list], NA, ADM 101/250, p. 5).

53. McClure (1856), p. 180; Armstrong (1857), pp. 322–23; Ford's diary (May 13, 1851), KML, 18500119Arctic1xx.

54. Armstrong (1857), p. 324; Neatby (1967), p. 111.

55. McClure (1856), pp. 180–81; Armstrong (1857), p. 326–27; Piers's journal (May 20, 1851), NMM, JOD/102.

56. McClure (1856), p. 181; Ford's diary (May 20, 1851), KML, 18500119Arctic1xx; Armstrong (1857), p. 327; Piers's journal (May 20, 1851), NMM, JOD/102.

57. Piers's journal (May 20 and June 13, 1851), NMM, JOD/102. Miertsching wrote that Cresswell reached lat. 74° 16' N. and long. 117° 40' W. (Neatby [1967], p. 122); Armstrong (1857), p. 472; Manning (1956), p. 69. Cresswell created a watercolor sketch of the scene (Cresswell, *Cliff at North West Extremity of Banks Land & Cape Hamilton May 8th 1851*, NRO, WMH 3/1/D4/1). Cresswell left a notice dated April 21, 1851, in a canister at Russell Point. The note and canister were retrieved by V. Stefansson, commander of the Canadian Arctic Expedition 1913–18, on July 26, 1917, and transferred to the Public Archives by the Department of the Naval Service in 1920 (LAC, R6790–0–8-E).

58. McClintock and Haughton, p. 206–07. McClintock's journey lasted from April 15 to July 4, 1851 (Holland [1994], p. 232).

59. Piers's journal (May 20, 1851), NMM, JOD/102; Armstrong (1857), pp. 327–28.

60. Armstrong (1857), pp. 328–29.

61. Armstrong's journal (Sick List/ A List of Men who have received Wounds or Hurts, during the Period of the Journal), NA, ADM 101/250, pp. 5 and 91. Facey was granted an Ordinary Certificate for Hurts: "Severely frostbitten in feet & hands in May 1851 when employed with a travelling party in Polar Regions which ultimately entailed the loss of distal phalanges of right index finger & right great toe together with small portions of several others." Ellis Griffiths was also granted an Ordinary Certificate for Hurts: "Similarly frostbitten when similarly employed ashore mentioned above [as with Joseph Facey] underwent amputation of distal phalanges of left great toe necessary & part of right [?]."

62. Armstrong (1857), pp. 329–30;

Piers's journal (May 21, 1851), NMM, JOD/102. McClure wounded the bear in the spine, evidently paralyzing his hind legs. Armstrong took credit for finishing the creature off with a ball to the head, but Piers indicated, "at the Captain's desire Newton went close to him and put a shot through his head, which at once finished the work," and Stone confirms this: "our old ice-man went out with a gun and finished him" (Wood, p. 76).

63. Armstrong (1857), p. 331; Ford's diary (May 21, 1851), KML, 18500119Arctic1xx; Piers' journal (May 21, 1851), NMM, JOD/102.

64. Piers's journal (May 21, 1851), NMM, JOD/102.

65. Armstrong (1857), p. 331; Neatby (1967), p. 112 and fn.

66. Armstrong (1857), pp. 331–32; Neatby (1967), p. 112; Piers's journal (May 24, 1851), NMM, JOD/102; Ford's diary (May 24, 1851), KML, 18500119Arctic1xx.

67. Armstrong (1857), p. 332. Piers's version of events mirror's Armstrong's account (Piers's journal [May 24, 1851], NMM, JOD/102); Wood, p. 77; "Last night there were 2 polar bears close to the ship; a few men chased them as far as to the islands but could not get them. On the way back to the ship they followed older bear tracks which lead close to the ship, where they found a tin can with some old raisins etc. With those tracks of a bear in the snow, it was to be seen, that the bear that was shot near the ship a time ago, had filled his stomach here with tainted raisins, tobacco etc.—So the riddle was solved. At 6 in the evening Mr. Sainsbury went with 4 men to Prince Albert's Land for a week in the tent; and Newton with 4 men to Baring's Land. The captain gave order to bring all waste from the ship to one single pile close to the ship—for that the polar bears would not poisoning themselves!—as the seamen said" (Miertsching's May 25, 1851, entry, omitted in Neatby's translation; M. Opel to Stein, personal communication, October 4, 2014).

68. Armstrong (1857), p. 332; McClure (1856), p. 184.

69. Ford's diary (May 29, 1851), KML, 18500119Arctic1xx; Piers's journal (May 29 and June 13, 1851), NMM, JOD/102—on the latter date, Piers wrote that Haswell reached lat. 70° 37' N. and long. 115° 36' W.; Armstrong (1857), p. 334; McClure (1854a), p. 39. There are slight variances in the coordinates listed for Haswell's farthest between the latter source (McClure's dispatches), Piers, McClure (1856), p. 185, and Armstrong; McGoogan (2002), p. 135; Rich and Johnson, p. 187; Rae was on a HBC search mission from August 2, 1850–September 26,

1851, and although he did not discover any definite traces of Franklin's expedition, Rae explored over 620 miles (1,000 km) of new coastline along southern Victoria Island (Holland [1994], pp. 234–35).

70. McClure (1854a), p. 39; Armstrong (1857), pp. 334–35; McClure (1856), p. 185; Piers's journal (May 29, 1851), NMM, JOD/102; Condon, p. 22. After visiting them, Miertsching wrote, "Unlike the Eskimos of Cape Bathurst these people have *not* pierced the under lip for bright stones, which apparently have the same purpose as the pierced ear-lobe in Europe, from which stones, glass, metal, etc., are hung" (Neatby [1967], p. 116). Miertsching stated Haswell's party observed five tents (Neatby [1967], p. 112), while McClure also saw five tents on his visit (McClure [1856], p. 186).

71. McClure (1854a), p. 39.

72. Piers's journal (May 29, 1851), NMM, JOD/102.

73. McClure (1854a), p. 39; Piers's journal (May 29, 1851), NMM, JOD/102; Armstrong (1857), pp. 341–42; Armstrong's journal (Sick List/A List of Men who have received Wounds or Hurts, during the Period of the Journal), NA, ADM 101/250, pp. 5 and 91. Hulott was granted a Pension Certificate for Hurts on June 1, 1853: "Severely frostbitten when employed with travelling party Pr. of Wales Strait on 30 May 1851, which rendered some amputation of all the toes on the right foot & greater portion of left great toe" (Neatby [1967], p. 113). On June 30, Miertsching wrote, "Today the sick Hewlett [Hulott] had seven toes amputated. Facey and Griffiths have lost a few fingers by frost-bite" (Neatby [1967], p. 124).

74. Armstrong (1857), p. 342.

75. McClure (1854a), p. 39; Neatby (1967), p. 115.

76. Neatby (1967), p. 115.

77. McClure (1856), p. 188; Neatby (1967), pp. 116–17; Condon, p. 26; Kangiryuarmiut, http://en.wikipedia.org. McClure theorized that the forefathers of these Eskimos probably crossed the Hudson Strait, and eventually made their way along the coastline of Victoria and Wollaston Lands, accounting for the purity of their language. He wrote, "I certainly should have considered it my duty to endeavour deciding this point by detaching a boat through the Dolphin and Union Straits; but I feel assured that service has been accomplished by Dr. Rae last year, as he evidently was not in this direction" (McClure [1854a], p. 41). Rae of course, had only recently been in the vicinity.

78. Point Parry is indicated on a contemporary map, which was drawn after an Admiralty chart (*Wellington Strait, North Polar Sea*, 1852).

79. Neatby (1967), pp. 116–17. According to McClure: "[A] large sheet of paper which I brought for the purpose, continuing a sketch which Mr. Miertsching had made from the ship to their tents, which they immediately comprehended." A tracing of this sketch map accompanied McClure's dispatches (McClure [1854a], p. 40).

80. McClure (1854a), pp. 40–41.

81. McClure (1854a), p. 40; Armstrong (1857), pp. 340–41. The name Copper Inuit "derives from the groups' traditional practice of manufacturing hunting tools and other implements out of native copper, which is found in great abundance in certain areas of Copper Inuit territory" (Condon, p. xv).

82. Neatby (1967), p. 117.

83. Ibid., p. 118. The *Enterprise* wintered during 1851–52 at Winter Cove (Walker Bay, entrance of the Prince of Wales Strait), and her people had very friendly relations with these same Eskimos. In early November, "among these men we found a small axe and part of a pemmican tin, which showed they were the party who had met with the *Investigator*'s people in the spring" (Collinson [1889], p. 172).

84. Ibid., pp. 118–20; McClure (1854a), p. 40.

85. Armstrong (1857), pp. 337, 342; Piers's journal (June 5, 1851), NMM, JOD/102; Armstrong's journal (Sick List), NA, ADM 101/250, p. 5. It's interesting to note that Whitefield was on the sick list for exhaustion and snow blindness from May 8–17, while Gauen appeared on the list for snow blindness from May 25–29, so was released the very day he joined McClure's sled party (Armstrong's journal [Sick List]), NA, ADM 101/250, p. 5); Nelson (vol. 1, June 5, 1851), SPRI, MS 748/1; Neatby (1967), p. 120, 124.

86. Armstrong (1857), pp. 337–38; Neatby (1967), p. 117 and fn.

87. McClure (1854a), p. 40; McClure (1856), pp. 185–89.

88. Armstrong (1857), pp. 342–43; Piers's journal (June 1, 5, 1851), NMM, JOD/102. Armstrong wrote that the first rain was "so light as to be barely perceptible" (Armstrong [1857], p. 336).

89. Ford's diary (June 2, 1851), KML, 18500119Arctic1xx; Neatby (1967), p. 120; Piers's journal (May 29–June 10, 1851), NMM, JOD/102—June 10: "M! Ford, Carpenter, and two of his men went with a tent & provisions, to the island, where they are to remain a few days to paint & repair the whale boat which it is intended to leave there with the provisions landed in the spring." On June 12, Armstrong wrote, "I made my last visit to the island with Mr. Court, when some observations were completed with the theodolite [surveying instrument], and we re-

turned in the evening to the ship" (Armstrong [1857], p. 349).

90. McClure (1854a), p. 40; McClure (1856), p. 189. In both sources, the date Wynniatt reached his furthest point is May 26, however, Armstrong wrote May 24 (Armstrong [1857], p. 343), and Inglefield's chart shows the same date (Inglefield, 1853); dead reckoning, https://en.wikipedia.org; Piers's journal (June 7, 13, 1851), NMM, JOD/102. The naming history of Wynniatt Bay requires some explanation. Though shown as Beaufort Bay (Inglefield, *Chart Shewing the North West Passage, etc.*, 1853), Collinson sledded there in May 1851 and named it Glenelg Bay (Barr [2007], p. 128). This name appears in McClure's book, on the chart Osborn corrected (Osborn, *Chart to Illustrate the Narrative of the Accomplishment of the North West Passage by H.M. Ship "Investigator," etc.*, 1856). Although sometimes known as Glenelg Bay through recent times, it's properly Wynniatt Bay (Neatby [1967], p. 120). Five days after his return, Wynniatt fell victim to an irritable ulcer, which kept him in sick bay for 44 days (Armstrong's journal [Sick List], NA, ADM 101/250, p. 6).

91. McClure (1854a), p. 40; Neatby (1967), p. 120.

92. Ford's diary (June 7, 1851), KML, 18500119Arctic1xx; Neatby (1967), p. 120; McClure (1856), p. 189; Osborn (1852), pp. 170–71; Inglefield, *Chart Shewing the North West Passage, etc.* (1853); Osborn, *Chart to Illustrate the Narrative of the Accomplishment of the North West Passage by H.M. Ship "Investigator," etc.* (1856). "At the same time Mr Sherard Osborn and Mr Wynniatt of *Investigator* were only thirty miles from each other" (Barr [2007], p. 74). May 23 is stated by Armstrong to have been Osborn's furthest west (Armstrong [1857], p. 344), and the same is shown on Inglefield's chart (Inglefield, *Chart Shewing the North West Passage, etc.* [1853]); however, this was the date he started back, after having backtracked off the sea ice.

93. Private King was born in February 1824, at Bury St. Edmunds, Suffolk, and was illiterate when he joined the Royal Marines on April 9, 1842 (he signed for his Arctic Medal with an "X" on May 9, 1857). King was discharged dead in the infirmary at Woolwich on April 1, 1859 (attestation papers, NA, ADM 158/53, and Arctic Medal 1818–1855 Roll, NA, ADM 171/9, p. 50). At Bury St. Edmunds, witch trials were intermittently conducted between 1599 and 1694. "Two specific trials in 1645 and 1662 became historically well known. The 1645 trial "facilitated" by the Witch-finder General Matthew Hopkins saw 18 people executed in one day. The judgment by the future Lord

Chief Justice of England and Wales, Sir Matthew Hale, in the 1662 trial acted as a powerful influence on the continuing persecution of witches in England and similar persecutions in the American colonies" (Bury St. Edmunds witch trials, https://en.wikipedia.org).

94. Armstrong's journal (Sick List), NA, ADM 101/250, p. 6; periostitis, https://en.wikipedia.org. Five days after getting off the sick list, King was back on it for 122 days with osteitis necrosis, wherein a bone becomes inflamed due to infection, trauma or degeneration, resulting in the death of most or all of the cells or tissues due to disease or injury, especially in a specific area of the body (Armstrong's journal [Sick List], NA, ADM 101/250, p. 6; Medical Dictionary, http://medical-dictionary.thefreedictionary.com).

95. McClure recorded Cresswell's farthest on this occasion as lat. 71° 10' N. and long. 123° 4' W. (McClure [1854a], p. 40).

96. Piers's journal (June 10, 1851), NMM, JOD/102. Cresswell left a record in a cylinder within a cairn he built on a low beach near Cape Lambton. This cape is referred to as Cape Hamilton (McClure [1854a], p. 41 and McClure [1856], p. 202), and shown on Osborn's 1856 map as "C. Lambton or Hamilton." Manning attributes the error to a probable slip in McClure's notes (Manning [1956], pp. 69, 72, 73 and fn). There is a Cape Vesey Hamilton on the northeastern coast of Banks Island, and Manning confuses this place and Cape Lambton on p. 69.

97. McClure (1854a), p. 41.

98. Piers's journal (June 13, 1851), NMM, JOD/102.

99. Ford's diary (June 14, 1851), KML, 18500119Arctic1xx; Piers's journal (July 4, 1851), NMM, JOD/102). A copper cylinder containing a report of the voyage thus far (dated June 15, 1851), and a map of newly discovered lands, were placed three days later in a large cairn erected on the cape of one of the Princess Royal Islands. Now held by the British Library, the report contains the same designation for *Investigator* found in the Letter & Order Book, "This Staff and Cairn were erected by a Party from Her Majesty's Discovery Ship Investigator." It goes on to state, "No intelligence whatever has been found which can throw the least light upon the fate of the missing expedition under Sir John Franklin" (Neatby [1967], p. 123 & BL, ADD. 35308).

## *Chapter 10*

1. Piers's journal (June 13, 1851), NMM, JOD/102.

2. Piers's journal (July 4, 1851), NMM, JOD/102.

3. Ibid.; McClure (1854a), p. 41; Great Britain (1850a), p. 84 (Appendix 4). McClure stated his intentions to the Secretary of the Admiralty in a July 20, 1850 letter, that he "might push more directly for Banks Land, which I think is of the utmost importance to thoroughly examine," and "it would be my anxious desire to get to the northward of Melville Island, and resume our search along its shores" (McClure [1856], pp. 43–44).

4. Piers's journal (June 13, 1851), NMM, JOD/102. Two days later was the anniversary of the 1815 Battle of Waterloo, and Piers wrote, "Waterloo day—I trust 'the good old Duke' is living and in good health to meet as usual the veterans who seconded him in that glorious victory" (Piers's journal [June 15, 1851], NMM, JOD/102).

5. Piers's journal (June 19–July 1, 1851), NMM, JOD/102; Ford's diary (June 29, 1851), KML, 18500119Arctic1xx; Armstrong stated the ice decreased somewhat less (2 feet 2 1/2 inches) over the same period (Armstrong [1857], p. 351); Ford: "Since I left home I have spent my Sundays & evenings reading the following religious books (for which I return thanks to those who introduced a library on board ship) Mark's Sailor's Hope, Retrospect, the Reformation of the Church, Beckersteth on Prayer, Scripture Help, Church in Navy & Army, Abbot's Young Christian, Scripture Truths, Bishop Tailor's Guide to Christianity, the Bible through, besides tracts of different sorts, which have taught me more of my dependence on & duty to my Maker than I have learned in all my life before, & I thank God for this opportunity" (Ford's diary [July 6, 1851], KML, 18500119Arctic1xx).

6. Ford's diary (June 27, 1851), KML, 18500119Arctic1xx; Piers's journal (July 9, 1851), NMM, JOD/102. Though noted as "Ralph" by Piers, this surely was Relfe, an *alias* for the name "Rolfe" previous to joining *Investigator* on December 26, 1849 (service record, NA, ADM 29/57; *Investigator*'s Muster, NA, ADM 38/1026). He signed "Samuel X his mark Relfe" for his Arctic Medal, so was illiterate, and this could have played into the confusion about his surname (Arctic Medal 1818–55 Roll, NA, ADM 171/9, p. 76). For a year and a half (from 1845 to 1847), he was shipmates on HMS *Ocean* with Isaac Stubberfield (service records, NA, ADM 29/57; 139/348/34759); Neatby (1967), p. 125.

7. Relfe's service record, NA, ADM 29/57; Hornby was appointed to the *Formidable* at mate on May 5, 1841 (*The New Navy List*, No. 11, [August 1842], p. 78); *Terror*'s Muster (March–May

1845, June 30, 1845), NA, ADM 38/1962.

8. McClure (1854a), p. 42; Piers's journal (July 7–14, 1851), NMM, JOD/102. "On Saturday, the 5th, a piece of copper, weighing nine pounds, was taken off the bow of the ship, from which it was nearly detached, curiously corrugated from pressure of the ice" (Piers's journal [July 7, 1851], NMM, JOD/102): Neatby (1967), p. 126.

9. Ford's diary (July 22, 1851), KML, 18500119Arctic1xx.

10. McClure (1854a), p. 42; Armstrong (1857), p. 356. Blasting was tried on the 19th, but to no useful result (Piers's journal [July 19, 1851], NMM, JOD/102; Neatby [1967], p. 127).

11. Neatby (1967), p. 128; McClure (1856), p. 198. The problems with the compasses may have been attributable to magnetic anomalies. Miertsching wrote on August 14 that "the compass is also useless, due to the nearness of the [North] Magnetic Pole" (Neatby [1967], p. 130). However, between 1831 and 1904, the North Magnetic Pole was located some 500 miles to the southeast, on the Boothia Peninsula's southwestern coast (Magnetic North Pole Positions, https://en.wikipedia.org).

12. Armstrong (1857), pp. 361–62; Piers's journal (July 28, 1851), NMM, JOD/102; Ford's diary (July 28, 1851), KML, 18500119Arctic1xx; M. Opel to Stein, personal communication, May 23, 2014—from Miertsching's *Travel Narrative of a North Pole Expedition*, etc.; Concertina, http://en.wikipedia.org; July 29, 1851; "Today the doctor operated on a seaman who had a circular carbuncle (struma) [a swelling of the thyroid gland] beneath the chin for 2 years. That thing had the shape of a hen's egg, but only a bit larger; it was put in spirits" (M. Opel to Stein, personal communication, October 16, 2014—from Miertsching's *Travel Narrative of a North Pole Expedition*, etc.).

13. Piers's journal (August 5, 1851), NMM, JOD/102.

14. Ford's diary (August 6, 1851), KML, 18500119Arctic1xx.

15. Neatby (1967), p. 130; Piers's journal (August 14, 1851), NMM, JOD/102.

16. Neatby (1967), pp. 130–31; McClure (1854a), p. 43; Ford's diary (August 15, 1851), KML, 18500119Arctic1xx. The spanker boom is a long spar extending from the lower part of the mizzenmast, to which the spanker sail is attached.

17. McClure (1856), p. 199. The coordinates are in slight variance to those recorded in McClure's dispatch, lat. 73° 13' 43" N. and long. 115° 32' 30" W. (McClure [1854a], p. 43).

18. Piers's journal (August 16, 1851), NMM, JOD/102.

19. Armstrong (1857), p. 376.

20. McClure (1854a), p. 43.

21. Neatby (1967), p. 131.

22. Armstrong (1857), p. 378.

23. Herrnhut is a municipality in Görlitz district in eastern Saxony, Germany. Herrnhut is also the name of the largest town in the municipality (Herrnhut, http://en.wikipedia.org). After fleeing from persecution in Bohemia, the Moravians established their headquarters at Herrnhut in the 18th century (Johann August Miertsching, www.biographi.ca).

24. At 10:00 p.m. that evening, Piers stated the ship was making six knots (Piers's journal [August 16, 1851], NMM, JOD/102).

25. Armstrong (1857), pp. 378–79.

26. Armstrong (1857), p. 379; Neatby (1967), p. 132. McClure identifies Cape Lambton as "Cape Hamilton" in his dispatch (McClure [1854a], p. 44 [see Appendix 6]; McClure [1854a], p. 44). One of the smaller rivers was the Atitok River, and the "one considerable river" was the Masik River (Map of Banks Island, 1956).

27. Neatby (1967), p. 132, fn.

28. McClure (1854a), p. 42.

29. McClure (1856), p. 202; Neatby (1967), p. 133; Armstrong (1857), pp. 381–82; McClure (1854a), p. 44.

30. McClure (1854a), p. 44; Piers's journal (August 19, 1851), NMM, JOD/102; Armstrong (1857), pp. 389–90; Inglefield, Chart Shewing the North West Passage, etc. (1853).

31. According to Manning, the earliest map showing Haswell Point is the 1854 Admiralty chart (Manning [1956], pp. 72–73); Discoveries in the Arctic Sea by the Squadrons Under the Orders of Capt⁺ Sir Edw⁺ Belcher C.B. H.M.S. Assistance, etc. (1855a); The Arctic Navy List (1875), p. 21; Map of Central Arctic America showing the track of H.M.S. Enterprise and Investigator in 1850–54 (1889); The Canadian Topographic Map Source, www.canmaps.com; McClure (1856); Armstrong (1857); Osborn, Chart to Illustrate the Narrative, etc. (1856); Haswell's service record, ADM 196/1/548.

32. Discoveries in the Arctic Sea by the Squadrons Under the Orders of Capt⁺ Sir Edw⁺ Belcher C.B. H.M.S. Assistance, etc. (1855a); McClure (1856); Armstrong (1857); Collinson (1889); Map of Central Arctic America showing the track of H.M.S. Enterprise and Investigator in 1850–54 (1889); The Canadian Topographic Map Source, www.canmaps.com; "Henry Foster Collins, Second Master, was educated at Greenwich Hospital School. He entered the Merchant Service on July 4th, 1832, and the Royal Navy on September 30th, 1843. Commander Fitzjames found him to be a most pleasant companion. His portrait is in the Royal Naval Museum" (Cyriax [1939], p. 210).

33. Cyriax (1939), p. 208.

34. Cyriax (1958), pp. 179, 183. A document found on King William Island in 1859 by Lieutenant William Robertson Hobson, RN, second-in-command of the Fox, included a reference to "the late Commander Gore."

35. Piers's journal (August 20, 1851), NMM, JOD/102; Ford's diary (August 20, 1851), KML, 18500119Arctic1xx. Ford notes in the evening that a cask with dispatches was landed on a hill. On Osborn's chart as "Ballast Beach (Petrified Trees)." In the days that followed, Armstrong, Piers, and Miertsching also noted the collection of petrified and fresh wood as natural history specimens. The nearly seven-foot section of petrified tree mentioned by Ford found its way to the Museum of the Royal Dublin Society (Armstrong [1857], p. 397; Seward, pp. 196–97; Osborn, Chart to Illustrate the Narrative of the Accomplishment of the North West Passage by H.M. Ship "Investigator," etc. [1856]; Armstrong [1857], pp. 395–402; Piers's journal [August 20–22, 1851], NMM, JOD/102; Neatby [1967], p. 135).

36. Piers's journal (August 20, 1851), NMM, JOD/102. Piers walked into the hills with Cresswell and Court to collect more petrified wood, and with scientific curiosity they remarked to one another that many places they had visited "contained wood in various states of decay and petrification, and in very large quantities—beds or layers, one on another, in the hills, giving to their sides a stratified appearance. The stone found with the wood we thought looked as if it had undergone the action of fire. The quantity of wood is far too large to be attributed to the drift of wood from the American coast on this shore. Whether the climate of this part of the world was once more temperate & fertile than it is at present; whether this island was ever connected with America and this part of it formed the delta of one of its large rivers; only what other means the wood was deposited here, Geological theorists may some day speculate upon" (Piers's journal [August 22, 1851], NMM, JOD/102).

37. Piers's journal (August 20, 1851), NMM, JOD/102.

38. Ibid. (August 21, 1851). "Bruin proved to be a young she Bear, with a remarkably fine white fur, and a depth of blubber upwards of two inches; but not a trace of food was in his [sic] stomach.... The flesh of the Bear we have eaten—it is coarse, oily, and I may say almost tasteless—whatever it does possess of flavor is not agreeable, and to hungry men only could such diet have been acceptable" (Armstrong [1857], pp. 407–08, 410). Ford wrote this was the fourth bear killed as of late (Ford's diary [August 21, 1851], KML, 18500119Arctic1xx).

39. Ford's diary (August 19–21, 1851), KML, 18500119Arctic1xx; Neatby (1967), pp. 135–36; Piers's journal (August 23–25, 1851), NMM, JOD/102: "From the gang way to the shore is 74 yards." Armstrong (1857), pp. 384, 391, 412–14; McClure (1856), p. 195. Piers identified the fish as salmon, whereas Armstrong stated they were trout.

40. Ford's diary (August 25, 1851), KML, 18500119Arctic1xx; Armstrong (1857), pp. 414–16.

41. Neatby (1967), p. 137; Piers's journal (August 29, 1851), NMM, JOD/102; Armstrong (1857), pp. 417–18.

42. A whip crane is a simple form of crane on the principle of the wheel and axle.

43. Piers's journal (August 29, 1851), NMM, JOD/102.

44. Armstrong (1857), pp. 418–19; McClure (1854a), p. 45; Piers's journal (August 29, 1851), NMM, JOD/102. Piers wrote that "all the carpenters with the smith [Stone] were set to work upon it, so that by the evening it was well repaired & lashed up astern."

45. Armstrong (1857), pp. 419–20; McClure (1854a), p. 45.

46. McClure (1854a), p. 45; "A charge of twenty-six pounds of powder was placed deep in its substance.... Some smaller charges were then used with similar results, and although the mass remained immovable as a rock, the little damage it had effected rendered it, in our opinion, less formidable" (Armstrong [1857], p. 420).

47. Piers's journal (August 29, 1851), NMM, JOD/102.

48. McClure (1856), p. 206; McClure (1854a), p. 45; Neatby (1967), 138.

49. McClure (1854a), pp. 45–46. "I cannot forbear from alluding to the admirable manner in which the ship resisted the pressure to which she was exposed, which was entirely owing to the excellent and scientific principles on which she was strengthened by William M. Rice, Esq., the present talented master-shipwright of Woolwich Dockyard, by whose plan and under whose superintendence the 'Investigator' was fitted for Polar service. This gentleman's name was frequently mentioned with grateful feelings during our long and eventful voyage, when our safety so often depended on the strength of the ship" (Armstrong [1857], p. 423, fn); William McPherson Rice (1796–1868): "I entered the School of Naval Architecture at Portsmouth; out of my time December 1819; then went to Deptford yard as student; 1820 removed to Sheer-

ness as student, and employed a portion of the time under the civil engineer in charge of the works, and under the master shipwright repairing ships; 1822 employed as draughtsman at Somerset House for 11 months. About 1823 went to sea for 12 months to Rio to put a mast together for the Sparshute [HMS *Spartiate*]; about 1824, after a short time at Woolwich, was appointed foreman of the yard at Chatham on 250£.; and was there 19 years as foreman; 1844 made assistant master shipwright at Portsmouth; 1852 made master shipwright at Pembroke; 1853 removed to Woolwich yard" (Memorial Inscriptions for the Parish of St. Clements, Halton, in the County of East Sussex, www.rootschat. com; Great Britain [1859], p. 240); HMS *Spartiate* (Vale, p. 142). Rice was tasked with refloating the *Terror* after she returned badly damaged by Arctic ice (Back to Rice [September 18, 1837], NMM, RCE/2).

50. Armstrong (1857), pp. 423–24. "The charges varied from 2 to 42 lbs. according to circumstances."

51. Armstrong (1857), p. 424; Neatby (1967), p. 139.

52. Neatby (1967), p. 139.

53. Piers's journal (September 1, 1851), NMM, JOD/102.

54. McClure (1856), pp. 210–11. The crew collected 55 tons of ballast (Armstrong [1857], p. 425); McClure (1854a), p. 46; Piers's journal (September 1–4, 1851), NMM, JOD/102; Neatby (1967), p. 140.

55. Piers's journal (September 10, 1851), NMM, JOD/102; Armstrong (1857), pp. 427–28 and fn. Armstrong wrote glowingly of Henry May: "This fine old fellow as the patriarch and Mentor of our crew, had served in former Expeditions, where he proved himself as invaluable as he did to us, by his correct and steady conduct, and the influence of his good example amongst the men. He has since served with me in H.M.S. 'Cornwallis,' where he well maintained the character he had previously earned, of being one of the most respectable and trustworthy petty officers in Her Majesty's Navy"; McClure (1854a), p. 46; Piers's journal (September 11, 1851), NMM, JOD/102.

56. Armstrong (1857), p. 428; McClure (1856), pp. 212–13.

57. "Ice blink is the white light seen on the horizon, especially on the underside of low clouds, resulting from reflection of light off a field of ice immediately beyond" (Ice blink, http://en.wikipedia.org).

58. Armstrong (1857), p. 428, 435. Armstrong wrote Point Colquhoun, which was subsequently called Cape Colquhoun, and is identified both ways in various sources (*Map of Banks Island*, 1956); McClure [1856], pp. 212–

13; Piers's journal [September 11, 1851], NMM, JOD/102; McClure [1854a], p. 46). Armstrong incorrectly wrote "Sunday, the 19th," when it was Sunday, September 14 (Armstrong [1857], p. 434).

59. Ford's diary (September 11, 1851), KML, 18500119Arctic1xx.

60. Ford's diary (September 13, 1851), KML, 18500119Arctic1xx. "Open water. Afternoon began to blow up the ice & after using about 400 lbs of powder we gave it up as we could not move the ship altho' only about 60 yards from open water, which will give some idea of the substance & state of the ice we have to contend with. One charge of powder consisted of 255 lb. in a cask, exploded about 30 yds. from the ship. It even lifted the ship & blew up & split the ice but nothing more. Other charges varied from 60 lb downwards in barricoles [?] & jars"; Armstrong (1857), p. 434.

61. Armstrong (1857), p. 435.

62. Neatby (1967), p. 142.

63. Armstrong (1857), p. 438–39.

64. Ibid., pp. 439–41. See Appendix 2 to understand Armstrong's writings as sources.

65. Piers's journal (September 19–20, 1851), NMM, JOD/102, marginal note dated February 1852.

66. Neatby (1967), p. 143; Piers's journal (September 18, 1851), NMM, JOD/102.

67. Armstrong (1857), pp. 443, 449; McClure (1854a), p. 47. Cape Wrottesley was a "point of land about ninety feet high," named after English Astronomer John Wrottesley, 2nd Baron Wrottesley, FRS, FRAS (August 5, 1798–October 27, 1867) (Armstrong [1857], p. 444; John Wrottesley, 2nd Baron Wrottesley, http://en.wikipedia.org).

68. Armstrong (1857), pp. 446, 449. Armstrong incorrectly wrote "Sunday morning the 20th," when it was Sunday, September 21; Neatby (1967), p. 144. According to Miertsching, "the captain said that we must have Divine Service before getting under way," but Armstrong and Piers both wrote that the ship got underway at 5:00 a.m., was delayed ice, and at 11:00 A.M.—after church service—the ice opened up, and sail was made again (Armstrong [1857], p. 446; Piers's journal [September 21, 1851], NMM, JOD/102).

69. Armstrong (1857), p. 448. There are two additional Cape Crozier geographical place names, one in the Arctic (western extreme of King William Island), and the other in the Antarctic (western extreme of Ross Island): Arrowsmith, *Map of a Portion of the Arctic Shores of America to Accompany Capt.ᵗ Mc Clintock's Narrative* (1859); *The Ross Sea Quadrant* (2003). Crozier's Arctic Medal 1818–55 was not issued in the

19th century, but was claimed by his great-great-nephew, Mr. Rawdon Crozier, and presented to him on August 5, 1988 (Poulsom and Myres [2000], p. 150); McClure [1854a], p. 48.

70. Armstrong's journal, NA, ADM 101/250, p. 125.

71. Ibid., pp. 127–28.

72. McClure (1854a), p. 48; Armstrong (1857), p. 454; Ford's diary (September 23, 1851), KML, 18500119 Arctic1xx; Piers' journal (September 23, 1851), NMM, JOD/102.

73. Neatby (1967), p. 147.

74. McClure (1854a), pp. 48–49.

75. Piers's journal (September 23, 1851), NMM, JOD/102, marginal note; Miertsching wrote that "it was the captain's intention to sail from here through the ice to Melville Island and there winter in the very bay where Captain Parry had wintered thirty years ago" (Neatby [1967], p. 149).

76. The recorded time the ship struck the shoal varies among sources: "About 6.30" (Neatby [1967], p. 147); "6.45" (Piers's journal [September 23, 1851], NMM, JOD/102); "At 7 p.m. while standing on the forecastle with a few other officers" (Armstrong [1857], p. 457); "7:30" (McClure [1854a], p. 49); "just before 8 P.M." (Ford's diary [September 23, 1851], KML, 18500119 Arctic1xx).

77. Three 15 fathom soundings are noted just north of this point on Court's chart (Court [1853]. Armstrong mentioned Point Providence, which is shown on Court's chart at lat. 74° 7' N. and long. 118° 15' W. (well within Mercy Bay). McClure wrote that *Investigator* anchored approximately one-quarter mile south of this point, "in four fathoms, latitude 74° 6' N., longitude 117° 54' W." Inglefield's chart shows a similarly named Providence Point, several miles to the northwest (McClure to Ross [April 1853], NA, BJ2/10; Armstrong [1857], pp. 454, 459, fn; Court, *Chart Shewing the land discovered by H.M. Ship Investigator. Between September 1850 and October 1851, etc.* [1853]; McClure [1854a], p. 59; Inglefield, *Chart Shewing the North West Passage Discovered by Capt. R. Le Mᶜ Clure, H.M. Ship. Investigator* [1853]).

78. Armstrong (1857), pp. 457–58. "The second master (Mr. Court), had previously been dispatched to sound, and reported deep water everywhere about the ship, except where she had struck"; McClure (1854a), p. 49.

79. Armstrong (1857), p. 458; Piers's journal (September 23, 1851), NMM, JOD/102.

80. McClure (1854a), p. 49; Armstrong (1857), p. 457.

81. Armstrong (1857), pp. 461–62; Piers' journal (September 24, 1851), NMM, JOD/102. "The extreme depth

of the bay appears to be about 7 miles, but at the bottom it is divided in two by a tongue [wording obscured] jutting out and forming a peninsula.... About 2 or 3 miles from the bottom of the bay, and at nearly equal distances from the opposite shores, are two small rocky islands, with a passage of about 500 yards between them, and deep water close to, so that a ship might be alongside" (Piers's journal [October 7, 1851, and marginal note], NMM, JOD/102). Armstrong wrote in his journal in August 1852, "The bay in which we were, had been previously called the 'bay of Mercy' was irregularly funnel shaped in form, extending inwards for about fifteen miles, and was about nine miles broad at its entrance, where there were numerous shoals, and about which the ice was grounded" (Armstrong's journal, NA, ADM 101/250, p. 146). In his book, Armstrong stated the bay was "seven [miles] broad at its entrance" (Armstrong [1857], p. 540).

82. McClure (1854a), p. 49; Ford wrote that the ice was about four inches thick (Ford's diary [September 27, 1851], KML, 18500119Arctic1xx).

## Chapter 11

1. Armstrong (1857), pp. 463–65.
2. Armstrong's journal, NA, ADM 101/250, p. 126.
3. Armstrong (1857), pp. 461–62.
4. McClure (1854a), p. 49; Court, *Chart Shewing the land discovered by H.M. Ship Investigator. Between September 1850 and October 1851, etc.* (1851).
5. Ford's diary (September 24, 1851), KML, 18500119Arctic1xx.
6. Neatby (1967), p. 149, fn.
7. Ibid., p. 149. The following day Miertsching wrote, "The sea was covered with ice as far as the eye could reach" (Neatby [1967], p. 151).
8. Piers's journal (September 24, 1851), NMM, JOD/102. Piers finished this entry with, "The pack during the day has been drifting before the N. W[ly] wind into the bay, but without touching us."
9. Brown manuscript, GM, M-141, p. 16.
10. Piers's journal (September 25, 1851), NMM, JOD/102.
11. Nelson (vol. 1, October 1851), SPRI, MS 748/1.
12. Armstrong (1857), pp. 467–68. The loss sustained in the accident upon first entering the ice was nearly 3,700 lbs. (see chapter 6, endnote 6), while three months' provisions were left on the larger of the Princess Royal Islands (McClure in Neatby [1967], p. 103; McClure [1854a], p. 38).
13. Armstrong (1857), pp. 468–69.

14. Letter & Order Book (October 1, 1851), RGS, SSC/106.
15. Ibid; Some quantities and items shown issued were at variance with the L&O Book's scale and/or Armstrong's published victualling scale, indicating there was need for adjustments after McClure's order, and Armstrong also noted the following: ½ lb. of preserved meat averaged about 6 oz.; salt meat consisted of beef and pork with bone, ½ lb. averaged about 6 oz.; 4 oz. of carrots averaged about 1 oz.; suet issued in lieu of flour, ½ oz. of the former equal to 1 oz. of the latter; no cranberries or soup after the first year; deficiency in preserved meat from jelly, and in salt meat from bone (Armstrong [1858], p. 14).
16. Evidently, biscuits were issued a bit longer. "The ship's co[mpany] commenced bread, instead of biscuit, to day—the allowance of four being ⅔ lb (head 13-⅓ oz.)" (Piers's journal [November 1, 1851], NMM, JOD/102).
17. Suet, the hard white fat on the kidneys and loins of cattle, sheep, and other animals, was used to make foods including puddings, pastry, and mincemeat.
18. Armstrong's journal provides a list of game killed from October 1850 to April 1853, and while there is a slight variance with some of the figures appearing in the list in his book, Armstrong's journal summation is telling: "The total quantity of edible meat comprising [musk] Oxen, Deer, Ptarmigan, Hares & wild fowl procured amounted to 9793 lbs. affording 66 men 1 lb. of meat per man per diem for 148 days." One pound per day, per man, for five months, which was unevenly spread over 2-½ years. "No regular account was kept of the Foxes that were shot or captured, which may have amounted to 50, and the number of wild-fowl is estimated at a low average" (Armstrong's journal, NA, ADM 101/250, p. 138 & Armstrong [1857], p. 601); "These creatures [foxes] are not required to be turned into the common stock" (Neatby [1967], p. 166).
19. Armstrong (1857), p. 469.
20. Ibid., p. 470.
21. Piers's journal (October 1, 1851), NMM, JOD/102; "Commenced to day lighting the Ship's (Sylvester), Gun-room and Sick-bay stoves: the Captain's has been lit some time. The temperature in the Gun-room has lately been 28° or 29°; and in the Officer's cabins 15° and 16°, in the day time. The allowance of coal for the galley fire is 70 lb. daily; for Sylvester's stove, which is intended to warm the whole ship, 40 lb.; Captain's stove, 16 lb., besides 2 lb. of lignum vitæ [a very hard, heavy wood of any of several tropical American guaiacums—evergreen trees]; Gun-room stove, 12

lb.; and Sick-bay, 7 lb." (Piers's journal [October 6, 1850], NMM, JOD/102).
22. Miertsching's former trade came in handy October 1: "I was shoemaker today, and re-soled my own and the captain's boots" (Neatby [1967], p. 153).
23. Ford's diary (October 4, 1851), KML, 18500119Arctic1xx. The identity of "Sam" is unknown, but may have been Ford's brother.
24. Armstrong (1857), pp. 471–72; McClure (1854a), p. 49; Piers' journal (October 4, 7, 1851), NMM, JOD/102; Neatby (1967), p. 153.
25. Ford's diary (October 7, 1851), KML, 18500119Arctic1xx; Armstrong (1857), pp. 472–73.
26. Armstrong (1857), p. 473. "Court saw a great deal of open water to sea-ward,[X] and had a view of Melville Is. from the cliffs. The ice along the shore was thrown up 30 and 40 ft high, so that the men were obliged to carry the sledge on their shoulders along the beach.[X] There was open water as far as he could see in the direction of Melville Island" (Piers's journal [October 7, 1851], NMM, JOD/102).
27. See Neatby's comments, Neatby (1967), pp. 149–50, fn. Neatby also noted: "It may be significant that Miertsching, who was much attached to the captain and no friend of Armstrong's, omits to mention that immediately beyond Point Back (only eight miles from the ship) Court found open water extending east as far as he could see, a confirmation of the surgeon's assertion, previously noted" (Neatby [1967], p. 153, fn). However, it should be kept in mind that Miertsching was not a seaman and did not have experience in ice navigation.
28. Armstrong (1857), pp. 474–76; McClure (1856), p. 218; Piers's journal (October 8, 1851), NMM, JOD/102; Miertsching: "Many scholars, and also Dr. Richardson, the famous Arctic traveller, claim that the whole wildlife of the polar areas will retreat to the mainland in autumn etc.—here we are more than 700 kilometers [435 miles] away from the mainland but, still, there is reindeer here; maybe these are delayed or out of their reckoning." *Investigator* was in the Prince of Wales Strait, January 14, 1851; this entry was omitted in Neatby's translation (M. Opel to Stein, personal communication, September 11, 2014).
29. Armstrong (1857), pp. 474–75; McClure (1856), pp. 219–20.
30. Piers's journal (October 9, 1851), NMM, JOD/102; Evans was admitted to sick bay with a sprained knee the following day, and returned to duty on October 19. Two days later, Joseph Paine went into sick bay for 42 days with "Spinal debility & Stricture Spasm." The surgeon wrote that Paine

was "a subject not usually of a weak attenuated habit of body & lax fibre [strength of character] and who at a former period had been much debilitated by disease and service in warm climates" (Armstrong's journal [Sick List], NA, ADM 101/250, pp. 5, 91).

31. Piers's journal (October 9, 11, 1851), NMM, JOD/102.

32. The composition of Sainsbury's party is not revealed in sources, but was probably made up of six or seven men. McClure (1854a), p. 49; Armstrong (1857), pp. 480 & 485; Piers's journal (October 10–12, 15, 1851), NMM, JOD/102. "Two deer killed by Sam! Mc Kenzie of C's party, were brought on board this afternoon [October 11]: their carcasses weighed 80 and 55 lb." (Ford's diary [October 15, 1851], KML, 18500119Arctic1xx).

33. McClure (1854a), p. 49; Armstrong (1857), p. 481; Piers's journal (October 11, 1851), NMM, JOD/102; Ford wrote: "The travelling party returned having found the river to extend about 16 miles inland" (Ford's diary [October 11, 1851], KML, 18500119Arctic1xx).

34. Letter & Order Book, RGS, SSC/106 (undated transcription of cairn note)—mention of this cairn is not found in any other sources.

35. Piers's journal (October 17, 1851), NMM, JOD/102.

36. *Herald*'s Description Book (1845–1851), NA, ADM 38/8269; *Investigator*'s Musters (1849–50), NA, ADM 38/1026; Fateful Voyage, www.fatefulvoyage.com; Davies first went to sea in 1836, and appears as "Jonathan/John Davis" and "John Davies" in various official records. Notably his seaman's register ticket no. 365.364 (issued January 16, 1850), has "Davies" (Registry of Shipping and Seamen: Register of Seamen's Tickets, NA, BT 113/183).

37. *Investigator*'s Musters (1849–50), NA, ADM 38/1026; McDonald's service record, NA, ADM 139/178/17722; *Thalia*'s Description Book (1841–1845), NA, ADM 38/9171; Sugden's service record, NA, ADM 29/73 & 188/9/42634; *Constance*'s Description Book (1846–49), NA, ADM 38/7837.

38. *Constance*'s Description Book (1846–49), NA, ADM 38/7837; See Tiffeny in Chapter 3 and endnote 97 for the transition of his rating. He appears as "Tiffeny," "Tiffney," and "Tiffeney" in various official records; Jackson's service record, NA, ADM 139/425/2430A; *Investigator*'s Musters (1849–50), NA, ADM 38/1026; Jackson also served as an ordinary seaman for 10 months (1845–46) with future Investigator, Ordinary Seaman Charles Steel, in HMS *Penelope* (*Albatross*'s

Description Book [1846–50], NA, ADM 38/7487).

39. Piers's journal (October 17, 18, 23, 1851), NMM, JOD/102, and marginal note dated February 1852. "On Saturday evening, when the Marines & our men were missing, Wynniatt & his party also lost their way on the ice, on their return to the ship, and were obliged to pitch their tent within, as they found the following morning, a mile of her; and the Captain, knowing that they would [be] coming off at the time, had a gun fired every half hour from about 6 to 9 P.M." (Piers's journal [October 23, 1851], NMM, JOD/102).

40. Piers's journal (October 19, 21, 23, 1851), NMM, JOD/102. "There were killed altogether by the party 26 hares, 11 ptarmigan and 2 foxes."

41. Piers's journal (October 26, 1851), NMM, JOD/102; Nelson (vol. 1, October 1851), SPRI, MS 748/1.

42. Armstrong (1857), pp. 487.

43. Ford's diary (October 18, 22, 1851), KML, 18500119Arctic1xx.

44. Piers's journal (November 1, 3, 1851), NMM, JOD/102. On December 13, Miertsching wrote: "The previous winter we received weekly three tallow candles per man, and this winter we receive three for fourteen days" (Neatby [1967], p. 157).

45. Ford's diary (November 5, 1851), KML, 18500119Arctic1xx.

46. McClure (1856), pp. 220–21; Piers's journal (November 3, 1851), NMM, JOD/102.

47. Piers's journal (November 1851), NMM, JOD/102; Nelson (vol. 1, November 1851), SPRI, MS 748/1; Armstrong (1857), pp. 490–93; Neatby (1967), p. 155. "Numbers of [the gun wads] got into circulation, were passed from hand to hand like Bank of England notes; in short, became the currency in all monetary transactions, and were duly honoured when presented for payment on our return to England" (Armstrong [1857], p. 491).

48. Armstrong (1857), p. 492; Nelson (vol. 1, November 1851), SPRI, MS 748/1–2; Piers's journal (November 13, 1851), NMM, JOD/102; Neatby (1967), p. 156.

49. Ford's diary (November 24, 1851), KML, 18500119Arctic1xx. On November 30, Ford wrote: "Morning performed divine service as usual. I wish I had some person in the ship to sympathise with & converse on religion to gain instruction, but I am afraid to broach to any one as all appear too formal in their manners in Church in my opinion." Ford may have shied away from approaching Miertsching, as he was a foreigner and part of the Moravian Church. In addition to studying scripture, the following month, Ford began studying algebra (Ford's diary

[December 8, 1851], KML, 18500119 Arctic1xx).

50. Armstrong (1857), pp. 493–94; McClure (1856), pp. 221–22. The ice measured 2'5" at the beginning of December (Ford's diary [December 1, 1851], KML, 18500119Arctic1xx).

51. Piers's journal (December 4, 1851), NMM, JOD/102.

52. Neatby (1967), p. 156.

53. Armstrong's description of Bradbury's case: "One Case of 'Epilepsy' occurred, in a man of previously dissipated [overindulging] habits but in which he had no opportunity of indulging to any extent under present circumstances, but on this occasion, he had become intoxicated and imprudently exposed himself to a low degree of cold on the upper deck, and from his statement, it would appear to have been the first attack. He was a man disposed to be plethoric [excessive], the fit was severe about twenty minutes duration and the cold 'domestic' man had [come] to with admirable results, after which by restoring the sensations which had become considerably deranged & improving the general health, there was no return of the attack & the case terminated favorably" (Armstrong's journal, NA, ADM 101/250, pp. 92, 153, & Sick List, p. 5); Descriptions of epileptic seizures can be traced alongside the history of humankind, and British medical science made important contributions to understanding the disease during the 19th century (Magiorkinis, Sidiropoulou & Diamantis, pp. 131, 140–41).

54. Piers's journal (December 16, 1851), NMM, JOD/102; Armstrong (1857), p. 495. Several more foxes were afterward also trapped (Piers's journal [December 23, 1851; January 7, February 2 and 21, 1852], NMM, JOD/102).

55. Smithfield, London, http://en.wikipedia.org.

56. Piers's journal (December 24, 1851), NMM, JOD/102.

57. Ibid. (December 25, 1851). Nelson wrote of venison and plum pudding being served on Christmas Day, and unlike the many of the holiday's celebrations he had seen on warships, Nelson noted that *Investigator* was "entirely free from rioting or drunkenness," and the crew's behavior was so good as to draw high praise from McClure. Miertsching, on the other hand, called it "a festival of gluttony and wine-bibbing.... The captain himself took part in the sports of his boisterous crew" (Nelson [vol. 1, Christmas Day 1851], SPRI, MS 748/1; Neatby [1967], p. 157).

58. Ford's diary (January 1, 1852), KML, 18500119Arctic1xx; Piers' journal (January 1, 1852), NMM, JOD/102.

59. Neatby (1967), p. 157.

60. Armstrong (1857), pp. 496–97.

61. Neatby (1967), pp. 157–58; Neatby commented: "This is the only instance where Miertsching takes sides and betrays a personal dislike. The quarrel may have related to the reduced ration to which the surgeon was opposed, though on grounds of prudence McClure could make out a good case. If Armstrong's "Falschheit" [intentional deception] lay in suppressing for two years his antipathy to the captain, he made handsome amends later in his *Personal Narrative*. One wishes that McClure had not fallen out with Paine in the presence of the crew. The officer administering a reduced ration had a cruelly difficult task" (Neatby [1967], p. 158 fn[1]).

62. "[B]ut once or twice while I was on the lower deck, forward, from several messes singing different songs at the same time, there was a perfect 'cat's serenade'" (Miertsching) (Piers's journal [Jan. 1, 1852], NMM, JOD/102); Nelson (vol. 1, January 1, 1852), SPRI, MS 748/1.

63. Piers's journal (January 1, 7, 1852), NMM, JOD/102; Armstrong (1857), pp. 497–99; Ford's diary (January 3–7, 1852), KML, 18500119Arctic 1xx; Piers's journal (January 29, 1852, marginal note), NMM, JOD/102; Armstrong's journal (Sick List), NA, ADM 101/250, p. 6. Others suffers at this time included: E. Griffiths (frostbite and laryngitis, 62 days), Facey (frostbite and amputation, 43 days), and Ross (debility and stricture [an abnormal narrowing of a bodily passage, as from inflammation, cancer, or the formation of scar tissue], 58 days). Ross went back to duty on February 15, only to be put back on the sick list one month later for 48 days, suffering from stricture and irritable bladder.

64. Neatby (1967), p. 158. Neatby rightly commented: "The flogging of three half-starved men for taking the portion of Mongo, the ship's mascot, seems revolting; but McClure dared not, in this crisis, overlook a breach of regulations, whatever the circumstances. By this apparent ruthlessness he was spared the necessity to which the American arctic traveler, Greely, was reduced, some years later, of ordering his sergeants to shoot a thieving comrade in cold blood" (Neatby [1967], p. 158 fn[2]).

65. Armstrong (1857), pp. 497–98, 601; Piers's journal (January 14, 28, 29, 1852), NMM, JOD/102 (Piers notes Newton's face was severely frostbitten on January 14); Ford's diary (January 28, 1852), KML, 18500119Arctic1xx.

66. Armstrong (1857), pp. 499–500, fn.

67. McClure's book features the incorrect date of January 4, an error which was copied by Douglas-Morris, and afterward by the present author in his paper on special medals to the *Investigator*'s crew. Armstrong's book also has the wrong date: February 9 (McClure [1856], p. 228; Douglas-Morris [1987], p. 413; Stein [December 2008], p. 307; Armstrong [1857], p. 499).

68. Up until this time, sources showed Anderson as an able seaman, but Ford referred to him at this time as "the black gunroom cook," and Piers wrote "Cha! Anderson, our cook," while Nelson wrote, "Warrant Officers cook." Evidently, Anderson had taken over Sugden's cooking chores, and the latter functioned more as the officers' and/or subordinate officers' steward (Ford's diary [February 4, 1852], KML, 1850 0119Arctic1xx; Piers's journal [February 4, 1852], NMM, JOD/102; Sugden's service record, NA, ADM 29/73; McClure [1856], p. xxxiv); Piers's journal (February 4, 5, 1852), NMM, JOD/102; Nelson (vol. 1, February 1852), SPRI, MS 748/1.

69. Piers's journal (February 4, 5, 1852), NMM, JOD/102; Ford's diary (February 4, 1852), KML, 18500119Arctic1xx; Armstrong (1857), pp. 499–503; McClure (1856), pp. 228–31; Neatby (1967), p. 159; Nelson (vol. 1, February 1852), SPRI, MS 748/1. Wynniatt's party had come across the track of the missing men, and followed it to the spot where Anderson was rescued, and then returned to the ship at two in the morning. Lieutenant Haswell's party was back onboard by 4:00 a.m. (Armstrong [1857], p. 503; Ford's diary [February 4, 1852], KML, 18500119Arctic1xx).

70. Piers's journal (February 5, 1852), NMM, JOD/102; Nelson (vol. 1, February 1852), SPRI, MS 748/1.

71. Armstrong (1857), p. 503; Anderson's Pension Certificate for Hurts—"Ordinary Certificate granted" —age 24—"Was frostbitten on several occasions in toes & fingers in the winter of 1851–52 & 53 in Bay of Mercy from effects to cold when employed hunting for the Ship, which ultimately caused for the removal of distal phalanges of both great toes & a portion of that of the little finger" (Armstrong's journal & Sick List, NA, ADM 101/250, pp. 6 & 90). "When frostbites existed as in this case, the recovery was more protracted, being of sufficient severity as to cause sloughing, and in this way, he lost a portion of left ala of nose, the soft parts of several toes & fingers & partially of the cheeks, together with the distal phalanx of right little finger. The frostbites in the other cases, were of a more partial nature & less severe, but such was the general character, which these cases of exhaustion presented" (Armstrong's journal, NA, ADM 101/250, p. 157).

72. Armstrong (1857), p. 503; Piers's journal (March 19, 1852), NMM, JOD/102.

73. Historian Leslie H. Neatby suggested that Anderson was "a fugitive slave, no doubt," but until now, evidently neither he nor anyone else ever sought out evidence to support such a claim (Neatby [1970], p. 162).

74. Anderson's seaman's register ticket no. 365.365 was issued January 16, 1850; Registry of Shipping and Seamen: Register of Seamen's Tickets, NA, BT 113/183; *Investigator*'s Musters, NA, ADM 38/1026; *Investigator*'s Musters (1849–50), NA, ADM 38/1026; Port Robinson, Ontario, www.wikipedia. org; Underground Railroad in Canada, www.pc.gc.ca; Concentrations of Underground Railroad refugee settlers in Ontario circa 1850, http://hrsbstaff. ednet.ns.ca/devrob/CDN%20History-%2011/underground_railroad_in_ cana.htm—The author spoke with Port Robinson resident Laurie Richards, owner of 3 R's Used Books, who said that today there are no black families in the town (personal communication, February 18, 2010); Winks, p. 152; Jackson, p. 68. Port Robinson historian Tom Russell mentioned the Colored Corps in conversation with the author (Stein and Russell, personal communication, February 26, 2010).

75. Slavery Abolition Act of 1833, http://en.wikipedia.org, 2014; "A small number of African slaves were forcibly brought as chattel by Europeans to New France, Acadia and the later British North America (see chattel slavery) during the 17th century. Those in Canada came from the American colonies, as no shiploads of human chattel came to Canada directly from Africa. The number of slaves in New France is believed to be in the hundreds. They were house servants and farm workers. There were no large-scale plantations in Canada, and therefore no large-scale plantation slave work forces of the sort that existed in most European colonies in the southerly Americas, from Virginia to the West Indies to Brazil" (Slavery in Canada, http://en.wikipedia.org, 2014).

76. Armstrong (1857), p. 500, fn; Piers's journal (March 19, 1852), NMM, JOD/102; Anderson's seaman's register ticket no. 365.365, NA, BT 113/183; Neatby (1967), p. 15; Ford referred to Anderson as "the black gunroom cook," and Piers wrote "Cha! Anderson, our cook," and finally, Nelson wrote, "Charles Anderson the Warrant Officers cook" (Ford's diary [February 4, 8, 1852], KML, 18500119Arctic1xx; Piers's journal [February 4, 1852], NMM, JOD/102; Nelson [vol. 1, February 1852], SPRI, MS 748/1).

77. Armstrong (1857), pp. 503–04. "The Aurora Borealis so frequently present, was, by no means, as brilliant as we had seen it in the Strait of Prince

of Wales" (Armstrong [1857], pp. 504); Piers's journal (February 2, 1852), NMM, JOD/102; Armstrong's journal, NA, ADM 101/250, p. 94.

78. Armstrong (1857), p. 504; Ford's diary (February 17, 1852), KML, 18500119Arctic1xx. "This voyage of ours will baffle all the naturalists in England in our getting deer this time of the year as they all say that they emigrate to the southward in the winter but it has pleased the Almighty to order it otherwise with us, as its His mercy towards us in providing us with fresh food" (Ford's diary [March 16, 1852], KML, 18500119Arctic1xx). "The few white foxes and lemmings that are caught or shot on land, and are not assigned to the ship as game, are devoured with the greatest relish" (Neatby [1967], pp. 159–60).

79. Piers's journal (February 16, 1852), NMM, JOD/102. In recounting the daily routine, Piers notes an evident dislike for Haswell: "4. The 'dinner pennant' is again hoisted, to let every one within sight of the ship know the time, and the men retire below again for the day. Court & I at the same time meet on deck; he to keep his watch and I to take exercise—Haswell too frequently joins us for half an hour."

80. Piers's journal (February 16, 1852), NMM, JOD/102.

81. Ford's diary (March 1, 1852), KML, 18500119Arctic1xx; Armstrong (1857), p. 504.

82. Piers's journal (March 1–10, 1852), NMM, JOD/102. Haswell killed the hare on March 10, when the temperature range was −35°F below zero (high), −52°F (low), and −45.2°F (average). According to Armstrong, it was the coldest day of the season (Armstrong [1857], p. 505).

## Chapter 12

1. Piers's journal (March 11, 1852), NMM, JOD/102.

2. Ibid.

3. Nelson (vol. 1, March 1852), SPRI, MS 748/1.

4. Armstrong (1857), pp. 505, 509–10. "A Deer was shot by one of the men (Wm. Whitfield): the novelty of the decoy used on the occasion, was a new feature in our sport, and was practiced afterwards by others with success. On sighting the herd, he took from his neck a red comforter, fastened it to his ramrod, which he planted in the snow, and lay down about twenty yards distant. Three of the animals immediately approached, and while turning it about in play, a shot was fired, which killed one and wounded another, which ultimately became a prize."

5. Piers's journal (March 18, 1852, and a marginal note), NMM, JOD/102; Nelson (vol. 1, March 1852), SPRI, MS 748/1–2; Ford's diary (March 17, 1852), KML, 18500119Arctic1xx; In considerable variance, Miertsching assigned February 28 as the date Brown and Gibbs went missing (Neatby [1967], p. 160).

6. Piers's journal (March 18, 1852, and a marginal note), NMM, JOD/102.

7. Piers's journal (March 18, 1852), NMM, JOD/102.

8. Ibid. McClure and everyone else reached the ship at 1:30 p.m. Haswell had picked up the lost men's trail and followed it in the direction of the ship, until he felt they were safe; he then took a route he knew through the hills, and arrived back at 9:00 p.m. bringing five hares onboard. Wynniatt returned at 12:50 a.m. also having found the tracks of the missing men. "W. himself was much exhausted, having a staggering gait, and having some time before experienced giddiness, tendency to sleep & coldness, and been obliged to rest several times. The men offered to go ahead & fetch a sledge for him, or to assist him by carrying his gun, or with their arms; with which kind attention—for the men must have been much fatigued themselves—he pretended afterwards to be highly indignant."

9. Brown manuscript, GM, M-141, p. 17. Armstrong took the opportunity to make an insulting reference toward Anderson in relation to Stone, Brown and Gibbs losing their ways: "The display of fortitude and endurance manifested by these men, contrast most forcibly to their advantage with the man spoken of on on the 4th of February" (Armstrong [1857], p. 508).

10. When Private 3rd Class Bancroft joined the Royal Marines in 1842, he was a 22-year-old laborer, and native of the village of Box, Wiltshire. Therefore, Bancroft had quite probably worked on the Box Tunnel, between Bath and Chippenham, the last completed portion of the London to Bristol Great Western Railway line. Work on the 1¾-mile-long tunnel took place between early 1836 and the spring of 1841, and completely changed the nature of the village (Bancroft's attestation form, NA, ADM 57/1131; Box, Wiltshire, http://en.wikipedia.org).

11. Nelson (vol. 1, April 1852), SPRI, MS 748/1; Armstrong's journal (Sick List), NA, ADM 101/250, pp. 6–7; Investigator's Musters (1849–50), NA, ADM 38/1026); Morgan's seaman's register ticket no. 302.723, NA, BT 113/152. Veils had been served out in mid–March, as the sun was then beginning to get strong for the eyes, and on April 7, Miertsching wrote that "a number of sailors have become snowblind: a more emphatic order from the captain: 'wear dark-colored glasses.'" In spite of this, throughout April and May there were 16 cases of snow blindness admitted to Sick Bay (Ford's diary [March 13, 1852], KML, 18500119Arctic1xx; Neatby [1967], p. 161).

12. Armstrong (1857), pp. 510–11; Ford's diary (April 6, 1852), KML, 18500119Arctic1xx; McClure to Ross (April [no day written] 1853), NA, BJ2/10; McClure (1856), pp. 232–34; Neatby (1967) p. 161.

13. Armstrong (1857), p. 511; McClure (1856), pp. 233–34.

14. McClure (1856), p. 234; McClure (1854a), p. 50; Armstrong (1857), p. 513; McClure (1854a), p. 60. According to Miertsching, the maximum temperature on April 11 was 8°F, minimum −6°F, and mean 2°F (Neatby [1967], p. 162).

15. McClure (1854a), pp. 57–60. "Dated on board her Britannic Majesty's Discovery Ship 'Investigator,' frozen in, in the Bay of 'Mercy,' latitude 74° 6' N., longitude 117° 54' W., April 12th, 1852," the date evidently being transcribed and printed in error. The accompanying chart is in all probability Court's *Chart Shewing the land discovered by H.M. Ship Investigator. Between September 1850 and April 1852,* or a copy of the same (UKHO, L9304).

16. Ibid., pp. 59–60.

17. Ibid., p. 60. A postscript read: "Unless there is a vessel now at Melville Island it is not my intention to revisit it, but make the best of my way down the Straits [*sic*—Viscount Melville Sound].—R. M'C."

18. Barr (2007), pp. 101, 107, 280.

19. Collinson (1889), pp. 182–85. None of these parties found any traces of Franklin's expedition.

20. Ibid., pp. 182–83, 207. Jago was following Haswell's track from 1851, and recorded in his sled journal that he "left intelligence at the following places: on an island bearing from Point Wollaston S.S.E. about 25 miles; the island where the *Investigator*'s cairn was in lat. 70° 33' N., and long. 114° 10' W.; and at my furthest in lat. 70° 34', and long. 110° 15' W."

21. Collinson (1889), p. 187.

22. Collinson, who was following Wynniatt's track from 1851, crossed the mouth of a major bay he named Richard Collinson Inlet, and went on to another bay he dubbed Glenelg Bay, which was afterwards named Wynniatt Bay (Barr [2007], p. 128).

23. Parks was promoted from midshipman to mate, having passed his lieutenant's examination on December 19, 1848, and was promoted to acting lieutenant aboard *Enterprise* on August 15, 1850, and then confirmed with seniority on April 11, 1851. Parks's medals were once in the Douglas-Morris Collection—Abyssinia Medal 1867–68 (officially embossed on the reverse: LIEUT. M.T. PARKS, R.N. TRANST. SERVE.)

and Arctic Medal 1818–55 (privately engraved on the edge: LIEUT. M.T. PARKS, H.M.D.S. ENTERPRIZE) (Douglas-Morris [1994], p. 214). At the National Maritime Museum is a head and shoulders miniature watercolor on ivory of Commander Parks, within an oval silver suspension locket, with reverse inscription: MURRAY THOMAS PARKS/1855/B.1827 D.1877 (F9511, NMM, www.rmg.co.uk). A descendant, also named Murray Parks, published an article which begins, "My interest in the North-west Passage was first aroused by the discovery among family papers of a faded journal, written in pencil in the Arctic more than a hundred years ago by a forbear of mine (Lieut. Parks), then a junior officer serving under Captain Richard Collinson, H.M.S. *Enterprise*" (Parks [1954], p. 609).

24. Armstrong (1857), p. 513; Ford's diary (April 11, 1852), KML, 18500119 Arctic1xx; Armstrong stated McClure carried 28 days' provisions, Ford indicated 30 days, and Miertsching 32 days (Neatby [1967], p. 162).

25. "The month was in every respect more favourable than that of the previous year—the mean temperature was 1.4° below zero, upwards of three degrees higher—and the wind was less in force being 2.5. Snow fell more abundantly—no less than fifteen days out of the thirty; and heavier in character than before" (Armstrong [1857], p. 515).

26. Ford's diary (April 12–22, 1852), KML, 18500119 Arctic1xx; Armstrong (1857), p. 513, 601—game in April: 19 deer, 18 hares, 14 ptarmigan; Neatby (1967), p. 162.

27. Armstrong's journal (Sick List), NA, ADM 101/250, p. 7. Fawcett spent 24 days in sick bay; Armstrong (1857), pp. 514–15; Millar to Stein, personal communication, May 31, 2015, in reference to Millar, Bowman, Battersby and Welbury (submitted for publication 2015); Letter and Order Book (October 1, 1851), RGS, SSC/106; Armstrong's journal, NA, ADM 101/250, p. 138; Armstrong (1857), p. 601.

28. Wooden sailing vessels were inherently buoyant, and tall masts made them extremely top-heavy. Ballast stones were added or removed as the weight of cargo, supplies, or ordnance changed.

29. Ford's diary (April 29–May 10, 1852), KML, 18500119 Arctic1xx; McClure (1854a), p. 50. Watering was completed on June 12, having been "obtained from a lake about a mile from the ship, by boring through seven feet ten inches of ice, and cutting a reservoir to receive it." Armstrong's Sick List shows 11 men, not 14, as of April 30 (Armstrong's journal [Sick List], NA, ADM 101/250, pp. 6, 7). Nelson wrote that McClure blamed his men's snow blindness on their carelessness in not

wearing eye protection, and threatened to "make 'Abstainers' of us all if we are not more careful" (Nelson [vol. 1, May 1852], SPRI, MS 748/1).

30. McClure (1856), p. 234; Armstrong (1857), pp. 516–19, incorrectly stated McClure's arrival date as April 20. The surgeon was incensed about the lack of known information regarding Franklin in the message: "*[B]ut not one word did it contain of the important intelligence, that traces of Franklin had been discovered by these ships the previous year at Beechey Island.* We might have been making fruitless efforts in other directions, had been in a fit state; but everything of the kind would have been avoided, if we had been informed of what had occurred"; McClure (1854a), p. 50.

31. McClure to Ross (April 1853), NA, BJ2/10.

32. Neatby (1967), p. 163; McClintock wrote: "The 'Winter Harbour' of Parry was reached, and the record I deposited there was found by M'Clure, just one year after. As is well known, he had approached from Behring's Straits; so that this communication of mine to him was the first ever made through the North-West passage" (McClintock and Haughton [1858], pp. 200–01).

33. Armstrong (1857), p. 518; McClure, "The North-West Passage, etc." (1853), p. 673. "The following letter [dated April 10, 1853] from Commander M'Clure to his sister [*sic*—half-sister], Mrs. Thomas E. Wright, of Dublin, has been communicated to a Dublin paper by Dr. Wilde".

34. Holland (1994), pp. 232–33.

35. McClure (1854a), p. 50; Armstrong (1857), p. 520; McClure's dispatch, Ford and Armstrong's journal all have that McClure returned on May 9, but Armstrong's book has May 7 (likely a misprint), and McClure's book has May 11 (McClure [1854a], p. 50; Armstrong's journal, NA, ADM 101/250, p. 95; Armstrong [1857], p. 515; McClure [1856], p. 236; Ford's diary [May 9, 1852], KML, 18500119 Arctic1xx). Thompson and Gibbs entered the sick list with snow blindness on May 10 and 11 respectively (Armstrong's journal [Sick List], NA, ADM 101/250, p. 7). According to Ford: "We get now instead of [a] half lb. of pork 1 lb. venison, man per week, & 1 lb. of venison instead of ½ lb. of preserved meat, which makes 3 venison days per week" (Ford's diary [May 14, 1852], KML, 18500119 Arctic1xx).

36. Barr (2007), p. 135. "It is highly unlikely, though not impossible, that there were any Inuit on Melville Island at this time. One wonders whether Parkes [*sic*] and his men had heard a wolf pack howling."

37. Collinson (1889), pp. 185, 213.

Parks's sled journal entry concluded with: "I also filled up one of the bottle or tide papers, merely saying who the cylinder was left by, and that I had endeavoured to reach Winter Harbour, but had failed. I judge the lat. of the pile to be 74° 32', from which I could see Point Hearne distinctly."

38. Collinson (1889), pp. 246; French's service record, NA, ADM 139/322/32191. French turned 25 just ten days before sledding to Melville Island, and was only five months older than Cresswell. An unnamed Arctic Medal 1818–55, attributed to French, was sold at Status International Auctions, Public Auction 267, May 29, 2010, lot 10485, gdVF [claw reattached and non-swiveling ball and ring suspension above star], "With research notes, including vendor notes on family provenance." French's Arctic Medal was sent to HMS *Wellesley* on June 8, 1857 (Status International Auctions, www.statusint.com & Arctic Medal 1818–55 Roll, NA, ADM 171/9, p. 30).

39. Nelson (vol. 1, May 1852), SPRI, MS 748/1.

40. Armstrong (1857), pp. 513, 521–22.

41. Ford's diary (June 1, 1852), KML, 18500119 Arctic1xx.

42. McClure (1854a), p. 50; Armstrong (1857), p. 524. Armstrong noted "that in the pond from which we obtained our water, [the thickness] was seven feet ten inches; which may perhaps be considered a fair estimate of the difference existing between fresh and salt water freezing."

43. Neatby (1967), pp. 164–66; Armstrong (1857), p. 525. On July 22, Miertsching "caught fourteen beautiful bright butterflies," and on the 31st wrote, "I am on land every night, and collect plants, grasses, moss, etc., and whatever I can find of interest. Various types of small birds are found in the moss-covered swamps which were known to me in Labrador" (Neatby [1967], pp. 167–68).

44. Ford's diary (June 3, 4, 8, 1852), KML, 18500119 Arctic1xx; Nelson (vol. 1, June-July 1852), SPRI, MS 748/1; Armstrong (1857), pp. 525–26, 601.

45. Neatby (1967), p. 165. "With the inspection of the provisions, much of the preserved meat was rotten and thrown away." This line was omitted in Neatby's translation (M. Opel to Stein, personal communication, November 2, 2014).

46. McClure (1854a), p. 50; Armstrong (1857), p. 530. From Miertsching's June 30, 1852, entry: "Today we got gifts from the government again. Everybody got 1 solid jacket, 1 solid trousers, 1 pair of water-proofed boots, 2 pairs of woolen stockings, 2 pair of woolen gloves, 2 shawls and a Sou'wester." This line was omitted in Neatby's trans-

lation (M. Opel to Stein, personal communication, November 2, 2014).

47. McClure (1854a), pp. 50–51.

48. Armstrong (1857), p. 532. The relevant passage by Osborn in McClure's book is a thorough whitewash: "The long absence of [a] fresh vegetable diet might have predisposed these men to this disease; but, considering the quantity of fresh animal food that had so happily been procured for them throughout the past winter and at that time also, it appears quite likely that the anxious feelings awakened at finding neither provisions nor a vessel at Melville Island, or indeed even a promise of any, had quite as much, if not more, to do in developing the seeds of this disease, than either the nature of their diet or the slight labour of preparing the ship for sea, by ballasting and watering her" (McClure [1856], p. 237). The final comment about "slight labour" is a direct contradiction to McClure's "heavy labour in ballasting and watering."

49. Armstrong's journal, NA, ADM 101/250, pp. 144–45.

50. Armstrong's journal, NA, ADM 101/250, p. 145. This passage was toned down in Armstrong's book: "To these suggestions, Captain MᶜClure declined to accede, or to make any addition whatever to the then scanty allowance of provisions" (Armstrong [1857], p. 532).

51. Nelson (vol. 1, June-July 1852), SPRI, MS 748/1; Armstrong (1857), pp. 532, 601: game in July (minus musk ox): 3 deer (197 lbs. of meat), 2 seals, 14 hares, 40 ptarmigan, and 109 wild fowl. On July 23, Piers shot one seal, and Miertsching clubbed the other one (Armstrong [1857], p. 538; Neatby [1967], p. 167).

52. Armstrong (1857), p. 533; McClure (1854a), p. 51. According to Nelson, the larger musk ox was a cow, while the other was a bull (Nelson [vol. 1, July 8, 1852], SPRI, MS 748/1).

53. McClure (1854a), p. 51; Nelson recorded a slightly different version of events at this stage. Woon attempted to reload, but was astonished to find he was without ammunition, having evidently lost his ammunition pouch during the recent encounter. Though it was quite probably close by, there was no time to search for it (Nelson [vol. 1, July 8, 1852], SPRI, MS 748/1).

54. A native of Millbrook, Devon, the unmarried, 5'5½", blue-eyed Samuel Bounsall was about 26 years old at the time, and sported intriguing tattoos of a "pair of Epaulettes on each arm." He is also shown as Samuel Bonnsall and Samuel/George Bounsell in various official records. Shipmate Able Seaman William Batten was also from Millbrook (*Investigator*'s Musters [1849–50], NA, ADM 38/1026; *Asia*'s De-

scription Book [1847–51], NA, ADM 38/7567; *Asia*'s and *Cockatrice*'s [tender to *Asia*] Muster [1850], NA, ADM 38/2531).

55. Armstrong (1857), p. 534; Armstrong's journal (Sick List), NA, ADM 101/250, p. 7; McClure (1854a), p. 51.

56. Armstrong (1857), p. 537.

57. McClure (1856), p. 240; Neatby (1967), p. 167.

58. Armstrong's journal and Sick List, NA, ADM 101/250, pp. 7, 153–54. Armstrong wrote in detail about Bradbury's condition and his treatment of it.

59. Sorrel, http://en.wikipedia.org; Hatfield, p. 303; Neatby (1967), pp. 168–69 and fn; Armstrong (1857), pp. 538–39. In his journal, Armstrong wrote the sorrel and scurvy grass appeared "early in July," but in his book wrote, "Towards the middle of July" (Armstrong's journal, NA, ADM 101/250, p. 145); Miertsching found the sorrel on August 1, but not unusual for his writings, the date may have been off (see Appendix 2).

60. McClure (1854a), p. 51. McClure wrote that sorrel "could not withstand this rigorous summer beyond the 15th of the month [August]." Neatby (1967), pp. 169, 170: Miertsching's August 2, 1852, entry reads in part: "The captain gave orders for 4 men to go tomorrow to collect this weed, to cure the men suffering from scurvy," and on August 29, "According to the two doctors, the health condition in this month is much better, because of the daily ingestion of the sorrel." These lines were omitted in Neatby's translation (M. Opel to Stein, personal communication, November 2, 2014); Nelson (vol. 1, June-July 1852), SPRI, MS 748/1.

61. Armstrong (1857), pp. 539–40.

62. Neatby (1967), pp. 168–69; Armstrong (1857), p. 601: August—5 hares, 31 ptarmigan, 55 wild fowl, and 1 seal, and September—just 19 ptarmigan. Nelson wrote that a fishing party with a net caught 28 lbs. of flavorful salmon one day (evidently from a river), and 61 lbs. of fish the following day. On August 21, Miertsching wrote, "In four days 173 little fish of an unknown species were caught" (Nelson [vol. 1, August 10, 11, 1852], SPRI, MS 748/1; Neatby [1967], p. 169–70); McClure's journal (May 31, 1850), RGS, SSC/106; Armstrong's journal (Sick List), NA, ADM 101/250, p. 7. Taylor was in Sick Bay from July 15 to August 8.

63. Neatby (1967), p. 169.

64. Armstrong (1857), pp. 538, 540; Neatby (1967), p. 169.

65. McClure (1856), pp. 240–41; beacon at lat. 74° 6' 48" N. and long. 118° 15' W.

66. Ibid.

67. Neatby (1967), p. 169; Arm-

strong (1857), p. 541; McClure (1856), pp. 241–42; McClure (1854a), p. 51.

68. Nelson (vol. 1, August 22, 1852), SPRI, MS 748/1; Armstrong's journal (Sick List), NA, ADM 101/250, p. 7: Davies (August 16–October 10) and Ramsay (August 17–October 17); Neatby (1967), p. 170.

69. Neatby (1967), p. 171.

70. McClure (1854a), p. 51.

71. Neatby (1967), pp. 171–72.

72. Armstrong (1857), pp. 544–45. "From this date, the 8th September, the provisions were still further reduced, chiefly in vegetables—two and a half ounces of which was the daily issue; the quantity of meat issued was eight ounces daily, but making due allowance for bone in the salt, and jelly in the fresh meat, the average weight did not exceed six ounces, which with ten ounces of flour constituted the allowance on which we had lived for the previous twelve months; the articles tea, cocoa and sugar were issued in fractional parts of an ounce." See the full scale of victualling for September 1852–June 1853 (Armstrong [1858], p. 14).

73. McClure (1854a), p. 51.

74. Armstrong's journal, NA, ADM 101/250, p. 147.

75. None of the sources are in complete agreement as to the total number of men to have been sent in both parties, with the figures stated here being from Armstrong's book.; Armstrong's journal, NA, ADM 101/250, p. 147; Armstrong (1857), pp. 542–44; McClure (1854a), p. 51; McClure (1856), pp. 243–44 and fn, 257; McClure (1856), pp. 243–44 and fn; Neatby (1967), p. 172 and fn. Miertsching is the only one who indicated Haswell's destination was Port Leopold, although McDougall wrote that Haswell "was to proceed to Cape Spencer, and either remain till the breaking up of the ice, or push forward to Port Leopold, and taking the launch left there by Sir James Ross in 1848-9, coast along the west shore of Baffin's Bay, in hope of meeting the whalers" (McDougall, p. 216). From this, it appears McDougall did not know about the boat at the Cape Spencer depot.

76. Armstrong (1857), p. 543.

77. Armstrong's journal, NA, ADM 101/250, p. 147; Armstrong (1857), pp. 542–44; McClure (1854a), p. 51, 56; McClure (1856), pp. 243–44 and fn; Neatby (1967), pp. 172, 179; Holland (1994), p. 244. McClure wrote to James Ross that he was glad he made the trip to Winter Harbour in April–May 1852, "as it has prevented my sending the party I am about to dispatch upon a service which would probably have starved them" (McClure to Ross [April {no day written} 1853], NA, BJ2/10). Neatby also commented: "The supplies would certainly have proved insufficient

to carry the travelling parties to their respective destinations. In 1851 McClintock with a fresh and carefully selected crew had taken eighty days to make a round trip of 760 miles on a route which largely coincided with the course assigned to Haswell and his twenty-six invalids. McClure did not know this, but he was aware that in the same season Lieutenant Cresswell had spent thirty-four days, out and back, on a route corresponding to but rather shorter than the one he was now to cover one way in thirteen days with a party of near cripples" (Neatby [1967], p. 184, fn). McClintock had six men with him in HM Sled *Perseverance* for the 760 miles in 80 days, and reached lat. 74.38° W. and long. 114.20°N (Captain Horatio Austin's dispatch [August 12, 1851], Report of Proceeding, Naval Correspondence, Indexes and Digests for 1793–1913, NA, ADM 12).

78. Armstrong (1857), p. 544. Armstrong used nearly the identical wording in his journal, which is something of a contradiction about what he knew on March 2, 1853, when he wrote, "Captain McClure made known to me, his intention of dispatching the weaker half of our crew from the ship." This may be the result of the surgeon's having written in retrospect; see Appendix 2 (Armstrong's journal, NA, ADM 101/250, pp. 147, 161; Armstrong [1857], p. 558).

79. McClure (1854a), p. 51; Ross (1994), p. 306. See the latter part of Chapter 9 for a full explanation concerning McClure's misleading opinion about the land area between Point Peel and Cape Walker.

80. McClure (1854a), pp. 51–52; McClure to Ross (April [no day written] 1853), NA, BJ2/10; McClure, "The North-West Passage, etc." (1853), p. 673.

81. Ibid., p. 52.

82. McClure (1856), p. 244.

83. McClure to Ross (April [no day written] 1853), NA, BJ2/10. The steadfast loyalty of Sergeant Woon and his Marines on this occasion may have contributed to the later awards of a unique "Arctic Gallantry Medal" to Woon, a special "Arctic Meritorious Service Medal" to Private Biggs, and promotions upon returning home for Corporal Farquharson and Private Parfitt. In Parfitt's case, he notably also received "an excellent certificate from Captain McClure for nearly 5 years Service in HMS Investigator" (Douglas-Morris [1987], pp. 412–14; Farquharson's attestation form, NA, ADM 157/35; Parfitt's attestation form, NA, ADM 157/56).

84. Neatby (1967), p. 172.

85. McClure to Ross (April 1853), NA, BJ2/10. McClure wrote that he "detailed the circumstance to the Admi-

ralty," but the author has never seen or heard of any official correspondence on this subject.

86. McClure (1854a), p. 52.

87. Nelson (vol. 1, September 1852), SPRI, MS 748/1–2; Armstrong (1857), pp. 545, 601. However, on his list of game, Armstrong shows two deer were shot in October.

88. Neatby (1967), p. 172; Nelson (vol. 1, October 1852), SPRI, MS 748/1; Armstrong's journal (Sick List), NA, ADM 101/250, p. 7.

89. McClure (1856), p. 245, October 16, 1852; Neatby (1967), p. 172. According to Miertsching: "Our reserves of food and also of coal has been checked and weighed; it is found that it will last to November 1853, at the present daily ration."

90. Armstrong's journal, NA, ADM 101/250, p. 148, stated October 5; Armstrong (1857), p. 548, stated October 4, and finished with, "to their application, Captain McClure refused to accede"—leaving out the word "peremptorily"; Miertsching stated October 18 (Neatby [1967], p. 174).

91. Neatby (167), pp. 174–75 and fn. Neatby wrote: "Presumably occasional gifts from his private stock were accepted as a fulfillment of his promise; the organized protest was not repeated [so far as is known]."

92. McClure (1856), pp. 244, 246; Neatby (1967), pp. 174–76.

93. "The cold between decks is more severely felt in the months of Sept. and October, than any other period of the year, the hatchways being still kept open, favour the rapid condensation of the vapour generated below, when there is not a sufficient amount of artificial warmth to dissipate it, the consequence is, the air becomes, cold, moist, and impure, and in men whose power of generating heat are feeble, when the body is weak and attenuated, becomes a fertile source for the production of disease" (Armstrong's journal, NA, ADM 101/250, p. 149).

94. Nelson (vol. 1, October 1852), SPRI, MS 748/1; Armstrong (1857), pp. 548–49; Armstrong's journal, NA, ADM 101/250, pp. 148–49; Neatby (1967), p. 173.

95. Armstrong's journal (Sick List), NA, ADM 101/250, pp. 7–8.

96. Neatby (1967), pp. 173–75. Since Miertsching had to reconstruct most his journal, he likely wrote "Lieutenant" Wynniatt as a result of the latter's promotion in absentia; Wynniatt was on the sick list from October 13, 1852 to April 15, 1853, a total of 184 days (Armstrong's journal [Sick List], NA, ADM 101/250, p. 8).

97. Armstrong's journal, NA, ADM 101/250, pp. 154–55. Armstrong wrote in detail about Wynniatt's condition

and his treatment of it. Nelson (vol. 1, May 2, 1853), SPRI, MS 748/1.

98. See Chapter 6. While *Investigator* was on the northern coast of Russian America, Piers wrote of how "the Officers were on the ice, which we could step on from the Ship, and Wynniatt set one of his musical boxes playing on it" (Piers's journal [August 16, 1850], NMM, JOD/102).

99. Armstrong's journal, NA, ADM 101/250, p. 154.

100. Ibid.

101. "The Dissolution of the Monasteries, sometimes referred to as the Suppression of the Monasteries, was the set of administrative and legal processes between 1536 and 1541 by which Henry VIII disbanded monasteries, priories, convents and friaries in England, Wales and Ireland, appropriated their income, disposed of their assets, and provided for their former members and functions" (The Dissolution of the Monasteries, http://en.wikipedia.org).

102. Burke (1871), pp. 1564–65; Walford, p. 1061; Ancestry.com, www.ancestry.com.

103. Hart (1840), p. 235; 83rd (County of Dublin) Regiment of Foot, http://en.wikipedia.org; Gethyn-Jones, p. 72.

104. Misstoricalfiction, "Wreckless horseman, wild horses or just plain bad luck?"

105. Lutz and Chartrand (2011); cydlee61, "Eldon House."

106. Ibid. Eldon House is now a museum, and the oldest surviving private residence in London, Ontario, and the story of Lieutenant Wenman Wynniatt and Sarah Harris continues to be told to visitors to this day.

107. Armstrong's journal, NA, ADM 101/250, p. 155. That said, Raymond Priestley, a veteran of two British Antarctic expeditions in the early 20th century, commented on "polar madness" (depression, sleep disruption, anger, irritability): "It is a well-established fact that men unsuited for polar exploration are liable to suffer from temporary mental aberration, either during or immediately after an expedition. Cases have occurred in nearly all recent expeditions where real hardships have been incurred. The most extraordinary hallucinations afflict the patient and for the time being he is quite irresponsible. It is a merciful fact that this aberration is apparently temporary only, though in extreme cases it may last for months or even years.... Scarcely an expedition has returned without having to record at least one case of this disease. And there are many cases of which the world at large does not hear" (Priestley, SPRI, MS 1097/16/1, p. 26; MS 1097/16/2, p. 28).

108. Armstrong (1857), pp. 546, 601. "The salt beef or port issued by the

clerk-in-charge as a day's ration is in like manner impartially divided and distributed by lot, whereupon each man puts his little portion in cold water to draw out the salt, and, in order not to shrink it by cooking, devours it raw with as much zest as if it were the best roast.!'" Neatby commented: "¹Armstrong protested that raw salt meat aggravated scurvy, but McClure declined the risk of again exerting his authority which had already been challenged once (p. 546)" (Neatby [1967], p. 176 and fn.). Armstrong wrote "Thomas Scurvy [age] 28 A.B.," and by the age, this could have been either Thomas Carmichael or Thomas Toy (Armstrong's journal [Sick List], NA, ADM 101/250, p. 8).

109. Armstrong's journal (Sick List), NA, ADM 101/250, p. 8.

110. Armstrong (1857), p. 547.

111. "Two cases of 'Hernia' occurred, both oblique inguinal, [one for Dr. Armstrong and] one in the person of the Carpenter, Mr. Geo. James Ford, who had received a similar injury, while serving on the Comet [sic—*Contest*] of[f] Africa at a former period, on the left side, for which he was compelled to wear a truss. On this occasion it occurred when he was engaged in assisting to lift a heavy skylight on the 10th of November [1852] preparatory to housing in for the winter, when from the motion entailed in doing so a right Inguinal Hernia resulted, rendering the use of a double truss necessary which accordingly was issued, and to him, I have given a Certificate of the recurrence of the injury" (Armstrong's journal, ADM 101/250, p. 159; Ford's service record, NA, ADM 29/23/531); "Ordinary Certificate granted"—age 31—"When employed lifting the after hatchway preparatory to housing in for the winter on the 10th November 1852 received an oblique Inguinal Hernia on right side" (Armstrong's journal and Sick List, ADM 101/250, pp. 8, 90).

112. Nelson (vol. 1, December 1852), SPRI, MS 748/1; McClure (1854a), p. 52; Armstrong (1857), pp. 549–50, 601; Neatby (1967), pp. 175–767. The ice was 3'1" thick by the end of November.

113. Nelson (vol. 1, December 1852), SPRI, MS 748/1; Neatby (1967), p. 177; Armstrong (1857), pp. 551–52, 601. The extreme temperatures made it very difficult to ram the ball ammunition all the way down the barrels due to frostbite, consequently the guns burst when fired on at least two occasions. Armstrong's numbers conflict as to the total deer for December. His journal and book have 9 deer for 874 lbs. of meat, but his chart in the latter only indicates 6 deer for 557 lbs. of meat (to which was added 3 hares and 9 ptarmigan). Dr. Armstrong's Pension Certifi-

cate for Hurts—"Ordinary Certificate granted"—age 33—"An oblique Inguinal Hernia left side received when engaged in Reindeer hunting for provisioning for ship on the 17th December 1852 by falling down a precipitous Snow bank, in the dark weather. Temp. –40°" (Armstrong's journal and Sick List, ADM 101/250, pp. 8, 90, full details on p. 159).

114. Neatby (1967), pp. 177–78. This line was omitted from Neatby's translation of the December 25, 1852, entry (M. Opel to Stein, personal communication, November 2, 2014); Nelson (vol. 1, December 1852), SPRI, MS 748/1–2; Armstrong (1857), p. 552; McClure (1854a), p. 52.

115. Osborn wrote, "The old-fashioned English plum pudding was still to be seen on Christmas-day [1852], not a very rich one, may be, but good appetite compensated for what it lacked in that respect." Given what Miertsching wrote on November 30, 1852, one wonders if this was why the plum pudding was "not a very rich one": "This winter the cook [evidently Stubberfield] prepares our vegetables in the most original manner; the beans are broken up with a hammer, ground in a coffee mill, converted into a dough with water, then they are cooked in water in a bag, like a pudding, and this mass is brought to the table without fat or butter, and the portions distributed by lot to the hungry crew" (McClure [1856], p. 248; Neatby [1967], p. 176).

116. Neatby (1967), p. 178; McClure (1854a), p. 52.

117. This line was omitted in Neatby's translation (M. Opel to Stein, personal communication, November 2, 2014).

118. McClure (1856), p. 249; Neatby (1967), p. 193.

119. As far as the author is aware, "Arctic Cooking" has not previously been published. "Arctic Cooking" (undated), Mumford's journal, LAC, MG24-H80. Nelson and William Mumford, Carpenter's Crew/Mate onboard *Resolute*, became friends, and several of Nelson's poems are preserved within Mumford's journal (see Appendix 2). The "grinding the peas" is surely a reference to Miertsching's writings about the cook's original "pudding" (Neatby [1967], p. 176). Mumford's Arctic Medal 1818–55 exists, and is privately engraved on the edge: W.I MUMFORD H.M.S. RESOLUTE 1852–54 (Purves, p. 50, Plate 3; Scheeres to Stein, personal communication, June 18, 2006).

120. McClure (1854a), p. 52.

121. Nelson (vol. 1, December 1852), SPRI, MS 748/1; Neatby (1967), pp. 176–78.

## Chapter 13

1. Neatby (1967), p. 178.

2. Armstrong (1857), p. 554. "In the month of January, the temperature fell lower than has ever been experienced by any former Expedition—to 65° below zero, and in the interval of the usual period for taking observations it fell to –67°." Armstrong also wrote that the monthly average was –43.87°F, the lowest the expedition had known, and (he believed) colder than any other polar voyage; McClure (1856), p. 255; Neatby (1967), p. 179.

3. Neatby (1967), p. 179.

4. Ibid., p. 180; Armstrong's journal (Sick List), NA, ADM 101/250, pp. 8–9.

5. Armstrong's journal (Sick List), NA, ADM 101/250, pp. 8–9. Ascites is the accumulation of fluid in the peritoneal cavity (a potential space between the parietal peritoneum and visceral peritoneum, that is, the two membranes that separate the organs in the abdominal cavity from the abdominal wall), http://en.wikipedia.org. Some of the more prominent cases in January were: Gibbs (rheumatism and debility, 30 days), Carmichael (rheumatism, 25 days), Williams (debility, 18 days), Mackenzie (debility, 26 days), Morgan (dysentery, 18 days), Stone (intermittent fever, 42 days), Parfitt (dysentery and debility, 22 days), Taylor (rheumatism and debility, 18 days).

6. Armstrong's journal, NA, ADM 101/250, p. 156.

7. Armstrong (1857), p. 555; syncope (medicine), http://en.wikipedia.org; Neatby (1967), p. 180.

8. Neatby (1967), p. 180; Armstrong (1857), p. 601.

9. Neatby (1967), pp. 180–81. Of the other two cooks—Anderson and Stubberfield—Anderson was a "a very good, well-conducted man," and Stubberfield had "Very Good" conduct during the expedition (Armstrong [1857], p. 500, fn; Stubberfield's service record, NA, ADM 139/348/34759).

10. Neatby (1967), p. 182; Armstrong (1857), pp. 300, 555, 601. The hunters also brought in 9 hares and 10 ptarmigan in February; Nelson (vol. 1, February 1853), SPRI, MS 748/1; McClure (1856), p. 256. Miertsching wrote on February 22: "Our daily ration had been changed again; now we get per man daily: 10 loth of meat, 16 loth of bread und 2 loth of oatmeal as vegetables" [1 loth = 14.6 g]. This line was omitted in Neatby's translation (M. Opel to Stein, personal communication, December 3, 2014).

11. McClure (1854a), p. 53; Neatby (1967), p. 182.

12. Some of the notable inductions on the sick list in February: Steel

(dysentery and debility, 62 days), Kerr (ascites, dysentery and debility, 64 days, until death), Tiffeny (ascites, dysentery and debility, 61 days), Evans (ascites, 34 days), Mark Griffiths (scurvy, 30 days) (Armstrong's journal [Sick List], NA, ADM 101/250, p. 9).

13. Neatby (1967), p. 183.

14. Ibid.; Armstrong's journal (Sick List), NA, ADM 101/250, p. 9.

15. Armstrong (1857), p. 556.

16. Armstrong's journal, NA, ADM 101/250, p. 160.

17. Ibid.

18. Armstrong's journal, NA, ADM 101/250, p. 161.

19. Armstrong's journal, NA, ADM 101/250, p. 161; Armstrong (1857), p. 558. Only in his book did Armstrong specifically state that he placed on record his and Piers's opinions "by letter"—and if so, presumably the writings were signed by both doctors. It seems Armstrong and Piers would have kept copies of such an important document; although neither the original letter nor any copies have been discovered, large portions of the journals for McClure and Piers are missing, which is also the case with the *Investigator*'s Letter & Order Book (see Appendix 2); Neatby (1967), p. 185.

20. McClure (1854a), p. 53. The numbers for the sled parties were set at 26 (Haswell) and eight (Cresswell). However, for unexplained reasons, McClure's published account showed a change to 15 men for each party. In addition, Cresswell's destination was altered from the Mackenzie to the Coppermine River. Both of these "changes" were evidently errors in the published work, since Lieutenant Pim (*Resolute*) was told that the greater number was set to leave for Cape Spencer, while the rest would try to reach the Mackenzie. Also, McClure again noted the Mackenzie River in his official dispatch (Pim [1855a], p. 657; McClure [1856], p. 257; McClure [1854a], p. 53).

21. Nelson (vol. 1, March 1853), SPRI, MS 748/1. Later on Nelson had a change of heart, and though difficult to say exactly why, perhaps the reality of situation sunk in; Neatby (1967), p. 185.

22. Nelson (vol. 1, March 1853), SPRI, MS 748/1; McClure (1854a), p. 53; Armstrong's journal, NA, ADM 101/250, p. 161. According to McClure and Armstrong, the full allowance of food began on March 15, whereas Nelson wrote March 12; Neatby (1967), p. 183. Also see chapter 12, endnote 77, regarding the insufficient amount of supplies allotted for Haswell's and Cresswell's sled parties.

23. Nelson (vol. 1, March 1853), SPRI, MS 748/1; Armstrong (1857), pp. 556–57, 601. The first wolf "was a fine specimen, with a skin of spotless white; weighed eighty pounds, was five feet ten inches in length, and three feet four inches in height. The meat when cooked was excellent—much resembling in taste that of Fox—and we considered it preferable to Bear's flesh." The second wolf weighed 70 lbs.; McClure (1856), pp. 258–59; McClure to Ross (April [no day written] 1853), NA, BJ2/10.

24. Armstrong's journal and Sick List, NA, ADM 101/250, pp. 7, 9, 152; *Brilliant*'s Description Book (1846–49), NA, ADM 38/7678; scrofula, www.britannica.com.

25. British surgeon Julius Jeffreys (1800–77) invented a mask, which he called a "Respirator." As the wearer exhaled, moisture and warm air were captured in a fine wire mesh. In turn, inhaled air was warmed and moistened as it passed through the same mesh, and so gave some relief from lung diseases. The Respirator became very popular, and Elizabeth Gaskell, William Makepeace Thackeray and Charles Dickens were among the writers who mentioned the device in their writings (Julius Jeffreys, http://en.wikipedia.org).

26. Armstrong (1857), p. 559; Nelson (vol. 1, March 1853), SPRI, MS 748/1–2; Neatby (1967), p. 185; Armstrong's journal (Sick List), NA, ADM 101/250, p. 9.

27. Neatby (1967), p. 186; Nelson (vol. 1, April 1853), SPRI, MS 748/1–2.

28. Ibid. and fn. This was Miertsching's last entry in his reconstructed journal. The balance of his writings, from April 7, 1853 to November 10, 1854, are the journal's only original day-by-day record (see Appendix 2).

29. McClure (1854a), pp. 31, 53–54; Neatby (1967), p. 187. Miertsching's April 7, 1853, entry recorded events of April 6; McClure wrote to James Ross that he was glad he made the trip to Winter Harbour in April–May 1852, "as it has prevented my sending the party I am about to dispatch upon a service which would probably have starved them. (McClure to Ross [April {no day written} 1853], NA, BJ2/10).

30. McClure to Back (April [no day written] 1853), RGS, JMS/17/28. According to a notation at the top, Back read this to the RGS on November 14, 1853, however, Back's commentary and draft article on the letter is dated August 1854, and it was afterwards published (in edited form) in *The Journal of the Royal Geographical Society*, where the year of reading is incorrect, "Communicated by Sir George Back, R.N. Read November 14, 1854" (Back [August 1854]; Back [undated]; McClure [1854]).

31. "*McClure required 53 days to complete his time for promotion at this date. P.S. It is evident that this letter was written previous to Lieut! Pim's arrival at the 'Investigator,' with the joyful information of Captain Kelletts being at 'Dealy' island with two vessels. [signed] G Back" (McClure to Back [April {no day written} 1853], RGS, JMS/17/28).

32. McClure to Back (April [no day written] 1853), RGS, JMS/17/28.

33. Armstrong's journal and Sick List, NA, ADM 101/250, pp. 9, 161. Boyle is on the sick list with "scurvy & diarrhea"; Armstrong (1857), p. 559; Armstrong (1858), pp. 48–49.

34. Armstrong (1857), p. 559; Armstrong (1858), pp. 48–52. These pages contain the published version of Armstrong's journal entries regarding Boyle's case (Armstrong's journal, NA, ADM 101/250, p. 161, 169–70).

35. Nelson (vol. 1, April 1853), SPRI, MS 748/1; Neatby (1967), p. 193; McClure (1856), p. 271; McClure also wrote to his uncle about "having only lost one man who accidentally poisoned himself" (McClure to his uncle [the Rev. Richard W. Elgee] [April [no day written] 1853], LAC, R6790–0–8-E; Armstrong (1857), p. 559; Armstrong's journal and Sick List, NA, ADM 101/ 250, pp. 9, 161, 169–70.

36. Neatby (1967), p. 34; Armstrong (1857), p. 559.

37. Nelson wrote that the condition of the ground meant it would take two days to dig a grave four feet deep (Nelson [vol. 1, April 1853], SPRI, MS 748/1).

38. Armstrong (1857), p. 560; McClure (1856), pp. 272–73. The black face came from cooking smoke in tents (McClure to Uncle Elgee [the Reverend W. Elgee), LCA, R6790–0–8-E).

39. McClure (1856), pp. 273–74; *Resolute*, 61 men and *Intrepid*, 30 men (Belcher [vol. 1], p. 13); Pim later gave admirable credit to his dog team during the trip to Mercy Bay and back during March and April 1853: "I cannot finish this letter without mentioning the extraordinary performance of the dogs. These useful animals dragged about 1000 lbs. and travelled with that load as fast as a man could walk; two men were attached to the sledge, but their services were only required over hummocky ice, where, of course, it would have stopped but for their assistance" (Great Britain [1855a], p. 650).

40. Ibid.

41. Harrod, p. 81.

42. Holland (1994), pp. 241–43; Belcher (vol. 1), pp. 2–3.

43. McClure (1856), pp. 261–67.

44. As a midshipman, George Mecham served in the schooner HMS *Constance* from 1846 to 1848, with future Investigators Henry Sugden, James McDonald, Robert Tiffeny, and James Jackson (deserted at Honolulu, July 3–4, 1850) (Markham [1875], pp.

35; Sugden, NA, ADM 29/73/42634; McDonald, NA, ADM 139/178/17722; Tiffeny, *Constance*'s Description Book, NA, ADM 38/7837; Jackson, NA, ADM 139/425/2430A; *Investigator*'s Musters [1849–1850], NA, ADM 38/1026).

45. Vice-Admiral Sir George Strong Nares, KCB, FRS (1831–1915). Nares went on to become an accomplished marine surveyor, and commanded HMS *Challenger* during most of her historic around the world oceanographic voyage (1872–76), leaving the ship in November 1874 to return to England and take command of the Arctic expedition of HMS *Alert* and *Discovery* during 1875–76. His honors included: Knighted (1876), Knight Commander of the Bath (KCB/civil/1876), Fellow of the Royal Society (FRS), RGS Founder's Gold Medal (1877), Paris Geographical Society's Gold Medal (1879). Nares was one of just five individuals entitled to both the Arctic Medal 1818–55 (Mate/*Resolute*/1852–54), and Arctic Medal 1875–76 (Captain and expedition commander/*Alert*/1875–76) (see Appendix 7). He retired as vice-admiral in 1892 (Deacon and Savours, pp. 127–41; Stein [2010], p. 87).

46. The motto of HM Sled *Fearless* could not be found. In McDougall, under the officers' sleds, is Nares' *Perseverance* (motto—"Dum spiro spero"/"While I breathe, I hope"), which he commanded for two journeys in the spring of 1853 (Great Britain [1855a], p. 490; McDougall, pp. 286, 522, 526).

47. Holland (1994), p. 242; Markham (1875), pp. 35, 37—This wrongly shows Mecham as "MECHAM, FREDERICK G."; McDougall, p. 522; Had Haswell left *Investigator* as planned and headed toward Cape Spencer along the northern shore of Viscount Melville Sound, he would have encountered *Resolute* and *Intrepid* at Dealy Island. In *Fatal Passage*, McGoogan inexplicably wrote, "In April 1853, mere days before [McClure] acted on this plan, a searcher from HMS *Resolute*, trapped sixty miles away, chanced upon the *Investigator*" (McGoogan [2002], p. 261).

48. Lady Franklin made Pim's sled flag, which was also flown on Pim's other command during the expedition, HM Sled *Murchison*. The flag is preserved in the collections of the National Maritime Museum, Greenwich (Tomlinson [2009], p. 217; McDougall, p. 526).

49. Bidgood attended the 50th anniversary of Franklin's departure on May 20, 1895, and is listed as "Bidgood (dog-driver), *Resolute*, 1852–54" ("The Franklin Commemoration" [1895], p. 40, fn). Bidgood and Hoile signed for their Arctic Medals spelling both of their names as shown, while Armstrong incorrectly recorded "Thomas Bidgood and Robert Hoyle" (Arctic Medal 1818–55 Roll, NA, ADM 171/9, pp. 12, 41; Armstrong [1857], p. 564).

50. Cape Dundas, Melville Island, lat. 74° 30' N. and long. 113° 45' W. (Dawson, p. 47).

51. Holland (1994), p. 242; McDougall, pp. 200, 217, 520. Who wrote that a young puppy accompanied the party, and Nelson afterward noted six dogs (Nelson [vol. 1, April 1853], SPRI, MS 748/1–2); Pim (1855a), pp. 647–48, 654–56, 660.

52. Armstrong (1857), p. 564.

53. McDougall, p. 520; "[John J. Barrow, Jr.] has been frequently confused with his father by subsequent writers and even by some of his contemporaries. He served in the Admiralty from 1825 to 1857, and during this time acquired his father's interest in Arctic exploration; probably he contributed to the results more than any other man not actually employed on the expeditions." (Roberts, p. 368); Kellett to Barrow, Jr. (April 12, 1853), NMM, MSS/86/033.

54. McClure to Admiralty (June 1, 1853), McClure (1855a), p. 107; McClure (1856), pp. 276–77; Pim (1855a), p. 657; Nelson (vol. 1, April 1853), SPRI, MS 748/1; Armstrong (1857), pp. 564–65; April 5, 1853—"Mr. Payne [*sic*] (clerk in charge), who had been a great invalid from rheumatism until this last winter, when he has made a most rapid and wonderful recovery, and at present is in the enjoyment of more robust health than when he quitted England" (McClure [1854a], p. 53).

55. Kellett's description of McClure's arrival at *Resolute*: "19ᵗʰ April 1853 This is really a Red Letter day in my Voyage and shall be kept as a Holy Day by my Heirs and Successors for ever at 9 O Clock this day our look out man made the Signal for a party coming in from the Westward all went out to meet them and assist them in a second party was then seen Doctor Domville was the first person I met I cannot describe to you my feelings when he told me that Captⁿ McClure was amongst the next party I was not long in reaching him and giving him many hearty shakes No Purer were ever given by two men in the world." A note in the top left side margin in Kellett's hand reads, "not time to get one yet" (Kellett to Barrow, Jr. [April 12, 1853], NMM, MSS/86/033).

56. Pim (1855a), pp. 647–48, 657–58 & 669; Nelson (vol. 1, April 1853), SPRI, MS 748/1; Kellett to Barrow, Jr. (April 12, 1853), NMM, MSS/86/033; Barr (1992), p. 125, 263, 266; McClure to the Senior Officer of HM Ships & Vessels at Wahou, Letter & Order Book (July 1, 1850), RGS, SSC/106; Court's service record, NA, ADM 196/77.

57. McClure's recording of dates in April 1853 is problematic. Between April 8 and 19 he was on the sledding trail, and it is highly unlikely he wrote correspondence under such conditions. Yet, both an official dispatch and letter to his half-sister are dated April 10, and a letter to his wife Mary has April 15. Two other letters, a reply to his uncle's letter (the Reverend Richard W. Elgee) and James Ross, were simply dated "April 1853"—without days. By their content, they were obviously written after Pim's arrival. In the letters to his uncle and half-sister, McClure incorrectly wrote that he left *Investigator* on April 7, and edited versions of these letters appeared in *The Nautical Magazine* (McClure, "The North-West Passage, etc." [1853], pp. 670–75). Two letters from McClure to the Reverend Richard W. Elgee (April 1853 and September 26, 1854), three letters for Lady Wilde and an unsigned letter from Richard Elgee, all regarding McClure's estate, plus a typewritten letter from the Geological Survey of Canada (December 14, 1966), acknowledging copies of the present letters in the National Archives of Canada, were sold at Adam's, April 20, 2010, lot 482 (Adam's, www.adams.ie).

58. McClure (1854a), pp. 60–61.

59. McClure to Ross (April [no day written] 1853), NA, BJ2/10; Markham (1875), p. 6.

60. McClure to Ross (April [no day written] 1853), NA, BJ2/10.

61. McClure to his uncle [the Rev. Richard W. Elgee] (April [no day written] 1853) LCA, R6790-0-8-E; McClure, "The North-West Passage, etc." (1853), p. 673; McClure to wife Mary (April 15, 1853), PBA Galleries, www.pbagalleries.com; McClure to Reynolds (April [no day written] 1853), NRO, BL/MC 5/17—McClure singed this letter "Your attached & affectionate friend."

62. McClure to his uncle [the Rev. Richard W. Elgee] (April [no day written] 1853) LCA, R6790-0-8-E. "As regards Sir John Franklin," wrote McClure to Sir George Back in April, "I have arrived at the conclusion that, all hopes expired in 1850:– when it was far from expected that we could have penetrated so far to the East" (McClure to Back [April {day not written} 1853], RGS, JMS/17/28).

63. McClure to wife Mary (April 15, 1853), PBA Galleries, www.pbagalleries.com; McClure to Back (April [no day written] 1853), RGS, JMS/17/28.

64. Armstrong's journal, NA, ADM 101/250, pp. 167, 171, 173; Armstrong (1857), pp. 564–66. The dates of death for Boyle, Ames, and Kerr are from Armstrong's journal, but there are discrepancies in the official and unofficial sources regarding the exact dates, and

sometimes there is conflict within the same source (Claims by Executors and Next-of-Kin for Back Pay for Ratings, A/2361, B/8909, K/2120, NA, ADM 44); Miertsching wrote that Kerr was buried April 10 and Ames April 13, but if anything, it seems likely these dates should be reversed (Neatby [1967], pp. 191–92).

65. Neatby (1967), pp. 191–92.

66. Armstrong's journal, NA, ADM 101/250, p. 162. Armstrong listed "24 Seamen & marines"; "Mr. Wyniatt [sic] in his diseased condition still cannot properly understand that he is to leave the ship. Ah, it will indeed be a trying journey," wrote Miertsching. He afterward wrote on April 15 that Nelson "gave me as a souvenir sixteen hymns and songs of his composition, and as I left the cabin where I had spent so many lonely and gloomy, but also so many blessed and happy days, and came on deck, there stood my friend, the poet Nelson"—but Nelson left with Mc-Clure's party on April 8 (Neatby [1967], pp. 192–93; Nelson [vol. 1, April 1853], SPRI, MS 748/1).

67. Armstrong's journal and Sick List, NA, ADM 101/250, pp. 9, 59, 162; Harrod (2000), pp. 81–82. Cresswell wrote: "Shortly after leaving the ship, Corporal Farquarson [sic] and Joseph Facey broke down and I was obliged to let them fall out from the drag ropes, the former having pains in his chest, the latter suffering from a fall he had shortly before leaving the ship." Private James Biggs was rated corporal on this day, evidently because Corporal Farquhar-son left with Cresswell's party (McClure [1856], p. xxxv). Miertsching's April 30 entry notes Anderson and Ross as being on sleds, and Richard Ross was still a scurvy patient when he left the ship (Armstrong's journal [Sick List], NA, ADM 101/250, p. 9).

68. This must have been Bradbury, and the cause of his frostbitten fingers (Armstrong's journal, NA, ADM 101/250, p. 57).

69. Harrod (2000), pp. 84–86. On April 27, Cresswell took 112 lbs. of bacon from a cache and gave it to his men. "The Capt. of my sledge, [Henry May,] an Old Quartermaster that had been some 30 years at sea informed me that it was a day he should remember to the day of his death" (May's service record, NA, ADM 139/219/21814); Armstrong's journal, NA, ADM 101/250, p. 57; Neatby (1967), p. 196. "The ship Intrepid—200 paces from the Res-olute—has been set up as a hospital for the sick, and twenty-two men of our company placed there immediately. We six sound men remain on the com-modore's ship, Resolute" (Neatby [167], p. 197). Several of McClure's men had previously served with the men of Res-

olute and Intrepid, especially during the 1848–49 expedition.

70. Armstrong's notation at the end of Dr. Domville's medical survey of the men in Cresswell's party reads: "The second Lieutenant in command of the party, the mate, Assistant Surgeon and Interpreter were not examined. I may here state, the three first were much debilitated on leaving "Investigator" and the mate was also insane, the Inter-preter was in fair health but had lost flesh. A.A." (Armstrong's journal, NA, ADM 101/250, pp. 56–57).

71. Armstrong's journal, NA, ADM 101/250, pp. 56–57; Kellett to Barrow, Jr. (April 12, 1853), NMM, MSS/86/033; Edema, www.mayoclinic.org.

72. Kellett to McClure, Domville and Armstrong (May 5, 1853), Arm-strong's journal, NA, ADM 101/250, p. 57.

73. Armstrong's journal, NA, ADM 101/250, p. 163; Armstrong (1857), p. 571.

74. A copy of "Order № 1" on the subject of volunteers—Kellett to McClure (May 5, 1853)—is, however, contained in the Court Martial Pro-ceedings of October 17, 1854 (NA, ADM 1/5645, pp. 85–86); Armstrong's journal, NA, ADM 101/250, p. 163; Neatby (1967), pp. 245–46.

75. Barr (1992), pp. 126–27; Nelson (vol. 1, May 1853), SPRI, MS 748/1; Neatby (1967), p. 198. With the same vagueness displayed in his writing to the Admiralty about his reason for coming to see Kellett, McClure explained the "arrangements" with his senior officer in equally hazy terms: "Having entered into all the arrangements which our position peculiarly required, upon the evening of May the 5th [we] took our departure, accompanied by Dr. Domville with a sledge, reaching this Bay on the 21st" (McClure to Admi-ralty [June 1, 1853], McClure [1855a], p. 107).

76. Harrod (2000), pp. 86–87, 90, 100. According to Cresswell's May 5, 1853, journal entry: "Capt. Kellett hav-ing placed the Investigator's dispatches in my charge for conveyance to England." Later, in a speech Cresswell gave at a civic reception in King's Lynn on October 26, 1853: "I volunteered, as I had good health myself, to go on [to North Star] and take a chance of any ship that might come out there"; "Lieu-tenant Cresswell of the 'Investigator,' whom I appointed from the 'North Star' as supernumerary to this ship [Phoenix], is charged with the letters and journals of Commander M'Clure. As his journal is of considerable length, I will endeavour to acquaint you with the substance of it, that their Lordships may thus be early informed of the lead-ing features of the 'Investigator's' dis-

coveries" (Inglefield to Admiralty [October 4, 1853], Great Britain [1854a], p. 11); (Neatby [1967], p. 82; Markham [1875], p. 46; "The Arctic Searching Expedition" (1852), p. 201; McClure [1856], p. 290).

77. Armstrong stated in his journal that McClure's party returned to Inves-tigator on May 19, but afterward wrote that Kellett's orders regarding volun-teers "were accordingly read on the quarter deck on Sunday 22nd the day fol-lowing their arrival." This error was repeated in his published account (Armstrong's journal, NA, ADM 101/250, p. 163; Armstrong [1857], pp. 569, 572).

78. A few onboard still continued avidly hunting, but the deer had nearly disappeared from the area, and only two of the animals (180 lbs. of meat) and 6 ptarmigan were brought in in April 1853 (Armstrong [1857], pp. 568, 601).

79. Armstrong (1857), p. 569; Arm-strong's journal (Sick List), NA, ADM 101/250, p. 9.

80. Ford's diary (July 25, 1853), KML, 18500119Arctic1xx; Armstrong (1857), p. 572.

81. Ford's diary (July 25, 1853), KML, 18500119Arctic1xx; McClure included a negative allusion to Ford in his official dispatch of June 1, 1853: "[B]esides the officers, who I am happy I having the opportunity of stating, ten-dered their services and were desirous of remaining, with the solitary excep-tion of one person. Had I been aware that at the last moment he would have failed, I certainly should not have dis-charged the carpenter's mate." Carpen-ter's Mate Henry Gauen was over on Resolute, but Carpenter's Crew William Whitefield was still onboard (McClure [1855a], p. 107; Armstrong's journal, NA, ADM 101/250, pp. 57, 59).

82. Armstrong's journal, NA, ADM 101/250, pp. 58–59; McClure to Admi-ralty (June 1, 1853), McClure (1855a), p. 107 and marginal note; James Nel-son's health: "In good health, has just returned as one of Capt. M'Clure's trav-elling party from Melville Island, which has improved him, lividity and tumidity of gums." Notably, he is the only one in this medical survey for which there is no indication of whether he volun-teered or not.

83. Davies was promoted to quarter-master on April 15, 1853, the day Quar-termaster Henry May left with Cresswell's party left for Resolute (Mc-Clure [1856], p. xxxiii; May's service record, NA, ADM 139/219/21814).

84. Brown manuscript, GM, M-141, p. 19.

85. The officers in better health: McClure—"Good health but slight ane-mia of gums"; Haswell—"In apparent good health, but scorbutic taint manifest

with lividity of gums, with line of demarcation [a band of inflammatory reaction separating gangrenous from healthy tissue]"; Armstrong—"Good health—Left inguinal Hernia since embarkation"; Court "Good health" (Armstrong's journal, NA, ADM 101/250, p. 59).

86. Armstrong's journal, NA, ADM 101/250, pp. 58–61.

87. McClure (1856), p. 284; Armstrong's journal and Sick List, NA, ADM 101/250, pp. 9–10, 163–64. Between May 24 and 26, Newton, Ford, Kennedy, Woon, Mackenzie, and Bancroft were all put on the sick list due to diarrhea and other ailments, but none stayed on more than six days.

88. Armstrong's journal and Sick List, NA, ADM 101/250, pp. 9, 164; Armstrong (1857), p. 575; McDougall, pp. 249–50.

89. McClure to Admiralty (June 1, 1853), McClure (1855a), pp. 107–08 (concerning Copy of Notice left at the Bay of Mercy, June 1, 1853), p. 109 includes a detailed list of provisions, slops, stores, etc., that make up the depot. A marker was erected (presumably at the mouth of the bay), and a notice placed therein stated: "A large depôt of stores has been left on shore nine miles S.W. of this (four months for 66 men)," which also listed depots left by Kellett at Dealy Island, Assistance Harbour, Cape Cockburn, Winter Harbour, and Point Hotham." According to McClure's book, only one boat was left ashore (McClure [1856], p. 288).

90. Condon, pp. 29–30.

91. McClure to Admiralty (June 1, 1853), McClure (1855a), pp. 107–08; Nelson (vol. 1, May 1853), SPRI, MS 748/1; Armstrong (1857), p. 575. According to Armstrong: "On the 30th, we performed the last sad duty to our departed shipmates, by erecting a tablet to their memory."

92. Armstrong (1857), p. 576; "I asked Com.ᵗ M.ᶜClure if the numerous specimens of Natural History, which I had collected during the voyage could be taken, to which a negative answer was returned, and I regret to say, that all were left behind, embracing as they did, anything that my opportunities afforded me the means of collecting, as illustrative of the Natural History of the country in the various branches of Zoology, Ornithology, Icthyology [sic], Geology and Botany, and which I had hoped would have occupied a place with museums of our country" (Armstrong's journal, NA, ADM 101/250, p. 164). Not surprisingly, Armstrong omitted Miertsching's considerable contributions to the natural history collection (Neatby [1967], pp. 167–68).

93. Ford—"Inguinal Hernia on both sides, one of which occurred on board, and the other previous, has also varicose

veins,—in apparent health, but anemia of the gums & line demarcation very apparent." Newton—"Tumidity and lividity of gums, painful mastication [chewing] and looseness of the teeth, many of which are decayed, reduced in health & strength" (Armstrong's journal, NA, ADM 101/250, p. 59). Given McClure's prior lack of faith in the ice mate, he was probably being dismissive of Newton by not including him.

94. Ford's diary (July 25, 1853), KML, 18500119Arctic1xx. The day after departing from *Investigator*, Ford was promoted in absentia to carpenter 2nd class (Ford's service record, NA, ADM 29/23/531); Armstrong wrote that "a few words, not complimentary, were addressed to the men" by McClure (Armstrong [1857], pp. 576).

95. Armstrong (1857), p. 576.

96. Ibid., p. 577; "Very warm & very hard travelling but as we are provided with sails it helps us considerably. We capsize now & then with the sails on the large floes. We are in sight of Melville Island" (Ford's diary [June 8, 1853], KML, 18500119Arctic1xx).

## Chapter 14

1. McClure (1856), p. 288.

2. Ford's diary (July 2, 1853), KML, 18500119Arctic1xx.

3. Presumably McClure disposed of his officers' sled journals before he left the ship.

4. Sub-Lieutenant Emile Frédéric de Bray, Imperial French Navy (1829–79), was one of just two French naval officers entitled to the Arctic Medal 1818–55. De Bray offered his services to the Admiralty and was assigned to the *Resolute*. "De Bray was the only living Frenchman ever to receive the Arctic Medal. It had been Queen Victoria's intention to honour him with an even higher decoration, namely that of the Order of the Bath (de Bray, G., 1926:4). But since this could be awarded only to officers of high rank, it was agreed that this honour should be deferred until de Bray reached the appropriate rank. In fact, his premature death denied him this honour." De Bray was made a Knight of the Legion of Honor by Emperor Napoleon III on August 12, 1854, and on June 11, 1857, his Arctic Medal was sent for distribution to Captain John Washington, Hydrographer of the Navy. De Bray's friend Jules Verne relied heavily on him for technical details in writing a two-part novel inspired by the Franklin Search, about the adventures of Captain Hatteras in the Arctic (Barr [1992], pp. ix, xix, xx, 189, 191, 197, 198; Arctic Medal 1818–55 Roll, NA, ADM 171/9, p. 23).

5. Neatby (1967), p. 201.

6. McClure to Admiralty (June 25, 1853), McClure (1855a), p. 109. According to McClure, "every arrangement that kindness could suggest was made for our reception and comfort, so that without the slightest confusion each officer was at once domiciled in his allotted cabin and every man appointed to his respective berth, either here or in the 'Intrepid,' and in a few minutes all were apparently as much at home as if in their own ship."

7. Ibid.; Armstrong (1857), p. 584.

8. Armstrong (1857), p. 585.

9. "On [Dealy Island] is erected a cairn in shape like a pyramid; diameter at base 14 ft., height 14 ft., diameter at bottom of top 7 ft, with a hole in the center, with 5 casks over it to make it look large so that it may be seen at a distance. A board with the names of the men (which is all Investigators) who built it also on it" (Ford's diary [August 2, 1853], KML, 18500119Arctic1xx).

10. Ford's diary (August 22, 1853), KML, 18500119Arctic1xx.

11. Inglefield to Admiralty (October 4, 1853), Great Britain (a), p. 12; Markham (1875), p. 16; Midshipman Noel Osborn (Sherard Osborn's brother), was originally serving in the transport *Diligence* (which went no further than Disco, Greenland), but transferred to the *Phoenix*, and then joined *North Star* as a mate on August 8, 1853. "From various sources it appears that *Phoenix* was accompanied for part of the way of this voyage by the transport *Diligence* with Inglefield's senior Lieutenant, James Elliott, possibly in command" (Holland, "Sherard Osborn," www.biographi.ca; Poulsom and Myres, pp. 78, 263).

12. Lieutenant Joseph-René Bellot, Imperial French Navy (1826–53). Bellot was a naval cadet on the corvette *Berceau*, and on June 15, 1845, he was seriously wounded in a joint English-French attack on the port of Tamatave (Madagascar); as a result he was made a Knight of the Legion of Honor. During 1851–52, Bellot was second-in-command of the *Prince Albert*, a private search expedition sponsored by Lady Franklin. His posthumous Arctic Medal was sent for distribution to Captain John Washington, Hydrographer of the Navy (Holland, "Joseph-René Bellot," www.biographi.ca; Arctic Medal 1818–55 Roll, NA, ADM 171/9, p. 117).

13. Harrod (2000), pp. 91–92. The two who returned with news of Bellot's death were William Johnson, Able Seamen/Captain of the Forecastle, *North Star* and *Phoenix*, and David Hook, Sailmaker's Mate/Able Seaman, *North Star* and *Phoenix*; a third man was William Harvey, Boatswain's Mate/Captain of the Maintop, *North Star* and *Phoenix* (Belcher [vol. 2], pp. 3–4; Barr

[1992], p. 280; Poulsom *and Myres*, pp. 74, 75, 77); Johnson and Hook safely returned the dispatches, and Commander Pullen left it up to Cresswell to interview the two regarding the details of the incident (Pullen to Inglefield [August 20, 1853], Great Britain [1854a], p. 19).

14. Harrod (2000), p. 92.

15. Ibid; Inglefield to Admiralty (October 4, 1853), Great Britain (1854a), p. 14. The wreck of the *Breadalbane*, with two of her three masts still standing, was located using side-scan radar in August 1980 by Undersea Research Ltd. (Dr. Joseph B. MacInnis). The ship was in perfect condition and became the northernmost known shipwreck in the world (MacInnis, pp. 124–27).

16. Inglefield to Admiralty (October 4, 1853) (Great Britain [1854a], p. 15).

17. Harrod (2000), p. 98.

18. "Plymouth Man Who Searched for the Explorer" (1914); (Cray to Stein, personal communication, March 9, 2012); According to *Phoenix's* Log, a brief stop was made on October 4, 1853: "P.M.—Standing along the land for Thurso Harbour 1:30 Shortened sail, stopped, lowered boat, Captain Inglefield & Lieutenant Cresswell landed, boat returned less ditto. 2 Made sail & proceeded at full speed on the 2nd stop. Stopped occasionally ship overrunning the screw. Standing for Hoy Head" (*Phoenix's* Log [October 4, 1853], NA, ADM 53/4335).

19. McClure to Admiralty (April 10, 1853), McClure (1854a), p. 60; Admiralty to McClure (October 7, 1853), Great Britain (1854a), p. 62.

20. Admiralty to McClure (October 7, 1853), Great Britain (1854a), p. 62; On October 29, *The Illustrated London News* reported that the Admiralty had published McClure's dispatches, and went on (misleadingly) about how "the skill, fortitude, and heroism which have just been crowned by so large a measure of success, in the completion of the North-West Passage" ("H.M.S. 'Investigator,' in the Arctic Regions" [1853], p. 361).

21. Harrod (2000), pp. 98, 101. The caption of an illustration of the Civic Reception between pages 96 and 97 states it was held on October 28, whereas the text has October 26. In 1953, "in the strong room at Lynn there is a large silver cup, heavily chased, and engraved with these words: 'To Lieutenant Samuel Gurney Cresswell, from the Ladies of Lynn'" (Harrod [1953]).

22. Harrod (2000), pp. 102–03; Cresswell (1854).

23. Harrod (2000), pp. 101–02; . On March 2, 1854, the *Morning Herald* used Cresswell's appointment to the *Archer* to explain why he did not accept the *Talbot* appointment: "We therefore presume that Mr Cresswell has declined the appointment of Lieutenant Commander under Captain Inglefield, and the whole Naval service will applaud Lieut. Cresswell for his spirit. As an officer and a gentleman it would be most distasteful for Lieut. Cresswell to serve as a lieutenant under the officer who was promoted for bringing home those despatches of which he, Lieut. Cresswell was the bearer; he (Lt Cresswell) having been the officer who actually made the North-West Passage under Captain M'Clure. The whole affair is most discreditable to the Admiralty" (Harrod [2000], p. 102). His service record hints at the conflict by stating in one place that he was assigned to the *Archer* on February 21, but March 1 in another (Cresswell's service record, NA, ADM 196/36); Clowes (vol. 6), p. 393.

24. Clowes (vol. 6), p. 399; Harrod (2000), p. 107.

25. Wynniatt's service record, NA, ADM 196/37. Promoted to lieutenant in absentia on February 25, 1852, on January 22, 1856, he was "refused sea-time as Lieutenant, while borne as Mate of the Investigator" (Clowes [vol. 6], p. 419).

26. Armstrong (1857), p. 586. Byam Martin Island, lat. 74° 49' 35" N. and long. 105° 42' W.

27. Neatby (1967), pp. 206–07.

28. Ford's diary (August 27, 1853), KML, 18500119Arctic1xx; Armstrong (1857), p. 586. Armstrong stated "latitude 70° 41', longitude 101° 22' W.," but this is in error, as the latitude was likely 74°.

29. Neatby (1967), pp. 209–10.

30. Ford's diary (October 26, November 5, 1853), KML, 18500119Arctic1xx. Also known as Guy Fawkes Day, Bonfire Night and Firework Night, this is a yearly commemoration of November 5, 1605, when Guy Fawkes was arrested while guarding explosives that had been placed beneath the House of Lords by members of the Gunpowder Plot (Guy Fawkes Night, https://en.wikipedia.org). One might correctly assume the ill treatment and jealousy directed toward the Investigators was the result of the realization by Kellett's men of the fame from the North-West Passage discovery that would come the way of McClure's people once they reached England.

31. Neatby (1967), pp. 212–13.

32. The first stanza of "The Resolution" (October 10, 1853), Mumford's journal, LAC, MG24-H80.

33. Sainsbury was promoted to lieutenant in absentia on December 10, 1852, and then his seniority backdated to October 26, 1850, on October 23, 1854. His arrears of full pay amounted to £25.6.10, which was paid to his father, Henry Sainsbury (Romsey, Hants.), on June 28, 1855. "Hubert" was a poem published in his memory in 1858 (Sainsbury's service record, NA, ADM 196/37; Great Britain [1855a], p. 111. Claims by Executors and Next-of-Kin for Back Pay for Officers, NA, ADM 45/33; Tatham, p. 210).

34. Nelson (vol. 1, July 14, 1853), SPRI, MS 748/1; Ford's diary (November 4, 1853), KML, 18500119Arctic1xx; Charles Steel had been released from the sick list on April 10, having suffered 62 days with dysentery and debility (Armstrong's journal [Sick List], NA, ADM 101/250, p. 9); Sainsbury was buried on the 16th, and when "the few preparations required were completed; the funeral service was read on board, in a most impressive manner, by Captain Kellett, and the mournful procession then wended its way to the grave, a hole in the ice, about 250 yards from the ship. The day was cold (–20° [–4°F]), and misty, and never shall I forget the scene on the ice, as the body, sewn in canvas, with weights attached, was launched through the narrow opening, and disappeared to our view. Within an hour, Nature had placed an icy slab over the grave of our departed messmate" (McDougall, pp. 340–41); Barr (1992), p. 276).

35. Barr (1992), pp. 152–53. Aboard *Intrepid* on December 22, Master Frederick Krabbé performed magic tricks, while two Intrepids performed the play *Box and Cox*. "During the intermissions we had several comical songs, and a group of negroes produced a great effect. The leader of the group (the solitary real negro) [Charles Anderson again] played the castanets while the others, who were admirably made up, accompanied themselves on tambourines." McClure, Haswell, Mecham, Pim, Krabbé and Nares performed in *The Two Bonnycastles* (Ford's diary [November 30, 1853], KML, 18500119Arctic1xx).

36. Nelson (vol. 1, December 1853), SPRI, MS 748/1; Barr (1992), pp. 152–54. De Bray wrote on December 30, 1853: "For several days I had been working with Mr Hamilton at putting our electric telegraph in order; once everything was ready the men were employed in erecting snow pillars at regular intervals between ourselves and *Intrepid* for carrying the conductor wire, and that evening we were in communication."

37. Ford's diary (February 8, 18, 24, 1854), KML, 18500119Arctic1xx. February 24, 1853: "Scale of provisions since Sepr. 16th: bread of flour ¾ lb 14 times fortnight; salt beef ¾ lb 6 times a fortnight; pork or bacon ¾ lb 4 times, preserved meat ¾ lb 2 times, ox cheek soup ¾ lb 2 times; potatoes 4 oz. 4 times & 2 oz 1 time; preserved vegetables in canisters, 8 oz 3 times & spirits 10 ½ gills a fortnight; peas 1 gill 4 times; rice 2 oz 2 times; dried vegetables 2 oz 3 times; tea ¼ oz. 7 times; coco ¾ oz 14

times & sugar for it 1½ oz. 14 times; pickles, lemon juice & sugar 1 oz each 14 times; cranberries 4 oz 1 time; & apples 1½ oz 1 time; & sugar for it 1 oz 2 times a fortnight up to April."

38. Kellett wrote of Court: "This officer was with Sir James Ross, and will execute this service zealously and well" (Great Britain [1855a], p. 77).

39. Great Britain (1855a), pp. 77–78.

40. Neatby (1967), p. 219.

41. Krabbé came from a naval background, his father was Danish-born Assistant Surgeon Charles Frederick Krabbé, and according to Greenwich Hospital School records, at various times prior to 1816, he had been a prisoner of both the French and the Americans while serving with the Royal Navy (Charles Brehmer Krabbé [brother] and Frederick John Krabbé, Royal Greenwich Hospital: School Admission Papers, NA, ADM 73/276).

42. Krabbé's service record, NA, ADM 196/21; Markham (1875), pp. 27–28.

43. Krabbé (1855a), p. 707; Great Britain (1855a), p. 87.

44. Krabbé (1855a), p. 707.

45. Ibid.; Great Britain (1855a), p. 87; McClure (1856), p. 302.

46. Neatby (1967), p. 220; McClure (1856), p. 299.

47. April 10—Haswell, Paine, Ford and Newton, with 19 Investigators, two sleds, and 15 days' provisions; April 11—Pim, Armstrong, and Kennedy, with five Resolutes and 12 Investigators, two sleds, and 15 days' provisions; April 14—McClure, Piers and Miertsching, with 17 men, three sleds, and 15 days' provisions (Barr [1992], pp. 166–67; McDougall, pp. 384–86; Ford's diary [April 10, 1854], KML, 18500119Arctic1xx.

48. Neatby (1967), p. 222. Miertsching noted prior to these lines: "It has been good for us all that in love and friendship we could conduct ourselves differently from the crews of these ships; the 'pietistic Investigators' have often been mocked and have suffered much unfriendly handling which, with ordinary seamen, would have caused much unpleasantness, and demanded retaliation and reprisal; but in this as in other matters our sailors show themselves grateful for the love and friendship they have enjoyed, and apologize when any unintentional fault has been committed." "[Captain McClure] has brought a letter from Captn. Kellett, certifying to the uniform good conduct of our crew,—which was read on the quarter-deck of the North Star. This is very gratifying and I am quite sure will be appreciated by us all" (Nelson [vol. 1, April 23, 1854], SPRI, MS 748/1); Great Britain [1855a], p. 803; Ford's

diary [April 23, 1854], KML, 18500119 Arctic1xx.

49. McDougall, p. 386.

50. Barr (1992), p. 281.

51. Mills (vol. 1), p. 75; Neatby (1958), p. 161; Savours (1999), p. 266.

52. Barr (1992), pp. 167, 169; McDougall, p. 388; DeBray wrote that he arrived onboard *North Star* May 25, but McDougall wrote May 19, and Commander Pullen's journal seems to indicate he arrived on May 20 (Barr [1992], p. 170; McDougall, p. 404; Great Britain [1855a], p. 803). "The health of the Investigators, is with the exception of Morgan, very satisfactory" (Nelson [vol. 1, February 2, 1854], SPRI, MS 748/1).; Kellett's squadron had suffered a total of five deaths: Private Thomas Mobley, RM (*Resolute*, October 19, 1852), Captain of the Forecastle George Drover (*Intrepid*, December 12, 1852), Stoker John Coombs (*Intrepid*, May 12, 1853), Private Thomas Hood, RM (*Intrepid*, January 2, 1854), Ice Quartermaster James Wilkey *alias* Stoneman (*Intrepid*, February 2, 1854) (McDougall, pp. 148, 166, 241–42, 363, 365; Poulsom and Myres, pp. 74, 335).

53. McDougall, p. 391 and facing page.

54. Neatby (1967), p. 228.

55. Great Britain (1855a), p. 804; Ford's diary (May 22, 1854), KML, 18500119Arctic1xx; From May 20 to 29, a medical survey of all officers and men of the squadron by Drs. David Lyall, Alexander Armstrong and William Domville, showed the following conditions for 53 of the 56 Investigators: 24 "Good"; 8 "Fair"; 1 "Very Indifferent"; 6 "Indifferent"; 11 "Debilitated"; 1 "Imbecile"; 2 "Bad" (Report of Examination of Officers and Men in HMS *North Star* at Beechey Island, May 20–29, 1854, SPRI, MS 1523/4/3).

56. Great Britain (1855a), pp. 803–04.

57. Great Britain (1855a), pp. 89, 804–05. "McClintock, who until Mecham's return held the record for the longest sledge trip on the Franklin search, was delighted at his achievement; 'Mecham's journey is a most splendid feat, topping all previous ones in speed & probably in distance. His sledging amounts to 1,157 [geographic] miles (mine to 1,148 & with walking examinations to 1,210) but Mecham is absent only sixty-nine days; his marches average eighteen miles. The longest one is thirty miles'" (Barr [1992], p. 283).

58. Krabbé (1855a), pp. 707–22. Upon reaching Cape Hamilton on May 4, Krabbé could not find a cairn here, or at any place up to that point (even though Cresswell left one at this place in May 1851). Krabbé did bring back the medicines, as well as a few botanical and

zoological specimens, and some books. Several plant specimens attributed to Miertsching exist at Kew Gardens (M. Opel to Stein, personal communications, March 13 and May 28, 2011); Neatby (1967), p. 230.

59. Armstrong (1857), p. 593.

60. Barr (1992), pp. 176–77.

61. Ford's diary (August 27, 1854), KML, 18500119Arctic1xx. To include the crews of the *Pioneer* and *Intrepid*.

62. Barr's notation just after Ford's August 28 entry: "Cross-written over 3 pages."

63. Neatby (1967), p. 234; Ford's diary (September 10, 1854), KML, 18500119Arctic1xx.

64. Neatby (1967), p. 90 (November 2, 1850).

65. Douglas-Morris (1987), p. 411. The NA reference for this correspondence is listed as ADM 12/592–85a, but McClure's letters of September 1, 1854 (Capt M.157 ) and October 6, 1854 (Capt M.177) are both noted by Douglas-Morris as missing from the archives. The Admiralty response regarding the medal was dated November 7, 1854. On November 14, McClure replied to an Admiralty letter, writing in part: "Sir, it only remains for me to add, that the promotion which has been awarded to the whole of the officers [*sic*], and the rewards that have been bestowed upon the men most entitled to receive them, have left me nothing further to ask, or their Lordships to grant" (McClure to Admiralty [November 14, 1854], Great Britain [1855a], p. 112). In fact, Armstrong was the only one *not* promoted (Great Britain [1855a], p. 111), and on October 31 he requested to be promoted to deputy inspector, "also stating that Their Lordships had promoted every Officer engaged in the discovery of the North West passage." The reply four days later: "Their Lordships are favorably impressed by his services in general & especially on the recent polar voyage, but that it is not usual to promote to the rank of Deputy Inspector of Hospitals solely on account of meritorious Services, but only when the actual requirements of the Service call for such appointments & that My Lords have directed a note to be made of Dr. Armstrong's services for favorable consideration whenever a suitable opportunity may offer." Armstrong was subsequently promoted to staff surgeon (April 21, 1857), and deputy inspector-general of hospitals and fleets (July 19, 1858) (Armstrong's service record, NA, ADM 104/23).

66. This medal was an adaptation of the Anchor-Type Naval Long Service and Good Conduct Medal.

67. Douglas-Morris (1987), p. 412.

68. Stein (Part 1, September 2008), pp. 153–54.

69. McClure (1854a), p. 53.

70. Neatby (1967), p. 72; Milner's service record, NA, ADM 29/64.

71. McClure (1855a), p. 107 (marginal notation).

72. Armstrong's journal, NA, ADM 101/250, pp. 58–59.

73. Douglas-Morris (1987), pp. 411–14. Douglas-Morris wrote that the Admiralty Digest books do not contain any correspondence regarding this award, but a clue to it being an official reward was found within the recommendation of the Royal Marines Meritorious Service Medal in November 1859: "This exemplary non-commissioned officer has been favourably recommended to their Lordships by Captain Sir Robert McClure, C.B., for services in the Arctic regions" (ADM 191/22/318–9). McClure had also recommended Woon's promotion to color sergeant in a letter dated April 10, 1853, which was received by the Admiralty on October 13, 1853 (presumably via Cresswell), and Woon was appointed color sergeant on February 17, 1854 (Douglas-Morris [1987], p. 414; Woon's attestation form, NA, ADM 157/40).

74. Stein (Part 1, December 2008), pp. 307–08; McClure (1854a), p. 51.

75. McClure to his uncle [the Rev. Richard W. Elgee] (September 26, 1854), LAC, R6790-0-8-E.

76. Barr (1992), p. 180; McClure to Ross (October 3, 1854), NA, BJ2/10); McClure to Ross (May 3, 1860), NA, BJ2/10; McClure was "allowed to reckon sea-time as Captain from 18 Decr 1850, to 17 October 1854, when he was paid off in 'Investigator'" (October 13, 1854), and "Seniority as Captain altered to 18 December 1850" (October 23, 1854) (McClure's service record, NA, ADM 196/1/395).

77. Neatby (1967), p. 239 and fn. Since the *Investigator*'s departure in 1850, there had been notable introductions into the Royal Navy: "Reserve Half Pay" (1851), Continuous Service (1853), and the beginning of regular uniforms for seamen (1853) (Lewis, pp. 255, 276). The day before the court-martial, McClure's first cousin gave birth to a boy, whom Jane Francesca Elgee (Lady Wilde) named Oscar Wilde (Captain Sir Robert John Le Mesurier McClure, www.priaulxlibrary.co.uk).

78. The officers and men present at the court-martial are listed (with several of their names spelled incorrectly), "except Lieutenant Cresswell on Service in the Baltic, Mr. Pierse [*sic*] Assistant Surgeon who was sick on Shore, Mr. Wynniatt on Service in the Baltic, Mr. Sainesbury [*sic*] Mate now deceased Mr. Miertscheing [*sic*] absent on Admiralty leave, William Carrall [*sic*] absent Mark Bradbury Sick in Hospital and Thomas Toy and Elias Bone [*sic*] absent without leave and Thomas Morgan now

deceased were brought into Court and the Witnesses and Audience admitted." Toy's post-expedition history is unknown, and Bow's service record is unblemished (Court Martial Proceedings of Capt. Robt. J. Le M. McClure and Officers and Crew of HMS *Investigator*, NA, ADM 1/5645, pp. 78–89; Bow's attestation form, NA, ADM 157/156).

79. President—The Hon. William Gordon, Vice Admiral of the Blue and Commander in Chief of HM's Ships and Vessels in the River Medway and at the Buoy of the Nore; Members—Captain Sir Thomas Sabine Pasley (HMS *Royal Albert*), Captain Christopher Wyvill (HMS *Wellesley*), Captain John Jervis Tucker (HMS *Formidable*), Captain Hon. Keith Stewart (HMS *Nankin*), Captain George Henry Seymour (HMS *Cumberland*), Captain Edward Gennys Fanshawe (HMS *Cossack*); Deputy Judge Advocate William W.W. Hayward (Court-Martial Proceedings of Capt. Robt. J. Le M. McClure and Officers and Crew of HMS *Investigator*, NA, ADM 1/5645, pp. 83, 89).

80. Court-Martial Proceedings of Capt. Robt. J. Le M. McClure and Officers and Crew of HMS *Investigator*, NA, ADM 1/5645, pp. 78–89

81. A *copy* of this order is contained in the court-martial proceedings (NA, ADM 1/5645, pp. 85–86).

82. McClure had written to Ross one month before: "Kellett however thought we had persisted sufficiently long & left it to the men to volunteer or not, four only were willing to remain" (McClure to Ross [September 15, 1854], NA, BJ2/10).

83. Court-Martial Proceedings of Capt. Robt. J. Le M. McClure and Officers and Crew of HMS *Investigator*, NA, ADM 1/5645, pp. 86–89. A *copy* of the "Report of the State of health of the Officers & Crew of Her Majesty's Discovery Ship Investigator, etc.," of May 23, 1853, formed part of the court-martial record. Henry Bluff is omitted from this copy (Armstrong's journal, NA, ADM 101/250, pp. 58–59).

84. Barr (1992), pp. 181, 289.

85. A copy of the minutes was sent to the Secretary of the Admiralty by Deputy Judge Advocate William W.W. Hayward from the Precinct, Rochester, on October 21 (Court-Martial Proceedings of Capt. Robt. J. Le M. McClure and Officers and Crew of HMS *Investigator*, NA, ADM 1/5645, p. 82).

86. McGoogan (2002), pp. 181, 191–97; Barr to Stein, personal communication, March 24, 2012. On January 19, 1854, the Admiralty announced that if intelligence regarding the officers and crews of *Erebus* and *Terror* being alive was not received on or before March 31, they would "be considered as having

died in Her Majesty's Service" (LG, January 20, 1854, no. 21515, p. 174).

87. 1 guinea = £1 1s.

88. "The Arctic Explorers—Testimonial to Dr. Armstrong" (1854). O'Byrne (1855), p. 103. The gold chronometer and chain were valued at 70 guineas; "Some Relics of the Late Sir Alexander Armstrong, M.D., K.C.B., F.R.S." (1906), p. 341.

89. "The Arctic Explorers—Testimonial to Dr. Armstrong" (1854).

90. Ibid.

91. McClure was not present, and there is no indication that any other *Investigator* officers that may have been available were in attendance.

92. "The Arctic Explorers—Testimonial to Dr. Armstrong" (1854).

93. Wilcox died c. February 24, 1855; Bradbury died April 16, 1855; Flynn's Arctic Medal was sent to his widow on June 3, 1857; Whitefield is shown as discharged dead on the medal roll, and the Arctic Medal was collected by his widow on October 12, 1857; King was discharged dead in the infirmary (presumably at Woolwich) on April 1, 1859; Wynniatt died on November 29, 1860 (Claims by Executors and Next-of-Kin for Back Pay for Ratings, W/7/39, B/9030, NA, ADM 44; Arctic Medal 1818–55 Roll, NA, ADM 171/9, pp. 30, 100; Royal Marines' Description Books, NA, ADM 158/53; *The Annual Register* [1862], p. 424; Markham [1875], p. 165).

94. Harrod (2000), pp. 184, 187–88. Cresswell died at home on August 14, 1867. After Cresswell's appointment to command HMS *Scylla* in September 1863, McClure's writings to him harked back to the conflict on *Investigator*: "Don't let the authority out of your own hands, delegate a sufficient amount to yr. 1st Lt. to uphold Discipline and not to be always referring to you in small matters. Recollect that you must always be the Big Joss, always have the Defaulters before you at the morning Quarters, which ought to be the Parade of the Day when all offences should be brought before you and (except in cases of Mutiny) only receive complaints at that time. It will save many upsets as officers will have time for reflection. And you yourself upon such subjects take the night to sleep over it, your judgement will generally then be correct. Be courteous but not too intimate with yr. officers, support your 1st Lt. if you have confidence in him, if not you had better part. Be careful of the Officers Messes, and to the Mids., impress upon them to avoid bad company and not get into debt. This will generally keep them straight" (Harrod [2000], p. 181).

95. McClure to Barrow, Jr. (January 1, 1855), BL, Add.35308.

96. McClure to Barrow, Jr. (January 11, 1855), BL, Add.35308.

97. Barrow Bequest, BL, Add. 35308.

98. Ibid.

99. Collinson (1889), p. 344; Barr (2007), p. ix.

100. "The rejoicing over the safe arrival of the *Enterprise* in England in May 1855 was soured by her captain's insistence that some of her officers should be court-martialled for the disorders of which they had been guilty. The Admiralty, sympathetic to the nervous strain of prolonged Arctic service, knew that the squabbles bound to arise among a small group of men penned up for months of darkness and discomfort, if aired in court, might make both prosecutor and accused appear ridiculous, and did its best to pacify him. When Collinson consented to soften his charges, Their Lordships absentmindedly took them as withdrawn and, by immediate promotion of the offending officers, put judicial proceedings out of the question" Barr (2007), p. x; (Neatby [1970], pp. 225–26).

101. Barr (2007), p. 209—July 4, 1854.

102. Collinson (1889), pp. 243, 260, 263, 267–68; Of three artifacts brought back by Collinson, only one evidently came from either *Erebus* or *Terror*. It was part of a fir door frame that had a copper latch bearing the Queen's broad arrow mark, having been found on a beach on the eastern side of the Finlayson Islands (Dease Strait, southwest of Cambridge Bay) in July 1853 (Great Britain [1855d], p. 30; Barr (2007), pp. 234–35). On September 7, 2014, in confirmation of Eskimo oral history, HMS *Erebus* was found somewhere southwest of King William Island (in the Queen Maud Gulf), 36 feet (11 meters) below the surface, upright and in very good condition ("Lost Franklin expedition ship found in the Arctic," www.cbc.ca.com; Chase, "Fate of Franklin's ship and gold will be decided by 1997 Canada-U.K. deal," www.theglobeandmail.com; Kylie, "It's *Erebus*!: Prime Minister Stephen Harper reveals identity of found Franklin ship during Question Period," www.canadiangeographic.ca).

103. Great Britain (1855d), p. ii. Select Committee members: Mr. Mackinnon, Mr. Wilson, Lord Stanley, Admiral Walcott, Mr. Edward Ellice, Sir Thomas Herbert, Mr. Ker Seymer, Mr. Jackson, Mr. Gordon, Sir Thomas Acland, Captain Scobell, Mr. Isaac Butt, Mr. Stephenson, Mr. Talbot, Sir Robert Peel. Five members were necessary for a quorum, and the Committee had powers to send for persons, papers and records, and report to the House of Commons its observations and minutes of evidence taken before it.

104. Ibid., pp. xviii, xix, 4, 7, 10, 11, 12, 19, 20, 21.

105. Great Britain (1855d), p. 12.

106. Oddly, John Ross's 1829–33 expedition in the private ship *Victory* does not appear on the list of North-West Passage expeditions in Table 20 (Mills [vol. 2], p. 476); Holland (1994), pp. 202–03, 225, 234–35, 245–46; Potter, "Who 'discovered' the Northwest Passage?"; McGoogan (2002), pp. 190, 264; Potter and McGoogan disagree as to navigability off the eastern side of King William Island. Potter wrote: "A 'navigable' passage, yes—but not for ships of the sort which the British Admiralty had been sending." In contrast, McGoogan stated that Rae "correctly identified the only Northwest Passage navigable by ships of the time."

107. Great Britain (1855d), pp. 2, 5, 17.

108. Ibid., pp. 14, 16, 29. Even prior to this testimony, McClure had stated: "I had imagined that Captain Collinson had preceded me into the ice, and was anxious to follow him."

109. Ibid., pp. 9, 16, 25; William Baillie-Hamilton, https://en.wikipedia.org.

110. Armstrong's service record, NA, ADM 104/23.

111. This was Sainsbury [who had been promoted in absentia], but he died much later, on November 14, 1853 (Sainsbury's service record, NA, ADM 196/37).

112. Great Britain (1855d) p. 24. Inexplicably, Neatby commented that "Dr. Domville was permitted by what seems to have been a pro-McClure committee to be cautious and non-committal in his evidence as to the condition of the *Investigator*'s crew when the order to abandon ship was given" (Neatby [1967], p. 246). To his credit, McClure afterwards declared: "Perhaps I may be allowed to say a word with respect to Dr. Domville. When I went over with my men to the 'Resolute,' they were immediately placed under Domville's charge, and he paid the greatest possible attention to them in their enfeebled state; and I think that some tribute is due to Dr. Domville for his great attention to them" (Great Britain [1855d], p. 27).

113. Ibid., pp. iii & vi; An embarrassing reminder cropped up when the *Resolute* drifted into Davis Strait, where it was salvaged by Captain James M. Buddington, of the American whaler *George Henry*, in September 1855 (Barr [1992], pp. 182–85).

114. Haydn, p. 490; Holland (1994), p. 185; www.measuringworth.com provides rough comparisons of the value of a person's spending money between the years 1855 and 2013.

115. Great Britain (1855d), p. vi.

116. www.measuringworth.com.

117. Great Britain (1855d), p. vi.

118. Douglas-Morris (1987), pp. 416, 418. All of these rewards were issued by the end of October 1855, and although John Davies was advanced to quartermaster on April 15, 1853, the Admiralty determined he would share as an able seaman.

119. Great Britain (1855d), p. vii; Seventeen years later, Back was still appalled for his friend, but somewhat exaggerated Collinson's accomplishments, writing that he "nearly, if not actually crossed the track of the Erebus & Terror, and then completed the North-West passage!—(on shipboard)…. Collinson, returned by Behring Strait and brought his Ship to England. M⁽ᶜ⁾Clure got £5,000 reward, & was Knighted—and got a command.—Collinson got nothing!" (Back's notes on Collinson to Back [January 27, 1872], RGS, ar RGS/SGB/1/26).

120. Great Britain (1855d), p. viii.

121. Great Britain (1855d), p. xviii; Gore actually left two very similar documents at different locations in May and June 1847, but only one had a second entry written on it. Both were found in 1859 by Lieutenant William Robertson Hobson, RN, second-in-command of the *Fox* (Cyriax [1958], pp. 179–89).

122. McGoogan (2005), pp. 381, 385.

123. McClure to Barrow, Jr. (February 6, 1860), BL, Add.35309.

124. McClure to Ross (May 3, 1860), NA, BJ2/10.

125. It was "'on the following morning I was startled by receiving a letter from the Lord Chamberlain's Office directing me to render the Fees of Honour upon receiving the Honour of Knighthood of £104–0–2d.'" McClure then sought to be repaid from the Treasury, and his request was assisted by royal command—but only after he demonstrated he was not flourishing financially—and fumed how "'it is scarcely necessary, Sir, to add that £100 taken from the above is a most serious inconvenience'" (Douglas-Morris [1987], p. 416); "Names of Individuals to Whom the Royal Premium Has Been Awarded," p. ix; Obituary. "Sir Robert M'Clure, C.B. A Memoir," p. 355; "Testimonial to Captain Sir Robert M'Clure."

126. McClure's service record, NA, ADM 196/1/395—Admiralty dissatisfaction was noted on March 31, 1860, and February 28, 1861; MID, LG, February 16, 1858, no. 22097, p. 771, in command of the 3rd Division ashore (with Captain Sherard Osborn under his command); MID (twice), LG, February 26, 1858, no. 22104, pp. 1023, 1028, made a sortie against the North Gate & Major General Straubenzee expressed his admiration; Companion

of the Bath—military/May 20, 1859/ capture of Canton, 1857 (McClure, NMM, MCCLU/14); Cresswell's service record, NA, ADM 196/36; Court's service record, NA, ADM 196/77; Woon's attestation papers, NA, ADM 157/40; Winton, p. 174. McClure previously wrote from the *Esk*, while cruising off Bahia, Brazil, that "the crew are getting into decent trim, the Marines being part of the last batch which were not paid off, were a troublesome and disorganized lot, but having surprised a few of them with four dozen [lashes] each, the venom has been considerably eradicated & they are behaving much better" (McClure to Barrow, Jr. [July 16, 1856], BL, Add.35309).

127. McClure's service record, NA, ADM 196/1/395—Good Service Pension (September 21, 1863); "I have now done with 'Service Afloat' & only want the G.S. Pension to enable me to live comfortably away from War's Alarms, if you have any means of slipping a word in for me, you might do me good Service, I am not intimate with any of the present Lords" (McClure to Barrow, Jr. [December 22, 1860], BL, Add.35309).

128. McClure's service record, NA, ADM 196/1/395; According to Dunlop (1972, p. 17) Constance Ada Tudor was the daughter of Richard H. Tudor, of Birkenhead, and she married McClure in 1869, but Dunlop (1977, p. 41) shows "the late Mr. Richard H. Tudor," and gives the year of marriage as 1867. Lady McClure died October 13, 1909 (Pollock & Co. to Secretary of the RGS [December 6, 1909], McClure, RGS, CB7).

129. Obituary, "Sir Robert M'Clure, C.B. A Memoir," p. 356.

130. McClure's service record, NA, ADM 196/1/395; Obituary, "Sir Robert M'Clure, C.B. A Memoir," p. 356. "When McClure died in October 1873 McClintock was shocked to learn that the Admiralty was quibbling about paying his widow a pension. He wrote to Sophia Cracroft [Lady Jane's niece] to enlist her help, telling her that he and other naval officers were trying to secure Mrs McClure a Civil List pension" (Murphy, p. 163).

131. Obituary, "Sir Robert M'Clure, C.B. A Memoir," pp. 356; "Sir Robert McClure, C.B.," p. 325; Lord John Hay (Royal Navy admiral of the fleet), http://en.wikipedia.org; Rodney Mundy, https://en.wikipedia.org. It was later reported in the *New York Times* that "there are now only four surviving officers of the English expedition which discovered the North-west Passage," naming Armstrong, Haswell, Piers, and Paine ("Foreign Notes" [1873]).

132. "The North-West Passages," pp. 38–39; Kensal Green Cemetery Online, www.kensalgreencemetery.com.

133. Holland, "Sherard Osborn,"

www.biographi.ca. Osborn died May 6, 1875, three weeks before Nares left England; Mills (vol. 2), pp. 408, 448; "Obituary. Sir Alexander Armstrong, KCB, RN, FRS, Sometime Director-General of the Royal Navy Medical Department," p. 181.

134. Johann August Miertsching, www.biographi.ca; Neatby (1967), pp. 240, 244.

135. UAC Protocols, 1855 & 1856 (MAH); Miertsching, Handwritten notes by Miertsching; Zuber (1975), p. 97; M. Opel to Stein, personal communications, November 7, 2010, March 13 and 20, April 7, 2011, February 1, 2014.

136. Mills (vol. 2), p. 448; "Obituary. Sir Alexander Armstrong, KCB, RN, FRS, Sometime Director-General of the Royal Navy Medical Department," p. 181. See "Report of the Scurvy Committee," *The Geographical Magazine*, pp. 145–47.

137. Barr, "A Warrant Officer in the Arctic," pp. 122–23. Soon after Ford's death, "his widow wrote to Dr Armstrong, requesting that she might be awarded 'the special instead of an ordinary pension,' in the light of the fact that Ford had died due to 'extraordinary exposure' on duty, citing the [two] hernias received in the Arctic and the reduced vision and paralysis resulting from his experience on board Steam Launch No. 7. On 8 March 1877 she was granted a pension of £25 per annum, backdated to 15 January. She herself died on 20 January 1909"; Woon's attestation papers, NA, ADM 157/40; Feather, pp. 9, 12. Woon died from acute rheumatism and cardiac disease; LG, September 16, 1859, no. 22307, p. 3425; Hart, p. 301g.

138. David, p. 156. The exhibition opened May 2, 1891.

139. *Royal Naval Exhibition, 1891. Official Catalogue & Guide* (exhibit no. 5353, *The Arctic Regions*), p. 516.

140. David, p. 156. See *The Illustrated London News*, May 9, 1891, p. 614; May 16, p. 631; June 6, p. 751; and *The Times*, May 2, 1891, p. 9; *Royal Naval Exhibition, 1891. Official Catalogue & Guide* (item no. 139), p. 11.

141. *Antarctica: The Extraordinary History of Man's Conquest of the Frozen Continent*, p. 296.

142. Edward Fawcett, "A Veteran Explorer" (letter to the editor), *Norfolk Daily Standard*, August 1895. In 1895, there existed the *Norfolk Daily Standard* and the *Norfolk Weekly Standard and Argus*. In the newspaper clipping in the possession of descendant Jane Inglesby, Fawcett referred to the July 30, 1895, issue of "*The Standard*" in his letter to the editor—which was a Tuesday—and the *Norfolk Weekly Standard and Argus* was published on Saturdays (*The Newspaper Press Directory*, p. 154).

143. Just Plain Folks, http://justplain-folks.co.uk; Inglesby to Stein, personal communication, July 17, 2013.

144. Just Plain Folks, http://justplain-folks.co.uk; Haswell's service record, NA, ADM 196/1/548; Piers's service records, NA, ADM 104/29; Obituary, "Henry Piers, M.R.C.S. ENG., L.S.A., Deputy Inspector-General of Hospitals and Fleets (Retired)." Piers retired on June 12, 1873, at age 55, and "was allowed to assume the honorary rank of Deputy Inspector General (i.e., having at least 25 years' service, and of distinction)" (Savours [1990], p. 38).

145. *Portrait and Biographical Album of Warren County, Illinois*, p. 372; The IGI shows a daughter named Fanny was born in 1856, in Landport, Somerset, and died in 1857, but the date of birth does not appear correct (International Genealogical Index, www.familysearch.org); 1903 Historical Encyclopedia of Illinois (Warren County), www.usgennet.org.

146. "In the Frozen Ocean. The Only Living Man Who Has Been Around the Americas," p. 26. An editor evidently took literary license when writing the headline.

147. Ibid.; Calder's Arctic Medal 1818–55 was not issued until October 25, 1870, when it was delivered to his sister, Elizabeth Calder (Arctic Medal 1818–55 Roll, NA, ADM 171/9, p. 16).

148. International Genealogical Index, www.familysearch.org; Warren County Illinois Genealogical Society, Deaths and Obituaries, 1902–06, p. 63; The Gjøa Expedition (1903–1906), www.frammuseum.no.

## Epilogue

1. Martin, "Exclusive: Historic Northwest Passage Wreckage Discovered Beneath Beaufort Sea," *Calgary Herald*, July 28, 2010, www.calgaryherald.com.

2. Anderson, "The shipwreck hunter," *Canadian Geographic*, July–August 2013, http://canadiangeographic.ca/magazine.

3. Ibid. In 1908 there were false reports that *Investigator* was discovered in Mercy Bay ("Looks Like an Arctic Fake," p. 6).

4. Martin, "Exclusive: Historic Northwest Passage Wreckage Discovered Beneath Beaufort Sea," *Calgary Herald*, July 28, 2010, www.calgaryherald.com.

5. Ibid.; Struzik, "Hunt for the HMS Investigator," *The Montreal Gazette*, July 26, 2010, www.montrealgazette.com; Woods, "The Saga of the Northwest Passage," *Archaeology*, March-April 2012, www.archaeology.org.

6. Woods, "The Saga of the Northwest Passage," *Archaeology*, March-April 2012, www.archaeology.org.

7. Anderson, "The Shipwreck Hunter," *Canadian Geographic*, July-August 2013, http://canadiangeograph ic.ca/magazine.

## *Appendix 2*

1. Neatby (1967), p. 186.

2. Letter & Order Book (April 21, 1851), RGS, SSC/106; McClure (1854a), p. 57.

3. Letter & Order Book, RGS, RMC, SSC/106; McClure, 1854a & 1855a; Wheeler to Stein, personal communication, October 4, 2013, and October 9, 2014.

4. *Enterprise* and *Investigator* Logs, NA, ADM 55/45 and ADM 55/80. At the top of the first two pages of *Enterprise*'s log is written "Log, N̅ 2"; presumably there was/is another volume that covers the ship's 1848–49 voyage.

5. McClure, RGS, ar RMC, SSC/106; Carrington to Stein, personal communication, July 3, 2007; Wheeler to Stein, personal communication, October 4, 2013.

6. Miertsching, October 14, 1850; Neatby (1967), p. 82; This was only one week before the North-West Passage sled journey.

7. McDougall, p. 213; Barr (1992), p. 126.

8. Osborn (1852), p. 10. Preface is dated February 15, 1852.

9. Great Britain (1855a), pp. 624, 626–27.

10. Great Britain (1855a), pp. 624, 633–44; Belcher (vol. 2), p. 338.

11. Barr (1992), p. 126; Harrod (2000), pp. 86–87; Inglefield to Admiralty (October 4, 1853), Great Britain (1854a), pp. 11, 12, 15; *Phoenix*'s Log (October 4, 1853), NA, ADM 53/4335.

12. Great Britain (1854a), p. 62.

13. Markham, "Sherard Osborn" (obituary), p. 163.

14. McClure (1856), p. 76.

15. McClure (1856), pp. xxix, xxx; Harrod (2000), p. 69.

16. McClure (1856).

17. Markham, "Sherard Osborn" (obituary), pp. 163–64; McClure (1856), pp. xxviii, xxx. In the 1857 second edition, Osborn pointed out the additional material: "My gallant friend Captain F.L. M'Clintock has placed me under deep obligations for the kind manner in which his valuable observations upon the Fauna of the Arctic Archipelago were made available. They are embodied with my own in an entirely new chapter. To Sir Roderick Murchison my thanks are also due, on behalf of the 'Investigators' as well as from myself, for his valuable papers of

General Remarks upon the Geological Specimens and Fossils brought home by Captain Sir Robert M'Clure. My opinions upon the abandonment of our ships in the Arctic Regions have been mistaken for those of Captain Robert M'Clure. I have therefore erased them from this work—the more willingly as it has been shown to me that the record of the greatest achievement of our day can be rendered perfect without connecting it in any way with the saddest tale in Naval History" (McClure [1857], pp. vii-viii).

18. Dunlop (1972), p. 17; Murphy, p. 161; H.F. McClintock to Scott-Keltie (February 2, 1910), McClure, RGS, CB7. "I saw some of these journals (original ones) at the Lawyer's"; Pollock & Co. to Secretary of the RGS (December 6 & 20, 1909), McClure, RGS, CB7; John Scott Keltie, http://en.wikipedia.org.

19. Secretary of the RGS to Pollock & Co. (January 19, 1910); Pollock & Co. to Secretary of the RGS (February 3, 1910); Pollock & Co. to Secretary of the RGS (February 5, 1910); Secretary of the RGS to H.F. McClintock (February 3, 1910); McClure, RGS, CB7. "The solicitors submitted a whole lot of manuscript volumes belonging to the late Sir Robert McClure, most of them official letters connected with his service on [*sic*] China and other parts of the world" (Secretary of the RGS to H.F. McClintock (February 3, 10, 1910).

20. H.F. McClintock to Scott-Keltie (February 10, March 16 (presumed), April 21, 1910); Secretary of the RGS to H.F. McClintock (April 22, 1910, McClure, RGS, CB7). Lady Richards (Admiral Sir George Richards's widow and Lady McClure's friend) was also offered the manuscripts.

21. Cresswell, NMM, BGR/15.

22. Harrod (2000), p. 8.

23. Harrod (2000), pp. 67–69, 81, 97–98.

24. Harrod (2000), pp. 61–63, 68.

25. Cresswell (1854), reprinted by the Arctic Press in 1998, limited to an edition of 200 numbered sets.

26. D. Harrod to Stein, personal communication, July 3, 2006.

27. Armstrong (1857). The pagination is flawed as follows: pages 1–128, 145–160, 145–616.

28. Armstrong (1857), p. v.

29. Armstrong's journal and Sick List, NA, ADM 101/250, p. 176.

30. Armstrong's journal and Sick List, NA, ADM 101/250. Much detailed medical information within the handwritten journal saw print in *Observations on Naval Hygiene and Scurvy, More Particularly as the Latter Appeared During a Polar Voyage* (Armstrong [1858]).

31. Neatby (1967), p. 201, fn. It might prove interesting to compare

Armstrong's Arctic journal to the writing style in his following journal: "Vice Adml. Sir E. Owen stated that Dr. Armstrong had been ordered to keep a Journal relating to the Scientific part of the proceedings of the Expedition to the River Xanthus, & he trusted their Lordships would give that gentleman credit for the intelligence & zeal with which he had fulfilled that order" (March 28, 1844—Armstrong's service record, NA, ADM 104/23).

32. Armstrong (1857), pp. 583–84.

33. Bevan to Stein, personal communication, October 7, 2013.

34. Piers's journal, NMM, JOD/102. This manuscript was examined on microfilm, and words are sometimes obscured by irregularly shaped shadows on the right sides of pages; this was most likely caused by someone's hand holding down the pages during the photographing process. During the author's transcriptions, words presumed to be obscured were placed in brackets.

35. Piers's journal, NMM, JOD/102. The accession document shows the manuscript original reference number was MS/67/103.

36. Bevan to Stein, personal communication, July 21, 2006.

37. McClure (1856), p. 203.

38. Wellcome Library, http://wellcomelibrary.org, MS.5990 & MS.6110.

39. Ford's diary, KML, 18500119Arctic1xx. Barr sent the transcription to the author in July 2008, after a telephone conversation with Barr, during which he first heard about the existence of Ford's writings for the first time (Barr to Stein, personal communication, July 7, 2008).

40. Cross writing is writing longhand on a sheet of paper, then turning it over and writing page two, and then going back to page one, rotating the paper 90 degrees, and writing over it again to save paper.

41. Barr to Stein, personal communication, July 7, 2008; Barr's introduction to his transcription of Ford's diary, KML, 18500119Arctic1xx.

42. Armstrong (1857), p. 576; Ford's diary (July 25, 1853), KML, 18500119 Arctic1xx; Neatby (1967), pp. 212–13.

43. Neatby (1967), p. xii; Stein to B. Jannasch, personal communication, May 24, 2005; Barbara Jannasch also has his Arctic Medal 1818–55, which is unnamed as issued, and retains a long length of original ribbon. The medal was signed for by "W Mallalieu Friar of Moravian Mission," who was Brother Mallalieu, of the Moravian Brotherhood in London (E. Jannasch to Stein, personal communication, Jan-uary 5, 2006; Arctic Medal 1818–55 Roll, ADM 171/9; Neatby [1967], p. 240).

44. Neatby (1967), p. xii.

45. Neatby (1967), pp. 192, 198, 201.

46. Miertsching (1855, 1856).

47. M. Opel to Stein, personal communications, August 12 and December 2, 2010.

48. Benham (1854); Cherbuliez (1857); Miertsching (1861); Neatby (1967).

49. M. Opel to Stein, personal communications, August 7, 12, 15, 2010; May 14, August 11, September 11 and October 4, 2014.

50. Neatby (1967), p. 148, fn.

51. Copybook: an exercise book containing models of penmanship, used in teaching handwriting.

52. Nelson (1967), p. 753 & 768.

53. Nelson, SPRI, MS 748/1–2.

54. Mumford's journal, LAC, MG24-H80. The letter lacks a year, as Nelson only put "9ᵗʰ Septᵗ" on it. By the wording, it appears to have been written some years after their return from the Arctic.

55. Nelson to Mumford (September 9 [no year]), Mumford's journal, LAC, MG24-H80. Nelson's humorous postscript: "Have you much time on hand? if so I wish you would exert yourself for a season and build me a sledge!"

56. Brown manuscript, GM, M-141.

57. Krabbé (1855a), p. 715.

58. Neatby (1967), p. 201.

59. Asplin to Stein, personal communication, October 13, 2013; Documents relating to Arctic Expeditions, NA, ADM 7/198, 199; Krabbé (1855a), p. 715; Neatby (1967), p. 230.

60. The North Star's log indicated that Krabbé's sled party arrived onboard June 13 (North Star's Log [March 9–September 11, 1854], NA, ADM 53/4536).

61. Archives Hub, http://archiveshub.ac.uk.

62. Farmerie to Stein, personal communication, August 10, 2013.

63. Stein to Irvine-Fortescue, personal communication, September 22, 2013; England and Wales, National Probate Calendar (Index of Wills and Administrations), 1858–1966, http://search.ancestry.com; Genes Reunited, www.genesreunited.co.uk; Haswell, Admiral William, Last Will and Testament, HM Courts and Tribunals Service.

64. HM Courts and Tribunals Service; Haswell's service record, NA, ADM 196/1/548.

65. Armstrong (1857), p. v.

66. Haswell, Elizabeth, Last Will and Testament, HM Courts and Tribunals Service; Haswell, Clara, Last Will and Testament, HM Courts and Tribunals Service; Haswell, Lieutenant George, Last Will and Testament, HM Courts and Tribunals Service; The Old Vicarage, http://rshawker.co.uk; Asplin to Stein, personal communication, October 25, 2013.

67. Stein to Wellby, personal communication, September 23, 2013; Mort to Stein, personal communication, September 24, 2014; Whitehead to Stein, personal communication, October 2, 2013; Thomas to Stein, personal communication, November 5, 2013.

## Appendix 7

1. Markham (1901), p. 226.

2. Sainthill (1857), p. 27; Back to Sainthill (November 15, 1856), Glenn M. Stein Collection.

3. Markham (1901), pp. 226–27.

4. McDougall, p. 520.

5. Kellett to Barrow, Jr. (April 12, 1853), NMM, MSS/86/033.

6. Noble Numismatics, July 22–24, 2008, Sale 88, lot 679; "Arctic Search Good Conduct Medal," SPRI, Y:54/20/6.

7. Great Britain (1854a), p. 62; "H.M.S. 'Investigator,' in the Arctic Regions"; Armstrong (1857), p. 594.

8. Harrod (2000), p. 103.

9. McClintock (1859), p. 116.

10. Obituary, "Richard Sainthill"; "Biographical Memoir of the Late Capt. Richard Sainthill, R.N."; Sainthill (1844), pp. i–iv. William Wyon was Leonard's father, and with "the accession of Queen Victoria the preparation of the coronation medal was entrusted to Pistrucci, and in 1837 and 1838 a newspaper controversy as to the respective merits of the work (and nationality) of Pistrucci and [William] Wyon excited public interest. Pistrucci was stoutly defended by William Richard Hamilton [q.v.], while Wyon was supported by Richard Sainthill the numismatist and by Edward Hawkins" (Lee [vol. 58; 1900], p. 270).

11. Sainthill (1855), p. 3.

12. Ibid., p. 6.

13. Great Britain (1855d), pp. ii, vi.

14. Great Britain (1855d), p. vii.

15. Kellett to Barrow, Jr. (April 12, 1853), NMM, MSS/86/033.

16. Great Britain (1855d), pp. vii–viii. McClure wrote to James Ross that September, sending a proof of the Committee's Report, adding: "The medals I am assured will be given, and [the] report [says a] Knighthood is to be conferred upon me" (McClure to Ross [September 5, 1855 {?}], SPRI, MS 1226/18/4). The year of 1855 is presumed correct, since McClure received the honor of a knighthood from the hands of Sir George Grey on November 21, 1855 (Douglas-Morris [1987], p. 416).

17. Great Britain (1855d), p. viii.

18. Sainthill (1857), pp. 35–36.

19. Royal Archives VIC/MAIN/B/14/91, Sir Charles Wood to Queen Victoria, 20 October 1855. "I have checked our index to Queen Victoria's Journal, but cannot find any reference to the Arctic Medal there" (Clark to Stein, personal communication, October 4, 2011).

20. "Once the Battles and Actions to be commemorated by the award of the Military (1801–1814) and Naval (1793–1840) War Medals [MGS and NGS] and respective clasps had been selected, the claimants verified and medals issued, the responsible 'Board of General Officers' and 'Flag Officers' Committee' were disbanded (circa 1851–1853). Thereafter, the War Office assumed control of arrangements for the institution of all new campaign medals and clasps, except the Baltic Medal, until 1894. In that year the Admiralty obtained the right to approach the Sovereign direct to institute certain awards, leading to the issue of those rare clasps to the East and West Africa Medal for minor actions by river gun-boats" (Douglas-Morris [1994], p. 3).

21. RA VIC/MAIN/B/14/93, Queen Victoria to Sir Charles Wood (draft), 4 November 1855.

22. Great Britain (1856), pp. 451–52. Admiral Walcott's Naval General Service Medal 1793–1840, with Centaur 26 Augᵗ 1808 clasp, exists, and is officially impressed: J.E. WALCOTT, MASTER'S MATE.

23. Admiralty to Ross (March 20, 1856), SPRI, MS 1226/12/2. The author has confirmed that only 29 of Ross's men were entitled to the Arctic Medal, over a third of whom were lost with the Franklin Expedition. However, a mere bureaucratic hurdle did not stop one Antarctic officer from recognizing himself: an Arctic Medal exists to Second Master Henry Yule, privately engraved: "H.B. YULE, EREBUS" (Glendining's, January 27, 28, 1910, lot 230).

24. Great Britain (1857), p. 1487.

25. Back to Sainthill, November 15, 1856 (Glenn M. Stein Collection).

26. Attwood to Stein, personal communication, April 27, 1995. Philip Attwood is currently the Keeper of the British Museum's Coins and Medals Department. At the time of his letter, Attwood was in the relatively early stages of his work on Leonard Wyon's diary, which in 2014 resulted in Hard at Work: The Diary of Leonard Wyon 1853–1867 (British Numismatic Society Special Publication No. 9).

27. Harrod (2000), p. 103.

28. Stein (Winter 1994), pp. 301–03; Stein (Winter 1995), p. 306.

29. Lithograph of HMS Terror (Back [1838], facing p. 274); oil painting of HMS Terror (Smyth, NMM, BHC3655).

30. Cresswell, NRO, WMH 3/1/D4/1; Armstrong (1857), p. 444; Neatby (1967), p. 122.

31. Back to Sainthill, November 15, 1856 (Glenn M. Stein Collection).

32. Back to Sainthill, November 15, 1856 (Glenn M. Stein Collection).

33. Sainthill (1857), pp. 41–43.

34. Ibid., pp. 85–87.

35. Ibid., p. 87. Sainthill proposed: "A Subscription therefore, limited to 300 Medals in Bronze, at 12s. each Medal, will give the £180—and the Dies will remain the property of the Society. The Subscription Money to be paid in advance, to the Society as Treasurer, and by whom the Medals will be issued to the Subscribers, thus, guarding the Society against any outlay of money, and securing to the Subscribers, the delivery of their Medals."

36. RA VIC/MAIN/E/49/13, Sir Charles Wood to Queen Victoria, 23 May 1856; RA VIC/MAIN/E/49/14, Sir Charles Wood to Queen Victoria, 27 May 1856.

37. Poulsom (1968), frontispiece—Alec Purves Collection; Purves, p. 157; Hocking, p. 167.

38. This piece was acquired on eBay and is now in a private collection.

39. Queen to Wood (May 30, 1856), BIA, HAL A.4/73.

40. A special Sea Gallantry Medal (Foreign Services), see Stein (March 2012).

41. RA VIC/MAIN/E/49/16, Sir Charles Wood to Queen Victoria, 10 June 1856.

42. Queen to Wood (June 11, 1856), BIA, HAL A.4/73. The Crimea Medal was 36 mm.

43. RA VIC/MAIN/B/15/69, Sir Charles Wood to Queen Victoria, 16 June 1856; Queen to Wood (June 20, 1856), BIA, HAL A.4/73. The request was sent to Wyon the following day (Baring to Wyon [copy] [June 21, 1856], BIA, HAL A.4/73).

44. Cole-Mackintosh, pp. 159–60.

45. Ibid.

46. Poulsom (1968), frontispiece.

47. Graham was Master of the Royal Mint from 1855–69, being the last person to hold this position. When Graham filled the position, the general perception was that he would look upon the post as a cushy job, but in fact he took the job so seriously that he halted his chemical research for several years to organize the Mint's operation. Previous to this post, he held the office of Assayer, whose duty it was to ensure uniform scientific control over all bullion presented for coinage at the Mint (Thomas Graham (chemist), http://en.wikipedia.org; Lane and Solon; Timbs (1857), p. 3).

48. Graham to Wood (October 17, 1856), BL, Add Mss 49559; Queen to Wood (October 20, 1856), BIA, HAL A.4/73; Wood to Graham (copy) (October 22, 1856), BL, Add Mss 49599.

49. Wyon to Acland (November 8, 1856), DCRO, Acland Political & Family Papers, Bundle 4, 51/12/4/10.

50. Queen to Wood (November 13, 1856), BIA, HAL A.4/73.

51. Mint to Admiralty (December 12, 1856), BL, Add Mss 49559, folio 119.

52. RA VIC/MAIN/E/49/18, Sir Charles Wood to Queen Victoria, 13 December 1856. It important to keep in mind that Graham was a chemist—not a medalist—and the addition of this Pole Star (or North Star), while visually pleasing, created a dilemma of its own, since the connections above and below the star were fragile and susceptible to breaking. (A similarly ill-advised suspension design was repeated in the use of a crown with the Abyssinian War Medal 1867–68, and given that Graham was Master of the Mint until his death on September 16, 1869 (Lane and Solon), one wonders if he also had a hand in its design.

53. Wood to Graham (December 18, 1856), BL, Add Mss 49566, p. 159.

54. DNW, May 18, 2011, lot 453.

55. Stroud Auction Rooms, April 10, 2013, lot 482, and afterwards a private collection.

56. Graham to Trevelyan (February 12, 1857), NA, T 1/6054A/2674. The final total was £157.10.

57. Arctic Medal 1818–55 Roll, NA, ADM 171/9, p. 61. "Sent Party, May 6th 1902 Issue No 1835".

58. "Arctic Medal for Winnipeg Resident"; Inuvialuit Pitqusiit Inuuniarutait: Inuvialuit Living History, www.inuvialuitlivinghistory.ca; Robert J. Bilow wrote: "My Great Great Grandfather Robert [sic] MacFarlane was awarded this medal, too. Our family (McKinnon) history reports that this medal was awarded to Robert for his participation in the search for Sir John Franklin. Our family tradition has established that this medal is to be passed on to the oldest grandson on his 40th birthday. It is now in my possession" ("For Arctic Discoveries' Medal," November 22, 2011, www.bbc.co.uk).

59. Arctic Medal 1818–55 Roll, NA, ADM 171/9, pp. 1, 122; Callahan, p. 404.

60. Myres (1986), p. 149.

61. List of officers and men of the Royal Navy and Royal Marines employed on Arctic service, NA, ADM 171/10.

62. Ibid.

63. Ibid., RA VIC/MAIN/E/49/20, Sir Charles Wood to Queen Victoria, 10 January 1857; On February 5, 1857, there was also a request by the Admiralty for "Specimens of The 'Baltic' & 'Arctic' Medals, to form part of a collection for the Queen," and the medals were forwarded on February 25 (Admiralty to Mint, Royal Mint Register [February 5, 1857], NA, MINT 21/6).

64. Accountant General to Admiralty (January 12, 1857), NA, ADM 1/5685; Holland, pp. 202, 233.

65. Accountant General to Admiralty (January 12, 1857), NA, ADM 1/5685.

66. Jones (1992), pp. 229–42; Markham (1875), pp. 12, 13, 48; Poulsom and Myres, p. 25; Ramsland (2014); *Cove* (December 1835–September 1836) is NA, ADM 37/8947.

67. Admiralty to Treasury (January 17, 1857), NA, T 1/6054A/2674.

68. Mint to Admiralty, Royal Mint Register (February 6, 1857), NA, MINT 21/6; Mint to Accountant General, Royal Mint Register (draft) (February 25, 1857), NA, MINT 21/6.

69. Douglas-Morris (1987), p. 416.

70. LG, January 30, 1857, p. 320.

71. LG, May 5, 1857, p. 1580.

72. Arctic Medal 1818–55 Roll, NA, ADM 171/9, pp. 120, 121, 125—AO 5022 (September 22, 1859), AO 5331 (November 20, 157), AO 469 (January 28, 1859); Sailing Master Allen W. Young received his medal from McClintock that September day, and 18 years later was issued the Arctic Medal 1875–76 for having commanded the yacht *Pandora* in Arctic waters in 1876 (Arctic Medal 1875–76 Roll, NA, ADM 171/38, p. 13).

73. RA VIC/MAIN/E/49/13, Sir Charles Wood to Queen Victoria, 23 May 1856; Queen to Wood (May 30, 1856), BIA, HAL A.4/73.

74. Graham to Wood (October 17, 1856), BL, Add Mss 49559.

75. Ibid.

76. Dorling, p. 52.

77. Admiralty to Mint, Royal Mint Register (February 5, 1857), NA, MINT 21/6; Mint to Admiralty, Royal Mint Register (February 6, 1857), NA, MINT 21/6.

78. Murawski to Stein, personal communication, November 17, 2014; Harris (2001), pp. 8, 22. STA.2 (3-year medal), the correct ribbon is 38 mm, with plum edges and a 19 mm gold center stripe.

79. Deacon and Savours (1976), pp. 128, 134, 138; Nares was one of only five individuals who appear entitled to both the Arctic Medal 1818–55 and Arctic Medal 1875–76, though evidently only four actually received both medals (Stein [June 2010], p. 87).

80. Sainthill (1855), p. 6.

81. Great Britain (1855d), p. viii.

82. Sainthill (1857), pp. 49–50.

83. Great Britain (1857), p. 1487.

84. Stein (June 2010), p. 90. Rae's Arctic Medal, along with his RGS Founder's Medal, were on display at the Scottish Geographical Society's 50-year remembrance of Franklin in 1895. Both medals are now in the care of the National Museums of Scotland (Edinburgh).

85. Sotheby's, June 28, 1984 ; ex–Glenn M. Stein Collection.

86. Stein (Spring 1991), pp. 16–17.

87. Wyon to Fremantle (November 18, 1876), NA, MINT 16/76; Charles W. Fremantle, Deputy Master of the Royal Mint.

88. Stein (Winter 1994), p. 303.

89. Yelverton (2000), p. 166. The photograph was of Lieutenant Albert B. Armitage's Western Reconnaissance Party ready to start on September 11, 1902.

90. Purves, p. 156.

# Bibliography

## Abbreviations

| | |
|---|---|
| BIA | Borthwick Institute for Archives |
| BL | The British Library |
| DCRO | Devon County Record Office |
| DUM | *The Dublin University Magazine* |
| ER | *The Edinburgh Review* |
| FO | Foreign Office |
| GM | Glenbow Museum |
| IGI | International Genealogical Index |
| ILN | *The Illustrated London News* |
| KML | Karpeles Manuscript Library |
| LAC | Library and Archives Canada |
| LG | *The London Gazette* |
| MAH | Moravian Archives (Herrnhut, Germany) |
| MID | Mention in Dispatches |
| MINT | Royal Mint |
| NA | The National Archives (UK) |
| NHCRA | Naval Historical Collectors and Research Association |
| NMM | National Maritime Museum |
| NPG | National Portrait Gallery |
| NRO | Norfolk Record Office |
| OMRS | Orders and Medals Research Society |
| RA | The Royal Archives |
| RGS | Royal Geographical Society |
| SPRI | Scott Polar Research Institute |
| T | Treasury |
| UKHO | United Kingdom Hydrographic Office |

## Unpublished Sources and Archives Consulted

### Borthwick Institute for Archives (University of York, UK):

Thomas Baring to Leonard Wyon (copy). June 21, 1856 (HAL A.4/73).

Queen Victoria. Correspondence to Sir Charles Wood, May–December 1856 (HAL A.4/73).

### The British Library (London, UK):

Arctic Medal 1818–55 Correspondence, October 1855–October 1856—Thomas Graham to Sir Charles Wood (Add Mss 49559); Mint to Admiralty (Add Mss 49559); Sir Charles Wood to Thomas Graham (letter book, Add Mss 49566); Sir Charles Wood to Queen Victoria (letter book, Add Mss 49566); Sir Charles Wood to Graham (copy, Add Mss 49599).

Barrow Bequest. "An Abstract of the Principal Voyages Undertaken by the Different Maritime Nations of Europe, Either Under the Orders of Their Respective Governments, or Through Private Enterprise, for the Purpose of Discovering a Passage Between the Atlantic & Pacific Oceans; Commencing with John Cabot, in the Reign of Henry the Seventh, and Terminating with that of [Captain M<sup>c</sup>Clure, the Officers, & Crew of—handwritten addition] Her Majesty's Ship Investigator, Whose Crew Discovered the Long-Sought-for Opening in October 1850, in the 13th Year of the Reign of Her Most Gracious Majesty, Victoria the First," printed, c. April 1855 (Add.35308).

_____. "Brief Statement of Captain McClure's Services in Her Majesty's Ship 'Investigator,'" printed, c. April 1855 (Add.35308).

_____. McClure, Robert J. Letter distributed to each member of the House of Commons (which accompanied his abstract of principal voyages, memorial, and brief statement of service), printed, April 24, 1855 (Add.35308).

_____. McClure, Robert J. Letters to John Barrow, Jr., 1855–61 (Add.35308 & Add.35309).

_____. "Memorial of Captain Robert McClure, R.N., on behalf of Himself and the Officers and Crew of H.M. Ship 'Investigator,'" printed, c. April 1855 (Add.35308).

### Devon County Record Office:

Sir Thomas Acland Political & Family Papers, Bundle 4, 1839–1900.

### Glenbow Museum (Calgary, Alberta, Canada):

Brown, George. "The Manuscript of My Grandfather the Late Mr. George Brown of His Naval Service from 1841 to His Retirement in 1876," undated (M-141). Note: A 1968 photocopy of a typewritten manuscript by Brown's grandson, the latter being a transcription of Brown's handwritten manuscript from c. 1876.

### HM Courts & Tribunals Service (London, UK):

Haswell, Clara Standbridge. Last Will and Testament, August 11, 1905.

Haswell, Elizabeth Ann Gray. Last Will and Testament, April 9, 1891.

Haswell, Commander George Gray. Last Will and Testament, November 18, 1897.

Haswell, Admiral William H. (retired). Last Will and Testament, March 11, 1895.

## Library and Archives Canada (Ottawa, Ontario):

McClure, Robert J. Photographs and transcriptions of two letters to McClure's uncle [the Rev. Richard W. Elgee], (a) HMS *Resolute*, Dealy Island, Barrow's Strait, April [no day written] 1853, (b) HMS *Phoenix*, 100 Miles off Cape Clear, September 26, 1854 (R6790–0–8–E).

Mumford, William T. "Private Journal of an Expedition to the Arctic Regions to ascertain the fate of Sir John Franklin and his Crews, under the Command of Captain Sir Edward Belcher K! C.B., Consisting of Her Majesty's Ships Assistance, Resolute, Pioneer, Intrepid, and North Star in the Years 1852.3.4" (MG24-H80).

Record left by a traveling party from HMS *Investigator* [Lieutenant S.G. Cresswell] at Point John Russell on Banks Island on April 21, 1851, and found by member of the 1913–18 Canadian Arctic Expedition, July 26, 1917 (R6790–0–8–E).

## The National Archives (London, UK):

*Arctic Records, Claims by Executors, Court-Martial & Service Records:*

Claims by Executors and Next-of-Kin for Back Pay for Ratings: (ADM 141, Series AF and Series EC, ADM 44).

Claims by Executors and Next-of-Kin for Back Pay for Officers: (ADM 141, Series ED, ADM 45).

Coastguard Service Records (ADM 175).

Continuous Service engagement books (ADM 139).

Court-Martial Proceedings of Capt. Robt. J. Le M. McClure and Officers and Crew of HMS *Investigator* (*copy* of the Minutes of Proceedings) (ADM 1/5645).

Documents relating to Arctic Expeditions (ADM 7/198, ADM 7/199, ADM 7/200).

List of officers and men of the Royal Navy and Royal Marines employed on Arctic service (ADM 171/10).

Naval Officers' Service Records (ADM 104, ADM 107, ADM 196).

Records of the Admiralty, Naval Forces, Royal Marines, Coastguard, and related bodies—Correspondence and Papers, Original Series (2nd group), 1840–1913 (ADM 1/5685 & ADM 1/7847).

Register of Mates (ADM 11/22).

Registers of Deceased Ratings (ADM 154).

Registers of Officers' Effects (ADM 45).

Registers of Seamen's Effects (ADM 44 & ADM 141).

Registers of Seamen's Services (ADM 29, ADM 188).

Registry of Shipping and Seamen: Alphabetical Index to Registers of Seamen's Tickets (BT 114).

Registry of Shipping and Seamen: Register of Seamen's Tickets (BT 113).

Royal Greenwich Hospital: School Admission Papers (ADM 73).

Royal Marines' Attestation Forms (ADM 157).

Royal Marines' Description Books (ADM 158).

Succession Book of Mates, Midshipmen, Admiralty Midshipmen, etc. (ADM 11/29).

Warrant Officers' Service Records (ADM 29).

*Foreign Office:*

Foreign Office, Political and Other Departments: General Correspondence before 1906, British Medals awarded for saving life at sea, 1839–82 (FO 83/769).

Foreign Office, Political and Other Departments: Miscel-

lanea, Series II, Entry books of presents given for assistance to ships in distress, etc., 1841–61 (FO 96/140).

Foreign Office, Records of Embassies, Legations, Consulates, etc.: Miscellaneous, 1855 (FO 115/162), and United States Government, Consuls, Naval and Colonial, 1856 (FO 115/172).

*Journals:*

Armstrong, Alexander. Journal of HMS *Investigator*, January 1, 1850–June 1, 1853; including a *copy* of the Daily Sick List, along with the following sections (some of which contain *copy* documents): medical surveys and reports (and related correspondence), plus meteorological and natural history observations, and observations of the Eskimos on the North American coast (ADM 101/250).

Charlton, John F. Medical journal of HMS *Phoenix*, March 1–October 25, 1853 (ADM 101/112/7).

Hornby, Rear Admiral Sir Phipps, Journal of the Commander-in-Chief of the Pacific Station, September 6, 1847–May 14, 1851 (ADM 50/253).

*Letters:*

From Admirals Pacific, 1851 (ADM 1/5609).

In-letters and papers from Admirals (1850–59), January 1–December 31, 1850 (ADM 1/5602).

McClure, Robert J. Correspondence and papers; letters to Sir James Clark Ross (BJ2/10). Note: Also included in this file is correspondence to Ross from Edward Ommaney and J.H. Kay.

Naval Correspondence. Indexes and Digests for 1793–1913 (ADM 12).

Promiscuous, 1850 (ADM 1/5606).

*Medal Rolls:*

Arctic Medal 1818–55 Roll (ADM 171/9).

Arctic Medal 1875–76 Roll (ADM 171/38).

Baltic Medal 1854–55 Roll (ADM 171/19–22).

China Medal 1840–42 Roll (ADM 171/12).

Crimea Medal 1854–55 Roll (ADM 171/26–28, Royal Navy).

St. Jean d'Acre Medal 1840 Roll (ADM 171/14).

*Royal Mint:*

Correspondence, Arctic Medal [1876] (MINT 16/76).

Royal Mint Register, 1856–57 (MINT 21/6).

*Ships' Musters, Log Books and Descriptions Books:*

*Albatross*—C,D,O, November 12, 1846–September 28, 1850 (ADM 38/7487).

*Amphitrite*—Log, February 12–September 27, 1849 (ADM 53/2094).

*Apollo*—C,D,O, October 30, 1841–February 7, 1845 (ADM 38/7532).

*Asia*—D, August 25, 1847–May 24, 1851(ADM 38/7567).

*Asia* & *Cockatrice* (tender to *Asia*)—M, July 1, 1850–December 31, 1850 (ADM 38/2531).

*Bittern*—C,D,O, May 5, 1841 May 5–July 18, 1845 (ADM 38/7634).

*Brilliant*—C,D,O, February 28, 1846–October 9, 1849 (ADM 38/7678).

*Calypso*—C,D,O, December 12, 1845–September 24, 1849 (ADM 38/7736).

*Cambridge*—D, August 9, 1856–February 28, 1862 (ADM 38/7743).

*Carysfort*—D, December 28, 1841–June 26, 1845 (ADM 38/7769).

*Castor*—C,D, April 29, 1843–November 16, 1847 (ADM 38/7771).

*Columbia*—C,D,O, May 4, 1842–January 12, 1848 (ADM 38/7820).

*Constance*—D, April 23, 1846–December 8, 1849 (ADM 38/7837).

*Cornwallis*—D&O, February 2, 1855–August 13, 1856 (ADM 38/7855).

*Cove*—M, December 1835–September 1836 (ADM 37/8947).

*Enterprise*—C,D,O, January 31, 1848–November 26, 1849 (ADM 38/8041).

*Enterprise*—Log, December 14, 1849–August 7, 1851 (ADM 55/45).

*Erebus*—M, April 8, 1839–September 23, 1843 (ADM 38/8045).

*Erebus*—M, March 3–May 19, 1845 (ADM 38/672).

*Excellent*—M, April 1–June 30, 1849 (ADM 38/3332).

*Gorgon*—C,D,O, March 29, 1848–February 4, 1852 (ADM 38/8198).

*Herald*—C,D,O, February 8, 1845–June 16, 1851 (ADM 38/8269).

*Inflexible*—M, January 1–December 31, 1847 (ADM 38/1022).

*Investigator*—C,D,O, March 1, 1848–November 26, 1849 (ADM 38/8387).

*Investigator*—Log, December 17, 1849–June 30, 1850 (ADM 55/80).

*Investigator*—M, December 17, 1849–June 30, 1850 (ADM 38/1026).

*North Star*—C,D,O, February 24, 1852–October 23, 1854 (ADM 38/8622).

*North Star*—Log, March 9–September 11, 1854 (ADM 53/4536).

*Phoenix*—Log, February 15–October 25, 1853 (ADM 53/4335).

*Plover*—C,D,O, November 20, 1847–April 25, 1855 (ADM 38/8740).

*Prometheus*—C&D, May 15, 1844–September 2, 1847 (ADM 38/8783).

*Rodney*—M, January 1–March 31,1848 (ADM 38/1617).

*Snake*—C,D,O, January 10, 1846–May 7, 1848 (ADM 38/9047).

*Spy*—C,D,O, August 8, 1848–November 18, 1850 (ADM 38/9091).

*Superb*—D&B, December 7, 1844–November 28, 1848 (ADM 38/9119).

*Swift*—C,D,O, June 25, 1849–January 29, 1853 (ADM 38/9133).

*Terror*—M, May 11, 1839–September 23, 1843 (ADM 38/9162).

*Terror*—M, March 3–May 17, 1845; June 30, 1845 (ADM 38/1962).

*Thalia*—C,D,O, August 28, 1841–November 27, 1845 (ADM 38/9171).

*Winchester*—M, July 1–September 30, 1845 (ADM 38/2278).

*Treasury:*
Correspondence with Admiralty and Mint (T 27/148T (*copy*), 1/6054A/2467)

## National Maritime Museum (Greenwich, UK):

Admiralty plans of HMS *Investigator*, Devonport Dockyard, July 26, 1848 (S.6837).

Collinson, Richard. Journal of HMS *Enterprise*, August 16, 1850–April 8, 1855 (CLS/20/1–3).

_____. Amended fair copy the "Private Journal" kept by Capt. Richard Collinson onboard HMS *Enterprise* (CLS/20/1–3).

_____. Official and unofficial letters to and by Richard Collinson, 1835–55 (CLS/47 1835).

Cresswell, Samuel G. Biographical notes and *copies* of letters of Captain Samuel Gurney Cresswell (d.1867) compiled by Mrs. Cresswell [mother] c. 1870; bound with McClure's *The Discovery of the North West Passage*, 4th edition (BGR/15).

Kellett, Henry. *Copy* of a private dispatch to John Barrow, Jr. April 12, 1853 (MSS/86/033).

McClintock, Francis L. Journal of HMS *Enterprise*, May 1848–November 1849 (MCL/9).

McClure, Sir Robert John Le Mesurier, Vice-Admiral, 1807–73 (MCCLU).

_____. Naval service and conduct ratings by captains (1824–37) and physical characteristics (MCCLU/1). Note: This document has no source reference, and it is in variance with ADM 107/62; the latter is surely the more accurate of the two for the 1824–30 period of McClure's service.

Piers, Henry. Journal of HMS *Investigator*, 1849–53 (JOD/102). Note: The start date is December 2, 1849, and the microfilm copy of the journal stops in the middle of the last entry on March 31, 1852.

Rice, William McPherson (Master Shipwright) (RCE/3).

Stone, Edward. Record of naval service (ADM 359/51A/223).

W.J.A. "Sonnet to Capt. McClure, R.N.—the discoverer of the North West Passage," Lyme Regis, December 1854 (MCCLU/6).

## Norfolk Record Office:

McClure, Robert J. Letter to Mrs. Reynolds (*copy*), April [no day written] 1853 (BL/MC 5/17).

## Private Collections and Sources:

Back, George. Letter to Richard Sainthill, November 15, 1856 (Glenn M. Stein Collection).

Church book, Gröditz, Baruth Parish, Upper Lusatia.

Fawcett, Edward. Painting of Edward Fawcett with his great-grandson, Robert George Williams (c. 1894), photograph James Williams and Edward Fawcett, almost certainly taken on the dunes at Winterton (c. 1890s) (great-great-great-grandaughter Jane Inglesby, Wednesbury, West Midlands, UK).

Ford, George J. Diary of HMS *Investigator*, January 10, 1850–June 8, 1852 and May 26, 1853–September 21, 1854, Karpeles Manuscript Library, Santa Barbara, California (18500119Arctic1xx).

McClure to wife Mary. April 15, 1853, HMS *Investigator*, Mercy Bay. PBA Galleries, www.pbgalleries.com, Fine Books and Manuscripts, April 30, 2009, Sale 402, lot 199. Note: Letter contained within an early folder from Parke-Bernet Galleries, in which it was auctioned c. 1930s, along with inner folder with typed description, and lot number tag 365.

Miertsching, Johann A. Handwritten notes by Miertsching (Barbara Jannasch, Nova Scotia, Canada).

_____. *Travel Narrative of a North Pole Expedition in Search of Sir John Franklin and for the Discovery of the Northwest Passage in the Years 1850–1854* (Barbara Jannasch, Nova Scotia, Canada).

Okak Diary, northern Labrador (R 15 kb 5e, MAH).

St. Mary Magdalen Church, Woolwich, UK. 1813–37 baptisms.

Skead, Francis. *Private Journal of F. Skead 2nd Master. H.M.S. "Enterprise" 1850–/51–/52* [January 1850–March 1852, August 1854] (transcribed by Thomas Skead from original manuscript at SPRI, MS 1161).

UAC Protocol. 1850, 1854, 1855, 1856 (MAH).

Warren County Illinois Genealogical Society. Deaths and Obituaries, 1902–06.

Williams, James. Certificate of Service, Mariner's Register Ticket, Images—gravestone in Winterton churchyard, portrait photograph taken at Yarmouth (c. 1880s), photograph of James Williams and Edward Fawcett, almost certainly taken on the dunes at Winterton (c. 1890s) (great-great-granddaughter Jane Inglesby, Wednesbury, West Midlands, UK).

The Royal Archives (Windsor Castle, UK):

Clark, Pamela M. (Registrar). Letter to Glenn M. Stein, October 4, 2011.

Correspondence between Sir Charles Wood and Queen Victoria, 1855–57 (RA VIC/MAIN/B/14/91; RA VIC/MAIN/B/14/93; RA VIC/MAIN/B/15/69; RA VIC/MAIN/E/49/13; RA VIC/MAIN/E/49/14; RA VIC/MAIN/E/49/15; RA VIC/MAIN/E/49/16; RA VIC/MAIN/E/49/18; RA VIC/MAIN/E/49/20).

Royal Geographical Society (London, UK):

The Back Collection (ar GB 402 SGB).

Back, George. Draft article with commentary based on McClure to Back, April [day not written] 1853, August 1854 (JMS/17/28).

_____. Draft article with commentary based on McClure to Back, April [day not written] 1853, for Beaufort, undated (JMS/17/28).

Collinson, Richard. Letter to George Back, January 27, 1872 (ar RGS/SGB/1/26).

Findlay, A.G. *Chart of Part of the Arctic Regions as known in 1845, being a copy of the Chart supplied to the Franklin Expedition.* London: E. Stanford, 1858 (Canada S/D.61).

Franklin, Jane. Letter to George Back, November 28, 1849 (SGB/1/34).

Matthews, John. Journal onboard HMS *Herald* and *Plover*, September 1850–April 1855 (ar 62,1993).

McClure, Robert J. Correspondence regarding Lady Constance A. McClure's Estate (original and evidently carbon copies): (1) RGS Patron's Gold Medal and Paris Geographical Society Gold Medal to the RGS; (2) acquisition by the RGS of four manuscript volumes: (a) Journal of HMS *Terror*, 1836–37, (b) Journal of HMS *Investigator*, 1850—one volume, (c) Letter and Order Book of HMS *Investigator*, 1850–51—one volume, and (d) signed copy of McClure's dispatches to the Admiralty, August 1850–April 1853; December 6, 1909–April 22, 1910 (RGS/CB7).

_____. Journal of HMS *Investigator*, January 20–September 30, 1850 (ar RMC, SSC/106).

_____. Letter & Order Book of HMS *Investigator*, December 29, 1849–October 1, 1851 (ar RMC, SSC/106).

_____. Letter to George Back [copy—in Back's hand], April [day not written] 1853 (JMS/17/28). Note: A notation incorrectly indicates, "Read November 14. 53"; Back communicated this to the RGS on November 14, 1854.

_____. Private journal onboard HMS *Terror*, June 1836–September 1837 (ar RMC, MG387B).

Shaw, Norton. Letter to Rear Admiral Sir Francis Beaufort, July 29, 1854 (JMS/17/28).

Scott Polar Research Institute (Cambridge, UK):

Admiralty to Captain Sir James C. Ross. March 20, 1856, Aston Abbott House, Aylesbury (MS 1226/12/2).

Arctic Search Good Conduct Medal (Y:54/20/6).

Armstrong, Alexander. Letter to John Richardson, January 6, 1850, Greenhithe (MS 1503/41/1).

_____. Letter to John Richardson, August 22, 1850; received May 13, 1863 (MS 1503/42/3). Note: Included, but absent from the archival description, are two additional letters to Richardson (one cross written over the other), August 29, 1850 (off Cape Bathurst) and August 30, 1850.

Barrow, John, Jr. Five letters to George Back, 1849–1855 (MS 395/37/1–5).

McClintock, Francis L. "The Private Journal of F.L. McClintock, Commander, H.M. Steamer Intrepid, 1852–54" (MS 1).

McClure, Robert J. Four letters to Sir James Clark Ross, 1849–1855, written from HMS *Enterprise* and *Investigator* (MS 1226/18/1–4).

MacFarlane, Roderick. Letter to John Richardson, July 14, 1862, Fort Anderson Mackenzie River District (MS 1503/65/9).

MacKenzie, W.G. August 1967 report on copper sheets and nails found at O'Reilly Island, being evidence to suggest the wreck in Queen Maud Gulf may be HMS *Investigator*, not HMS *Erebus* or HMS *Terror* (MS 978).

Nelson, James H., Certificate of service, 1849–54 (MS 748/3).

_____. "Voyage H.M.S. Investigator In Search of Sir J. Franklin and Resulting in the Discovery of the North West Passage" (2 vols.), 1850–54 (MS 748/1–2). Note: Both volumes are *photocopies* of draft manuscripts written in the forms of a journal.

Priestley, Raymond E. "The Polar Exploration as a Psychological Study," 1955 lecture (MS 1097/16/2).

_____. "The Psychology of Exploration," 1914 lecture (MS 1097/16/1).

Report of Examination of Officers and Men in HMS *North Star* at Beechey Island, May 20–29, 1854 (MS 1523/4/3).

Richard Collinson Collection (GB 15).

## Visual Material

### Charts and Maps:

Note: Not all appear within the text.

Armstrong, Alexander. 1857. *Chart Illustrating the Discovery of The North West Passage by H.M. Ship Investigator. Arranged and Corrected from Official Charts and Documents by Dr. Armstrong, R.N., F.R.G.S.* Scale not given. London: Hurst & Blackett, 1857. In Alexander Armstrong, *A Personal Narrative of the Discovery of the North-West Passage; with Numerous Incidents of Travel and Adventure During Nearly Five Years' Continuous Service in the Arctic Regions While in Search of the Expedition Under Sir John Franklin.* London: Hurst and Blackett. Facing p. xxii.

Arrowsmith, John. 1859. *Map of a Portion of the Arctic Shores of America to Accompany Capt[a]. Mc Clintock's Narrative.* Scale not given. In Francis L. McClintock, *In the Arctic Seas: A Narrative of the Discovery of the Fate of Sir John Franklin and His Companions.* Philadelphia: Porter & Coates. End of book.

Court, Stephen. 1851. *Chart Shewing the land discovered by H.M. Ship Investigator. Between September 1850 and October 1851. Robert M'Clure Commander.* Scale not given. NA, MFQ 1/346. Note: Hand drawn, UKHO, L9302. It appears there were a total of three copies of this chart showing *Investigator*'s discoveries, all being copies of a single chart, and one of which covers "September 1850 and April 1852" (see Manning [1956], p. 65).

_____. 1852. *Chart Shewing the land discovered by H.M. Ship Investigator. Between September 1850 and April 1852. Robert M'Clure Commander.* Scale not given. UKHO, L9304.

_____. 1853. *Harbour of Mercy. Surveyed by Mr. Stephen Court, Second Master. H.M. Ship Investigator. Commanded by Robert M'Clure Esqʳ Commander 1853.* 3½ inches to 2 nautical miles. London: UKHO, D1073.

Cresswell, Samuel G. 1854. *Chart of the Route* [of the voyage of HMS *Investigator* during the discovery of the North-West Passage]. Scale not given. Plate IX in *A Series of Eight Sketches in Colour (together with a Chart of the Route) by Lieut. S. Gurney Cresswell, of the Voyage of H.M.S. Investigator (Captain M'Clure), During the Discovery of the North-West Passage.* Colored lithographs. London: Day & Son and Ackerman & Co.

*Discoveries in the Arctic Sea by the Squadrons Under the Orders of Captᵗ Sir Edwᵈ Belcher C.B. H.M.S. Assistance, Captᵗ Kellett C.B. H.M.S. Resolute, Captᵗ Collinson C.B. H.M.S. Enterprise and Captᵗ McClure H.M.S. Investigator up to MDCCCLIV.* 1854–55. Scale not given. In *Papers relative to the recent Arctic expeditions in search of Sir John Franklin and the crews of H.M.S. "Erebus" and "Terror."* Scale not given. House of Commons, Sessional Papers, Accounts and Papers. 35(1898) (1855a)

Falconer, George. 1958. Map of the Beaufort Sea "Ice Stream" and its effects on the expeditions of Parry (first expedition), Franklin, McClure and Collinson. 15/16" to 100 miles. In Leslie H. Neatby, *In Quest of the Northwest Passage: The Adventures of Brave Men in Forlorn Lands.* New York: Thomas Y. Crowell Company, pp. 82–83

Findlay, A.G. 1858. *Chart of Part of the Arctic Regions as known in 1845, being a copy of the Chart supplied to the Franklin Expedition.* Scale not given. London: E. Stanford.

Inglefield, Edward A. 1853. *Chart Shewing the North West Passage Discovered by Capt. R. Le MᶜClure, H.M. Ship. Investigator: Also The Coast Explored in Search of Sir John Franklin* [search expeditions, 1848–53, and approved] *by E.A. Inglefield, Commander, H.M.S. Phoenix.* Scale not given. Drawn by Second Master William Henry Fawckner. London: Admiralty Hydrographic Department, October 14.

*Map of Banks Island.* 1956. ½ inch to 20 miles. In Thomas H. Manning, "Narrative of a Second Defence Research Board Expedition to Banks Island, With Notes on the Country and Its History," *Arctic* 9(1–2): 2.

*Map of Central Arctic America showing the track of H.M.S. Enterprise and Investigator in 1850–54. Taken from the Admiralty Charts on the scale of 2½° Longitude to one inch and corrected to 1882.* 1889. Scale not given. London: Sampson Low, Marston, Searle,& Rivington, 1889. In Richard Collinson, *Journal of H.M.S. Enterprise, on the Expedition in Search of Sir John Franklin's Ships by Behring Strait. 1850–55.* London: Sampson Low, Marston, Searle, & Rivington. Facing p. 153.

Morse, Charles W. 1856. *Chart Showing the Recent Search for a North-West Passage. Also the Coast Explored in Search of Sir John Franklin between the Years 1848 and 1854.* Scale not given. In *Morse's General Atlas of the World. Containing Seventy Maps, Drawn And Engraved From The Latest And Best Authorities By Charles W. Morse. With Descriptions And Statistics Of All Nations To The Year 1856,* by Charles Colby, A.M. New York: D. Appleton.

Osborn, Captain Sherard. 1856. *Chart to Illustrate the Narrative of the Accomplishment of the North West Passage by H.M.*

*Ship "Investigator." Captᵗ Sir Robert Le M.M' Clure R.N. with latest corrections by Captᵗ Sherard Osborn R.N. C.B.* Scale not given. In Robert J. McClure and Sherard Osborn (editor), *The Discovery of the North-West Passage by H.M.S. "Investigator" Capt. R. M'Clure 1850, 1851, 1852, 1853, 1854, Edited by Commander Sherard Osborn From The Logs and Journals of Capt. Robert Le M. M'Clure.* Scale not given. London: Longman, Brown, Green, and Longmans, & Roberts. Facing p. 1.

*The Ross Sea Quadrant.* 2003. 7/8 inch to 300 miles. In *Exploring Polar Frontiers: A Historical Encyclopedia* (Volume 1) Santa Barbara: ABC-CLIO, Inc., p. xxix.

*Wellington Strait, North Polar Sea.* 1852. 1 inch to 100 miles. In: *Papers and Despatches Relating to the Arctic Searching Expeditions of 1850–51–52. Together with a Few Brief Remarks as to the Probable Course Pursued by Sir John Franklin.* 2nd edition. London: Francis & John Rivington, p. 5.

## Illustrations and Paintings:

Note: Not all appear within the text.

Adams, Edward. c. 1854. *HMS Enterprise in winter quarters, Camden Bay, Alaska, 1853–54.* Watercolor. SPRI, Accession No. 83/11/35.

Bedwell, Frederick. 1889. *H.M.S. Enterprise Entering Dolphin and Union Strait, September 1852.* In Richard Collinson, *Journal of H.M.S. Enterprise, on the Expedition in Search of Sir John Franklin's Ships by Behring Strait. 1850–55.* London: Sampson Low, Marston, Searle, & Rivington. Facing title page.

Browne, W.H. (late of HMS *Enterprise*). 1850. *The Devil's Thumb, Ships Boring and Warping in the Pack.* Colored lithograph by Charles Haghe, after the original by W.H. Browne. London: Ackermann & Co. NMM, PAD6191.

Cresswell, Samuel G. 1834–58. Album containing 59 mounted drawings (colored watercolors, monochrome watercolors and ink sketches) and one engraved print, plus one loose watercolor between the end leaves at the back of the volume, and a loose sheet of interleaved notes. NRO, Personal and Family Papers of Lady Wilhelmine Harrod, WMH 3/1/D4/1.

_____. 2000. Renderings related to Arctic Expeditions 1848–49 & 1850–54. In Dominick Harrod (editor), *War, Ice & Piracy: The Remarkable Career of a Victorian Sailor The Journals and Letters of Samuel Gurney Cresswell.* London: Chatham Publishing, between pp. 96 and 97.

_____. 1854. *A Series of Eight Sketches in Colour (together with a Chart of the Route) by Lieut. S. Gurney Cresswell, of the Voyage of H.M.S. Investigator (Captain M'Clure), During the Discovery of the North-West Passage.* Colored lithographs. London: Day & Son and Ackerman & Co.

King, Horatio. c. 1872–73. *Sir Robert McClure.* CDV. Horatio N. King, photographer, 188 Regent Street, London.

Pearce, Stephen. 1855. *Sir Robert McClure.* Oil on canvas. National Portrait Gallery, NPG 1210. (An engraving after this portrait was executed by J. Scott and published by Henry Graves & Company on February 15, 1856.)

Smyth, William. 1838. "The Crew of H.M.S. Terror Saving the Boats and Provisions on the Night of the 15th March [1837]." In George Back, *Narrative of an Expedition in H.M.S. "Terror", Undertaken With a View to Geographical Discovery on the Arctic Shores, in 1836–37.* London: John Murray. Facing p. 274.

_____. n.d. *Perilous position of H.M.S. Terror, Captain Back, in the Arctic Regions in the summer of 1837.* NMM, BHC3655

## Published Sources

Parliamentary Papers:

Great Britain, Parliament. 1846. *Correspondence on The Slave Trade, with Foreign Powers, Parties to Treaties, Under Which Captured Vessels are to be Tried by Mixed Tribunals; from 1st January to 31st December 1845, inclusive.* House of Lords, Sessional Papers, Accounts and Papers. 16.
_____. *Copies and Extracts of Correspondence and Proceedings of the Admiralty, in reference to the Arctic Expedition.* House of Commons, Sessional Papers, Accounts and Papers 1847–48. 1848a. 41 (284).
_____. 1847. *Slave Trade,* House of Commons, Sessional Papers, Accounts and Papers 19th January to 23rd July 1847. 67.
_____. 1850a. *Arctic Expedition. Return to an Order of The Honourable The House of Commons, dated 5 February 1850, etc.* House of Commons, Sessional Papers, Accounts and Papers. 35(107).
_____. 1851a. *Papers relating to the Arctic Relief Expeditions. Return to an address of The Honourable The House of Commons, dated 7 February 1851, etc.* House of Commons, Sessional Papers, Accounts and Papers. 33(97).
_____. 1854a. *Papers relative to the recent Arctic expeditions in search of Sir John Franklin and the crews of H.M.S. "Erebus" and "Terror."* House of Commons, Sessional Papers, Accounts and Papers. 42(1725).
_____. 1855a. *Further papers relative to the recent Arctic expeditions in search of Sir John Franklin and the crews of H.M.S. "Erebus" and "Terror."* House of Commons, Sessional Papers, Accounts and Papers, 1854–55. 35(1898).
_____. 1855d. *Report of the Select Committee on Arctic Expedition; together with the proceedings of the Committee, Minutes of Evidence and Appendix. Ordered by the House of Commons to be printed, 20 July 1855.* House of Commons, Sessional Papers, Accounts and Papers. 1854–55. 7(409):i–38.
_____. 1857. *Hansard's Parliamentary Debates: Third Series, Commencing with the Ascension of William IV.* 1856. 140, 144.
_____. 1859. *Navy. Dockyard Economy. Minutes of Evidence taken before the Committee of Inquiry on the Economy of Her Majesty's Dockyards, assembled at Woolwich.* House of Commons, Sessional Papers, Accounts and Papers. 18.
Krabbé, Frederick J. 1855a. "Journal of the Proceedings of Her Majesty's Sledge 'Newton,' detached from Her Majesty's Ship 'Resolute,' between 3d April and 13th June 1854, under the Command of Mr. F.J. Krabbé, Master." *Papers relative to the recent Arctic expeditions in search of Sir John Franklin and the crews of H.M.S. "Erebus" and "Terror."* House of Commons. Sessional Papers, Accounts and Papers 1854–55. 35(1898): pp. 707–22.
McClure, Robert. 1854a. "Proceedings of Captain M'Clure, of Her Majesty's Discovery Ship 'Investigator,' in search of the Expedition under Sir John Franklin, from August 1850 to April 1853, and reporting the Discovery of the North-West Passage." *Papers relative to the recent Arctic expeditions in search of Sir John Franklin and the crews of H.M.S. "Erebus" and "Terror."* House of Commons, Sessional Papers, Accounts and Papers. 42(1725): pp. 23–61.
_____. 1855a. "Proceedings of Captain M'Clure, of Her Majesty's Discovery Ship 'Investigator.'" *Further papers relative to the recent Arctic expeditions in search of Sir John Franklin and the crews of H.M.S. "Erebus" and "Terror."* House of Commons, Sessional Papers, Accounts and Papers, 1854–55. 35(1898): pp. 107–12.
Pim, Bedford C.T. 1855a. "Journal of Proceedings of Her Majesty's Sledge 'John Barrow,' dispatched from H.M. Ship 'Resolute,' between 10th March and 19th April 1853, under the command of Bedford C.T. Pim, Lieutenant." *Papers relative to the recent Arctic expeditions in search of Sir John Franklin and the crews of H.M.S. "Erebus" and "Terror."* House of Commons, Sessional Papers, Accounts and Papers, 1854–55. 35(1898): pp. 646– 60.

Periodicals:

Allen, Joseph. 1854. "The New Navy List and General Record of the Service of Officers of the Royal Navy and Royal Marines."
"Anecdote of an Arctic Officer." 1861. *The Sunday at Home: A Family Magazine for Sabbath Reading* 8: p. 11.
"The Arctic Expedition." 1854. *The Illustrated London News,* October 7.
"The Arctic Expedition." 1876. *The Illustrated London News,* December 16.
"The Arctic Explorers—Testimonial to Dr. Armstrong." 1854. *The Illustrated London News,* October 28.
"Arctic Literature—The M'Clure Discovery." 1858. *The Dublin University Magazine,* 51(302): pp. 189–97.
"Arctic Medal for Winnipeg Resident." 1902. *Manitoba Morning Free Press,* June 14.
"The Arctic Searching Expedition." 1852. *The Nautical Magazine and Naval Chronicle,* 21(4): p. 201.
Barr, William. 1992. "Franklin in Siberia?—Lieutenant Bedford Pim's Proposal to Search the Arctic Coast of Siberia, 1851–52." *Arctic,* 45(1): pp. 36–46.
_____. 1999. "A Warrant Officer in the Arctic: The Journal of George Ford, 1850–1854." *Pacific Empires: Essays in Honour of Glyndwr Williams,* Alan Frost & Jane Samson (editors), pp. 101–23.
_____. 2009. "The Use of Dog Sledges during the British Search for the Missing Franklin Expedition in the North American Arctic Islands, 1848–59." *Arctic,* 62(3):257–72.
Barrett, W. Bowles. 1907. "The Burning Cliff at Holworth, Near Weymouth." *Notes & Queries for Somerset and Dorset,* 10: p. 18.
Battersby, William, and Peter Carney. 2011. "Equipping HM Ships *Erebus* and *Terror.*" *International Journal for the History of Engineering & Technology,* 81(2): pp. 159–81.
"Biographical Memoir of the Late Capt. Richard Sainthill, R.N." 1830. *The United Service Journal and Naval and Military Magazine* (Part I).
"British Adventure." 1849. *The Illustrated London News,* October 13.
Bruemmer, Fred. 1992. "Last of the Umiaks." *Natural History,* 101(10).
"Captain Austin's Arctic Expedition." 1850. *The Illustrated London News,* May 11.
"Captain Cresswell, R.N." 1867. *The Illustrated London News* (Supplement), August 24.
"Captain M'Clure, R.N." 1853. *The Illustrated London News,* November 5.
"Captain M'Clure, R.N." 1854. *The Dublin University Magazine,* 48(5): pp. 334–58.
Carr, H.G. 1941. "Sledge-Flags, Their Origin and Development." *Mariner's Mirror,* 7(1): pp. 5–13.
Church, William C. 1890. "John Ericsson, The Engineer—July 31, 1803–March 8, 1889" (Part 2), *Scribner's Magazine,* March 7(3): pp. 336–61.
Coghlan, Tom.2013. "Navy Bans Historic Toast to the Wives and Sweethearts." *The Times,* June 22.
Cole-Mackintosh, Ronnie. 2006. "The Obverse Portraits on

Medals of Queen Victoria." *The Journal of the Orders and Medals Research Society*, 45(3): pp. 158–63.

Cooper, Thompson. 1883. *Men of Mark: A Gallery of Contemporary Portraits of Men Distinguished in the Senate, the Church, in Science, Literature, and Art, the Army, Navy, Law, Medicine, Etc.* London: Sampson Low, Marston, Searle, and Rivington.

Cyriax, Richard J. 1942. "Sir James Clark Ross and the Franklin Expedition." *Polar Record*, 3(24): pp. 528–40.

Dawson, George M. 1887. "Notes to Accompany a Geological Map of the Northern Portion of the Dominion of Canada, East of the Rocky Mountains." *Annual Report*, Geological and Natural History Survey of Canada (Vol. 2). Alfred R.C. Selwyn, Director, pp. 35–62.

_____. 1963. "Arctic Sledge Travelling by Officers of the Royal Navy, 1819–49." *Mariner's Mirror*, 49 (2): pp. 127–42.

_____. 1958. "The Two Franklin Expedition Records Found on King William Island." *Mariner's Mirror*, 44 (3): pp. 179–89.

Dawson, George M., and James M. Wordie. 1945. "Centenary of the Sailing of Sir John Franklin with the *Erebus* and *Terror*." *The Geographical Journal*, 106: pp. 169–97.

Deacon, Margaret, and Ann Savours. 1976. "Sir George Strong Nares (1831–1915)." *Polar Record*, 18(13):127–41.

"Discovery of the North-West Passage. By Commander R. M'Clure, of H.M.S. 'Investigator' (Gold Medallist)." 1854. *The Journal of the Royal Geographical Society*, 24: pp. 240–45.

"Expedition in Search of Sir John Franklin." 1848. *The Illustrated London News*, May 13.

Fawcett, Edward. 1895. "A Veteran Explorer" (letter to the editor). *Norfolk Daily Standard*, August.

Feather, Frederick. 1977. "John Woon: A Hero Who Might Have Been Forgotten." *Essex Police Magazine,* 5(10): pp. 5–12.

"Fete on Board H.M.S. 'Vindictive.'" 1843. *Colonial Times*, January 3.

"Foreign Notes." 1873. *New York Times*, November 8.

"The Franklin Commemoration." 1895. *The Geographical Journal*, (1): pp. 31–45.

"The Franklin Commemoration." 1895. *The Scottish Geographical Magazine*, (7): pp. 362–64.

Gledhill, Vince. 2003. "Baptism of Ice for Memorial Arctic Journey." *The Evening Chronicle*, April 5.

"Good News for the Navy." 1861. *Punch*, (41): p. 236.

"Greenwich Royal Hospital Schools." 1848. *The Illustrated London News*, February 19.

Harrod, Wilhelmine. 1886. "Lieut. Cresswell of Lynn." *The Lynn News and Advertiser*, October 26.

Hart, H.G. *The New Army List* (various years).

Hoag, Elaine. 2000. "Shipboard Printing on the Franklin Search Expeditions: A Bibliographical Study of the *Plover* Press." 38(1): pp. 7–71.

_____. 2001. "Caxtons of the North: Mid-Nineteenth Century Arctic Shipboard Printing." *Book History* (Vol. 4). Ezra Greenspan and Jonathan Rose (editors): pp. 81–114.

Hodak, George. 2010. "Congress Bans Maritime Flogging." *ABA Journal*, 96(9): p. 72.

"In the Frozen Ocean. The Only Living Man Who Has Been Around the Americas." 1891. *Chicago Tribune*, January 18.

Ingram, Winnington. 1886. "Journal of H.M.S. *Talbot* in October and November, 1840, During Operations on the Coast of Syria." *The Illustrated Naval and Military Magazine*, 3:30–37.

"H.M.S. 'Investigator,' in the Arctic Regions." 1853. *The Illustrated London News*, October 29.

Jones, A.G.E. 1958. "The Halkett Boat and Other Portable Boats." *The Mariner's Mirror*, 45(2): pp. 154–57.

_____. 1971. "Sir James Clark Ross and the Voyage of the *Enterprise* and *Investigator*, 1848–49." *The Geographical Journal*, 137(2): pp. 165–79.

Kellett, Henry. 1898. "Proceedings of Captain Kellett, C.B., H.M. Discovery Ship 'Resolute.' *Further papers relative to the recent Arctic expeditions in search of Sir John Franklin and the crews o f H.M.S. "Erebus" and "Terror."* House of Commons, Sessional Papers, Accounts and Papers, 1854–55 (1855a), 35: pp. 69–106.

Kendall, E.J. 1958. "Scurvy During Some British Polar Expeditions, 1875–1917." *Polar Record*, 7(51): pp. 467–85.

"A Kings County Hero." 1938. *Toronto Globe and Mail*, September 14.

"The Late Captain S. Gurney Cresswell, R.N." 1867. *The Lynn Advertiser*, August.

Lenn, Yueng-Djern. 2009. "How the Atlantic Water Is Cooled in the Arctic Refrigerator." *Ocean Challenge*, 16(3): pp. 28–31.

Lewis-Jones, Huw. 2009. "'Nelsons of Discovery': Notes on the Franklin Monument in Greenwich." *The Trafalgar Chronicle*, pp. 78–105.

"Lieutenant-General John Le Mesurier." 1844. *The Military Annual for 1844*, pp. 444–45.

"Lieut. Gurney Cresswell, R.N." 1853.*The Illustrated London News*, November 5.

"List of Objects Shown at the Franklin Commemoration Meeting, Edinburgh, On 4th June 1895, and on Subsequent Days." 1895. *The Scottish Geographical Magazine*, 11(8): pp. 410–16.

*The London Gazette* (various years).

"Looks Like an Arctic Fake." 1908. *The Sun* (New York), April 9.

Lushington, Vernon. 1860. "Her Majesty's Ship Himalaya. Salvage—Proportion Awarded—Distribution." *The Law Times Reports*, 35: p. 307.

Lutz, Roxanne, and Alex Chartrand. 2011. "New Light Shed on Chilling Tale." *The London Free Press*, May 2.

Mackinnon, C.S. 1985. "The British Man-Hauled Sledging Tradition." *The Franklin Era in Canadian Arctic History 1845–1859*, Patricia D. Sutherland (editor). Ottawa: National Museums of Canada, pp. 130–37.

Magiorkinis, E., K. Sidiropoulou, and A. Diamantis. 2011. "Hallmarks in the History of Epilepsy." *Epilepsy in Antiquity Novel Aspects on Epilepsy*, Prof. Humberto Foyaca-Sibat (editor). Maastricht, Netherlands: Institute for New Technologies, pp. 131–56.

Manning, Thomas H. 1953. "Narrative of an Unsuccessful Attempt to Circumnavigate Banks Island by Canoe in 1952." *Arctic*, 6(3): pp. 171–97.

_____. 1956. "Narrative of a Second Defence Research Board Expedition to Banks Island, with Notes on the Country and Its History." *Arctic*, 9(1–2): pp. 2–77.

Markam, Clements R. (editor). 1875. "Sherard Osborn." (obituary). *The Geographical Magazine*, 2: pp. 161–70.

_____. 1895. "Captain Parker Snow." *The Geographical Journal*, 5(5): pp. 500–01.

_____. 1901. "In Commemoration of the Reign of Her Late Majesty, Queen Victoria, Empress of India, President's Address in Commemoration of Her Late Majesty." *The Geographical Journal*, 17(3): pp. 225–52.

_____. 1908. "Admiral Sir Leopold M'Clintock, K.C.B." *The Geographical Journal*, 31(1): pp. 1–11.

McClintock, F.L. 1875. "On Arctic Sledge-travelling." *Proceedings of the Royal Geographical Society of London*, 19(7): pp. 464–75.

_____. 1889. "Notes on Blasting Thin Ice, as Usually Practised in Arctic Expeditions." *Journal of H.M.S. Enterprise, on the Expedition in Search of Sir John Franklin's Ships by Behring Strait. 1850–55*, Richard Collinson, pp. 430–31.

McClintock, F.L., and S. Haughton. 1858. "Reminiscences of Arctic Ice-Travel in Search of Sir John Franklin and His Companions." *Journal of the Royal Dublin Society*, 1: pp. 183–250.

McClure, Robert. 1853. "The North-West Passage.—Brief Summary of Captain M'Clure's Passage in the 'Investigator' from the Behring Strait to the Bay of Mercy, Banks Land." *The Nautical Magazine and Naval Chronicle*, 22(12): pp. 617–75.

_____. 1854. "Discovery of the North-West Passage." *The Journal of the Royal Geographical Society*, 24: pp. 240–45.

McKenzie, W.G. 1969. "A Further Clue in the Franklin Mystery." *The Beaver*, 49(2): pp. 28–32.

_____. 1970. "Able Seaman James Nelson." *North*, 17(5): pp. 14–18.

"Memorial Pillar on Beechey Island." 1854. *The Illustrated London News*, October 28.

Miertsching, Johann A. 1861. "Notes from an Arctic Diary." *The Sunday at Home: A Family Magazine for Sabbath Reading* 8: pp. 65, 97, 165, 197, 209, 225, 241.

Millar, K., Bowman, A.W., Battersby, W., Welbury, R.R. 2015. "The Health of Six Arctic Discover Ships Sent in Search of the Franklin Expedition: Implications for the Crews of *Erebus* and *Terror*" (submitted for publication).

Myres, J.A.L. 1986. "The Franklin Expedition: A Long-Delayed Presentation." *The Journal of the Orders and Medals Research Society*, 25(3): pp. 147–49.

"Names of Individuals to Whom the Royal Premium Has Been Awarded." 1858. *The Journal of the Royal Geographical Society*, 28: p. ix.

*The Navy List* (various years).

Nelson, J.H. 1967. "The Last Voyage of HMS Investigator, 1850–53, and the Discovery of the North West Passage." *Polar Record*, 13(87): pp. 753–68.

*The New Navy List* (various years).

"The North-West Passages." 1874. *The Shipwrecked Mariner*, 81(21): pp. 37–40.

Obituary. 1870. "Richard Sainthill." *The Art-Journal*, 9: p. 182.

Obituary. 1873. "Sir Robert M'Clure, C.B. A Memoir." *Ocean Highways: The Geographical Review* (December): pp. 353–56.

Obituary. 1895. "The Late Captain Parker Snow. An Arctic Veteran." *Hampshire Telegraph and Sussex Chronicle* (Portsmouth), March 23.

Obituary. 1895. Major-General Richard Hugh Stotherd. *Minutes of the Proceedings of the Institution of Civil Engineers*, 121: pp. 343–44.

Obituary. 1901. "Henry Piers, M.R.C.S. ENG., L.S.A., Deputy Inspector-General of Hospitals and Fleets (Retired)." *The Lancet*, 2(2): p. 1706.

"Obituary. Henry Piers, Deputy Inspector-General of Hospitals and Fleets." 1901. *The Philadelphia Medical Journal*, Foreign News and Notes, 8(26): p. 1113.

"Obituary. Sir Alexander Armstrong, KCB, RN, FRS, Sometime Director-General of the Royal Navy Medical Department." 1899. *The British Medical Journal*, , 2(2011): p. 181.

Osborn, Sherard, and George F. McDougall (editors). 1852. "Facsimile of The Illustrated Arctic News, Published on Board H.M.S. Resolute: Captn. Horatio T. Austin. C.B. in Search of the Expedition Under Sir John Franklin."

"The Outbreak of Scurvy in the Arctic Expedition." 1877. *The British Medical Journal* (March 10): pp. 297–98.

Parks, Murray. 1954. "Discovery of the North-West Passage." *The Listener*, 51(1310): pp. 609–10.

Pearson, Michael. 1995. "Sledges and Sledging in Polar Regions." *Polar Record*, 31(176): pp. 3–24.

"Plymouth Man Who Searched for the Explorer" (transcription). 1914. *Western Daily Mercury*, May 23.

"The Queen's Regulations and the Admiralty Instructions for the Government of Her Majesty's Naval Service." 1862.

"Report of the Scurvy Committee." 1877. *The Geographical Magazine*, 4: pp. 145–47.

Reviews. 1858. *The Natural History Review, and Quarterly Journal of Science*, 5.

Roberts, Brian. 1940. "Notes on the Barrow Collection of Arctic Equipment." *The Geographical Journal*, 95(5): pp. 368–80.

"Royal Geographical Society." 1855. *The Illustrated London News*, June 16.

Sainthill, Richard. 1856. "Suggestions for a Medal to Record 'The Discovery of the Passage by The North Pole.'" Reprinted from "Numismatic Crumbs." London: Nichols and Sons; printed for private distribution; Cork: J. Crowe [1855].

Savelle, James M. 1855. "Effects of Nineteenth Century European Exploration on the Development of the Netsilik Inuit Culture." *The Franklin Era in Canadian Arctic History 1845–1859*, Patricia D. Sutherland (editor) [1985], pp. 192–214.

Savours, Ann. 1990. "The Diary of Assistant Surgeon Henry Piers, HMS *Investigator*, 1850–54." *Journal of the Royal Naval Medical Service*, 76(1): pp. 33–38.

Savours, Ann, and Deacon, Margaret. 1981. "Nutritional Aspects of the British Arctic (Nares) Expedition of 1875–76 and Its Predecessors." In *Starving Sailors: The Influence of Nutrition Upon Naval and Maritime History*. J. Watt, E.J. Freeman, and W.F. Bynum (editors), International Symposium at the National Maritime Museum, Greenwich, April 16–18, 1980.

"Sir Robert McClure, C.B." 1873. *Ocean Highways: The Geographical Review* (November): p. 325.

"*Sketches from My Life.* By the late Hobart Pasha. London: 1886" (review). 1887. *The Edinburgh Review*, 165: pp. 166–67.

"Some Relics of the Late Sir Alexander Armstrong, M.D., K.C.B., F.R.S." 1906. *The Lancet* (August 4): p. 341.

Stein, Glenn M. 1991. "Arctic Oddity." *The Journal of the Orders and Medals Research Society*, 30(1): pp. 16–17.

_____. 1994. "Design Origins of the First and Second Arctic Issues." *The Journal of the Orders and Medals Research Society*, 33(4): pp. 301–03; and a note regarding same, Winter 1995, 34(4): pp. 306.

_____. 1996. "Past Meets Present: Ice Quartermaster Peter Finnecy and the Aftermath of the 1875–76 Arctic Expedition." *The Review*, Naval Historical Collectors & Research Association, 8(4): pp. 4–9.

_____. 2007. "Scattered Memories and Frozen Bones: Revealing a Sailor of the Franklin Expedition, 1845–48." *The Journal of the Orders and Medals Research Society*, 46(4): pp. 224–32.

_____. 2008. "The Voyage of HMS *Investigator* (1850–54): Solving the Mysteries of the Arctic Meritorious Service and Gallantry Medals." *The Journal of the Orders and Medals Research Society*, Part 1, 47(3):pp. 148–55; and Part 2, 47(4): pp. 245–49.

_____. 2010. "The Franklin Expedition 50th Anniversary Commemorations: Arctic Veterans and Medals from the Frozen Zone." *The Journal of the Orders and Medals Research Society*, 49(2): pp. 84–92.

_____. 2012. "British and American Awards to the American Second Grinnell Arctic Expedition of 1853–55." *The Journal of the Orders and Medals Research Society*, 51(1): pp. 13–24.

Stotherd, R.H. 1872. "Electrical Ignition of Explosives." *Journal of the Society of Telegraph Engineers, Including Original Communications on Telegraphy and Electrical Science*, 1: pp. 209–24.

Taylor, Geoffrey. 1981. Clinical Manifestations of Vitamin Deficiencies." In *Starving Sailors: The Influence of Nutrition Upon Naval and Maritime History*. J. Watt, E.J. Freeman, and W.F. Bynum (editors), International Symposium at the National Maritime Museum, Greenwich, April 16–18, 1980.

"Testimonial to Captain Sir Robert M'Clure." 1856. *The Illustrated London News*, June 14.

Tomlinson, Barbara. 2009. "Chivalry at the Poles: British Sledge Flags." The XIX International Congress of Vexillology, York, July 23–27, 2001, *Proceedings*: pp. 215–21.

Urban, Sylvanus. 1844. "The Xanthian Expedition." *The Gentleman's Magazine and Historical Review*, 21: pp. 191.

_____. 1854. Notes of the Month. *The Gentleman's Magazine and Historical Review*, 41: pp. 605–06.

_____. 1860. Deaths. *The Gentleman's Magazine and Historical Review* (July 9): p. 97.

"A Veteran Explorer. To the Editor of The Standard." 1895. *The Standard*, August.

"William Fitzwilliam Owen (1774–1857)." 1894. *Collections of the New Brunswick Historical Society*, 1: pp. 217–20.

"The Work of the Arctic Expedition." 1875. *The Geographical Magazine*, 2: pp. 65–71.

Yelverton, David E. 1996. "Sir James Clark Ross (1800–1862)." *The Journal of the Orders and Medals Research Society*, , 35(3): pp. 235.

Zubor, A. 1975. "Jan Awgust Měrćink—K jeho 100. posmjertninam 30. měrca 1975." *Serbska Protyka*, p. 97.

## Reference Works:

Abbott, P.E., and J.M.A. Tamplin. 1981. *British Gallantry Awards*. London: Nimrod Dix.

*The Annual Register: A Review of Public Events at Home and Abroad for the Year 1900*. 1901. London: Longmans, Green.

*The Annual Register, or a View of the History and Politics of the Year 1860*. 1861. London: Woodfall and Kinder.

*Antarctica: The Extraordinary History of Man's Conquest of the Frozen Continent*. Surry Hills: Reader's Digest (Australia) Pty. Limited, 1990.

*The Arctic Dispatches Containing An Account of the Discovery of the North-West Passage by Captain Robert Maclure, Commanding H.M.S. Investigator. with a Narrative of Proceedings of H.M.S. Resolute, Capt. Kellett, C.B., and the Dispatches of Capt. Sir Edward Belcher, C.B., Capt. Inglefield and Commr. Pullen. with a Map of the Discoveries in the Arctic Regions*. 1854. Reprinted from *Nautical Magazine* 22, December 1853. London: J.D. Potter, undated, but presumed.

Armstrong, Alexander. 1858. *Observations on Naval Hygiene and Scurvy, More Particularly as the Latter Appeared During a Polar Voyage*. London: John Churchill.

_____. 1857. *A Personal Narrative of the Discovery of the North-West Passage; with Numerous Incidents of Travel and Adventure During Nearly Five Years' Continuous Service in the Arctic Regions While in Search of the Expedition Under Sir John Franklin*. London: Hurst and Blackett, Note: The pagination is flawed as follows: 1–128, 145–160, 145–616. Consequently, the researcher needs to be aware of this anomaly when referencing this source.

Asplin, Kevin J. 2004. *China Medal Roll 1856–60: Royal Navy*. London: Savannah.

Back, George. 1838. *Narrative of An Expedition in H.M.S. "Terror", Undertaken with a View to Geographical Discovery on the Arctic Shores, in 1836–37*. London: John Murray.

Barr, William. 2007. *Arctic Hell-Ship: The Voyage of HMS Enterprise 1850–1855*. Edmonton: University of Alberta Press.

_____ (translator and editor). 1992. *A Frenchman in Search of Franklin: De Bray's Arctic Journal, 1852–1854*. Toronto: University of Toronto Press.

_____ (editor). 1999. *Searching for Franklin: The Land Arctic Searching Expedition, 1855. James Anderson's and James Stewart's Expedition Via the Back River*. London: The Hakluyt Society.

Baynham, Henry. 1971. *Before the Mast: Naval Ratings of the Nineteenth Century*. London: Hutchinson.

Beattie, O., and J. Geiger. 1987. *Frozen in Time: Unlocking the Secrets of the Franklin Expedition*. New York: E.P. Dutton.

Beechey, Frederick W. 1843. *A Voyage of Discovery Towards the North Pole, Peformed in His Majesty's Ships Dorothea and Trent, Etc.* London: Richard Bentley.

Belcher, Edward. 1855. *The Last of the Arctic Voyages; Being a Narrative of the Expedition in H.M.S. Assistance, Under the Command of Captain Sir Edward Belcher, C.B., in Search of Sir John Franklin, During the Years 1852–53–54* (vols. 1 and 2). London: Lovell Reeve.

Benham, Daniel. 1854. *Sketch of the Life of Jan August Miertsching, Interpreter of the Esquimaux Language to the Arctic Expedition on Board H.M.S. "Investigator," Captain M'Clure, 1850, 1851, 1852, 1853*. London: William Mallalieu.

Berton, Pierre. 1988. *The Arctic Grail: The Quest for the North West Passage and the North Pole, 1818–1909*. New York: Viking Penguin.

Bilcliffe, John. *Irreproachable Character: The Award of the Royal Marine Meritorious Medal*. Portsmouth: Royal Marine Historical Society, 2005.

Bockstoce, John (editor). 1988. *The Journal of Rochfort Maguire 1852–52* (2 vols.). London: The Hakluyt Society.

Bolster, W. 1997. Jeffrey. *Black Jacks: African American Seamen in the Age of Sail*. Cambridge: Harvard University Press.

Bourne, John. 1855. *A Treatise on the Screw Propeller, with Various Suggestions for Improvement*. London: Longman, Brown, Green, and Longmans.

Bunyan, Ian, et al. 1993. *No Ordinary Journey: John Rae, Arctic Explorer 1813–1893*. Edinburgh: National Museums of Scotland.

Burke, Sir Bernard. 1871. *A Genealogical and Heraldic Dictionary of the Landed Gentry of Great Britain and Ireland* (vol. 2, 4th edition). London: Harrison, 1863; (vol. 2, 5th edition) London: Harrison.

Burridge, Kate. 2010. *Gift of the Gob: Morsels of English Language History*. Sydney: ABC Books/HarperCollins.

Callahan, Edward W. 1901. (editor). *List of Officers of the United States of the Navy and of the Marine Corps from 1775 to 1900, Comprising a Complete Register of All Present and Former Commissioned, Warranted, and Appointed Officers of the United States Navy, and of the Marine Corps, Regular and Volunteer*. New York: L.R. Hemersly.

Cherbuliez, J. 1857. *Journal De M. Miertsching Interprète Du Capitaine Mac Clure Dans Son Voyage Au Pôle Nord* (3d edition). Genève.

Choris, Louis. 1822. *Voyage Pittoresque Autour Du Monde, Avec Des Portraits De Sauvages d'Amérique, d'Asie, d'Afrique, Et Des Iles Du Grand Ocean; Des Paysages, Des Vues Maritimes, Et Plusieurs Objets D'histoire Naturelle.* Paris: Firmin Didot.

Clowes, Sir William Laird. 1903. *The Royal Navy: A History from Earliest Times to the Death of Queen Victoria* (vols. 4, 5, 6 & 7). London: Sampson Low, Marston, 1899, 1900, 1901.

Coad, J.G. 1983. *Historic Architecture of the Royal Navy: An Introduction.* London: Victor Gollancz.

Collins, John. 1823. *A Dictionary of Spanish Proverbs, Compiled from the Best Authorities in the Spanish Language, Translated into English; with Explanatory Illustrations from the Latin, Spanish, and English Authors.* London: S. Brook.

Collinson, Richard. 1889. *Journal of H.M.S. Enterprise, on the Expedition in Search of Sir John Franklin's Ships by Behring Strait. 1850–55.* London: Sampson Low, Marston, Searle, & Rivington.

Condon, Richard G., with Julia Olgina and the Holman Elders. 1996. *The Northern Copper Inuit: A History.* Norman: University of Oklahoma Press.

*Conference on Missions Held in 1860 at Liverpool: Including the Papers Read, the Deliberations, and the Conclusions Reached; with a Comprehensive Index Shewing the Various Matters Brought Under Review.* 1860. London: James Nisbet.

Cowan, James. 1983. *The New Zealand Wars: A History of the Maori Campaigns and the Pioneering Period* (3d edition, vol. 1, 1845–64). Wellington: P.D. Hasselberg.

Cyriax, Richard J. 1939. *Sir John Franklin's Last Arctic Expedition.* London: Methuen.

David, Robert G. 2000. *The Arctic in the British Imagination 1818–1914.* Manchester: Manchester University Press.

Dickerson, Mark O. 1993. *Whose North? Political Change, Political Development, and Self-Government in the Northwest Territories.* Vancouver: University of British Columbia Press.

Dodge, Ernest S. 1973. *The Polar Rosses: John and James Clark Ross and Their Explorations.* London: Faber and Faber.

Dorling, H. 1974. Taprell. *Ribbons and Medals: The World's Military and Civil Awards.* New Enlarged Edition. New York: Doubleday.

Douglas-Morris, Kenneth. 1976. *The Life of Vice-Admiral Sir Robert John Le Mesurier McClure, C.B.: Arctic Explorer and Discovery of the North West Passage (1807–1873).* Salisbury: M.O. Collins.

_____. 1982. *the Naval General Service Medal Roll 1793–1840.* London: privately printed).

_____. 1991. *Naval Long Service Medals 1830–1990.* London: privately printed.

_____. 1987. *Naval Medals 1793–1856.* London: privately printed.

_____. 1994. *Naval Medals 1857–1880.* London: privately printed.

Dunlop, Andrew. 1972. *Memorabilia of the McClures.* Salisbury: M.O. Collins.

Egerton, Mary Augusta Phipps. 1896. *Admiral of the Fleet Sir Geoffrey Phipps Hornby G.C.B.: A Biography.* Edinburgh and London: William Blackwood and Sons.

Firth, Edith C. 1963. (compiler). *The North West Passage 1534–1859: A Catalogue of An Exhibition of Books and Manuscripts in the Toronto Public Library.* Toronto: Baxter.

Ford, Herbert. 1996. *Pitcairn—Port of Call* (1st edition). Angwin: Hawser Titles.

Forgey, William W.1999. *Basic Essentials Hypothermia* (2d edition). Billings: Falcon Press.

Franklin, John. 1823. *Narrative of a Journey to the Shores of the Polar Sea, in the Years 1819, 20, 21 and 22.* London: John Murray.

_____. 1828. *Narrative of a Second Expedition to the Shores of the Polar Sea, in the Years 1825, 1826, and 1827.* London: John Murray.

Gethyn-Jones, Eric. 1966. *Dymock Down the Ages.* Dymock, UK: privately published.

Giesbrecht, G.G., and J.A. Wilkerson. 2006. *Hypothermia, Frostbite, and Other Cold Injuries: Prevention, Survival, Rescue, and Treatment* (2d edition). Seattle: Mountaineers Books.

Giffard, Edward. 1852. *Deeds of Naval Daring: Or Anecdotes of the British Navy.* London: John Murray.

Gough, Barry M. (editor). 1973. *To the Pacific and Arctic with Beechey: The Journal of Lieutenant George Peard of H.M.S. 'Blossom' 1825–1828.* Cambridge: The Hakluyt Society.

Griffiths, George (compiler). 1890. *Chronicles of the County Wexford, Being a Record of Memorable Incidents, Disasters, Social Occurrences, and Crimes, Also Biographies of Eminent Persons, &C., &C., Brought Down to the Year 1877.* Enniscorthy: The "Watchman" Office.

Harris, David A. 2001. *A Guide to Military Temperance Medals.* Ontario: Stewart.

Harrod, Dominick (editor). 2000. *War, Ice & Piracy: The Remarkable Career of a Victorian Sailor—The Journals and Letters of Samuel Gurney Cresswell.* London: Chatham.

Harter, Jim. 1979. *Animals: 1419 Copyright-Free Illustrations of Mammals, Birds, Fish, Insects, Etc. a Pictorial Archive from Nineteenth-Century Sources.* New York: Dover.

Hatfield, Gabrielle. *Encyclopedia of Folklore Medicine: Old World and New World Traditions.* Santa Barbara: ABC-CLIO, 2004.

Haydn, Joseph, and Benjamin Vincent. 1883. *Haydn's Dictionary of Dates and Universal Information Relating to All Ages and Nations* (17th edition). New York: Harper & Brothers.

HMSO. 1862. *The Queen's Regulations and the Admiralty Instructions for the Government of Her Majesty's Naval Service.* London: HMSO.

Hocking, William J. 1910. *Catalogue of the Coins, Tokens, Medals, Dies, and Seals in the Museum of the Royal Mint* (vol. 2: *Dies, Medals, and Seals*). London: Darling & Son.

Holland, Clive. 1994. *Arctic Exploration and Development C. 500 B.C. to 1915: An Encyclopedia.* New York: Garland.

Holzer, Harold (editor). 2009.*Lincoln and New York.* New York and London: New-York Historical Society & Philip Wilson Publishers.

Howell, Raymond C. 1987. *The Royal Navy and the Slave Trade.* Beckeham: Croom Helm.

Hughes-Hughes, W.O. 1893. *The Register of Tonbridge School, from 1820–1893.* London: Richard Bentley and Son.

Hurd, Douglas. 1967. *The Arrow War: An Anglo-Chinese Confusion 1856–1860.* New York: Macmillan.

Jackson, John N. 1997. *The Welland Canals and Their Communities: Engineering, Industrial, and Urban Transformation.* Toronto: University of Toronto Press.

Jacob, John. 1830. *Annals of Some of the British Norman Islands, Constituting the Bailiwick of Guernsey, as Collected from Private Manuscripts, Public Documents and Former Historians* (Part 1). Carrefour, Guernsey: T. Greenslade.

Jones, A.G.E. 1992. *Polar Portraits: Collected Papers.* Whitby, UK: Caedmon of Whitby.

Kane, Elisha K. 1856. *Arctic Explorations: The Second Grinnell Expedition in Search of Sir John Franklin, 1953, '54, '55* (2 vols.). Philadelphia: Childs & Peterson.

Kingston, W.H.G. 1854. *Blue Jackets Or, Chips of the Old Block. A Narrative of the Gallant Exploits of British Seamen, and of the Principal Events in the Naval Service, During the Reign of Her Most Gracious Majesty Queen Victoria*. London: Grant and Griffith.

Knight, Charles (editor). 1856. *The English Cyclopædia: A New Dictionary of Universal Knowledge* (vol. 1: *Biography*). London: Bradbury and Evans.

Lansing, Alfred. 1959. *Endurance: Shackleton's Incredible Voyage*. New York: McGraw-Hill.

Lavery, Brian. 1989. *Nelson's Navy: The Ships, Men and Organisation 1793–1815*. Annapolis: Naval Institute Press.

Lee, Sidney (editor). 1909. *Dictionary of National Biography*. London: Smith, Elder, 1900.

Lehane, Brenda, and the editors of Time-Life Books. 1981. *The Northwest Passage*. Alexandria: Time-Life Books.

Levere, Trevor H. 1993. *Science and the Canadian Arctic: A Century of Exploration, 1818–1918*. Cambridge: Cambridge University Press.

Lewis, Michael. 1965. *The Navy in Transition: A Social History 1814–1864*. London: Hodder and Stoughton.

Librarian and Keeper of the Papers, Foreign Office (compiler). 1846. *British and Foreign State Papers, 1824–1825* (vol. 12). London: James Ridgway and Sons.

Lloyd, Christopher. 1968. *The British Seaman 1200–1860: A Social Survey*. London: Collins.

_____. 1949. *The Navy and the Slave Trade: The Suppression of the African Slave Trade in the Nineteenth Century*. London: Longmans, Green.

Lyon, David. 1993. *The Sailing Navy List 1688–1860*. London: Conway Maritime Press.

Lyon, George F. 1824. *The Private Journal of Captain G.F. Lyon, of H.M.S. Hecla, During the Recent Voyage of Discovery Under Captain Parry*. London: John Murray.

McCandless, B., and G. Grosvenor. 1917. *Flags of the World*. Washington, DC: National Geographic Society.

McClintock, Francis L. 1859. *In the Arctic Seas: A Narrative of the Discovery of the Fate of Sir John Franklin and His Companions*. Philadelphia: Porter & Coates.

McClure, James A. 1914. *The McClure Family*. Petersburg, VA: Frank A. Owen.

McClure, Robert J. 1853. *The North-West Passage. Capt. M'Clure's Despatches from Her Majesty's Discovery Ship, "Investigator," Off Point Warren and Cape Bathurst*. London: John Betts.

McClure, Robert J., and Sherard Osborn (editor). 1856 [1969]. *The Discovery of the North-West Passage by H.M.S. "Investigator" Capt. R. M'Clure 1850, 1851, 1852, 1853, 1854, Edited by Commander Sherard Osborn from the Logs and Journals of Capt. Robert Le M. M'Clure* (1st edition). Longman, Brown, Green, and Longmans, & Roberts; reprint, Rutland: Charles E. Tuttle; 2d edition, London: Longman, Brown, Green, and Longmans, & Roberts, 1857; 4th edition, London: William Blackwood and Sons, 1865.

McCormick, Robert. 1884. *Voyages of Discovery in the Arctic and Antarctic Seas, and Round the World: Being Personal Narratives of Attempts to Reach the North and South Poles; and of An Open-Boat Expedition in Search of Sir John Franklin and Her Majesty's "Erebus" and "Terror", Etc.* (2 vols.). London: Sampson Low, Marston, Searle, and Rivington.

McDougall, George F. 1857. *The Eventful Voyage of H.M. Discovery Ship Resolute to the Arctic Regions in Search of John Franklin and the Missing Crews of H.M. Discovery Ships "Erebus" and "Terror."* London: Longman, Brown, Green, Longmans, & Roberts.

McGoogan, Ken. 2002. *Fatal Passage: The Story of John Rae, the Arctic Hero Time Forgot*. New York: Carroll & Graf.

_____. 2005. *Lady Franklin's Revenge: A True Story of Ambition, Obsession, and the Remaking of Arctic History*. Toronto: HarperCollins.

MacInnis, Joe. 1985. *The Land That Devours Ships: The Search for the Breadalbane*. Toronto: CBC Enterprises.

MacMechan, Archibald. 1916. *The Winning of Popular Government: The Union of 1841*. Chronicles of Canada, No. 27. Toronto: Glasgow, Brook.

Mair, Charles. 1908. *Through the Mackenzie Basin: A Narrative of the Athabasca and Peace River Treaty Expedition, 1899 ... Also, Notes on the Mammals and Birds of Northern Canada*. Toronto: William Briggs.

Markham, Clements R. 1875. *the Arctic Navy List; Or, a Century of Arctic & Antarctic Officers, 1773–1873*. London: Griffin.

_____. 1909. *Life of Admiral Sir Leopold McClintock*. London: John Murray.

Marshall, John. 1835. *Royal Naval Biography* (vol. 4, part 2). London: Longman, Rees, Orme, Brown, Green and Longman.

Maxwell, William H. 1854. *History of the Irish Rebellion in 1798 with Memoirs of the Union, & Emmett's Insurrection in 1803* (4th edition). London: H.G. Bohn.

Melville, Herman. 1992. *Billy Budd*. New York: Tom Doherty Associates.

Mennell, Philip. 1892. *The Dictionary of Australasian Biography: Comprising Notices of Eminent Colonists from the Inauguration of Responsible Government Down to the Present Time* [1853–1892] London: Hutchinson.

Miertsching, Johann A. 1856. *Reise-Tagebuch Des Missonars Joh. Aug. Miertsching, Welcher Als Dolmetscher Die Nordpol-Expedition Zur Aussuchung Sir John Franklin Auf Dem Schiff Investigator Begleitete in Dem Jahren 1850 Bis 1854* (1st edition, Gnadau, Germany: H.L. Menz, 1855; 2d edition.

Mills, William J. 2003. *Exploring Polar Frontiers: A Historical Encyclopedia* (vols. 1 and 2). Santa Barbara: ABC-CLIO.

Murphy, David. 2004. *The Arctic Fox: Francis Leopold McClintock*. Toronto: Dundurn.

Murray, Thomas B. 1860. *Pitcairn: The Island, the People and the Pastor*. London: Spottiswoode.

Myers, Norma. 1996. *Reconstructing the Black Past: Blacks in Britain C.1780–1830*. London: Routledge.

Neatby, Leslie H. 1967. (translator and editor). *Frozen Ships: The Arctic Diary of Johann Miertsching 1850–1854*. Toronto: John Deyell.

_____. 1958. *In Quest of the Northwest Passage: The Adventures of Brave Men in Forlorn Lands*. New York: Thomas Y. Crowell.

_____. 1970. *Search for Franklin: The Story of One of the Great Dramas of Polar Exploration*. London: Arthur Baker.

Nelson, Edward W. 1899. *The Eskimo About the Bering Strait*. Washington, DC: Bureau of American Ethnology.

*The Newspaper Press Directory* (vol. 60). 1905. London: C. Mitchell.

O'Byrne, Robert. 1855. *O'Byrne's Naval Annual for 1855*. London: Piper, Stephenson, & Spence.

O'Byrne, William R. 1849. *A Naval Biographical Dictionary: Comprising the Life and Services of Every Living Officer in Her Majesty's Navy, from the Rank of Admiral of the Fleet to That of Lieutenant, Inclusive. Compiled from Authentic and Family Documents* (vol. 1). London: John Murray.

Osborn, Sherard. 1860. *The Career, Last Voyage and Fate of Capt. Sir John Franklin*. London: Bradbury and Evans.

_____. 1852. *Stray Leaves from an Arctic Journal; Or, Eighteen Months in the Polar Regions, in Search of Sir John Franklin's Expedition, in the Years 1850–51.* New York: George P. Putnam.

Oswalt, Wendell H. 1999. *Eskimos and Explorers.* Lincoln: University of Nebraska Press.

Parry, William E. 1821. *Journal of a Second Voyage for the Discovery of a North-West Passage from the Atlantic to the Pacific; Performed in the Years 1819–20, in His Majesty's Ships Hecla and Griper.* London: John Murray.

_____. 1824. *Journal of a Second Voyage for the Discovery of a North-West Passage from the Atlantic to the Pacific; Performed in the Years 1821–22–23, in His Majesty's Ships Fury and Hecla.* London: John Murray.

Payne, A.A. 1911. *A Handbook of British and Foreign Orders, War Medals and Decorations Awarded to the Army and Navy.* Sheffield: J.W. Northend.

Penn, Geoffrey. 1955. *Up Funnel, Down Screw! The Story of the Naval Engineer.* London: Hollis and Carter.

Philbrick, Nathaniel. 2000. *In the Heart of the Sea: The Tragedy of the Whaleship* Essex. New York: Penguin.

Phillips-Birt, Douglas. 1971. *A History of Seamanship.* Garden City: Doubleday.

Pineau, Roger (editor). 1968. *The Japan Expedition 1852–1854: The Personal Journal of Commodore Matthew C. Perry.* Washington, DC: Smithsonian Institution Press.

Porsild, Alf E. 1955. *The Vascular Plants of the Western Canadian Arctic Archipelago.* Ottawa: Cloutier.

*Portrait and Biographical Album of Warren County, Illinois, Containing Full Page Portraits and Biographical Sketches of Prominent and Representative Citizens of the County*, etc. 1886. Chicago: Chapman Brothers.

Potter, Russell A. 2007. *Arctic Spectacles: The Frozen North in Visual Culture, 1818–1875.* Seattle: University of Washington Press.

Poulsom, N.W. 1968. *The White Ribbon: A Medallic Record of British Polar Expeditions.* London: B.A. Seaby.

Poulsom, N.W., and J.A.L. Myres. 2000. *British Polar Exploration and Research: A Historical and Medallic Record with Biographies 1818–1999.* London: Savannah.

Power, John Carroll. 1875. *Abraham Lincoln: His Life, Public Services, Death, and Great Funeral Cortege, with a History and Description of the National Lincoln Monument.* Springfield: Edwin A. Wilson.

Proctor, David. 1992. *Music of the Sea.* London: HMSO.

Purves, Alec J. 1978. *Collecting Medals and Decorations* (3d edition). London: Seaby.

Ramsland, John. 2014. *From Antarctica to the Gold Rushes: In the Wake of the Erebus.* Melbourne: Brolga.

Rich, E.E., and A.M. Johnson. 1853. *John Rae's Correspondence with the Hudson's Bay Company on Arctic Exploration, 1844–1855.* London: Hudson's Bay Record Society.

Riffenburgh, Beau. 1994. *The Myth of the Explorer: The Press, Sensationalism, and Geographical Discovery.* Oxford: Oxford University Press.

Robertson-Lorant, Laurie. 1998. *Herman Melville: A Biography.* Amherst: University of Massachusetts Press.

Robinson, Michael F. 2006. *The Coldest Crucible: Arctic Exploration and American Culture.* Chicago: University of Chicago Press.

Rockley, Joan. 2008. *Antiquarians and Archaeology in Nineteenth-Century Cork.* Oxford: Archaeopress.

Rodger, N.A.M. 1988. *Naval Records for Genealogists.* London: HMSO.

Romkey, Bill. 2003. *The Story of Labrador.* Montreal: McGill-Queen's University Press.

Roscoe, Henry E. 1906. *The Life & Experiences of Sir Henry Enfield Roscoe.* London and New York: Macmillan.

Ross, M.J. 1994. *Polar Pioneers: John Ross and James Clark Ross.* Montreal: McGill-Queen's University Press.

_____. 1982. *Ross in the Antarctic: The Voyages of James Clark Ross in Her Majesty's Ships* Erebus & Terror, *1839–1843.* Whitby, UK: Caedmon of Whitby.

*Royal Naval Exhibition, 1891. Official Catalogue & Guide.* 1891.London: W.P. Griffith & Sons.

Rutter, Owen. 1986. *The Pirate Wind: Tales of the Sea-Robbers of Malaya.* Oxford: Oxford University Press.

Sainthill, Richard. 1857. *Numismatic, and Other Crumbs.* Cork: John Crowe, for private distribution only.

_____. 1855 [1856]. *Numismatic Crumbs.* London: Nichols and Sons, for private distribution only; reprinted by John Crowe, Cork.

_____. 1844. *An Olla Podrida; Or, Scraps, Numismatic, Antiquarian, and Literary.* London: Nichols and Son.

Sargent, Epps. 1857. *Arctic Adventure by Sea and Land.* Boston: Phillips, Sampson.

Savours, Ann. 1999. *The Search for the Northwest Passage.* New York: St. Martin's.

Scott, Barry E. n.d. *Songs and Ditties of the Royal Navy & Royal Marines.* Unpublished manuscript.

Seemann, Berthold. 1853. *Narrative of the Voyage of H.M.S. Herald During the Years 1845–51, Under the Command of Captain Henry Kellett, R.N., C.B.; Being the Circumnavigation of the Globe, and Three Cruizes in the Arctic Regions in Search of Sir John Franklin* (vols. 1 and 2). London: Reeve.

Seward, Albert C. 1919. *Fossil Plants: A Text-Book for Students of Botany and Geology* (vol. 4). Cambridge: Cambridge University Press.

Shay, Frank. 1924. *Iron Men and Wooden Ships.* Garden City: Doubleday.

Tatham, Emma. 1858. *The Dream of Pythagoras and Other Poems* (3d edition; originally published in 1854). London: Hamilton.

Timbs, John. 1857. *The Year-Book of Facts in Science and Art: Exhibiting the Most Important Discoveries and Improvements of the Past Year; in Mechanics and the Useful Arts; Natural Philosophy; Electricity; Chemistry; Zoology and Botany; Geology and Mineralogy; Meteorology and Astronomy.* London: David Bogue.

United States Department of State. 1868. *Russian America. Message from the President of the United States, in Answer to a Resolution of the House of 19th of December Last, Transmitting Correspondence in Relation to Russian America.* Washington, DC: Government Printing Office.

Vale, Brian. 2001. *A Frigate of King George: Life and Duty on a British Man-Of-War.* London: I.B. Tauris.

Vaux, W.S.W. 1851. *Handbook to the Antiquities in the British Museum: Being a Description of the Remains of Greek, Assyrian, Egyptian, and Etruscan Art Preserved There.* London: John Murray.

Verne, Jules. 2005. *The Adventures of Captain Hatteras.* William Butcher, translator. Oxford: Oxford University Press.

Walford, Edward. 1869. *The County Families of the United Kingdom or Royal Manual of the Titled and Untitled Aristocracy of Great Britain and Ireland.* London: Robert Hardwicke.

Ward, Robert DeCourcy. 1908. *Climate, Considered Especially in Relation to Man* New York: G.P. Putnam's Sons.

Washington, John (compiler). 1850. *Eskimaux and English Vocabulary, for the Use of the Arctic Expeditions.* London: John Murray.

_____. 1853. *Greenland-Eskimo Vocabulary, for the Use of the Arctic Expeditions.* London: John Murray.

Webb, William. 1976. *Coastguard! An Official History of HM Coastguard.* London: HMSO.

Whitaker, Capt. A.E. 1890. *British War Medals and Decorations.*

White, Adam. 1850. *A Popular History of Mammalia; Comprising a Familiar Account of Their Classification and Habits.* London: Reeve and Benham.

White, William. 1878. *History, Gazetteer and Directory of the County of Hampshire, Etc.* (2d edition). London: Simpkin, Marshal.

Wilkins, Philip A. 1904. *The History of the Victoria Cross.* London: Archibald Constable.

Wills, James W., and Freeman Wills. 1876. *The Irish Nation: Its History and Its Biography.* Dublin: A. Fullarton.

Winks, Robin W. 1997. *The Blacks in Canada: A History* (2d edition). Montreal: McGill-Queen's University Press.

Winton, John. 1977. *Hurrah for the Life of a Sailor! Life on the Lower-Deck of the Victorian Navy.* London: Michael Joseph Ltd.

Wood, Walter. 1932. *Survivors' Tales of Famous Shipwrecks.* London: Geoffrey Bles.

Woodman, David C. 1991. *Unravelling the Franklin Mystery: Inuit Testimony.* Montreal: McGill-Queen's University Press.

Yelverton, David E. 2000. *Antarctica Unveiled: Scott's First Expedition and the Quest for the Unknown Continent.* Boulder: University Press of Colorado.

Young, Lambton. 1872. *Acts of Gallantry.* London: Sampson Low.

Internet:

Adam's. 2014. www.adams.ie.

Ames (surname). 2013. http://en.wikipedia.org.

Amukta Pass. 2014. https://en.wikipedia.org.

Ancestry.com. 1997–2014. www.ancestry.com.

Anderson, Mark. July-August 2013. "The Shipwreck Hunter." *Canadian Geographic,* http://canadiangeographic.ca/magazine.

Archives Hub. n.d. http://archiveshub.ac.uk.

Ascites. 2014. http://en.wikipedia.org.

Attucks, Crispus. 2001. www.africawithin.com.

Baillie-Hamilton, William. 2014. https://en.wikipedia.org.

Battersby, William. November 29, 2009. "The Remarkable Background of Lt. Graham Gore." Web blog post. *Hidden Tracks.*

Box, Wiltshire. 2014. http://en.wikipedia.org.

Bruin. 2013. http://en.wikipedia.org.

Builder's Old Measurement. 2011. http://en.wikipedia.org.

Bury St. Edmunds Witch Trials. 2010. https://en.wikipedia.org.

Camber, East Sussex. 2010. http://camber.east-sussex.co.uk.

Campbell, Richard (editor). April 2009. "The Voyage of HMS *Erebus* and HMS *Terror* to the Southern and Antarctic Regions. Captain James Clark Ross, R.N. 1839–1843." *The Journal of the Hakluyt Society,* Parts 1, 2 & 3.

Canadian Confederation. 2014. http://en.wikipedia.org.

The Canadian Topographic Map Source. 2009–2010. www.canmaps.com.

Chase, Steven. September 10, 2014. "Fate of Franklin's Ship and Gold Will Be Decided by 1997 Canada–U.K. Deal." *The Globe and Mail,* www.theglobeandmail.com.

Clydesite & TugTalk. n.d. www.clydesite.co.uk.

Concentrations of Underground Railroad Refugee Settlers in Ontario, circa 1850. n.d. http://hrsbstaff.ednet.ns.ca/devrob/CDN%20History%2011/underground_railroad_in_cana.htm.

Concertina. 2014. http://en.wikipedia.org.

Congreve Rocket. 2010. www.wikipedia.org.

County Museum Dundalk. www2009.dundalkmuseum.ie.

Cresswell, Samuel Gurney. n.d. www.runctonweb.co.uk.

Christmas Pudding. 2014. http://en.wikipedia.org.

cydlee61. May 19, 2011. "Eldon House." Web blog post. *Creative Cynchronicity.*

Damon, Samuel C. 2012. www.wikipedia.org.

Dead Reckoning. 2014. https://en.wikipedia.org.

Descendants of Thomas Ames (www.fadedgenes.co.uk/ThomasAMESDescendants.html, 2014)The Dissolution of the Monasteries. 2014. http://en.wikipedia.org.

Dixons Medals. 2014. www.dixonsmedals.co.uk.

The Dysplastic Brain. 2010. http://dysplastic-brain.blogspot.com.

Edema. 1998–2014. www.mayoclinic.org.

83rd (County of Dublin) Regiment of Foot. 2014. http://en.wikipedia.org.

1861 England Census. 2010. www.ancestry.co.uk.

1881 British Isles Census. 2008. www.familysearch.org.

Elliot, George (1784–1863). 2010. www.wikipedia.org.

HMS *Enterprise* (1848). 2010. www.wikipedia.org.

Ericsson, John. 2014. https://en.wikipedia.org.

Fateful Voyage. 2012. www.fatefulvoyage.com.

Fix (position). 2013. https://en.wikipedia.org.

"For Arctic Discoveries' Medal." 2014. www.bbc.co.uk.

Free Settler or Felon? 2003–14. www.jenwilletts.com.

Friendly Society. 2013. https://en.wikipedia.org.

Gavin, Philip. 2000. "Irish Potato Famine." www.historyplace.com.

Genes Reunited. 2013. www.genesreunited.co.uk.

GenForum. 2009. http://genforum.genealogy.com.

Gill (unit). 2014. http://en.wikipedia.org.

The *Gjøa* Expedition (1903–1906). 2014. www.frammuseum.no.

Gorgon. 2013. https://en.wikipedia.org.

Graham, Thomas (chemist). 2014. http://en.wikipedia.org.

Great Havana Hurricane of 1846. 2010. www.wikipedia.org.

Guy Fawkes Night. 2014. https://en.wikipedia.org.

Hansard 1803–2005: Commons Sittings in the 19th Century. 2005. http://hansard.millbanksystems.com.

Haswell Family, London (Middlesex). 2007. http://genforum.genealogy.com.

Hay, Lord John (Royal Navy admiral of the fleet). 2014. http://en.wikipedia.org.

Hernnhut. 2013. http://en.wikipedia.org.

The Historical Maritime Society. 2008. www.hms.org.

History of the Black Cultural Centre for Nova Scotia. 2008. www.bccns.com.

Holland, Clive. 2003–14. "Joseph-René Bellot." www.biographi.ca.

_____. 2003–14. "Sherard Osborn." www.biographi.ca.

Hypothermia. 2010. www.wikipedia.org.

Ice Blink. 2014. http://en.wikipedia.org.

Imperial Units. 2013. http://en.wikipedia.org.

Index of 19th Century Naval Vessels and a Few of Their Movements. n.d. http://freepages.genealogy.rootsweb.ancestry.com.

International Genealogical Index. 2008. www.familysearch.org.

Inuit Contact and Colonization. 2009. www.inuitcontact.ca.

Inuktitut. 2010. www.wikipedia.org.

Inuit. 2013. http://en.wikipedia.org.

Iñupiat people. 2013. http://en.wikipedia.org.
Inuvialuit Pitqusiit Inuuniarutait: Inuvialuit Living History. n.d. www.inuvialuitlivinghistory.ca.
Inuvialuktun. 2010. www.wikipedia.org.
HMS *Investigator* (1848). 2010. www.wikipedia.org.
Irish Rebellion of 1798. 2010. www.wikipedia.org.
Isle of Sheppey. 2008. www.wikipedia.org.
Jeffreys, Julius. 2014. http://en.wikipedia.org.
Just Plain Folks. n.d. http://just-plain-folks.co.uk.
Kangiryuarmiut. 2014. http://en.wikipedia.org.
Keltie, John Scott. 2014. http://en.wikipedia.org.
Kensal Green Cemetery Online. 2006. www.kensalgreen cemetery.com.
Kew, Royal Botanic Gardens. n.d. www.kew.org.
King, Horatio Nelson. n.d. www.photolondon.org.uk.
Kylie, Aaron. 2014. "It's *Erebus*!: Prime Minister Stephen Harper Reveals Identity of Found Franklin Ship During Question Period." www.canadiangeographic.ca.
Labrador Retriever. 2013. http://en.wikipedia.org.
Lane, D. and J. Solon. 1992. "Thomas Graham," Woodrow Wilson Leadership Program in Chemistry, The Woodrow Wilson National Fellowship Foundation. www.woodrow.org.
Late 18th, 19th and early 20th Century Naval and Naval Social History Index. n.d. www.pbenyon.plus.com/Naval.html.
Le Mesurier-Foster, Ray. 2010. "The Rough Index to the Le Mesurier Family, 2010" (4'th edition). www.guernsey-society.org.uk.
Le Vesconte Family Tree. n.d. http://jamcnairn.com/Genealogy/LeVesconteFamilyTree.htm.
Line-crossing Ceremony. 2012. http://en.wikipedia.org.
List of Ship Names of the Royal Navy (I–L). 2014. https://en.wikipedia.org.
*London Gazette*. n.d. www.thegazette.co.uk.
Loney, William, RN—Victorian naval surgeon. n.d. http://home.wxs.nl/~pdavis/Loney.htm.
"Long Forgotten Grave of Franklin Expedition Search Ship Revealed. 2007. www.vancouvermaritimemuseum.com.
"Lost Franklin Expedition Ship Found in the Arctic." September 9, 2014. www.cbc.ca.com.
MacFarlane, Roderick. 2008. www.collectionscanada.gc.ca.
MacFarlane, Roderick Ross. 2013. www.clanmacfarlanegen ealogy.info.
Martin, Don. uly 28, 2010. "Exclusive: Historic Northwest Passage Wreckage Discovered Beneath Beaufort Sea." *Calgary Herald*, Jwww.calgaryherald.com.
McClure, Captain Sir Robert John Le Mesurier. n.d. http://www.priaulxlibrary.co.uk.
McClure, Sir Robert John Le Mesurier. 2008. www.biographi.ca.
Magnetic North Pole Positions. 2012. http://en.wikipedia.org.
Maritime Memorials. 2008. www.nmm.ac.uk.
MeasuringWorth. 2011. www.measuringworth.com.
Medical Dictionary. 2014. http://medical-dictionary.the freedictionary.com.
Memorial Inscriptions for the Parish of St. Clements, Halton, in the County of East Sussex. 2013. www.rootschat.com.
Merchant Seamen Research—General. 2014. www.poheri tage.com.
Misstoricalfiction (Roxanne Lutz). November 15, 2011. "Wreckless Horseman, Wild Horses or Just Plain Bad Luck?" Web blog post. *MisstoricalFiction*.
Moravian Church. 2010. www.wikipedia.org.
Morton & Eden. www.mortonandeden.com.

Mundy, Rodney. 2014. https://en.wikipedia.org.
National Maritime Museum. 2014. www.rmg.co.uk.
National Museums of Scotland. n.d. http://nms.scran.ac.uk.
Naval Warfare in the American Revolution. 2004. www.hmsrichmond.org.
Navy Song, "Working Song." 2014. http://myweb.tiscali.co.uk.
Neatby, Leslie H. 2013. "Sir Alexander Armstrong." www.biographi.ca.
_____. 2013. "Sir Henry Kellett." www.biographi.ca.
Nelsonøya. 2013. https://en.wikipedia.org.
Newfoundland (dog). 2013. https://en.wikipedia.org.
1903 Historical Encyclopedia of Illinois (Warren County). 1998–2014. www.usgennet.org.
Noble Numismatics. 2014. www.noble.com.au.
Okidaitōjima. 2013. http://en.wikipedia.org.
The Old Vicarage. 2013. http://rshawker.co.uk.
Osborn, Sherard. 2003–2014. www.biograhi.ca.
Oxford Dictionaries. 2013. http://oxforddictionaries.com.
Pacific Station. 2013. https://en.wikipedia.org.
Partridge, Victoria. November 17, 2011. "Cecil Higgins and the Arctic Explorer." Web blog post. *The Higgins*.
PBA Galleries. 2009. www.pbagalleries.
Periostitis. 2013. https://en.wikipedia.org.
Pitcairn Island Encyclopedia. 2009. http://library.puc.edu/pitcairn.
Port Robinson, Ontario. 2008. www.wikipedia.org.
Potter, Russell. March 21, 2009. "Who 'Discovered' the Northwest Passage?" Web blog post. *Visions of the North*.
Pullen, Hugh F. 2003–13. "William John Samuel Pullen." www.biographi.ca.
*Punch*. September 21, 2010.
Purser William Paine, RN. 2010. www.britishmedals.us.
Ravens, Ralph. 2013. http://en.wikipedia.org.
Rao, Joe. 2010. "The Myth of Arctic Daylight and Darkness Exposed." Web blog post.
Rebellions of 1837. 2014. http://en.wikipedia.org.
Red Ensign. 2013. http://en.wikipedia.org.
remedianetwork. January 28, 2013. "Specimen: Memento Mori." Web blog post. *Remedia*.
Reynard. 2013. http://en.wikipedia.org.
Reynard the Fox. 2013. www.britannica.com.
RootsWeb.com. 2014. www.rootsweb.ancestry.com.
The Rough Index to the Le Mesurier Family (4th edition). 2010. www.guernsey-society.org.uk.
The Royal Navy & Marine Customs and Traditions. 2004. www.hmsrichmond.org.
Royal Navy Hulks Overseas, 1800–1976. 2001. www.gwpda.org.
Sailing Navies 1650–1850. 2009. www.sailingnavies.com.
Scrofula. 2014. www.britannica.com.
Scurvy—Symptoms. N.d. www.nhs.uk.
Seguam Pass. 2013. http://en.wikipedia.org.
Slavery Abolition Act of 1833. 2014. http://en.wikipedia.org.
Slavery in Canada. 2014. www.wikipedia.org.
Smithfield, London. 2014. http://en.wikipedia.org.
Sorrel. 2014. http://en.wikipedia.org.
Sotheby's. 2014. www.sothebys.com.
Spink. 2014. www.spink.com.
Spur, John W., and Donald M. Schurman. 2008. "Williams Sandom." www. biographi.ca.
Status International Auctions. 2010. www.statusint.com.
Stroud Auction Rooms. n.d. http://stroudauctions.co.uk, undated.
Struzik, Ed. July 26, 2010. "Hunt for the HMS Investigator." *Montreal Gazette*, www.montrealgazette.com.

HMS *Superb* (1842). 2013. www.wikipedia.org.

Syncope (medicine). 2014. http://en.wikipedia.org.

Tenby Museum & Art Gallery. 2013. www.tenbymuseum.org.uk.

Timeanddate.com. 2011. www.timeanddate.com.

Traditional Music Library. n.d. www.tradionalmusic.co.uk.

Traditional Nautical Terms & Sayings. 1993–2013. www.goat-locker.org.

*Traditional Watch System.* 2013. http://en.wikipedia.org.

*Twilight.* 2013. www.wikipedia.org.

UK Genealogy Archives. 2014. http://ukga.org/index.html.

Umiak. 2013. http://en.wikipedia.org.

Underground Railroad in Canada. 2005. www.pc.gc.ca.

Understanding Pleurisy—The Basics. 2005–13. www.webmd.com.

The Wayfarer's Bookshop. 2010. www.wayfarersbookshop.com.

Webb, Dix Noonan, formerly Buckland Dix Wood. n.d. www.dnw.co.uk.

Wellcome Library. 2014. http://wellcomelibrary.org.

Whiteley, William. 2014. "Johann August Miertsching." www.biographi.ca.

Woods, Allan. March-April 2012. "The Saga of the Northwest Passage." *Archaeology*, www.archaeology.org.

Wrottesley, John, 2nd Baron Wrottesley. 2014. http://en.wikipedia.org.

# Index

Numbers in *bold italics* indicate pages with photographs.